RHCE™ Red Hat® Certified Engineer Linux Study Guide

Exam (RH302)

FOURTH EDITION

Michael Jang

McGraw-Hill/Osborne

New York Chicago San Francisco Lisbon London Madrid
Mexico City Milan New Delhi San Juan Seoul Singapore Sydney Toronto

The McGraw·Hill Companies

McGraw-Hill/Osborne
2100 Powell Street, 10th Floor
Emeryville, California 94608
U.S.A.

To arrange bulk purchase discounts for sales promotions, premiums, or fund-raisers, please contact **McGraw-Hill**/Osborne at the above address. For information on translations or book distributors outside the U.S.A., please see the International Contact Information page immediately following the index of this book.

RHCE™ Red Hat® Certified Engineer Linux Study Guide (Exam RH302), Fourth Edition

1234567890 DOC DOC 01987654

Book p/n 0-07-225366-5 and CD p/n 0-07-225367-3
parts of
ISBN 0-07-225365-7

Publisher
Brandon A. Nordin

**Vice President &
Associate Publisher**
Scott Rogers

Acquisitions Editor
Timothy Green

Project Editor
Jody McKenzie

Acquisitions Coordinator
Jessica Wilson

Technical Editor
Elizabeth Zinkann

Copy Editor
Lunaea Weatherstone

Proofreader
Susie Elkind

Indexer
Jack Lewis

Composition
Apollo Publishing Services

Illustrators
Kathleen Edwards and
Melinda Lytle

Series Design
Roberta Steele and
Peter Hancik

Cover Series Design
Peter Grame

This book was composed with Corel VENTURA™ Publisher.

ABOUT THE CONTRIBUTORS

Author

Michael Jang (RHCE, LCP, Linux+, MCSE) is currently a full-time writer, specializing in operating systems and networks. His experience with computers goes back to the days of jumbled punch cards. He has written other books on Linux certification, including *Linux+ Exam Cram* and *Sair GNU/Linux Installation and Configuration Exam Cram*. His other Linux books include *Mastering Red Hat Linux 9*, *Mastering Linux Second Edition*, and *Linux Networking Clearly Explained*. He has also written or contributed to books on Microsoft operating systems, including *MCSE Guide to Microsoft Windows 98* and *Mastering Windows XP Professional, Second Edition*.

In his previous life as a Boeing engineer, Michael worked a variety of jobs, including project manager for the first FAA type certified In-Seat Video Entertainment systems.

Technical Editor

Elizabeth Zinkann is a logical Linux catalyst, a freelance technical editor, and an independent computer consultant. She was a contributing editor and review columnist for *Sys Admin Magazine* for ten years. (Her most recent reviews have taken refuge at www.equillink.com.) Her articles have also appeared in *Performance Computing, Linux Magazine,* and *Network Administrator* magazines. As an independent computer consultant, she has built Linux servers; maintained computers utilizing Linux, Solaris, Macintosh, and Windows environments; programmed databases; and taught Linux, Unix, computer hardware basics, and Internet essentials. In a former life, she also programmed communications features, including ISDN at AT&T Network Systems.

LearnKey

LearnKey provides self-paced learning content and multimedia delivery solutions to enhance personal skills and business productivity. LearnKey claims the largest library of streaming-media training content that engages learners in dynamic media-rich instruction complete with video clips, audio, full motion graphics, and animated illustrations. LearnKey can be found on the Web at www.LearnKey.com.

CONTENTS AT A GLANCE

CONTENTS

ACKNOWLEDGMENTS

I personally would like to thank the following people:

- **Nancy E. Cropley, R.N. (d. 2002)** As a political activist, you fought for what you believed in: social justice, peace, and universal health care. You were never afraid to go to jail to support your beliefs. Your example is helping me find a backbone for life.

    As a nurse for the homeless, you helped so many who are less fortunate. You worked tirelessly in the clinics, in the shelters, and on the streets. Your efforts eased the pain of so many people. And you saved lives. Nancy, you are my hero.

    As an Internet entrepreneur, you showed me how to be happy pursuing a life working from home. You made it possible for me to have the freedom to be, instead of getting stuck in the corporate world.

    Nancy, you were my partner, my lover, my soul mate. You helped me find joy in this world. I take your lessons with me. I hold your spirit in my heart. I thank you for the best seven years of my life.

- All the incredibly hard-working folks at McGraw-Hill/Osborne: Brandon Nordin, Scott Rogers, Gareth Hancock, Tim Green, Jessica Wilson, Jody McKenzie, Lunaea Weatherstone, Susie Elkind, and Jack Lewis for their help in launching a great series and being solid team players.

PREFACE

L inux is thriving. Red Hat is at the forefront of the Linux revolution. And Red Hat Certified Engineers are making it happen.

Even in the current economic recovery, business, education, and governments are cost conscious. They want control of their operating systems. Linux—even Red Hat Enterprise Linux—saves money. The open source nature of Linux allows users to control and customize their operating systems. While there is a price associated with Red Hat Enterprise Linux (RHEL), it includes support and updates. As I describe shortly, there are freely available "rebuilds" of RHEL 3 that you can get without support from Red Hat.

A "rebuild" is software that is built by a third party from the same source code. On the other hand, a "clone" is built from different source code.

Major corporations, from Home Depot to Toyota, and governments such as Germany, the Republic of Korea, and Mexico have made the switch to Linux. When faced with a Microsoft audit for licenses, the Portland, Oregon, school system switched to Linux. Major movie studios such as Disney and Dreamworks use Linux to create the latest motion pictures. IBM has invested more than a billion dollars in this "free" operating system—just in 2001—and constantly features Linux in its advertising. HP has reported 2.5 billion dollars in Linux-related revenue in 2003.

Security is another reason to move toward Linux. The U.S. National Security Agency has developed its own version of the Linux kernel; RHEL 3 has incorporated many of these improvements.

While there are Linux distributions available from a number of companies, Red Hat is far and away the market leader. Therefore, the RHCE provides the most credibility to you as a Linux professional.

The RHCE exam is difficult. Historically, about 60 percent of the candidates pass this exam. The pass rate is lower for people taking the exam for the first time. But do not be intimidated. While there are no guarantees, this book can help you prepare for and pass the Red Hat Certified Engineer exam.

To study for this exam, you should have a network of at least two Linux or Unix computers. You need to install RHEL 3 on at least one of these computers. That will allow you to configure Linux and test the results. After configuring a service, it's important to be able to check your work from another computer.

Getting Red Hat Enterprise Linux 3

The Red Hat exams are based on your knowledge of Red Hat Enterprise Linux 3. When you take the RHCE exam, it'll be on a "standard" PC with Intel 32-bit (or compatible) personal computers. The CPU should have a speed of at least 700MHz, and the PC should have at least 256MB of RAM. There are four major versions of this operating system available; the price depends on your hardware and the amount of support you need.

- RHEL 3 Advanced Server (AS) includes varying levels of support for high-end and mission-critical systems.
- RHEL 3 Entry-level Server (ES) includes varying levels of support suitable for smaller or mid-range servers.
- RHEL 3 Workstation (WS) includes varying levels of support suitable for desktop computers and workstations.
- Red Hat Professional Workstation (RHPW) includes all software from RHEL 3 WS, without any support. The difference between RHPW and RHEL 3 ES is minimal. With a few downloadable RPM packages, you can use this to prepare for the RHCE exam fairly inexpensively. I describe the freely available packages that you need shortly.

If you want to prepare for the RHCE exam with the official RHEL 3 server operating system, you can purchase RHEL 3 ES, Basic Edition. This edition allows you to download the four binary CDs associated with this operating system, in ISO format, with quarterly updates, as well as access to downloads through the Red Hat Update Agent. Naturally, as this is the least expensive server option, it does not include any other official level of support.

But you don't have to pay for the operating system to prepare for the RHCE exam. As of this writing, there are four efforts to build freely available "rebuilds" of Red Hat Enterprise Linux 3. The source code for almost all RHEL 3 RPM packages is released under the Linux General Public License (GPL) or related licenses. This gives anyone the right to build Red Hat Enterprise Linux 3 from the Red Hat released source code.

The source code is released in Source RPM package format, which means the RPM packages can be built using the **rpm** commands described in Chapter 4. The four groups have all revised the source code to remove Red Hat trademarks. Some have used and added different versions of a limited number of RPM packages. As of this writing, the first three groups have consolidated the RHEL 3 software in three CDs. You can select and download the rebuild that most closely meets your needs. I have only tried the rebuild as developed by the cAos group. However, there are good reports about all of these rebuilds. These rebuilds are free; however, you should have a high-speed Internet connection. These rebuilds do not use 100 percent RHEL 3 software, so be careful:

- **Community Linux** The rebuild developed by the cAos group at www.caosity.org appears solid. As of this writing, this seems closest to the original RHEL 3 software.

- **TaoLinux** The folks behind TaoLinux are based at Alfred University. You can find out more about TaoLinux at www.taolinux.org.

- **White Box Linux** This group was first with a "final" rebuild of RHEL 3. As of this writing, they've documented the different sources that they've used on their first CD. You can find out more about this distribution at www.beau.org /~jmorris/linux/whitebox/.

- **RHEL-Rebuild** This group is based out of the University of Innsbruck, Austria. While their rebuild of RHEL 3 is not available as of this writing, they have a complete HOWTO for rebuilding RHEL from source at www2.uibk.ac.at/zid/software/unix/linux/rhel-rebuild.htm.

Alternatively, you can work from RHEL 3 WS or RHPW. There are four binary CDs associated with RHEL 3 ES and RHEL 3 WS (or RHPW). The software on the final three CDs are identical. The first RHEL 3 ES CD includes 22 additional RPM packages, naturally related to a number of servers. Thus you can install RHPW, without support or updates from Red Hat, and then build the software for the following servers from the source code:

- Domain Name Service (DNS)
- Dynamic Host Configuration Protocol (DHCP)
- Very Secure FTP (vsFTP)
- Network Information Service (NIS)

Using the techniques described in Chapter 4, you can download the Red Hat Enterprise Linux source RPMs at ftp.redhat.com, process them into binary RPMs, and then install them on your computer.

In This Book

This book is organized to serve as an in-depth review for the RHCE exam for both experienced Linux and Unix professionals. Each chapter covers a major aspect of the exam, with an emphasis on the "why" as well as the "how to" of working with and supporting RHEL 3 as a systems administrator or engineer. As the actual RHCE study points change with every release of RHEL, refer to www.redhat.com for the latest information.

This book includes relevant information from Red Hat Enterprise Linux 3 (RHEL 3). There are more than 100 major new features when compared to Red Hat Enterprise Linux 2.1. A few of the key features of RHEL 3 include:

- A strong stable Linux kernel. While the version is 2.4.21-4.EL, it includes features "backported" from the latest 2.6 kernel, as well as features that improve stability of the operating system environment.

- A new NPTL (Native Posix Threading Library) which improves the performance of multi-threaded applications.

- Improved support for Logical Volume Management (LVM).

- Performance and stability improvements for NFS.

- Support in high-performance enterprise computing environments.

- Tight integration and support of a number of enterprise-level applications by IBM, Oracle, Veritas, and more.

- Samba version 3.0, which allows Linux to act as a Microsoft Windows PDC, as well as a member server on an Active Directory network.

- A substantial number of GUI configuration utilities developed by Red Hat.

There are many more key features; those that I believe are relevant to the RHCE exam are also included in this book.

While it's not the best practice in service, it is fastest to administer RHEL 3 during the exam by logging into the root user account. The command prompt and PATH assumes use of that account. When you're logged into the root account, you'll see a command line prompt similar to:

```
[root@Enterprise3 root]#
```

As the length of this prompt would lead to a number of broken and wrapped code lines throughout this book, I've normally abbreviated the root account prompt as:

```
#
```

Be careful. The hash mark (#) is also used as a comment character in Linux scripts and programs; for example, here is an excerpt from /etc/inittab:

```
# Default runlevel. The runlevels used by RHS are:
```

When logged in as a regular user, the prompt is slightly different; for user michael, it would typically look like the following:

```
[michael@Enterprise3 michael]$
```

Similarly, I've abbreviated this as:

```
$
```

There are a number of command lines and code interspersed throughout the chapters.

On the CD

For more information on the CD-ROM, please see Appendix A.

Exam Readiness Checklist

At the end of the Introduction, you will find an Exam Readiness Checklist. This table has been constructed to allow you to cross-reference the official exam objectives with the objectives as they are presented and covered in this book. The checklist also allows you to gauge your level of expertise on each objective at the outset of your studies. This should allow you to check your progress and make sure you spend the time you need on more difficult or unfamiliar sections. References have been provided for the objective exactly as the vendor presents it, the section of the study guide that covers that objective, and a chapter and page reference.

In Every Chapter

We've created a set of chapter components that call your attention to important items, reinforce important points, and provide helpful exam-taking hints. Take a look at what you'll find in every chapter:

■ Every chapter begins with the **Certification Objectives**—what you need to know in order to pass the section on the exam dealing with the chapter topic. The Objective headings identify the objectives within the chapter, so you'll always know an objective when you see it.

■ **Exam Watch** notes call attention to information about, and potential pitfalls in, the exam. These helpful hints are written by authors who have taken the exams and received their certification—who better to tell you what to worry about? They know what you're about to go through!

EXERCISE

■ **Practice Exercises** are interspersed throughout the chapters. These are step-by-step exercises that allow you to get the hands-on experience you need in order to pass the exams. They help you master skills that are likely to be an area of focus on the exam. Don't just read through the exercises; they are hands-on practice that you should be comfortable completing. Learning by doing is an effective way to increase your competency with a product. Remember, the RHCE exam is entirely "hands-on;" there are no longer any multiple choice questions on this exam.

■ **On the Job** notes describe the issues that come up most often in real-world settings. They provide a valuable perspective on certification- and product-related topics. They point out common mistakes and address questions that have arisen from on-the-job discussions and experience.

■ **Inside the Exam** sidebars highlight some of the most common and confusing problems that students encounter when taking a live exam. Designed to anticipate what the exam will emphasize, getting inside the exam will help ensure you know what you need to know to pass the exam. You can get a leg up on how to respond to those difficult-to-understand labs by focusing extra attention on these sidebars.

■ **Scenario & Solution** sections lay out potential problems and solutions in a quick-to-read format.

SCENARIO & SOLUTION

James must be available to troubleshoot the computers in any office in the four buildings of the company that he works for…	Implement a roaming profile for James so that he can access his desktop no matter what computer he is using. This is especially handy since his roaming profile can include the mapping to a network drive that holds his diagnostic tools.

■ The **Certification Summary** is a succinct review of the chapter and a restatement of salient points regarding the exam.

Q&A

- The **Two-Minute Drill** at the end of every chapter is a checklist of the main points of the chapter. It can be used for last-minute review.

- The **Self Test** offers questions similar to those found on the certification exams. The answers to these questions, as well as explanations of the answers, can be found at the end of each chapter. By taking the Self Test after completing each chapter, you'll reinforce what you've learned from that chapter while becoming familiar with the structure of the exam questions.

- The **Lab Questions** at the end of the Self Test section offers a unique and challenging question format that requires the reader to understand multiple chapter concepts to answer correctly. These questions are more complex and more comprehensive than the other questions, as they test your ability to take all the knowledge you have gained from reading the chapter and apply it to complicated, real-world situations. Most importantly, the RHCE exam contains only lab type questions. I've tried to make these questions a bit more difficult than what you will find on the exam. If you can answer these questions, you have proven that you know the subject!

Some Pointers

Once you've finished reading this book, set aside some time to do a thorough review. You might want to return to the book several times and make use of all the methods it offers for reviewing the material:

1. *Reread all the Exam Watch notes.* Remember that these notes are written by authors who have taken the exam and passed. They know what you should expect—and what you should be on the lookout for.

2. *Review all the Scenario & Solution sections* for quick problem solving.

3. *Retake the Self Tests.* Taking the tests right after you've read the chapter is a good idea. Focus on the labs, as there are no multiple choice questions on the RHCE exam. I've included multiple choice questions just to test your mastery of the practical material in each chapter.

4. *Complete the exercises.* Did you do the exercises when you read through each chapter? If not, do them! These exercises are designed to cover exam topics, and there's no better way to get to know this material than by practicing. Be sure you understand why you are performing each step in each exercise. If there is something you are not clear on, reread that section in the chapter.

The RHCE Exam Challenge

This section covers the reasons for pursuing industry-recognized certification, explains the importance of your RHCE certification, and prepares you for taking the actual examination. It gives you a few pointers on how to prepare, what to expect, and what to do on exam day.

Leaping Ahead of the Competition!

The RHCE certification exam is a hands-on exam. As such, it is respected throughout the industry as a sign of genuine practical knowledge. If you pass, you will be head and shoulders above the candidate who has passed only a "standard" multiple-choice certification exam.

There are two parts to the RHCE exam, as follows. The requirements are detailed in the Exam Readiness Checklist later in this Introduction.

■ **Section I** Troubleshooting and System Maintenance: 2.5 hours. As described in the Red Hat Exam Prep guide, RHCE candidates need to meet the requirements for both Red Hat certifications. RHCE candidates must complete *all five* RHCT Troubleshooting and System Maintenance problems within the first hour. RHCEs must also "successfully complete enough additional RHCE items to earn a score of 80 or higher overall on the section." As there are five "optional problems," you'll need to complete three of five of these RHCE-level problems as well. For simplicity, I refer to Section I throughout the book as the "Troubleshooting and System Maintenance" exam.

■ **Section II** Installation and Configuration: 3.0 hours. As described in the Red Hat Exam Prep guide, RHCE candidates need to meet the requirements for both the RHCT and RHCE. RHCE candidates must get a grade of 70 or higher on *both* the RHCT and RHCE components of the Installation and Configuration exam. For simplicity, I refer to Section II throughout the book as the "Installation and Configuration" exam.

Why a Hands-On Exam?

Most certifications today are based on multiple-choice exams. These types of exams are relatively inexpensive to set up and easy to proctor. Unfortunately, many people without real-world skills are good at taking multiple-choice exams. This results in problems on the job with "certified" engineers, who have an image as "paper tigers" who do not have any real-world skills.

In response, Red Hat wanted to develop a certification program that matters. For the most part, they have succeeded with the RHCE.

Linux administrators frequently debug computers with problems. The challenges on the Troubleshooting and System Maintenance exam are based on real-world problems. As the typical Linux administrator has to work through multiple challenges on a daily basis, the RHCE Troubleshooting and System Maintenance exam provides a credible measure of real-world skills.

Linux administrators sometimes have to install Linux on a computer. Depending on the configuration, they may need to install Linux from a central source through a network. Installing Linux is not enough to make it useful. Administrators need to know how to configure Linux: add users, install and configure services, create firewalls, and more.

The overall pass rate for RHCE exam candidates has historically hovered around 60 percent. However, this includes candidates who are taking the exam for the first time and the second time (and later). In other words, the actual first-time pass rate may be well under 50 percent.

I've taken the RHCE course (RH300) and exam. Everyone in my class has practical experience administering Linux and/or Unix servers. However, I think the pass rate in my class closely matched the published statistics.

on the **job**

This exam is a **Red Hat exam. Knowledge of System V or BSD-based Unix is** *certainly helpful, as well as experience with services like Apache, SMB, NFS, DNS,* iptables, *and DHCP. But it is important to know how to set up, configure, install, and debug these services under* **Red Hat Enterprise Linux 3.**

Preparing for the RHCE Exam

Work with Red Hat Enterprise Linux 3. Install it on a computer that you don't need for any other purpose. Configure the services described in this book. Find ways to make Linux unbootable, study the characteristics of the problem, and find different ways to fix the problem.

As you go through this book, you'll have the opportunity to install RHEL 3 several times. If you have more than one computer, you'll be able to install RHEL 3 over a network connection. Then you can work with the different network services. Test out each service as you configure it, preferably from another computer on your network. Testing your work becomes especially important when you start working with the security features of Linux.

Red Hat Certification Program

Red Hat offers several courses that can help you prepare for the RHCE. Most of these courses are four or five days long. In some cases, you can take parts of an individual course on an electronic basis. Table 1 illustrates the available hands-on, instructor-led courses that can also help you prepare for the RHCE exam.

Should You Take a RHCE Course?

This book is intended as a substitute for the Red Hat "crash course" (RH300/301). It covers the material described in the RHCE Rapid Track Course Outline, available at www.redhat.com. However, RH300 is an excellent course. The Red Hat instructors who teach this course are highly skilled. If you feel the need for classroom instruction, read this book, and then take the course.

TABLE 1	Course	Description
Red Hat Courses	RH033	Introduction to Linux: basic pre–system administration skills
	RH131	Basic system administration skills for installation and configuration (RH133 without the RHCT exam)
	RH133	Basic system administration skills for installation and configuration; includes the RHCT exam
	RH202	The RHCT exam
	RH253	Basic network and security administration; requires a basic knowledge of LANs/WANs and TCP/IP
	RH300	The crash course plus the RHCE exam
	RH301	The crash course without the RHCE exam
	RH302	The RHCE exam

If you're not sure if you're ready for this course or book, read Chapter 1. It is a rapid overview of the prerequisites for the Red Hat certification courses. If you find the material in Chapter 1 to be overwhelming, consider one of the books noted near the start of the chapter, or one of the other RHCE courses. However, if you are just less familiar with a few of the topics covered in Chapter 1, you're probably okay. Even experienced Linux administrators aren't familiar with everything. Just use the references noted at the beginning of Chapter 1 to fill in any gaps in your knowledge.

Alternatively, you may already be familiar with the material in this book. You may have the breadth and depth of knowledge required to pass the RHCE exam. In that case, use this book as a refresher to help you focus on the skills and techniques you need to pass the RHCE exam.

Signing Up for the RHCE Course and/or Exam

Red Hat provides convenient Web-based registration systems for the courses and test. To sign up for any of the Red Hat courses or the RHCE exam itself, navigate to www.redhat.com, click the link for Training and the RHCE/RHCT Program, and select the desired course or exam. Alternatively, contact Red Hat Enrollment Central at (866) 626-2994.

Final Preparations

The RHCE exam is grueling. Once you have the skills, the most important thing that you can take to the exam is a clear head. If you're tired or frantic, you may miss the easy solutions that are often available. Get the sleep you need the night before the exam. Eat a good breakfast. Bring snacks with you that can keep your mind in top condition.

Remember, the RHCE exam is five and a half hours long. That is twice the length of a world-class marathon!

As I describe in Chapter 1, this is an advanced book. It is not designed for beginners to Unix or Linux. As Red Hat does not cover prerequisite skills in its prep course for the RHCE exam (RH300), I've only covered the tools associated with these skills briefly—mostly in Chapter 1. If you need more information on these prerequisite skills, please read the reference books I've cited in that chapter.

The RHCE exam requires that you master RHCT and RHCE skills, and assumes that you already have the prerequisite skills. I've cited them separately, as is done in the current version of the Red Hat Exam Prep guide. Watch for updates at www.redhat.com/training/rhce/examprep.html and www.redhat.com/training/rhce/courses/rhexam.html.

Exam RH302

Exam Readiness Checklist						
Official Objective	**Certification Objective**	**Ch #**	**Pg #**	**Beginner**	**Intermediate**	**Expert**
Red Hat Exam Prerequisite Skills						
Use standard command line tools (e.g., **ls**, **cp**, **mv**, **rm**, **tail**, and **cat**) to create, remove, view, and investigate files and directories	Basic Commands	1	16			
Use **grep**, **sed**, and **awk** to process text streams and files	Basic Commands	1	16			
Use a terminal-based text editor, such as vi/vim, to modify text files	Basic Linux Knowledge	1	5			
Use input/output redirection	Shells	1	24			
Understand basic principles of TCP/IP networking, including IP addresses, netmasks, and gateways	Basic TCP/IP Networking	1	36			
Use **su** to switch user accounts	System Administration	1	31			
Use **passwd** to set passwords	Basic Security	1	27			
Use **tar**, **gzip**, and **bzip2v**	System Administration	1	31			
Configure an e-mail client on Red Hat Enterprise Linux	Basic Graphical Applications	6	409			
Use Mozilla and/or links to access HTTP/HTTPS URLs	Basic Graphical Applications	6	409			
Use **lftp** to access FTP URLs	The Very Secure FTP Service	7	453			
RHCT Troubleshooting and System Maintenance Skills						
Boot systems into different run levels for troubleshooting and system maintenance	The linux rescue Environment	11	671			
Diagnose and correct misconfigured networking	Network Configuration	4	260			

Exam Readiness Checklist

Official Objective	Certification Objective	Ch #	Pg #	Beginner	Intermediate	Expert
Diagnose and correct hostname resolution problems	DNS/BIND	9	545			
Configure the X Window System and a desktop environment	X Window System (entire chapter)	6	369			
Add new partitions, filesystems, and swap to existing systems		1, 2, 3	1, 73, 155			
Use standard command-line tools to analyze problems and configure (your) system		all				
RHCE Troubleshooting and System Maintenance Skills						
Use the rescue environment provided by first installation CD	The linux rescue Environment	11	671			
Diagnose and correct boot loader failures arising from boot loader, module, and filesystem errors	The linux rescue Environment	11	671			
Diagnose and correct problems with network services (see the following Installation and Configuration skills for a list of these services)		7, 8, 9, 10	425, 483, 543, 601			
Add, remove, and resize logical volumes		3, 11	155, 661			
RHCT Installation and Configuration Skills						
Perform network OS installation	Configuring a Network Installation, The Installation Process	2	87, 110			
Implement a custom partitioning scheme	The Installation Process	2	110			
Configure printing	Print Services	8	516			
Configure the scheduling of tasks using **cron** and **at**	The cron System	5	349			

Exam Readiness Checklist

Official Objective	Certification Objective	Ch #	Pg #	Beginner	Intermediate	Expert
Attach system to a network directory service, such as NIS or LDAP	Configuring Directory Clients and NIS Servers	10	603			
Configure **autofs**	Filesystem Management and the Automounter	4	237			
Add and manage users, groups, and quotas	Adding, Deleting, and Modifying User Accounts	4	220			
Configure filesystem permissions for collaboration	Red Hat User Private Group Scheme	11	664			
Install and update RPMs	The Red Hat Package Manager Command and Utility, RPM Sources	4	245, 256			
Properly update the kernel RPM	Kernel, cron, and User Administration (multiple sections)	5	295			
Modify the system boot loader		2, 3, 11	73, 155, 661			
Implement software RAID at install-time and runtime		2, 3	73, 155			
Use /proc/sys and **sysctl** to modify and set kernel runtime parameters		5, 10	295, 601			
RHCE Installation and Configuration Skills						
For SMB, install, configure to start on reboot, for basic operation, and host- and user-based security	Samba Networking	8	485			
For HTTP/HTTPS, install, configure to start on reboot, for basic operation, and host- and user-based security	Apache	7	427			
For NFS, install, configure to start on reboot, for basic operation, and host- and user-based security	Network File System	9	563			

Exam Readiness Checklist

Official Objective	Certification Objective	Ch #	Pg #	Beginner	Intermediate	Expert
For FTP, install, configure to start on reboot, for basic operation, and host- and user-based security	The Very Secure FTP Service	7	453			
For Web proxy, install, configure to start on reboot, for basic operation, and host- and user-based security	Easy Squid Configuration	7	449			
For SMTP, install, configure to start on reboot, for basic operation, and host- and user-based security	Mail Services	7	459			
For IMAP/IMAPS/POP3, install, configure to start on reboot, for basic operation, and host- and user-based security	Mail Services	7	459			
For SSH, install, configure to start on reboot, for basic operation, and host- and user-based security	The Secure Shell Package	11	692			
For DNS, install, configure to start on reboot, for basic operation, and host- and user-based security	DNS/BIND	9	545			
Configure hands-free installation using Kickstart	Automated Installation with Kickstart	3	188			
Implement logical volumes at install-time	The Installation Process	2	110			
Use PAM to implement user-level restrictions	The Pluggable Authentication Module (PAM) System	10	614			

1

RHCE
Prerequisites

T he Red Hat exams are an advanced challenge. As both the RHCE and RHCT courses have a number of prerequisites, this book assumes that you know some basics about Linux. This chapter covers the prerequisite topics for Red Hat's RH300 course in a minimum of detail, with references to other books and sources for more information. It also covers the related prerequisites as defined in the Red Hat Exam Prep guide. Unlike in other chapters and other books in this series, the questions include a number of "zingers" that go beyond this chapter's content. That is the only way to see if you have the prerequisite skills necessary for the remaining chapters.

If you're serious about the RHCE or RHCT exams, this chapter should be just a review. In fact, this chapter is far from comprehensive. However, it is okay if you do not feel comfortable with a small number of topics in this chapter. In fact, it's quite natural that many experienced Linux administrators don't use every one of the prerequisite topics in their everyday work. Many candidates are successfully able to fill in the gaps in their knowledge with some self-study and lots of practice.

If you're new to Linux or Unix, this chapter will not be enough for you. It's not possible to detail the commands listed in this chapter, at least in a way that can be understood by newcomers to Linux and other Unix-based operating systems. Such descriptons require several hundred pages in other books, and would take away from the skills that you need for the Red Hat exams. If after reading this chapter you find a need for more detailed information, please refer to one of the following guides:

- *Red Hat: The Complete Reference, Enterprise Linux & Fedora Edition,* by Richard Petersen and Ibrahim Haddad (McGraw-Hill/Osborne, 2004), provides a detailed step-by-step guide to every part of this operating system. After reading the book you have in your hands, if you want additional exercises in Red Hat Enterprise Linux, this Complete Reference is the book.

- *Hacking Exposed Linux, Second Edition: Linux Security Secrets and Solutions,* by Brian Hatch and James Lee (McGraw-Hill/Osborne, 2003), gives you a detailed look at how you can secure your Linux system and networks in every possible way.

- *Linux Programming: A Beginner's Guide,* by Richard Peterson (McGraw-Hill/ Osborne, 2001), takes a fundamental look at the scripts you need to administer

Linux professionally and customize tools such as the GNOME and KDE GUIs for your users.

■ *Mastering Red Hat Linux* 9, by Michael Jang (Sybex, 2003), also provides a detailed guide to the operating system that provides the foundation for Red Hat Enterprise Linux 3.

Critical to a Linux administrator is knowledge of one or more text editors to manage the many configuration files on a Linux system. The Linux filesystem hierarchy organizes hardware, drivers, directories, and, of course, files. You need to master a number of basic commands to manage Linux. Printer configuration can be a complex topic. Shell scripts enable you to automate many everyday processes. Security is now a huge issue that Linux can handle better than other operating systems, both locally and on larger networks such as the Internet.

As an administrator, you need a good knowledge of basic system administration commands, TCP/IP configuration requirements, and standard network services. While the RHCE and RHCT exams are by and large not hardware exams, some basic hardware knowledge is a fundamental requirement for any Linux administrator.

This is not a book for beginners to Linux/Unix-type operating systems. Some of what you read in this chapter may be unfamiliar. Use this chapter to create a list of topics that you may need to study further. In some cases, you'll be able to get up to speed with the material in other chapters. But if you have less experience with Linux or another Unix-type operating system, you may want to refer to the aforementioned books.

If you're experienced with other Unix-type operating systems such as Solaris, AIX, or HP-UX, you may need to leave some defaults at the door. When Red Hat developed their Linux distribution, they did a number of things that may not seem completely consistent with Unix standards. When I took RH300, some students with these backgrounds had difficulties with the course and the RHCE exam.

For the purpose of this book, I'll be running most commands as the Linux administrative user, root. Logging in as the root user is normally discouraged unless you're administering a computer. However, since the RHCE and RHCT exams tests your administrative skills, it's appropriate to run commands in this book as the root user.

There are several additional prerequisite skills as defined in the Red Hat Exam Prep guide. They are straightforward, but belong in other chapters. In Chapter 6, I'll show you how to configure an e-mail client and use Mozilla to browse online. In Chapter 7, I'll show you how to use the **lftp** command as a client.

INSIDE THE EXAM

Prerequisite Skills

For the RHCE and RHCT exams, the skills outlined in this chapter are generally minimum requirements. For example, while you might not see a question on the vi editor, you will need to know how to use vi on at least the Troubleshooting and System Maintenance exam. While it's not a requirement to know how to pipe the output of **dmesg** to the **less** command, it's a very useful tool that can help you identify problems on the Troubleshooting or Installation portions of either exam.

But remember, there is more than one way to do most everything in Linux. While it's a good idea to learn all of these "prerequisite" skills, you don't have to know everything in this chapter. In most cases, it's okay if you have other ways to edit or otherwise configure your RHEL 3 system. As there is no longer a multiple choice component to the Red Hat exams, don't worry about the dozens of switches for certain commands. Focus on results, not trivia.

Using Other Versions of Red Hat

For the purpose of this chapter, you can use Red Hat Linux 9 or Fedora Linux 1 to test your knowledge of basic commands. There are trivial variations in a few commands. For example, fdisk now interprets the size of a partition slightly differently. (For more information, see the RELEASE-NOTES-i386-en file in the /usr/share/doc/redhat-release-3 directory or the RHEL 3 documentation at www.redhat.com.)

For those of you with more advanced hardware, the Red Hat exams are based on PCs built with Intel 32-bit CPUs. That means you'll be using the Linux kernel and associated software that has been customized for this CPU.

In future chapters, I will highlight some of the differences between Red Hat Enterprise

Linux 3 (RHEL 3) and Red Hat Linux 9. This should help students who are using the freely available Red Hat Linux 9 distribution to study for the RHCE and RHCT exams. Generally, you'll be able to update your Red Hat Linux 9 system to the RHEL 3 software. If you're using Fedora Linux 1 or above, the process may be more difficult, as RHEL 3 is based on Red Hat Linux 9.

Fortunately, there is a freely available version of RHEL 3 from the Community Linux group, at www.caosity.org. It's available as packages processed from the source code or as a three-CD set of ISO images. It includes all available non-proprietary packages from Red Hat Enterprise Linux 3 server.

CERTIFICATION OBJECTIVE 1.01

Basic Linux Knowledge

Linux and Unix are managed through a series of text files. Linux administrators do not normally use graphical editors to manage these configuration files. Editors such as WordPerfect, StarOffice, and yes, even Microsoft Word normally save files in a binary format that Linux can't read. Popular text editors for Linux configuration files include emacs, pico, joe, and vi.

The Visual Editor

While emacs may be the most popular text editor in the world of Linux, every administrator needs at least a basic knowledge of vi. While emacs may be more popular and flexible, vi may help you save a broken system. If you ever have to restore a critical configuration file using an emergency boot floppy, vi is probably the only editor that you'll have available.

In reality, RHEL 3 uses an enhanced version of the vi editor, known as vim. It adds color to different types of variables in key configuration files such as /etc/fstab. All regular vi commands work in the vim editor. While you can remove the coloring in the vim editor with the **:nohl** command, this detail does not affect your ability to manage your Linux system.

You need to know how to restore your system from a rescue floppy, which does not have enough room to carry any editor other than vi. However, the Red Hat Exam Prep guide suggests that you need to be able to "use the rescue environment provided by the first installation CD," which does include other console editors. If you use the joe text editor, it's available when you boot from the rescue floppy.

on the Job

This section provides only the briefest of introductions to the vi editor.

You should know how to use the two basic modes of vi: command and insert. When you use vi to open a file, it opens in command mode. Some of the commands start insert mode. Opening a file is easy: just use the **vi *filename*** command. By default, this starts vi in command mode. An example of vi with the /etc/passwd file is shown in Figure 1-1.

FIGURE 1-1

The vi editor

```
root:x:0:0:root:/root:/bin/bash
bin:x:1:1:bin:/bin:/sbin/nologin
daemon:x:2:2:daemon:/sbin:/sbin/nologin
adm:x:3:4:adm:/var/adm:/sbin/nologin
lp:x:4:7:lp:/var/spool/lpd:/sbin/nologin
sync:x:5:0:sync:/sbin:/bin/sync
shutdown:x:6:0:shutdown:/sbin:/sbin/shutdown
halt:x:7:0:halt:/sbin:/sbin/halt
mail:x:8:12:mail:/var/spool/mail:/sbin/nologin
news:x:9:13:news:/etc/news:
uucp:x:10:14:uucp:/var/spool/uucp:/sbin/nologin
operator:x:11:0:operator:/root:/sbin/nologin
games:x:12:100:games:/usr/games:/sbin/nologin
gopher:x:13:30:gopher:/var/gopher:/sbin/nologin
ftp:x:14:50:FTP User:/var/ftp:/sbin/nologin
nobody:x:99:99:Nobody:/:/sbin/nologin
rpm:x:37:37::/var/lib/rpm:/sbin/nologin
vcsa:x:69:69:virtual console memory owner:/dev:/sbin/nologin
nscd:x:28:28:NSCD Daemon:/:/sbin/nologin
sshd:x:74:74:Privilege-separated SSH:/var/empty/sshd:/sbin/nologin
rpc:x:32:32:Portmapper RPC user:/:/sbin/nologin
rpcuser:x:29:29:RPC Service User:/var/lib/nfs:/sbin/nologin
nfsnobody:x:65534:65534:Anonymous NFS User:/var/lib/nfs:/sbin/nologin
"/etc/passwd" 37L, 1680C
```

The following is only a brief introduction to the vi editor. For more information, there are a number of books available, as well as an extensive manual formatted as a HOWTO available from the Linux Documentation Project at www.tldp.org.

vi Command Mode

In command mode, you can do everything you need to do to a text file except edit it. The options in command mode are broad and varied, and they are the subject of a number of book-length texts. Using vi requires seven critical command skills:

- **Open** To open a file in the vi editor from the command line interface, run the **vi** *filename* command.

- **Search** Start with a backslash, followed by the search term. Remember, Linux is case sensitive, so if you're searching for "Michael" in /etc/passwd, use the **/Michael** (not **/michael**) command.

- **Write** To save your changes, use the **w** command. You can combine commands; for example, **:wq** writes the file and exits vi.

- **Close** To leave vi, use the **:q** command.

- **Abandon** If you want to abandon any changes that you've made, use the **:q!** command.

- **Edit**   You can use a number of commands to edit files through vi, such as **x**, which deletes the currently highlighted character, **dw**, which deletes the currently highlighted word, and **dd**, which deletes the current line. Remember, **p** places text from a buffer, and **U** restores text from a previous change.

- **Insert**   A number of commands allow you to start insert mode, including **i** to start inserting text at the current position of the editor, and **o** to open up a new line immediately below the current position of the cursor.

Basic Text Editing

In modern Linux systems, editing files with vi is easy. Just use the normal navigation keys (arrow keys, PAGE UP, and PAGE DOWN), and then one of the basic commands such as **i** or **o** to start vi's insert mode, and type your changes directly into the file.

When you're finished with insert mode, press the ESC key to return to command mode. You can then save your changes, or abandon them and exit vi.

EXERCISE 1-1

Using vi to Create a New User

In this exercise, you'll create a new user by editing the /etc/passwd file with the vi text editor. While there are other ways to create new Linux users, this exercise helps you verify your skills with vi and at the command line interface.

1. Open a Linux command line interface. Log in as the root user, and type the **vi /etc/passwd** command.

2. Navigate to the last line in the file. As you should already know, there are several ways to do this in command mode, including the DOWN ARROW key, the PAGE DOWN key, the **G** command, or even the K key.

3. Make one copy of this line. If you're already comfortable with vi, you should know that you can copy an entire line to the buffer with the **yy** command. This "yanks" the line into buffer. You can then restore, or put that line as many times as desired with the **p** command.

4. Change the username, user ID, group ID, user comment, and home directory for the new user. If you understand the basics of Linux or Unix, you'll understand their locations on each line in the /etc/passwd file. For example, in Figure 1-2, this corresponds to tb, 501, 501, Tony Blair, and /home/tb. Make sure the username also corresponds to the home directory.

FIGURE 1-2

Adding a
new user in
/etc/passwd

```
rpm:x:37:37::/var/lib/rpm:/sbin/nologin
vcsa:x:69:69:virtual console memory owner:/dev:/sbin/nologin
nscd:x:28:28:NSCD Daemon:/:/sbin/nologin
sshd:x:74:74:Privilege-separated SSH:/var/empty/sshd:/sbin/nologin
rpc:x:32:32:Portmapper RPC user:/:/sbin/nologin
rpcuser:x:29:29:RPC Service User:/var/lib/nfs:/sbin/nologin
nfsnobody:x:65534:65534:Anonymous NFS User:/var/lib/nfs:/sbin/nologin
mailnull:x:47:47::/var/spool/mqueue:/sbin/nologin
smmsp:x:51:51::/var/spool/mqueue:/sbin/nologin
pcap:x:77:77::/var/arpwatch:/sbin/nologin
xfs:x:43:43:X Font Server:/etc/X11/fs:/sbin/nologin
ntp:x:38:38::/etc/ntp:/sbin/nologin
gdm:x:42:42::/var/gdm:/sbin/nologin
desktop:x:80:80:desktop:/var/lib/menu/kde:/sbin/nologin
apache:x:48:48:Apache:/var/www:/sbin/nologin
webalizer:x:67:67:Webalizer:/var/www/usage:/sbin/nologin
squid:x:23:23::/var/spool/squid:/sbin/nologin
postfix:x:89:89::/var/spool/postfix:/sbin/nologin
named:x:25:25:Named:/var/named:/sbin/nologin
netdump:x:34:34:Network Crash Dump user:/var/crash:/bin/bash
mj:x:500:500::/home/mj:/bin/bash
tb:x:501:501::/home/tb:/bin/bash
~
```

5. Return to command mode by pressing the ESC key. Save the file with the **wq** command.

6. As the root user, run the **passwd** *newuser* command. Assign the password of your choice to the new user.

CERTIFICATION OBJECTIVE 1.02

Linux Filesystem Hierarchy and Structure

Everything in Linux can be reduced to a file. Partitions are associated with *filesystem device nodes* such as /dev/hda1. Hardware components are associated with node files such as /dev/modem. Detected devices are documented as files in the /proc directory. The Filesystem Hierarchy Standard (FHS) is the official way to organize files in Unix and Linux directories. As with the other sections, this introduction provides only the most basic overview of the FHS. More information is available from the official FHS home page at www.pathname.com/fhs.

Linux Filesystems and Directories

Several major directories are associated with all modern Unix/Linux operating systems. These directories organize user files, drivers, kernels, logs, programs, utilities, and more into different categories. The standardization of the FHS makes it easier for users of other Unix-based operating systems to understand the basics of Linux.

Every FHS starts with the root directory, also known by its symbol, the single forward slash (/). All of the other directories shown in Table 1-1 are subdirectories of the root directory. Unless they are mounted separately, you can also find their files on the same partition as the root directory.

Mounted directories are often known as volumes, which can span multiple partitions. However, while the root directory (/) is the top-level directory in the FHS, the root user's home directory (/root) is just a subdirectory.

on the **Job**

In Linux, the word "filesystem" has several different meanings. For example, a filesystem can refer to the FHS, an individual partition, or a format such as ext3. A filesystem device node such as /dev/sda1 represents the partition on which you can mount a directory.

Media Devices

Several basic types of media are accessible to most PCs, including IDE hard disks, floppy drives, CD/DVD drives, and the various standards of SCSI devices. Other media are accessible through other PC ports, including serial, parallel, USB, and IEEE 1394. You can use Linux to manage all of these types of media.

Most media devices are detected automatically. Linux may require a bit of help for some devices described in Chapter 2. But in the context of the Linux FHS, media devices, like all others, are part of the /dev directory. Typical media devices are described in Table 1-2.

Making Reference to Devices in /dev

Take a look at the files in the /dev directory. Use the **ls -l /dev | more** command. Scroll through the long list for a while. Are you confused yet? Well, there's a method to this madness. Some devices are linked to others, and that actually makes it easier to understand what is connected to what. For example, the virtual device files /dev/mouse and /dev/modem are easier to identify than the true device files. Generally, these devices are

TABLE 1-1	Directory	Description
Basic Filesystem Hierarchy Standard Directories	/	The root directory, the top-level directory in the FHS. All other directories are subdirectories of root, which is always mounted on some partition.
	/bin	Essential command line utilities. Should not be mounted separately; otherwise, it could be difficult to get to these utilities when using a rescue disk.
	/boot	Includes Linux startup files, including the Linux kernel. The default, 100MB, is usually sufficient for a typical modular kernel and additional kernels that you might install during the RHCE or RHCT exams.
	/dev	Hardware and software device drivers for everything from floppy drives to terminals. Do not mount this directory on a separate partition.
	/etc	Most basic configuration files.
	/home	Home directories for almost every user.
	/lib	Program libraries for the kernel and various command line utilities. Do not mount this directory on a separate partition.
	/mnt	The mount point for removable media, including floppy drives, CD-ROMs, and Zip disks.
	/opt	Applications such as the WordPerfect or OpenOffice.org Office suites.
	/proc	Currently running kernel-related processes, including device assignments such as IRQ ports, I/O addresses, and DMA channels.
	/root	The home directory of the root user.
	/sbin	System administration commands. Don't mount this directory separately.
	/tmp	Temporary files. By default, Red Hat Enterprise Linux deletes all files in this directory periodically.
	/usr	Small programs accessible to all users. Includes many system administration commands and utilities.
	/var	Variable data, including log files and printer spools.

automatically linked to the actual device files during Linux installation. For example, if you have a mouse and modem installed, the following commands illustrate possible links between these components and the actual device files:

```
# ls -l /dev/mouse
lrwxrwxrwx  1 root  root  5 Apr 18 12:17 /dev/mouse -> psaux
# ls -l /dev/modem
lrwxrwxrwx  1 root  root  5 Apr 18 12:17 /dev/modem -> /dev/ttyS0
```

TABLE 1-2	Media Device	Device File
Media Devices	Floppy drive	First floppy (Microsoft A: drive) = /dev/fd0 Second floppy (Microsoft B: drive) = /dev/fd1
	IDE hard drive IDE CD/DVD drive	First IDE drive = /dev/had Second IDE drive = /dev/hdb Third IDE drive = /dev/hdc Fourth IDE drive = /dev/hdd
	SCSI hard drive SCSI CD/DVD drive	First SCSI drive = /dev/sda Second SCSI drive = /dev/sdb ... Twenty-seventh SCSI drive = /dev/sdaa and so on
	Parallel port drives	First IDE drive = /dev/pd1 First tape drive: /dev/pt1
	USB drives	Varies widely
	IEEE 1394 drives	IEEE 1394 (a.k.a. FireWire, iLink) is actually a SCSI standard, so these are controlled in Linux as SCSI devices

The first output shows that /dev/mouse is linked directly to the PS/2 device driver port, and that /dev/modem is linked directly to the first serial port, which corresponds to COM1 in the Microsoft world.

Filesystem Formatting and Checking

Three basic tools are available to manage the filesystem on various partitions: fdisk, mkfs, and fsck. They can help you configure partitions as well as create, and then check and repair, different filesystems. As with the rest of this chapter, this section covers only the very basics; for more information, see the man page associated with each respective command tool.

fdisk

The Linux fdisk utility is a lot more versatile than its Microsoft counterpart. But to open it, you need to know the device file associated with the hard drive that you want to change. Identifying the hard disk device file is covered in Chapter 2. Assuming you want to manage the partitions on the first SCSI hard disk, enter the following command:

```
# fdisk /dev/sda
```

INSIDE THE EXAM

Running as Root

Throughout the book, I'm assuming that you're running commands after having logged in as the root user. While it may not be the best practice on the job, it can save you a little bit of time on the RHCT and RHCE exams. For example, if you've logged in as a regular user, you'd start fdisk with the **/sbin/fdisk** command. This applies even if

you've taken administrative privileges with the **su** command. (I know, you could take administrative privileges with the root user PATH with the **su - root** command, but time is of the essence on these exams.) On the other hand, if you log in as the root user, the default root $PATH variable, means all you need to type is **fdisk**.

As you can see in Figure 1-3, the fdisk utility is flexible. Some key fdisk commands are described in Table 1-3.

FIGURE 1-3

Linux fdisk commands; p returns the partition table

```
[root@berkeley root]# fdisk /dev/sda

Command (m for help): m
Command action
   a   toggle a bootable flag
   b   edit bsd disklabel
   c   toggle the dos compatibility flag
   d   delete a partition
   l   list known partition types
   m   print this menu
   n   add a new partition
   o   create a new empty DOS partition table
   p   print the partition table
   q   quit without saving changes
   s   create a new empty Sun disklabel
   t   change a partition's system id
   u   change display/entry units
   v   verify the partition table
   w   write table to disk and exit
   x   extra functionality (experts only)

Command (m for help): p

Disk /dev/sda: 4294 MB, 4294967296 bytes
255 heads, 63 sectors/track, 522 cylinders
Units = cylinders of 16065 * 512 = 8225280 bytes

   Device Boot    Start      End    Blocks   Id  System
/dev/sda1   *         1       13    104391   83  Linux
/dev/sda2            14      474   3702982+  83  Linux
/dev/sda3           475      522    385560   82  Linux swap

Command (m for help):
```

TABLE 1-3	fdisk Command	Description
Important fdisk Options	a	Allows you to specify the bootable Linux partition (with /boot).
	l	Lists known partition types; fdisk can create partitions that conform to any of these filesystems.
	n	Adds a new partition; works only if there is free space on the disk that hasn't already been allocated to an existing partition.
	q	Quits without saving any changes.
	t	Changes the partition filesystem.

mkfs

To format a Linux partition, apply the **mkfs** command. It allows you to format a partition to a number of different filesystems. To format a typical partition such as /dev/hda2 to the current Red Hat standard, the third extended filesystem, run the following command:

```
# mkfs -t ext3 /dev/hda2
```

The **mkfs** command also serves as a "front-end," depending on the filesystem format. For example, if you're formatting a Red Hat standard ext3 filesystem, **mkfs** by itself automatically calls the **mkfs.ext3** command. Therefore, if you're reformatting an ext3 filesystem, the following command is sufficient:

```
# mkfs /dev/hda2
```

on the job

Be careful with the mkfs command. First, back up any data on the subject partition and computer. This command erases all data on the specified partition.

fsck

The **fsck** command is functionally similar to the Microsoft **chkdsk** command. It analyzes the specified filesystem and performs repairs as required. Assume you're having problems with files in the /var directory, which happens to be mounted on /dev/hda7. If you want to run **fsck**, unmount that filesystem first. In some cases, you may need to go into single-user mode with the **init 1** command before you can unmount a filesystem. To unmount, analyze, then remount the filesystem noted in this section, and run the following commands:

```
# umount /var
# fsck -t ext3 /dev/hda7
# mount /dev/hda7 /var
```

The **fsck** command also serves as a "front-end," depending on the filesystem format. For example, if you're formatting an ext2 or ext3 filesystem, **fsck** by itself automatically calls the **e2fsck** command (which works for both filesystems). Therefore, if you're checking an ext3 filesystem, once you unmount it with the **umount** command, the following command is sufficient:

```
# fsck /dev/hda7
```

Multiple Partitions with One Filesystem

The Logical Volume Manager (LVM) enables you to set up one filesystem on multiple partitions. For example, assume you're adding more users and are running out of room in your /home directory. You don't have any unpartitioned space available on your current hard disk.

With the LVM, all you need to do is add another hard disk, configure some partitions, back up /home, and use the LVM tools to combine the new partition and the one used by /home into a volume set. You may need to install the LVM rpm package. Once it is installed, the steps are fairly straightforward, as described in the following exercise:

EXERCISE 1-2

Creating a New LVM Partition

Logical Volume Management (LVM) is new to RHEL 3 and is more important than the prerequisite skills covered in most of this chapter. The latest available Red Hat Exam Prep guide includes LVM requirements on both parts of the RHCE exam. For more information on LVM, see Chapters 3 and 11.

1. Add a new hard disk.

2. Create new partitions. Assign the Linux LVM filesystem to one or more of these partitions. This can be easily done with the Linux **fdisk** utility.

3. Back up /home. Assign the LVM filesystem to that partition.

4. Scan for Linux LVM filesystems with the **vgscan** utility, to create a database for other LVM commands.

5. Create volumes for the set with the **pvcreate** */dev/partition* command.

6. Add the desired volumes to a specific volume group with the **vgcreate** *groupname* */dev/partition1* */dev/partition2* ... command.

7. Now you can create a logical volume. Use the **lvcreate -L-xyM -n** *volname* *groupname* command, where *xy* is the size of the volume, and *groupname* is the volume group name from the previous step.

8. Finally, you can format the logical volume with the **mkfs** command for the desired filesystem (usually ext2 or ext3), using the device name returned by the **lvcreate** command.

Mounting Partitions

The **mount** command can be used to attach local and network partitions to specified directories. Mount points are not fixed; you can mount a CD drive or even a Samba share to any empty directory where you have appropriate permissions.

There are standard mount points based on the FHS. The following commands mount a floppy with the VFAT filesystem, a CD formatted to the ISO 9660 filesystem, and a Zip drive. The devices may be different on your system; if in doubt, look through the startup messages with **dmesg | less**.

```
# mount -t vfat /dev/fd0 /mnt/floppy
# mount -t iso9660 /dev/cdrom /mnt/cdrom
# mount /dev/sdc
```

exam
watch

The following section covers only the most basic of commands that you can use in Linux. It describes only a few of the things that you can do with each command. Unfortunately, a full discussion would require several hundred more pages. Expect to know considerably more about commands for the RHCE and RHCT exams. If you feel a need for a more solid grounding in basic commands, get more information by reading **Red Hat: The Complete Reference, Enterprise Linux & Fedora Edition,** *by Richard Petersen and Ibrahim Haddad.*

CERTIFICATION OBJECTIVE 1.03

Basic Commands

Linux was developed as a clone of Unix, which means that it has the same functionality with different source code. And the essence of both operating systems is at the command line. Basic commands for file manipulation and filters are available to help you do more with a file.

Basic File Operations

Two basic groups of commands are used to manage Linux files. One group helps you get around Linux files and directories. The other group actually does something creative with the files. Remember, in any Linux file operation, you can take advantage of the HISTORY (this is capitalized because it's a standard environment variable) of previous commands, as well as the characteristics of command completion, which allow you to use the TAB key almost as a wildcard to complete a command or a filename, or give you the options available in terms of the absolute path.

Almost all Linux commands include switches, options that allow you to do more. Few are covered in this chapter. If you're less familiar with any of these commands, use their man pages. Study the switches. Try them out! Only with practice, practice, and more practice can you really understand the power behind some of these commands.

Basic Navigation

Everything in Linux can be reduced to a file. Directories are special types of files that serve as containers for other files. Drivers are files. As discussed earlier, devices are special types of files. The nodes associated with USB hardware are just files. And so on. To navigate around these files, you need some basic commands to tell you where you are, what is there with you, and how to move around.

The Tilde (~)　But first, every Linux user has a home directory. You can use the tilde (~) to represent the home directory of any currently logged on user. For example, if your username is tb, your home directory is /home/tb. If you've logged in as the root user, your home directory is /root. Thus, the effect of the **cd ~** command depends on your username. For example, if you've logged in as user mj, the **cd ~** command brings you to the /home/mj directory. If you've logged in as the root user, this command brings you to the /root directory.

Paths   There are two path concepts you need to know when you work with Linux directories: absolute paths and relative paths. An absolute path describes the complete directory structure based on the top level directory, root (/). A relative path is based on the current directory, also known as the present working directory. Relative paths do not include the slash in front.

The difference between an absolute path and a relative one is important. Especially when you're creating a script, absolute paths are essential. Otherwise, scripts executed from other directories may lead to unintended consequences.

pwd   In many configurations, you may not know where you are relative to the root (/) directory. The **pwd** command, which is short for present working directory, can tell you, relative to root (/). Once you know where you are, you can know if you need to move to a different directory.

cd   It's easy to change directories in Linux. Just use **cd** and cite the absolute path of the desired directory. If you use the relative path, just remember that your final destination depends on the present working directory.

ls   The most basic of commands is to list the files in the current directory. But the Linux **ls** command, with the right switches, can be quite powerful. The right kind of **ls** can tell you everything about a file, such as creation date, last access date, and size. It can help you organize the listing of files in just about any desired order. Important variations on this command include **ls -a** to reveal hidden files, **ls -l** for long listings, and **ls -i** for inode numbers.

Looking for Files

There are two basic commands for file searches: **find** and **locate**.

find   The **find** command searches through directories and subdirectories for a desired file. For example, if you wanted to find the directory with the XF86Config GUI configuration file, you could use the following command, which would start the search in the root directory:

```
# find / -name XF86Config
```

But this search on my older laptop computer with a 200 MHz CPU took several minutes. Alternatively, if you know that this file is located in the /etc subdirectory tree, you could start in that directory with the following command:

```
# find /etc -name XF86Config
```

locate   If this is all too time-consuming, RHEL 3 includes a default database of all files and directories. Searches with the **locate** command are almost instantaneous. And **locate** searches don't require the full filename. The drawback is that the **locate** command database is normally updated only once each day, as documented in the **/etc/cron.daily/slocate.cron** script.

Getting into the Files

Now that you see how to find and get around different files, it's time to start reading, copying, and moving the files around. Most Linux configuration files are text files. Linux editors are text editors. Linux commands are designed to read text files. If in doubt, you can check the file types in the current directory with the **file *** command.

cat   The most basic command for reading files is **cat**. The **cat** *filename* command scrolls the text within the *filename* file. It also works with multiple filenames; it concatenates the filenames that you might list as one continuous output to your screen.

less and more   Larger files demand a command that can help you scroll through the file text at your leisure. Linux has two of these commands: **more** and **less**. With the **more** *filename* command, you can scroll through the text of a file, from start to finish, one screen at a time. With the **less** *filename* command, you can scroll in both directions through the same text with the PAGE UP and PAGE DOWN keys. Both commands support vi-style searches.

head and tail   The **head** and **tail** commands are separate commands that work in essentially the same way. By default, the **head** *filename* command looks at the first 10 lines of a file; the **tail** *filename* command looks at the last 10 lines of a file. You can specify the number of lines shown with the **-n***xy* switch. Just remember to avoid the space when specifying the number of lines; for example, the **tail -n15 /etc/passwd** command lists the last 15 lines of the /etc/passwd file.

Creating Files

A number of commands are used to create new files. Alternatively, you can let a text editor such as vi create a new file for you.

cp   The **cp** (copy) command allows you to take the contents of one file and place a copy with the same or different name in the directory of your choice. For example, the **cp** *file1 file2* command takes the contents of *file1* and saves the contents in *file2*. One of the dangers of **cp** is that it can easily overwrite files in different directories, without prompting you to make sure that's what you really wanted to do.

mv   While you can't rename a file in Linux, you can move it. The **mv** command essentially puts a different label on a file. For example, the **mv** *file1 file2* command changes the name of *file1* to *file2*. Unless you're moving the file to a different partition, everything about the file, including the inode number, remains the same.

ln   You can create a linked file. As discussed earlier, linked files are common with device files such as /dev/modem and /dev/mouse. They're also useful to make sure that multiple users have a copy of the same file in their directories. Hard links include a copy of the file. As long as the hard link is made within the same partition, the inode numbers are identical. You could delete a hard-linked file in one directory, and it would still exist in the other directory. For example, the following command creates a hard link from the actual Samba configuration file to smb.conf in the local directory:

```
# ln smb.conf /etc/samba/smb.conf
```

On the other hand, a soft link serves as a redirect; when you open up a file created with a soft link, you're directed to the original file. If you delete the original file, the file is lost. While the soft link is still there, it has nowhere to go. The following command is an example of how you can create a soft link:

```
# ln -s smb.conf /etc/samba/smb.conf
```

File Filters

Linux is rich in commands that can help you filter the contents of a file. There are simple commands to help you search, check, or sort the contents of a file. And there are special files that contain others; these container files are known colloquially as "tarballs," which is an alternative to the Red Hat Package Manager.

on the *job*

Tarballs are a common way to distribute Linux packages. They are normally distributed in a compressed format, with a .tar.gz or .tgz file extension, consolidated as a package in a single file. In this respect, they are similar to Microsoft-style compressed zip files.

sort

You can sort the contents of a file in a number of ways. By default, the **sort** command sorts the contents in alphabetical order depending on the first letter in each line. For example, the **sort /etc/passwd** command would sort all users (including those associated with specific services and such) by username.

grep and egrep

The **grep** command uses a search term to look through a file. It returns the full line that contains the search term. For example, **grep 'Michael Jang' /etc/passwd** looks for the name of this author in the /etc/passwd file.

The **egrep** command is more forgiving; it allows you to use some unusual characters in your search, including +, ?, |, (, and). While it's possible to set up **grep** to search for these characters with the help of the backslash, the command can be awkward.

on the Job

*The locate **command is essentially a specialized version of the** grep **command, which uses the** slocate **command-based database of files on your Linux computer.***

wc

The **wc** command, short for word count, can return the number of lines, words, and characters in a file. The **wc** options are straightforward; for example, **wc -w** *filename* returns the number of words in that file.

sed

The **sed** command, short for stream editor, allows you to search for and change specified words or even text streams in a file. For example, the following command changes the first instance of the word "Windows" with "Linux" in each line of the file opsys, and writes the result to the file newopsys:

```
# sed 's/Windows/Linux' opsys > newopsys
```

However, this may not be enough. If there's more than one instance of "Windows" in a line in the opsys file, it does not change the second instance of that word. But you can fix this by adding a "global" suffix:

```
# sed 's/Windows/Linux/g' opsys > newopsys
```

awk

The **awk** command, named for its developers (Aho, Weinberger, and Kerrigan), is more of a database management command. It can identify lines with a key word, and read out the text from a specified column in that line. A common example is with the /etc/ passwd file. For example, the following command will read out the username of every user with a "Mike" in the comment column:

```
# awk '/Mike/ {print $1}' /etc/passwd
```

Administrative Commands

You'll work with a number of administrative commands in this book. But every budding Linux administrator should be familiar with at least two basic administrative commands: **ps** and **who**.

ps

It's important to know what's running on your Linux computer. The **ps** command has a number of critical switches. When trying to diagnose a problem, it's common to get the fullest possible list of running processes, then look for a specific program. For example, if the Mozilla Web browser were to suddenly crash, you'd want to kill any associated processes. The **ps aux | grep mozilla** command could then help you identify the process(es) that you need to kill.

who and w

If you want to know what users are currently logged into your system, use the **who** command or the **w** command. This can help you identify the usernames of those who are logged in, their terminal connections, their times of login, and the processes that they are running.

If you suspect that a username has been compromised, use the w command to check currently logged-on users. Look at the terminal. If the user is in the office but the terminal indicates a remote dial-in connection, be suspicious. The w command can also identify the current process being run by that user.

Wildcards

Sometimes you may not know the exact name of the file or the exact search term. That is when a wildcard is handy. The basic wildcards are shown in Table 1-4.

Wildcards are sometimes known in the Linux world as globbing.

TABLE 1-4	Wildcard	Description
Wildcards in the Shell	*	Any number of alphanumeric characters (or no characters at all). For example, the **ls ab*** command would return the following filenames, assuming they exist in the current directory: ab, abc, abcd.
	?	One single alphanumeric character: For example, the **ls ab?** command would return the following filenames, assuming they exist in the current directory: abc, abd, abe.
	[]	A range of options. For example, the **ls ab[123]** command would return the following filenames, assuming they exist in the current directory: ab1, ab2, ab3. Alternatively, the **ls ab[X-Z]** command would return the following filenames, assuming they exist in the current directory: abX, abY, abZ.

CERTIFICATION OBJECTIVE 1.04

Printing

As of this writing, printers are not always connected or configured during the installation of Red Hat Enterprise Linux. You may have to install printers yourself. The default Red Hat Enterprise Linux 3 print daemon is CUPS, the Common Unix Printing System.

There are two basic ways to configure a printer: first, you can edit the configuration files in the /etc/cups directory with a text editor, which can be a difficult process. These files are long, and the language is somewhat obscure, at least on the surface.

Though its support of the Internet Printing Protocol (IPP), CUPS is more suited toward managing printers on a network. CUPS also includes a fairly reliable front-end configuration tool that you can call up in a browser, using TCP/IP port 631.

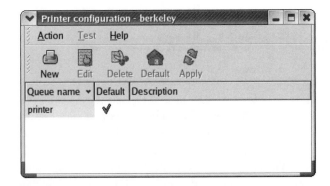

FIGURE 1-4

The Red
Hat Printer
Configuration tool

The other method in RHEL 3 is using the Red Hat Printer Configuration tool, which I describe in Chapter 8.

Adding Printers

The easy way to add a printer is with the Red Hat Printer Configuration tool, which is also known by the command used to start it from a terminal, **redhat-config-printer**. I recommend that you learn to use this GUI tool. Unless you're a CUPS expert, it's a faster way to configure printers on the RHCT or RHCE exams. I show you how to use this utility in Chapter 8.

It's fairly easy to configure printers with this tool; just click New as shown in Figure 1-4 (the computer name is berkeley) and follow the prompts.

Print Commands

Three basic commands are associated with printing in Linux, as described in Table 1-5.

TABLE 1-5

Linux Print
Commands

Command	Description
lpr	The basic print command. **lpr** *filename* prints that file.
lpq	Query the print queue for status. **lpr -l** lists print job numbers.
lprm	Remove a specific job, usually specified by job number, from the printer queue.

CERTIFICATION OBJECTIVE 1.05

Shells

A *shell* is a user interface. The Linux command shell is the prompt that allows you to interact with your computer with various system commands. With the right file permissions, you can set up commands in scripts to run when you want, even in the middle of the night. Linux shells can process commands in various sequences, depending on how you manage the input and output of each command. The way commands are interpreted is in part determined by variables and parameters associated with each shell. Some of these variables make up the environment that is carried over even if you change from one shell to another.

The default shell in Linux is bash, also known as the Bourne Again Shell. A number of other shells are available that are popular with many users. As long as you have installed the appropriate RPMs, users can start any of these shells. As desired, you can change the default shell for individual users in the /etc/passwd file.

Basic Shell Programming

"Real" Linux administrators program their own scripts. They create scripts because they don't want to sit at their computers all of the time. Scripts can allow Linux to automatically back up directories when nobody is in the office. Scripts can help Linux process databases when few people are using the system.

If you're not a programmer, don't worry—this is not as difficult as it sounds. For example, utilities related to the **crontab** command automate the creation of a number of different scripts. The cron system is discussed in more detail in Chapter 5.

If you're at all familiar with shell commands and programming expressions, you can find some examples of Red Hat Enterprise Linux shell programs in the /etc/cron.daily directory.

Script Execution and Permissions

Any Linux file can be set up as an executable file. Then if the file includes a series of commands that can be interpreted by the shell, the commands in that file are executed. If you want Linux to run a script that you've created, you need to assign executable permissions. For additional information on executable files, read the information under the "Basic Security" objective later in this chapter.

Variables and Parameters

Variables can change. Parameters are set. The bash shell includes a number of standard environment variables. Their default values are shown in the output to the **env** command. One critical variable is the value of PATH, which you can check at the command line with the **echo $PATH** command. The directories listed in PATH are automatically searched when you try to run a command. For example, if you want to run the **fdisk** command from the /sbin directory, you could do it with the following command:

```
$ /sbin/fdisk
```

However, if the /sbin directory were in your PATH, you don't need the leading /sbin to call out the command; the following would work:

```
$ fdisk
```

You can easily change the PATH variable. For example, if you want to add the /sbin directory to your PATH, just run the following commands:

```
# PATH=$PATH:/sbin
# export PATH
```

The /sbin directory is in the default PATH for the root user. The most common parameters are the settings associated with Linux configuration files, which are mostly located in the /etc directory. For example, the /etc/resolv.conf file uses the nameserver parameter to represent the DNS servers for your network. This is normally set to the IP address for that DNS server.

EXERCISE 1-3

Checking the PATH

In this exercise, you'll examine the path for a regular and the root user.

1. Log into the Linux command line interface as a regular user. If you're in the GUI, you can get to a command line login with the CTRL-ALT-F2 command. From the command prompt, run the following command and note the result:

```
$ echo $PATH
```

2. From the regular user command line interface, log in as the superuser. You'll need the root user's password.

```
$ su
Password:
#
```

3. Run the following command again and note the result. Compare it to the result as a regular user. Is there a difference? By default there is no difference on regular Red Hat Linux. There is a slight difference when you repeat this process on Red Hat Enterprise Linux.

```
# echo $PATH
```

4. Log out of Linux. If you followed steps 1, 2, and 3, you'll need to type the **exit** command twice to log out.

5. Now log into Linux as the root user. At the command prompt, run the following command again and note the result:

```
# echo $PATH
```

6. Observe the difference. You'll see more directories in the PATH for the root user. Now you can see why many Linux gurus who are doing heavy-duty administrative work log in as the root user. And that is why I also recommend that you log in as the root user during the RHCE or RHCT exams.

Inherited Environment

It's easy to move from shell to shell. While the default Linux shell is bash, many experienced Unix users prefer the Korn shell. Once set, with the **set** command, environment variables stay the same from shell to shell. In contrast, shell variables such as **umask** may change when you move from shell to shell, or even from user to user. For example, **umask** is typically different for regular users and the root user.

Piping, Input/Output, Error, and Redirection

Linux uses three basic data streams. Data goes in, data comes out, and errors are sent in a different direction. These streams are known as standard input (stdin), standard output (stdout), and standard error (stderr). Normally, input comes from the keyboard and goes out to the screen, while errors are sent to a buffer. Error messages are also sent to the display (as text stream 2). In the following example, *filename* is stdin to the **cat** command:

```
# cat filename
```

When you run **cat** *filename*, the contents of that file are sent to the screen as standard output.

You can redirect each of these streams to or from a file. For example, if you have a program named database and a datafile with a lot of data, the contents of that datafile can be sent to the database program with a left redirection arrow (**<**). As shown here, datafile is taken as standard input:

```
# database < datafile
```

Standard input can come from the left side of a command as well. For example, if you need to scroll through the boot messages, you can combine the **dmesg** and **less** commands with a pipe:

```
# dmesg | less
```

The output from **dmesg** is redirected as standard input to **less**, which then allows you to scroll through that output as if it were a separate file.

Standard output is just as easy to redirect. For example, the following command uses the right redirection arrow (**>**)to send the standard output of the **ls** command to the file named filelist.

```
# ls > filelist
```

You can add standard output to the end of an existing file with a double redirection arrow with a command such as **ls >> filelist**.

If you believe that a particular program is generating errors, redirect the error stream from it with a command like the following:

```
# program 2> err-list
```

CERTIFICATION OBJECTIVE 1.06

Basic Security

The basic security of a Linux computer is based on file permissions. Default file permissions are set through the **umask** shell variable. SUID and SGID permissions can give all users access to specific files. Ownership is based on the default user and group IDs of the person who created a file. Managing permissions and ownership involves commands such as **chmod, chown,** and **chgrp.**

Users and groups own files. Users and groups have passwords. Security can be enhanced if you configure users and groups in the Shadow Password Suite.

File Permissions

Linux file permissions are straightforward. Take the following output from **ls -l /sbin/ fdisk**:

```
-rwxr-xr-x  1 root  root     80236 Sep  1  18:26    /sbin/fdisk
```

The permissions are shown on the left-hand side of the listing. Ten characters are shown. The first character determines whether it's a regular or a special file. The remaining nine characters are grouped in threes, applicable to the file owner (user), the group owner, and everyone else on that Linux system. The letters are straightforward: r=read, w=write, x=execute. These characters are described in Table 1-6.

Key commands that can help you manage the permissions and ownership of a file are **chmod**, **chown**, and **chgrp**. The **chmod** command uses the numeric value of permissions associated with the owner, group, and others. In Linux, permissions are assigned the following numeric values: r=4, w=2, and x=1. For example, if you were crazy enough to give read, write, and execute permissions on fdisk to all users, you would run the **chmod 777 /sbin/fdisk** command. The **chown** and **chgrp** commands adjust the user and group owners associated with the cited file.

Users, Groups, and umask

Linux, like Unix, is configured with users and groups. Everyone who uses Linux is set up with a username, even if it's just "guest." Take a look at /etc/passwd. One version of this file is shown in Figure 1-5.

As you can see, all kinds of usernames are listed in the /etc/passwd file. Even a number of Linux services such as mail, news, nfs, and apache have their own usernames. In any case, the /etc/passwd file follows a specific format, described in more detail in Chapter 4. For now, note that the only users shown in this file are mj and tb, their user IDs (UID) and group IDs (GID) are 500 and 501, and their home directories match their usernames. The next user gets UID and GID 502, and so on.

TABLE 1-6	Position	Description
Description of File Permissions	1	Type of file; - = regular file, d=directory, b=device, l=linked file
	234	Permissions granted to the owner of the file
	567	Permissions granted to the group owner of the file
	890	Permissions granted to all other users on the Linux system

FIGURE 1-5

/etc/passwd

```
rpcuser:x:29:29:RPC Service User:/var/lib/nfs:/sbin/nologin
nfsnobody:x:65534:65534:Anonymous NFS User:/var/lib/nfs:/sbin/nologin
mailnull:x:47:47::/var/spool/mqueue:/sbin/nologin
smmsp:x:51:51::/var/spool/mqueue:/sbin/nologin
pcap:x:77:77::/var/arpwatch:/sbin/nologin
xfs:x:43:43:X Font Server:/etc/X11/fs:/sbin/nologin
ntp:x:38:38::/etc/ntp:/sbin/nologin
gdm:x:42:42::/var/gdm:/sbin/nologin
desktop:x:80:80:desktop:/var/lib/menu/kde:/sbin/nologin
apache:x:48:48:Apache:/var/www:/sbin/nologin
webalizer:x:67:67:Webalizer:/var/www/usage:/sbin/nologin
squid:x:23:23::/var/spool/squid:/sbin/nologin
postfix:x:89:89::/var/spool/postfix:/sbin/nologin
named:x:25:25:Named:/var/named:/sbin/nologin
netdump:x:34:34:Network Crash Dump user:/var/crash:/bin/bash
mj:x:500:500:Michael Jang:/home/mj:/bin/bash
tb:x:501:501:Tony Blair:/home/tb:/bin/bash
~
~
~
~
~
~
```

Users can change their own passwords with the **passwd** command. The root user can change the password of any user. For example, the **passwd mj** command allows the root user to change user mj's password.

umask

The way **umask** works in Red Hat Enterprise Linux may surprise you, especially if you're coming from a different Unix style environment. You cannot configure **umask** to automatically allow you to create new files with executable permissions. This is a recent change that promotes security; if fewer files have executable permissions, fewer files are available for a cracker to use to run programs to break through your system.

In the world of Linux, a hacker is a good person who simply wants to create better software. A cracker is someone who wants to break into your system for malicious purposes.

Every time you create a new file, the default permissions are based on the value of **umask**. In the past, the value of **umask** cancelled out the value of numeric permissions on a file. For example, if the value of **umask** is 000, the default permissions for any file created by that user are 777 – 000 = 777, which corresponds to read, write, and execute permissions for all users.

When you type the **umask** command, you get a four-number output such as 0245. As of this writing, the first number in the **umask** output is always 0 and is not used.

In the future, this first number may be usable to allow for new files that automatically include the SUID or SGID bits.

Also, no matter what the value of **umask**, new files in Red Hat Enterprise Linux can no longer be automatically created with executable permissions. In other words, a **umask** of 0454 leads to identical permissions on new files as a **umask** of 0545. You need to use commands such as **chmod** to specifically set executable permissions on a file.

SUID and SGID

Permissions can be a risky business. But you need to give all users access to some programs. To set full read, write, and execute permissions for all users on a Linux system can be dangerous. One alternative is setting the SUID and the SGID permission bits for a file. When active, these bits allow you to configure appropriate permissions on the subject file. For example, one common practice is to set the SUID bit for the KPPP Internet Connection Utility so all users can use it to dial in to the Internet. You can set the SUID bit on this utility with the following command:

```
# chmod u+s /usr/sbin/kppp
```

SGID permissions can be useful when you're setting up a special group of users who need to share files on a specific task or project. This process is discussed in more detail in Chapter 11.

Shadow Passwords

When you look at the default /etc/passwd file, you should see an "x" in the second column. Older versions of Linux had an encrypted version of user passwords in this column. As /etc/passwd is accessible to all users, a cracker could copy this file and decrypt everyone's password on a Linux computer. This problem led to the development of the Shadow Password Suite.

Shadow Password Suite

Historically, all that was needed to manage Linux users and groups was the information included in the /etc/passwd and /etc/group files. These files included passwords and are by default readable by all users.

The Shadow Password Suite was created to provide an additional layer of protection. It is used to encrypt user and group passwords in shadow files (/etc/shadow and /etc/gshadow) that are readable only by users with root privileges.

The Shadow Password Suite is now enabled by default in Red Hat Enterprise Linux. Standard commands for creating new users and groups automatically set up encrypted passwords in the Shadow Password Suite files. These commands are described in more detail in Chapter 4.

But if you're restoring a system, you may not have access to these special commands. The old way of creating new users and groups is by editing the /etc/passwd and /etc/group files directly. Four commands allow you to convert passwords to and from the /etc/shadow and /etc/gshadow files:

- **pwconv**   Converts passwords from /etc/passwd. This command works even if some of the passwords are already encrypted in /etc/shadow.

- **pwunconv**   Opposite of **pwconv**.

- **grpconv**   Converts passwords from /etc/group. This command works even if some of the passwords are already encrypted in /etc/gshadow.

- **grpunconv**   Opposite of **grpconv**.

CERTIFICATION OBJECTIVE 1.07

System Administration

Most system administration tasks require root or superuser privileges. You should already be familiar with a number of basic Linux system administration commands and files. Standard user files are stored in /etc/skel. Daemons are processes that run in the background and run various Linux services. cron is a special daemon that can run scripts when you want. It's especially useful for setting up backup jobs in the middle of the night. Logging is a key part of monitoring Linux and any services that you choose to run.

Superuser

Generally in Linux, a system administrator does everything possible as a normal user. It's a good practice to use superuser privileges only when absolutely necessary. But one time where it's appropriate is during the Red Hat exams. Good administrators will return to being normal users when they're done with their tasks. Mistakes as the root user can disable your Linux system.

There are two basic ways to make this work:

- **su** The superuser command, **su**, prompts you for the root password before logging you in with root privileges. A variation, **su -c**, sets up root privileges for one specific command. Many Red Hat GUI utilities are set up to prompt for the root password before they can be started. One more variation, **su - root**, sets up root privileges with the root user PATH. (Remember to have a space on both sides of the dash in this command.)

- **sudo** The **sudo** command allows users listed in /etc/sudoers to run administrative commands. You can configure /etc/sudoers to set limits on the root privileges given to a specific user.

However, Red Hat Enterprise Linux provides some features that make working as root somewhat safer. For example, logins using the **ftp** and **telnet** commands to remote computers are disabled by default.

e x a m

ⓦ a t c h   *On the RHCE and RHCT exams, time is of the essence. In general, I recommend that you don't bother logging in as a regular user during these exams. It's faster to log in as the root user. You don't* *have to remember to invoke the su or sudo commands, and you gain the advantages of a more liberal PATH variable. While you just save a few seconds with each command, that time can add up.*

/etc/skel

Basic configuration files for individual users are available in the /etc/skel directory. This directory includes a number of hidden files. For a full list, run the **ls -a /etc/skel** command. If you want all future users to get specific files in their home directories, include them here.

The next time you create a regular user, check that person's home directory. For example, if you just created a user named elizabeth, run the **ls -a /home/elizabeth** command. Compare the results to the previous command on the /etc/skel directory.

Daemons

A *daemon* is a process that runs in the background. It is resident in your computer's RAM and watches for signals before it goes into action. For example, a network daemon such as httpd, the Linux Web server known as Apache, waits for a request from a browser before it actually serves a Web page.

Daemons are often configured to start automatically when you start Linux. This process is documented at various runlevels in the /etc/rc.d directory. Alternatively, you can use a tool such as ntsysv to identify and manage the daemons that are started at various Linux runlevels. This is discussed in more detail in Chapter 4.

Network Service Daemons

Networks don't always work. Sometimes you need to restart a network daemon to implement a configuration change. Red Hat Enterprise Linux provides an easy way to control network service daemons through the scripts in /etc/rc.d/init.d. This directory includes scripts that can control installed Linux network services (and more) for everything from the Network File System (NFS) to sendmail. The actual daemon itself is usually located in the /sbin or /usr/sbin directory.

With these scripts, it's easy to start, stop, status, reload, or restart a network daemon. This is useful to implement or test changes that you make to a specific configuration file. For example, if you make a change to the Apache Web server configuration file in /etc/httpd/conf/httpd.conf, you can implement the change right away with the **/etc/rc.d/init.d/httpd reload** command. Other switches to these scripts allow you to **stop**, **start**, or **status** these services. Network service management is discussed in more detail in Chapter 9.

e**x**a m
watch   *In Red Hat Enterprise*   *is with the service **command. For example,** Linux, a simpler way to reload or restart*   *to restart the httpd service, you could run* a service in the /etc/rc.d/init.d directory*   *the service httpd restart **command.***

cron

Perhaps the most important daemon is cron, which can be used to execute a command or a series of commands in a script, on a schedule. Red Hat Enterprise Linux already includes a series of scripts that are executed by cron on committed schedules in the /etc/cron.hourly, /etc/cron.daily, /etc/cron.weekly, and /etc/cron.monthly directories.

System crontab

The easiest way to set up your own cron jobs is through the crontab file, which can be managed through the **crontab** command. Users can edit their own crontab files with the **crontab -e** command; the root user can configure the crontab for a specific user with the **crontab -u** *username* **-e** command.

The general format for a crontab file can be found in the /etc/crontab script, which is used to run the scripts in the aforementioned schedule-related directories. A typical crontab entry from that file is

```
42 4 1 * * root run-parts /etc/cron.monthly
```

Five schedule fields appear on the left-hand side of each crontab entry: minute, hour, day of month, month, and day of week. The preceding line is executed at 4:42 A.M. on the first of every month, no matter what day of the week it is.

Backup and Restore

Hard drives include spinning disks and magnetic media. These are mechanical parts. By definition, all mechanical hard drives will eventually fail. If you're administering a Linux system with multiple users, you do not want to have to hear the complaints of people who know that their data is more important than yours, because you'll know that they are right. Configuring backups involves a number of strategic choices that go beyond Linux.

Using full backups, you can back up the entire drive; using incremental backups, you back up just the data that has changed since the last backup. A wide variety of media are available for backups, including tape drives, writable CD/DVDs, and other hard drives in various RAID configurations. You can back up data locally or over a network. Linux includes a number of quality tools for backups.

It's common to back up through a network to a dedicated backup server. Since you're transferring at least substantial portions of a hard drive during a backup, backups can degrade network performance for other users. So it is best to perform backups when few people are using your Linux system, which in most cases is during the middle of the night. For this reason, it's a common practice to automate backups using the previously discussed cron daemon.

Tape Backups

Using magnetic tape in Linux depends on the ftape system, using "tarballs" to group directories into single compressed backup files. Once it is mounted, it's easy to test a tape drive; just use the **mt -f /dev/*tapedevice*** command to status, rewind, or eject the tape. If it's a SCSI tape drive, use the **st** command instead.

Unlike when using regular media, you don't mount a tape; you can actually use switches with the **tar** command to write or restore directly from the tape device. Just cite the appropriate /dev/*tapedevice* in the command. Just make sure you can also restore from the backup you've made.

CD Backups

Backups to CDs are made in a similar fashion, using "iso" files instead of tarballs. The **mkisofs -J -r -T -o /tmp/backhome.iso /home** command can consolidate regular users' home directories from /home onto a single file. You can then record this file onto the CD with a command such as:

```
# cdrecord -v speed=2 dev=0,0,0 /tmp/backhome.iso
```

You can then store the CD and later restore the files from it just by mounting it as you would any regular CD.

Hard Drive (RAID) Backups

Hard drive–based backups are based on the system known as the Redundant Array of Independent Disks, or RAID, which is covered in more detail in Chapter 5. There are several versions of RAID that can automatically restore data once you've replaced a broken hard disk.

tar

The **tar** command was originally developed for archiving data to tape drives. However, it's commonly used today for collecting a series of files, especially from a directory. For example, the following command backs up the information from the /home directory in the home.tar.gz file:

```
# tar czvf home.tar.gz /home
```

This is one of the few commands that does not require a dash in front of the switch. This particular command creates (**c**) an archive, compresses (**z**) it, in verbose (**v**) mode, with the filename (**f**) that follows. Alternatively, you can extract (**x**) from that file with the following command:

```
# tar xzvf home.tar.gz /home
```

gzip and bzip2

The **gzip** and **bzip2** commands are similar—they compress and decompress files, using different algorithms. If you wanted to compress a big picture file, you could do so with one of the following commands:

```
# gzip big.jpg
# bzip2 big.jpg
```

It adds a .gz or a .bz2 extension. You can uncompress from these files with the **-d** switch:

```
# gzip -d big.jpg.gz
# bzip2 -d big.jpg.bz2
```

System Log File Management

Log files are controlled by the syslogd daemon and organized in the /etc/syslog.conf file. It is important to use log files to understand the behavior of your Linux system; deviations may be a sign of problems with recently installed service or a security breach. Basic log files are organized in the /var/log directory. For more information on system logs, see Chapter 10.

CERTIFICATION OBJECTIVE 1.08

Basic TCP/IP Networking

TCP/IP is a series of protocols organized in layers, known as a protocol suite. It was developed for Unix and eventually adopted as the standard for communication on the Internet. With IP addresses, it can help you organize your network. Then, there are a number of TCP/IP tools and configurations that can help you manage your network.

As with the previous sections in this chapter, the statements here are oversimplifications. So if you find this section overwhelming, read the references cited at the beginning of the chapter. Linux is built for networking, and there is no practical way to pass either the RHCT or the RHCE exams unless you understand networking in some detail.

IP Numbers and Classes

Every computer that communicates on a network needs its own IP address. Some addresses are assigned permanently to a particular computer; these are known as *static* addresses. Others are leased from a DHCP server for a limited amount of time; these are also known as *dynamic* IP addresses.

Two standards for IP addresses are in use today, IP version 4 (IPv4) and IP version 6 (IPv6). IPv4 addresses have 32 bits and are set up in octets in dotted decimal notation. The range of possible IPv4 addresses is between 0.0.0.0 to 255.255.255.255. While over four billion IP addresses are available, that is not nearly enough for the current Internet.

IPv6 addresses have 128 bits and are set up in hexadecimal notation. An IPv6 address is normally organized in eight groups of four hexadecimal numbers each, and it may look like 4abe:03e2:c132:69fa:0000:0000:c0b8:2148. More than 340,000,000,000,000,000,000,000,000,000,000,000,000 IPv6 addresses are available.

To ease the transition, specific IPv6 addresses have been assigned for every one of the four billion IPv4 addresses. There are still over 3.4×10^{38} addresses left over. While actual routing on the Internet now commonly uses IPv6, network configuration in Linux is still normally based on IPv4 addresses.

IPv4 addresses are organized into five different classes, as shown in Table 1-7. The academics among you may note that this is different from the official addresses in each IPv4 class as specified in RFC 1518 from the Internet Engineering Task Force (www.ietf.org). The *assignable* address range includes those IP addresses that can be assigned to a specific computer on a network.

In addition, there are a number of private IP addresses that are not to be assigned to any computer that is directly connected to the Internet. They are associated with network addresses 10.0.0.0, 172.168.0.0, and 192.168.0.0 through 192.168.255.0.

TABLE 1-7	Class	Assignable Address Range	Note
IP Address Classes	A	1.1.1.1–126.255.255.254	Allows networks of up to 16 million computers
	B	128.0.0.1–191.255.255.254	Allows networks of up to 65,000 computers
	C	192.0.0.1–223.255.255.254	Allows networks of up to 254 computers
	D	224.0.0.1–239.255.255.254	Reserved for multicasts
	E	240.0.0.1–255.255.255.254	Reserved for experimental use

IP Addresses Define a Network

Three key IP addresses define a network: the network address, the broadcast address, and the subnet mask. The network address is always the first IP address in a range; the broadcast address is always the last address in the same range. The subnet mask helps your computer define the difference between the two addresses. You can assign IP addresses between the network and broadcast addresses (not including these addresses) to any computer on the network.

As an example, let's define the range of addresses for a private network. Start with the private network address 192.168.122.0. Use the standard subnet mask for a class C network, 255.255.255.0. Based on these two addresses, the broadcast address is 192.168.122.255, and the range of IP addresses that you can assign on that particular network is 192.168.122.1 through 192.168.122.254.

If this is confusing to you in any way, please refer to the IP Sub-Networking Mini-HOWTO of the Linux Documentation Project at www.tldp.org.

Tools and Commands

You have a substantial number of tools available to manage the TCP/IP protocol suite on your Linux computer. Three of the more important commands are **ping**, **ifconfig**, and **netstat**.

ping

The **ping** command allows you to test connectivity—locally, within your network, and on the Internet. For the purpose of this section, assume your IP address is 192.168.122.43, and the gateway address on your network is 192.168.122.99. If you're having problems connecting to a network, you should use the **ping** command in the following order. The first step is to test the integrity of TCP/IP on your computer:

```
# ping 127.0.0.1
```

Normally, **ping** works continuously on Linux; you'll need to press CTRL-C to stop this command. If you need to see if you're properly connected to your LAN, you should **ping** your own IP address:

```
# ping 192.168.122.43
```

If that works, **ping** the address of another computer on your network. Then start tracing the route to the Internet. **ping** the address for your gateway, in this case, 192.168.122.99.

If possible, **ping** the address of your network's connection to the Internet. And finally, **ping** the address of a computer that you know is *active* on the Internet.

You can substitute host names such as www.google.com for an IP address. If the host name doesn't work, there's a problem with the database of host names and IP addresses, more commonly known as a DNS, BIND, or nameserver.

ifconfig

The **ifconfig** command can help you check and configure network adapters. Run the **ifconfig** command by itself to see the detected adapters on your computer. You can also use **ifconfig** to assign IP address or hardware port information as well. For example, if you want to assign IRQ 10 to the second Ethernet adapter, run the following command:

```
# ifconfig eth1 irq 10
```

For more information on **ifconfig**, refer to Chapter 4.

netstat

The **netstat** command is versatile; it can help you see the channels available for network connections, interface statistics, and more. One important version of this command, **netstat -r**, displays routing tables that can tell you if your computer knows where to send a message. More information on this command is available in Chapter 4.

Name Resolution

When I used a static IP address on my high-speed Internet connection, I could sometimes memorize those numbers. But how can anyone memorize the IP addresses of every Web site you need on the Internet? Using four configuration files, Linux can help you translate computer host names to IP addresses.

/etc/hosts

The first database of host names and IP addresses was set up in a static text file, /etc/hosts. When there were just a few nodes on the network that eventually turned into the Internet, it was possible to maintain identical /etc/hosts files on each computer. Here's a typical line in /etc/hosts, which lists the IP address, fully qualified domain name, and alias for one computer connection:

```
192.168.132.32    linux1.mommabears.com   laptop
```

/etc/resolv.conf

There are millions of hosts on the Internet. Even if it were possible to collect all domain names and IP addresses into a /etc/hosts file, the file would overwhelm every computer. And it would overwhelm every network administrator who would have to make sure that all the /etc/hosts files on the Internet match—and get updated every time a new Web site appears. That's why the Domain Name System (DNS) was developed, based on the Berkeley Internet Name Domain (BIND). In /etc/resolv.conf, the IP address of each DNS server is listed with a simple line similar to:

```
nameserver 192.168.0.1
```

/etc/host.conf

Many networks configure an /etc/hosts file for the local network and a DNS server for other networks and/or the Internet. When your computer looks for an IP address, this file determines whether it searches through /etc/hosts or DNS first. This is usually a one-line file:

```
order hosts,bind
```

A computer with this line looks through /etc/hosts first. If it can't find the computer name that you want in that file, it next looks to the DNS server (bind) for the computer name.

/etc/nsswitch.conf

This file relates to the configuration on a network of Linux- and Unix-type computers, which are configured to communicate using the Network File System (NFS). When it is used in concert with the Network Information System (NIS), networks can maintain a single database of usernames and passwords for all NFS-enabled computers on that network.

CERTIFICATION OBJECTIVE 1.09

Standard Network Services

Linux is built for networking. The code associated with many standard networking services is integrated into the Linux kernel. A basic understanding of the functionality of standard Linux networking services is essential. Many themes throughout this book assume that you already understand the purpose of network communication protocols, mail services, host name and IP address management, Web services, and more.

In Red Hat Enterprise Linux, network services are often installed separately. Some include different packages for clients and servers. Some network services are activated through /etc/xinetd.conf, which reads activation files in the /etc/xinetd.d directory. Others are activated directly with scripts in the /etc/rc.d/init.d directory. I briefly examine some key RHEL network services in the following sections.

Network File System

The first network system on Unix and Linux computers is the Network File System (NFS). Ideally, this leads to a seamless Linux interface; for example, you can set up one /home directory for all users on your network on one server. Remember, you need NFS on both server and client computers on your network.

First, make sure NFS support is part of the kernel, as documented in /proc/filesystems. If it isn't there, you may need to activate the nfs and related modules (nfsd, lockd, sunprc) in the kernel. Inspect installed modules with the following command:

```
# lsmod | more
```

Make a list of the modules that aren't included in the list. Run a **modprobe** command (for example, **modprobe nfs**) on any missing modules. With a standard Red Hat Enterprise Linux installation, this should add the modules to the lsmod list, and then add them to the kernel, as listed in /proc/filesystems.

Once you've shared an NFS directory, you can then activate the NFS daemon with the **service nfs start** command. I illustrate an example where you can share the Red Hat Enterprise Linux installation files through NFS in Chapter 2.

Once NFS is configured, you can find shared directories on the server's /etc/exports file, and then mount them with a command similar to the following:

```
# mount -t nfs nfsserver:/home /mhome
```

For more information on NFS, see Chapter 9.

sendmail

There are some who suggest that sendmail is the biggest test for Linux system administrators. The sendmail configuration files, sendmail.cf and submit.cf, are complex. But it should not be intimidating. With the help of the corresponding .mc files, it's easier to define the features you want, the protocols you need, and the way mail is sent and received on your network.

More information on sendmail is available in Chapter 7.

POP and IMAP

The Post Office Protocol (POP) and the Internet Mail Access Protocol (IMAP) are each a set of rules for delivering e-mail from a server such as sendmail to an e-mail client such as Netscape, elm, or pine. While POP3 is the current standard for e-mail that is sent to clients, IMAP4 is more flexible for users such as those who access their mail using different computers. POP3 and IMAP4 configuration is addressed in Chapter 7.

File Transfer Protocol (FTP)

Perhaps the most basic file sharing protocol still in common use is the File Transfer Protocol (FTP). It is set up specifically for file transfers; you might already know that file transfers using FTP are generally faster than with any other protocol.

As with NFS and Samba, you need a server and a client. FTP servers can be anonymous, which means they accept connections from anyone, or they can be configured to require a specific username and password. Generally, Linux FTP servers share files from the /var/ftp directory. Red Hat Enterprise Linux now comes with the Very Secure FTP daemon (vsFTPd) as the only FTP server.

The original FTP client works from the command line. Most Linux navigational commands work for FTP; just remember that the **get** and **put** commands download and upload specific files. FTP is covered in more detail in Chapter 7.

Domain Name Service (DNS)

If there were a practical way to list all of the domain names and IP addresses of every Web site on the Internet in a single file, we would not need the Domain Name Service (DNS). The DNS system allows us to set up different parts of this database on different servers around the world. If a DNS server does not have the answer, you can configure it to ask other DNS servers for help. DNS is covered in more detail in Chapter 9.

Dynamic Host Configuration Protocol (DHCP)

IP version 4 addresses are scarce. The Dynamic Host Configuration Protocol (DHCP) was designed to help ration IP addresses. A DHCP server leases a specific IP address to a computer network card for a limited, but renewable, amount of time. DHCP servers can lease IP addresses on different LANs using the BOOTP protocol. More information on setting up DHCP clients and servers is available in Chapter 9.

Samba

The network system originally developed for networks with Microsoft and IBM computers is based on the Server Message Block (SMB) format. SMB, also known as Samba, is the basis for Microsoft Windows Workgroup and Domain-based network communication. When you install Samba on a Linux computer, you can make it part of one of these Microsoft-style networks. It can share files just like any other member of a workgroup network. It can act as a server. Current versions of Samba can even be configured as a Windows NT–style Primary Domain Controller or a member server on a Windows 2000/XP–based network.

Separate packages are available to set up your Linux computer as a Samba client and as a Samba server. Once shares are configured in /etc/samba/smb.conf, other Samba-enabled Linux clients can mount these directories with a command similar to the following:

```
# mount -t smbfs -o username=user //servername/sharename /mountpoint
```

You can also set up the **smbmount** command for this purpose. Samba and the associated configuration tools are discussed extensively in Chapter 8.

Web Services

Apache is by far the most popular Web server in use on the Internet. It's a standard part of the Red Hat Enterprise Linux server installation. The main configuration file is /etc/httpd/conf/httpd.conf. Configuration is based on an extensive array of modules in the /etc/httpd directory. Basic HTML files, icons, and CGI applets are installed in the /var/www directory. The main Apache log files are part of the /var/logs/httpd directory. Daily log files for the largest Web sites can grow into the GB range. Apache is covered in more detail in Chapter 7.

A substantial number of other Web servers are available for Red Hat Enterprise Linux, such as Sun's iPlanet and Zeus's Web server.

Network Information Service (NIS)

The Network Information Service was formerly known as the "yellow pages," as it is a centralized database of usernames and passwords on a network with Linux and other Unix-style computers. NIS can be configured as a centralized database for a number of other configuration files in the /etc directory. Anything that can standardize the configuration of different computers on a network helps the system administrator. For more information on NIS, see Chapter 10.

CERTIFICATION OBJECTIVE 1.10

Basic Network Security

I divide network security in Linux into four basic categories. Security by computer can help you manage what computers can send messages into and out of your network. Security by port can help you manage the services that others can use to break into your network. Security by address translation can help you hide the computers inside your network. And finally, security by rule can help you manage the type of data allowed into your network in excruciating detail. Red Hat Enterprise Linux includes two different tools to help you configure a firewall on your computer, lokkit and redhat-config-securitylevel (also known as the Red Hat Firewall Configuration tool). Security issues are discussed in more detail in Chapter 10.

Allowing and Denying

The /etc/hosts.allow and /etc/hosts.deny files can help you manage what computers are allowed into your network. You can specify computers by name, IP address, network, or domain name in each file. This can help you limit access to a trusted few computers such as those within your company, or it can protect you from computers that you know may pose a problem.

Port Security

TCP/IP has 65,536 ports, which work sort of like TV channels. If you leave all ports open, you're leaving a lot of options for a cracker who wants to break into your network. With a firewall, you can create a solid barrier and then open only the ports that you need.

Network Address Translation

Most LAN administrators set up Network Address Translation (NAT) as a matter of course on an IPv4 network. Since IPv4 addresses are scarce, it is typical to use private IP addresses inside a LAN, with a regular IP address only on the gateway computer that is directly connected to an outside network such as the Internet.

For example, when a computer inside a LAN wants access to a Web page, NAT sends the IP address of the gateway to the Internet. Nobody outside the LAN need know the real source of the Web page request.

iptables

There are two basic services for filtering information in and out of a network, based on the **ipchains** and **iptables** commands. Red Hat has recently implemented **iptables** as the firewall tool of choice in RHEL 3. Once you've configured a firewall and loaded it, the rules are stored in the /etc/sysconfig/iptables file.

The **iptables** command has three basic ways to look at a data packet: input, output, or forward. Within these and other parameters, you can set up your firewall with instructions to let the packet pass, let it drop, or direct it someplace else.

iptables is covered in more detail in Chapter 10.

CERTIFICATION OBJECTIVE 1.11

Basic Hardware Knowledge

While customized Red Hat distributions are available for such diverse platforms as the Alpha, Itanium, and S/390 CPUs, the RHCE and RHCT exams are focused on computers built to the Intel-based 32-bit architecture (or similar 32-bit CPUs such as those built by AMD and National Semiconductor/Cyrix).

The architecture of a personal computer defines the components that it uses as well as the way that they are connected. In other words, the Intel-based architecture describes much more than just the CPU. It includes standards for other hardware such as the hard drive, the network card, the keyboard, the graphics adapter, and more. All software is written for a specific computer architecture, such as the Intel-based 32-bit architecture.

Even when a manufacturer creates a device for the Intel platform, it may not work with Linux. Therefore, it's important to know the basic architecture of an Intel-based computer.

While it is important to know how Linux interacts with your hardware, the RHCE and RHCT exams are not hardware exams. As of this writing, *while the RH133 and RH300 courses do address hardware issues, there are no hardware components listed in the Red Hat Exam Prep guide.*

Intel Communications Channels

Three basic channels are used to communicate in an Intel architecture PC: interrupt request (IRQ) ports, input/output (I/O) addresses, and direct memory address (DMA) channels. An IRQ allows a component such as a keyboard or printer to request service from the CPU. An I/O address is a memory storage location for communication between the CPU and different parts of a computer. A DMA channel is used when a device such as a sound card has an independent processor and can bypass the CPU.

With the plug and play features built into RHEL 3, these channels are generally not a problem, but are included because they are on the prerequisite list for the RH300 course, as described in www.redhat.com/training/rhce/courses/rh300_prereq.html.

IRQ Settings

An *IRQ* is a signal that is sent by a peripheral device (such as a network card, graphics adapter, mouse, modem, or serial port) to the CPU to request processing time. Each device you attach to a computer may need its own IRQ port. Normally, each device needs a dedicated IRQ (except for USB and some PCI devices). The Intel architecture is currently limited to 16 IRQs (0–15), which is often not enough for modern PCs with network cards, modems, hard drives, sound cards, printers, and more.

If you run out of IRQs, some PCI devices can share IRQs. USB devices can share IRQs. This support is available in most PCs manufactured after the year 2000.

on the **Job** *If you're having a problem with your USB ports or PCI cards, check your BIOS first. Many BIOS menus include options that enable PCI sharing and support USB connections.*

Planning the IRQ Layout: Standard IRQs

IRQs are a precious commodity on a PC. IRQ conflicts are common when you're connecting a lot of devices. If your printer doesn't work after you've connected a second network card, it can help to know the standard IRQ for printers. You can then assign a different IRQ to that network card. If you don't have any free IRQs to assign to that network card, you may be able to sacrifice a component that uses a standard IRQ. For example, if you always connect to a server remotely, that server PC may not need a keyboard. If you can boot a computer with a CD-ROM, you may not need a floppy drive.

Some IRQs are essential to the operation of a PC and just can't be changed. These are reserved by the motherboard to control devices such as the hard disk controller and the real-time clock. Do not use these interrupts for other devices or there will be conflicts! Other IRQs are normally assigned to common devices such as a floppy disk and a printer. In Linux, you can check /proc/interrupts to see which interrupts are being used and which are free for new devices.

Input/Output Addresses

Every computer device requires an *input/output (I/O) address.* It's a place where data can wait in line for service from your CPU. I/O addresses are listed in hexadecimal notation, where the numbers are 0, 1, 2, 3, 4, 5, 6, 7, 8, 9, a, b, c, d, e, and f. Some typical I/O addresses include those for the basic serial ports, known in the Microsoft world as COM1, COM2, COM3, and COM4. These ports normally use the following I/O addresses: 03f8, 02f8, 03e8, and 02e8.

You can find a list of assigned I/O addresses in your /proc/ioports file.

Direct Memory Addresses

A *direct memory address (DMA)* is normally used to transfer information directly between devices, bypassing the CPU. Many components don't need a CPU. For example, many sound cards include their own processor. This allows your PC to set up a DMA channel between a hard drive and a sound card to process and play any music files that you may have stored.

While DMA channels bypass the CPU, devices that use DMA are still configured with IRQ ports. There are eight standard DMA channels (0–7); DMA 4 is reserved and cannot be used by any device.

You can find a list of assigned DMA addresses in your /proc/dma file.

RAM Requirements

Red Hat nominally requires that you install Red Hat Enterprise Linux on a computer with at least 256MB of RAM. While I've installed RHEL 3 on computers with less RAM, 256MB is the minimum that is required if you've purchased the appropriate version of RHEL 3 and want contracted tech support from Red Hat.

The maximum amount of memory your system will use is the sum of all of the memory requirements of every program that you will ever run at once. That's hard to compute. Therefore, you should buy as much memory as you can afford. Extra RAM is usually cost-effective when compared to the time you would spend trying to tune an underpowered system. Limitations are few; on Red Hat Enterprise Linux 3 Advanced Server, you can use up to 64GB of RAM.

If you're installing RHEL 3 on a computer with between 16GB and 64GB of RAM, you'll need to use the "hugemem" kernel, which I describe in a bit more detail in Chapter 5.

on the job *If you're setting up Linux as a server, RAM requirements increase with the number of users who may need to log in simultaneously. The same may be true if you're running a large number of programs or have memory-intensive data such as that required by a database.*

Hard Drive Options

Before your computer can load Linux, the BIOS has to recognize the active primary partition on the hard drive. This partition should include the Linux boot files. The BIOS can then set up and initialize that hard drive, and then load Linux boot files from that active primary partition. You should know the following about hard drives and Linux:

- The standard Intel architecture PC is configured to manage up to four IDE (Integrated Drive Electronics) hard drives.

- Depending on the SCSI (Small Computer Systems Interface) hardware that you have, you can attach up to 31 different SCSI hard drives.

- While you can use as many IDE or SCSI drives as your hardware can handle, you need to install the Linux boot files from the /boot directory on one of the first two hard drives. If Linux is installed on a later drive, you'll need a boot floppy.

- Although you can install Linux on USB (Universal Serial Bus) or IEEE 1394 (Institute of Electrical and Electronics Engineers standard 1394, also known as FireWire or iLink) hard drives, as of this writing, you can't load Linux boot files directly from these drives. However, it is possible to set up a boot floppy to start Linux from these drives.

CERTIFICATION OBJECTIVE 1.12

Hardware Compatibility

Now it's time to explore in detail the hardware that Red Hat Enterprise Linux can handle. While some manufacturers now include their own Linux hardware drivers, most Linux hardware support comes from third parties. Fortunately, there is a vast community of Linux users, many of whom produce drivers for Linux and distribute them freely on the Internet. If a certain piece of hardware is popular, you can be certain that Linux support for that piece of hardware will pop up somewhere on the Internet and will be incorporated into various Linux distributions, including Red Hat Enterprise Linux.

Be careful when purchasing a new computer to use with Linux. Though Linux has come a long way the last few years, and you should have little problem installing it on most modern PCs, you shouldn't assume Linux will run on *any* PC, especially if the PC in question is a state-of-the-art laptop computer. Laptops are often designed with proprietary configurations that work with Linux only after some reverse engineering.

Fortunately, there are a number of major manufacturers who support RHEL 3 out of the box for their workstations and servers. Check the Red Hat Hardware Compatibility List, as discussed in the section of the same name, for the latest information.

Other kinds of hardware, such as "winmodems" and "winprinters," are designed to use Microsoft Windows driver libraries. Integrated hardware (such as video chips that share system RAM) and parallel port devices can also be problematic. While Linux drivers exist for many of these devices, do your research.

Linux runs very well on lower-end computers. This is one of Linux's strong points over other operating systems, such as Microsoft's Windows XP. Linux runs fine on 64MB of RAM, although more is always better, especially if you want to run any graphical applications.

on the job *While it is important to know how to select and configure hardware components to get to a smoothly running Linux computer, the RHCE exam is not a hardware exam.*

Linux Hardware Documentation

There are many resources available to help you select the best hardware for Linux. Thousands of Linux gurus are available online in areas such as mailing lists and newsgroups. Perhaps the best places to look are the Linux Documentation Project (LDP) or the Red Hat Hardware Compatibility List. The LDP is a global effort to produce reliable documentation for all aspects of the Linux operating system, including hardware compatibility.

Linux Hardware HOWTO

The Linux Hardware HOWTO is a document listing most of the hardware components supported by Linux. It's updated irregularly with added hardware support, so it is a relatively up-to-date source of information. As of this writing, various LDP HOWTOs are supplied on the documentation CD-ROM in text format and in various languages, in the /HOWTOS directory. The official up-to-date list can be found at the LDP www.tldp.org.

The Red Hat Hardware Compatibility List

The Red Hat Hardware Compatibility List is different from the one you'll find in the Linux Hardware HOWTO. It specifies name brand hardware that has been tested with RHEL and Red Hat Linux (versions 9 and below). If you've purchased RHEL 3, Red Hat will provide some level of installation support for any certified or compatible hardware. Some hardware that has been tested by Red Hat has specifically been found not to work with Red Hat Linux or RHEL and is therefore not supported. Red Hat hasn't tested all PC hardware; as a courtesy, they also include a list of hardware that others have tested with Red Hat Enterprise Linux, as "Community Knowledge" hardware. These four categories of hardware are described in Table 1-8.

Like the Linux Hardware HOWTO, the Red Hat Hardware Compatibility List draws upon the efforts of volunteers. If you want to check if any of the "latest" hardware (such as USB) will run on your Linux system, it's probably best to consult the Red Hat support site first, then maybe LDP's Linux Hardware HOWTO. However, if you want the option of being able to contact Red Hat for support, you should stay within the "supported" list of the Red Hat Hardware Compatibility List.

Check the documentation for your hardware. Find a component such as a modem or a network card. Cross-check this component against the Red Hat and LDP hardware compatibility lists (HCLs). Find the Red Hat lists by starting at www.redhat.com. Find their HCL in their support area. Find the LDP Hardware HOWTO by starting at www.tldp.org. Find this list in the LDP section on HOWTOs. Compare the results. While in most cases the results are identical, it's good to know how to search through both sources just in case.

As part of this process, find a component listed on one or both of these HCLs as incompatible with Linux. Do a search on your favorite search engine or the newsgroups based on the name and model of the product. Don't forget to include "linux" in your list of search terms. You might be pleasantly surprised. As of this writing, a searchable newsgroup database is available at groups.google.com.

TABLE 1-8	**Status**	**Description**
Red Hat Hardware Compatibility Categories	Certified	Approved by Red Hat, Inc., through the Red Hat Hardware Certification Program.
	Compatible	Reviewed by Red Hat, and known to be supported.
	Not Supported	Reviewed by Red Hat, and known not to work with Red Hat Linux or RHEL.
	Community Knowledge	Untested by Red Hat; others have reported some degree of compatibility with Red Hat Linux and RHEL.

CPU and SMP Support

Red Hat Enterprise Linux for Intel supports computers with Intel and compatible processors. It is "Itanium-ready," which means that it will be able to support this 64-bit Intel CPU when it is finally released.

Linux is commonly used as a server operating system. Many server applications can take advantage of the flexibility provided by multiple CPUs. This is known as symmetric multiprocessing (SMP) support. Linux began supporting multiple CPUs with the release of the 2.4 kernel back in 2001.

on the *Some of the developers hope to increase the SMP limit to 128 CPUs. If you're*
job *running Linux on a SMP computer, keep up to date with the latest kernel developments at www.kernel.org.*

exam

watch   *Red Hat Enterprise Linux   believe that you'll need to install the 2.6*
was released with Linux Kernel version 2.4.21.   kernel for the RHCE or RHCT exams. As
While it includes a number of features, or   always, monitor the Red Hat syllabus and
"backports," from Linux Kernel 2.6, I don't   requirements for the latest information.

Plug and Play

Plug and play (PnP) refers to the capability of an operating system to automatically allocate hardware ports or addresses to specific devices such as hard drives, sound cards, or modems. Linux's ability to work with plug and play devices is somewhat less than perfect. For example, if you have the right network modules installed with the kernel, Linux may be able to automatically detect and install the drivers for a new network card in a PCMCIA slot. However, Linux does not automatically detect all printers; in this case, you may need to use the techniques discussed in Chapter 8 to install the appropriate print driver.

A plug and play system has three parts: the BIOS, the device, and the operating system. Unless all three work perfectly, problems can arise with plug and play. The BIOS has to allow the operating system to find the devices on your computer. Plug and play devices have to accept port and channel assignments from the operating system. And a plug and play operating system is constantly searching each connection for new hardware. Red Hat developed the kudzu utility to look for and configure any hardware changes when you boot Linux.

Plug and Play Support in Linux

The unfortunate truth is that Linux doesn't handle plug and play as well as we may want. The main problem lies with plug and play support for devices that run on an ISA bus. ISA is a legacy technology from older IBM PCs, created without plug and play in mind, so support for it is complex.

PCI hardware is a different story. As Linux loads, device drivers can easily find PCI devices. However, conflicts may still arise with ISA devices. While Linux works well with many USB and IEEE 1394 devices, support for the latest USB 2.0 and IEEE 1394 hardware is still officially "experimental" as of this writing.

Plug and Play Conflicts

The Linux plug and play subsystem may have problems with the newest computer devices or some very old ones. If you're having problems with the newest computer equipment, various Web sites are dedicated to offering help. For example, www.linmodems.org can help you configure many so-called "winmodems," and www.linux-usb.org can help you configure the latest USB equipment on Linux.

Many hardware conflicts with relatively old equipment are fairly simple to eliminate. There are three possible areas of conflict:

- A physical hardware jumper is conflicting with another card.
- Your ISA plug and play cards are not properly configured.
- You are out of IRQs or other resources to add to your new device.

You can use the /proc files to check the currently used IRQ ports, I/O addresses, and DMA channels. For example, to check the occupied IRQs, the following command lists the devices that *are* loaded by the kernel:

```
# cat /proc/interrupts
```

If there is a conflict, the device is not loaded. You can quickly scan over the left side to see what interrupts are available. To get a list of used I/O addresses and DMA channels, issue the following commands:

```
# cat /proc/ioports
# cat /proc/dma
```

The kernel included with Red Hat Enterprise Linux 3 and above should keep plug and play configuration problems to a minimum. When problems arise, two or more devices are probably trying to use the same IRQ, I/O, and/or DMA. In that case, one or both devices may not be loaded. It may take a little detective work to identify the troubled hardware; conflicts may prevent it from being listed in one of the associated /proc directory files. Then select one of the devices, and change its IRQ, I/O, and/or DMA to a free location.

This is usually a two-step process: first, change the settings on the card itself through physical jumpers or a diagnostic disk, as described in the next section. If Linux doesn't detect your changes, use the appropriate configuration utility, such as **redhat-config-mouse**, **ifconfig**, **modprobe**, or **redhat-config-network**, to change the settings on your device.

Generally, Linux should not have problems with PCI plug and play cards or USB devices. Linux should recognize them and set them up with appropriate IRQ ports, I/O addresses, and DMA channels. If you cannot see what your PCI cards are set to, you can type **cat /proc/pci**. If a PCI card that you're concerned about does not show up here, you may be out of IRQs. If you run out of IRQs, you may want to look into alternatives such as IEEE 1394 (also known as FireWire or iLink) or USB devices.

ACPI and APM

Closely related to plug and play are the latest computer power management standards, known as Advanced Configuration and Power Interface (ACPI) and Advanced Power Management (APM). Both are efforts to manage PC power consumption. As such, they are important tools to extend the lifetime of battery-operated devices such as laptop computers.

Microsoft has driven developments in both areas toward computers that can be easily suspended and reactivated from a minimum power state. Red Hat has incorporated some ACPI features from the 2.6 kernel in RHEL.

If you have problems with an ACPI computer, you can deactivate ACPI support with the **acpi=off** command to the kernel during the Red Hat Enterprise Linux boot or installation process.

CERTIFICATION OBJECTIVE 1.13

Configuring External Devices

You can install many devices externally to your computer. These devices are sometimes known as peripherals. Generally, peripheral devices fall into five categories: serial, parallel, USB, IEEE 1394, and PC Cards. A device attached to a serial port, such as a mouse or a modem, uses the device associated with that port. Devices attached to parallel, USB, or IEEE 1394 ports normally use their own device files. PC Cards are a special case normally associated with laptop computers.

While Linux normally recognizes basic devices attached to serial or USB ports, such as a mouse during installation, configuring other devices may take additional work.

Serial Ports

In many cases, configuring a device for a serial port is as simple as linking to the driver of the associated port. For example, if you have an external modem connected to the only serial port on your computer, the Linux plug and play subsystem may have already linked the device for that port with the device for your modem. Run the **ls -l /dev/modem** command. If it shows something like the following output, you know that Linux has already linked your modem driver with the second serial port:

```
lrwxrwxrwx   1 root    root    10 Apr 4 11:28 /dev/modem -> /dev/ttyS1
```

Otherwise, you can use the **ln** command to create a link to the appropriate port. If you have a serial mouse, you should find the same type of link from /dev/mouse.

Parallel Ports

Configuring devices attached to a parallel port can be more complex. For example, Linux doesn't always recognize plug and play printers that are attached to a parallel port such as /dev/lp0. Further configuration with tools such as the CUPS Web-based tool or the Red Hat Printer Configuration tool may be required. You can find the device associated with your CUPS printer in the /etc/cups/printers.conf file.

If you're connecting an external hard drive to a parallel port, you'll want to install the paride module and the module associated with your device, whether it is a hard drive, a tape drive, or a CD-ROM. Similar steps are required for other parallel port devices. Detailed information on configuring parallel port devices is available from the Linux Parallel Port Web site at www.torque.net/linux-pp.html.

USB

Linux support for USB is growing with the evolution of the latest kernels. While the latest versions of Red Hat Enterprise Linux supports USB hot-swapping, support for the higher-speed USB 2.0 standard is still "experimental," as are Linux drivers for many USB devices. For the latest information, see the Linux USB Web site at www.linux-usb.org. You may be able to download your driver and install it using the techniques discussed in Chapter 4.

IEEE 1394

The Institute of Electrical and Electronics Engineers (IEEE) has developed the IEEE 1394 specifications for very high speed data transfer applications, such as digital movies. Equipment designed to these standards is often known by its trade names: FireWire and iLink. The current status is similar to USB; in other words, some IEEE 1394 equipment works with Linux, and development continues. For the latest information, see the Linux IEEE 1394 Web site at linux1394.sourceforge.net/hcl.php.

PC Card (PCMCIA)

Linux has one package called Card Services that deals exclusively with PC cards. This package includes all the kernel modules you'll need to manage PCMCIA cards and a set of drivers for specific cards. The package also includes a daemon that handles hot-swapping for most PC cards.

While development of the Card Services package is ongoing, there is often a period where there is no support for the proprietary configurations especially common on laptops. For this reason, the latest laptop is often not the best choice for a Linux installation. However, support for Linux on most name brand laptops is now common even when the laptop is first released. In fact, several companies sell laptops with Linux installed.

Supported PCMCIA Controllers

According to the Linux PCMCIA Information page at pcmcia-cs.sourceforge.net, Linux now supports all common PCMCIA controllers. If you have a problem with a specific PCMCIA card, focus on finding a driver for the card itself. A current list of supported PCMCIA controllers can be found on the Hardware HOWTO.

Supported Cards

The Card Services package comes bundled with a file named SUPPORTED.CARDS. You can probably find it on your Linux computer with the **locate SUPPORTED.CARDS** command. Also, you can check the PCMCIA HOWTO or the Red Hat Hardware Compatibility List for supported cards. Alternatively, the Linux PCMCIA Information Page may also be helpful.

on the Job

During your career as a computer professional, there will be times you'll be asked to research a specific product or technology. To get an idea of how hard or easy this can be, call a major computer retailer or manufacturer and inquire about their latest laptop. Ask them if it supports Linux. What kind of answer do you get? Ask them if they have any earlier models that will. Do you believe the answers you receive are reliable? Check out the company's Web page, if you can, and find out if they provide any information about the product on the Internet. Doing this kind of research can be very trying, with or without success. Before deciding what kind of hardware you want to install Linux on, you should have a good understanding of what will and will not work. Start early and build a good base of reliable references you can use to find out new computer information. Web sites, such as the Linux Documentation Project, as well as magazines like Linux Journal, Linux Format (UK), Sys Admin Magazine, *and* Linux Magazine, *will help you stay informed.*

CERTIFICATION OBJECTIVE 1.14

Preparing to Install Linux

Installing Linux on most Intel-based computers is pretty straightforward. In many cases, most installation proceeds without problems. Generally, if you are installing Linux on one modern computer, it should be okay to just install Linux without worrying too much about your hardware.

However, if you have problems, you'll save yourself a lot of time and frustration by knowing exactly what hardware you have. Before you start installing Red Hat Enterprise Linux, it's helpful to be familiar with the following components of your system:

- **Drives** Check to see if you are using SCSI or IDE drives. You should know the manufacturer, model number, and capacity of the drive. In addition, if it's a SCSI drive, make sure you know its SCSI ID number. (As of this writing, if you're installing Red Hat Enterprise Linux on a VMWare machine, emulated SCSI drives don't work; you'll have to configure an emulated IDE hard drive.)

- **Hard drive controller** Know the manufacturer and model number of the drive controller. If this data is hard to find, at least try to find the chipset of the controller. If it's an IDE controller, the documentation is associated with the computer motherboard. If it's a SCSI controller, see the documentation associated with that controller.

■ **CD-ROM**   For most standard SCSI or IDE CD-ROMs, the standard drivers should work without problems. However, if you are using a CD-ROM with a proprietary interface, you should know the manufacturer, as well as the model of the drive and controller card.

■ **Mouse**   You should know the type of mouse that you have—such as PS/2, serial, or USB. If your mouse uses a serial port, it helps if you know which port. For example, if you're converting a computer that's running Microsoft Windows, a serial mouse is associated with a serial port, typically COM1, COM2, COM3, or COM4. The corresponding Linux device files are /dev/ttyS0, /dev/ttyS1, /dev/ttyS2, and /dev/ttyS3. And the number of buttons on a mouse may not be obvious; if you have a two-button mouse with a scrolling wheel that you can click, you actually have a three-button mouse.

■ **Graphics card**   If you will be running the Linux graphical user interface (GUI), also known as X or X11, you will need the manufacturer, the model number, the chipset, and the amount of video memory. If it's a fairly common graphics card and you can't find the chipset or memory, you should be able to select a generic or older version of the card from the X installation database.

■ **Sound, video, and game adapters**   If you want to set up sound on your system, you should know the manufacturer and model number of the sound card. If plug and play doesn't work for your sound card, you'll also need the default IRQ port, I/O address, and DMA channel(s). Especially on laptops, this information may be stored in your BIOS.

■ **Network adapters**   If you are going to network your Linux system, you should know the manufacturer and model number of the network adapter. If plug and play doesn't work for your network adapter, you should find its default IRQ port and I/O address.

■ **Monitor**   If you will be running the Linux GUI, based on the Linux implementation of the X Window System (www.xfree86.org), you will need the manufacturer, model number, available resolutions, and refresh frequencies of the monitor.

o n   t h e
!
ⓘ o b

Be especially careful with older monitors or laptop displays. Exceeding the frequency refresh capabilities of such monitors could easily overload the display system. Replacing a laptop display is not a pleasant exercise!

Not all hardware will work with Linux. After you've collected information about your system, you should consult the Red Hat Hardware Compatibility List (HCL) or LDP Hardware HOWTO to determine if your components are compatible with the current version of Red Hat Enterprise Linux.

CERTIFICATION SUMMARY

The RHCE and RHCT exams are not for beginners. This chapter covers the prerequisites for the RHCE exam and thus the elementary skills that you need for the remainder of this book. If the explanations in this chapter are too brief, you may need to refer to sources such as those I cite at the beginning of this chapter. While these exams are based on RHEL 3, you can use Red Hat Linux 9 to study for these exams, with the tips I provide throughout this book.

This chapter provides an overview of many Linux fundamentals. While the RHCE and RHCT hands-on exams may not explicitly test the skills you learn in this chapter, you need to know many of these fundamentals to solve the problems presented on those exams. However, you may see some questions related to this chapter on the multiple-choice portion of the RHCE exam.

Before you start planning your Linux installation, you need a basic degree of knowledge of PC hardware, specifically the Intel-based architecture. A basic understanding of IRQ ports, I/O addresses, DMA channels, and hard drive systems can help you plan how Linux manages and connects every component in your PC.

But not all hardware is supported by Linux. You should now have enough information to find the hardware that fits your needs. Alternatively, you now know about the resources that help you determine what other hardware you need that also works with Linux. Planning your Linux installation makes it easier to handle a wide variety of hardware.

✔ TWO-MINUTE DRILL

Here are some of the key points from the certification objectives in Chapter 1.

Basic Linux Knowledge

❑ Linux is managed through a series of text configuration files.

❑ Even though Red Hat Enterprise Linux now has a rescue CD with text editors such as emacs, you need to know how to restore a system from a rescue floppy, which normally includes just the vi editor. Therefore, you need to know how to use vi.

Linux Filesystem Hierarchy and Structure

❑ Linux directories are organized to the Filesystem Hierarchy Standard (FHS).

❑ In the FHS, devices such as mice and hard drives are grouped in the /dev directory. Some /dev files have logical names such as mouse and modem and are linked to the actual device files.

❑ FHS partitions can be managed and formatted with the **fdisk**, **fsck**, and **mkfs** commands.

❑ The Logical Volume Manager allows you to consolidate multiple partitions in one filesystem, on one directory.

❑ Once configured, Linux directories can be mounted on a partition through /etc/fstab or directly with the **mount** command.

Basic Commands

❑ Linux administrators need to know how to use the command line interface.

❑ Basic commands allow you to navigate, find the files that you need, read file contents, create new files, and more.

❑ File filters allow you to search through the files themselves for specific citations or other file characteristics.

❑ Administrative commands allow you to manage Linux in a number of ways, including running processes and logged-in users.

Printing

❑ The default Red Hat Enterprise Linux print system is CUPS.

❑ You can configure printers by directly editing the files in the /etc/cups directory, or by running the Red Hat Printer Configuration tool, **redhat-config-printer**.

Shells

❑ Command lines are based on a shell.

❑ With the right permissions, you can set up shell programs in executable scripts.

❑ The way a shell works depends on the settings in its variables and parameters. Some variables and parameters are grouped in the inherited environment, which maintains settings from shell to shell.

❑ With stdin, stdout, and stderr, you can manage different data streams.

Basic Security

❑ Basic security within Linux is based on file permissions, users, groups, and **umask**.

❑ The SUID and SGID bits allow you to share owner-level permissions with different users and groups.

❑ Shadow passwords hide user authentication data. The Shadow Password Suite protects user and group passwords in files that should be accessible only to the root user.

System Administration

❑ While it's normally best to log in as a regular user, it's faster to log in as the root user for the RHCE and RHCT exams.

❑ Standard files for new users are kept in /etc/skel.

❑ Daemons are processes that run in the background.

❑ Network service can be controlled through scripts in the /etc/rc.d/init.d directory.

❑ The cron daemon helps you schedule different jobs, including backup and restore jobs, which should be done when network use is at a minimum.

❑ When you have problems, system log files, as organized by /etc/syslog.conf, provide important clues to the causes.

Basic TCP/IP Networking

❑ Most of the work in TCP/IP networking is with configuring IP addresses.

❑ There are three different sets of private IPv4 addresses suitable for setting up TCP/IP on a LAN.

❑ Tools such as **ping, ifconfig**, and **netstat** can help you diagnose problems on that LAN.

❑ Name resolution configuration files determine how your computer finds the right IP address.

Standard Network Services

❑ There are a number of standard network services. They include NFS, sendmail, POP, IMAP, FTP, DNS, DHCP, Samba, Apache, and NIS.

❑ Each of these services, when installed, can be configured to start and stop through the scripts located in the /etc/rc.d/init.d or /etc/xinetd.d directories.

Basic Network Security

❑ Basic network security settings can depend on allowing or denying access to different computers by their IP addresses or by the desired TCP/IP port.

❑ Computers behind a firewall can be protected through Network Address Translation or various **iptables** commands.

Basic Hardware Knowledge

❑ The focus of the RHCE exam is on computers built with an Intel-based architecture.

❑ An Intel-architecture PC has three basic communications channels: IRQ ports, I/O addresses, and DMA channels.

❑ The latest version of Red Hat Enterprise Linux as certified requires at least 256MB of RAM.

❑ You can set up Linux on IDE, SCSI, USB, or IEEE 1394 hard drives. However, the BIOS of a PC can load Linux boot files only from the first two IDE or SCSI hard drives or a boot floppy.

Hardware Compatibility

❑ Linux has come a long way the last few years, and you should have little problem installing it on most modern PCs.

❑ You may not be able to install Linux on every PC; there are occasional problems on newer laptop computers.

❑ The best places to look for compatible hardware are the Hardware HOWTO of the Linux Documentation Project or the Red Hat Hardware Compatibility List.

❑ Red Hat Enterprise Linux has a very capable plug and play service that can configure most current hardware.

❑ Closely related to plug and play are the ACPI and APM power management standards.

Configuring External Devices

❑ There are five basic categories of external devices: serial, parallel, USB, IEEE 1394, and PCMCIA.

❑ Serial port devices are usually linked to specific device files. For example, /dev/modem is often linked directly to a specific serial device file.

❑ Parallel port device configuration can be more complex. For example, a separate configuration utility is required to recognize devices such as printers.

❑ While Linux supports USB and IEEE 1394, support for many specific USB and IEEE 1394 devices is still in the works.

❑ Linux supports PCMCIA cards, also known as PC Cards, through the Card Services package, which includes drivers for the PCMCIA adapter and individual cards.

Preparing to Install Linux

❑ Installing on most Intel-based computers is pretty straightforward, but you can save yourself much time and frustration by knowing exactly what hardware you have.

❑ It can help to know the make and model number for each of the following components: hard drive controllers, network adapters, graphics cards, and sound adapters.

❑ If possible, also find the resolution and horizontal and vertical refresh rates of your monitor.

SELF TEST

The following questions will help you measure your understanding of the material presented in this chapter. Read all the choices carefully, as there may be more than one correct answer. Don't focus exclusively on these questions. There are no longer any multiple choice questions on the Red Hat exams. These questions exclusively test your understanding of the chapter. While the topics in this chapter are "prerequisites," it is okay if you have another way of performing a task. Getting results, not memorizing trivia, is what counts on the Red Hat exams.

Choose all correct answers for each question.

Basic Linux Knowledge

1. If you're editing the /etc/inittab file, which of the following vi commands would you use to copy the currently highlighted line?

A. p

B. c

C. yy

D. cw

Linux Filesystem Hierarchy and Structure

2. Which of the following commands would you use to mount an MS-DOS floppy disk?

A. mount -t /dev/fd0 /mnt/floppy

B. mount -t ext2 /dev/fd0 /mnt/floppy

C. mount -t ext3/dev/fd0 /mnt/floppy

D. mount -t vfat /dev/fd0 /mnt/floppy

Basic Commands

3. Which of the following commands returns the actual number of times user mj is logged into your Linux computer?

A. wc -l

B. who | grep mj

C. who | wc -l

D. who | grep mj | wc -l

Printing

4. You're maintaining a large queue of print jobs on your network, and you need some job numbers to make sure the engineers get highest priority on the printer. Which of the following commands lists print job numbers?

A. lpr -l

B. lpq -l

C. lprm -l

D. lpd

Shells

5. Which of the following commands would you use to add the /usr/sbin directory to your PATH?

A. $PATH=$PATH:/usr/sbin

B. $PATH=PATH:/usr/sbin

C. PATH=$PATH:/sbin

D. PATH=$PATH:/usr/sbin

Basic Security

6. When you run the **umask** command, you see the following result: 0000. The next time you create a file, what will be the permissions?

A. drwxrwxrwx

B. ----------

C. -rwxr-xr-x

D. -rw-rw-rw-

System Administration

7. Based on the following line from a user's crontab file, when will the Berkeleylives program be run?

```
0 1 2 3 * Berkeleylives
```

A. At 1:23 A.M. every day

B. At 1:00 A.M. on March 2

C. At 1:00 A.M. on February 3

D. At 2:00 A.M. on March 2

Basic TCP/IP Networking

8. Which of the following sets of numbers, in order, correspond to an appropriate network address, subnet mask, and broadcast address?

- **A.** 192.168.14.255, 255.255.255.0 192.168.14.0
- **B.** 192.168.14.0, 255.255.255.0 192.168.14.255
- **C.** 255.255.255.0 192.168.14.255, 192.168.14.0
- **D.** 192.168.14.0, 192.168.14.255, 255.255.255.0

Standard Network Services

9. Which of the following services works to connect Linux to a Microsoft Windows–based network?

- **A.** NFS
- **B.** SMB
- **C.** DNS
- **D.** Windows for Workgroups

Basic Network Security

10. Which of the following commands are associated with a Red Hat Enterprise Linux firewall configuration utility?

- **A.** lokwall
- **B.** lokkit
- **C.** redhat-config-securitylevel
- **D.** firewall-lokkit

Basic Hardware Knowledge

11. You've checked your /proc/interrupts file and find that you don't have any leftover IRQ ports. Nevertheless, you want to install another printer and network card. Which of the following actions would let you keep your current devices?

- **A.** You need to make some hard decisions on what devices you need to remove from your computer before installing anything new.
- **B.** Use the free PCI slots or USB connectors in your PC for new devices. The PCI system allows all PCI and USB devices to share a single IRQ.
- **C.** Look through /proc/ioports and /proc/dma. Find free I/O addresses and DMA channels for your new devices. Then IRQ conflicts are not a problem.
- **D.** Just install the new devices. The Linux plug and play system can make sure that extra devices share the appropriate IRQ ports.

Hardware Compatibility

12. When you look through the Red Hat Hardware Compatibility List, you find that a number of devices in your computer are listed as "community knowledge." What should you do about these devices before installing Linux?

   A. Replace those devices with hardware that you know is compatible.

   B. Examine the LDP Hardware HOWTO.

   C. Check the Web sites of the manufacturers of each community knowledge device.

   D. Look at the documentation for each device and remove any winmodems from your PC.

Configuring External Devices

13. How would you know if your serial mouse is properly attached to a serial port?

   A. Run the **ls -l /dev/mouse** command. You should see a file link to the appropriate serial port.

   B. Check the physical connection. If the connection is not solid, Linux may not be receiving signals from your mouse.

   C. Run the **ls -l /dev/ttys0** command. You should see a file link to your serial mouse.

   D. Run the redhat-config-mouse utility and make sure you have a serial mouse.

Preparing to Install Linux

14. What kind of information should you collect about your PC's video system if you want to install Linux with a graphical user interface?

   A. Model and manufacturer of the graphics card

   B. Horizontal and vertical refresh rates of the monitor

   C. Video memory

   D. Maximum monitor resolution

LAB QUESTIONS

Lab 1

You have 18 computers on a LAN behind a firewall. Diagram your computers on a sheet of paper. Connect them together in a "star" configuration. Assign a private IP address to each computer. Take one computer and draw a second connection to the Internet.

   While this is a fairly simple exercise, Linux is built for networking. To understand what you can do with Red Hat Enterprise Linux, you need to think in terms of the role of your computer on a network.

Lab 2

In the next two labs, we'll be experimenting with the /etc/inittab file. So before you begin, back it up to a file such as /etc/inittab.bak, or back up a copy to your home directory.

1. Use the vi editor to open the /etc/inittab file in your computer.

2. Take a look at your id variable. If it's set to 3, change it to 5, and vice versa.

3. Reboot your computer and see what happens.

4. Restore your original /etc/inittab file.

Lab 3

In this lab, we'll experiment a bit more with the /etc/inittab configuration file.

1. If you haven't already done so, create a backup for /etc/inittab.

2. Press CTRL-ALT-F2. You should see a virtual console text login screen.

3. Return to the original text console with CTRL-ALT-F1 or the GUI console with CTRL-ALT-F7.

4. In the /etc/inittab file, identify the lines related to the virtual login consoles.

5. Try experimenting with these lines with the **mingetty** commands. Add a comment character (**#**) in front of the second line with the **mingetty** command.

6. Run the **init q** command to make Linux reread this file.

7. Try pressing CTRL-ALT-F2 again. What happens?

8. Restore your original /etc/inittab configuration file.

SELF TEST ANSWERS

Basic Linux Knowledge

1. ☑ **C.** The **yy** command copies the entire line associated with the current location of the cursor. You can then use the **p** command to insert that line into the file.

   ☒ **A** is incorrect, since the **p** command only takes data from the buffer. **B** is incorrect, since there is no **c** command. **D** is incorrect, since it places only one word into the buffer.

Linux Filesystem Hierarchy and Structure

2. ☑ **D.** Current MS-DOS floppy disks are usually formatted to VFAT, which supports long filenames.

   ☒ **A** is not correct, since you need to specify a file type with the **-t** switch. **B** and **C** are not correct, since ext2 and ext3 are unusable file types for an MS-DOS disk.

Basic Commands

3. ☑ **D.** While this level of piping isn't covered in this chapter, this should be a straightforward question if you're sufficiently familiar with basic command line tools. The **who** command returns every active login of every user. Piping the result returns just the lines associated with the logins of user mj. Piping that result to **wc -l** returns the actual number of lines.

   ☒ **A** is not correct, as the **wc** command needs a file or other input to read first. **B** is not correct, as it returns the lines associated with the logins of user mj. While you could count the number of lines, that does not address the requirements of the question. **C** is not correct, as it would return the number of times all users are logged into this system.

Printing

4. ☑ **B.** The **lpq -l** command checks print queues. If you get an error message from this command, you may need to install a printer first.

   ☒ **A** is incorrect, as **lpr** is a print command, and its **-l** switch tells **lpr** to expect a binary file. **C** is incorrect, as **lprm** is for removing print jobs. **D** is incorrect, as **lpd** is the line print daemon. While this must be running before you can check a print queue, **lpd** does not itself check print queues.

Shells

5. ☑ **D.** The variable is PATH. When you input $PATH, the value of that variable, in this case, the directories in your path, are substituted in this equation.

    ☒   **A** and **B** are not correct, since $PATH is not itself a variable. **C** is not correct, since /sbin is the wrong directory.

Basic Security

6. ☑   **D**. The effect of **umask** has changed. Even if you try to set it to allow execute permissions, Red Hat won't let you do this anymore. You'll need to set execute permissions on each file after creation.

    ☒   **A** is not correct, since the file is not necessarily a directory, and execute permissions are no longer set up by default. **B** is not correct, as this would correspond to a **umask** value of 0666 or 0777. **C** is not correct, as execute permissions are no longer set up by default.

System Administration

7. ☑   **B**. This is based on the convention for the first five entries in a crontab line: minute, hour, day of month, month, and day of week.

    ☒   **A**, **C**, and **D** are incorrect, as they are readings of the cited crontab line that don't correspond to the convention.

Basic TCP/IP Networking

8. ☑   **B**. By convention, a network with a 192.168.14.0 address with a 255.255.255.0 subnet mask uses a 192.168.14.255 broadcast address.

    ☒   **A** is not correct, as there cannot be a network that starts with a broadcast address. **C** is not correct, as there cannot be a network that starts with a subnet mask. **D** is not correct, as 255.255.255.0 is not a qualified broadcast address.

Standard Network Services

9. ☑   **B**. The Server Message Block (SMB) file system, also known as Samba, is the standard way to connect Linux as a member of a Microsoft Windows– or IBM OS/2–based network.

    ☒   **A** is not correct. While it is possible to set up "Services for Unix" on some Microsoft Windows computers, that would no longer be a Microsoft Windows–based network. **C** is not correct, since the Domain Name System has nothing to do with protocols necessary to connect operating systems. **D** is not correct, since Windows for Workgroups is not an available service in Linux.

Basic Network Security

10. ☑   **B** and **C** are both current Red Hat Enterprise Linux firewall configuration utilities.

    ☒   **A** and **D** are not valid Red Hat Enterprise Linux commands.

Basic Hardware Knowledge

I I. ☑ **B.** The PCI system really does make sure that installed PCI devices share IRQ ports, as needed. This works as well for any USB or IEEE 1394 devices on your system.

☒ **A** is incorrect because it is possible for PCI devices to share IRQ ports. In fact, USB devices can also share an IRQ port. **C** is incorrect because all devices need CPU service. **D** is incorrect because no plug and play system by itself can compensate for a lack of available IRQs.

Hardware Compatibility

12. ☑ **B and C.** Red Hat Enterprise Linux community knowledge hardware lists devices that have not been tested by Red Hat. But others in the Linux community have tested such hardware, and the results are often documented in the LDP's Hardware HOWTO. Many device manufacturers now include any special installation instructions that you may need to install their devices on Linux.

☒ **A and D** are both incorrect. Most devices are compatible with Linux. It would be a waste to remove hardware from your PC that Red Hat Enterprise Linux would recognize without any problems. While winmodems are a special case, some winmodems can be made to work with Red Hat Enterprise Linux.

Configuring External Devices

13. ☑ **A.** As with modems, the /dev/mouse file is linked to the port used by your mouse.

☒ **B** is incorrect since the question addresses device filenames in Linux, not any hardware issue. **C** is incorrect, since you don't know which serial port is attached to your mouse. **D** is incorrect, since you shouldn't have to reconfigure your mouse just to find the serial port to which it is attached.

Preparing to Install Linux

14. ☑ **A, B, C, D.** Most Linux installation programs allow you to specify the model and manufacturer of the graphics card. This information is correlated as part of the Linux installation database to provide information on other needed settings, including chipset and video memory. You do want to make sure Linux does not exceed the horizontal or vertical refresh capabilities of the monitor, to minimize the risk of damage. The video memory allows you to verify what the Red Hat Enterprise Linux installation program reads from your system. If you exceed the resolution capabilities of the monitor, the graphics may degrade.

☒ There are no incorrect answer choices.

LAB ANSWERS

Lab 1

There are many ways to configure the IP addresses on a LAN. But it is generally best to do it by setting up a network from one of the private IP address ranges. When you configure networking on your LAN, pay particular attention to the computer that also has a connection to the Internet. The IP address of its connection to your network will be the gateway address for every other computer on your LAN. It's also the logical location for any firewall that you may wish to configure.

Lab 2

When you troubleshoot a Red Hat Enterprise Linux computer, one of the things you'll be working through are critical configuration files. One key file in the boot process is /etc/inittab. One thing that I can do in this book is to illustrate the behavior of potential problems. The more problems that you're familiar with, the easier it is to troubleshoot or debug a problem during the RHCT and RHCE exams. However, there is often more than one way to solve a problem. I present one method. You may be able to find others.

To go through this lab, I'd take the following steps:

1. Log in as the root user. You can do this from either the GUI or the text login interface.

2. Run the **cp /etc/inittab /root/inittab** command. This backs up the subject configuration file in the root user's home directory.

3. Open the subject file with the **vi /etc/inittab** command.

4. Scroll down until you see the following line:

   ```
   id:3:initdefault
   ```

5. The number after the **id** command identifies your starting runlevel. If it's 3, Linux starts in text mode; if it's 5, Linux starts in the GUI.

6. Change this number from 3 to 5 (or 5 to 3).

7. Save your changes and exit from the vi editor with the **:wq** command.

8. Reboot your computer with the **reboot** command.

9. Linux should now start in your new runlevel (3 or 5).

10. Restore your original settings in /etc/inittab. You can do this by opening /etc/inittab with the vi editor. Alternatively, you can copy your backup from the /root directory with the **cp /root/inittab /etc/inittab** command.

Lab 3

In this lab, we experiment with deactivating a specific virtual console. By default, six virtual text login consoles are configured in the /etc/inittab configuration file. In this lab, we deactivate the second of the six consoles.

1. Log in as the root user. You can do this from either the GUI or the text login interface. If you're in the GUI, open a text console. Right-click on the desktop and click New Terminal in the pop-up menu.

2. Run the **cp /etc/inittab /root/inittab** command. This backs up the subject configuration file in the root user's home directory.

3. Open the subject file with the **vi /etc/inittab** command.

4. Scroll down until you see the following line:

        2:2345:respawn:/sbin/mingetty tty2

5. Press CTRL-ALT-F2. This should start a text login interface. You should be able to log in at the prompt with your username and password.

6. If you logged into the GUI, press CTRL-ALT-F7 to return to the GUI. If you logged into the text interface, press CTRL-ALT-F1 to return to your original screen.

7. Turn the **subject** command in /etc/inittab into a comment. Add a comment character in front of the line as shown:

        #2:2345:respawn:/sbin/mingetty tty2

8. Close and save this change to /etc/inittab with the **:wq** command.

9. Make Linux reread /etc/inittab with the **init q** command.

10. Press CTRL-ALT-F2. This should start a text login interface. Try logging in again. You'll see that it's not possible. Now you can see how adding a comment character to the right line in /etc/inittab deactivates the second virtual console.

11. If you logged into the GUI, press CTRL-ALT-F7 to return to the GUI. If you logged into the text interface, press CTRL-ALT-F1 to return to your original screen.

12. Restore your original settings in the /etc/inittab file.

2

Installation

I nstallation is one of the two parts of both the RHCE and the RHCT exams. To pass this part of each exam, you'll need to know a lot more than just the basic GUI installation process for a single computer! Once you've studied the installation chapters (Chapters 2 and 3), you'll be able to install Red Hat Enterprise Linux (RHEL) in a number of ways: over a network, directly from the CD, using boot disks, and with automated Kickstart-based tools.

While this chapter covers the "basics," they are important. You'll learn the nuances of disk partitions. You'll learn to select between available installation classes. Both **fdisk** and Disk Druid are useful tools for configuring your hard drives. Both GRUB and LILO are popular and flexible options as boot loaders. And it's faster to install RHEL over most networks on the RHCE exam, as well as in real life on a group of computers on a LAN.

All you need to get started is sufficient unformatted free disk space (as well as 256MB of RAM). The easiest way to get this is by adding a new disk drive to your system. While the mechanics of adding a drive and setting your PC to boot from your CD-ROM bootable is beyond the scope of this book, neither operation is complicated. Once the new drive is installed and your system is configured to boot from the CD-ROM, just stick the first Red Hat Installation CD-ROM into the CD drive and reboot. Accept the defaults during the installation process and see what happens; it will probably just install, dual-boot automatically (assuming another operating system is already installed), and voilà! You are ready to play!

Time is of the essence on the Red Hat Installation and Configuration exams. You may be asked to install and configure some or all of the services described on the Red Hat Exam Prep guide (www.redhat.com/training/rhce/examprep.html). Use this chapter to understand the services that you can install with RHEL. The fastest way to install RHEL is in text mode.

However, there are two reasons why you may wish to install RHEL in the regular graphical screen. Text mode does not allow you to configure Logical Volume Management (LVM) partitions. It does not allow you to customize individual packages in the package groups that you may want to install.

This book assumes you're using Red Hat Enterprise Linux (RHEL) version 3. If you're using Fedora Linux or Red Hat Linux 9 to simulate an RHEL installation, select a Custom installation for the RHCE exam, and a Workstation installation for the RHCT exam.

INSIDE THE EXAM

Focus During Installation

Both the RHCE and RHCT exams include an installation section. You'll have to do more than just install Linux. You'll have a series of instructions. You'll be told to configure certain services. You may also have to configure different partitions.

Time limits are severe on these exams. Install and configure as much as you can when you install Red Hat Enterprise Linux on your computer. While you can configure and install most anything after Linux is installed, that can take more time than you have.

On the other hand, don't install everything. It takes time to install gigabytes of software over a network. If it's software that you don't need, that's time you can't get back during the exam.

As you read this chapter, learn every part of the installation process. Know what you need to install. For example, if you see a requirement to set up Apache and Samba servers, you'll want to install the Web Server and Windows File Server package groups when you install RHEL 3.

Studying for the Installation Exam

You can use Red Hat Linux 9 to study for the Installation portion of the RHCE and RHCT exams. The steps required are essentially identical to those for Red Hat Enterprise Linux 3. If you haven't been able to get RHEL 3 from Red Hat or another source such as cAos, I've set

up Appendix B on the CD-ROM as a pictorial-only guide to the RHEL 3 installation process. You can verify for yourself that the steps are essentially identical to those required to install Red Hat Linux 9.

CERTIFICATION OBJECTIVE 2.01

Disk Partitions and Block Devices

A disk drive requires a partition table. The *partition* is a logical sequence of cylinders on the disk, while a *cylinder* represents all the sectors that can be read by all heads with one movement of the arm that contains all these heads. While it's possible to create more, RHEL 3 will recognize only up to 16 partitions on any individual SCSI or an IDE hard drive. But don't be too concerned about these details; I think it's highly unlikely that you'll have to create so many partitions on either exam.

on the **Job**

The main Linux partition utility is fdisk. As you'll see in Chapter 3, it won't allow you to create more than 16 partitions on each physical hard disk.

Normally, you should create several partitions when preparing your hard drive to install Linux. This is a good idea for various reasons. First, RHEL 3 is normally configured with at least two filesystems: a Linux native filesystem and a Linux swap filesystem. Second, if you want to install RHEL 3 and another operating system on the same computer, you will have to configure separate partitions for each operating system. You can configure software RAID partitions on different hard drives during the RHEL 3 installation process. However, if you have a hardware RAID system, you'll need to configure it after RHEL 3 is installed.

exam

Watch

During the Installation and Configuration exam, pay careful attention to the instructions. Make sure that the partitions you create while installing RHEL *match any instructions you might see. It's much more difficult and much more time-consuming to revise partitions with utilities such as fdisk after RHEL is installed.*

Naming Conventions

Linux has a simple naming standard for disk partitions: three letters followed by a number. The first letter identifies the type of drive (h is for IDE/EIDE, s is for SCSI). The second letter is d for disk, and the third letter represents the relative position of that disk, starting with "a." In other words, the first IDE drive is hda, followed by hdb, hdc, and hdd.

The number that follows is based on the relative position of the partition. There are primary, extended, and logical partitions. Primary partitions can contain the boot files for an operating system. Hard drives can also be configured with one extended partition, which can then contain up to 12 logical partitions.

You are limited to four primary partitions on each hard disk. But four partitions are often not enough. If you need more partitions on an IDE drive, substitute an extended partition for one primary partition. You can then configure the logical partitions that you need within the extended partition.

You can't install files directly in an extended partition. You must first allocate some extended partition space to at least one logical partition. You can then configure up to 11 logical partitions within that extended partition. In all cases, the first logical partition on the first IDE drive is hda5.

on the

job

While you can actually configure more than 11 logical partitions in an IDE extended partition, that's as many as RHEL 3 will accept.

Each partition is associated with a Linux device file. At least this is straightforward; for example, the device filename associated with the first logical partition on the first IDE drive is /dev/hda5.

exam

watch

You should know the device name associated with each partition, as well as the starting names and numbers of any logical partitions created on any basic disk drive. Also remember that logical partitions on an IDE hard drive always start with number 5; on the first IDE hard drive on a PC, that is hda5.

EXERCISE 2-1

Partitioning

You may never have had to plan partitions on a basic Microsoft Windows desktop computer. On a real server, whether you're using Windows or Linux, you should preplan your disk usage and partitions very carefully. This is a preliminary exercise; be prepared to think more deeply about partitions later in this chapter and in Chapter 3.

1. On a piece of paper, draw a rectangle to represent each hard drive on your computer.

2. Label them in order just as Linux would (Hard Drive 1: /dev/hda, Hard Drive 2: /dev/sda, Hard Drive 3: /dev/sdb).

3. Use this diagram to plan how you are going to partition each drive. While this is a preview of future chapters, you should already know that Linux is set up in multiple directories. Each of these directories can be set up in its own partition. Think about how much space you want to allocate to several major directories, such as /home, /var, /usr, /boot. Don't forget to allocate some area for a swap partition.

Using this method, you can organize your data, keeping system or users' files together, as well as strategically plan where to place your swap partition(s).

Stability and Security

Linux is organized in a Filesystem Hierarchy Standard (FHS) which includes a number of directories described in Chapter 1. You can organize these directories into a few or many hard drive partitions. During the installation process, RHEL is by default organized into three partitions: the root directory, /, the /boot directory, and a swap partition. One recommended configuration for a Linux server includes separate partitions for each of the following directories: /, /boot, /usr, /tmp, /var, and /home. Other partitions may be appropriate for corporate data, database services, and even the Web and FTP sites if they are expected to be large.

Partitioning the hard drive in this manner keeps system, application, and user files isolated from each other. This helps protect the disk space used by the Linux kernel and various applications. Files cannot grow across partitions. For example, an application such as a Web server that uses huge amounts of disk space can't crowd out space needed by the Linux kernel. Another advantage is that if a bad spot develops on the hard drive, the risk to your data is reduced, as is recovery time. Stability is improved.

Security is also improved. Multiple partitions give you the ability to set up certain directories as read-only filesystems. For example, if there is no reason for any user (including root) to write to the /usr directory, mounting that partition as read-only will help protect those files from tampering.

While there are many advantages to creating many disk partitions, it isn't always the best solution. When hard drive space is limited, the number of partitions should be kept to a minimum. For example, if you have a 2GB hard drive and want to install 1500MB during RHEL installation, you may not want to dedicate extra space to the /var directory. You need room for swap space, additional programs, and your own personal files on other directories.

on the
Ⓙob
If you think you may need to reconfigure your Linux partitions in the future, learn more about Logical Volume Management (LVM) configuration. It can allow you to resize Linux partitions after installation.

e**x**a m
ⓦatch
It can take considerable time to set up LVM partitions. Unless you know the process very well, the fastest way is through the RHEL installation program in graphical mode, which is available when installing from CD or from an NFS server. (LVM configuration is not available via text mode RHEL installation.) Learn the process well, just in case you need to set up LVM during the Installation part of the exam.

Basic Space Requirements

Linux is a very flexible operating system. While a full installation of RHEL 3 requires several gigabytes of space, the Red Hat 1.44MB rescue disk that you can create during installation is also a complete operating system (in a minimalist fashion). Depending on your needs, you can install RHEL comfortably, without the GUI, on any hard drive larger than 1GB.

In Chapter 3, you'll learn about the different ways you can allocate space on partitions to several different Linux directories.

There is a Linux distribution on CD which can even be used to diagnose hard disk failures on Microsoft Windows PCs. For more information, see www.knoppix.net. But you won't be able to use the Knoppix CD on the Red Hat exams.

You should size your Linux partitions according to your needs and the function of the computer. For example, a mail server will require more space in /var, because mail files are stored in /var/spool/mail. You could create a separate partition for /var or even /var/spool/mail. In almost every case, it's a good idea to configure at least the /boot directory on a separate partition.

Example: File Server

If the Linux system you are installing is to be a file server, then you could configure your partitions as shown in Table 2-1.

The /usr filesystem is large enough to include key services such as Samba and the Linux graphical user interface. Most of the disk space has been allocated to /var, for the log files and for FTP and Web services, to /home for individual user files, and to /home/shared for common files. Of course, this is only an example. The amount of disk space you allocate for file sharing will depend on factors such as the number of users and the type of files they work on.

TABLE 2-1	Filesystem	Size (MB)	Mounted Directory
Example Partition Configuration for a Linux File Server	/dev/sda1	100	/boot
	/dev/sda2	400	/
	/dev/sda5	2000	/var
	/dev/sda6	300	/usr
	/dev/sda7	60	Swap space
	/dev/sda8	1000	/home
	/dev/sda9	3000	/home/shared

Linux Swap Space

Linux uses the swap space configured on one or more hard drive partitions to store infrequently used programs and data. Swap space can extend the amount of effective RAM on your system. However, if you don't have enough actual RAM, Linux may use the swap space on your hard drive as virtual memory for currently running programs. Because hard drive access can be 1/100,000th the speed of RAM, this can cause significant performance problems.

But you can't just buy extra RAM and eliminate swap space. Linux moves infrequently used programs and data to swap space even if you have gigabytes of RAM.

Normally, Linux (on a 32-bit Intel-style computer) can use a maximum 4GB of swap space, in partitions no larger than 2GB. This 4GB can be spread over a maximum of eight partitions. The typical rule of thumb suggests that swap space should be two to three times the amount of RAM. However, at larger amounts of RAM, the amount of swap space that you need is debatable.

The way Red Hat assigns default swap space is based on the amount of RAM on your system and the space available in your hard drive. As discussed in Chapter 1, Red Hat requires at least 256MB of RAM on RHEL 3. If there's room available on your hard drives, Anaconda configures a swap partition of at least 512MB. For Intel 32-bit systems, Red Hat requires a swap partition at least equal to the amount of RAM on your system.

on the **job** *Red Hat RAM and swap space requirements vary if you're installing RHEL 3 on computers with non-Intel 32-bit CPUs.*

In any case, you want to make the swap space you create as efficient as possible. Swap partitions near the front of a hard disk, thus on a primary partition, have faster access times. Swap partitions on different hard drives attached to separate disk controllers gives Linux flexibility on where to send swap data. Linux can start a program through one hard drive controller, and move files to and from swap space on a separate hard drive controller simultaneously.

BIOS Limits

Some computers built before 1998 may have a BIOS that limits access to hard disks beyond the 1,024th cylinder. Some older BIOSes report only 1,024 cylinders on a hard drive no matter how many actual cylinders there are. Computers that are subject to this limit can't see partitions beyond this cylinder. In this case, you should configure the

exam

ⓦatch   *Problems due to hardware*   *limitations as you can, including the 1,024-*
limitations are common and difficult to   *cylinder limit inherent in some older PC*
troubleshoot if you don't know about them.   *models. But don't overdo it; the Red Hat*
Familiarize yourself with as many hardware   *exams are focused on Linux, not PC hardware.*

Linux /boot directory on its own partition. Make sure that partition is located within the first 1,024 cylinders of the hard drive. Otherwise, the BIOS won't be able to find the partition with the Linux kernel.

Logical Block Addressing (LBA)

Most PCs manufactured after 1998 have a built-in fix called *logical block addressing*, or *LBA*. A system that can report LBA will adjust the cylinder, head, and sector numbers such that the entire disk is available using these logical addresses.

Multiple Controllers

It is possible and desirable to use more than one disk controller interface card at the same time on the same PC. This is a common method to increase throughput on your system by reducing your read/write bottlenecks to the only disk.

You can use both SCSI and EIDE controllers in the same machine, but you should be aware of a few snags. The BIOS may only have access to the first two EIDE hard drives. Also, SCSI disks may not be accessible if EIDE drives are installed. The BIOS might have a setting to allow you to boot from SCSI hard disks. Make sure you understand which drives the BIOS will be able to access. If you install /boot on an inaccessible drive, the BIOS won't be able to find your Linux boot files.

on the
ⓙob   *Many servers are set up with SCSI and EIDE hard drives. If you have one SCSI and two EIDE hard drives, and your computer is set up to boot Linux from a SCSI disk, the BIOS assigns the number 0x80 to /dev/sda (the SCSI disk) and 0x81 to /dev/hda (the first EIDE drive). Linux, however, assigns 0x80 to /dev/hda, 0x81 to /dev/hdb (the second EIDE disk), and 0x82 to the SCSI disk. There is a disagreement between the BIOS and the boot loader. Your boot loader (GRUB or LILO) will not find the boot sector on /dev/sda and, therefore, will not be able to boot Linux.*

Partitioning Utilities

Many disk-partitioning utilities are available for Linux—even utilities that do not run under Linux. The basic Linux partitioning utility is **fdisk**. During installation, Red Hat gives you access to Disk Druid. They all work toward the same end, but Red Hat recommends you use Disk Druid during the installation. It is safer than fdisk, and it has an easier-to-read graphical interface. But Disk Druid is not available after RHEL is installed.

on the job

As it's not cited in any of the Red Hat requirements for the exams, I do not cover the parted utility. However, it is a viable option for managing your partitions.

CERTIFICATION OBJECTIVE 2.02

Downloading the Red Hat Installation CD-ROMs

To study for the RHCE or RHCT exam, you need to practice with a copy of a Red Hat Linux distribution. Ideally, you should work with a copy of Red Hat Enterprise Linux 3. Unfortunately, it is expensive. But assuming you have a high-speed connection, there are options.

RHEL 3 is based on Red Hat Linux 9. If you install and update this operating system, you can use Red Hat Linux 9 to study for the exams. Just be sure that you have the appropriate version of any software that you're studying. Alternatively, you could even use the version of Fedora Linux (Yarrow) released in November 2003. It's a mixed bag; that Fedora Linux release includes some updates that are in RHEL 3, and others that go beyond RHEL 3.

If you don't have a high-speed connection, downloading the gigabytes of files associated with the latest versions of RHEL can take several days. If Red Hat Linux 9 or Fedora Linux is all that you can or want to afford, and you can accept the differences with Red Hat Enterprise Linux 3, you can purchase downloaded CDs from a source such as CheapBytes (www.cheapbytes.com) or buy a book with the publisher's edition of Red Hat Linux 9. Alternatively, there are third parties who have built RHEL 3 from the publically available source RPMs. I describe these options in more detail in the Introduction to this book.

Generally, these downloaded CDs are available in ISO format, which you can process and write to CDs using the methods I describe in this section.

Red Hat Enterprise Linux

As described in the introduction to this book, you can buy a copy of RHEL. Assuming you have a PC with an Intel-style 32-bit CPU, you can purchase the most inexpensive version of this server, Red Hat Enterprise Linux ES. As of this writing, you can purchase the Basic Edition with a one-year subscription to the Red Hat Network for $349. At this price, RHEL ES 3 is available only by download in ISO format; for all practical purposes, this requires a high-speed connection.

While there are versions of RHEL available with packaged CDs, they are significantly more expensive. Once again, let me repeat my belief that you can use Red Hat Linux 9 or the RHEL rebuilds to study for the RHCE and RHCT exams based on RHEL 3.

Red Hat Enterprise Source RPMs

Red Hat provides free access to the source RPMs for Red Hat Enterprise Linux 3 (RHEL). You can download these source RPMs from ftp.redhat.com (or an FTP mirror site) for free. You can then build your own copy of RHEL using the instructions as described in the Red Hat Enterprise Linux Rebuild mini-HOWTO, available online from www2.uibk .ac.at/zid/software/unix/linux/rhel-rebuild.htm. My understanding is that once you've downloaded and prepared the source RPMs, it takes a couple of days for an average PC to process the source code into binary RPM packages which you can then install on your computer.

While I am not a lawyer, I understand that this is legal because the source code for almost all of the software included with RHEL 3 has been released through the Linux General Public License (GPL).

Third-Party Red Hat Enterprise Linux

As I've described in the introduction to this book, there are third-party versions of RHEL 3 available. They are built from the source code RPMs that Red Hat has made freely available, under the Linux General Public License (GPL). While I am not a lawyer, my understanding is that these third parties have complied with the following guidelines:

- Software in RHEL 3 that is not licensed under the GPL must not be included. As I understand it, this includes some packages supplied by IBM and not covered on the Red Hat exam.

- All software in the third-party version of RHEL 3 must be built from the source code (despite what you might see on eBay, my understanding is that you can't just resell copies of the RHEL binary RPMs, especially the installation CDs).

- References to "Red Hat" must be removed from the software.

- Binary updates, such as through **up2date** or the Red Hat Network, are not allowed. However, this does not exclude updates from revised GPL source code.

As I've described in the introduction, there are three major groups working on a rebuild of RHEL 3. As of this writing, each of these groups have made their work available in ISO format through their Web sites (and mirrors), which you can write to CDs using the techniques I describe shortly.

on the *Job* *The work of these third parties are known as "rebuilds" because their versions of RHEL 3 are built from source RPMs. They are not "clones," as they use the same basic source code used and released by Red Hat.*

Red Hat Linux 9 or Fedora

RHEL 3 is based on Red Hat Linux 9. It includes some improvements that are included in the first release of Fedora Linux in late 2003. Therefore, you could prepare for the RHCE or RHCT exams using one or both of these operating system distributions.

However, these operating systems are not identical. For example, while Red Hat Linux 9 uses the samba-2.2.7 RPM package for sharing with Microsoft Windows computers, RHEL 3 uses the samba-3.0.0 RPM package. With the current Red Hat development model, Red Hat will use Fedora to test *some* future changes to RHEL. Today, the differences between RHEL 3, Red Hat Linux 9, and the Fedora Linux released in late 2003 are fairly small. However, I believe that the differences between RHEL 4 and Fedora (or its successor) will be more substantial. I'm guessing RHEL 4 will be released in 2005.

If you don't have a copy of Red Hat Enterprise Linux 3, I recommend that you study with one of the third-party rebuilds of RHEL 3.

e x a m

w a t c h   *If you're using Red Hat Linux 9 or Fedora Linux to simulate the conditions of RHEL 3, you may want to download and install some of the RHEL 3 source RPMS. If you want to install the version of Samba associated with RHEL 3*   *(3.0.0-14.3E), for example, you can download the Samba source RPM from a Red Hat Rawhide server at ftp.redhat.com or one of the mirrors listed at www.redhat.com/download/ mirror.html.*

An Overview of the Download Process

If you have a high-speed connection, downloading Red Hat operating system CD-ROMs is fairly easy. If you've purchased Red Hat Enterprise Linux, follow the Red Hat Network download instructions. If you want to download the Red Hat Linux 9 or Fedora Installation CDs, just connect to ftp.redhat.com or one of the many mirrors such as Tucows Linux (www.tucows.com) or www.linuxiso.org, and start your download. If you're downloading a third-party rebuild of RHEL 3, navigate to their Web sites for more information. Since FTP is optimized for file transfer, FTP clients are the best way to download a Linux distribution.

There are two ways to download and prepare Red Hat Installation files: as individual files or as ISO packages. You can install from ISO packages on a hard drive. You can also install from ISO packages or a directory of RPM files on an HTTP, FTP, or NFS server.

Once you've downloaded the installation files or ISOs, you're ready to install the Red Hat operating system, possibly with the help of the appropriate boot disk as described later in this chapter.

Downloading Installation Files

If you have 2GB of available disk space, you can download the Red Hat operating system installation files. Create a RedHat directory or subdirectory on your hard disk, and copy the files from the /RedHat directory on the FTP server. I'll show you shortly how you can use this to set up a network installation server.

On your computer, direct the download to a /RedHat directory (or subdirectory). Organize the files in the /RedHat directory with the same subdirectories that you can find on a Red Hat installation CD. Make sure to include both the /base and /RPMS subdirectories. When you perform the download, make sure you also copy the hidden .discinfo file on the first installation CD.

Downloading Red Hat Linux on ISO Files

An ISO is a single file that is associated with a large package of files, usually on a CD. Once you download an ISO, you can use a number of tools to extract the files to a CD-ROM. There are four binary installation ISOs associated with Red Hat Enterprise Linux 3. Alternatively, the third-party rebuilds (as of this writing) have consolidated the RHEL 3 software on three binary installation ISOs.

As long as you have a high-speed connection, it's easy to download the appropriate ISOs. I describe the **lftp** client in Chapter 7. Once you've downloaded the three Red Hat installation ISOs, use the tool of your choice to extract the contents to a writable CD. For example, the following command records the /tmp/RedHat/rhcd1.iso file, at 2x speed, to a blank writable CD on the first CD drive on your computer:

```
# cdrecord -v speed=2 dev=0,0,0 /tmp/RedHat/rhcd1.iso
```

If you need more information on recording CDs, refer to the CD-Writing HOWTO available from www.tldp.org. Alternatively, you can mount the ISO as if it were a CD. For example, the following command mounts the aforementioned ISO file:

```
# mount -t iso9660 -ro loop /tmp/RedHat/rhcd1.iso /mnt/cdrom
```

You don't even need to extract the files from the ISO. Just use the /mnt/cdrom directory as if it were a real CD.

It's easy to check the integrity of each installation CD. Reboot your computer with the first Red Hat Enterprise Linux installation CD. Type **linux mediacheck** at the prompt; the RHEL 3 installation program takes you to the screen shown in Figure 2-1 where you can test each CD.

e x a m

ⓦatch

As you prepare for the RHCE or RHCT exams, remember to think in terms of what is practical. While it is important to know how to download and set up a Red Hat installation CD, it wouldn't be practical for a group of test candidates to all be downloading the Red Hat installation CDs during an actual exam.

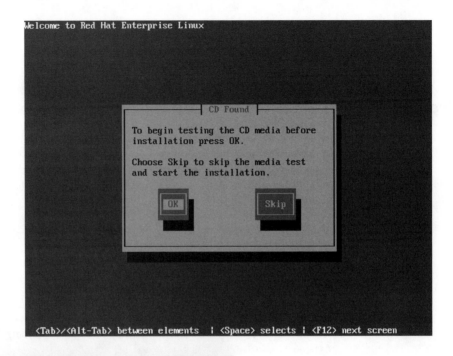

Configuring a Network Installation

Most Linux users can install Red Hat Enterprise Linux from a CD-ROM. During the installation portion of the Red Hat exam, you'll probably want to save time by installing RHEL 3 over a network on an NFS, HTTP, or FTP server. As you'll want to practice network installations, you'll want to set up a network server. For completeness, you can also install RHEL from ISO images on a local hard disk.

Configuring a Network Installation Server

Once you have the Red Hat installation CDs, configuring a network installation server is a fairly easy process. All you need to do is copy the files from each CD's /RedHat directory to a common directory, configure sharing on the directory, and then activate the NFS, FTP, or HTTP network.

Before you set up a network installation source, you'll need a partition with about 2GB of free space (or more). I'll illustrate the process for an NFS server, and explain the variations for FTP and HTTP servers.

Creating an NFS Installation Server

In the following steps, I'll show you how to create a shared directory, copy the Red Hat installation files, and then set up the share through NFS. As NFS is the most efficient way to share files between Linux and Unix computers, I think it's the most likely option for network installations during the exam. You'll need the Red Hat Enterprise Linux installation CDs, or at least the ISO files associated with those CDs.

1. Create a directory for your installation files. With the following command, I can create the /mnt/inst directory:

   ```
   # mkdir /mnt/inst
   ```

2. Insert the first Red Hat Enterprise Linux installation CD into its drive. Mount it with the following command. (If all you have are the ISO files, say in the /tmp directory, substitute **mount -t iso9660 -ro loop /tmp/*firstcd*.iso /mnt /cdrom**.)

   ```
   # mount /mnt/cdrom
   ```

3. Copy the required files from the first Red Hat Enterprise Linux installation CD.

   ```
   # cp -ar /mnt/cdrom/RedHat /mnt/inst
   ```

4. Copy the .discinfo file from the first Red Hat Enterprise Linux installation CD. This is required if you want to use **redhat-config-packages** (also known as the Red Hat Package Management tool) to add software using this installation server after Linux is installed. (While there are a number of other files on the first RHEL 3 installation CD, .discinfo is the only file that's absolutely required for an installation server.)

   ```
   # cp /mnt/cdrom/.discinfo /mnt/inst
   ```

5. Unmount the first Red Hat Enterprise Linux installation CD.

   ```
   # umount /mnt/cdrom
   ```

6. Repeat steps 2, 3, and 5 with the remaining Red Hat Enterprise Linux installation CDs.

7. Set up an NFS share. Add the following line to /etc/exports. You can do it with a text editor such as vi or the **redhat-config-nfs** utility (also known as the NFS Server Configuration tool) described in Chapter 9.

```
/mnt/inst        *(ro,sync)
```

8. Export the shared directory.

```
# exportfs -a
```

9. Make sure there's nothing blocking access to NFS. The default Red Hat Enterprise Linux firewall blocks access to an NFS server. While inelegant, the following command "flushes," or turns off the standard Linux firewall from the local computer. I'll describe the **iptables** command in more detail in Chapter 10.

```
# iptables -F
```

10. Now you can activate the NFS service. The following commands assume that it's already running (which you can check with the **service nfs status** command):

```
# service nfs stop

# service nfs start
```

11. Finally, you can check the status of your share. If it's working, you should see the contents of the /etc/exports directory when you run the following command:

```
# showmount -e
```

When you install Red Hat Enterprise Linux from an NFS server, you'll need the name of the installation directory, in this case, /mnt/inst.

on the
Ob

For an NFS connection, you don't need to copy the files from a CD. If you've downloaded ISOs of the RHEL installation CDs, all you need to do is copy them to the shared NFS directory, in this case, /mnt/inst. However, this does not work for FTP or HTTP servers.

Configuring Another Network Installation Server

The Red Hat exams test your knowledge of Linux. The most efficient way to share files between Linux computers is NFS. If you have a choice on the exams, install Red Hat Enterprise Linux over a network connection, using NFS. However, it's possible that you'll want or need to install Red Hat Enterprise Linux using one of the two other available protocols: HTTP or FTP.

HTTP Installation Server

The most popular Web server on the Internet is Apache, which you can easily install with Red Hat Enterprise Linux. The basic steps are the same as for the NFS server. The details are slightly different. I'm assuming that you've already installed the Apache Web server as described in Chapter 7. The basic Apache share directory corresponds to the DocumentRoot variable, which is by default the /var/www/html directory. In other words, you'd copy the Red Hat Installation files to a subdirectory of this directory. For the purpose of this chapter, I've created the /var/www/html/test directory. Here are the detailed steps:

1. Create a directory for your installation files. With the following command, I'm creating the /var/www/html/test directory. (If you get an error message, Apache may not be properly installed.)

   ```
   # mkdir /var/www/html/test
   ```

2. Insert the first Red Hat Enterprise Linux installation CD into its drive. Mount it with the following command. (If all you have are the ISO files, say in the /tmp directory, you can mount the first Red Hat Enterprise Linux installation CD with the **mount -t iso9660 -ro loop /tmp/firstcd.iso /mnt/cdrom** command.)

   ```
   # mount /mnt/cdrom
   ```

3. Copy the required files from the first Red Hat Enterprise Linux installation CD.

   ```
   # cp -ar /mnt/cdrom/RedHat /var/www/html/test/
   ```

4. Copy the .discinfo file from the first Red Hat Enterprise Linux installation CD. This is required if you want to use **redhat-config-packages** (also known as the Red Hat Package Management tool) to add software using this installation server after Linux is installed. (While there are a number of other files on the first RHEL 3 installation CD, .discinfo is the only file that's absolutely required for an installation server.)

   ```
   # cp /mnt/cdrom/.discinfo /var/www/html/test/
   ```

5. Unmount the first Red Hat Enterprise Linux installation CD.

   ```
   # umount /mnt/cdrom
   ```

6. Repeat steps 2, 3, and 5 with the remaining Red Hat Enterprise Linux installation CDs.

7. Make sure there's nothing blocking access to your Apache server. While inelegant, the following command "flushes," or turns off the standard Linux

firewall from the local computer. I'll describe the **iptables** command in more detail in Chapter 10.

```
# iptables -F
```

8. Now you can activate the Apache service, **httpd**. The following commands assume that it's already running (which you can check with the **service httpd status** command):

```
# service httpd stop
```

```
# service httpd start
```

When you install Red Hat Enterprise Linux from an Apache HTTP server, you'll need to remember the directory with the Red Hat installation files. For an HTTP server, the right directory is relative to the DocumentRoot variable, /var/www/html. With these steps, the installation files are in /var/www/html/test; therefore, the correct directory is /test.

FTP Installation Server

One of the oldest protocols still in common use on the Internet is FTP, the File Transfer Protocol. It's efficient, it's easy to use, and now that Red Hat has implemented the very secure FTP (vsFTP) service on its systems, it's relatively secure.

The basic steps are the same as for the NFS server. I'm assuming that you've already installed the vsFTP server, as described in Chapter 7. The basic FTP share directory is /var/ftp/pub. In other words, you'd copy the Red Hat Installation files to a subdirectory of this directory. For the purpose of this chapter, I've created the /var/ftp/pub/test directory. Here are the detailed steps:

1. Create a directory for your installation files. With the following command, I'm creating the /var/ftp/pub/test directory. (If you get an error message, Apache may not be properly installed.)

```
# mkdir /var/ftp/pub/test
```

2. Insert the first Red Hat Enterprise Linux installation CD into its drive. Mount it with the following command. (If all you have are the ISO files, say in the /tmp directory, you can mount the first RHEL installation CD with the **mount -t iso9660 -ro loop /tmp/firstcd.iso /mnt/cdrom** command.)

```
# mount /mnt/cdrom
```

3. Copy the required files from the first Red Hat Enterprise Linux installation CD.

```
# cp -ar /mnt/cdrom/RedHat /var/ftp/pub/test
```

4. Copy the .discinfo file from the first Red Hat Enterprise Linux installation CD. This is required if you want to use **redhat-config-packages** (also known as the Red Hat Package Management tool) to add software using this installation server after Linux is installed. (While there are a number of other files on the first RHEL 3 installation CD, .discinfo is the only file that's absolutely required for an installation server.)

```
# cp /mnt/cdrom/.discinfo /var/www/html/test/
```

5. Unmount the first Red Hat Enterprise Linux installation CD.

```
# umount /mnt/cdrom
```

6. Repeat steps 2, 3, and 5 with the remaining Red Hat Enterprise Linux installation CDs.

7. Make sure there's nothing blocking access to your Apache server. While inelegant, the following command "flushes," or turns off the standard Linux firewall from the local computer. I'll describe the **iptables** command in more detail in Chapter 10.

```
# iptables -F
```

8. Now you can activate the FTP server, vsFTP. The following commands assume that it's already running (which you can check with the **service vsftpd status** command):

```
# service vsftpd stop
```

```
# service vsftpd start
```

When you install Red Hat Enterprise Linux from an FTP server, you'll need to remember the directory with the Red Hat installation files. For an FTP server, the right directory is relative to the basic /var/ftp directory. With these steps, the installation files are in /var/ftp/pub/test; therefore, the correct directory is /pub/test.

Requirements for Network Installations

Now that you've set up the Red Hat Enterprise Linux installation files on a network server, let's look at what else you'll need on the computer where you'll be installing Linux. Once Linux detects your network card, you'll need to configure that card to be a part of your network. It'll be done by a DHCP (Dynamic Host Configuration Protocol) server or by static IP addressing.

If there's a DHCP server for your network, this process is easy. All you'll need to do is set the Linux installation program to ask for your IP address information from that DHCP server. As long as there are no active firewalls between your computer and the DHCP server, you should not have any problems.

Otherwise, you'll need to configure your computer with static IP addresses. In this case, you'll need a valid, unused IP address, the local network mask, the default gateway IP address (if the installation files are on a different LAN), and optionally, the primary DNS IP address, a domain name such as example.com, and the hostname to use for the local computer.

As you can see in Figure 2-2, Anaconda allows you to get your IP address information from a DHCP server or enter the static IP address information yourself.

FIGURE 2-2

Configuring
TCP/IP on your
network card
during installation

```
Welcome to Red Hat Linux




                       ┤ Configure TCP/IP ├
         Please enter the IP configuration for this machine. Each
         item should be entered as an IP address in dotted-decimal
         notation (for example, 1.2.3.4).

              [ ] Use dynamic IP configuration (BOOTP/DHCP)

                IP address:            _____
                Netmask:               _____
                Default gateway (IP):  _____
                Primary nameserver:    _____


                 ┌────────┐              ┌────────┐
                 │   OK   │              │  Back  │
                 └────────┘              └────────┘




        <Tab>/<Alt-Tab> between elements  ¦ <Space> selects ¦ <F12> next screen
```

You'll also need the hostname or IP address of the Red Hat Enterprise Linux installation server. If you have the hostname, you'll also need the IP address of the DNS server for the network used for the exam. As shown in Figure 2-2, this is also known as the *Primary nameserver*. If the DNS server is not on the LAN, you'll also need the *Default gateway* IP address.

on the
job *If you're installing Red Hat Enterprise Linux from files on a network server, check the firewall on that server. The standard RHEL 3 and Red Hat Linux 9 firewalls cut off network communication to whatever FTP, HTTP, or NFS server you might be using to store the /RedHat directory tree.*

CERTIFICATION OBJECTIVE 2.04

Customizing Your Installation

Before we install Red Hat Enterprise Linux on a computer, we'll look at some of the critical decisions that you'll need to make during the Red Hat exams. Time is of the essence on these exams. While you could just install everything, that could easily cost you 15 minutes or more. That may be the time that you need to configure the critical services required to pass the exam. By the time you're done with this section, you'll have the tools to select just the software that you need.

Red Hat Enterprise Linux includes its own installation program, known as Anaconda. RHEL 3 Workstation and RHEL 3 Server include different sets of default RPM packages. With Fedora Core 1 or Red Hat Linux 9, you can simulate these installations using the Workstation or Custom installation options. Naturally, RHEL Workstation is associated with the RHCT exam; RHEL Server is associated with the RHCE exams.

exam

Watch *Even RHCEs need to know how to configure the X Window, as they are often expected to configure workstations for users who need graphical applications.*

As the RHCE exam includes RHCT components, you may also need to configure your computer as a workstation. Don't be surprised if you install applications associated with the X Window System and GNOME or KDE desktop environments.

Depending on your needs, you can set up a system with anywhere from about 600MB to 4GB of files. In the real world, you'll need lots of additional room for user files, log files, and any additional applications that you may want to install in the future.

The essence of each installation is in the installed package groups. As you examine each of the options, focus on the associated package groups. First, there are basic package groups that are included with every installation. Then, there are the package groups that you can select during the installation process.

Baseline Packages

Every installation of Red Hat Enterprise Linux gets a series of packages, organized into the Core and Base package groups. You can find a list of these on the first Red Hat Enterprise Installation CD-ROM in /RedHat/base/comps.xml, at the top of this text file. I've modified this file slightly, as shown in Figure 2-3, to list the first few base packages specified in this file.

FIGURE 2-3

Red Hat
Enterprise Linux
base packages

```
<group>
  <id>core</id>
  <name>Core</name>
  <default>true</default>
  <description>Smallest possible installation</description>
  <uservisible>false</uservisible>
  <packagelist>
    <packagereq type="default">ash</packagereq>
    <packagereq type="mandatory">basesystem</packagereq>
    <packagereq type="mandatory">bash</packagereq>
    <packagereq type="mandatory">coreutils</packagereq>
    <packagereq type="mandatory">cpio</packagereq>
    <packagereq type="mandatory">e2fsprogs</packagereq>
    <packagereq type="mandatory">ed</packagereq>
    <packagereq type="mandatory">efibootmgr</packagereq>
    <packagereq type="mandatory">elilo</packagereq>
    <packagereq type="mandatory">file</packagereq>
    <packagereq type="mandatory">filesystem</packagereq>
    <packagereq type="mandatory">glibc</packagereq>
    <packagereq type="mandatory" basearchonly="true">grub</packagereq>
    <packagereq type="mandatory">hdparm</packagereq>
    <packagereq type="mandatory">hotplug</packagereq>
    <packagereq type="mandatory">initscripts</packagereq>
    <packagereq type="mandatory">iproute</packagereq>
    <packagereq type="mandatory">iputils</packagereq>
    <packagereq type="mandatory">kbd</packagereq>
    <packagereq type="mandatory">kernel</packagereq>
    <packagereq type="mandatory">libgcc</packagereq>
    <packagereq type="mandatory">libtermcap</packagereq>
    <packagereq type="mandatory">losetup</packagereq>
    <packagereq type="mandatory">passwd</packagereq>
    <packagereq type="mandatory">procps</packagereq>
    <packagereq type="mandatory">raidtools</packagereq>
    <packagereq type="mandatory">readline</packagereq>
```

Default Packages

The RHEL 3 server installation process installs about 1.4GB of software by default. This includes several package groups that are suitable for some uses. If this is good enough for the requirements as presented on your particular exam, activate the Accept The Current Package List option and click Next to continue. In most cases, you'll want to select the Customize The Set Of Packages To Be Installed option.

As shown in Figure 2-4, they include the package groups described in Table 2-2. They actually include three other package groups, Graphical Internet, Text Internet, and Printing Support. I include a basic description of these Package Groups in Table 2-2 as well.

There are actually more default package groups, which you can review in the aforementioned comps.xml file. They include the following package groups: Printing Support, Dialup Networking Support, and Text-based Internet.

on the
()ob

When you install RHEL 3, the Dialup Networking Support package group is automatically installed during the regular installation process. You're not even allowed to deselect it through the default version of Anaconda.

FIGURE 2-4

Red Hat
Enterprise Linux
default package
groups

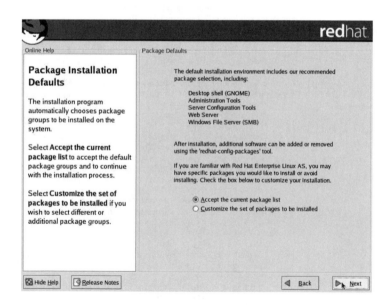

TABLE 2-2	Package Group	Description
Default Package Groups	Desktop shell (GNOME)	The default Red Hat Enterprise Linux GUI desktop. While it may not be required on the job for many servers, it is very likely that you'll need to install GNOME during the Red Hat exams.
	Administration Tools	Includes Red Hat's basic GUI administration tools. Useful if you're going to configure Red Hat from the GUI.
	Server Configuration Tools	Adds Red Hat's basic GUI configuration tools for many major servers.
	Web Server	Installs basic packages associated with the Apache Web Server. Includes the Tux Web Server.
	Windows File Server (SMB)	Includes the Samba client and server packages.
	Graphical Internet	Graphical tools for connections and communication on TCP/IP networks.
	Text Internet	Text-based tools for connections and communication on TCP/IP networks.
	Printing Support	Basic software required to connect this computer to a printer and set it up as a print server.

Customizing Package Installation

In most cases, it will be best to customize the packages that you'll install during the Red Hat exams. Alternatively, you can use the **redhat-config-packages** (Red Hat Package Management) tool, described in more detail in Chapter 4. This section focuses on package groups. If you see requirements on your exam for a mail server, graphics applications such as The GIMP, and to recompile the kernel, you'll want to select the Mail Server, Graphics, and Kernel Development package groups.

on the *The general option to select individual RPM packages during the Linux*
ⓙob *installation process is no longer available in RHEL (or in Fedora Linux). However, you can select some individual RPM packages as part of RHEL package groups during the graphical installation process.*

Red Hat package groups are organized logically; for example, all of the packages associated with the GNOME desktop environment belong to one Red Hat package group. It's important to pick only the package groups you need. Fewer installed packages means more room for personal files for you and your users, as well as the log files you need to monitor your system and actually get some use from your applications. On the exam, fewer installed packages leaves more time to configure the required services.

on the
Job *Understanding how these package groups work is important in a Kickstart installation, which is described in more detail in Chapter 3.*

Package Groups

This section includes the briefest possible overview of each of the packages you can select during the RHEL installation process. Remember, some of these packages depend on others; for example, if you want to install the GNOME Desktop Environment package group, the Red Hat installation program will make sure that you install the X Window System package group as well.

For complete details of the RPMs associated with each package, go to the first RHEL installation CD, and read the comps.xml file in the /RedHat/base directory in the text editor or Web browser of your choice.

These packages, as well as the order in which they are presented, are based on Red Hat Enterprise Linux 3. If you're using Fedora, some other version of Red Hat Linux, or even one of the third-party rebuilds, the packages may vary. In any case, the best way to study what's in each package group is through the graphical installation.

For example, Figure 2-5 illustrates the RHEL 3 installation, with a focus on the Mail Server package group. As you can see, two major mail servers, sendmail and postfix, are both installed by default when you select this package group.

Take some time with this screen. Examine the packages within each package group. You'll learn about the kinds of packages that are installed by default. If you don't add them during the installation process, it isn't the end of the world. You can still add them with the **rpm** commands described in Chapter 3, or the **redhat-config-packages** (Red Hat Package Management) tool described in Chapter 4. What you learn here can help you select the package groups to install during the RHCE or RHCT exam.

In the following sections, I describe each package group in more detail, based on what you see during the RHEL ES 3 Server graphical installation process. You won't see all of these package groups during a RHEL 3 Workstation or Red Hat Professional Workstation installation.

FIGURE 2-5

Red Hat
Enterprise Linux
Mail Server
package group
details

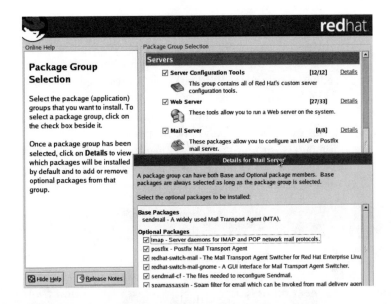

INSIDE THE EXAM

During the Installation Exam

Even if you're taking the RHCE exam, pay attention to the software associated with the Linux desktop environment. The RHCE exam includes RHCT components, which means that you'll also be tested on setting up Linux as a workstation.

That means you'll be installing a number of package groups that you would not install on a computer that's just being used as a server. When you take the exam, read the configuration requirements carefully. I would not be surprised if you see a requirement to install software

such as sound software and the OpenOffice.org suite.

But don't install everything. If you don't need to install the OpenOffice.org suite, you can save several minutes during the Installation and Configuration exam. The time you save could allow you to configure a few more services, which could determine whether you pass the exam.

And if you make a mistake during the installation process, don't panic. You can use the **redhat-config-packages** tool after installation to add any package groups that you missed.

X Window System

This package group includes a number of basic Linux GUI fonts, libraries, and critical tools such as the Red Hat GUI Display Settings tool, which you can start with the **redhat-config-xfree86** command. It's required if you install the GNOME or KDE desktop environments.

As a Linux administrator, you may have confidence in your ability to configure Linux from the command line. In practice, you may install Linux on a number of computers without the GUI. However, even the RHCE exam includes an RHCT component, which tests your ability to create a Linux workstation for your users, which almost invariably includes a GUI.

ⓦ a t c h *Since the RHCT exam requires you to configure a workstation, and you have to meet all RHCT*	*requirements during the RHCE exam, expect to install the GUI during the Installation and Configuration exam.*

GNOME Desktop Environment

The GNOME group includes the basic packages required to install the GNOME Network Object Model Environment. While GNOME is the default GUI for RHEL 3, read the instructions on your exam carefully. It's possible that you'll be asked to install the other major GUI, the K desktop environment.

When you choose to install the GNOME Desktop Environment package group, all GNOME packages are installed by default.

KDE Desktop Environment

The KDE group includes the basic packages required to install the K Desktop Environment, which is the main alternative GUI for RHEL 3. It is the default GUI for a number of other Linux distributions.

When you choose to install the KDE Desktop Environment package group, not all of the KDE packages are installed by default. However, unless you're familiar and

ⓦ a t c h *Read the instructions on the RHCE and RHCT installation exam carefully. As an example, if it requires you*	*to set up only KDE, it's a waste of time to accept the default GNOME desktop environment!*

feel that you can use the KDE Administrative tools to help you configure RHEL, you won't need to change the defaults associated with this package group.

Editors

These include the basic text editors associated with Linux: vi and emacs. It also includes **nedit**, a Macintosh-style text editor. While it's essential that you know vi to use the Linux rescue mode, the emacs text editor may be the most popular text editor in the world of Linux and Unix. It also requires an extensive series of packages, which makes it impossible to include emacs on a rescue floppy that is limited to 1.44MB.

Engineering and Scientific

RHEL includes a group of packages for mathematical and scientific purposes, such as **gnuplot**, **pvm**, and **units**.

Graphical Internet

Linux now includes a number of different GUI clients for Internet access, including the Mozilla Web browser, the **xchat** and **gaim** instant message utilities, and the Evolution personal information manager.

Text-Based Internet

Linux includes a number of different text-based clients for Internet access, including the **elinks** Web browser, and the **fetchmail** and **mutt** e-mail readers. This is closely related to the Graphical Internet package group.

Office/Productivity

This group includes the emerging standard for Linux office suites, OpenOffice.org, as well as related packages such as PDF viewers. It includes about 300MB of software. If you don't need these tools on your Linux computer, you should consider leaving this out of the installation.

exam
watch

Time is of the essence on the Red Hat exams. Unless specifically required on your exam, don't install the Office/Productivity package group. This can save you several minutes which you could use to meet other requirements on your exam.

Sound and Video

Not surprisingly, the Sound and Video group installs the packages required to allow you to use sound cards and interconnect the basic components of your sound and video system: sound card, speakers, microphone, and CD/DVD drive.

Don't dismiss this package group out of hand; I've heard that some people are asked to configure a sound card during the RHCE exam. Therefore, it's possible that you'll want to install this package group when you configure the Linux desktop environment.

Authoring and Publishing

The Authoring and Publishing group includes support for several documentation systems, such as DocBook and TeX.

Graphics

This package group automatically incorporates the X Window package and a number of graphical applications. This includes the most prominent Linux graphics application, The GIMP. Depending on whether you also install GNOME and/or KDE, this also installs graphical packages associated with each of these GUIs.

Games and Entertainment

Be careful with this package group. Do you really want to install games on a business computing system? Some believe that computer games are useful to help newer users become comfortable with Linux. While I doubt that you'll ever have to install this package group during the RHCE or RHCT exams, read the instructions that come with your exam.

Server Configuration Tools

Red Hat has developed a series of GUI server configuration tools. For expert users, it's faster to configure most services from the command line interface. In fact, I encourage you to learn to configure all Linux services in this way; you'll be a better administrator.

However, these tools are installed by default in RHEL 3. As the RHCE exam requires you to configure servers, I encourage you to install this package group. It includes about 6MB of files, so the time penalty during the installation process is trivial. If you're less certain about your skills in one or more of these services—or if nerves affect your skills during an exam—these GUI tools can be a lifesaver:

- **redhat-config-bind**   Domain Name Service (DNS) configuration tool
- **redhat-config-httpd**   HTTP (Apache) configuration tool
- **redhat-config-network**   Network Configuration tool

- **redhat-config-nfs** NFS Server Configuration tool
- **redhat-config-printer** Printer Configuration tool
- **redhat-config-samba** Samba Server Configuration tool
- **redhat-config-securitylevel** Security Level Configuration tool
- **redhat-config-services** Service Configuration tool

Web Server

The Web Server group installs Apache, Squid, and the extensive array of supporting modules and configuration files. It's installed by default for RHEL 3. It's quite possible that you'll have to configure at least a Web server for the RHCE exam.

Mail Server

This group includes the packages required to configure a sendmail-based IMAP or a postfix mail server. While it is not installed by default, it is quite possible that you'll have to configure a mail server such as sendmail or postfix during the RHCE exam.

Windows File Server

This group includes the Samba packages required to set up Linux as a client and as a server on a Microsoft Windows-based network. It is installed by default, and it's quite possible that you'll have to configure Samba during both the RHCT and RHCE exams. RHEL 3 includes the Samba 3.0 file server; if you're using Red Hat Linux 9 to study for your exam, you'll have to upgrade accordingly from the RPM source code, using the techniques described in Chapter 4.

While I haven't seen any Microsoft Windows computers at Red Hat, it is possible to configure and test Samba clients and servers, using a second Linux computer as a client.

DNS Name Server

The DNS Name Server group includes the tools you need to configure and maintain a Domain Name System server on the local Linux computer. In the Linux world, a DNS server is also known as a nameserver, based on the Berkeley Internet Name Domain (bind). While it is not installed by default, it is quite possible that you'll have to configure a DNS server during the RHCE exam.

FTP Server

This includes the default Red Hat FTP server, the Very Secure FTP Daemon (**vsftpd**). While it is not installed by default, it is quite possible that you'll have to configure an

FTP server during the RHCE exam. It also happens to be the server that Red Hat uses for its own FTP sites.

SQL Database

The Structured Query Language (SQL) is one of the basic database languages. This group includes support for the PostgreSQL database system. It is not installed by default. As there is no reference to SQL or databases in any materials related to the RHCT or RHCE exams, I don't believe that you'll have to install this package group during either exam.

MySQL Database

The Structured Query Language (SQL) is one of the basic database languages. This group includes support for the MySQL database system. It is not installed by default. As there is no reference to SQL or databases in any materials related to the RHCT or RHCE exams, I don't believe that you'll have to install this package group during either exam.

News Server

This is a simple group, incorporating the inn (Internet Network News) server. It is not installed by default, and there is no reference to a News Server in the Red Hat Exam Prep guide.

Network Servers

This package group includes a number of smaller servers that are useful for running a network, including those associated with DHCP (Dynamic Host Configuration Protocol) and NIS (Network Information Service). It is not installed by default. When you select this package group during the RHEL 3 installation process, Red Hat installs DHCP and the NIS server.

However, if you're asked to install other components of this package group during the RHCE Installation and Configuration exam, you may want to customize details during the Anaconda installation process. You can then select the required servers as shown in Figure 2-6. Alternatively, you can just use the **rpm** command as described in Chapter 4 to install the appropriate packages after RHEL is installed. Servers with similar functionality are included in the Legacy Network Servers package group.

Legacy Network Servers

There are several legacy network servers. While some Linux gurus discourage their use due to security concerns, they remain popular. They include packages that allow you to install an RSH (Remote Shell), Telnet, and TFTP (Trivial File Transfer Protocol) server.

FIGURE 2-6

Network Servers
package group

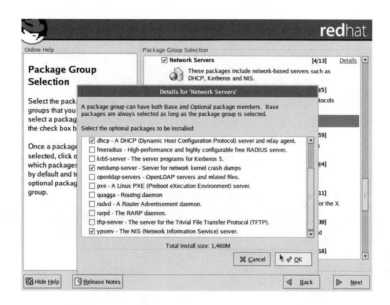

Development Tools

This group includes a large number of development tools. Additional development tools
are included when you install other packages such as GNOME Development, Graphics,
Web Server, News Server, and more. As there is no reference to Development Tools
packages in any materials related to the RHCT or RHCE exams, I don't believe that
you'll have to install this package group during either exam.

Kernel Development

This group includes the very large Kernel source packages, which currently require
over 500MB of disk space. There is no longer a specific requirement to recompile the
Linux kernel during the Red Hat exams. As this group requires over 500MB of software,
don't install this package group unless required on your specific exam.

X Software Development

The X Software Development group includes the basic packages such as XFree86-devel
required to develop additional GUI applications. As there is no reference to X Software
Development packages in any materials related to the RHCT or RHCE exams, I don't
believe that you'll have to install this package group during either exam.

GNOME Software Development

The GNOME group includes the basic packages required to develop additional GTK+ and
GNOME GUI applications. As there is no reference to GNOME Software Development

packages in any materials related to the RHCT or RHCE exams, I don't believe that you'll have to install this package group during either exam.

KDE Software Development

The KDE group includes the basic packages required to develop additional QT and KDE GUI applications. As there is no reference to KDE Software Development packages in any materials related to the RHCT or RHCE exams, I don't believe that you'll have to install this package group during either exam.

Legacy Software Development

Red Hat makes it possible to develop software on RHEL 3 for older versions of Red Hat Linux. The Legacy Software Development group includes support for older C and C++ language compilers. As there is no reference to these software development packages in any materials related to the RHCT or RHCE exams, I don't believe that you'll have to install this package group during either exam.

Administration Tools

Red Hat has developed a series of GUI administration tools. For expert users, it's faster to configure most services from the command line interface. In fact, I encourage you to learn to configure all Linux services in this way; in the long run, you'll be a better administrator.

However, these tools are installed by default in RHEL 3. For the purposes of the RHCE and RHCT exams, I encourage you to install this package group. If you're less certain about your skills in one or more of these services—or if nerves affect your skills during an exam—these GUI tools can be a lifesaver:

- **redhat-config-authentication**   Supports configuration of NIS and Samba clients and more; also known as the Authentication Configuration tool.
- **redhat-config-date**   Allows you to configure the time and date of your system; also known as the Date/Time Properties tool.
- **redhat-config-keyboard**   Lets you select a different keyboard; also known as the Keyboard configuration tool.
- **redhat-config-kickstart**   Opens a GUI for customizing a Kickstart file; also known as the Kickstart Configurator.
- **redhat-config-language**   Supports configuration of the GUI in different languages; also known as the Language Selection tool.

- **redhat-config-nfs** Allows configuration of an NFS server; also known as the NFS Server Configuration tool.
- **redhat-config-packages** Lets you install packages after RHEL is installed. Very important; also known as the Package Management tool.
- **redhat-config-proc** Opens a GUI for customizing the kernel. Functionally similar to Microsoft's Registry Editor; also known as the Kernel Tuning tool.
- **redhat-config-rootpassword** Allows you to change the root password (no special name).
- **redhat-config-soundcard** Automatically configures most sound cards (no special name).
- **redhat-config-users** Supports creating and modifying users and groups; also known as the Red Hat User Manager.
- **redhat-logviewer** Provides a GUI for viewing standard log files; also known as the System Logs configuration tool.

System Tools

This package group includes a varied array of tools, from the ethereal network traffic reader to the zsh shell. This package group is not installed by default, and I believe it's unlikely that you'll have to install this package group during either exam. While the Samba client is part of this package group, you can also install it through the Windows File Server package group.

However, it's a good idea to review the details of this package group during your studies, just in case you need one of these packages during your exam.

Printing Support

Red Hat Enterprise Linux currently includes support for the Common Unix Printing System (CUPS). It supports the next-generation printing protocol, known as IPP. Once installed, it can help detect network printers, with the help of the **redhat-config-printers** (Printer Configuration) tool.

on the
job

Red Hat no longer includes the Line Print Daemon (LPD) in the latest Linux distributions (RHEL 3 and Fedora Linux).

CERTIFICATION OBJECTIVE 2.05

Required Disk Space

Most new computers come with very large disks, easily supporting even the 4GB of files associated with a full installation of Red Hat Enterprise Linux. If you do not have this much space available, you should carefully consider the space requirements associated with each type of installation. When considering the following options, remember to leave adequate room for swap space, personal files, log files, and any applications that you may want to install after RHEL installation is complete.

It's common to install Linux on older computers with limited hard disk space. Linux functions quite well on older computers. It's common to configure such computers as servers for DNS, DHCP, NIS, and more. However, RHEL 3 does require at least Pentium-level 200 MHz CPU support, so you can't install it on the oldest computers

How Much More Space Is Needed?

The question of disk space needed over and above operating system needs is always relevant. Make sure to have extra room. The absolute minimum for a Red Hat Enterprise Linux OS is around 600MB of disk space, if you install Linux with few server services and without the X Window System. With 1000MB, you could probably sneak in the X Window, but you still wouldn't have enough room for more than a few server services. You still should have at least 100MB or more to work with. And if you want GNOME or KDE, you'll need another 200MB or so.

You'll also need to add room for swap space. By default, Red Hat usually configures a swap partition that is about twice the amount of RAM on your computer. The minimum requirement in RHEL 3 is a swap partition that equals the amount of RAM on your system. The actual swap partition size depends on the RAM and the size of the hard disk on your system.

The actual amount of swap space that you may need is a highly debatable issue. Some suggest that Linux computers can use a swap partition that is up to three or even four times the amount of available RAM. Others suggest that at higher levels of RAM, 100MB of swap space is more than sufficient.

Filesystems

By default, the RHEL installation program configures multiple volumes—separate volumes associated with different directories. The advantage of separate partitions for certain directories is that it limits the risks to your system. For example, many Webmasters configure their Web sites to write daily log files with data relating to all users who visit their sites. These files can become quite large, especially for large online merchants.

Before you decide how to set up partitions, you need to know about each of the major Linux directories. Linux directories are organized according to something known as the Filesystem Hierarchy Standard (FHS).

Filesystem Hierarchy Standard

The FHS is a standard for organizing directories for Linux- and Unix-based systems. Every FHS-compliant operating system starts with a top directory, root, symbolized by the forward slash. All other directories are subdirectories of root. The major FHS directories are described in Table 1-1 in Chapter 1.

Why Separate Filesystems?

Unix was developed when disk space was miniscule by today's standards. As Unix became an operating system for larger companies and universities, administrators had access to multiple, separate physical disks for each Unix computer. They took advantage of the space by splitting up the filesystem into smaller, more manageable pieces. Different directories were mounted on different physical drives.

This has a number of advantages. Smaller partitions are easier to maintain. Smaller partitions are easier to back up and restore. The size of a partition can limit the space taken by any specific directory. You can set up specific partitions as "read-only" for additional security.

There is at least one case where you should not mount different Linux directories on different partitions. If you're limited to a smaller hard drive, you need all of the spare room that you can get. This may apply to an older laptop computer, or an older computer that you're using for a dedicated purpose, such as a DNS server or a gateway router.

Configuring Linux Filesystems on Different Partitions

When you set up an RHEL Server filesystem, you can let Red Hat configure the partitions for you. By default, Red Hat configures a root directory (/) and a /boot directory partition.

Additional filesystems can be mounted on separate partitions to meet additional or specific needs of related groups of users. Some examples include: /home, /usr, /var, /development, /dbms, /financials, /inventory. The /tmp directory is often also mounted on a separate partition, to limit the space allocated to what should be temporary storage.

As befits a standard Linux server, it's quite possible that you'll need to configure several filesystems on different partitions during the Installation and Configuration exam.

Other Possible Separate Filesystems

Dedicated services are also good candidates for separate filesystems. For example, specific applications such as Web and FTP services can take up gigabytes of data. They store files in the /var/www/html and /var/ftp/pub directories.

You want to protect the rest of your computer if problems arise with a specific service. File and print sharing services such as NFS and Samba present security risks because they expose shared directories to other users. If you don't mount these services on separate partitions, anyone who uploads a large number of files could conceivably fill your hard disk.

If the number of files and users are large, you may even want to spread shared files over several partitions on different physical drives. In this situation, not every user will want data from the same drive all of the time. The load is shared by the different drives. Performance is improved.

CERTIFICATION OBJECTIVE 2.07

The Installation Process

You have many interrelated questions to answer during installation, just as you have many ways to access installation files, and many options on how to install the operating system. The following installation outline is designed to get you through the process in as simple a fashion as possible, with just enough detail to keep you going. While other sections and chapters address the special situations that you're more likely to encounter on the RHCE and RHCT exams, you need to know how to install Red Hat Enterprise Linux before you can work through the other installation scenarios.

During the RHCE or RHCT exams, you'll have access to the installation files. There are four methods that you can use to install RHEL Workstation or Server:

■ From a copy of the Red Hat Enterprise Linux installation CDs

■ Booting from the first RHEL installation CD

■ Booting from a special RHEL boot CD

■ Booting from a floppy designed to start the RHEL installation process

The last three options generally assume that you're going to install RHEL over a network. It's very possible that you'll see this option during the exam, which is why I described how to create a network installation server earlier in this chapter.

Avoid installing RHEL 3 from the CDs if at all possible. The basic installation takes a longer time. And the way the RHEL 3 installation packages are organized, you'll have to remove and insert your CDs several times.

Booting from the First CD-ROM

Most current Intel-based PC hardware systems allow you to boot directly from the CD drive. You can start the installation process by booting from the first Red Hat Enterprise Linux CD. The same basic process also works with older versions of Red Hat Linux as well as Fedora Linux.

If You Need an Installation Floppy or CD

If you don't have the first installation CD, you can start a network installation from a specialized boot floppy or CD. While one may be provided for you on the RHCE or RHCT exams, you'll need to know how to create one in order to practice for the exam.

It's easy to create an installation floppy or CD. You can do so from one of the files on the images directory on the first installation CD:

■ **bootdisk.img**   For a boot floppy

■ **boot.iso**   For a boot CD

The boot.iso file is small enough to fit on a credit-card sized CD. It contains all of the information in the bootdisk.img file as well as the driver images shown next.

Otherwise, if you create a boot floppy, you'll likely also need one or more of the following driver images on a floppy disk:

- **pcmciadd.img**   Additional support for PCMCIA adapters
- **drvblock.img**   Additional drivers for special hardware
- **drvnet.img**   Additional network card drivers

Creating Boot Floppies

There are two easy ways to project the boot images from the first Red Hat Installation CD-ROM onto a 1.44MB floppy disk.

In a Microsoft Windows–based operating system, open an MS-DOS window. Navigate to the drive associated with your CD. For example, if your CD is drive E: on your Microsoft-based system, change to that drive and enter the following command:

```
E:\> \dosutils\rawrite.exe
```

The RAWRITE.EXE program prompts you for the filename to write to the floppy disk. Next, it prompts you for the target drive, normally the A: drive. At the first prompt, enter the full path to the desired filename as follows:

```
E:\images\filename.img
```

You can view the files on any of the floppies that you create with MS-DOS commands. You also must repeat this process for each image file you wish to create. Once the boot image is transferred to disk, you can use standard MS-DOS commands such as **dir** to read the file list.

Creating Diskette Images with Any Unix/Linux System

You can also create diskette images with the **dd** command from any running Unix or Linux computer, along with the desired image files on the CD-ROM. For example, the following commands mount the appropriate CD and "disk dumps" the image into a disk on a floppy drive.

```
# mount /mnt/cdrom
# dd  if=/mnt/cdrom/images/bootdisk.img  of=/dev/fd0
```

Alternatively, you can just **cat** the disk image of your choice directly to a floppy drive device. For example, the following command reads the laptop driver disk directly to the first floppy drive:

```
# cat /mnt/cdrom/images/pcmciadd.img  > /dev/fd0
```

You can also create a boot CD from the boot.iso file in the /images directory. With Linux, you can do this with the following command:

```
# cdrecord -v speed=1 dev=0,0,0 /mnt/cdrom/images/boot.iso
```

You may need to find a different setting for the *dev* switch; you'll get the information that you need from the **cdrecord --scanbus** command. The advantage to a boot CD is that all available boot drivers are included; you won't need separate floppy disks for your drivers.

Know how to create the right boot disk for your system. If you have a problem, the installation boot disk can also serve as a rescue disk. At the boot prompt, the linux rescue *command will eventually bring you to a rescue mode that can help you mount your partitions or recover specific files or directories. I describe this process in Chapter 11.*

Almost Ready to Install

Now you have the boot and driver media that you need. Your system is now configured to boot either from the CD-ROM directly or from one of the boot floppies created in the previous section. Now install your first RHEL Installation CD-ROM or boot disk, and reboot your computer.

Bootable CD-ROM

Most newer computers can be set to boot directly from the CD-ROM. Just after your computer reboots, go into your computer's BIOS menu. You should be able to change the boot order to look to the CD-ROM drive first. If this option is not available, you're just going to have to use an installation boot floppy.

CD-ROM or Boot Diskette Starts Installation

Now your PC should boot from the CD-ROM or the installation boot floppy. After a few files are opened and decompressed, a Red Hat Enterprise Linux installation screen should appear, with the following prompt:

```
[F1-Main] [F2-Options] [F3-General] [F4-Kernel] [F5-Rescue]
boot:
```

You are finally beginning to install Red Hat Enterprise Linux! Press the F2 key. As you can see in Figure 2-7, a number of options are available to you when you start the process.

FIGURE 2-7

Red Hat Installer
boot options

```
                        Installer Boot Options

 -  To disable hardware probing, type: linux noprobe <ENTER>.

 -  To test the install media you are using, type: linux mediacheck <ENTER>.

 -  To enable rescue mode, type: linux rescue <ENTER>.
    Press <F5> for more information about rescue mode.

 -  If you have a driver disk, type: linux dd <ENTER>.

 -  To prompt for the install method being used on a CD-ROM install,
    type linux askmethod <ENTER>.

 -  If you have an installer update disk, type: linux updates <ENTER>.

 [F1-Main] [F2-Options] [F3-General] [F4-Kernel] [F5-Rescue]
 boot: _
```

If you're working from installation CDs that you downloaded through the Internet, your first step should be to check the media. While Red Hat provides checksums that you can use for this purpose, the easiest way to check your CDs is with the **linux mediacheck** option. Type in that command at the boot: prompt, and you'll see an option to test the media as shown back in Figure 2-1. Follow the prompts to check your CDs.

on the **Job**

If you have a problem with your graphics hardware, press F3 from the first screen. As described under the General Boot Help screen, you can try to force installation with a specific resolution with a command such as linux resolution=800x600.

To start the installation process from the boot: prompt, there are three basic options:

- **Graphical mode**   By default, Red Hat is installed from the CDs in graphical mode. If you're installing from the CDs, just press the ENTER key at the boot: prompt. If you're installing over a network, graphical installations are supported over an NFS connection.

- **Text mode**   The **linux text** option starts a low-intensity graphical installation known as text mode that all but the most graphically challenged computers can handle. If your computer can't even handle text mode, consider upgrading for RHEL.

- **Network installation**   You can use the installation CD or boot floppy to install RHEL over a network connection. If you're booting from the installation CD, enter **linux askmethod** at the boot: prompt. This tells the RHEL installation CD to ask you whether you want to install from the CD or from a network server.

It's also possible to install from files or ISOs on the local hard drive. For example,
if you're dual-booting with another version of Linux, you can copy the files
or ISOs to a specific directory on a specific partition. You can then use the
*linux askmethod **command to get Anaconda to look for files on a certain directory***
on that partition. If you don't know the partition device, such as /dev/hda8,
some trial and error may be required.

Basic Installation Overview

The basic RHEL installation is straightforward and should already be well understood
by any RHCE candidate. The differences between the RHEL 3 and Red Hat Linux 9
installation process are almost trivial. Most of the steps are described here for reference;
it's useful to remember this process as you work on advanced configuration situations such
as Kickstart files, which are described in Chapter 5. I've detailed the RHEL 3 installation
process in screenshots in Appendix B on the CD-ROM.

On the exam, you'll have a computer where you'll install RHEL 3. Therefore,
I'm assuming that you're installing RHEL as the only operating system on the local
computer (in other words, no dual-boots with Microsoft Windows). If you don't have
a separate computer that you can use for testing purposes (that is, where you don't
need any data), one very useful option is VMWare, which you can download from
www.vmware.com. It allows you to set up RHEL 3 on a Virtual Machine, configured
on a Linux or a Microsoft Windows 2000/XP computer.

As of this writing, you'll need to set up a virtual IDE drive on VMWare before
installing Red Hat Enterprise Linux 3 on that type of Virtual Machine.

The most efficient, and thus in my opinion, the most likely way you'll install
Red Hat Enterprise Linux during the RHCE and RHCT exams is with a graphical
installation from a remote NFS server. Therefore, the instructions I present are based
on that scenario. You'll have the opportunity to install RHEL from a CD and from
remote FTP or HTTP servers in exercises or labs later in this chapter.

1. Boot your computer from the first RHEL CD or a boot floppy.

2. When you see the boot: prompt, enter the **linux askmethod** command. This
   temporarily starts the installation process in text mode (which is actually a low
   resolution graphical mode), as shown in Figure 2-8. Use the TAB key to switch
   between options.

*While the linux askmethod **command isn't required to start a network installation***
from a boot floppy, it still works as described.

FIGURE 2-8

Starting the
installation
process

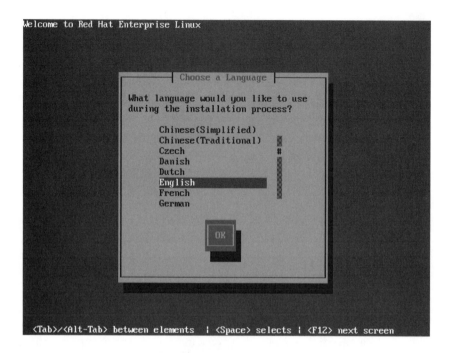

```
Welcome to Red Hat Enterprise Linux

                 ┌───────┤ Choose a Language ├───────┐
                 │ What language would you like to use │
                 │ during the installation process?    │
                 │                                     │
                 │         Chinese(Simplified)  ▓      │
                 │         Chinese(Traditional) ▓      │
                 │         Czech                ▓      │
                 │         Danish                      │
                 │         Dutch                       │
                 │         English                     │
                 │         French                      │
                 │         German                      │
                 │                                     │
                 │            ┌──────┐                 │
                 │            │  OK  │                 │
                 │            └──────┘                 │
                 └─────────────────────────────────────┘



 <Tab>/<Alt-Tab> between elements  ¦  <Space> selects  ¦  <F12> next screen
```

3. Select a language to use during the installation process. English is the default; 19 options are available.

4. Select a keyboard type; the default depends on the language you selected.

5. Choose your installation method. Earlier in this chapter, I described how to configure an NFS installation server. Therefore, select the NFS image option (the steps for installing from an HTTP or FTP server vary slightly).

   a. If you started with a boot floppy, you'll probably have to insert a driver disk. Follow the prompts associated with the Use A Driver Disk option, and insert a driver floppy that you created earlier.

6. Configure your IP address information, as shown in Figure 2-9. If you have a DHCP server on your network, the default should be sufficient. Otherwise, deselect the Use Dynamic IP Configuration option, and enter at least an IP address and Netmask. (A Netmask is also known as an IPv4 Subnet Mask or a network mask.)

7. Next, you'll direct your computer to the remote NFS server. As shown in Figure 2-10, you can enter the hostname or IP address of the NFS server, as

FIGURE 2-9

Configuring TCP/
IP for installation

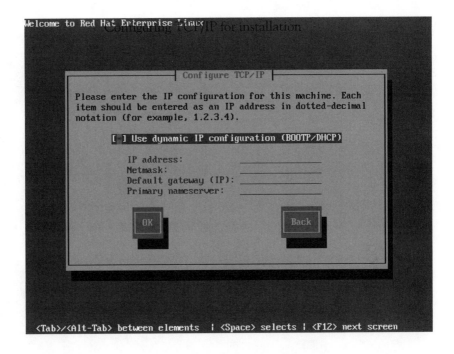

well as the shared directory. (If you enter a hostname, you'll need a working DNS server on your network.) If you set up an NFS installation server with the instructions earlier in this chapter, enter /mnt/inst in the Red Hat directory text box. (The corresponding HTTP and FTP figures are shown in Figures 2-11 and 2-12.)

8. Now you'll see the first Red Hat Enterprise Linux graphical installation screen. Click Next to continue. Since you've already selected a Keyboard and Language, RHEL skips those graphical screens that you'd otherwise see when installing from a CD.

If you're installing from an HTTP or FTP Server, installation proceeds in text mode. Red Hat Enterprise Linux 3 does not incorporate Fedora's ability to run graphical installations from these types of servers. Next, you'll get to select a mouse (or pointing device) for your system. If you have a mouse with a center wheel, press on it. If it clicks, you have a middle mouse button and need not select the Emulate 3 Buttons option. Make your selection and click Next to continue.

FIGURE 2-10

Connecting to
an NFS Server

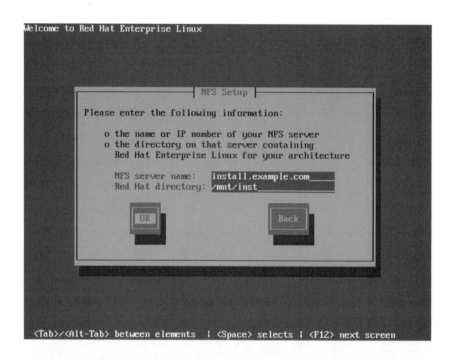

FIGURE 2-11

Connecting to
an HTTP Server

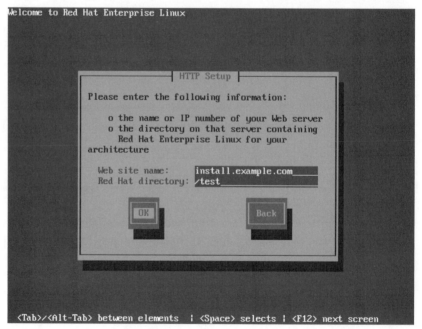

FIGURE 2-12

Connecting to
an FTP Server

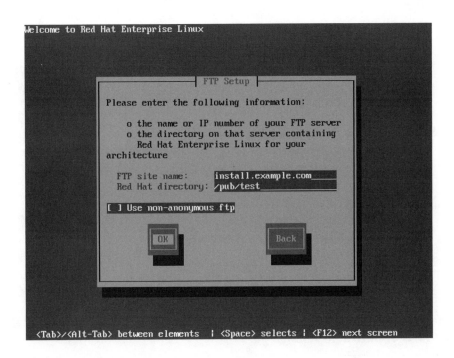

If you're installing Red Hat Linux 9, the installation program checks for a previous version of Linux and then allows you to select between a Personal Desktop, Workstation, Server, or Custom installation.

9. Now you can select between automatic and manual partitioning. If you select Automatically Partition, you'll get the partition scheme described in Table 2-3 (small variations of a few MB do not matter). Chances are good that won't match the requirements on your RHCE or RHCT installation exam. Select the Manually Partition With Disk Druid option and click Next to continue.

TABLE 2-3

Result When
You Partition
Automatically

Location	Size
/boot	100MB
Swap	Twice available RAM (assuming sufficient hard drive space)
/	Remaining space on the drive

10. Now you can set up the partitions as desired. The graphical Disk Druid screen is shown in Figure 2-13. This is a good opportunity to run the following exercises, to see all that you can do with Disk Druid. Once you complete the exercises, you can continue with step 11. If you choose to do any or all of the exercises later, you'll need to repeat the first ten steps of the installation process.

on the job

Disk Druid brings up a menu that allows you to format your RAID system to the ext2, ext3, Linux swap, or VFAT filesystems. It also allows you to configure your partitions to RAID 0, RAID 1, or RAID 5.

exam watch

Learn how to use all features of Disk Druid. It's quite possible that you'll have to create all sorts of partitions during your

exam. The following three exercises are designed to help you practice and learn the major features of this disk configuration tool.

FIGURE 2-13

Disk Druid

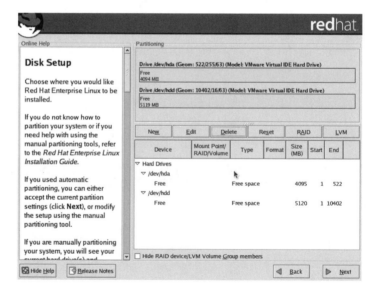

EXERCISE 2-2

Basic Partitioning

This is an excellent opportunity to see how you can create a RAID array with what you can do with Disk Druid. In this exercise, you'll practice adding partitions to a computer with two hard drives. (If you don't have two hard drives, or a single hard drive with at least 9GB of free space, do your best. You may need to assign different sizes to each partition. That is okay. The point is to practice working with Disk Druid.)

This illustrates what you would do if you are asked to create a /boot partition of 100MB, a /tmp partition of 500MB, a /var partition of 1000MB, a /home partition of 2000MB, and a swap partition of 512MB. Assign the remaining space to the root directory (/) partition. This starts with the scenario shown in Figure 2-13. The /boot partition must be a primary partition.

Before you get to step 1 in this exercise, you'll have to run the first ten steps of the Installation process described earlier in this section. When you're done, you should be able to reboot your computer with the CTRL-ALT-DEL command; alternatively, you can turn off your computer during the middle of the installation process.

1. In the Disk Druid Menu, click New. This opens the Add Partition window shown in Figure 2-14.

2. Enter **/boot** in the Mount Point text box. Enter **100MB** in the Size(MB) text box. Select the Force To Be A Primary Partition option and click OK.

FIGURE 2-14

Adding a partition

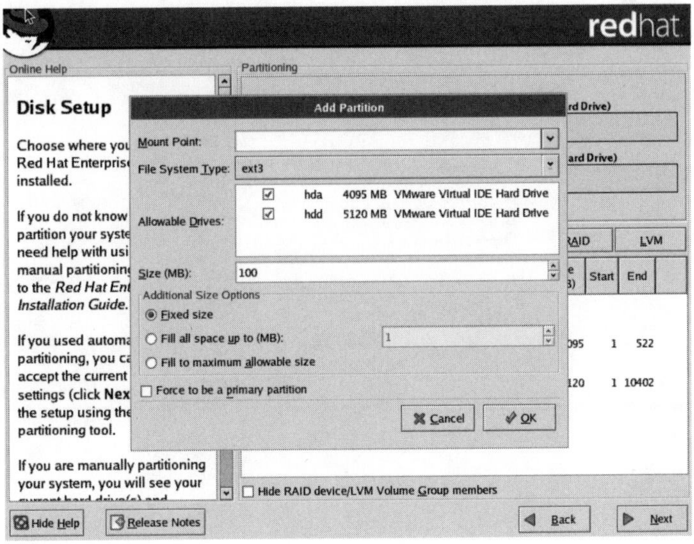

3. Repeat the basic process described in step 1 with the other noted partitions: /tmp, /var, and /home. As described earlier, these need not be primary partitions.

4. Now create a swap partition. Click New to open the Add Partition window. Click the File System Type drop-down box and select Swap. As you'll see, the Mount Point text box is now grayed out. Enter the required size (**512MB**) in the Size(MB) text box and click OK.

5. Allocate the remaining space to the root directory (/) partition. Click New to open the Add Partition window. Enter **/** in the Mount Point text box. Under Additional Size Options, select Fill To Maximum Allowable Size and click OK.

6. Observe the result in the Disk Druid screen. Note that Disk Druid may not follow your instructions exactly. For example, as shown in Figure 2-15, I end up with a /boot partition of 102MB. The error is trivial and depends on the geometry of your hard drive.

7. At this point, you have three options: continue with the next two exercises, continue the installation process with step 11, or stop the installation process completely by shutting down your computer.

FIGURE 2-15

Disk Druid
Exercise 2-2
results

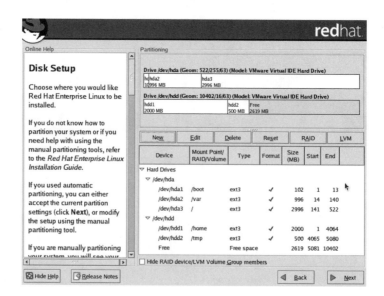

RAID Partitioning

In this exercise, you'll follow up by setting up a RAID 1 software array. As described in Chapter 4, this is a disk mirror, where the same data is copied to both partitions in this array. For an effective RAID system, each partition in the array should be located on different physical hard drives. In that way, if one hard drive fails, you do not lose all of the data in the array.

I'll start by working with the results shown in Figure 2-15. Your situation may be different. While not recommended in practice, it's okay if you don't have two physical hard drives on your computer. It's certainly possible that you'll be asked to set up a RAID array on a computer with one physical hard drive during the exam. The point of this exercise is to learn how to set up a RAID array with Disk Druid.

on the

Job

In the real world, you should never configure different parts of a RAID array on the same hard drive. If you do, the failure of any single hard drive can lead to the loss of all of your data on that array.

In this exercise, I'll set up a RAID 1 software array of 100MB for the /home/mj directory. In the case shown in Figure 2-15, I first need to make some room on the first hard drive, as represented by /dev/hda. In that way, I'll have free space on the two hard drives on this computer.

Before you get to step 1 in this exercise, you'll have to run the first ten steps of the Installation process described earlier in this section. When you're done, you should be able to reboot your computer with the CTRL-ALT-DEL command; alternatively, you can turn off your computer during the middle of the installation process.

1. Highlight the root directory partition on the first hard drive (/dev/hda) and click Edit. This opens the Edit Partition window, which is functionally identical to the Add Partition window shown back in Figure 2-14.

2. In the Size(MB) text box, enter a size for the root directory (/) partition smaller than what's currently configured. I've allocated 500MB for this purpose, leaving a root directory (/) partition size of 2500MB. Make sure the Fixed Size option is selected and click OK.

3. Click RAID. This opens the RAID Options menu shown here.

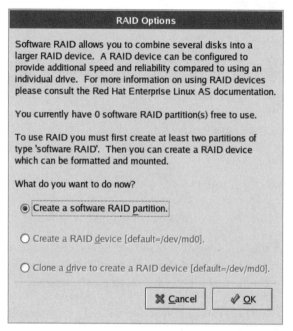

4. Select the Create A Software RAID Partition option and click OK. This opens the Add Partition window with a Software RAID File System Type. Select the first physical hard drive in the Allowable Drives list. Make sure that the size of this partition is fixed at 100MB. Click OK.

5. Repeat steps 2 and 3, making sure that the second RAID partition is located on the other physical hard drive.

6. Click RAID. Now you'll be able to select the Create A RAID Device [default=/dev/md0] option. Do so and click OK. This opens the Make RAID Device window shown next. As you can see, the size of the RAID members need not be identical.

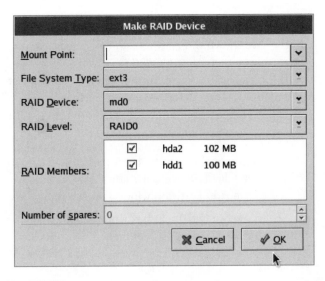

7. Enter **/home/mj** in the Mount Point text box. Click the RAID Level drop-down box and select RAID1. If you had more than three RAID partitions, you could assign one as a spare. Click OK. Congratulations! You've just created a RAID array.

8. At this point, you have three options: continue with Exercises 2-2 and 2-4, continue the installation process with step 11, or stop the installation process completely by shutting down your computer.

EXERCISE 2-4

LVM Partitioning

In this exercise, you'll follow up by setting up a Logical Volume Management (LVM) system. As described in Chapter 4, this allows you to resize partitions after Linux is installed.

I'll start by working with the results shown previously in Figure 2-15. Your situation may be different. It's okay if you don't have two physical hard drives on your computer. The point of this exercise is to learn how to set up an LVM system with Disk Druid.

In this exercise, I'll set up an LVM system of 100MB for the /home/angels directory. In the case shown in Figure 2-15, I first need to make some room on the first hard drive, as represented by /dev/hda.

Before you get to step 1 in this exercise, you'll have to run the first ten steps of the Installation process described earlier in this section. When you're done, you should be able to reboot your computer with the CTRL-ALT-DEL command; alternatively, you can turn off your computer during the middle of the installation process.

1. Highlight the root directory partition on the first hard drive (/dev/hda) and click Edit. This opens the Edit Partition window, which is functionally identical to the Add Partition window shown previously in Figure 2-15.

2. In the Size(MB) text box, enter a size for the root directory (/) partition smaller than what's currently configured. I've allocated 500MB for this purpose, leaving a root directory (/) partition size of 2500MB. Make sure the Fixed Size option is selected and click OK.

3. Click New. In the Add Partition window that opens, click the File System Type drop-down box. Select Physical Volume (LVM). Select the first physical hard drive in the Allowable Drives list. Make sure that the size of this partition is fixed at 100MB. Click OK.

4. Repeat step 2. Repeat until you have four LVM partitions, two on each physical hard drive.

5. Click LVM. This opens the Make LVM Volume Group window shown here. Note that all of the available LVM partitions are selected in the Physical Volumes To Use text box. You're free to select or deselect the LVM partitions of your choice.

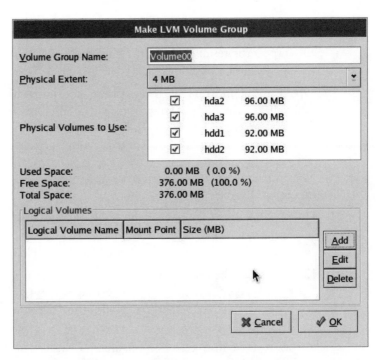

6. Click Add. This opens the Make Logical Volume window shown here. Enter **/home/angels** in the Mount Point text box. You can change the Logical Volume Name and Size as desired. Click OK.

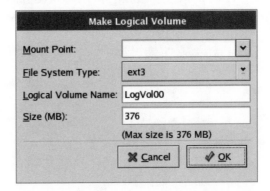

Do not set up the /boot directory on an LVM volume. Unless you have the /boot directory on a regular partition, you won't be able to start other LVM volumes.

7. Inspect the result in the Make LVM Group window. Click OK.

8. Inspect the result in the Disk Druid window. Congratulations! You've just created an LVM system.

9. At this point, you have three options: continue with Exercises 2-2 and 2-3, continue the installation process with step 11, or stop the installation process completely by shutting down your computer.

Now that you've reviewed the exercises, continue with the installation steps you started before Exercise 2-2.

11. You should now be more comfortable with the Disk Druid process and be able to create the kinds of partitions that are required on the Red Hat exams. Once you've finished creating the desired partitions, click Next to continue.

12. Next, you'll be able to configure the boot loader as shown in Figure 2-16. It can help you configure how your BIOS finds Linux (and possibly other operating systems) on your computer. GRUB is the default, which I describe in more detail in Chapter 3.

   a. If you're instructed to configure LILO instead of GRUB (or no boot loader at all) during your exam, click Change Boot Loader.

   b. You can also set up a boot loader password as shown in Figure 2-16.

   c. If you select Configure Advanced Boot Loader Options, you're taken to a different menu before the next step, where you can place the boot loader

FIGURE 2-16

Configuring
a boot loader

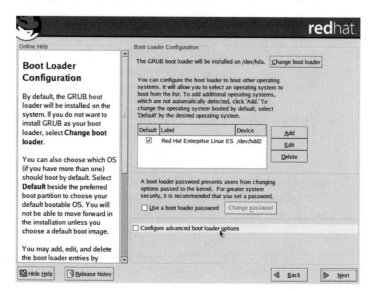

on the first sector of the boot partition, force LBA32 addressing, needed for some older hard drives.

    d. You can also add kernel parameters of your choice with the Advanced Boot Loader Configuration menu.

13. Now you'll be able to configure this computer on your network. Assuming you've set up installation from a remote computer on the network, you'll see the settings that you previously entered in Figure 2-9. You can either configure the IP address information shown manually, or you can leave this task to a DHCP server. Some DHCP servers can assign hostnames as well. Make your selections and click Next to continue.

e x a m
w a t c h

For the RHCE and RHCT Installation and Configuration exam, follow the IP address instructions carefully. If there's a DHCP server on your exam room's network, make sure that the Network Configuration points to a DHCP server. In either case, you may get instructions to set up a specific hostname for your computer.

14. Next, you'll be able to configure a standard firewall for your computer. Generally, you won't need to configure a firewall for a workstation inside a LAN. Firewalls are generally located on computers that serve as junctions, or routers between networks such as a LAN and the Internet. Figure 2-17 illustrates a configuration

FIGURE 2-17

Configuring a firewall

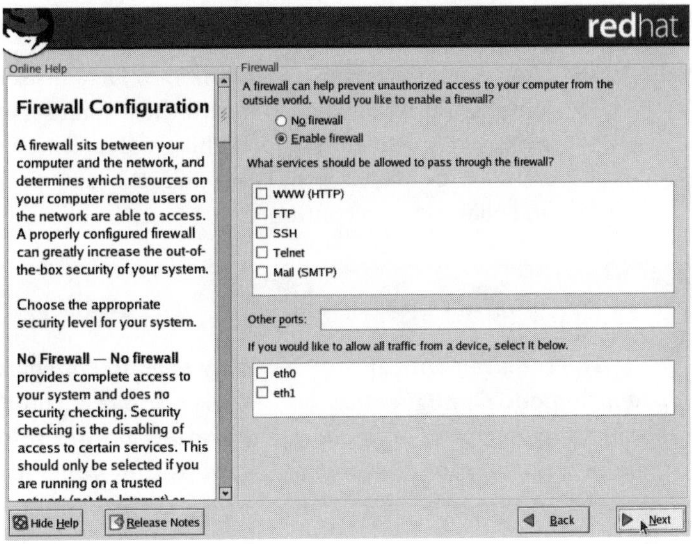

with two network cards, which are presumably connected to different networks. The options you see here are identical to those shown in the **redhat-config-securitylevel** (Security Level Configuration) tool, which I describe in Chapter 10.

on the job *In older versions of Anaconda, from Red Hat Linux 9 and before, you used to be able to configure a firewall with a high or medium level of security. Those options are no longer available through the GUI. For more information on customizing your firewall, read about iptables in Chapter 10.*

15. In the Additional Language Support screen, you'll be able to add from a large number of different language sets, which is reflected on the command line and the GUI after installation. Make your selections and click Next to continue.

16. In the Time Zone Selection screen, select your time zone. Assuming this is the only operating system on this computer, activate the System Clock Uses UTC option. (This option causes problems on a computer that also has Microsoft Windows.) Make any needed changes and click Next to continue.

17. Type in the password that you'll use for the root user account in the text boxes provided and click Next to continue.

exam **Watch** *If you get special instructions for the root user password, follow them carefully! A grader who can't* *get into your root user account will have trouble grading your work and giving you the credit you deserve on the exam.*

18. Now you'll see a Package Installation Defaults screen, similar to what you saw previously in Figure 2-4, with the default set of package groups associated with your installation. Unless this group meets *all* of the requirements of your particular exam, select the "Customize the set of packages to be installed" option and click Next to continue.

exam **Watch** *The requirements of the Red Hat Installation and Configuration exam vary. Some may need to configure a Windows File Server and sound; others* *may need to configure mail and print servers. On your exam, read your instructions carefully before selecting the package groups that you'll install.*

19. In the Package Group Selection screen shown in Figure 2-18, select the package groups that you'll need for the requirements of your particular Installation exam. Make your selections and click Next to continue.

20. Finally, you're taken to a summary screen. You can click Back in this screen (or just about any time during the process) to return to a previous step. Otherwise, click Next to start the installation process.

21. Once the installation process is complete, you're taken to a screen where you can create a customized boot disk. On the job, this is an excellent idea. However, during the exam, unless specifically required, this takes time that you might not have. You can still create a custom boot floppy disk after installation with the following command:

```
# mkbootdisk --device /dev/fd0 `uname -r`
```

exam
watch

While installation proceeds, you'll have a bit of "dead time." You can use this time to start configuring your RHEL 3 system. Just press the CTRL-ALT-F2 command and you'll see a shell. You'll *find the standard root directory (/) mounted on the /mnt/sysimage subdirectory during the installation process. You can edit the files of your choice as soon as they're installed.*

FIGURE 2-18

Selecting Package
Groups

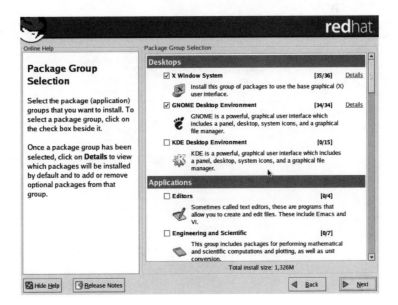

e**x**am

watch
Unless specifically required by your Installation and Configuration exam, don't create a boot floppy. This takes time that you may not have. You can use an installation boot floppy or the first installation CD as a rescue disk, as described in Chapter 11. While it's a good idea to create a custom boot floppy in real life, not all real life practices are consistent with doing your best on the Red Hat exams.

22. Assuming you've installed GUI components such as the GNOME desktop, you'll get to configure your video card, as shown in Figure 2-19. A large number of different manufacturers, models, and generic options are available. You can also set the available memory in your video card, as shown in the Graphical Interface (X) Configuration screen.

23. In the Monitor Configuration screen, you can set the make and model of your monitor. If you don't see your monitor in the list, there are also a large variety of generic CRT (standard) and LCD (flat panel/laptop) monitors available.

24. There is one more step in the installation process. In the Customize Graphics Configuration screen shown in Figure 2-20, *be careful*! While the default color depth and screen resolution should suffice, the login type is a critical choice during the Red Hat exams. If you select a graphical login by default, you'll have to go through the First Boot process described in later steps.

FIGURE 2-19

Configuring your graphics system

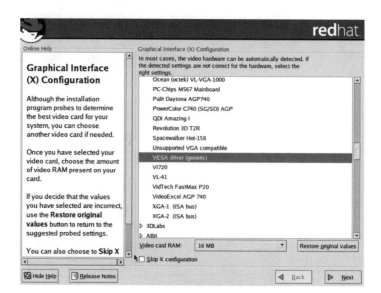

FIGURE 2-20

Customizing the graphics setup of your Linux system

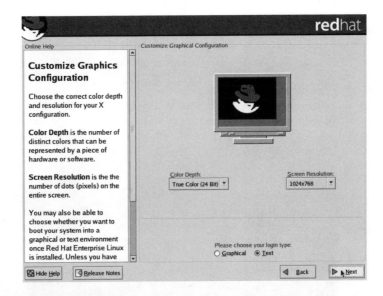

You'll see the Customize Graphics Configuration screen near the end of the installation process. Unless your exam requires going through the First Boot process, *select a Text login type. Otherwise, you'll be wasting time on the Installation and Configuration exam that you could use to meet other requirements.*

25. RHEL now reboots your computer. Red Hat Enterprise Linux is now installed! If you've selected a Text login type, you'll see something similar to the following login screen.

```
Red Hat Enterprise Linux ES release 3 (Taroon)
Kernel 2.4.21-4.EL on an i686

Enterprise3 login:
```

If you selected a Graphical login, I'd say congratulations, but you're not done yet.

26. The first time your computer boots into RHEL, you'll see the process known as First Boot. You'll get to configure a few more components during this process; they're summarized in the left pane of Figure 2-21. You may not see all of the options shown in the figure; for example, if your computer does not have a sound card, you won't see that option.

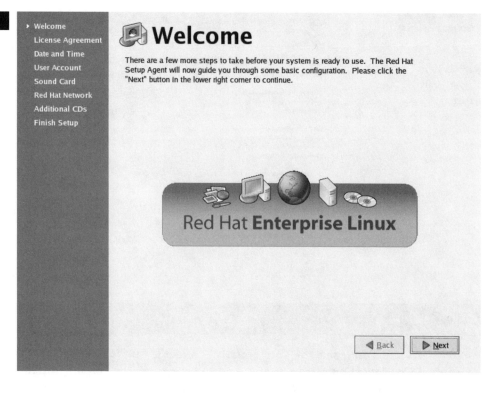

27. If you're running RHEL 3, you'll need to agree to the license agreement. If you do not agree, you're prompted to shut down your system and uninstall the operating system.

28. In the Date and Time screen, you can set the date and time for your system. If you select the Enable Network Time Protocol option, you can synchronize your computer with a Network Time Protocol server. Red Hat provides two: clock.redhat.com and clock2.redhat.com. If you're not sure, you can return

exam
w a t c h

The Red Hat exams are closed book. While you can use available documentation such as the man pages, don't expect a connection to the Internet during your exam. Therefore, I also believe it's highly unlikely that you'll have to connect to Internet sites such as a Red Hat time server or the Red Hat Network.

to this configuration screen with the redhat-config-time utility. Make any selections required by your exam and click Next.

29. In the User Account screen, you can configure a regular account. You may be required to create regular users with a specific password during your exam. You can create additional users with the **redhat-config-users** (Red Hat User Manager) tool described in Chapter 3. Create a user if required and click Next.

e x a m

w a t c h

If you're required to set up users over a network, pay attention to the requirements of your exam. Click the Use Network Login button and study the Authentication Configuration window.

Are these users on a central NIS server or a Samba Primary Domain Controller (PDC)? For more information on the Authentication Configuration window, read Chapter 10.

30. Normally, Red Hat automatically detects sound cards. If successful, you can click the Play Test Sound button to confirm. Click Next to continue.

31. If you want to register with the Red Hat Network, select Yes and you'll see the Red Hat Network configuration screen where you can set up a connection. The defaults are generally sufficient. Alternatively, you can set up a Red Hat Network connection using the **up2date** utility described in Chapter 4.

32. Finally, if you have more software to install, such as from a Red Hat documentation CD, you'll get to do so in the Additional CDs window. Don't do so unless required by your particular exam. Click Next to continue.

33. You'll now see the Finish Setup screen, which tells you that "Your system is now set up and ready to use." Click Next to finish the process.

34. Congratulations! Installation is now complete. With the exception of the firewall security configuration options, the basic installation process for Red Hat Linux 9 is almost identical to RHEL 3, so you can use that freely available operating system to practice for the exam.

o n t h e

o b

If you don't install the GUI during the installation process, make sure that you don't configure your system to boot from the GUI. If you do, you'll need to use the linux rescue *mode discussed in Chapter 11 to boot into your system. Then you can edit /etc/inittab to make sure that you boot into text mode in the future.*

Caveat Emptor on Installation

Do not worry if you make a mistake the first time you practice installing Linux on a test computer. Just redo the installation; it will be significantly faster and easier than trying to correct a problem. There are so many options and possibilities in the overview just presented that it is not possible to name them all or take them all into account. In most cases, the default is sufficient if you do not understand the question posed. You'll want to practice installing RHEL more than once.

If you have to reinstall Linux on the RHCE Installation and Configuration exam, you may not have time to configure services as required. You are not allowed to reinstall Linux on the RHCE or RHCT Troubleshooting and System Maintenance exam.

Although you have finished the installation and have worked with the concepts of partitioning (and possibly multiple operating system boots), there are still a few more details to note, such as GRUB configuration, LILO errors, BIOS issues, and others, all described in the following sections.

A Note on Boot Disks

One major danger with a floppy is the chance of damaging that boot disk. You may want to make multiple copies to minimize possible problems. You can use the **dd** command to make multiple copies of the disk. Here is an example of the commands needed to create a copy of the original diskette to a local file and how to create duplicates from this local file:

```
# dd if=/dev/fd0 of=diskboot.img # stores a copy of diskette
# dd if=/diskboot.img of=/dev/fd0  # makes the copy
```

As described earlier, the **mkbootdisk** utility can help you create a custom boot diskette from your running system with the required root and /boot partitions. In Red Hat Linux 9, this command does not require the **--device** switch. While this command needs the name of the running kernel, you can have the command line shell generate that for you and insert it into the command line with the following command:

```
# # to create a boot disk for the 'current kernel number'
# mkbootdisk --device /dev/fd0 `uname -r`
```

on the job *If you have the prerequisite experience for this book, you should already understand the effects of double, single, and back quotes in the shell. Regular double quotes interpret only variables within before processing the result as standard input. Single quotes do not interpret the enclosed commands or variables. Back quotes process the enclosed command even if it's further contained within double quotes.*

CERTIFICATION OBJECTIVE 2.08

Sample Installation Exercises

The following exercises are meant to provide you with a step-by-step set of progressively more complex installation exercises that cover everything from basic workstations to very specific and advanced server installations.

on the job *You should do these exercises on test machines only. One possible option is a virtual machine that can simulate a computer inside your operating system. An example of this is VMWare, available from www.vmware.com.*

Introduction to Installation Exercises

All these exercises assume you have a basic PC available at your disposal to work with as a learning station. You do not want any important data on that PC. You do not need a network connection, nor do you need to know how to configure X for these exercises—you can simply select the default answers, in most cases.

These exercises are designed to provide progressive development to help further your knowledge about installing Linux. If you're studying for the RHCT, you may not be able to go through all of the steps, especially with respect to server software that is not included on the RHEL 3 Workstation.

If you're using Fedora Linux or Red Hat Linux 9 to run these exercises, the Workstation option is fine for the first exercise in this section; the Custom option is best for the final two exercises in this section.

In these exercises, you will be asked to configure the installation for a specific usage and customize the disk partition table to meet the needs of the intended usage. This will require that you do a Custom installation in all but one of the exercises.

These exercises also assume your machine boots from the floppy during a normal reboot, that there is no pertinent information on these test machines, and that you realize all data will be overwritten on these machines.

EXERCISE 2-5

Advanced Workstation Installation

In this exercise, you will distribute your filesystem over more than just one partition. You will need to create the partitions on a 20GB or larger IDE hard disk (see Table 2-4).

1. Create a Linux installation floppy from the bootdisk.img image file, then reboot the system.

2. Select manual partitioning at the appropriate step.

3. Use Disk Druid to reconfigure the partition table.

4. Delete all partitions.

5. Create the first partition with 100MB of disk space, ext3, and assign to /boot.

6. Create the next primary partition, hda2, as Linux Swap, and assign to ID 83.

7. Create a third partition with about 5500MB of disk space, ext3, and assign it to the root directory, /.

8. Create an extended partition containing all the rest of the disk space. Make it *growable*.

TABLE 2-4	Partition	Size	Use	Comment
Custom Installation as a Workstation (No Other OS), 1.2 GHz Pentium, 20GB Single Disk, 256MB of Memory	hda1	100MB	/boot	Maintains boot files
	hda2	512MB	swap	Plenty of space
	hda3	5.5GB	/	The root directory
	hda4	14GB	Extended partition	Solely a container for logical partitions
	hda5	4GB	/var	For print spool files
	hda6	5GB	/home	User files—RAID 1
	hda7	5GB	/home	User files—RAID 1

9. Create the first logical partition, hda5, with about 4GB, and assign it to /var.

10. Create two more logical partitions, hda6 and hda7. Split the remaining space between these two partitions (about 5GB each). Set it up with a software RAID filesystem.

11. Make a RAID 1 device from the two new software RAID partitions, formatted to ext3, and assign it to /home.

on the
() o b

In the real world, you should never configure different parts of a RAID array on the same hard drive. If you do, the failure of any single hard drive can lead to the loss of all of your data on that array. However, it may be necessary if the computer on your exam has only one physical hard drive.

12. Continue with the installation process, using your best judgment.

13. When asked to select packages, make sure that the OpenOffice.org suite as well as the Graphics, Graphical Internet, and Games packages are selected.

14. Finish the Workstation installation normally.

15. Reboot the computer and log in as the root user.

EXERCISE 2-6

Disk Partitioning a Server Installation

In this exercise, you will install Red Hat Enterprise Linux 3 to create a basic server. You can create a very similar installation using Red Hat Linux 9's custom installation option. You will need to create the partitions on a 10GB or larger hard disk (see Table 2-5).

1. Create a Linux installation floppy from the bootdisk.img image file, then reboot the system.

2. Select manual partitioning at the appropriate step.

3. When prompted, select Disk Druid to edit partitions.

4. Delete all partitions.

5. Create the first partition with 100MB of disk space, formatted to ext3, and assign it to /boot.

TABLE 2-5	Partition	Size	Use	Comment
	hda1	100MB	/boot	Maintains boot files
Custom Installation as a Server, 2 GHz Pentium, 10GB Single Disk, 256MB Memory	hda2	500MB	swap	Probably plenty of space
	hda3	5GB	/	The root directory
	hda4	4500MB	Extended partition	Solely a container for logical partitions
	hda5	500MB	/var	For print spool files
	hda6	1000MB	/var/www	Web services
	hda7	2000MB	/home	No interactive users
	hda8	1000MB	/usr	Additional network services

6. Create the next primary partition, hda2, with about 500MB of disk space, as Linux Swap.

7. Create third partition with about 5GB disk space, Linux Native, and assign to the root directory, /.

8. Create an extended partition containing all the rest of the disk space, 4500MB.

9. Create the first logical partition, hda5, with about 500MB, formatted to ext3, and assign to /var.

10. Create the next logical partition, hda6, with about 1000MB, formatted to ext3, and assign it to /var/www.

11. Create the next logical partition, hda7, with about 2000MB, formatted to ext3, and assign it to /home.

12. Create the next logical partition, hda8, with about 1000MB, formatted to ext3, and assign to /usr.

13. Continue with the installation process, using your best judgment.

14. Choose to customize the package groups to be installed. On an exam, you may see a requirement to install a number of different services such as a Web server, communication with Windows PCs, an FTP server, as well as servers for DNS and DHCP.

15. Finish the installation normally.

16. Reboot when prompted and log in as the root user.

EXERCISE 2-7

Disk Partitioning Strategy for Database Server Installation

In this exercise, you will install Red Hat Enterprise Linux 3 to configure the partitions for an imaginary database server. You can create a very similar installation using Red Hat Linux 9's custom installation option. In this exercise, you will need to create the partitions on a 25GB or larger hard disk (see Table 2-6). The main use for such a system is as a database, file, and print server, with few interactive users.

1. Create a Linux installation floppy from the bootdisk.img image file, then reboot the system.

2. Select manual partitioning at the appropriate step.

3. When prompted, select Disk Druid to edit partitions.

4. Delete all partitions.

5. Create the first partition with 100MB of disk space, formatted to ext3, and assign it to /boot.

6. Create the next primary partition, hda2, with about 1000MB of disk space, as Linux Swap.

7. Create third partition with about 10GB disk space, Linux Native, and assign to / (root).

TABLE 2-6	Partition	Size	Use	Comment
Custom Installation as a Server (No Other OS), 2.4 GHz Pentium II, 25GB Single Disk, 512MB Memory	hda1	100MB	/boot	Maintains boot files
	hda2	1000MB	swap	Probably plenty of space
	hda3	10GB	/	The root directory
	hda4	14GB	Extended partition	Solely a container for logical partitions
	hda5	3GB	/var	For print spool files
	hda6	3.5GB	/opt	Database system using RAID 1
	hda7	3.5GB	/opt	Database system using RAID 1
	hda8	2GB	/usr	File services using RAID 0
	hda9	2GB	/usr	File services using RAID 0

8. Create an extended partition containing all the rest of the disk space, about 14GB.

9. Create the first logical partition, hda5, with about 3GB, formatted to ext3, and assign it to /var.

10. Create the next two logical partitions, hda6 and hda7 with about 3.5GB each. Format each to the software RAID filesystem.

on the Job

In the real world, you should never configure different parts of a RAID array on the same hard drive. If you do, the failure of any single hard drive can lead to the loss of all of your data on that array. However, it may be necessary if the computer on your exam has only one physical hard drive.

11. Use the Make RAID option to set up a RAID 1 array from these two partitions. Format it to ext3 and assign it to /opt.

12. Create the next two logical partitions, hda8 and hda9, with about 2GB each. Format each to the software RAID filesystem.

13. Use the Make RAID option to set up a RAID 0 array from these two partitions. Format it to ext3 and assign it to /usr.

14. Continue with the installation process, using your best judgment.

15. When asked to select packages, make sure to include the MySQL Database Server package group.

16. Finish the installation normally.

17. Reboot and log in as the root user.

CERTIFICATION SUMMARY

One of the three parts of the RHCE certification is an exam that tests your ability to install Linux in different situations. In this chapter, you learned to install RHEL over a network. You've also worked with the major configuration tools that are part of the installation process.

Generally, there is no easy way to resize a Linux partition. This makes hard drive partition planning quite important. How you assign partitions to directories depends on the size of your hard drives, what you plan to install, and the demands on the system.

Appropriately configured partitions can prevent overloads on key systems, allow for appropriate swap space, improve security on key files, and ensure that your BIOS can find the Linux /boot files.

It's easy to download the Red Hat CDs. Whether you're using Red Hat Linux 9, Fedora Linux, Red Hat Enterprise Linux, or Professional Workstation, the basic steps are the same. You'll download ISO files which you can then write to CDs.

In most cases, you'll install Red Hat Enterprise Linux over a network. I've shown you how to set up a network installation server in this chapter. The same basic lessons apply if you're studying for the RHCE or RHCT exams using Fedora Linux or Red Hat Professional Workstation.

There are a number of ways to customize your installation. The software is organized in package groups. Red Hat starts with baseline package groups, which are the minimum requirements for the operating system. These include default packages for a functional workstation or server. You can then customize by adding or subtracting the package groups of your choice. The selections you make are critical during the Red Hat installation exams.

Before you start your installation, you need to understand the relationship between the Filesystem Hierarchy Standard and Linux directories. You can then make intelligent decisions on what directories to mount on separate partitions.

Understanding the installation process is one of the keys to success on the RHCE exam. Find a spare computer. Practice every installation scenario that you can think of. Repeat this process as you work through the advanced installation scenarios in Chapter 3.

TWO-MINUTE DRILL

The following are some of the key points from the certification objectives in Chapter 2.

Disk Partitions and Block Devices

❑ Linux has a simple naming standard for disk partitions: three letters followed by a number. The first letter reflects the type of drive (h for IDE, s for SCSI). The second letter is d for drive. The third letter represents the relative position of the disk. The number that follows is based on the relative position of the partition on the disk.

❑ The first IDE drive would be hda and the next hdb, then hdc and hdd.

❑ It's helpful to configure separate partitions for important data such as Web services, databases, FTP sites, and e-mail.

❑ Unless you use LVM, there is no easy way to resize Linux partitions. Therefore, you need to consider your partition scheme carefully.

❑ Typically, swap space should be two to three times the amount of RAM. However, the amount of swap space you need is debatable when you have larger amounts of RAM.

Downloading the Red Hat Installation CD-ROMs

❑ Many candidates will want to study for the Red Hat exams using downloaded CDs.

❑ There are several distributions that you could use to study for the Red Hat exams. Ideally, you'll be able to get a copy of Red Hat Enterprise Linux for your studies.

❑ If you can't get a copy of RHEL, there are options, including the source RPMs, Red Hat Professional Workstation, Red Hat Linux 9, Fedora Linux, or one of the third-party "rebuilds."

❑ If you do download the Installation files, you can download the files themselves, or representations of installation CDs on special files known as ISOs.

Configuring a Network Installation

❑ It's quite possible that you'll end up installing Red Hat Enterprise Linux over a network during your exam.

❏ You can configure a Network Installation Server to work with an NFS, FTP, or HTTP connection.

❏ Network installations require static IP address information or a DHCP server on the network.

Customizing Your Installation

❏ There are baseline packages associated with every installation of RHEL, as defined by the /RedHat/base/comps.xml file on the first installation CD.

❏ There are default packages associated with and suitable for RHEL Server and Workstation.

❏ In most cases, it's likely that you'll need to customize the package groups for your installation—for the exam and in real life.

❏ The package groups you select is a critical choice during the Installation part of both Red Hat exams.

Required Disk Space

❏ Depending on your requirements, Red Hat Enterprise Linux installs between approximately 600MB and 4GB of files.

❏ When you plan space for any RHEL installation, remember to leave room for user data, additional applications, services, and a swap partition.

Filesystems

❏ To know how you want to set up partitions, you need to understand the Filesystem Hierarchy Standard (FHS).

❏ The FHS is a standard for organizing directories for Linux- and Unix-based systems.

❏ You can organize different directories within the FHS on different partitions. Such a configuration is easier to maintain and easier to secure.

❏ There are several filesystems that you should consider mounting on separate partitions: /tmp, /boot, /usr/local, /var, and /home.

❏ Depending on installed services such as Web, FTP, NFS, or Samba, it may be appropriate to configure other filesystems on separate partitions.

The Installation Process

❏ Boot disks are important but fragile; with the **dd** command, boot disks are easy to copy.

❏ You can usually start the RHEL 3 installation process directly from a bootable CD or an installation floppy.

❏ The installation process is fairly straightforward and self-explanatory.

❏ When you practice installing RHEL 3, don't worry if you make a mistake during the process. It is usually easiest to restart the process from the beginning.

Sample Installation Exercises

❏ One of the key decisions when you plan a Linux installation is partitioning. This section sets up a number of partitioning exercises for installing RHEL 3 in different scenarios.

SELF TEST

The following questions will help you measure your understanding of the material presented in this chapter. Read all the choices carefully, as there may be more than one correct answer. Don't focus exclusively on these questions. There are no longer any multiple choice questions on the Red Hat exams. These questions exclusively test your understanding of the chapter. It is okay if you have another way of performing a task. Getting results, not memorizing trivia, is what counts on the Red Hat exams.

Disk Partitions and Block Devices

1. Which of the following would be the Linux device name for the fourth logical partition on the second IDE drive?

   A. hdb4

   B. hdb8

   C. hdb5

   D. hdb9

Downloading the Red Hat Installation CD-ROMs

2. Which of the following commands would you use to write an ISO file to a CD?

   A. cdburn

   B. cdrecord

   C. isorecord

   D. xcdrecord

Configuring a Network Installation

3. Which of the following servers can you use to serve Red Hat Enterprise Linux installation files?

   A. NFS

   B. Samba

   C. HTTP

   D. FTP

4. During the installation, you are asked to configure static networking and access the installation source files from an NFS server. Assuming you already have the IP address and netmask for the local computer, what else do you need?

- **A.** DNS server IP, BOOTP server IP, NFS export name
- **B.** DNS export name, BOOTP server IP, NFS server IP
- **C.** DHCP server IP, DHCP name, NFS export name
- **D.** NFS export name, NFS server IP address

Customizing Your Installation

5. A Windows administrator is puzzled by the amount of swap space configured and wants to know what is recommended for Linux.

- **A.** The same as RAM memory.
- **B.** 40–90MB.
- **C.** The same as the server uses.
- **D.** Twice the amount of RAM.
- **E.** There is no recommended amount of swap space.

Required Disk Space

6. You have a computer with a 4GB hard drive. Should you install everything from Red Hat Enterprise Linux on your computer?

- **A.** Yes, it's good to have everything installed from the CDs.
- **B.** Yes, you'll still have plenty of room for other software.
- **C.** No, you won't have room for any other software.
- **D.** No, most users don't need many of the development packages included on the CDs.

Filesystems

7. Why would you organize different filesystems on different partitions?

- **A.** Because you barely have enough space to install Linux on your current hard drive
- **B.** To make it easier to back up and restore your data
- **C.** To limit the space taken by a specific directory
- **D.** For a dedicated single-use computer such as a DNS server or a gateway router

8. What other situations might be a good candidate for a separate filesystem?

    A. A Web server

    B. The /bin directory

    C. A group of shared files

    D. Users' home directories

The Installation Process

9. Which of the following steps can you take to test the integrity of your Installation CDs?

    A. Start the installation process with the **linux mediacheck** command.

    B. Start the installation process with the **linux md5** command.

    C. Nothing. You just have to run the installation CDs and hope there is no problem.

    D. Get an official boxed set of Red Hat Enterprise Linux Installation CDs.

10. You did not create a boot disk during the installation process. After installation, you want a boot disk customized for your installation. What can you do?

    A. Use the **dd** command to create a boot disk from the bootdisk.img disk image file on the first Red Hat installation CD.

    B. Use the **rawrite** command to create a boot disk from the bootdisk.img disk image file on the first Red Hat installation CD.

    C. Use the **mkboot --device /dev/fd0 `uname -r`** command.

    D. Use the **mkbootdisk --device /dev/fd0 `uname -r`** command.

LAB QUESTIONS

Lab 1

You need to test Red Hat Enterprise Linux 3 as a replacement for your current RH 7.2 installed Web server. But you do not want to lose the current 7.2 Web setup just yet. You just want to test RHEL 3 using the Web pages and CGI scripts to see if they will work. What can you do? (Note: Fresh installations from Red Hat Linux to RHEL 3 are recommended.)

Lab 2

You want to test the **linux rescue** option from a boot disk or Installation CD. To make this work, you'll need access to installation media locally (from a CD-ROM or hard disk) or over a network (from an NFS, FTP, or HTTP server). If required, create a boot disk from the bootdisk.img file described earlier in this chapter.

1. Insert the appropriate installation media (boot floppy or CD) into the drive.

2. Reboot your computer. If necessary, adjust the boot order in your computer's BIOS menu to boot from the appropriate media.

3. When you see the first RHEL installation screen, type **linux rescue** and then press ENTER.

4. Go through the text mode prompts for language and keyboard.

5. If you booted from the first installation CD, the following screen allows you to start networking on this system. While it can be helpful, it's not required here. Select No and press ENTER to continue.

   a. If you've started with a boot floppy, the next screen is entitled Rescue Method. Select the system (CD, hard disk, NFS, FTP, HTTP) with your installation media. (If you've started with the first RHEL installation CD, skip to step 7.)

6. Enter the data required to point the RHEL installation program at your installation media. The details vary with the method. For more information, refer to the appropriate sections earlier in this chapter.

7. You should now see a text mode Rescue screen. Select Continue and press ENTER to continue.

8. If successful, you'll see a message that "Your system has been mounted under /mnt/sysimage." Click OK to continue.

9. Run several commands to see what the rescue disk has done to your system: **df, ls -l /, ls -l /mnt /sysimage**. Observe the results.

10. Run the **vi /etc/inittab** command. This is a critical file. Observe the results. Why do you think the /etc/inittab file is empty?

11. Run the **chroot /mnt/sysimage** command. Run the commands shown in steps 9 and 10. What happened?

12. If you're feeling adventurous, repeat this process. At step 7, select Skip instead of Continue. What is the difference? Could you mount the partition with the root directory on the /mnt/sysimage directory? Remember, you can find partitions with the **fdisk** command and create directories with the **mkdir** command. (You might have to be adventurous during the Red Hat Troubleshooting and System Maintenance exams.)

Lab 3

You want to practice network installations. To do so, set up an FTP installation server on a different Linux computer using the instructions described earlier in this chapter. These instructions also work if you want to create an FTP installation server on Red Hat Linux 9.

If you don't have another Linux computer, you can set up an FTP server on Microsoft Windows 2000/XP Professional/2003 for this purpose.

For the purpose of this exercise, assume that you've been asked to install a Web server, a DNS server, an FTP server, and a mail server during the RHEL 3 installation process.

Lab 4

You want to practice network installations. To do so, set up an HTTP installation server on a Linux computer using the instructions described earlier in this chapter. These instructions also work if you want to create an HTTP installation server on Red Hat Linux 8 and 9.

If you don't have another Linux computer, you can set up an HTTP server on Microsoft Windows 2000/XP Professional/2003 for this purpose.

For the purpose of this exercise, assume that you've been asked to install a Samba server, a print server, and will need to recompile the kernel.

SELF TEST ANSWERS

Disk Partitions and Block Devices

1. ☑ **B.** By definition, the first logical partition on the second IDE drive on a computer is hdb5. Since logical partitions are then numbered in sequence, the fourth logical partition on this drive is hdb8.

   ☒ The other answers do not match the defined partition naming criteria for the fourth logical partition.

Downloading the Red Hat Installation CD-ROMs

2. ☑ **B.** The only valid command in the list is **cdrecord**.

   ☒ The other answers are not valid Linux commands.

Configuring a Network Installation

3. ☑ **A, C,** and **D.** You can install RHEL over an NFS, FTP, or HTTP server.

   ☒ **B.** You can't install Linux over a Samba network connection. (It was possible for older versions of Red Hat Linux.)

4. ☑ **D.** The IP address of the NFS server and the export directory name (as defined in /etc /exports). You must already have an IP address and netmask (as well as an optional gateway IP if the services are on another network).

   ☒ A DHCP or BOOTP server should share IP addresses to all computers on a given network. An active DNS server should share the names of all computers on the given network. You don't need the IP address of either type of server. Hence **A**, **B**, and **C** are all incorrect.

Customizing Your Installation

5. ☑ **D.** Generally, a swap partition equal to twice your RAM is standard; however, this is not an absolute rule.

   ☒ Technically speaking, all the other answers may be right, but **D** is the rule of thumb most commonly used.

Required Disk Space

6. ☑ **C** and **D.** There is 4GB of software on RHEL 3. If you install everything on a 4GB hard disk, you won't have room for anything else. And besides, most users don't need the development packages on the RHEL 3 CDs.

   ☒ **A** and **B.** Since 4GB leaves you no room, and includes software that you probably don't need, these answers are not correct.

Filesystems

7. ☑ **B and C.** Filesystems on different partitions allow you to back up and restore data, one partition at a time. The amount of space taken by a specific directory is limited by the size of the partition.

☒ **A and D** are incorrect. Extra partitions waste space. If you barely have enough space on the current hard drive, you may not be able to install Linux. If you have a dedicated single-use computer, the amount of data is small, so there is no reason for different partitions.

8. ☑ **A, C, and D.** Web servers take up lots of space, and the associated log files can grow quickly. Shared files on a separate partition reduce the security risk. A separate filesystem ensures that it won't crowd out other partitions.

☒ **B** is incorrect. If the /bin directory is mounted on a separate filesystem, you may not be able to get to the associated commands if you have to use a rescue disk.

The Installation Process

9. ☑ **A.** The **linux mediacheck** command adds a step where you can check the integrity of each of the RHEL installation CDs.

☒ **B, C, and D** are all wrong. There is no **linux md5** command. There is something you can do to check before you find a problem. And while official boxed sets are probably more reliable, getting such CDs does not by itself check their integrity.

10. ☑ **D.** Among the available choices, only the **mkbootdisk** command can create a boot disk customized to your installation.

☒ **A, B, and C** are not correct. The **dd** and **rawrite** commands, when applied to the standard bootdisk.img file, create a standard installation boot disk. The **mkboot** command is a little trickier, since that works in Debian (but not Red Hat) Linux.

LAB ANSWERS

Lab I

Scenario 1: Buy a new disk and add it to the system. Then do a custom install to create a new installation of RHEL 3 to partitions on the new disk, adding an entry to /etc/grub.conf to provide a boot option to both versions of Linux.

  Scenario 2: No space on server. Hmm … you've got to get creative and either find a test computer you can do the test install on *or* back up everything on the main server after taking it off line. Perform a new installation of RHEL 3. Copy your httpd.conf configuration file and see how it works. If it fails, you restore everything back to the way it was. Note: *Test your backups first* before overwriting an existing operating system.

Lab 2

This is a useful exercise in using the Linux rescue system. If the problem is relatively minor, the steps shown will create a RAM disk with some essential tools on the root (/) filesystem. You can use these tools to repair damaged filesystems or partitions on your hard disk. The man pages don't work right away, because what is normally your root (/) directory is actually mounted on /mnt/sysimage.

The **chroot /mnt/sysimage** command makes the /mnt/sysimage directory into your root (/) directory. Everything (such as man pages) should work normally now.

The other option, to skip the mount process during **linux rescue** setup, does not mount any of your partitions. You can now mount them individually. If you create a /mnt/sysimage directory, you can even mount them in the same way as you saw during the first part of this exercise. Since your partitions are not mounted, you can fix damaged filesystems with commands such as **fsck**.

Lab 3

As described earlier in this chapter, the standard Red Hat FTP server is vsFTP; the default location for download files is the /var/ftp/pub directory. You'll want to specify a subdirectory to copy the files from the /RedHat directory from the installation CDs.

As this is a book on RHEL, I do not describe the steps needed to create an alternate FTP server on a Microsoft Windows computer.

To install a Web server, a DNS server, an FTP server, and a mail server during the RHEL 3 installation process, you need to select the DNS Name Server, Web Server, FTP Server, and Mail Server package groups.

Lab 4

As described earlier in this chapter, the standard Red Hat HTTP server is Apache. The default location for download files is the /var/www/html directory. You'll want to specify a subdirectory to copy the files from the /RedHat directory from the installation CDs.

As this is a book on RHEL, I do not describe the steps needed to create an alternate HTTP server on a Microsoft Windows computer.

To install a Samba server, a print server, and the packages associated with recompiling the kernel during the RHEL 3 installation process, you need to select the Windows File Server, Printing Support, and Kernel Development package groups.

3

After Installation

I n this chapter, you will learn how to manage Linux in advanced installation and configuration scenarios. You'll see how to troubleshoot an installation in progress, as well as how to create automated installation scripts through the Kickstart process. You'll discover how to organize disks with fdisk. You'll find out how to manage boot loaders on Linux. You will learn how to implement a Redundant Array of Inexpensive Disks (RAID), as well as a Logical Volume Manager (LVM) disk system.

Remember, half of the RHCE and RHCT exams is based on how well you know the installation process. By the time you finish this chapter, you should be ready to install Linux in an automated fashion from a local boot disk or over a network from an NFS, FTP, or HTTP server.

As you study **fdisk**, RAID, LVM, and the GRUB boot loader, you'll also see how you might troubleshoot problems that can keep you from accessing a partition or even booting Linux completely. In other words, the skills you learn in this chapter can also help you on the Troubleshooting and System Maintenance exam.

INSIDE THE EXAM

Installation Skills

Both the RHCE and RHCT exams require you to install Linux in some configuration. You won't know the specifics until you see your exam. If you have problems during the installation process, the Installation Troubleshooting consoles can be a lifesaver. If you discover a bad network connection or unreadable installation CDs, you may discover that using the troubleshooting consoles can

help you identify the problem to the exam administrator.

It's easiest to configure partitions, set up RAID arrays, and create LVM groups during the installation process. However, when people get nervous on exams, they may forget details. All is not lost. You don't have to reinstall. You can use commands and configure key files to create new partitions, RAID arrays, and LVM groups.

Troubleshooting Skills

Troubleshooting skills are more difficult to learn. In many cases, you need to know what

looks right with installation files, with boot loaders, and more. Then you can observe the

INSIDE THE EXAM

symptoms of a problem, look at a critical file, say "Aha!" and fix whatever problems you

might encounter during the Troubleshooting and System Maintenance exam.

Using Other Versions of Red Hat

For the purpose of this chapter, you can use Red Hat Linux 9 to test your knowledge of what happens after installation. For what is covered in this chapter, the differences do not matter for the Red Hat exams. However, as described in Chapter 2, I've illustrated each of the installation screens for RHEL 3 in Appendix B on the CD-ROM.

For example, RHEL 3, unlike Fedora Linux, still uses a text-based GRUB configuration menu. It's the same version of GRUB used in Red Hat Linux 9. However, the kernel included with RHEL 3 no longer requires the **hdc=ide-scsi** command formerly required for most CD/RW drives.

CERTIFICATION OBJECTIVE 3.01

Installation Troubleshooting

There are actually many processes running and many parts to the installation. The system logs everything to an installation log file and separates related information between four of the five virtual console screens supported during the installation.

exam
ⓦatch

If your installation is trouble-free, you'll have a few minutes on your hands during the Installation and Configuration exam. I suggest that you use that time to plan how you'll configure the
services per the requirements of your particular exam. But pay attention to the following sections. If your installation gets stuck, the console screens described can quickly help you diagnose the problem.

The Console Installation Output Screens

There are up to six consoles available during the installation process. Each console tells a different story. What you see depends slightly on whether you install in text or graphical mode. A network graphical installation is something of a hybrid; it starts in text mode before connecting to the network source and proceeding to the graphical installation.

Text mode starts in the first virtual console. Graphical mode runs in the seventh virtual console (console number 6 is not used). You can switch between virtual consoles using the commands defined in Table 3-1. If you're in text mode, you don't need to use the CTRL key (but it does no harm). As you can see in the table, each console is associated with a function key.

The messages on the third and fourth consoles can scroll by quickly; fortunately, they're collected in dedicated files which I'll show you shortly.

Installation bash

You can find a bash shell on the second console. It can help you review what has been installed so far. Check it out for yourself with the CTRL-ALT-F2 command. You'll see the following installation boot prompt during the installation process:

```
-/bin/sh-2.05b#
```

This prompt allows you to run standard bash commands on the system as configured so far. Before Anaconda starts installing packages, you can inspect a number of things at this prompt. The installation files from the CD or network source will be mounted on the /mnt/source directory.

| TABLE 3-1 | Installation Virtual Consoles |

Command	Console and Function
CTRL-ALT-F1	Text installation display; if you're running in graphical mode, it includes the basic commands to start graphics drivers.
CTRL-ALT-F2	Accesses a bash shell prompt; available after the first few installation steps.
CTRL-ALT-F3	Lists the log of installation messages.
CTRL-ALT-F4	Displays all kernel messages, including detected hardware and drivers.
CTRL-ALT-F5	Installation displays partition formatting; not available until Anaconda formats the actual partitions.
CTRL-ALT-F7	Graphical installation display; active only if you're running the installation program in graphical mode.

While installation proceeds, you'll have a bit of "dead time." You can use this time to start configuring your RHEL 3 system. Just press the CTRL-ALT-F2 command and you'll see a shell. You'll find the standard root directory (/) mounted on the /mnt/sysimage subdirectory during the installation process. You can edit the files of your choice as soon as they're installed.

You can also find a number of interesting files in the /tmp directory; I've described the significant ones in Table 3-2.

If you're installing from a Kickstart configuration file, ks.cfg, you may be able to find it in the /tmp directory in the second virtual console during the installation process. It could be helpful to read this file during the Troubleshooting exam.

Other Consoles

The third console primarily lists detected hardware. If your computer is having problems with something critical, such as the CD drive or network card, you'll see it here.

The fourth console tells you more about detected hardware. However, you may need to be a detective to understand these messages. For example, if you see the following message:

```
<6>pcnet32: 1 cards_found.
```

TABLE 3-2 The /tmp Directory Contains Configuration Files During the Installation Process

File from installation /tmp	Description
anaconda.log	Contains a log of installation messages (from the third console).
ks.cfg	If you're installing from a Kickstart configuration file, it's stored in the /tmp directory.
modules.conf	Includes detected hardware that requires a driver module (frequently includes network cards).
netinfo	Contains IP address information for configured network cards.
syslog	Includes a log of kernel messages (from the fourth console).
XF86Config.test	Contains a temporary X Window configuration file.

you might not know there's a problem unless you remember that there are two network cards on this computer. On the fifth console, you can see what happens to your partitions; it lists the output of the **mke2fs** command, which can tell you if there's a problem with your partitions.

While Installing Software

Once Anaconda starts installing software, you'll see the Installing Packages screen, where you can watch as it actually installs Linux on your computer. Once this process starts, press the CTRL-ALT-F2 keys to return to the bash console. Now run the following command:

```
-/bin/sh-2.05b# cd /mnt/sysimage
```

You can now browse around the directory tree as it's being built.

CERTIFICATION OBJECTIVE 3.02

Postinstallation Validation

Red Hat Enterprise Linux 3 creates a number of files when installation is complete. These files essentially document what happened. The basic installation log file, /root/install.log, lists the packages that Anaconda installed on your system. The boot information is stored in the /var/log/dmesg file. The commands used by Anaconda to install Linux is stored in the /root/anaconda-ks.cfg file. This can serve as a template for the Kickstart process, which you can use to install RHEL 3 automatically on different computers. I describe Kickstart in more detail later in this chapter.

The Installation Log File

The installation log file, /root/install.log, provides a baseline. After you run Linux for some time, you've probably installed and upgraded a number of additional packages. You can refer back to this file to find the packages installed when Linux was installed on this computer.

dmesg Boot Messages

The /var/log/dmesg file contains boot messages duplicated from the console output as seen each time Linux boots. These messages contain hardware information, process initialization, and sequencing information, and more, as shown in Figure 3-1.

Graphical or Text Login Screen

After the installation process is complete, the installation script shuts down and reboots the computer. If you configured a graphical login, Linux starts in runlevel 5, the X Window login screen. Alternatively, if you configured a text login, Linux starts in runlevel 3.

on the job

If your X Window server is not configured properly, you can press CTRL-ALT-F2 to go back to a text-based login screen.

It's easy to shift runlevels. The **init** *x* command, where *x* represents the runlevel, modifies the Linux system accordingly. For example, if you have a text login, the **init 5** command should move Linux to a graphical login screen, assuming you have the appropriate packages such as GNOME and the X Window System installed. Alternatively, the **init 3** command moves Linux to a text login screen.

FIGURE 3-1	
dmesg boot messages	

```
OMB HIGHMEM available.
128MB LOWMEM available.
On node 0 totalpages: 32768
zone(0): 4096 pages.
zone(1): 28672 pages.
zone(2): 0 pages.
Kernel command line: ro root=LABEL=/ hdc=ide-scsi
ide_setup: hdc=ide-scsi
Initializing CPU#0
Detected 1193.754 MHz processor.
Console: colour VGA+ 80x25
Calibrating delay loop... 2359.29 BogoMIPS
Memory: 124308k/131072k available (1524k kernel code, 5288k reserved, 1086k data
, 164k init, 0k highmem)
zapping low mappings.
Dentry cache hash table entries: 16384 (order: 5, 131072 bytes)
Inode cache hash table entries: 8192 (order: 4, 65536 bytes)
Mount cache hash table entries: 512 (order: 0, 4096 bytes)
Buffer cache hash table entries: 8192 (order: 3, 32768 bytes)
Page-cache hash table entries: 32768 (order: 5, 131072 bytes)
CPU: L1 I cache: 16K, L1 D cache: 16K
CPU: L2 cache: 512K
Intel machine check architecture supported.
```

CERTIFICATION OBJECTIVE 3.03

Boot Loaders: GRUB and LILO

There are two main boot loaders associated with Red Hat Enterprise Linux: GRUB, the GRand Unified Bootloader, and LILO, the Linux Loader. Red Hat is moving toward making GRUB the only boot loader for its Linux distributions. You can't even install LILO during the Fedora Linux installation process.

There are a couple more clues. LILO is still included in the RHCE and RHCT exam requirements as of this writing. However, LILO is no longer included in the publically available outline for RH300, the main Red Hat prep course for the RHCE exam. But you'll need to come to your own conclusion on whether to study LILO for your exam.

on the   *You'll see the terms "bootloader" and "boot loader" used interchangeably.*
Job   *They both refer to software stored on the MBR of a hard disk which can load one or more operating systems. You may also see "Grand Unified Boot Loader" and "Grand Unified Bootloader" both referring to GRUB.*

Boot Loader Background

To understand the role of a boot loader, take a step back from Linux. When you boot your computer, the BIOS starts by detecting basic hardware, including your hard drives. Once it's done, it looks for the boot loader on the Master Boot Record of the first available disk. If you're working with an older PC, the BIOS can't find your boot loader unless it's located within the first 1,024 cylinders of the hard disk.

Newer BIOSes overcome this problem with Logical Block Addressing, which is also known as LBA mode. LBA mode reads "logical" values for the cylinder, head, and sector, which allows the BIOS to "see" a larger disk drive.

If you have multiple hard drives, there is one more caveat. If your drives are IDE hard drives, the /boot directory must be on a hard drive attached to the primary IDE controller. If your drives are all SCSI hard drives, the /boot directory must be located on a hard drive with SCSI ID 0 or ID 1. If you have a mix of hard drives, the /boot directory must be located on either the first IDE drive or a SCSI drive with ID 0. In other words, this is not an issue on the Red Hat exams unless the computer that you're tested on has more than two hard drives. And I believe that's less likely, as that would increase the cost of the exam.

GRUB, the GRand Unified Bootloader

Red Hat is moving toward GRUB, the GRand Unified Bootloader as the only way to start its Linux distributions. When you start your computer, your BIOS looks for the /boot directory and finds the GRUB menu, which will look similar to Figure 3-2. If you've configured your computer with multiple operating systems, you can use the GRUB menu to boot any operating system detected during the Linux installation process.

If you need to do something special with GRUB, you can edit the commands. If GRUB is password protected, you'll need to start with the **p** command. Use the **e** command to *temporarily* edit the file. You'll see a number of basic commands that you can use to modify GRUB, as shown in Figure 3-3 and Table 3-3. You can use these commands to test different GRUB configurations. They can help you troubleshoot problems with the GRUB configuration file without booting, editing, and rebooting your system. That could possibly help you save time during the Troubleshooting and System Maintenance exam. But once you find the solution, make sure to record the change in the GRUB configuration file, /etc/grub.conf.

You can also use GRUB to boot other operating systems, including various versions of Microsoft Windows. See Chapters 5 and 11 for more information, including a detailed line-by-line analysis of a dual-boot /etc/grub.conf file in Chapter 5.

FIGURE 3-2

The GRand
Unified
Bootloader
(GRUB)

```
GRUB   version 0.93   (638K lower / 194496K upper memory)

 Red Hat Enterprise Linux ES (2.4.21-4.EL)
 DOS




      Use the ↑ and ↓ keys to select which entry is highlighted.
      Press enter to boot the selected OS, 'e' to edit the
      commands before booting, 'a' to modify the kernel arguments
      before booting, or 'c' for a command-line.
```

FIGURE 3-3

Details of GRUB

If you've previously installed LILO and now want to install GRUB, edit the /etc/grub.conf file and then run the **grub-install /dev/xdy** command, where xdy represents the hard disk with your /boot directory.

on the **job**

The /etc/grub.conf file is linked to the actual GRUB configuration file, /boot/grub/grub.conf. When you edit /etc/grub.conf, changes are automatically reflected in /boot/grub/grub.conf.

TABLE 3-3   GRUB Editing Commands

Command	Description
b	Boot the currently listed operating system
d	Delete the current line
e	Edit the current line
o	Create an empty line underneath the current line
O	Create an empty line above the current line

INSIDE THE EXAM

Troubleshooting GRUB

If you're troubleshooting GRUB, the GRUB menu can help you experiment with changes quickly. However, if you find the solution in this way, you'll still need to change (and test) the GRUB configuration file, /etc/grub.conf.

If you find a problem with GRUB during the Troubleshooting and System Maintenance exam and are unsure about the solution, testing changes through the GRUB menu could save you time. However, until you record the change in the GRUB configuration file, /etc/grub.conf, you won't get credit for the work that you've done.

The LILO Alternative

The more traditional boot loader is LILO, the Linux Loader. It has been deprecated from RHEL 3 as well as Fedora Linux. Since it's no longer a part of the RH300 curriculum, I doubt that you'll see it on the RHCE exam. However, it is still a part of the RHCT prep course (RH133) curriculum as of this writing. You'll have to make your own judgment on whether you want to take the time to study LILO for your Red Hat exam.

The LILO configuration file is /etc/lilo.conf. If you edit this file, you need to implement these changes with the **lilo** command. The following shows a typical /etc/lilo.conf file:

on the *Job*   *If you've installed GRUB on your system, you can still find a LILO configuration file in /etc/lilo.conf.anaconda.*

```
prompt
timeout=50
default=linux
boot=/dev/hda
map=/boot/map
install=/boot/boot.b
message=/boot/message
linear

image=/boot/vmlinuz-2.4.21-3
        label=linux
```

```
                  initrd=/boot/initrd-2.4.21-3.img
                  read-only
                  append="hdc=ide-scsi root=LABEL=/"
       other=/dev/hda1
                  label=Win98
                  table=/dev/hda
```

Now here's the line-by-line interpretation of this file:

```
prompt
```

This forces the **lilo boot:** prompt to appear on the console.

```
timeout=50
default=linux
```

This forces LILO to wait five seconds (50 tenths of a second) before moving to the default operating system, labeled linux.

```
boot=/dev/hda
map=/boot/map
```

The system looks for boot and map information on the first IDE hard disk.

```
install=/boot/boot.b
```

This is the secondary boot loader.

```
message=/boot/message
```

This opens a graphical file that you see during the boot process.

```
linear
```

This uses linear addresses, and not standard hard disk geometry, to find the /boot directory.

```
image=/boot/vmlinuz-2.4.21-4
```

This is the actual virtual memory compressed kernel (version 2.4.21, with the -4 representing the Red Hat build number) used for this particular Linux system.

```
label=linux
```

This identifies the "boot option" label that appears if you press TAB at the LILO prompt.

```
initrd=/boot/initrd-2.4.21-4.img
```

This reveals the location of the second stage loader, the RAM disk.

```
read-only
```

During installation, the RAM disk filesystem is started in read-only mode. After the second stage is finished with a few tests, the RAM disk is unloaded from memory, and the real root partition is mounted from the filesystem, normally in read/write mode.

```
append="root=LABEL=/"
```

This adds a command to the kernel. The **root=LABEL=/** command points to the label associated with the root directory, which you can find with the **e2label** command described in Chapter 11.

The next section is another boot option—in this case, to boot Windows 98 on the first partition, /dev/hda1.

```
other=/dev/hda1
        label=Win98
        table=/dev/hda
```

The table is the location of the partition table to be used—in this case, the first physical IDE hard disk. If you edit this file, you need to run the **lilo** command to write the result to the appropriate boot record, usually the Master Boot Record (MBR) of your hard drive.

GRUB and LILO Parameters

To pass a parameter to GRUB, type the **a** command in the first GRUB menu. This allows you to append the command sent to the kernel. After typing the **a** command, you might see a command line similar to the following:

```
grub append> ro root=LABEL=/
```

You can add the command of your choice to the end of this command. For example, if you add "single" after the end of this line, Linux starts in single-user mode. If you're having trouble getting Linux to recognize all of the RAM on your computer, try adding **mem=**xyz**M** (where xyzM represents the amount of memory on your computer) to the end of the line.

LILO works in a similar way. At the LILO boot: prompt, type the parameter after the label name. For example, if you wanted to start your system in rescue mode, you would type **linux rescue**. If you wanted to start your system in single-user mode, type the following command at the prompt:

```
lilo boot: linux single
```

A wide variety of boot parameters are available; run the **man bootparam** command for more information.

Single-User Mode

Except for a normal boot of Linux, single-user mode is the most commonly used option. This is the system maintenance mode for experienced Linux administrators. It allows you to perform clean backups and restores to any partitions as needed from local hardware. It also allows you to run administration commands, recover or repair password and shadow password files, run filesystem checks, and so forth.

In some cases, to get out of single-user mode you just have to type **exit** and your system will go into multiuser mode. If you have made changes or repairs to any partitions, you should reboot the computer with the **reboot** command. If you've made changes during your exam, you'll want to test those changes with a reboot.

LILO Errors

The LILO first stage will also indicate some common and not-so-common problems:

```
(nothing)    did not get to lilo at all
L            first stage loaded and started
LI           second stage loaded from /boot
LILO         all of lilo is loaded correctly
```

Occasionally, there may be an error due to partition table changes, bad blocks, and so forth. On these rare occurrences, you will only get partial LILO prompts:

```
LIL          second stage boot loader is started
LIL?         Second stage loaded at an incorrect address
LIL-         the descriptor table is corrupt
```

CERTIFICATION OBJECTIVE 3.04

Partitioning Utilities

It's best to create partitions using Disk Druid during the installation process. This can save you grief as an administrator—and especially during the Red Hat exams. However, mistakes are made. You might forget to create a critical partition during the Installation and Configuration exam. You might need to create a larger /home directory partition for your users. For this purpose, the standard is still the **fdisk** utility, which I'll describe shortly.

Before you use fdisk to create or revise partitions, you should check your free space and the partitions that are currently mounted. You can do this with the **df** and **mount** commands. The following example illustrates how the **df** command displays the total, used, and available free space on all currently mounted filesystems.

Note the numbers under the 1k-blocks column. In this case, they add up to about 3GB of allocated space. (Don't include the space associated with /dev/hdc, which refers to a CD drive.) If your hard drive is larger, you may have unallocated space that you can use for another partition.

```
[root@Enterprise root]# df
Filesystem           1k-blocks     Used Available Use% Mounted on
/dev/hda8              932833     502478    382162  57% /
/dev/hda7               23300       2588     19509  12% /boot
/dev/hda1             1052064     914784    137280  87% /dosC
/dev/hda6             1052064     111648    940416  11% /home
none                    62828          0     62828 100% /dev/shm
/dev/hdc               556054     556054         0 100% /mnt/cdrom
[root@Enterprise root]#
```

The second command, **mount**, includes the filesystem type. In this case, we see the partition represented by device /dev/hda1 mounted with the VFAT file type on the / DosC directory. It provides direct access to the C: drive of the Windows operating system. I've set up the data shown from the **mount** command in columns for clarity; what you actually see in the RHEL 3 command line is less organized.

```
[root@Enterprise root]# mount
/dev/hda8 on /          type ext3 (rw)
none      on /proc      type proc (rw)
/dev/hda7 on /boot      type ext3 (rw)
/dev/hda1 on /dosC      type vfat (rw)
```

```
/dev/hda6 on /home      type vfat (rw)
none      on /dev/pts   type devpts (rw,mode=0620)
/dev/hdb  on /mnt/cdrom type iso9660 (ro)
[root@Enterprise root]#
```

 o n   t h e
j o b

As of this writing, RHEL 3 can reliably recognize NTFS partitions only in read-only mode. While support for write mode is available through the Linux kernel, it is noted as "dangerous" per the kernel help files.

One of the benefits is that you can move and copy files between the Linux and DOS partitions using standard Linux commands. You cannot, however, run many Microsoft Windows applications within Linux unless you run a DOS or Windows Emulation package such as WINE (www.winehq.org) or CrossOver Office (www.codeweavers.com).

The fdisk Utility

The **fdisk** utility is universally available and should be one of the first tools you get acquainted with. There are many commands, even an expert mode, but you only need to know a few, as discussed here.

Though you can modify the physical disk partition layout using many programs, we will be discussing the Linux implementation of fdisk. **FDISK.EXE** from DOS has the same name and is also used for creating partitions, but it doesn't incorporate any Linux-compatible features. It also includes a different interface.

Using fdisk: Starting, Getting Help, and Quitting

The following screen output lists commands that show how to start the **fdisk** program, how to get help, and how to quit the program. The /dev/hda drive is associated with the first IDE drive on a regular PC. Your computer may have a different hard drive; you can check the output from the **df** and **mount** commands for clues.

As you can see, once you start **fdisk**, it opens its own command line prompt.

```
# fdisk /dev/hda
Command (m for help): m
Command action
   a   toggle a bootable flag
   b   edit bsd disklabel
   c   toggle the dos compatibility flag
   d   delete a partition
   l   list known partition types
```

```
m    print this menu
n    add a new partition
o    create a new empty DOS partition table
p    print the partition table
q    quit without saving changes
s    create a new empty Sun disklabel
t    change a partition's system id
u    change display/entry units
v    verify the partition table
w    write table to disk and exit
x    extra functionality (experts only)

Command (m for help): q
```

Using fdisk: In a Nutshell

In the **fdisk** command line prompt, start with the print the partition table command
(**p**). This allows you to review the current entries in the partition table. Assuming you
have free space, you then create a new (**n**) partition, either primary (**p**) or logical (**l**). If
it doesn't already exist, you can also create an extended partition (**e**) to contain your
logical partitions. Remember that there are four primary partitions, which correspond
to numbers 1 through 4. One of the primary partitions can be redesignated as an extended
partition. The remaining partitions are logical partitions, numbered between 5 and
above. The Linux **fdisk** utility won't allow you to create more than 16 partitions on
the drive.

When you assign space to a partition, you're assigning a block of cylinders on that
hard disk. If you have free space, the fdisk default starts the new partition at the first
available cylinder. The actual size of the partition depends on disk geometry; do not
worry about exact size here.

Using fdisk: Deleting Partitions

In the following example, you will remove the only partition. The sample output
screen first starts fdisk. Then you print (**p**) the current partition table, delete (**d**) the
partition by number (1 in this case), write (**w**) the changes to the disk, and quit (**q**)
from the program. Needless to say, *do not perform this action on any partition where you
need the data.*

```
# fdisk /dev/hdb
Command (m for help): p
Disk /dev/hdb: 255 heads, 63 sectors, 525 cylinders
Units = cylinders of 16065 * 512 bytes
```

```
Device    Boot    Start        End    Blocks    Id  System
/dev/hdb1    *        1        525    4217031    6  FAT16
Command (m for help): d
Partition number (1-1): 1
```

This is the last chance to change your mind before deleting the current partition. If you want to quit without saving changes, exit from **fdisk** with the **q** command. If you're pleased with the changes that you've made and want to make them permanent, proceed with the **w** command:

```
Command (m for help): w
```

You did it! Now you have an empty hard disk or hard disk area where you can create the partitions you need.

Using fdisk: Creating Partitions

The following screen output sample shows the steps used to create (**n**) the first (/boot) partition, make it bootable (**a**), and then finally write (**w**) the partition information to the disk. (Note: Although you may ask for a 100MB partition, the geometry of the disk may not allow that precise size, as shown in the example.)

```
# fdisk /dev/hdb

Command (m for help): n
Command action
   e   extended
   p   primary partition (1-4)
p
Partition number (1-4):
First cylinder (1-256, default 1): 1
Last cylinder or +size or +sizeM or +sizeK (2-256,def 256): +100M

Command (m for help): a
Partition number (1-4): 1

Command (m for help): p
Disk /dev/hdb: 255 heads, 63 sectors, 256 cylinders
Units = cylinders of 16065 * 512 bytes
   Device Boot    Start        End    Blocks    Id  System
/dev/hdb1    *        1         12    98163     83  Linux

Command (m for help):
```

Repeat the previous commands as appropriate to create any other partitions that you might need. I illustrate one possible group of partitions here:

```
Command (m for help): p

Disk /dev/hdb: 255 heads, 63 sectors, 256 cylinders
Units = cylinders of 16065 * 512 bytes
   Device Boot    Start      End    Blocks   Id  System
/dev/hdb1            1        2     16044   83  Linux
/dev/hdb2            3       18     64176   82  swap
/dev/hdb3           19      169   1203300   83  Linux
/dev/hdb4          170      250    649782    5  Extended
/dev/hdb5          170      201    248682   83  Linux
/dev/hdb6          202      257    449232   83  Linux

Command (m for help): w
```

on the
Job

The number of blocks that you see may vary slightly depending on the size of your hard disk, the number of heads, sectors, and cylinders on that disk, as well as the version of fdisk that you're using.

Using fdisk: A New PC with No Partitions

After installing Linux on a new PC, you'll want to use **fdisk** to configure additional physical disks attached to the system. For example, if it's the first disk attached to the secondary IDE controller, run the **fdisk /dev/hdc** command.

Remember the limitations on partitions. If you need more than four partitions on the new physical disk, configure type Primary for the first three partitions, and then Extended for the rest of the disk as partition 4. You can then create logical partitions 5–16 within the extended partition.

Using fdisk: Creating a Swap Partition

You need to create a partition before you can reassign it as a swap partition. At the fdisk prompt, run the **L** command. You'll see a large number of file types, listed as hex codes. When you create a partition, fdisk creates a Linux Native type partition by default. As you can see from the output of the **L** command, the associated hex code is (83).

It's easy to reassign a partition as a swap partition. Run the **p** command. Remember the number of the partition you want to change. Make sure that partition doesn't have data that you want to save.

Now run the **t** command. Type in the number associated with the partition that you want to change. Type in the hex code for the type you want, in this case, 82 for a Linux swap partition. For example, I could run the following sequence of commands to set up a new swap partition on the second IDE hard drive. The commands that I type are in bold. The details of what you see depend on the partitions that you may have created. It'll be a 1GB swap space on the first primary partition (/dev/hdb1).

```
# fdisk /dev/hdb
Command (m for help): n
Command action
    e   extended
    p   primary partition (1-4)
p
Partition number (1-4): 1
First cylinder (1-10402, default 1):
Using default value 1
Last cylinder or +size or +sizeM or +sizeK (1-10402, default 10402): +1000M

Command (m for help): p

Disk /dev/hdb: 5368 MB, 5368709120 bytes
16 heads, 63 sectors/track, 10402 cylinders
Units = cylinders of 1008 * 512 = 516096 bytes

   Device Boot      Start         End      Blocks   Id  System
/dev/hdb1               1        1939      977224+   83  Linux

Command (m for help): t
Selected partition 1
Hex code (type L to list codes): 82
Changed system type of partition 1 to 82 (Linux swap)

Command (m for help): w
The partition table has been altered!

Calling ioctl() to re-read partition table.
Syncing disks.
#
```

The **fdisk** utility doesn't actually write the changes to your hard disk until you run the write (**w**) command. You have a chance to cancel your changes with the quit (**q**) command.

CERTIFICATION OBJECTIVE 3.05

RAID Configuration and Data Recovery

A Redundant Array of Independent Disks (RAID) is a series of disks that can save your data even if there is a catastrophic failure on one of the disks. While some versions of RAID make complete copies of your data, others use the so-called parity bit to allow your computer to rebuild the data on lost disks.

Linux RAID has come a long way. A substantial number of hardware RAID products support Linux, especially from name brand PC manufacturers. Dedicated RAID hardware can ensure the integrity of your data even if there is a catastrophic *physical* failure on one of the disks.

Depending on your definitions, RAID has nine or ten different levels, which can accommodate different levels of data redundancy. Only three levels of RAID are supported directly by RHEL 3: levels 0, 1, and 5. Hardware RAID uses a RAID controller connected to an array of several hard disks. A driver must be installed to be able to use the controller. Most RAID is hardware based; when properly configured, the failure of one drive in a RAID 1 or RAID 5 array does not destroy the data in the array. Linux, meanwhile, offers a software solution to RAID. Once RAID is configured on a sufficient number of partitions, Linux can use those partitions just as it would any other block device. However, to ensure redundancy, it's up to you in real life to make sure that each partition in a Linux software RAID array is configured on a different physical hard disk.

on the job

The RAID md device is a meta device. In other words, it is a composite of two or more other devices such as /dev/hda1 and /dev/hdb1 that might be components of a RAID array.

The following sections describe the basic RAID levels supported on Red Hat Enterprise Linux 3.

RAID 0

This level of RAID makes it faster to read and write to the hard drives. However, RAID 0 provides no data redundancy. It requires at least two hard disks.

Reads and writes to the hard disks are done in parallel, in other words, to two or more hard disks simultaneously. All hard drives in a RAID 0 array are filled equally. But since RAID 0 does not provide data redundancy, a failure of any one of the drives will result in total data loss. RAID 0 is also known as "striping without parity."

RAID 1

This level of RAID mirrors information to two or more other disks. In other words, the same set of information is written to two different hard disks. If one disk is damaged or removed, you still have all of the data on the other hard disk. The disadvantage of RAID 1 is that data has to be written twice, which can reduce performance. You can come close to maintaining the same level of performance if you also use separate hard disk controllers. That prevents the hard disk controller from becoming a bottleneck.

And it is expensive. To support RAID 1, you need an additional hard disk for every hard disk worth of data. RAID 1 is also known as disk mirroring.

RAID 4

While this level of RAID is not directly supported by current Linux distributions associated with Red Hat, it is still supported by the current Linux kernel. RAID 4 requires three or more disks. As with RAID 0, data reads and writes are done in parallel to all disks. One of the disks maintains the parity information, which can be used to reconstruct the data. Reliability is improved, but since parity information is updated with every write operation, the parity disk can be a bottleneck on the system. RAID 4 is known as disk striping with parity.

RAID 5

Like RAID 4, RAID 5 requires three or more disks. Unlike RAID 4, RAID 5 distributes, or "stripes," parity information evenly across all the disks. If one disk fails, the data can be reconstructed from the parity data on the remaining disks. RAID does not stop; all data is still available even after a single disk failure. RAID level 5 is the preferred choice in most cases: the performance is good, data integrity is ensured, and only one disk's worth of space is lost to parity data. RAID 5 is also known as disk striping with parity.

on the
Job

Hardware RAID systems should be "hot-swappable." In other words, if one disk fails, the administrator can replace the failed disk while the server is still running. The system will then automatically rebuild the data onto the new disk. If you configure different partitions from the same physical disk for a software RAID system, the resulting configuration can easily fail. Alternatively, you may be able to set up "spare disks" on your servers; RAID may automatically rebuild data from a lost hard drive on properly configured spare disks.

RAID in Practice

RAID is associated with a substantial amount of data on a server. It's not uncommon to have a couple dozen hard disks working together in a RAID array. That much data can be rather valuable.

If continued performance through a hardware failure is important, you can assign additional disks for "failover," which sets up spare disks for the RAID array. When one disk fails, it is marked as bad. The data is almost immediately reconstructed on the first spare disk, resulting in little or no downtime. The next example demonstrates

INSIDE THE EXAM

Creating RAID Arrays

During the Red Hat Installation and Configuration exam, it's generally easier to do as much as possible during the installation process. If you're asked to create a RAID array, it's easiest to do so with Disk Druid, which only works during installation. You can create RAID arrays once RHEL is installed, but as you'll see in the following instructions, it is more time consuming, and involves a process that is more difficult to remember.

However, if you're required to create a RAID array during your exam and forget to create it during the installation process, not all is lost. You can still use the tools I describe in this chapter to create and configure RAID arrays during the exam. And the skills you learn here can serve you well through your career.

The exam may use examples from RAID levels 0, 1, and or 5. However, if the PC that you're using on the exam includes only one physical hard disk, you may have to configure multiple RAID partitions on the same disk.

this practice in both RAID 1 and RAID 5 arrays. Assuming your server has four physical drives, with the OS loaded on the first, it should look something like this:

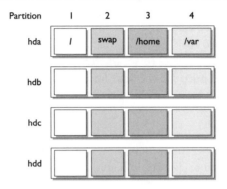

All four drives (hda, hdb, hdc, hdd) should be approximately the same size.

This first example shows how to mirror both the /home and the /var directories (RAID 1) on Drive 2 and Drive 3, leaving Drive 4 as a spare.

You need to create nearly identically sized partitions on Drives 2 and 3. In this example, four disks are configured with four partitions of the same size. If you use the Linux fdisk program, use the **t** command to toggle the drive ID type. You can then set the partition to type fd, which corresponds to the Linux raid autodetect filesystem. You'll get to test it out for yourself shortly in an exercise, as well as a lab at the end of this chapter.

In the partition table of the first drive is /dev/hda3 (currently mounted as /home) and /dev/hda4 (currently mounted as /var). The second drive includes /dev/hdb3 and /dev/hdb4. The third drive is set up with /dev/hdc3 and /dev/hdc4, while the last drive has /dev/hdd3 and /dev/hdd4. All of these partitions have been marked with partition IDs of type 0xFD.

e x a m
ⓦ a t c h

If you need to create a raidtab configuration file during the exam, it may be faster to start with one of the sample raidtab configuration files. There are several available in the following directory: /usr/share/doc/raidtools-1.00.3.

Next, update the configuration file /etc/raidtab. As shown in the following code, you'll see two different RAID 1 arrays (/dev/md0 and /dev/md1):

```
raiddev /dev/md0
raid-level 1

nr-raid-disks 2
nr-spare-disks 1
persistent-superblock 1
chunk-size 4

device   /dev/hdb3
raid-disk 0
device   /dev/hdc3
raid-disk 1
device   /dev/hdd3
spare-disk 0

raiddev /dev/md1
raid-level 1
nr-raid-disks 3
nr-spare-disks 1
persistent-superblock 1
chunk-size 4
 device   /dev/hdb4
raid-disk 0
device   /dev/hdc4
raid-disk 1
device   /dev/hdd4
spare-disk 0
```

Table 3-4 shows what some of the commands are, along with a brief description of what they do. If you haven't already done so, it's time to format these partitions and convert them to the default ext3 filesystem.

TABLE 3-4	Command	Description
Commands in raidtab	nr-raid-disks	Number of RAID disks to use
	nr-spare-disks	Number of spare disks to use
	persistent-superblock	Required for autodetection
	chunk-size	Amount of data to read/write
	parity-algorithm	How RAID 5 should use parity

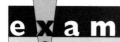

The Linux format command is **mkfs**; with the right switch, you can automatically set it up to ext3 with a journal. For example, the following command formats the /dev/hda4 partition:

```
# mkfs -j /dev/hda4
```

If the partitions in /etc/raidtab are new, repeat this command for all of those other partitions.

Partitions from older Linux computers may be formatted to the ext2 filesystem, which is essentially the same as ext3 without a journal. You can add journaling to an older partition with a command such as:

```
# tune2fs -j /dev/hda4
```

When a journal is added to the ext2 filesystem, it upgrades that partition to the ext3 filesystem.

on the
job
There are advantages to the ext3 journaling filesystem. If your system suffers a sudden power failure, it does not have to check every inode for file data; the information is already available in the journal.

The aforementioned /etc/raidtab file includes two RAID devices, /dev/md0 and /dev/md1. To start RAID 1 on those devices, run the following commands:

```
# mkraid -R /dev/md0
# mkraid -R /dev/md1
```

If it works, you'll see the result in the dynamic /proc/mdstat file. You can now mount the device and format it with the appropriate **mkfs** command, and finally mount it on the Linux directory of your choice. You can even set it up to be automatically mounted through /etc/fstab, as described in Chapter 4.

on the
job
Yes, when you configure a RAID device, you're formatting the same space twice. First, you format the partitions that make up the array. Once you've made RAID devices such as /dev/md0, you can then format those devices as if they were new partitions.

For a RAID 5 array on the /var partition (in order to preserve mail, print spools, and log files), the /etc/raidtab file should be modified as follows:

```
raiddev /dev/md0
raid-level 5
nr-raid-disks 3
nr-spare-disks 1
persistent-superblock 1
chunksize 32

parity-algorithm right-symmetric
device   /dev/hda4
raid-disk 0
device   /dev/hdb4
raid-disk 1
device   /dev/hdc4
raid-disk 2
device   /dev/hdd4
spare-disk 0
```

Now you can run **mkraid /dev/md0** to initialize this RAID 5 device. You can then format and mount this RAID array on the Linux directory of your choice.

Formatting the RAID Array

Now you can run the **mkfs** command to format each RAID array. It's fairly simple; now that you've created arrays such as /dev/md0 and /dev/md1, you can work with them as if they were any other hard drive partition. For example, you can format these arrays to the ext3 filesystems with the following commands:

```
# mkfs -j /dev/md0
# mkfs -j /dev/md1
```

The process is straightforward—for example, if you wanted to mount the /home/mj directory on the first RAID array, you'd run the following commands (assume the /hometmp directory exists):

```
# cp -r /home/mj /hometmp
# mount /dev/md0 /home/mj
# cp -r /hometmp /home/mj
```

Setting up RAID on a critical set of files such as a /boot directory partition is a bit trickier. Because of the importance of this data, manually copy the contents of the /boot directory (as well as the boot loader file, /etc/grub.conf or /etc/lilo.conf) to a different physical drive.

Implementing the RAID Array

But that's not the last step. You may not get full credit for your work on the exam unless the directory gets mounted on the RAID array when you reboot your Linux computer. Based on a standard RHEL 3 /etc/fstab configuration file, you might add the following line to that file:

```
LABEL=/home/mj   /home/mj   ext3      defaults   1 2
```

Before this line can work, you'll need to set the label for this directory with the following command:

```
# e2label /dev/md0 /home/mj
```

I describe the /etc/fstab file, including the meaning of the data in each these columns, in more detail in Chapter 4.

EXERCISE 3-1

Mirror the /home Partition with Software RAID

Don't do this exercise on a production computer. If you have a computer with Red Hat Enterprise Linux already installed with several different physical hard drives that you can use for testing, that is best. One alternative is to use virtual machine technology such as VMWare, which can allow you to set up these exercises with minimal risk to a production system. You can also set up several IDE and SCSI hard disks on a VMWare machine. When you're ready, use the Linux **fdisk** techniques discussed in Chapter 3 to configure the following two-drive partition scheme:

```
Drive 1:
hda1     256    /
hda2      64    swap
hda3     500    /home
hda4     256    /var

Drive 2:
hdb1    1200    /usr
hdb2      64    swap
hdb3     100    /tmp
hdb4     500    (not allocated)
```

Now with the following steps, you can create a mirror of hda3, which stores the /home directory, to the hdb4 partition. (The partition sizes do not have to be identical.)

If you're making fdisk changes on a production computer, back up the data in the /home partition first. Otherwise, all data on the current /dev/hda3 will be lost.

1. Mark the two partition IDs as type FD using the Linux fdisk utility.

```
# fdisk /dev/hda
Command (m for help) : t
Partition number (1-4)
3
Partition ID (L to list options): FD
Command (m for help) : w
# fdisk /dev/hdb
Command (m for help) : t
Partition number (1-4)
4
Partition ID (L to list options): FD
Command (m for help) : w
```

2. Update the configuration file /etc/raidtab with these lines of code:

```
# vi /etc/raidtab
raiddev /dev/md0
raid-level 1

nr-raid-disks 2
nr-spare-disks 0
persistent-superblock 1
chunk-size 4
device   /dev/hda3
raid-disk 0
device   /dev/hdb4
raid-disk 1
```

3. Now make the RAID device file md0 and format it this way:

```
# mkraid -R /dev/md0
# mkfs -j /dev/md0
```

4. All that's left is to restore the files to the device and mount it.

5. However, for the exam, you may not get full credit for your work unless your Linux system mounts the directory on the RAID device. Make sure to do so in the /etc/fstab configuration file. Run the **e2label** command as required to

make sure that the LABEL that you add to /etc/fstab is read properly the next time you boot Linux.

Logical Volume Management: Configuration and Administration

Logical Volume Management (LVM) can allow you to manage active partitions. Before LVM, there was no easy way to increase or reduce the size of a partition after Linux is installed.

on the *Job*

This isn't quite true; you can use the GNU Parted utility to manage the size of an active partition. However, while the Red Hat curricula does refer to fdisk, there is no reference as of this writing to Parted. For more information on Parted, see www.gnu.org/software/parted.

For example, if you find that you have extra space on the /home directory partition and need more space on your /var directory partition for log files, LVM will let you reallocate the space. Alternatively, if you are managing a server on a growing network, new users will be common. You may come to the point where you need more room on your /home directory partition. With LVM, you can add a new physical disk and allocate its storage capacity to an existing /home directory partition.

on the *Job*

While LVM can be an important tool to manage partitions, it does not by itself provide redundancy. Do not use it as a substitute for RAID. However, you can use LVM in concert with a properly configured RAID array.

LVM Concepts

The LVM system organizes hard disks into Logical Volume (LV) groups. Essentially, physical hard disk partitions (or possibly RAID arrays) are set up in a bunch of

INSIDE THE EXAM

Logical Volume Management

One of the critical decisions during the Installation and Configuration exam is whether you install in text or graphical mode. Text mode is faster. However, if you're required to create an LVM group during your exam, you can configure with Disk Druid *only* if you install RHEL in graphical mode.

I can't give you a concrete timesavings between graphical and text mode; it depends on the traffic demands (how many other users) and the hardware available during your exam. I can say that when I installed the standard RHEL server configuration in graphical mode, it took five minutes longer than the same process in text mode. If your computer has more than 256MB of RAM (and more than 16MB of video memory), I suspect the difference would decrease.

Alternatively, you can use the techniques I describe in this section to configure LVM groups during the exam. Even if you remember to configure LVM groups during the installation process, read through this section. During the exam, it'll allow you to confirm that the LVM groups were created correctly. And on the job, it'll allow you to create LVM groups for your users in the real world.

If you don't have to configure an LVM group during your Installation and Configuration exam, text mode saves you time. If you are asked to configure an LVM group during your exam, your choice depends on whether you can configure an LVM group more quickly during the graphical installation process or the techniques described in this chapter.

equal-sized chunks known as Physical Extents (PE). As there are several other concepts associated with the LVM system, let's start with some basic definitions:

- **Physical Volume (PV)** is the standard partition that you add to the LVM mix. Normally, a physical volume is a standard primary or logical partition. It can also be a RAID array.

- **Physical Extent (PE)** is a chunk of disk space. Every PV is divided into a number of equal sized PEs. Every PE in a LV group is the same size. Different LV groups can have different sized PEs.

- **Logical Extent (LE)** is also a chunk of disk space. Every LE is mapped to a specific PE.

- **Logical Volume (LV)** is composed of a group of LEs. You can mount a filesystem such as /home and /var on an LV.
- **Volume Group (VG)** is composed of a group of LVs. It is the organizational group for LVM. Most of the commands that you'll use apply to a specific VG.

As of this writing, there are two basic ways to create an LVM Volume Group in Red Hat Enterprise Linux. You can set up an LVM if you install RHEL 3 in graphical mode, using Disk Druid. Alternatively, you can use the basic LVM commands to create and manage Volume Groups after Linux is installed. As LVM is not much good unless you can add and delete specific LVs, you should know the basic LVM commands. But the first step is to create a PV.

Creating a Physical Volume

The first step to create an LVM is to start with a physical disk. If you have a freshly installed hard disk, you can set up a PV on the entire disk. For example, if that hard disk is attached as the third IDE hard disk (/dev/hdc), and you haven't configured partitions on the drive, you'd run the following command:

```
# pvcreate /dev/hdc
```

Alternatively, you can set up a new PV on a properly formatted partition. For example, assume that you've added a new partition, /dev/hdc2. You could then use **fdisk** or a similar tool to set it to the Linux LVM partition type. In fdisk, this corresponds to partition type 8e. The sequence of commands would look similar to the following:

```
# fdisk /dev/hdc
Command (m for help) : t
Partition number (1-4)
2
Partition ID (L to list options): 8e
Command (m for help) : w
```

Once your partition is ready, you can run the following command to create a new PV on that partition (/dev/hdc2):

```
# pvcreate /dev/hdc2
```

Creating a Volume Group

Once you have two or more PVs, you can create a Volume Group (VG). You can substitute the name of your choice for *volumegroup*.

```
# vgcreate volumegroup /dev/hdc2 /dev/hdd2
```

You can add more room to any VG. When you create a new partition that you want to add to the VG, just extend it with the following command:

```
# vgextend volumegroup /dev/sda1
```

Creating a Logical Volume

However, a new VG doesn't help you unless you can mount a filesystem on it. So you need to create a logical volume (LV), for this purpose. The following command creates an LV. You can add as many chunks of disk space (also known as Physical Extents or PEs) as you need.

```
# lvcreate -l number_of_PEs volumegroup -n logvol
```

This creates a device named /dev/*volumegroup*/*logvol*. You can format this device as if it were a regular disk partition, and then mount the directory of your choice on your new logical volume.

But this isn't useful if you don't know how much space is associated with each PE. You could use trial and error, using the **df** command to check the size of the volume after you've mounted a directory on it. Alternatively, you can use the **-L** switch to set a size in MB. For example, the following command creates an LV named flex of 200MB:

```
# lvcreate -L 200M volumegroup -n flex
```

Using a Logical Volume

But that's not the last step. You may not get full credit for your work on the exam unless the directory gets mounted on the LVM group when you reboot your Linux computer. Based on a standard RHEL 3 /etc/fstab configuration file, you might add the following line to that file:

```
LABEL=/home/mj   /home/mj    ext3     defaults    1 2
```

Before this line can work, you'll need to set the label for this directory with the following command:

```
# e2label /dev/volumegroup/logvol /home/mj
```

I describe the /etc/fstab file, including the meaning of the data in each these columns, in more detail in Chapter 4.

CERTIFICATION OBJECTIVE 3.07

Automated Installation with Kickstart

Kickstart is Red Hat's solution for an automated installation of Red Hat. All of the questions asked during setup can be automatically supplied with one text file. You can easily set up nearly identical systems very quickly. Kickstart files are very useful for quick deployment and distribution of Linux systems.

INSIDE THE EXAM

Kickstart and the Red Hat Exams

For the Troubleshooting and System Maintenance exam, it's possible that the exam proctor might configure your computer using a customized Kickstart configuration file. The file might be local or it might be stored on the server. Understanding Kickstart is a very useful skill that can help you install Linux on a number of different computers simultaneously. You can start the process and walk away. The options are rich and varied. The Red Hat Exam Prep guide suggests that you need to configure "hands-free installation using Kickstart."

In addition, as of this writing, there is a bug with respect to Kickstart installations that relies on a DHCP server (Red Hat Bugzilla #90774). I therefore doubt that you'll see or have to configure a Kickstart DHCP server on either exam, at least until this bug is closed. You can check the bug status for yourself at bugzilla.redhat.com.

Kickstart Configuration Concepts

There are two methods for creating the required Kickstart configuration file:

- Use the anaconda-ks.cfg file from the root user's home directory, /root.
- Use the graphical Kickstart Configurator, accessible through the **ksconfig** command or in the GUI, click Main Menu | System Tools | Kickstart.

The first option lets you use the Kickstart template file created for your computer by Anaconda, the Red Hat Enterprise Linux installation program. The second option, the Kickstart Configurator, is discussed in detail later in this chapter.

If you're installing RHEL 3 on a number of different computers, you will find the anaconda-ks.cfg file helpful. You can install RHEL 3 the way you want on one computer. You can then use the anaconda-ks.cfg file from that computer as a template to install RHEL on the other identical computers on your network. If the computers aren't identical, you can customize each anaconda-ks.cfg file as required, for elements such as a different hard disk size, host name, and so on.

Configuring a Kickstart Floppy

Once the Kickstart file is configured, the easiest way to use it is through the RHEL installation boot floppy. To do so, follow these basic steps:

1. Configure and edit the anaconda-ks.cfg file as desired. I'll describe this process in more detail shortly.

2. Insert and mount a 1.44MB installation floppy. If you need to create one, I describe the process in Chapter 2. You can then mount the floppy with the **mount /mnt/floppy** command.

on the Job

The mount /mnt/floppy command is not a complete command; however, it works in RHEL because of the settings in /etc/fstab, as described in Chapter 4.

3. Copy the Kickstart file to the floppy with the following command:

```
# cp /root/anaconda-ks.cfg /mnt/floppy/ks.cfg
```

4. Check the ks.cfg file on the floppy with the **vi /mnt/floppy/ks.cfg** command. If you don't see your entire ks.cfg file, you may not have enough room on your installation boot floppy. You can make room by deleting the snake.msg file from the floppy. If you don't need the description of options during the installation process, you can also delete the general.msg, options.msg, param.msg, and rescue.msg files without affecting the functionality of the installation boot floppy.

5. You should now be ready to try out the installation boot floppy on a different computer. You'll get to try this again shortly in an exercise.

At the time of this writing, boot disks still bring up the LILO boot: prompt. Use LILO's boot options to initiate the Kickstart file. To boot, and then perform the Kickstart installation from a floppy, type

```
boot: linux ks=floppy
```

As long as you have a DHCP server on your network, you may be able to use the same Red Hat Enterprise Linux installation boot floppy. Just boot each new Linux computer from that floppy, type in the **linux ks=floppy** command at the boot prompt, give the computer a moment to read the ks.cfg file, and insert the same floppy in the next new Linux computer.

During the troubleshooting exam, your exam proctor may set up a computer for you using a Kickstart floppy or CD. If it's a floppy, it's quite possible **that you'll also need a driver floppy, or first installation CD, which your proctor should provide.**

Configuring a Kickstart Server

Alternatively, you can configure a Kickstart configuration file on the DHCP/BOOTP server for your network. If you want to put the file on a DHCP/BOOTP server, open the /etc/dhcpd.conf configuration file on that server. Specify the Kickstart file. For example, if you've stored the appropriate Kickstart file in the /usr/install directory on the DHCP server, add the **filename "/usr/install/"** command to dhcpd.conf. That prompts Anaconda to look on the server in the /usr/install directory for a *client_ip*-kickstart file.

Alternatively, if the Kickstart file is stored on a different server, add the **next-server** *servername* option to the dhcpd.conf configuration file. In this case, the *servername* is the name of the computer with the Kickstart file.

Starting the Installation with a Kickstart File

No matter where you choose to put the Kickstart file, you can boot with a floppy or a specialized CD. You can put the Kickstart file on the Red Hat boot floppy, or with a bit more work, on a Red Hat boot ISO. Just mount the floppy and copy it as the ks.cfg file from wherever you've saved your Kickstart configuration file.

If you're booting from a Red Hat installation floppy, enter the following command at the boot: prompt:

```
boot: linux ks=floppy
```

If you're booting from the Red Hat installation CD-ROM, you can still refer to a Kickstart configuration file on a floppy disk with the following command:

```
boot: linux ks=hd:fd0:/ks.cfg
```

This assumes the Kickstart configuration file is called ks.cfg and is located on the first floppy disk on your PC. Alternatively, you can refer to the Kickstart configuration file on a hard disk with this command:

```
boot: linux ks=hd:hda2:/home/mj/ks.cfg
```

This assumes the Kickstart configuration file is called ks.cfg and is located on the second partition of the first IDE drive in the /home/mj directory. The syntax of this command certainly looks strange; it's been updated for Red Hat Linux 9 and RHEL 3.

You don't need to get a Kickstart file from a DHCP server. To boot from a specific NFS or HTTP server on the network, say with an IP address of 192.168.17.18, from the /kicks/ks.cfg file, type one of the following commands:

```
boot: linux ks=nfs:192.168.17.18:/kicks/ks.cfg
boot: linux ks=http:192.168.17.18:/kicks/ks.cfg
```

However, even if you've specified a static IP address in ks.cfg, this installation looks for IP address information from a DHCP server. If not found, Anaconda continues with a standard installation, not using the Kickstart file.

Sample Kickstart File

I've based this section on the anaconda-ks.cfg file created when I installed my RHEL 3 Server computer. I've added a number of comments. While you're welcome to use it as a sample file, be sure to customize it for your hardware and network. This section just scratches the surface on what you can do with a Kickstart file; your version of this file may vary.

While most of the options are self-explanatory, I've interspersed my explanation of each command within the file. This file illustrates just a small portion of available commands. For more information on each command (and options) in this file, read the RHEL 3 Configuration Guide, which is available online at www.redhat.com/docs /manuals/enterprise.

Follow these ground rules and guidelines to use when setting up a Kickstart file:

- Do *not* change the order of the options.
- You do not need to use all the options.
- If you leave out a required option, the user will be prompted for the answer during the installation process.
- For upgrades, you *must* have at least the following options defined:
  - Language
  - Installation method
  - Device specification
  - Keyboard setup
  - The upgrade keyword
  - Boot loader (GRUB or LILO) configuration

on the **Job**

If you leave out an option, you will be prompted to complete it. This is an easy way to see if your Kickstart file is properly configured. But as some Kickstart options change the partitions on your hard drive, even testing this file can delete all of the data on your computer. So make sure to have a test computer available to test your Kickstart configuration file.

Here is the code from my Kickstart file. The first line is a comment that tells me that this file was created during the installation process.

```
# Kickstart file automatically generated by anaconda.
```

The first command is simple; it starts the installation process. It defaults to the first available local media, in this case, the first RHEL installation CD or floppy.

```
install
```

However, if you want to specify an installation, you could add the source of your choice on the next line. It could be *cdrom*, or if you're installing from an NFS server, you can specify it as follows. If you have the name of the server, you can substitute it for the IP address.

```
nfs --server=192.168.30.4 --dir=/mnt/inst
```

You can also configure a connection to an FTP or HTTP server by substituting one of the commands shown here. The directories I specify are based on the FTP and HTTP installation servers created in Chapter 2:

```
url --url http://192.168.30.4/inst
```

or

```
url --url ftp://192.168.30.4/pub/inst
```

The **lang** command specifies the language to use during the installation process. It matters if the installation stops due to a missing command in this file. The **langsupport** command specifies the language to install with the operating system. The keyboard command is self-explanatory, as it specifies the keyboard to configure on this computer.

```
lang en_US.UTF-8
langsupport --default en_US.UTF-8 en_US.UTF-8
keyboard us
```

The **mouse** command specifies the pointing device associated with this computer. This particular command specifies a generic PS/2 mouse, connected to /dev/psaux, configured to emulate a middle mouse button.

```
mouse genericps/2 --device psaux --emulthree
```

The **xconfig** command specifies the graphical configuration for this system. The switches are nearly self-explanatory. The **--card** switch specifies the graphics card driver. The **--videoram** switch specifies the amount of RAM on the video card. The **--hsync** and **--vsync** switches specify horizontal sync and vertical refresh rates, respectively. The **--resolution** switch sets the default resolution for the monitor, with a given color **--depth** in bits. The **--defaultdesktop** switch is normally **gnome** or **kde**.

Due to typesetting limitations, we're showing the following code on *three* lines. Please note that all options for the **xconfig** command *must* be on *one* line. Line wrapping, if the options exceed the space in your editor, is acceptable.

```
xconfig --card "VESA driver (generic)" --videoram 16384
--hsync 31.5-37.9 --vsync 40-70 --resolution 800x600
--depth 24 --defaultdesktop gnome
```

The **network** command is a lot more straightforward if you have a DHCP server for your network; it would read **network --device eth0 --bootproto dhcp**. This particular

line configures static IP address information, with the specified network mask
(**--netmask**), gateway address (**--gateway**), DNS servers (**--nameserver**), and
computer name (**--hostname**).

Due to typesetting limitations, we're showing the following code on *three* lines.
Please note that all options for the **network** command *must* be on *one* line. Line
wrapping, if the options exceed the space in your editor, is acceptable.

```
network --device eth0 --bootproto static --ip 192.168.30.149
--netmask 255.255.255.0 --gateway 192.168.30.113
--nameserver 207.217.120.83,207.217.126.81 --hostname Enterprise3
```

You need to specify the root user password during the installation process. This
line specifies the password in encrypted format. You don't have to encrypt the root
password in this line. If needed, you can copy this password from /etc/shadow.

```
rootpw --iscrypted $1$5UrLfXTk$CsCW0nQytrUuvycuLT317/
```

As for security, in RHEL 3, the firewall is either **--enabled** or **--disabled**. By default,
the **authconfig** command sets up the Shadow Password Suite (**--enableshadow**) and
md5 encryption (**--enablemd5**).

```
firewall --enabled
authconfig --enableshadow --enablemd5
```

The **timezone** command is associated with a long list of time zones. If you've
installed the squirrelmail RPM, you can find a full list in /usr/share/squirrelmail
/locale/timezones.cfg. If you want to set the hardware clock to Greenwich Mean
Time, you can add the **--utc** switch.

on the
job

Linux uses the UTC acronym for Greenwich Mean Time. UTC is the French
acronym for this standard, which does not refer to a city in the United Kingdom.

```
timezone America/New_York
```

The default boot loader is GRUB, which is installed unless you add the **--useLilo** switch.
Naturally, it should normally be installed on the Master Boot Record (MBR) of a hard
drive. You can include an **--append** switch to specify commands for the kernel.

```
bootloader --location=mbr
```

By default, the commands that partition your hard drives are commented out of the anaconda-ks.cfg file. These options are a bit more complex, so I discuss them in more detail in the next section. If the commands work for you, don't forget to delete the comment character (#) to activate these commands.

```
# The following is the partition information you requested
# Note that any partitions you deleted are not expressed
# here so unless you clear all partitions first, this is
# not guaranteed to work

# clearpart --all --drives=hda
# part /boot --fstype ext3 --size=100 --ondisk=hda
# part / --fstype ext3 --size=1024 --grow --ondisk=hda
# part swap --size=256 --grow --maxsize=512 --ondisk=hda
```

The following is a list of package groups that are installed through this Kickstart configuration file. These names correspond to the names that you can find in the comps.xml file described in Chapter 2.

```
%packages
@ system-tools
@ base-x
@ web-server
@ smb-server
@ printing
@ text-internet
@ mail-server
@ legacy network server
@ dns-server
@ server-cfg
@ dialup
@ sound-and-video
@ admin-tools
@ news-server
@ gnome-desktop
@ ftp-server
@ network-server
@ kernel-development
@ graphical-internet
@ compat-arch-support
```

After the package groups are installed, you can specify postinstallation commands (**%post**) in the Kickstart installation file.

```
%post
```

Kickstart Partitioning

The partitioning options in the Kickstart file are a bit complex. They can give you full control of the partitioning options, too. You can clear all partitions with **clearpart --all**, or just clear any Linux-type partitions with **clearpart --linux**, or just add to the end of the current partitions. You can create partitions on more than one drive, but you need to identify each device specifically.

To add Linux partitions, use the **part** command with the following syntax:

```
part mount dir --size size [--grow] [--maxsize size]
```

The *size* is in megabytes. You can use the **--grow** option to allow the partition to expand and fill all remaining disk space (or share it with any other partitions marked "grow" on the same disk). This will not expand on the fly, but rather, when all fixed-size partitions are added, these "growable" partitions will use the rest of the space.

If you specify multiple partitions with the **--grow** option, their space will be divided evenly. You can also specify a **--maxsize**, which will allow the partition to grow only to the size specified in megabytes.

Therefore, the following commands from my Kickstart configuration file (with comment characters removed) perform the following tasks:

This **clearpart** command removes all of the partitions on the first IDE hard drive.

```
clearpart --all --drives=hda
```

This first **part** command configures the /boot directory to the ext3 filesystem with 100MB of space on the first IDE hard drive.

```
part /boot --fstype ext3 --size=100 --ondisk=hda
```

This second **part** command configures the root directory (/) to the ext3 filesystem with at least 1024MB of space on the first IDE hard drive. If more room is available, this partition expands to take the available space.

```
part / --fstype ext3 --size=1024 --grow --ondisk=hda
```

This third **part** command configures a swap partition to be at least 256MB, which corresponds to the amount of RAM available on this computer. If space is available on the hard drive, it's allowed to grow up to 512MB.

```
part swap --size=256 --grow --maxsize=512 --ondisk=hda
```

Creating a Sample Kickstart File from a Running System for a Second Similar System Installation

In this exercise, you will use the anaconda-ks.cfg file to duplicate the installation from one computer to another with identical hardware. This exercise simply installs all the exact same packages with the same partition configuration on the second computer. Assume that both computers use DHCP to set up their IP addresses. Add one /home partition of 2000MB with a 512MB swap partition. (This means you must have at least 2500MB of free space available. If you have more space, let it remain unused for now.) You want to install all the same packages as your current installation, so you do not need to make any package changes to the default Anaconda Kickstart file in the /root directory.

If you do not have multiple computers for this exercise, one alternative as discussed earlier is VMWare.

1. Review the /root/anaconda-ks.cfg file. Copy it to ks.cfg.

2. Create the boot disk and add this ks.cfg file to it:

```
dd if=/mnt/cdrom/images/bootdisk.img of=/dev/fd0
mount /dev/fd0 /mnt/floppy
cp ks.cfg /mnt/floppy
```

3. Prepare the second computer so that it has the same disk configuration, the same C: drive size if it was present, and same amount of unused and unpartitioned space as the first computer. Reboot the second computer with the Linux boot file with the Kickstart file in the floppy drive and the first binary CD in the CD-ROM.

4. At the Red Hat Installation menu boot prompt, enter the following startup command:

```
boot: linux ks=floppy
```

You should now see the system installation creating the same setup as the first system. Depending on how you installed Linux on the original computer, you may need a network connection to the same installation source or the other installation CDs.

EXERCISE 3-3

Modify the Packages to Be Installed (Optional Exercise)

Edit the ks.cfg file on the floppy and remove all the game packages you can find. Alternatively, set up an interactive installation so that you can test and observe the result on another computer.

The Red Hat exams test your skills on Red Hat Enterprise Linux. While many Unix skills are transferable to the exam, there are also many features unique to RHEL. While you can configure anything in Linux from the command line interface, Red Hat has created a number of administrative tools that you can use only in the GUI.

Based on the nature of the published Red Hat Exam Prep guide, you'll almost certainly be installing a GUI during the installation portion of the exam. When you

INSIDE THE EXAM

For Administrators from Other Unix-Style Distributions

Linux is not the only operating system developed in the style of Unix. There are a number of other Unix-style operating systems that are important in the computing world. These include, but are not limited to Solaris, HP-UX, AIX, IRIX, or even SCO UNIX. A substantial number of candidates for the RHCE learned their skills on these other operating systems.

You can then start the Red Hat tool of your choice from the command line; most of these utilities start with redhat-config-*. To see a full list, type **redhat-** at the command line and press the TAB key twice. Alternatively, you can start a number of these tools from the Main Menu button, under the System Settings and System Tools menus.

If you're confident in your skills editing the Linux text configuration files, don't bother with the GUI tools. It's faster to edit Linux text configuration files directly in any Unix-style operating system. If you get nervous on exams, however, or are uncertain of your skills where a GUI tool is available, learn the appropriate Red Hat GUI tools. They can be a lifesaver during the exam.

install the GUI, you'll also have access to the tools developed by Red Hat. You can also have access to the command line interface in the GUI. You can do so with a right-click, which starts a pop-up menu where you can start the New Terminal command. Alternatively, you can click on the Main Menu button (in the lower-left corner), click System Tools | Terminal to open the same command line interface, also known as GNOME terminal.

In the KDE desktop, the default command line terminal is konsole, which is slightly different from GNOME terminal.

The Kickstart Configurator

Now that you understand the basics of what goes into a Kickstart file, it's time to solidify your understanding through the graphical Kickstart Configurator. When you experiment with this GUI tool, you can learn more about what happens in the Kickstart configuration file.

To start the Kickstart Configurator, go into the Linux GUI. Open a command line interface shell and enter the **redhat-config-kickstart** command. Alternatively, click Main Menu | System Tools | Kickstart. The following sections should look familiar, as they are closely related to the RHEL installation menus.

The first screen in Figure 3-4 illustrates a number of basic installation steps. If you've installed RHEL or Red Hat Linux before, all of these steps should look familiar.

As you can see, there are a number of other options in the left pane, each associated with different Kickstart commands. To learn more about Kickstart, experiment with some of these settings. Use the File | Save command to save these settings in the filename of your choice, which you can then review in a text editor. Alternatively, you can run the File | Preview command to see the effect of different settings on the Kickstart file.

The following sections provide a brief overview of each option shown in the left pane. I believe it's unlikely that you'll have to know Kickstart in this level of detail on the Red Hat exams. However, an understanding of the Kickstart Configurator can help you understand the installation process, which is important on the installation part of each exam.

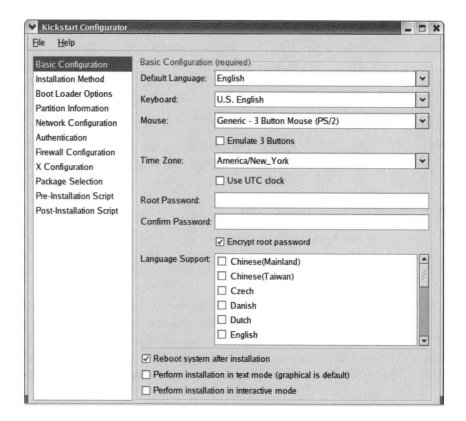

FIGURE 3-4

The Kickstart Configurator

Basic Configuration

In the Basic Configuration screen, you can assign settings for the following components:

■ Default Language for the installation; also set as the default language for the operating system

■ Keyboard

■ Mouse

■ Time Zone, which supports computers where the hardware clock is set to Greenwich Mean Time (also known as UTC)

■ Root Password, which can be encrypted in the Kickstart file

■ Language Support to be installed with the operating system

■ Reboot; adds the reboot command to the end of the Kickstart file

■ Perform Installation In Text Mode supports automated installation in text mode

Installation Method

The Installation Method options are straightforward. You're either installing Linux for the first time or upgrading a previous installation. The installation method and your entries are based on the location of the installation files. For example, if you select an NFS installation method, the Kickstart Configurator prompts you for the name or IP address of the NFS Server, and the shared directory with the RHEL installation files.

You can set up your Kickstart file to install RHEL 3 from a CD, a local hard drive partition, or one of the standard network servers: NFS, HTTP, or FTP.

Boot Loader Options

The next section lists Boot Loader Options. The two boot loaders available to Linux are GRUB and LILO. Unlike for Fedora Linux, LILO is still available as an option. With GRUB, you can set a password, which can provide an additional level of security during the boot process.

Linux boot loaders are normally installed on the MBR. If you're dual-booting with Windows NT/2000/XP with GRUB, you can set up the Windows boot loader (or an alternate boot loader such as Partition Magic or System Commander) to point to GRUB on the first sector of the Linux partition with the /boot directory. Kernel parameters allow you to pass commands to the kernel through the GRUB configuration file as described earlier in this chapter.

Partition Information

The Partition Information options determine how this installation configures the hard disks on the affected computers. While it supports the configuration of standard and RAID partitions, it does not yet support the configuration of LVM groups. The Clear Master Boot Record option allows you to wipe the MBR from an older hard disk that might have a problem there; it sets up the **zerombr yes** command in the Kickstart file.

Don't use the zerombr yes option if you want to keep an alternate on the MBR such as the NT Boot Loader.

You can remove partitions depending on whether they've been created to a Linux filesystem. If you're using a new hard drive, you'll want to initialize the disk label as well. Click the Add button to open the Partition Options menu. As you can see in Figure 3-5, this corresponds to the Anaconda Add Partition menu shown back in Chapter 2, Figure 2-13.

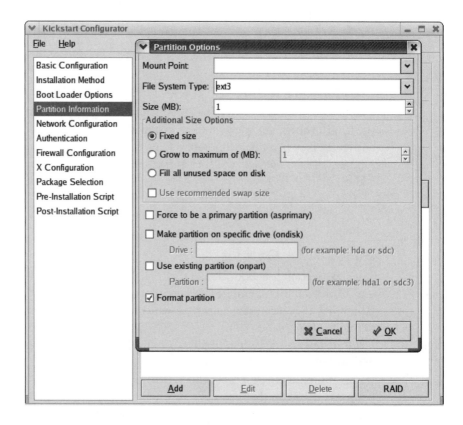

FIGURE 3-5

Using the
Kickstart
Configurator to
set up partitions

Network Configuration

The Network Configuration section enables you to set up IP addressing on the network cards on a target computer. You can customize static IP addressing for a specific computer, or you can configure the use of a DHCP server. You can also make Kickstart look for a BOOTP server, which is a specially configured DHCP server on a remote network.

Authentication

The Authentication section lets you set up two forms of security for user passwords: Shadow Passwords, which encrypt user passwords in the /etc/shadow file, and MD5 encryption. This section also allows you to set up authentication information for various protocols:

- ■ **NIS**   Network Information Service for one login database on a network with Unix and Linux computers on a network.
- ■ **LDAP**   The Lightweight Directory Assistance Protocol for certain types of databases such as directories.
- ■ **Kerberos 5**   The MIT system for strong cryptography to authenticate users on a network.
- ■ **Hesiod**   Associated with Kerberos 5.
- ■ **SMB**   Samba allows configuration of your Linux computer on a Microsoft Windows–based network.
- ■ **Name Switch Cache**   Associated with NIS for looking up passwords and groups.

Firewall Configuration

The Firewall Configuration section allows you to configure a default firewall for the subject computer. Generally, you'll want a firewall only for those computers that are connected to outside networks such as the Internet.

X Configuration

The X Configuration section allows you to configure the Linux GUI. While there is a lot of debate on the superiority of GUI- or text-based administrative tools, text-based tools are more stable. For this reason (and more), many Linux administrators don't even install a GUI. However, if you're installing Linux on a series of computers, it's likely that most of the users won't be administrators.

In this section, there are three tabs. Under the General tab, you can set a default color depth and resolution. Under the Video Card and Monitor tabs, you can set Linux to probe your hardware or specify the hardware from a list. If you want to do something fancy such as specifying multiple resolutions, you'll need to modify the ks.cfg file directly.

Package Selection

The Package Selection section shown in Figure 3-6 allows you to choose the package groups that are installed through this Kickstart file. It's a good idea to check the Automatically Resolve Dependencies option; if you miss a package or a package group, Anaconda can find the critical package and install it with your list.

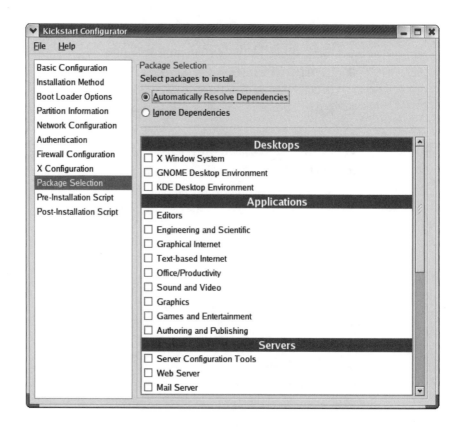

FIGURE 3-6

Configuring
package groups
with Kickstart

Installation Scripts

You can add preinstallation and postinstallation scripts to the Kickstart file. Postinstallation scripts are more common, and they can help you configure other parts of a Linux operating system in a common way. For example, if you wanted to install a directory with employee benefits information, you could add a postinstallation script that adds the appropriate **cp** commands to copy files from a network server.

CERTIFICATION SUMMARY

The Linux installation is extremely flexible. You can troubleshoot the installation process with several different consoles. Some provide useful messages; one console provides a bash shell prompt where you can inspect the current detailed status of the installation.

After Linux is installed, you can find out what happened. The /var/log/dmesg file helps you figure out what hardware was detected. The /root/install.log file lists the packages that were installed.

The default boot loader is GRUB. The GRUB configuration file, /etc/grub.conf, is highly customizable. You can use it to boot multiple operating systems. You can add commands to the boot sequence. You can customize GRUB to test different configurations. Red Hat is moving away from LILO as an alternative boot loader.

It's most efficient to configure partitions with Disk Druid during the installation process. However, if you forget something, you can use fdisk to help configure the partitions, RAID arrays, and LVM groups that you need on the exam and on production computers.

You can set up RAID level devices to mirror and stripe your drives. RAID levels 1 and 0 require that you have two or more drives, while RAID 4 and 5 require three or more. You can also set up linear mode to combine multiple physical hard disks into a single volume.

You can set up LVM groups to increase your flexibility. LVM allows you to set up partitions with the sizes you need and readjust them at will. While it's best to configure LVM groups using the graphical version of Disk Druid, you can do so with appropriately configured partitions and commands.

You can automate your entire installation of Red Hat Enterprise Linux with the Kickstart system. You have two ways to set up the Kickstart configuration file: from the anaconda-ks.cfg file based on your local installation or through the GUI Kickstart Configurator. In this way, you can automate the installation of Linux from a local source such as a CD-ROM, or through an NFS or HTTP network connection.

✓ TWO-MINUTE DRILL

The following are some of the key points from the certification objectives in Chapter 3.

Installation Troubleshooting

❑ When you start in graphical mode, you're taken to the seventh virtual console, which you can access with the CTRL-ALT-F7 command. A bash shell is on the second virtual console, an installation message log is on the third, kernel messages are on the fourth, and the output of format commands on each filesystem is displayed. If you want to see other screens, press the following key sequences at any time:

  ❑ CTRL-ALT-F1   Installation display; if you're running the installation process in text mode, this is the main display.

  ❑ CTRL-ALT-F2   The bash shell gives you access to limited system information.

  ❑ CTRL-ALT-F3   The Installation message log is displayed.

  ❑ CTRL-ALT-F4   Displays all kernel messages.

  ❑ CTRL-ALT-F5   The installation displays partition formatting.

Postinstallation Validation

❑ The file /var/log/dmesg contains boot messages duplicated from the console output, as seen each time you boot Linux.

❑ The /root/install.log file contains a list of the installed packages.

❑ The installation program reboots your computer when it's done. If you configured a graphical login, Linux starts in runlevel 5. Alternatively, if you configured a text login, Linux starts in runlevel 3.

Boot Loaders: GRUB and LILO

❑ The original Intel motherboard design provided a mechanism to start most any operating system. It would load a boot program from the Master Boot Record of the first available disk.

❑ The new default Red Hat boot loader is GRUB, the GRand Unified Boot Loader.

❑ You can edit GRUB directly during the boot process or pass commands to the kernel. For example, at the GRUB screen, if you add the word **single** to the end of the kernel argument, Linux starts in single-user mode.

❑ Single-user mode is the most commonly used option. This is the system maintenance mode for experienced Linux administrators.

Partitioning Utilities

❑ The **fdisk** utility is universally available and should be one of the first tools you learn as a Linux administrator.

❑ Disk Druid is the alternative to **fdisk** that is available only during the Red Hat installation process.

RAID Configuration and Data Recovery

❑ Software-based RAID can be set up on any number of physical partitions. Hardware-based RAID requires separate physical drives for each partition.

❑ You can set up software-based RAID through the Red Hat Enterprise Linux installation program.

❑ RAID has several different levels. Only three are currently supported by Red Hat Linux: levels 0, 1, and 5. Only RAID levels 1 and 5 offer true data protection against the failure of a single hard drive.

❑ RAID 0 and 1 require two or more drives, while RAID 5 requires three or more drives.

Logical Volume Management: Configuration and Administration

❑ Logical Volume Management allows you to manage the effective size of your active partitions.

❑ Once properly configured through **fdisk**, you can collect LVM chunks known as Logical Extents into Logical Volumes.

❑ Once Logical Volumes are collected into a Volume Group, it functions as a partition that you can resize as needed.

Automated Installation with Kickstart

❑ Kickstart is Red Hat's solution for an automated simultaneous installation of Red Hat Enterprise Linux on several computers.

❑ Kickstart installations can be configured to take installation files from a CD-ROM or an NFS, FTP, or HTTP server.

❑ There are two ways to create a Kickstart file: from the configuration from when you installed Linux as documented in the /root/anaconda-ks.cfg file, or from what you can configure with the GUI Kickstart Configurator.

SELF TEST

The following questions will help you measure your understanding of the material presented in this chapter. Read all the choices carefully, as there may be more than one correct answer. Choose all correct answers for each question. Don't focus exclusively on these questions. There are no longer any multiple choice questions on the Red Hat exams. These questions test your understanding of the chapter. Getting results, not memorizing trivia, is what counts on the Red Hat exams.

Installation Troubleshooting

1. While the installation is in progress, which of the following key combinations displays kernel messages?

    A. CTRL-ALT-F1

    B. CTRL-ALT-F2

    C. CTRL-ALT-F3

    D. CTRL-ALT-F4

Postinstallation Validation

2. Which of the following commands displays the messages that scrolled on your screen when you last booted Linux?

    A. cat /var/messages

    B. cat /var/log/dmesg

    C. cat /var/log/messages

    D. /sbin/messages

Boot Loaders: GRUB and LILO

3. In the GRand Unified Bootloader, what should you do if you wanted to start Linux in single-user mode for a quick repair?

    A. Enter **linux single** at the boot prompt.

    B. Run the **a** command and then add **single** at the end of the line that appears.

    C. Get a LILO boot disk and then run **linux sum** at the boot prompt.

    D. Boot Linux and edit the /etc/grub.conf file to automatically start Linux in single-user mode, then reboot.

4. When you see the **root=/dev/sda7** command in either GRUB or LILO, what does it mean?

    A. The root directory, /, is located on the third logical partition of the first SCSI hard disk.

    B. The /root directory is located on the third logical partition of the first SCSI hard disk.

    C. If it's GRUB, this represents the root directory, /. If it's LILO, this represents the /root directory. In either case, it is located on the third logical partition of the first SCSI hard disk.

    D. It is an error in either boot loader.

Partitioning Utilities

5. You are told to check the Web server drive table after installation. There are eight partitions. Your MIS manager asks how that can be. Her Microsoft Windows computer can include only one primary and one extended partition. How many IDE primary partitions can you configure using Red Hat Enterprise Linux?

    A. 4 primary, 1 of which is an extended partition, making for 16 total partitions

    B. 3 primary, 2 of which are extended, making for a total of 12 partitions

    C. 12 primary, with 1 an extended partition

    D. 16 extended partitions

6. Once you're in the **fdisk** utility, which command gives you the current partition table?

    A. m

    B. p

    C. x

    D. w

RAID Configuration and Data Recovery

7. You have a mirrored RAID system with three drives. The first two are mirrored and the third is supposed to be a spare. When you look at the /etc/raidtab file, you see that it says spare-disks 0. What does this entry tell you?

    A. The raidtab entry is set up correctly.

    B. Spare-disks support is turned off. To turn it on, change spare-disks to 1.

    C. Currently no spare disks are loaded.

    D. The mirror failed and had to use the spare disk.

8. Which of the following versions of RAID does not provide data redundancy?

    A. RAID 0

    B. RAID 1

    C. RAID 4

    D. RAID 5

Logical Volume Management: Configuration and Administration

9. Which of the following can be an LVM Physical Volume?

    A. A Volume Group

    B. A Logical Volume

    C. A Logical Extent

    D. A partition

Automated Installation with Kickstart

10. You're using the Kickstart Configurator to create a ks.cfg file for several computers. Which of the following lines allows for a **growable /var** partition with no limit on growth save the capacity of the hard disk?

    A. part /var --size 1000 --grow yes --maxsize no

    B. part /var --size 1000 --maxsize 0

    C. part /var --size 1000 --grow --maxsize 100000

    D. part /var --size 1000 --grow

LAB QUESTIONS

Lab 1

You just got hold of ten new PCs for the Human Resources department from a name brand PC manufacturer and you want to install Red Hat Enterprise Linux on each computer. You want to install Linux on all of them with an optimized set of packages, and you want to do it quickly.

Each of these computers has a standard 3Com network card that you know Linux has support for because you ordered the computers that way. They also each have one big 10GB disk that already contains Windows 98. You do not have time to install Red Hat Enterprise Linux 3 Workstation on each computer manually. What should you do?

Assume you need to configure each computer with static IP addresses.

Lab 2

This lab requires that you have one of the network installation servers described in Chapter 2 and a test computer where you're willing to reinstall RHEL 3. **This exercise erases any operating system that you currently have on a computer! Do not run this lab unless you can afford to lose all files and are willing to reinstall RHEL 3 on this computer.** You're going to move one of the critical files out of the installation source directory.

You could perform this lab on a new VMWare machine. Alternatively, you could run this on a computer with a standard configuration, where you can set up an automated reinstallation with a Kickstart configuration file. You've probably just seen this process in the answer to Lab 1.

1. Log into the remote network server with your RHEL 3 installation files.

2. Look at your comps.xml configuration file. It's stored in the RedHat/base/ subdirectory of the installation source. Open it in a text editor or a text reader such as the **less** command.

3. Browse through the list of packages in XML format. Pay attention to the packages in the Base and Core package groups.

4. Pick a RPM package from one of these groups. If you can't think of one, I've selected the filesystem-2.2.1-3.i386.rpm file.

5. Move that file to the home directory to some other directory on that network installation server. Make sure to use the **mv** command; the **cp** command leaves a copy on the installation source.

   If you have valuable data on this computer, STOP HERE! The following steps will delete the information at least on the Linux partitions on your computer—and possibly on the entire computer.

6. Return to your test computer, and proceed through the RHEL 3 installation process.

7. At some point, the RHEL 3 installation process will miss the RPM that you moved and stop with a message to that effect.

8. Press CTRL-ALT-F2. You should see a bash prompt. Look in the /mnt/sysimage directory. What is the directory tree in this directory?

9. Navigate to the /mnt/sysimage/root directory. Look at the files in this directory. Which file tells you about the RPMs that have been installed?

10. Run the **chroot /mnt/sysimage** command. If it doesn't work, your installation stopped before RHEL 3 had a chance to install the bash shell. With the RPM cited, this is the case.

11. Press CTRL-ALT-F3. Take a look at the messages. You should see the partitions you specified, mounted in some way. Where are they mounted?

12. Press CTRL-ALT-F4. Take a look at the messages. You should see various kernel messages. What types of messages do you see?

13. Press CTRL-ALT-F5. Take a look at the messages. You should see various partition messages. What commands do you see in this screen?

14. On the network server, restore the RPM that you moved.

15. Depending on whether you're installing in text or graphical mode, return to your installation screen with the CTRL-ALT-F1 or CTRL-ALT-F7 command.

16. Proceed with the installation of RHEL 3.

Lab 3

What would you do differently from Lab 2, assuming that you have configured a DHCP server for your network?

Lab 4

You want to set up a server for these new PCs. You want to configure that computer with the Red Hat Enterprise Linux 3 Server operating system. That server includes five separate SCSI physical hard drives of 10GB each. You'll install RHEL 3 on the first hard drive. How would you configure a RAID 5 array on the remaining hard drives? Assume you'll need 5GB from each of the 10GB hard drives.

Lab 5

On that server, you want to configure LVM in the remaining space. How would you set up the Physical Volumes (PVs)? How do you create a Volume Group (VG) from the PVs? Once you've created a VG, how would you set up a Logical Volume? Where would you mount a directory such as /home/flexuser?

SELF TEST ANSWERS

Installation Troubleshooting

1. ☑ **D.** The CTRL-ALT-F4 key combination accesses the screen with kernel messages during the Red Hat Linux installation process.

☒ **A**, **B**, and **C** are all incorrect, as they access the default text installation display, the bash shell, and the installation message log, respectively.

Postinstallation Validation

2. ☑ **B.** The /var/log/dmesg file contains boot messages.

☒ **A**, **C**, and **D** are all incorrect. The /var/log/messages file is significant as the location for service startup and shutdown messages.

Boot Loaders: GRUB and LILO

3. ☑ **B.** The **a** command in GRUB accesses the information passed to the kernel. The **single** command makes the kernel access single-user mode.

☒ **A**, **C**, and **D** are not correct. There is no boot prompt in GRUB. The **linux sum** command has no meaning at the LILO boot: prompt. While answer **D** could work, it is at best inefficient.

4. ☑ **A.** In both LILO and GRUB, the **root=/dev/sda7** command indicates that the root directory, /, is located on the third logical partition of the first SCSI hard disk.

☒ **B**, **C**, and **D** are not correct. In either boot loader, root represents the top-level / directory, not the home directory of the root user (/root). It is not an error in either boot loader.

Partitioning Utilities

5. ☑ **A.** 4 total, 3 that are called primary and 1 that is a primary partition that is configured as an extended partition. Extended partitions can contain up to 12 logical partitions. 12 + 4 = 16.

☒ **B**, **C**, and **D** are all incorrect configurations. The limitation described in the question applies to the Microsoft version of the FDISK.EXE utility.

6. ☑ **B.** The **p** command "prints" the current partition table to the screen.

☒ **A**, **C**, and **D** are all incorrect. The **m** command lists other available commands within fdisk. The **x** command exits from fdisk. The **w** command writes your changes to the partition table.

RAID Configuration and Data Recovery

7. ☑ **A.** The first spare-disks variable is number 0. Since we have one spare disk, the raidtab entry is set up correctly.
☒ **B, C,** and **D** are incorrect. There is no way to know from this file the status of the RAID disks, nor the current loading, as this is a configuration file, not a log of the running service.

8. ☑ **A and B.** RAID 0 does not include any parity data or any other way to recover data from a failed disk. RAID 1 includes an identical copy of data on two different disks. No parity data is required in this version of RAID.
☒ **C** and **D** are incorrect. Both RAID 4 and RAID 5 use parity bits. If one drive on either of these systems is lost, the data from that drive can be rebuilt from the parity bits.

Logical Volume Management: Configuration and Administration

9. ☑ **D.** An LVM Physical Volume is the physical partition or hard disk where you've applied the **pvcreate** command to set up Physical Extents.
☒ **A, B,** and **C** are incorrect. A Logical Extent is a chunk of disk space that maps to a Physical Extent. A Logical Volume is a group of Logical Extents. A Volume Group is composed of a group of Logical Volumes.

Automated Installation with Kickstart

10. ☑ **D.** The **--grow** switch alone is enough to accommodate a growable partition. If there is no **--maxsize** switch, that implies that you do not want to limit the size of this partition.
☒ **A, B,** and **C** are incorrect. Neither the **--grow** nor the **--maxsize** switch is associated with a yes or a no, so **A** is incorrect. A **--maxsize** switch alone without **--grow** is not meaningful, so **B** is incorrect. Answer **C** includes a limit on the size of the /var partition.

LAB ANSWERS

Lab 1

The solution is simple. The details are long. Each of the following steps are high level; for the nitty-gritty details of what you need to do, refer back to discussions in this chapter (as well as Chapter 2). If you're using these instructions to restore a RHEL 3 installation from Part 1, minimize the changes that you need to make to this file.

1. Set up the RHEL 3 Workstation installation files on a network source.

2. Install RHEL 3 Workstation over the network on one computer.

3. Edit the /root/anaconda-ks.cfg file as needed.

4. Modify this file with the **clearpart --all** command to wipe out all the old partitions, including the Windows 98 partitions. (This assumes you've backed up any needed data files first.)

5. Activate the command lines related to creating partitions. They are commented out by default in the anaconda-ks.cfg file.

6. In the Kickstart configuration file, make sure that the line after the **install** command points through the network to the source for the RHEL 3 Workstation installation files. If you're connecting through NFS, this starts with the **nfs** command; if you're connecting through FTP or HTTP, this starts with the **url** command.

7. Use this Kickstart file as a configuration file template for installing Linux on each of your computers.

8. Create a different file for each computer; you'll need to set a different IP address on the same subnet for each file.

9. Set up a different installation floppy for each computer. Each installation floppy will include the customized Kickstart file. You'll probably also need one or more driver floppies. Alternatively, you can set this up based on the boot.iso file. All of these disks can be created from images on your first RHEL 3 installation CD. This process is described in Chapter 2.

10. You can then set up a network installation on each computer. You'll probably also need the RHEL 3 network driver floppy described in Chapter 2. You can use the same driver floppy on each computer.

11. Now insert the appropriate installation floppy in each of your workstations. When prompted, add the driver floppy to load the appropriate network drivers.

12. Your installation should now proceed automatically on each workstation.

13. Save any installation boot and driver disks or CDs that you created in this lab for Part 2.

Lab 2

This lab should be fairly self-explanatory. It provides a specific problem that stops the installation of RHEL 3. It gives you an opportunity to examine the other consoles available during the installation process. Remember, you should not run this lab on any computer where you have valuable data. I've added some commentary which may clarify the steps you need to take in this lab.

The comps.xml file is located in the installation source. If you're using the same NFS installation source that I described in Chapter 2, it's on the /mnt/inst directory. Thus, the comps.xml file is located in the /mnt/inst/RedHat/base directory. If you already have an installed copy of RHEL 3 on an Intel-compatible 32-bit CPU computer, you can find another copy of this file in the /usr/share/comps/i386 directory.

The format of the comps.xml file might be confusing to anyone not familiar with the XML language. However, it's not as complex as it seems. For example, you can find the filesystem RPM in this file in the following format:

```
<packagereq type="mandatory">filesystem</packagereq>
```

When you browse higher on this file, you'll see that the filesystem RPM is part of the Core package group.

Once the installation stops at the problem you created, you can browse through the different consoles. The second console includes the bash prompt, even though bash commands aren't installed yet. You should also recognize the standard root directory (/) tree in the /mnt/sysimage directory.

In the third virtual console, you'll see messages that partitions such as /tmp/hda1 or /tmp/sda1 are mounted. For example, a partition mounted on the root directory is mounted on the /mnt/sysimage directory during the installation process. The partitions that you've created through Disk Druid are mounted on a temporary basis until installation is complete.

The kernel messages that you see in the fourth virtual console show hardware and filesystem messages. The fifth virtual console lists the messages you see when the filesystem is formatted.

Lab 3

The basic steps are the same. However, if the ten computers are connected to a network with a DHCP server, your task is easier. Modify the aforementioned Kickstart template file. Assuming it's the first Ethernet adapter on each computer, the key command will be **network --device eth0 --bootproto dhcp**.

Since you're getting network information from a DHCP server, you can use the same installation floppy for each of the workstations. You'll still need the driver floppy. Now insert the appropriate installation floppy in each of your workstations. When prompted, add the driver floppy to load the appropriate network drivers. You should be on your way!

Alternatively, you can create a customized boot CD based on the boot.iso file on the first RHEL 3 installation CD. Add the ks.cfg file when you burn your CD from boot.iso.

Lab 4

Now you're configuring a RAID 5 array for your workstations on a RHEL 3 server. With the given configuration, RHEL 3 will be installed on the first hard disk. The remaining four hard disks are available for other purposes. You'll use 5GB of each of those SCSI hard disks to create RAID 5 arrays. It's easiest to do so during the installation process. However, you can still do so after RHEL 3 is installed.

As they are SCSI hard disks, Linux represents them as /dev/sdb, /dev/sdc, /dev/sdd/, and /dev/sde. You can divide the 5GB on each of these hard disks into near equal parts (RAID does not require identical components in its arrays.). If you created 5GB partitions on each hard disk, you could set up a RAID 5 array with the first 3 partitions: /dev/sdb1, /dev/sdc1, and /dev/sdd1. You could then set up the partition on the final drive, /dev/sde1, as a spare. (While you could set up all four partitions as a RAID 5 array, it's useful to have a spare. If one drive fails, the RAID 5 software automatically begins rebuilding data on the spare drive.)

You can create a RAID array after RHEL 3 is installed, using the following basic steps. For detailed steps, refer back to the chapter.

1. Use the **fdisk** utility to create and size partitions from available space on the SCSI hard disks.

2. With the **t** switch, set these partitions as usable by RAID by setting them to the Linux RAID autodetect filesystem.

3. Format each partition, set up the array in /etc/raidtab, and use the **mkraid -R** command to create the RAID device.

4. Format the RAID device to the Linux ext3 filesystem.

5. Save any data from the directory that you want to mount on the RAID array.

6. Mount the directory of your choice to that filesystem, and finally, implement the change in /etc/fstab.

Lab 5

You can create LVM groups after RHEL 3 is installed, using the following basic steps. For detailed steps, refer back to the chapter.

1. Use fdisk to create partitions from the remaining available space on each of the last four SCSI drives. Make sure to set each partition to the Linux LVM filesystem.

2. Initialize each of these partitions with the **pvcreate** command.

3. Set up all of these partitions together as a Volume Group (VG) with the **vgcreate** command.

4. Now set up a Logical Volume from that VG with the **lvcreate** command. You can set it to a fixed number of Physical Extents or a fixed amount of space.

5. Take the directory of your choice. Back up any data currently on that directory.

6. Mount the directory on the LV. Copy the data from backup.

7. Finally, set up the mount in the /etc/fstab configuration file.

4

Basic Configuration and Administration

A fter installation is complete, you still have work to do. To customize the system to meet your needs, user accounts need to be set up, filesystems must be configured, and additional packages may need to be added or removed.

This chapter will get you started with the basics that every RHCE (and many RHCT) level administrator should know. At the end of this chapter, you should know how to manage user accounts and environments, configure and mount filesystems, use RPM to manage packages, manage system daemons, and configure virtual consoles, keyboards, and mice.

CERTIFICATION OBJECTIVE 4.01

Adding, Deleting, and Modifying User Accounts

The default Red Hat installation gives you just a single login account: root. You should set up some regular user accounts. Even if you're going to be the only user on the

INSIDE THE EXAM

Administrative Skills

When you take the Red Hat exams, as long as you don't cheat, it generally does not matter how you come to a solution. For example, you get the same credit whether you add users by directly editing /etc/passwd, using commands such as **useradd**, or using GUI tools such as the Red Hat User Manager (**redhat-config-users**). As in the real world, it is the result that matters.

When available, I present more than one method of configuring your Linux computer. Unless otherwise directed on the exam, the method you select is up to you. In general,

I believe it is better and faster to configure Linux directly from the command line interface. But if you get nervous on an exam and forget how to use **chkconfig** to enable a service at runlevels 3 and 5, it's okay to use Red Hat's GUI Service Configuration Utility. GUI tools just take more time to start, to manage, and to execute.

Many of the skills in this chapter apply only to the RHCE. If you're using this book to study for the RHCT, consult the syllabus for the Red Hat RH133 course at www.redhat.com for more information.

system, it's a good idea to create at least one nonadministrative account to do your day-to-day work. Then you can use the root account only when it's necessary to administer the system. Accounts can be added to Red Hat Enterprise Linux systems using various utilities, including the vi text editor (the manual method), the **useradd** command (the command line method), and the Red Hat User Manager utility (the graphical method).

e x a m

w a t c h

As discussed earlier, it's faster (but less safe) to log in as root (and not just the superuser). While you'll be doing most of the work on the Red Hat exams as root, it's quite possible that you'll be asked *to create accounts for regular users (and groups) to configure a workstation. As RHCT requirements are part of the RHCE exam, this applies to both exams.*

User Account Categories

There are three basic types of Linux user accounts: administrative (root), regular, and service. The administrative root account is automatically created when you install Linux, which has administrative privileges for all services on your Linux computer. A cracker who has a chance to take control of this account can take full control of your system.

Nevertheless, there are times when it is appropriate to log in as an administrator (that is, as the root user), such as during most of the Red Hat exams. Red Hat Enterprise Linux builds in safeguards for root users. Log in as the root user, and then run the **alias** command. You'll see entries such as:

```
alias rm='rm -i'
```

which prompt for confirmation before the **rm** command deletes a file. Unfortunately, a command such as **rm -rf directoryname** would supersede this safety setting.

Regular users have the necessary privileges to perform standard tasks on a Linux computer. They can access programs such as word processors, databases, and Web browsers. They can store files in their own home directories. Since regular users do not normally have administrative privileges, they cannot accidentally delete critical operating system configuration files. You can assign a regular account to most users, safe in the knowledge that they can't disrupt your system with the privileges they have on that account.

Services such as Apache, Squid, mail, games, and printing have their own individual service accounts. These accounts exist to allow each of these services to interact with your computer. Normally, you won't need to change any service account, but if you see that someone has logged in through one of these accounts, be wary. Someone may have broken into your system.

on the job

To review recent logins, run the utmpdump /var/log/wtmp | less command. If the login is from a remote location, it will be associated with a specific IP address outside your network.

Basic Command Line Tools

There are two basic ways you can add users through the command line interface. You can add users directly by editing the /etc/passwd file in a text editor such as vi. Alternatively, you can use text commands customized for the purpose.

exam watch

You'll probably need to know how to use the vi editor during the Troubleshooting and System Maintenance exam. Other editors such as joe, pico, or emacs are no longer available. I therefore focus on the vi editor throughout this book.

Adding Users Directly

Open the /etc/passwd file in the text editor of your choice. If you've added regular users to your system, you'll normally see them listed at the bottom of this file. Scroll around this file, and you should see a series of lines like the following:

```
mj:x:500:500:Michael Jang:/home/mj:/bin/bash
```

Each column in /etc/passwd, delineated by a colon, has a purpose, which I describe in Table 4-1.

You can create a new user in /etc/passwd by copying and then editing a line associated with an existing user. Just substitute the information of your choice to create the new user. Make sure that you at least assign a new username and user ID.

Assuming you've assigned a new home directory for your new user, you have to remember to create that directory. For example, if your new user is ez, you'll probably want to create the /home/ez directory. You'll also need to make sure that ez has ownership permissions on that directory and all of the files that you're going to put in that directory.

TABLE 4-1	The Anatomy of /etc/passwd	
Field	**Example**	**Purpose**
Username	mj	The user logs in with this name. Usernames can include hyphens (-) or underscores (_). However, they should not start with a number or include uppercase letters. RHEL limits usernames to 32 characters.
Password	x	The password. You should see either an "x," an asterisk (*), or a seemingly random group of letters and numbers. An "x" points to /etc/shadow for the actual password. An asterisk means the account is disabled. A random group of letters and numbers represents the encrypted password.
User ID	500	The unique numeric user ID (UID) for that user. By default, Red Hat starts user IDs at 500.
Group ID	500	The numeric group ID (GID) associated with that user. By default, Red Hat Enterprise Linux creates a new group for every new user. Some other Linux and Unix systems assign all users to the default Users group (GID=100).
User info	Michael Jang	You can enter any information of your choice in this field. Standard options include the user's full name, telephone number, e-mail address, or physical location. You can leave this blank.
Home Directory	/home/mj	By default, RHEL places new home directories in /home/*username*.
Login Shell	/bin/bash	By default, RHEL assigns users to the bash shell. You can change this to any legal shell that you have installed.

You can then populate that new user's home directory. A default environment is available in the /etc/skel directory. You can copy the contents of that directory to the new user's home directory. The /etc/skel directory is covered in more detail later in this chapter.

Adding Users to a Group

Every Linux user is assigned to a group. By default in RHEL 3, every user gets their own private group. By default, they are the only member of that group, as defined in the /etc/group configuration file. Open that file in the editor of your choice. You should see lines similar to the following:

```
mj:x:500:
vp:x:501:
managers:x:1000:mj,vp
```

TABLE 4-2	The Anatomy of /etc/group

Field	Example	Purpose
Groupname	mj	Each user gets their own group, with the same name as their username. You can also create unique groupnames.
Password	x	The password. You should see either an "x" or a seemingly random group of letters and numbers. An "x" points to /etc/gshadow for the actual password. A random group of letters and numbers represents the encrypted password.
Group ID	500	The numeric group ID (GID) associated with that user. By default, Red Hat Enterprise Linux creates a new group for every new user.
Group members	mj,vp	Lists the usernames that are members of the group. If blank, and there is a username that is identical to the groupname, that user is the only member of that group.

The contents are straightforward. The users mj and vp are members of their own groups, as well as the managers group. The four columns in each /etc/group line are described in Table 4-2.

Adding Users at the Command Line

Alternatively, you can automate this process with the **useradd** command. If you wanted to add a new user named pm, you could just type **useradd pm** to add this user to the /etc/passwd file. By default, it creates a home directory, /home/pm, adds the standard files from the /etc/skel directory, and assigns the default shell, /bin/bash. But **useradd** is versatile. It includes a number of command options, shown in Table 4-3.

TABLE 4-3	useradd Command Options

Option	Purpose
-u *UID*	Overrides the default assigned UID. By default, in RHEL this starts at 500 and can continue sequentially to 65536.
-g *GID*	Overrides the default assigned GID. By default, RHEL assigns the same GID and UID numbers to each user. The GID you assign must be either 100 (users) or already exist.
-c *info*	Enters the comment of your choice about the user, such as his or her name.
-d *dir*	Overrides the default home directory for the user, /home/*username*.
-s *shell*	Overrides the default shell for the user, /bin/bash.

Assigning a Password

You can now use the **passwd** *username* command to assign a new password to that user. For example, the **passwd pm** command lets you assign a new password to user pm. You're prompted to enter a password twice. RHEL is configured to discourage passwords that are based on dictionary words or are shorter than six characters for security reasons. Nevertheless, such passwords are legal, and such a password is accepted by the **passwd** command when you type it in a second time.

on the **job**

Good passwords are important. Any cracker who may have tapped into your network can try to match the password of any of your users. A password cracking program may be able to find dictionary word passwords in a matter of minutes. In contrast, it may take hours to crack a more complex password such as IIa451MS (which could stand for "I live at 451 Main Street").

The Red Hat User Manager

As of this writing, the Red Hat User Manager can be run only from the Linux graphical user interface (GUI). If you're not in a GUI, and have installed the needed software, the **startx** command moves you into the GUI, as shown in Figure 4-1.

FIGURE 4-1

The Red Hat
GNOME GUI

Pay attention to the figure of the Red Hat in the lower-left corner of the desktop; it starts program menus like the GNOME foot, the KDE K, or the Microsoft Windows Start buttons. Red Hat refers to it as the "Main Menu" button, which is the term I'll use throughout this book.

Red Hat has text-based versions of several of its graphical tools. I believe that they will develop text-based versions of GUI tools such as the Red Hat User Manager (redhat-config-users) sometime in the near future. But that does not help you on the current Red Hat exams.

If you're already in a Linux GUI, you can start the Red Hat User Manager in one of two ways. Enter **redhat-config-users** from a command line interface in the GUI, or click Main Menu | System Settings | Users and Groups. (This notation indicates you should click the Main Menu button—the "Red Hat"—in the lower-left corner of the Taskbar, then click System Settings followed by Users in the menus that appear.) Figure 4-2 shows the Red Hat User Manager window.

If you have not logged in as the root user, you'll be prompted for a root password before opening administrative tools such as the Red Hat User Manager.

FIGURE 4-2

The Red Hat User Manager

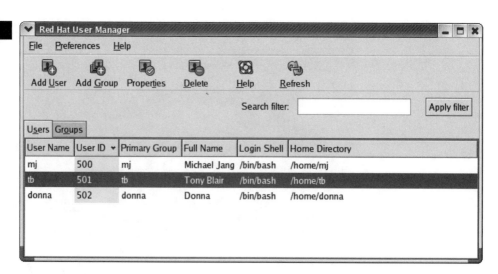

EXERCISE 4-1

Adding a User with the Red Hat User Manager

To add a user with the Red Hat User Manager:

1. Start the Red Hat User Manager. You can do this in one of two ways. Right-click on the desktop, and click New Terminal in the pop-up menu that appears. Type **redhat-config-users** in the command line terminal. Alternatively, click Main Menu | System Settings | Users and Groups.

2. In the Red Hat User Manager, click the Add User button, or click File | Add User. This will open the Create New User window, as shown here:

3. Complete the form. All entries are required, except Full Name. The entries are fairly self-explanatory; see the previous sections for more information on each field. The password should be at least six characters and should contain a mix of upper- and lowercase letters, numbers, and symbols to keep it more secure from the standard password cracking programs.

4. Enter the identical password in the Confirm Password field.

5. Click OK when you are done.

6. Repeat the process as desired for any additional new users you're expected to support.

User Account Management Tips

Although creating user accounts may seem to be a straightforward process, there are a few things that you should consider when configuring new users:

- By default, RHEL 3 configures individual private group IDs (GID) for each user. As this associates each user with their own exclusive group, this is also known as the Red Hat User Private Group scheme. In the default Red Hat scenario, everyone has a unique private GID (which corresponds to their UID), and regular users do not have access to other users' home directories. These users can still share access to special directories; see Chapter 11 for more information.

- If your configuration doesn't require each user to have his or her own GID, or if you have no need for the security associated with the User Private Group scheme, you can assign all of your users to the Users group, with a GID of 100. In many cases, this can make system administration easier.

- Discourage the use of shared accounts, where several people use a single account. Shared accounts are almost always unnecessary and are easily compromised.

- If you'll be using the Network File System (NFS), make sure all users have the same UID on every system on the network. This can be problematic. One alternative is the Network Information System (NIS). NIS supports a centralized database of users and passwords for users on all participating computers. For more information on NIS, see Chapter 9.

on the job

The Red Hat standard where every user is a member of his or her own exclusive group is known as the User Private Group scheme, which I describe in more detail in Chapter 11.

Deleting a User Account

Removing user accounts is a pretty straightforward process. The easiest way to delete a user account is with the **userdel** command. By default, this command does not delete that user's home directory. Alternatively, the **userdel -r** *username* command deletes that user's home directory along with all of the files stored in that home directory.

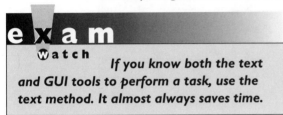

This is a lot faster than the GUI method, where you start the X Window System, open the Red Hat User Manager, select the user, and then click Delete. While it's probably easier for a less experienced user to remember the GUI method, text commands are faster.

Modifying a User Account

As a Linux administrator, you may want to add some limitations to your user accounts. The easiest way to illustrate some of what you can do is through the Red Hat User Manager. Start the Red Hat User Manager, select a currently configured user, and then click Properties to open the User Properties dialog box.

Click the Account Info tab for the account expiration information shown in Figure 4-3. As shown in the figure, you can limit the life of an account so that it expires on a specific date, or you can disable an account by locking it. Click the Password Info tab.

As shown in Figure 4-4, you can set several characteristics related to an individual user's password. Even when you set good passwords, frequent password changes can

FIGURE 4-3

Managing user account life

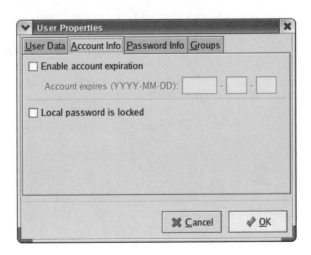

FIGURE 4-4

Configuring
password
information

help provide additional security. The categories shown in the figure are self-explanatory;
a 0 in any of these text boxes means that the limit does not apply.

Click the Groups tab. Users can belong to more than one group in Linux. Under
the Groups properties tab shown in Figure 4-5, you can assign the subject user to other
groups. For example, if you want to collect the files supporting the managers in your
company together in a directory, you can give access to these files to the group named
managers. Alternatively, you can then assign members of that project team to the
project group through the Groups tab.

FIGURE 4-5

Assigning groups

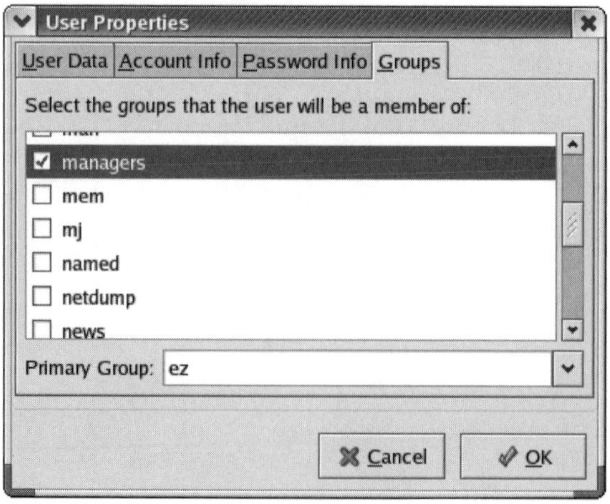

Regular User Management Commands

While the Red Hat User Manager GUI utility is convenient, it's often faster to perform the associated administrative functions at the command line interface. I've described some of these commands such as **useradd** and **userdel**. Two other key user administration commands are **usermod** and **chage**.

usermod

The **usermod** command modifies various settings in /etc/passwd. It also allows you to set an expiration date for an account or an additional group. For example, the following command sets the account associated with user test1 to expire on June 8, 2004:

```
# usermod -e 2004-06-08 test1
```

The following command makes user test1 a member of the special group:

```
# usermod -G special test1
```

chage

You can use the **chage** command to manage the expiration date of a password. Password aging information is stored in the /etc/shadow file. In order, the columns in /etc/shadow are shown in Table 4-4. The associated **chage** switch is shown with each description entry. For example, if you wanted to require that user test1 keep a password for at least two days, use the **chage test1 -m 2** command.

Limiting Access to su

As described earlier, I've recommended that you use the root account during the Red Hat exams. However, I assume you still need to configure Linux computers in real life. One security measure that can help is to limit regular users who can access the root account via the **su** command. This takes two basic steps.

| TABLE 4-4 | The Anatomy of /etc/shadow |

Column	Field	Description
1	Username	Username
2	Password	Encrypted password; requires an "x" in the second column of /etc/passwd
3	Password history	Date of the last password change, in number of days after January 1, 1970
4	mindays	Minimum number of days which you must keep a password (-m)
5	maxdays	Maximum number of days after which a password has to be changed (-M)
6	warndays	Number of days before password expiration - when a warning is given (-W)
7	inactive	Number of days after password expiration when an account is made inactive (-I)
8	disabled	Number of days after password expiration when an account is disabled (-E)

First, you'll need to add the users who you want to allow access to the **su** command. Make them a part of the wheel group. By default, this line in /etc/group looks like:

```
wheel:x:10:root
```

You can add the users of your choice to the end of this line directly, with the **usermod -G wheel** *username* command, or with the Red Hat User Manager.

Next, you'll need to make your Pluggable Authentication Modules look for this group. You can do so by activating the following command in your /etc/pam.d/su file:

```
# auth   required /lib/security/$ISA/pam_wheel.so use_uid
```

CERTIFICATION OBJECTIVE 4.02

The Basic User Environment

Each user on your Red Hat Enterprise Linux system has an *environment* when logged on to the system. The environment defines directories where Linux looks for programs to run, the look of the login prompt, the terminal type, and more. This section explains how you can configure the default environment for your users.

Home Directories and /etc/skel

By default, when you create a new user in RHEL 3, they get a default set of configuration files in their home directories. These defaults are hidden files stored in the /etc/skel directory.

Home Directories

The home directory is where users start when they first log on to a RHEL system. The home directory for most users is /home/*username,* where *username* is the user's login name. Users should normally have write permission in their own home directory, so they're free to read and write their own files. In Chapter 5, you'll learn how to configure disk quotas, so users don't take more than their fair share of disk space.

/etc/skel

The /etc/skel directory contains default environment files for new accounts. The **useradd** command and the Red Hat User Manager copy these files to the home directory when you create a new account. The contents of /etc/skel may vary depending on what you have installed. Standard files from my RHEL 3 /etc/skel are described in Table 4-5.

If you've installed more than the default software on RHEL, you may see additional configuration files in the /etc/skel directory. For example, if you've installed the appropriate RPMs, you may see configuration files associated with emacs and the z shell (zsh) in this directory.

TABLE 4-5   Default Home Directory Files from /etc/skel

Files	Purpose
.bashrc	The basic bash configuration file. May include a reference to the general /etc/bashrc configuration file. Can include commands you want to run when you start the bash shell, appropriate for aliases such as **rm='rm -i'.**
.bash_logout	A file executed when you exit a bash shell. Can include commands appropriate for this purpose, such as clearing your screen.
.bash_profile	Configures the bash startup environment. Appropriate place to add environment variables or modify the directories in your PATH.
.gnome*	Several directories that include startup settings for the GNOME desktop environment. For example, details of desktop icons such as Trash are stored in .gnome-desktop/Trash.
.gtkrc	Adds the Bluecurve theme for the default Red Hat GUI.
.kde	A directory that includes autostart settings for the K Desktop Environment. Not copied to user home directories if you haven't installed KDE on this computer.

on the job *Linux includes many hidden files, which start with a dot (.). To list these files, run the ls -a command. For example, if you wanted to list the files in the /etc/skel directory, run the ls -a /etc/skel command.*

As the system administrator, you can edit these files or place your own customized files in /etc/skel. When new users are created, these files are propagated to the new users' home directories.

on the job *Adding files to /etc/skel may be a convenient way to distribute files such as corporate policies to new users.*

Window Manager Configuration File Locations

RHEL 3 comes with several window managers. At some point, you will want to configure one or more of them for use on your system. Most window manager configuration files are stored in the /etc/X11/*windowmanager* directory, where *windowmanager* is the name of the specific window manager. This includes window managers such as twm (Tom's Window Manager), xdm (X Display Manager), and gdm (GNOME Display Manager). The exception is KDE, where the default window manager configuration files are stored in the /etc/kde/kdm directory.

on the job *Red Hat Linux 9 stores default KDE window manager configuration files in the /etc/skel/.kde directory.*

CERTIFICATION OBJECTIVE 4.03

Red Hat Filesystem Basics

There are as many, if not more, filesystem types as there are operating systems. RHEL 3 can work with many of these formats.

At the heart of every RHEL 3 installation are the filesystems on which it relies. Linux supports a rich variety of filesystem types. For Linux, we can divide filesystems into two categories: "standard" formatting and journaling. While this is an oversimplification, it suffices to describe the filesystems important to Linux. To me, a standard filesystem is an older Linux filesystem or more static systems.

on the
Job

There are a large number of filesystem types, well described in the Filesystems HOWTO at www.tldp.org. Strictly speaking, there is no "standard" filesystem, and in this book, I include a "balanced tree" filesystem (ReiserFS) as a journaling filesystem, just to be more consistent with the Red Hat outlines.

The filesystems I describe in this book are just a small list of those available for RHEL 3. If you have the kernel source RPMs loaded on your system, you can find a list of the filesystems supported by your kernel. Navigate to the /usr/src/linux-2.4 directory. Run the **make menuconfig** command and use your arrow keys to navigate to the filesystems section.

Standard Formatting Filesystems

Linux is a clone of Unix. The Linux filesystems were developed from the Unix filesystems available at the time. The first Linux operating systems used the Extended Filesystem (ext). Until the past couple of years, Red Hat Linux operating systems formatted their partitions by default to the Second Extended Filesystem (ext2).

I also include some other filesystems that you might see in RHEL 3. These "standard" filesystems don't include journaling features. I illustrate a sample of these filesystem types in Table 4-6.

TABLE 4-6   Linux Standard Filesystem Type

Filesystem Type	Description
ext	The first Linux filesystem, used only on early versions of that operating system.
ext2 (Second Extended)	The foundation for ext3, the default RHEL 3 filesystem. The ext3 filesystem is essentially ext2 with journaling.
swap	The Linux swap filesystem is associated with dedicated swap partitions. You've probably created at least one swap partition when you installed RHEL 3.
MS-DOS and VFAT	These filesystems allow you to read MS-DOS–formatted filesystems. MS-DOS lets you read pre–Windows 95 partitions, or regular Windows partitions within the limits of short filenames. VFAT lets you read Windows 9x/NT/2000/XP/2003 partitions formatted to the FAT16 or FAT32 filesystems.
ISO 9660	The standard filesystem for CD-ROMs. It is also known as the High Sierra File System, or HSFS, on other Unix systems.
NTFS	NTFS is the Microsoft Windows NT/2000/XP/2003 filesystem designed for username/password security. Currently supported as a read-only system.
/proc	The /proc filesystem is a Linux *virtual* filesystem. Virtual means that it doesn't occupy real disk space. Instead, files are created as needed. /proc is used to provide information on kernel configuration and device status.

TABLE 4-6	Linux Standard Filesystem Type *(continued)*

Filesystem Type	Description
/dev/pts	The /dev/pts filesystem is the Linux implementation of the Open Group's Unix98 PTY support.
NFS	The Network File System. This is the system most commonly used to share files and printers between Linux and Unix computers.
SMB	Server Message Block (SMB) is based on Microsoft and IBM network protocols. Linux can use SMB to share files and printers with Microsoft Windows operating systems. Works with Microsoft's Common Internet File System (CIFS).

Journaling Filesystems

As hard disks and partitions grow in size, Linux users are moving toward filesystems with journaling features. Journaling filesystems have two main advantages. First, it's faster to check them during the boot process. Second, if there's a crash, a journaling filesystem has a log (also known as a journal) which can be used to restore the metadata for the files on the relevant partition.

The default RHEL 3 filesystem is the Third Extended Filesystem, also known as ext3. However, it isn't the only journaling filesystem option available. I list a few of the options available for RHEL 3 in Table 4-7.

TABLE 4-7	Journaling Filesystems

Filesystem Type	Description
ext3	The default filesystem for RHEL 3.
JFS	JFS is IBM's journaled filesystem. This is commonly used on IBM enterprise servers.
ReiserFS	The Reiser File System is resizable and supports fast journaling. It's more efficient when most of the files are very small and very large. It's based on the concept of "balanced trees." While supported by RHEL 3, it is not the default Red Hat filesystem and is explicitly cited only in the RHCT course (RH133) syllabus. For more information, see www.namesys.com.
xfs	Developed by Silicon Graphics as a journaling filesystem. Supports very large files; as of this writing, xfs files are limited to 9×10^{18} bytes. Do not confuse this filesystem with the X Font Server; both use the same acronym.

CERTIFICATION OBJECTIVE 4.04

Filesystem Management and the Automounter

Before you can use the files in a directory, you need to mount that directory on a partition formatted to some readable filesystem. Linux normally automates this process using the /etc/fstab configuration file. When you boot Linux, specified directories are mounted on configured partitions. The mount options require some explanation, especially for removable media.

But there may be problems if connections are lost or media is removed. When you configure a server, you could be mounting directories from a number of remote computers. You could also want temporary access to removable media such as floppies or Zip drives. The automount daemon, also known as the Automounter or autofs, can help. It can automatically mount specific directories as needed. It can unmount a directory automatically after a fixed period of time.

/etc/fstab

Linux stores information about your local and remotely mounted filesystems in /etc /fstab. Open this file in the text editor of your choice. As you can see, different filesystems are configured on each line. A sample /etc/fstab might look like the following:

```
LABEL=/          /              ext3        defaults              1   1
LABEL=/boot      /boot          ext3        defaults              1   2
none             /dev/pts       devpts      gid=5,mode=620        0   0
none             /proc          proc        defaults              0   0
none             /dev/shm       proc        tmpfs                 0   0
/dev/hda3        swap           swap        defaults              0   0
LABEL=/usr       /usr           ext3        defaults              1   2
LABEL=/tmp       /tmp           ext3        defaults              1   2
LABEL=/var       /var           ext3        defaults              1   2
LABEL=/home      /home          ext3        defaults              1   2
/dev/cdrom       /mnt/cdrom     udf,iso9660    noauto,owner,kudzu,ro 0   0
/dev/floppy      /mnt/floppy    auto        noauto,owner,kudzu    0   0
```

As you can see, there are six fields associated with each filesystem, which I describe from left to right in Table 4-8. Remember, this is a configuration file. You can verify partitions that are actually mounted in /etc/mtab.

TABLE 4-8	Description of /etc/fstab by Column from Left to Right

Field Name	Description
Label	Lists the device to be mounted. If mounted, you can find the associated partition in /etc/mtab. For example, if you see /dev/hda2 in this file, you can verify its LABEL with the **e2label /dev/hda2** command.
Mount Point	Notes the directory where the filesystem will be mounted.
Filesystem Format	Describes the filesystem type. Valid filesystem types include ext, ext2, ext3, msdos, vfat, devpts, proc, tmpfs, udf, iso9660, nfs, smb, and swap.
Mount Options	Covered in the following section.
Dump Value	Either 0 or 1. A value of 1 means that data is automatically saved to disk by the dump(8) command when you exit Linux.
Filesystem Check Order	Determines the order that filesystems are checked by fsck(8) during the boot process. The root directory (/) filesystem should be set to 1, and other local filesystems should be set to 2. Removable filesystems such as /mnt/cdrom should be set to 0, which means that they are not checked during the Linux boot process.

Mount Options

Although **defaults** is the right mount option for most /etc/fstab filesystems, there are other options, as listed in Table 4-9. If you want to use multiple options, separate them by commas. Don't use spaces between options. The list in Table 4-9 is not comprehensive. You can find out more from the mount manual, which you can read by running the following command:

```
# man mount
```

TABLE 4-9	/etc/fstab Mount Options

Mount Option	Description
async	Data is read and written asynchronously.
atime	The inode associated with each file is updated each time the file is accessed.
auto	Searches through /etc/filesystems for the appropriate format for the partition; normally associated with a floppy or removable drive.
defaults	Uses default mount options: **rw**, **suid**, **dev**, **exec**, **auto**, **nouser**, and **async**.
dev	Permits access to character devices such as terminals or consoles and block devices such as drives.
exec	Allows binaries (compiled programs) to be run on this filesystem.

| TABLE 4-9 | /etc/fstab Mount Options *(continued)* |

Mount Option	Description
noatime	The inode associated with each file is not updated when accessed.
noauto	Requires explicit mounting. Common option for CD and floppy drives.
nodev	Devices on this filesystem are not read or interpreted.
noexec	Binaries (compiled programs) cannot be run on this filesystem so mounted.
nosuid	Disallows **setuid** or **setgid** permissions on this filesystem.
nouser	Only root users are allowed to mount the specified filesystem.
remount	Remounts a currently mounted filesystem. Also an option for the **mount** command.
ro	Mounts the filesystem as read-only.
rw	Mounts the filesystem as read/write.
suid	Allows **setuid** or **setgid** permissions on programs on this filesystem.
sync	Reads and writes are done at the same speed (synchronously) on this filesystem.
user	Allows nonroot users to mount this filesystem. By default, this also sets the **noexec**, **nosuid**, and **nodev** options.

Mounting Floppy Disks and Removable Media

To read floppy disks and other removable media, you need to mount the device. If RHEL detects your hardware, it adds the proper settings to /etc/fstab and default mount points to the /mnt directory. The default mount points are straightforward; for example, floppy disks are mounted on /mnt/floppy, CDs are mounted on /mnt/cdrom. If you're mounting an MS-DOS-formatted floppy, you can do so with the following command:

```
# mount -t vfat /dev/fd0 /mnt/floppy
```

The **-t** switch specifies the type of filesystem (vfat). The device file /dev/fd0 represents the first floppy drive; /mnt/floppy is the directory through which you can access the files on the floppy after mounting.

But the command that you actually need may be simpler. Take a look at your /etc /fstab configuration file. You'll probably see something like the following line:

```
/dev/fd0        /mnt/floppy        auto    noauto,owner,kudzu  0 0
```

This /etc/fstab line sets the default configuration for the first floppy drive (/dev/fd0). Normally, it's mounted on the /mnt/floppy directory. The format is auto, which means that the **mount** command searches through the /etc/filesystems configuration file. As long as vfat is part of this file, you do not need to specify the filesystem type. The **mount** command reads the filesystem on the floppy and mounts it with the correct filesystem automatically. So all you really need to mount the floppy is the following command:

```
# mount /dev/fd0 /mnt/floppy
```

But wait—if you know something about /etc/fstab, you know that the device and mount points are effectively linked. If you specify either, **mount** looks through /etc/fstab for the appropriate device, label, or mount point. Therefore, all you actually need to mount the floppy is either one of the following two commands:

```
# mount /dev/fd0
```

```
# mount /mnt/floppy
```

Similarly, the device for your CD-ROM is normally /dev/cdrom. To mount an ISO 9660 CD-ROM, run the following command:

```
# mount -rt iso9660 /dev/cdrom /mnt/cdrom
```

Now you can read the contents of /mnt/cdrom as if it were a normal filesystem on your system. You don't have to use the /mnt/floppy or /mnt/cdrom directories. They're part of the standard Linux filesystem as a matter of convenience. You can mount a floppy or CD on an empty directory of your choice.

But as with a floppy disk, the actual command that you need is simpler. Take a look at the relevant default line from /etc/fstab:

```
/dev/cdrom      /mnt/cdrom     udf,iso9660    noauto,owner,kudzu,ro    0 0
```

As you can see, iso9660 is already specified as the default CD filesystem, and CDs are mounted as read-only (ro) by default. Therefore, all you actually need to mount the CD is either one of the following two commands:

```
# mount /dev/cdrom
# mount /mnt/cdrom
```

To unmount a floppy or CD-ROM, use the **umount** command with the mount point as an argument. *Remember, the command is **umount**, not unmount.*

The following commands unmount both our floppy and our CD-ROM:

```
# umount /mnt/floppy
# umount /mnt/cdrom
```

It is important you unmount floppy disks before removing them. Otherwise, the data that you thought you wrote to the disk might still be in the cache. In that case, you would lose that data.

on the !job

Here's another example that I think you're unlikely to see on the Red Hat exams. Assume you're working with a Zip drive of 100MB. The device is set as /dev/hdd and formatted as a single partition (/dev/hdd1) with the Linux Native (ext3) filesystem. The directory /mnt/zip was created and an entry added to /etc/fstab. You can now manually mount, unmount, and eject the zip drive with the following commands:

```
# mount /dev/hdd1 /mnt/zip
```

The command to manually unmount the Zip drive:

```
# umount /dev/hdd1
```

The command to eject the Zip drive (which automatically unmounts it):

```
# eject /dev/hdd1
```

The Automounter

Once you run the **mount** command on a partition, it stays mounted until you unmount it or shut down or reboot your computer. This can cause problems. For example, if you've mounted a floppy and then physically removed the disk, Linux may not have had a chance to write the file to the disk. This situation also applies to Zip or other "hot-swap" removable drives.

Another example is with mounted NFS directories. If the remote computer fails or the connection is lost, your system may become slow or even hang as it looks for the mounted directory.

This is where the Automounter can help. It relies on the **autofs** daemon to mount configured directories as needed, on a temporary basis. In RHEL 3, the relevant configuration files are /etc/auto.master and /etc/auto.misc. If you use the Automounter, keep the /misc directory free. Red Hat configures automounts on this directory by default, and they won't work if there are local files or directories stored there.

/etc/auto.master

The standard /etc/auto.master file includes just a series of comments, with one sample command:

```
# /misc /etc/auto.misc  --timeout=60
```

You can activate the Automounter by activating this command (or adding a similar command). As you should already know as a Linux expert, the pound sign (#) is a comment character. When you delete the #, the command is activated. This command:

- Configures automounted filesystems on the /misc directory
- Points to /etc/auto.misc for detailed configuration
- Sets a timeout of 60 seconds; if the automounted directory is not used or accessed in this time, it is automatically unmounted

You can set up the Automounter on other directories. One popular option is to set up the Automounter on the /home directory. In this way, you can configure user home directories on remote servers, mounted on demand. Users are given access to their home directories upon login, and with the following command in /etc/auto.master, the home directory is automatically unmounted 60 seconds after that user logs off the system:

```
# /home /etc/auto.home  --timeout=60
```

This works only if you don't have a /home directory on your computer. You'll get a chance to test a variation of this in a lab at the end of this chapter.

/etc/auto.misc

Red Hat conveniently provides standard automount commands in comments in the /etc /auto.misc file. It's helpful to analyze this file in detail. I use the default RHEL 3 version of this file. The first four lines are comments, which I skip. The first command is:

```
cd    -fstype=iso9660,ro,nosuid,nodev  :/dev/cdrom
```

In RHEL, this command is active by default. In other words, if you have a CD in the /dev/cdrom drive, you can access its files through the Automounter with the **ls /misc/cd** command. The Automounter accesses it using the ISO9660 filesystem. It's mounted read-only (ro); set user ID permissions are not allowed (**nosuid**), and devices on this filesystem are not used.

With the command from /etc/auto.master, the CD is unmounted 60 seconds after the last time it's accessed. There are a number of other sample commands in comments. The first command allows you to set up a /misc/linux mount point from a shared NFS directory, /pub/linux, on the ftp.example.org computer.

```
#linux    -ro,soft,intr    ftp.example.org:/pub/linux
```

The next command assumes that the /boot directory is stored on the /dev/hda1 partition. With this command, you don't need to mount /boot when you start Linux. Instead, this command allows you to automount it with the **mount /misc/boot** command.

```
#boot    -fstype=ext2    :/dev/hda1
```

The following three commands apply to a floppy disk drive on your computer. The first command searches through /etc/filesystems to try to match what's on your floppy. The last two commands assumes that the floppy is formatted to the Second Extended (ext2) filesystem.

```
#floppy      -fstype=auto    :/dev/fd0
#floppy      -fstype=ext2    :/dev/fd0
#e2floppy    -fstype=ext2    :/dev/fd0
```

The next command points to the first partition on the third SCSI drive. The "jaz" at the beginning suggests this is suitable for an Iomega type "Jazz" drive.

```
#jaz      -fstype=ext2    :/dev/sdc1
```

Finally, the last command assumes that you want to apply the Automounter to the IDE drive connected as the slave on the secondary controller. The "removable" at the beginning suggests this is suitable for removable hard drives.

```
#removable  -fstype=ext2        :/dev/hdd
```

With the possible exception of the **floppy** commands, you'll probably need to modify these lines before activating them for your own hardware.

Activating the Automounter

Once you've configured the /etc/auto.master and related /etc/auto.misc configuration files, you can activate the Automounter. As it is governed by the autofs daemon, you can activate it with the following command:

```
# service autofs restart
```

With the default command in the /etc/auto.misc file, you should now be able to mount a CD on the /misc/cd directory, automatically, just by accessing the configured directory. Once you have a CD in the drive, the following command should work:

```
# ls /misc/cd
```

If you were to make /misc/cd your current directory, the Automounter would ignore any timeouts. Otherwise, /misc/cd is automatically unmounted according to the timeout, which according to the command in /etc/auto.master, is 60 seconds.

EXERCISE 4-2

Configuring the Automounter

In this exercise, you'll test the Automounter. You'll need at least a CD. Ideally, you should also have a floppy disk. But there are some preliminaries. You need to make sure that the **autofs** daemon is in operation, modify the appropriate configuration files, and then restart **autofs**. You can then test the Automounter for yourself.

Part of this exercise may be confusing. Where it refers to commands within a configuration file, a pound sign (#) in front indicates it's a comment. If it's on the command line interface, it refers to a command run by the root user, which I've signified in this section with the [root]# prompt. As with other exercises, I'm assuming that you've logged in as the root user.

1. From the command line interface, run the following command to make sure the **autofs** daemon is running:

   ```
   [root]# service autofs start
   ```

2. Open the /etc/auto.master configuration file in a text editor. Modify it if required to include the following line. If there's a pound sign (#) in front of the line, delete it. Save and exit from /etc/auto.master.

   ```
   /misc /etc/auto.misc  --timeout=60
   ```

3. Check the /etc/auto.misc configuration file in a text editor. Make sure it includes the following line (which should already be there by default). Save and exit from /etc/auto.misc.

   ```
   cd    -fstype=iso9660,ro,nosuid,nodev   :/dev/cdrom
   ```

4. Now restart the autofs daemon. (I know, this isn't the most efficient method, but it's a good habit to check the status of a service.)

   ```
   [root]# service autofs restart
   ```

5. The Automounter service is now active. Insert a CD into the drive on your computer and when you run the following command, you should see the contents of your CD:

```
[root]# ls /misc/cd
```

6. Run the **ls /misc** command immediately. You should see the cd directory in the output.

7. Wait at least one minute, and repeat the previous command. What do you see?

A Floppy Disk and the Automounter (Optional Exercise)

Now that you're more familiar with the Automounter, try using it on a floppy drive. If you don't have a floppy drive, experiment with some of the other commented commands in /etc/auto.misc.

CERTIFICATION OBJECTIVE 4.05

The Red Hat Package Manager Command and Utility

One of the major duties of a system administrator is software management. Applications are upgraded. Kernels are patched. Without the right tools, it can be difficult to figure out what software is on a system, what is the latest update, and what applications depend on other software. Worse, you may install a new software package only to find it has overwritten a crucial file from a currently installed package.

The Red Hat Package Manager (RPM) was designed to eliminate these problems. With RPM, software is managed in discrete "packages." An RPM *package* includes the software with instructions for adding, removing, and upgrading those files. When properly used, the RPM system can back up key configuration files before proceeding with upgrades and removals. It can also help you identify the currently installed version of any RPM-based application.

What Is a Package?

In the generic sense, an RPM package is a container of files. It includes the group of files associated with a specific program or application, which normally includes binary installation scripts, as well as configuration and documentation files. It also includes instructions on how and where these files should be installed and uninstalled.

An RPM package name usually includes the version, the release, and the architecture for which it was built. For example, the fictional penguin-3.4.5-26.i386.rpm package is version 3.4.5, build 26. The "i386" indicates that it is suitable for computers built to the Intel architecture.

on the job *Many RPM packages are CPU specific. You can identify the CPU type for your computer in the /proc/cpuinfo file. Some RPM packages, with the noarch label, can be installed on computers with all types of CPUs.*

What Is RPM?

At the heart of this system is the RPM database. Among other things, this database tracks the version and location of each file in each RPM. The RPM database also maintains an MD5 checksum of each file. With the checksum, you can use the **rpm -V** *package* command to see if any file from that RPM package has changed. The RPM database makes adding, removing, and upgrading packages easy, because RPM knows which files to handle, and where to put them.

RPM also manages conflicts between packages. For example, assume you have two different packages that use configuration files with the same name. Call the original configuration file /etc/*someconfig*. You've already installed package X. If you then try to install package Y, RPM backs up the original /etc/*someconfig* file before installing package Y.

Using RPM on Remote Packages

With the RPM system, you can even specify package locations just like an Internet address, in Uniform Resource Locator (URL) format. For example, if you want to apply the **rpm** command to the foo.rpm package on the /pub directory of the ftp.rpmdownloads.com FTP server, you can install this package with a command such as:

```
# rpm -i ftp://ftp.rpmdownloads.com/pub/foo.rpm
```

Assuming you're connected to the Internet, this particular **rpm** command logs onto the FTP server anonymously and downloads the file.

If the FTP server requires a username and password, you can use the following format: ftp://*username:password @hostname:port/path/to/remote/package/file*.rpm, where *username* and *password* are the username and password you need to log on to this system, and *port*, if required, specifies a nonstandard port used on the remote FTP server. Based on the preceding example, if the username is mjang and the password is Ila451MS, you could install an RPM directly from a server with the following command:

```
rpm -i ftp://mjang:Ila451MS@ftp.rpmdownloads.com/pub/foo.rpm
```

The key to this system is the **rpm** command. We'll cover the four most common modes associated with this command: query, install, upgrade, and remove. But first, in this age of insecure downloads, you should know how to validate the signature associated with an RPM, as well as verifying the files in a specific package.

Validating a Package Signature

RPM uses two methods of checking the integrity of a package: the MD5 checksum and the GPG signature. You can use the MD5 checksum to verify that the file is intact (no data was lost or corrupted while copying or downloading the file). You can then use the GPG signature to make sure the file is authentic. For example, you can use it to confirm that an RPM file is indeed an official Red Hat RPM. Red Hat provides a GPG public key for its RPM files; you can find it on each installation CD in the RPM-GPG-KEY file or in the /usr/share/rhn directory.

To authenticate your RPMs using the GPG system, import the key file using the following command (assuming it's a CD-based keyfile, mounted on the /mnt/cdrom directory):

```
# rpm --import /usr/share/rhn/RPM_GPG_KEY
```

Now if you wanted to check the integrity of some RPM such as pkg-1.2.3-4.noarch.rpm on a CD, run the following command:

```
# rpm --checksig /mnt/cdrom/RedHat/RPMS/pkg-1.2.3-4.noarch.rpm
```

This allows you to verify both the integrity and the authenticity of the RPM.

Verifying One or More Packages

Verifying an installed package compares information about that package with information from the RPM database on your system. The **--verify** switch checks the size, MD5 checksum, permissions, type, owner, and group of each file in the package. Here are a few examples:

- Verify all files. Naturally, this may take a long time on your system.

  ```
  # rpm --verify -a
  ```

- Verify all files within a package against an RPM file on a mounted CD-ROM.

  ```
  # rpm --verify -p /mnt/cdrom/RedHat/RPMS/inn-2.3.5-5.i386.rpm
  ```

- Verify a file associated with a particular package.

  ```
  # rpm --verify --file /bin/ls
  ```

If the files or packages check out, you will see no output. Any output means that a file or package is different from the original. There are eight tests. If there's a change, the output is a string of eight characters, each of which tells you what happened during each test.

If you see a dot (.), that test passed. The following example shows /bin/vi with an incorrect group ID assignment:

```
# rpm --verify --file /bin/vi
......G.   /bin/vi
```

Table 4-10 lists the failure codes and their meanings.

Looking for the Right RPM

Sometimes you need a file or a command, and just don't know what is the correct package to install. Red Hat provides a database that can associate the right RPM

TABLE 4-10	Failure Code	Meaning
rpm --verify Codes	5	MD5 checksum
	S	File size
	L	Symbolic link
	T	File modification time
	D	Device
	U	User
	G	Group
	M	Mode

package with a specific file. Naturally, this database can be installed from the rpmdb-redhat-* RPM. It's installed by default on RHEL 3. It enables you to find the RPM associated with any available file from the Red Hat installation CDs. For example, if you're looking for the package associated with /etc/passwd, run the following command:

```
# rpm --redhatprovides /etc/passwd
```

If you're using Red Hat Linux 9 to study for the exam, you'll have to install the rpmdb-redhat RPM after installation.

Adding and Removing RPM Packages

The **rpm** command makes it easy to add and remove software packages to your system. It maintains a database regarding the proper way to add, upgrade, and remove packages. This makes it relatively simple to add and remove software with a single command.

Install Mode

The install mode, as its name suggests, is used to install RPM packages on your system. You can install an RPM package with the **-i** option. For example, the following command installs the hypothetical penguin RPM:

```
# rpm -i penguin-3.4.5-26.i386.rpm
```

If the package is available on a remote FTP server, you could install it directly from that server. For example, the following command installs it from a hypothetical ftp.rpmdownloads.com server in its /pub directory.

```
# rpm -i ftp://ftp.rpmdownloads.com/pub/penguin-3.4.5-26.i386.rpm
```

Before installing the package, RPM performs several checks. First, it makes sure the package you're trying to install isn't already installed—normally, RPM won't let you install a package on top of itself. It also checks to make sure you aren't installing an older version of the package. Next, RPM does a dependency check. Some programs won't work unless others are already installed. In this example, you've just downloaded the latest RPM version of the Penguin utilities, and you now want to install it.

```
# rpm -i penguin-3.4.5-26.i386.rpm
failed dependencies:
iceberg >>= 7.1 is needed by penguin-3.26.i386.rpm
```

This error tells you that **rpm** did not install the Penguin package because it requires the iceberg RPM package, version 7.1 or later. You'll have to find and install the iceberg package, and any packages iceberg may require.

Finally, RPM checks to see if it would overwrite any configuration files when it installs a package. RPM tries to make intelligent decisions about what to do in this situation. If RPM chooses to replace an existing configuration file, it gives you a warning like:

```
# rpm -i penguin-3.26.i386.rpm
warning: /etc/someconfig saved as /etc/someconfig.rpmsave
```

It's up to you to look at both files and determine what, if any, modifications need to be made.

on the **job**

If you've already customized a package and upgraded it with rpm*, go to the saved configuration file. Use it as a guide to change the settings in the new configuration file. Since you may need to make different changes to the new configuration file, you should test the result in every way that package may be used in a production environment.*

Upgrade Mode

The **-U** switch is used to upgrade existing packages. For example, if Penguin utilities, version 3.25, is already installed, the following command:

```
# rpm -U penguin-3.26.i386.rpm
```

upgrades the old version of the package with the new one. In fact, if you've never installed this package before, the **-U** switch works just like **-i**. The package is simply installed for the first time.

Remove Mode

The **rpm -e** command removes a package from your system. But before removing a package, RPM checks a few things first. It does a dependency check to make sure no other packages need what you're trying to remove. If it finds dependent packages, **rpm -e** fails with an error message identifying these packages.

If you have modified any of the configuration files, RPM makes a copy of the file, adds an .rpmsave extension to the end of the filename, and then erases the original. Finally, after removing all files from your system and the RPM database, it removes the package name from the database.

on the **job**

Be very careful about which packages you remove from your system. Like many other Linux utilities, RPM may silently let you shoot yourself in the foot. For example, if you were to remove the packages for /etc/passwd or the kernel, that would devastate your system.

Adding Updates and Security Fixes

Red Hat Enterprise Linux is constantly being updated. As bugs or security problems are found, they are collected on Red Hat's errata Web page, currently located at www.redhat.com/apps/support/errata/. Additional errata associated with Red Hat Enterprise Linux is available through the Red Hat Network. If you've purchased RHEL 3, it's part of your subscription.

on the **job**

As of this writing, Red Hat has stated that it will discontinue errata for Red Hat Linux 9 in April of 2004. The people associated with the Fedora Legacy Project plan to continue support beyond that date. More information is available at www.fedoralegacy.org.

EXERCISE 4-4

Updating from the Red Hat Errata

The steps in this exercise assume that you're using Red Hat Enterprise Linux 3. If you are using Red Hat Linux 9 or earlier, you may not be able to do this exercise. Red Hat has stated that it will discontinue support for Red Hat Linux 9 after April 2004. However, you may be able to find errata through the Fedora project. If you find errata, here's a good checklist to follow whenever you review the errata page. The actual steps may vary widely for errata from the Fedora project:

1. Go to www.redhat.com/apps/support/errata. Find the Red Hat Errata link for your distribution.

2. The page you see includes links for security, bug fixes, and enhancements. The security alerts are especially important if your system is on a network. Click the security link. You may need to click the link associated with the alert. If you have a subscription to the Red Hat Network for RHEL 3, use your account. You may find additional errata here as well.

3. You may not have installed some of the affected packages. Use the **rpm -qi** *packagename* command to check. If you have installed an affected package on your system, consider the recommended upgrade.

4. Before replacing an affected package, consider the ramifications. You may need to bring the system down to single-user or perform a reboot, which can affect other users who are connected to your system. If a production computer is affected, you may want to test the changes on another computer first.

5. If you choose to make an upgrade, back up at least the relevant files on your current system. Upgrades do fail on occasion.

6. When performing the upgrade, watch for configuration file warnings. If your local configuration files are replaced with new files, you may need to change the new configuration files to reflect your current settings.

7. Thoroughly test the new package. Make sure you have it configured correctly.

8. If a package is listed in the errata but not installed on your system, chances are there's no reason to put it on your system now. Read the detailed errata entry for that package carefully, and only install it if needed.

Red Hat has included a Network Alert Notification Tool. You can use this to check for revised packages, new packages, errata, and other information. It comes as an entitlement with your purchase of Red Hat Enterprise Linux. There is no reference to this software in the syllabus for the RHCT (RH133) or RHCE (RH300) exams, or in the RHCE Exam Prep guide.

Seeing What Packages Are Installed

Without RPM, you'd need to search around your filesystems to figure out whether a particular software package is installed. RPM makes it easy for you to figure out what RPM packages are installed and get information about those packages.

Running RPM Queries

The **-q** switch is used to query packages. When you use RPM's query mode, you can learn if a specific package is installed or identify the files associated with that package. The **rpm -q** *packagename* command will return the installed version of a specified package. For example, to find the version number of an installed mutt text e-mail reader, run the following command:

```
# rpm -q mutt
lynx-1.4.1-3
```

If you want to see which installed package owns a file, use the **-f** modifier. Here we want to identify the package that owns /etc/passwd:

```
# rpm -qf /etc/passwd
setup-2.5.27-1
```

Likewise, if you want to generate a list of files belonging to a certain package, use the **-l** modifier.

```
# rpm -ql setup
/etc/bashrc
/etc/csh.cshrc
/etc/csh.login
/etc/exports
/etc/filesystems
/etc/group
/etc/gshadow
/etc/host.conf
/etc/hosts.allow
/etc/hosts.deny
/etc/inputrc
/etc/motd
/etc/passwd
/etc/printcap
/etc/profile
/etc/profile.d
/etc/protocols
/etc/securetty
/etc/services
/etc/shells
/usr/share/doc/setup-2.5.27
/usr/share/doc/setup-2.5.27/uidgid
/var/log/lastlog
```

One of the most common modifiers to **-q** is **-a**, a query for all installed packages on your system. As configured, my RHEL 3 system includes 700 packages. Here's a truncated output:

```
# rpm -qa
ghostscript-fonts-5.50-9
libmng-1.0.4-3
```

```
libtiff-3.5.7-13
ncurses-5.3-9.3
arts-1.1.3-2.2
...
commons-modeler-1.0-5
sendmail-cf-8.12.10-1
```

on the
job

It's common to use the rpm -qa *command as a searchable database. All you*
need to do is pipe the output with a search term through grep. *For example,*
the rpm -qa | grep kde *command makes it easy to identify all installed packages*
related to the K Desktop Environment.

For even more information about a specific package, use the **-i** (information)
modifier. Table 4-11 lists some of the most important entries from the package output.
Run the **rpm -qi** *packagename* command on the RPM of your choice and see the
result for yourself.

The Red Hat Package Management Utility

You can update packages with a graphical tool. The Red Hat Package Management
utility includes several advantages. It includes an interface similar to the Anaconda
Custom Installation screen. It allows you to install more than one package at a time.
It automatically installs any other dependent packages that may be needed.

There are two ways to start the Package Management utility. In the GNOME
or KDE desktop, click Main Menu | System Settings | Add/Remove Applications.
Alternatively, in a GUI text command window, run the **redhat-config-packages**
command. Either action opens the Package Management utility shown in Figure 4-6.

TABLE 4-11	Tag	Description
Information from the rpm -qi *packagename* Command	Name	The name of the package.
	Version	The version of the package.
	Release	The number of times this package has been released using the same version of the software.
	Install Date	When this package was installed on your system.
	Group	Your RPM database is divided into groups, which describe the functionality of the software. Every time you install a package, it will be grouped accordingly.
	Size	The total size in bytes of all the files in the package.
	License	The license under which the original software was released.

FIGURE 4-6

The Package
Management
utility

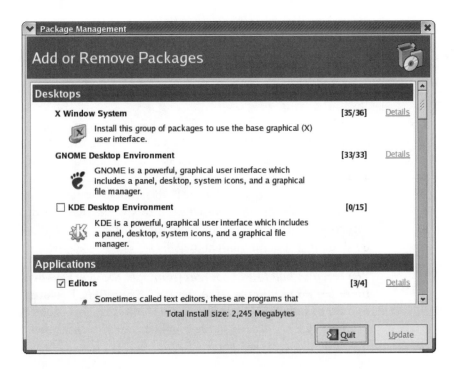

You can use it to add the package groups of your choice. The list shown is the same as what you saw during the installation process. Once you've selected a package group, you're allowed to customize the installation by clicking the associated Details link.

There's an important trick with the Package Management utility. With the right switch, you can connect it to a remote installation server, such as the one you created in Chapter 2. For example, if you've mounted the NFS installation source from Chapter 2 to the local /mnt/inst directory, you can link the Package Management utility to that source with the following command:

```
# redhat-config-packages --tree=/mnt/inst
```

For more information on mounting remote directories via Samba, see Chapter 8; to do the same via NFS, see Chapter 9.

exam
ⓦatch

If you need to install a group of packages during the Red Hat exams, you may not have access to all of the installation CDs. In that case, the redhat-config-packages **command can help. With the** --tree **switch, you can use the same network source that you used to install Red Hat Enterprise Linux.**

CERTIFICATION OBJECTIVE 4.06

RPM Sources

The RPMs that I've described so far are already in binary format. In other words, they're compiled and ready to install just like "tarballs" or Microsoft-style installation packages. But Linux goes back to the source code. Courtesy of the GPL, the source code is readily available.

In fact, if you're studying for the Red Hat exams using Red Hat Linux 9, the source code may be all you have available for the RHEL packages that you may need for this book. The source code includes the programs and configuration files that you need to set up and install the binary RPMs described earlier.

on the
job

You can also build RPM sources from a tar archive. However, as of this writing, there are no requirements in the RHCE and RHCT related course outlines related to building source RPMs from a tar archive. And the obsolete version of the RHCE exam prep guide suggests that you only need to be "familiar with the basic elements of" source RPMs.

Creating and Using Custom RPMs

A source RPM is, as the name indicates, a package of source code used to build architecture-specific packages. Properly labeled source RPMs include the "src" identifier as part of the filename, such as:

```
polarbear-2.07-2.src.rpm
```

Binary RPMs are built from source RPMs. The source RPM contains the source code and specifications necessary to create the binary RPM.

Before you continue with this section, install the rpm-build RPM package. For RHEL 3, if you're installing from a network source on the /mnt/inst directory, you'd run the following command:

```
# rpm -Uvh /mnt/inst/RedHat/RPMS/rpm-build-4.2.1-4.2.i386.rpm
```

If you're running Red Hat Linux 9, install the rpm-build package associated with that distribution. You can then use the **rpmbuild** command as described in the following sections.

*In RHEL 3, the rpmbuild **command has superseded the older** rpm **commands associated with building RPM packages from source code.***

Installing Source RPMs

Like normal RPMs, a source RPM (SRPM) is installed with the **-i** option. It does not install the package itself. This installs the contents of the SRPM within the /usr/src /redhat directory structure, which you can turn into a binary RPM. For the purpose of this section, I've installed the source for the Package Management utility, redhat-config-packages, from the freely available RHEL 3 source RPMs. I describe their availability later in this chapter.

The /usr/src/redhat/ Directory Structure

There are five subdirectories under the /usr/src/redhat directory, which I describe in Table 4-12.

When you build an SRPM, you will build it within this structure. If you install an SRPM, it is extracted into this structure. The redhat-config-packages source RPM that you installed in the previous section should now have a file in the /usr/src/redhat /SPECS directory, in the redhat-config-packages.spec file.

Changing Compile Options for a Source RPM

While most precompiled RPMs will serve your needs, at times you will want to modify the source code or compile options in the corresponding SRPMs. You can do so in the spec file that you get when you installed the source RPM.

The Spec File   To change the compile options in an SRPM, you must understand spec files. The spec file is stored in /usr/src/redhat/SPECS/*packagename*.spec. The spec file controls the way a package is built, and what actions are performed when it is installed or removed from a system. A spec file has ten different sections, as described in Table 4-13.

TABLE 4-12	Directory	Purpose
Build Directories from RPM Sources	/usr/src/redhat/SOURCES	Contains the original program source code
	/usr/src/redhat/SPECS	Contains spec files, which control the RPM build process
	/usr/src/redhat/BUILD	Source code is unpacked and built here
	/usr/src/redhat/RPMS	Contains the output binary RPM
	/usr/src/redhat/SRPMS	Contains the SRPM created by the build process

TABLE 4-13 | Build Directories for Source RPM Files

Section	Description
Preamble	Includes information shown with an **rpm -qi** command. This normally includes a summary, version, and group. It also includes a list of dependent packages.
Description	A basic package description.
Prep	Includes any preparatory commands required before building the source code, such as unpacking.
Build	Commands to actually compile the spec file and build sources.
Install	Commands to install the software on a system.
Install and uninstall scripts	This section contains scripts that will be run on the end user's system to install or remove the software. RPM can execute a script before the package is installed, after the package is installed, before the package is removed, and after the package is removed.
Verify	Although RPM takes care of most verification tasks, a script can be inserted here for any desired extra checks.
Clean	A script can be specified here to perform any necessary cleanup tasks.
Files	A list of files in the package.
Changelog	A list of revisions.

Several of the sections include commands that can be run as individual shell scripts. You won't see all of these sections in every spec file.

You can change the compile-time options for a package in the build section of the spec file. Here's a sample build section from a different spec file (this is not from the redhat-config-packages source RPM):

```
%build
rm -rf $RPM_BUILD_ROOT
mkdir -p $RPM_BUILD_ROOT/usr/bin $RPM_BUILD_ROOT/etc
./configure --prefix=/usr --exec-prefix=/
make CFLAGS="$RPM_OPT_FLAGS" LDFLAGS=-s
```

This section, a shell script, begins with some housekeeping, removing any files that may be left over from a previous build. A directory structure is created for the source files. Then the package is configured and compiled with a "make."

For a different package, you might modify the make command line to compile other components after LDFLAGS. The compile options from $RPM_OPT_FLAGS are defaults, set by RPM. Alternatively, you could use this variable to set other compile time options such as a different CPU.

on the *Job*

Perhaps the essential reference guide to the RPM system is a book called *Maximum RPM.* ***It's available online from Red Hat at www.redhat.com/docs*** ***/books/max-rpm.***

Building Custom Source and Binary RPMs

By now, you should understand where you should modify an SRPM spec file to change compile time options in the Build section. However, there's much more to building customized RPMs. Once you have modified the spec file, you need to tell RPM to build a new RPM and SRPM.

Starting a Build

You can build an RPM using the **rpmbuild** command, with the build switch, **-b**. By itself, **rpmbuild -b** calls the scripts specified in the Prep, Build, and Install parts of the spec file. Normally, you'll modify the **-b** with **a**, which makes RPM go through the build process, step by step. The RPM build operation is directed at a spec file. For example, the command

```
# rpmbuild -ba redhat-config-packages.spec
```

directs RPM to create binary and source RPMs from this spec file. Alternatively, if you just want the binary RPM, the following command will do the job:

```
# rpmbuild -bb redhat-config-packages.spec
```

Building Red Hat Enterprise RPMs

The SRPMs for RHEL 3 are freely available online from the Red Hat FTP site at ftp.redhat.com or mirror sites specified at www.redhat.com/download/mirror.html. As of this writing, the RHEL 3 SRPMs are located on the /pub/redhat/linux/enterprise/3 /en/os/i386/SRPMS directory.

If you're studying for the Red Hat exams using Red Hat Linux 9, you don't have to buy RHEL 3. You can build Red Hat Enterprise RPMs from the source code. For example, we can learn more about the Red Hat Package Management utility from the redhat-config-packages source code. To do so, take the following steps:

Navigate to ftp.redhat.com (or a mirror site) and navigate to the directory with RHEL 3 SRPMs. Then you can:

1. Download the RHEL 3 version of the package that contains the Package Management utility, redhat-config-packages-1.2.5-1.src.rpm.

2. Install the source RPM package. The **rpmbuild** commands described in the previous section do not install the package on your computer; it does set it up in your /usr/src/redhat tree.

CERTIFICATION OBJECTIVE 4.07

Network Configuration

The network is where the power of Red Hat Enterprise Linux really comes alive; however, getting there may not be trivial. As in all other things Linux, it's a learning experience. Most critical settings are stored in the /etc/sysconfig directory.

In most cases, you'll configure networking when you install RHEL 3 during each exam. However, if you have problems, you may need to diagnose networking problems, especially during the troubleshooting exams.

e**x**a m

ⓦatch
Learn the scripts in the /etc/sysconfig and /etc/sysconfig/network directories. These are crucial to the configuration of Red Hat Enterprise Linux. If you have a configuration to change or repair, it probably involves files in one of these directories. If you have a problem on the troubleshooting exam, you may find the solution in these files. Red Hat is consolidating a number of its key configuration files in its directories, so expect them to become even more important in the future.

The configuration file that provides the foundation for others in RHEL 3 networking is /etc/sysconfig/network. It can contain up to five variables, as described in Table 4-14.

TABLE 4-14	Variable	Description
/etc/sysconfig/ network Variables	NETWORKING	Can be yes or no, to configure or not configure networking.
	NISDOMAIN	If you're connected to an NIS network, this should be set to the name of the NIS domain.
	HOSTNAME	Sets the hostname of the local computer. If you don't see this variable, it may be set by a DHCP server.
	GATEWAY	Sets the IP address for the gateway for your network. If you don't see this variable, it may be set by a DHCP server.
	GATEWAYDEV	Sets the network device, such as eth0, that this computer uses to reach a gateway. You won't see this if you have only one network card on your computer.

If you don't see the variable in your /etc/sysconfig/network file, the situation does not apply. For example, if you don't see the GATEWAYDEV variable, you probably have only one network card on your computer.

The /etc/sysconfig/network-scripts Files

We'll start our tour in the /etc/sysconfig directory. This is where Red Hat Enterprise Linux stores and retrieves its networking information. With the various Red Hat configuration tools, you don't need to touch these files, but it's good to know they're there. A few representative files are shown in Table 4-15.

TABLE 4-15	/etc/sysconfig/network-scripts Files

File in /etc/sysconfig/network-scripts	Description
ifcfg-lo	Configures the loopback device, which is a virtual device that confirms proper installation of TCP/IP.
ifcfg-*	Each installed network adapter, such as eth0, gets its own **ifcfg-*** script. For example, eth0 gets **ifcfg-eth0**. This file includes the IP address information required to identify this network adapter on a network.
network-functions	This script contains functions used by other network scripts to bring network interfaces up and down.
ifup-* and ifdown-*	These scripts activate and deactivate their assigned protocols. For example, **ifup-ipx** brings up the IPX protocol.

| TABLE 4-16 | Other Network Configuration Commands |

Network Script	Description
ifup, ifdown	These scripts start and stop a network card such as eth0. Naturally, **ifup eth0** activates eth0; **ifdown eth0** deactivates this device.
dhclient	**dhclient** activates a connection to a DHCP server for your network. The function of a DHCP server is to lease an IP address. Normally activated during the boot process through the **ifcfg-*** script in the /etc/sysconfig/network-scripts directory. Supersedes scripts from previous versions of Red Hat Linux, including **pump** and **dhcpcd**.
ifconfig	The main network interface configuration utility. Can return or set the network parameters on a network device.

There are several closely related commands which can help you manage networking from the command line interface. I describe a few of these commands in Table 4-16.

Setting Up a Network Interface

In this section, I illustrate how you can configure networking on your computer with text commands as well as with the Red Hat GUI Network Configuration utility. Changes are written to various configuration files, including /etc/sysconfig/network, and file and related directories. There is a text mode version of this tool, in which you can modify your system name, as well as add, remove, and edit network interfaces. While you can start it with the **redhat-config-network-tui** command, it's officially an experimental interface for RHEL 3 and is not nearly as capable as the GUI tool.

on the
ⓞo b

With the redhat-config- GUI tools, Red Hat has developed a number of utilities that I believe will encourage Microsoft Windows administrators to make the switch to Linux. Unfortunately, I believe the lack of corresponding text-based tools has discouraged some Linux administrators from working with Red Hat.*

I illustrate how you can use the Network Configuration utility (see Figure 4-7) in the following exercise, and then illustrate how you can monitor and modify your network configuration with various text commands.

FIGURE 4-7

Network
Configuration
utility

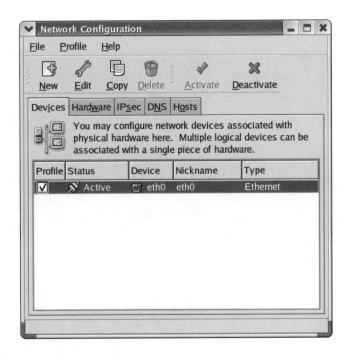

EXERCISE 4-5

Modifying Network Interfaces with redhat config-network

1. You can start the Network Configuration utility in one of two ways in the GUI. You can click Main Menu | System Settings | Network. Alternatively from a GUI terminal, run **redhat-config-network**. This opens the Network Configuration dialog box.

2. Select the Devices tab if required.

3. Select the adapter that you wish to modify, and then select Edit. If it is an Ethernet adapter, you'll see an Ethernet Device dialog box similar to the one shown here.

4. Pay attention to the "Allow all users to enable and disable the device" option. If you activate it, you'll change the USERCTL variable in the ifcfg-* script to yes.

Note: Record your current settings for this interface before proceeding.

5. Change the IP value to 192.168.1.11 and the network mask to 255.255.255.0.

Note: If your computer is on the 192.168.1.0 private network, use a different private IP address. It should isolate you from all other hosts on the local network. Test this after step 5 by using the **ping** command to try to connect to other hosts on your network.

6. Click File | Save and wait for the process to complete.

7. At the command prompt, run **ifconfig** to check your new IP settings.

8. Repeat steps 1–3 and then reset the values to your previous settings. Run **ifconfig** again to make sure you've restored your original network configuration.

Many values are associated with each network interface. At minimum, each network adapter requires a valid, unique IP address, as well as an appropriate network mask. The Network Configuration utility provides five convenient tabs which you can use to customize each network adapter:

- **Devices** This tab allows you to add a new network adapter or edit a configured adapter. You can revise the name of the adapter, IP address assignments, static routing, and hardware device information. Different devices are configured in the /etc/sysconfig files described earlier.

- **Hardware** This tab lets you modify the IRQ port, memory location, I/O address(es), and DMA channel(s) associated with the adapter. Hardware information is documented in different files in the /proc directory.

on the
()o b

Linux sometimes has trouble recognizing second network adapters; you may need to specify hardware addresses such as the IRQ port.

- **IPsec** This tab supports Virtual Private Network connections.

- **DNS** This tab lets you add the addresses of DNS servers available to network adapters on the given network, which is reflected in /etc/resolv.conf.

- **Hosts** This tab allows you to modify the name, alias, and IP address assigned to the specified adapter, which is shown in /etc/hosts.

In addition, if you run Profile | New, you can create different network configurations, which can be useful for flexible configurations. For example, if you have a laptop computer and a docking port, your configuration may change depending on whether the laptop is connected to the docking port.

If you want to use this tool, some trial and error is appropriate. Make some changes, and check the effect on the files I've described.

ifup/ifdown

For each installed network adapter, there is a corresponding ifcfg-* file in /etc/sysconfig /network-scripts. You can activate or deactivate that adapter with the **ifup** and **ifdown** commands. Either one of the following commands will activate the eth0 network adapter:

```
ifup ifcfg-eth0
ifup eth0
```

ifconfig

The **ifconfig** command is used to configure and display network devices. Here is some sample output from this command:

```
# ifconfig eth0
eth0      Link encap:Ethernet  HWaddr 00:50:56:40:1E:6A
          inet addr:192.168.30.2  Bcast:192.168.30.255  Mask:255.255.255.0
          UP BROADCAST RUNNING MULTICAST  MTU:1500  Metric:1
          RX packets:11253 errors:0 dropped:0 overruns:0 frame:0
          TX packets:1304 errors:0 dropped:0 overruns:0 carrier:0
          collisions:0 txqueuelen:100
          RX bytes:2092656 (1.9 Mb)  TX bytes:161329 (157.5 Kb)
          Interrupt:10 Base address:0x10a0
```

The preceding command requests configuration data for the first Ethernet device on the system, eth0. If you just specify eth0 (or another device), **ifconfig** displays information about only the specified interface. If you don't specify a device, **ifconfig** shows all network adapters, including the loopback adapter.

The **ifconfig** command can also be used to configure network interfaces. For example, you can assign a new IP address for eth0 with the following command:

```
# ifconfig eth0 207.174.142.142
```

The first parameter, eth0, tells us which interface is being configured. The next argument, 207.174.142.142, indicates the new IP address being assigned to this interface. If we want to make sure our change worked, we issue the **ifconfig** command again to view its current settings.

```
# ifconfig eth0
eth0      Link encap:Ethernet  HWaddr 00:50:56:40:1E:6A
          inet addr: 207.174.142.142  Bcast:207.174.142.255  Mask:255.255.255.0
          UP BROADCAST NOTRAILERS RUNNING MULTICAST  MTU:1500  Metric:1
          RX packets:11253 errors:0 dropped:0 overruns:0 frame:0
          TX packets:1304 errors:0 dropped:0 overruns:0 carrier:0
          collisions:0 txqueuelen:100
          RX bytes:2092656 (1.9 Mb)  TX bytes:161329 (157.5 Kb)
          Interrupt:10 Base address:0x10a0
```

Looking at the output of our command, we successfully changed the IP address on the eth0 interface to 207.174.142.142. But this is not enough, as you should realize that the broadcast address doesn't work with this IP address.

With the right switch, the **ifconfig** command can modify a number of other settings for your network adapter. Some of these switches are shown in Table 4-17.

TABLE 4-17   ifconfig Switches

Parameter	Description
up	Activates the specified adapter.
down	Deactivates the specified adapter.
netmask *address*	Assigns the *address* subnet mask.
broadcast *address*	Assigns the *address* as the broadcast address. Rarely required, since the default broadcast address is standard for most current networks.
metric N	Allows you to set a metric value of N for the routing table associated with the network adapter.
mtu N	Sets the maximum transmission unit as N, in bytes.
-arp	Deactivates the address resolution protocol, which collects network adapter hardware addresses.
promisc	Activates promiscuous mode. This allows the network adapter to read all packets to all hosts on the LAN. Can be used to analyze the network for problems, or to try to crack messages between other users.
-promisc	Deactivates promiscuous mode.
irq *port*	Assigns a specific IRQ port.
io_addr *address*	Assigns a specific I/O address.

netstat -r

The **netstat** command is used to display a plethora of network connectivity information. The most commonly used option, **netstat -r**, is used to display local routing tables. Here's a sample **netstat -r** output:

```
# netstat -nr
Kernel routing table
Destination      Gateway          Genmask        Flags MSS Window  irtt Iface
191.72.1.0       *                255.255.255.0  U     40  0          0 eth0
127.0.0.0        *                255.0.0.0      UH    40  0          0 lo
0.0.0.0          191.72.1.1       255.255.255.0  UG    40  0          0 eth0
```

Did you notice we used a **-n** flag? **-n** tells **netstat** to display addresses as IP addresses, instead of as hostnames. This makes it a little easier to see what's going on.

The Destination column lists networks by their IP addresses. The Gateway column indicates gateway addresses. If the destination is on the LAN, no gateway is required, so an asterisk is shown in this column. The Genmask column lists the network mask.

Networks look for a route appropriate to the destination IP address. The IP address is compared against the destination networks, in order. When the IP address is found to be part of one of these networks, it's sent in that direction. If there is a gateway address, it's sent to the computer with that gateway. The Flags column describes how this is done. Flag values are listed in Table 4-18.

arp as a Diagnostic Tool

The Address Resolution Protocol associates the hardware address of a network adapter with an IP address. The **arp** command displays a table of hardware and IP addresses on the local computer. With **arp**, you can detect problems such as duplicate addresses on the network, or you can manually add **arp** entries as required. Here's a sample **arp** command, showing all **arp** entries in the local database:

```
# arp
Address           HWtype  HWaddress          Flags Mask          Iface
192.168.0.121     ether   52:A5:CB:54:52:A2  C                   eth0
192.168.0.113     ether   00:A0:C5:E2:49:02  C                   eth0
```

If the arp table is empty, you haven't made any connections to other computers on your network. The address column lists known IP addresses, usually on the LAN. The HW Type column shows the hardware type of the adapter, while the HW Address column shows the hardware address of the adapter.

You can use the **-H** option to limit the output from **arp** to a specific hardware type, such as ax25, ether, or pronet. The default is ether, which is short for Ethernet.

The **arp** command can help you with duplicate IP addresses, which can stop a network completely. To remove the offending machine's arp entry from your arp table, use the **-d** option:

```
# arp -d bugsy
```

TABLE 4-18	Flag	Description
The netstat Flag Indicates the Route	G	The route uses a gateway.
	U	The network adapter (Iface) is up.
	H	Only a single host can be reached via this route.
	D	This entry was created by an ICMP redirect message.
	M	This entry was modified by an ICMP redirect message.

This removes all arp information for the host "bugsy." To add an arp entry, use the **-s** option:

```
# arp -s bugsy 00:00:c0:cf:a1:33
```

This entry will add the host bugsy with the given hardware address to the arp table. IP addresses won't work in this case.

DHCP Clients

You can set up your computer as a DHCP client. If the **redhat-config-network** configuration utility does not work, check the configuration file associated with your network card in the /etc/sysconfig/network-scripts directory. You should not need static IP configuration information, and you should see BOOTPROTO=dhcp.

In any case, if you have a working DHCP server on your network, you can connect your computer to it with the **dhclient** command.

on the job *Red Hat has used different commands to support DHCP clients in the past, including dhcpcd and pump.*

CERTIFICATION OBJECTIVE 4.08

The Basic Boot Process

Understanding how your system boots and shuts down will help you immensely as a Red Hat system administrator. Red Hat Enterprise Linux uses a boot process called System V init, which means that after the kernel is loaded, it starts a program called init, which then starts everything else. To understand the process better, let's go through the steps Red Hat Enterprise Linux takes to boot itself up to a usable system.

Once you understand the basic boot process, Red Hat Enterprise Linux provides two utilities that assist the system administrator in configuring and maintaining the commands that make up that startup and shutdown process. The **redhat-config-services** utility provides a GUI interface, while **chkconfig** provides a command line interface to manage services at different runlevels. Before we begin, it's important to understand Red Hat runlevels before reading about the boot process.

exam watch *The Red Hat course associated with the RHCT, RH133, explicitly requires that you understand what happens during the Linux boot process.*

Runlevels

There are six basic runlevels in Red Hat Enterprise Linux, as defined in /etc/inittab. Each runlevel is associated with a level of functionality. For example, in single-user mode, also known as runlevel 1, only one user is allowed to connect to that Linux system. X11 mode, also known as runlevel 5, starts Linux into a GUI login screen. The Red Hat definitions for System V init runlevels are shown in Table 4-19.

Making each runlevel work is the province of a substantial number of scripts. Each script can start or stop fundamental Linux processes such as printing (**cupsd**), scheduling (**crond**), Apache (**httpd**), Samba (**smbd**), and more. The starting and stopping of the right scripts becomes part of the boot process.

It should go without saying that if you set your initdefault to 0, your system will shut down when Linux tries to boot. Likewise, if you set the initdefault to 6, Linux will enter a continuous reboot cycle.

e**x**a m
ⓦatch

For the Troubleshooting and System Maintenance exam, it can be useful to back up and then modify critical configuration files such as /etc/inittab. But remember to do this on a test computer;

if you can't solve the problem, you may lose the data on that computer. Before you proceed, learn the rescue mode techniques described in Chapter 11.

The Boot Process

When you start your computer, the BIOS checks your system, and looks for a bootloader such as GRUB. It finds and installs the Linux kernel. Then Linux can start installing the services you have configured.

TABLE 4-19	Runlevel	Description
Red Hat Runlevels	0	Halt
	1	Single-user mode, for maintenance (backups/restores) and repairs
	2	Multiuser, without networking
	3	Multiuser, with networking
	4	Unused
	5	X11, defaults to a GUI login screen. Logins bring the user to a GUI desktop.
	6	Reboot (never set initdefault in /etc/inittab to this value!)

The kernel always starts by calling init. The init process in turn runs /etc/rc.d /rc.sysinit, which performs a number of tasks, including network configuration, keyboard maps, partition mounts, and hostnames. The init process then determines which runlevel it should be in by looking at the initdefault entry in /etc/inittab. A runlevel is defined as a group of activities. For example, the entry:

```
id:5:initdefault:
```

shows a default starting point in runlevel 5. Next, init starts the appropriate scripts associated with runlevel 5, from the /etc/rc.d directory. That directory includes the following subdirectories:

```
init.d
rc0.d
rc1.d
rc2.d
rc3.d
rc4.d
rc5.d
rc6.d
```

If the default runlevel is 5, init will look in /etc/rc.d/rc5.d and run each "kill" and "start" script it finds in that directory. A kill script is any file or symbolically linked file with a name that begins with a "K." Likewise, start scripts start with "S." If you run an **ls -l** command in this directory, you'll see only symbolic links to the actual scripts in /etc/rc.d/ init.d. Observe current examples of kill and start scripts at runlevel 5 in Figure 4-8.

What's going on here? System V init knows to go to the directory associated with a particular runlevel. Once there, init runs the scripts in that directory that start with a K and then the scripts starting with an S. The K scripts stop processes that

FIGURE 4-8	
Sample kill and start scripts in runlevel 5	

```
[root@Enterprise3 rc5.d]# \ls K*
K05innd         K20netdump-server  K34dhcrelay   K40smartd     K50vsftpd
K05saslauthd    K20nfs             K34yppasswdd  K45named      K70aep1000
K10psacct       K20rwhod           K35dhcpd      K50netdump    K70bcm5820
K15dc_client    K20spamassassin    K35smb        K50snmpd      K74ypserv
K15dc_server    K24irda            K35vncserver  K50snmptrapd  K74ypxfrd
K15httpd        K25squid           K35winbind    K50tux
[root@Enterprise3 rc5.d]# \ls S*
S00microcode_ctl  S12syslog      S25netfs       S58ntpd      S97rhnsd
S05kudzu          S13irqbalance  S26apmd        S59hpoj      S99local
S08arptables_jf   S13portmap     S28autofs      S80sendmail  S99mdmonitor
S08ip6tables      S14nfslock     S55cups        S85gpm
S08iptables       S17keytable    S55sshd        S90crond
S09isdn           S20random      S56rawdevices  S90xfs
S10network        S24pcmcia      S56xinetd      S95atd
[root@Enterprise3 rc5.d]# █
```

aren't supposed to operate in that runlevel. The S scripts start the processes associated with that runlevel. Within each category, scripts are run in numeric order; for example, K20nfs is run before K50tux, which is run before S10network.

Red Hat uses six different runlevels: 0, 1, 2, 3, 5, and 6. (Runlevel 4 is unused as of this writing.) Symbolic links allow the collection of all init scripts in one directory, /etc/init.d. Any changes to a start or kill script can be made in that directory.

You can run a start script yourself, with some key switches. For example, you can run the smbd (Samba) and sshd (secure shell daemon) scripts with the following options:

```
# /etc/rc.d/init.d/smb
Usage: /etc/rc.d/init.d/smb {start|stop|restart|reload|status|condrestart}
# service smb     # service is a shortcut to the management scripts
Usage: /etc/rc.d/init.d/smb {start|stop|restart|reload|status|condrestart}
# service sshd
Usage: sshd {start|stop|restart|reload|condrestart|status}
#
```

For example, the **/etc/rc.d/init.d/smb restart** command stops and starts Samba. See from the code how you can substitute the **service** command for /etc/rc.d/init.d in this command. It's one more timesaver that you can use on the Red Hat exams.

This is used by the scripts at each runlevel. In other words, if there is a K script for the smbd daemon, init runs **/etc/rc.d/init.d/smb stop**. And naturally, an S script for the ssh daemon runs **/etc/rc.d/init.d/sshd start**.

e x a m

⚙ a t c h   *Make sure you go through the /etc/rc.d hierarchy as well as the /etc/ inittab and /etc/rc.d/rc.sysinit files, and understand what's happening along the way. This is the key to understanding what's happening during the boot process.*

CERTIFICATION OBJECTIVE 4.09

Virtual Consoles

As Red Hat Enterprise Linux is a multiterminal operating system, you can log into Linux, even with the same user ID, several times. This is made possible through the use of virtual consoles.

It's easy to open up a new virtual console. Just use the appropriate ALT-function key combination. For example, pressing the ALT key and F2 at the same time brings you to the second virtual console. You can switch between adjacent virtual consoles by pressing ALT-RIGHT ARROW or ALT-LEFT ARROW. For example, to move from virtual console 2 to virtual console 3, press ALT-RIGHT ARROW.

/etc/inittab

Virtual consoles are configured in the init configuration file, /etc/inittab. By default, Red Hat Enterprise Linux is configured with six virtual consoles. You can add up to six more virtual consoles in /etc/inittab. Here are the default /etc/inittab entries for the first six virtual consoles:

```
1:2345:respawn:/sbin/mingetty tty1
2:2345:respawn:/sbin/mingetty tty2
3:2345:respawn:/sbin/mingetty tty3
4:2345:respawn:/sbin/mingetty tty4
5:2345:respawn:/sbin/mingetty tty5
6:2345:respawn:/sbin/mingetty tty6
```

Virtual consoles really bring the multiuser capabilities of Linux to life. You can be viewing a man page on one console, compiling a program in another, and editing a document in yet a third virtual console. Other users who are connected through a network can do the same thing at the same time.

The Graphical Console

The GUI is, in one way, just another console. By default, six virtual consoles are configured with Linux, so the GUI is next in line, at console 7. To switch from the GUI to a regular virtual console, press CTRL-ALT-F*x*, where *x* represents one of the other virtual consoles.

CERTIFICATION OBJECTIVE 4.10

Other Configuration Tools

There are a number of other key configuration files in the /etc/sysconfig directory. You can configure them with a text editor, with text commands, or in many cases, with a Red Hat graphical tool.

Time is of the essence on the Red Hat exams. It's fastest if you know how to configure these systems directly using text commands or by directly editing the key configuration file. However, if you forget how to manage one or two configuration commands or files, the Red Hat graphical tools can be a lifesaver.

I only address those systems that I believe are relevant on the Red Hat exams which are not already covered in other chapters.

Other /etc/sysconfig Files

Let's return to the /etc/sysconfig directory and discuss some of the non-network configuration files. I describe some of these files in Table 4-20. I cover only those files which might remotely be of interest on the Red Hat exams. I cover some of these files in other chapters. Some of these files can be edited directly; others can be configured with other Red Hat tools discussed in the following section.

TABLE 4-20   Key Non-network /etc/sysconfig Files

File in the /etc/sysconfig Directory	Description
clock	Contains defaults for the system clock, including time zone, UTC, and ARC (Alpha CPU-based) settings. If UTC=true, the BIOS is set to Greenwich Mean Time.
firstboot	If RUN_FIRSTBOOT=YES, then you can start the First Boot process with the **firstboot** command, if you're in runlevel 5.
gpm	Points to the mouse device, usually /dev/mouse.
grub	Lists the hard disk with your /boot drive, assuming you're using the GRUB boot loader.
harddisks	Supports settings for special hard disks.
hwconf	Lists peripherals detected by kudzu. Do *not* edit this file!
i18n	Sets the default language.
iptables	Includes the **iptables** firewall commands run when you boot Linux.
irda	Controls infrared devices
keyboard	Contains keyboard configuration data: KEYBOARDTYPE, usually "pc" and KEYTABLE, usually "us".

TABLE 4-20	Key Non-network /etc/sysconfig Files *(continued)*

File in the /etc/sysconfig Directory	Description
mouse	Contains mouse configuration data: FULLNAME describes the mouse type. MOUSETYPE lists the generic model such as IMPS2, msbm, or Microsoft. If XEMU3=yes, you have a two-button mouse set to emulate a third button. If WHEEL=yes, your mouse has a scroll wheel.
pcmcia	Contains PCMCIA configuration data. If PCMCIA=yes, Linux loads PCMCIA modules on boot.

GUI Configuration Utilities

It's best to know how to configure RHEL 3 by hand. It's the best way to control everything on your Linux system. It's faster on the Red Hat exams, where time is of the essence. There are a number of good GUI configuration tools available; almost all of them are "front-ends" which edit text configuration files, which you could edit directly.

However, there's a lot to learn about Linux. Learning how to edit *all* key Linux configuration files can be more than some can handle. While you should learn how to edit these files by hand, you may not have time. You may get nervous during the Red Hat exams and forget details. In these cases, the Red Hat GUI tools can be a lifesaver.

I cover a number of Red Hat GUI tools in this book. I summarize some other tools in RHEL 3 in this section. I cover only those tools which I believe can help you on the Red Hat exams in this section.

on the
ⓞob

The text mode setup tool is a front-end to a number of other tools you can view from the text console: authentication, firewall, mouse, network, printer, service, and time zone configuration. Unfortunately, they have not been updated for RHEL 3, and I therefore do not cover them in this book.

redhat-config-date

With the Date/Time Properties configuration tool, you can set the date, time, time zone, and NTP server for your system. You can start it in one of three ways in the GUI: run the **redhat-config-date** or **redhat-config-time** commands, or click Main Menu | System Settings | Date and Time. This opens the Date/Time Properties window shown in Figure 4-9.

FIGURE 4-9

The Date/Time
Properties tool

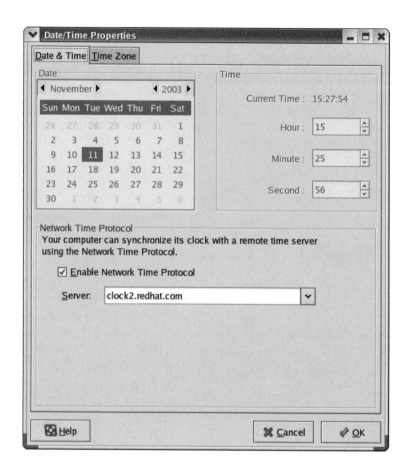

redhat-config-keyboard

The Keyboard configuration tool allows you to reselect the keyboard associated with
your system. You can start it in one of two ways in the GUI: run the **redhat-config-
keyboard** command or click Main Menu | System Settings | Keyboard. The options
are the same as you saw during the installation process. Results are recorded in /etc
/sysconfig/keyboard.

redhat-config-mouse

The Mouse Configuration tool allows you to reselect the pointing device associated with
your system. You can start it in one of two ways in the GUI: run the **redhat-config-
mouse** command or click Main Menu | System Settings | Mouse. The options are the
same as you saw during the installation process. Results are recorded in /etc/sysconfig
/mouse.

redhat-config-services

The Service Configuration tool shown in Figure 4-10 allows you to select the services that are to be activated in runlevels 3 (text login) and runlevel 5 (GUI login). You can start it in one of two ways in the GUI: run the **redhat-config-services** command or click Main Menu | System Settings | Server Settings | Services.

But it's faster to make these changes at the command line. The **chkconfig** command gives you a simple way to maintain different runlevels within the /etc/rc.d directory structure. With **chkconfig**, you can add, remove, and change services, list startup information, and check the state of a particular service. For example, you can check the runlevels where the sendmail service is set to start with the following command:

```
# chkconfig --list sendmail
sendmail 0:off 1:off 2:on 3:on 4:on 5:on 6:off
```

which indicates that sendmail is configured to start in runlevels 2, 3, 4, and 5. If you want to turn the sendmail service off for runlevel 4, execute the following command:

```
# chkconfig --level 4 sendmail off
```

Now sendmail is configured to run only on runlevels 2, 3, and 5. To turn it back on, you run the same command, substituting **on** for **off**. With **chkconfig**, you can also add

FIGURE 4-10

The Service
Configuration
utility

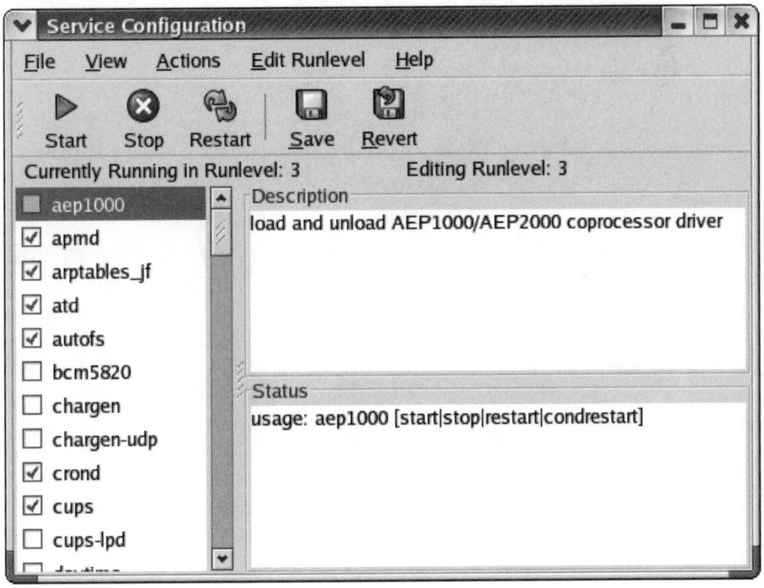

or delete services with the **--add** and **--del** switches. Installing a service sets up the appropriate links within the /etc/rc.d directory hierarchy. Uninstalling that service removes the associated links from the same hierarchy.

CERTIFICATION SUMMARY

This chapter covered basic configuration and administration of a Red Hat Enterprise Linux system. We learned the steps necessary to create a basic user, how to populate a user's home directory with the templates in /etc/skel, and where window manager configuration files are located. We also covered the different types of filesystems Linux uses, discussed how to mount them, and described what mount options to use with them.

This chapter covered the management of RPM packages. We learned the steps necessary to validate a package signature, how to add, remove, and upgrade packages, and how to add updates. We also talked about verifying packages and how to see what package a file belongs to. We finished the topic with a discussion on installing SRPMs and building RPMs from SRPMs and tar archives.

We addressed the configuration files in the /etc/sysconfig hierarchy. Some are important for networking; others are important for basic parameters such as the system clock, mouse, and keyboard. We also discussed a number of related networking commands, including **ifup**, **ifdown**, **ifconfig**, **netstat**, **arp**, and **dhclient**.

We concluded the chapter by describing some of the Red Hat GUI tools that you can use if you forget how to configure some key configuration files during the Red Hat exams.

TWO-MINUTE DRILL

Here are some of the key points from the certification objectives in Chapter 4.

Adding, Deleting, and Modifying User Accounts

❑ After installation, your system may have only a single login account: root. For most installations, you'll want to create more accounts, even if only for everyday use.

❑ Accounts can be added by directly editing /etc/passwd or with the **useradd** command. The advantage of **useradd** is that it automatically adds the new home directory as well as configuration files from /etc/skel.

❑ Accounts can be added with the Red Hat User Manager utility. You can also use this utility or related commands such as **chage** and **usermod** to further configure the account with parameters such as a password lifetime or a time limit on the account.

❑ Discourage the use of shared accounts, where several people use a single account. Shared accounts are almost always unnecessary, and they are easily compromised.

❑ If you'll be using the Network File System (NFS), it can help to make user accounts with the same UID across systems. The Network Information System (NIS) can serve this purpose by establishing one database for all systems on your network.

The Basic User Environment

❑ Each user on your system has an environment when logged on to the system.

❑ The home directory for each login account is the initial directory in which users are placed when they first log on. They start with files from /etc/skel.

❑ Window manager configuration files are often stored in /etc/X11/*windowmanager*, where *windowmanager* is the name of the window manager. KDE window manager files are stored in each user's home directory.

Red Hat Filesystem Basics

❑ Linux filesystems can be loosely defined as regular and journaling filesystems. While there are other filesystems available, this describes the essential difference between the older ext2 and the current default ext3 filesystems.

Filesystem Management and the Automounter

❑ If you have the kernel source RPMs installed, you can review supported filesystems.

❑ A number of mount options are available for /etc/fstab. The **defaults** option sets up a partition as rw (read/write), suid (superuser ID files allowed), dev (device files read), exec (binaries can be run), auto (automatic mounting), nouser (mountable only by root), and async (data is read asynchronously).

Using the Red Hat Package Manager Command and Utility

❑ The RPM database tracks where each file in a package is located, its version, and much more.

❑ Verifying an installed package compares information about that package with information from the RPM database on your system or the original package.

❑ The install mode of RPM, as its name suggests, is used to install RPM packages on your system.

❑ The upgrade mode of RPM will replace the old version of the package with the new one.

❑ The **rpm -e** command (erase) removes a package from your system.

❑ Using the **rpm** command query mode (**-q**), you can determine which packages are installed on your system or what file belongs to a particular package.

❑ You can use the Red Hat Package Management utility to install a group of packages from sources such as your installation CD. With the right **redhat-config-packages** command, you can even point to a network source.

RPM Sources

❑ Source RPMs are, as the name indicates, contain the source code used to build architecture-specific packages.

❑ The spec file is stored in /usr/src/redhat/SPECS/*packagename*.spec. It controls the way a package is built, and what actions are performed when it is installed or removed from a system.

❑ Run **rpmbuild -ba** *packagename* **spec** to build your RPM and SRPM.

Network Configuration

- ❑ Key network configuration files are in the /etc/sysconfig directory: the *network* file, and the networking and network-scripts subdirectories.
- ❑ You can start the Network Configuration utility with the **redhat-config-network** command.
- ❑ To manage network settings on each interface, use **dhclient** (dhcp/bootp client management), **ifup**, and **ifdown**.
- ❑ The **ifconfig** command is used to configure and display network devices.
- ❑ Use **ifup eth0** and **ifdown eth0** to activate and deactivate the eth0 interface.
- ❑ The **netstat** command is used to display a plethora of network connectivity information.
- ❑ The **arp** command is used to view or modify the local hardware address database.

The Basic Boot Process

- ❑ Red Hat uses a boot process called System V init, which means that after the kernel is loaded, it starts a program called init, which then starts /etc/rc.sysinit.
- ❑ Study the /etc/rc.d hierarchy and the /etc/inittab and /etc/rc.d/rc.sysinit files. This is the key to understanding what's happening during the boot process.
- ❑ The **chkconfig** command gives you a simple way to maintain the /etc/rc.d directory structure. The **redhat-config-services** command provides a GUI tool for the same purpose.

Virtual Consoles

- ❑ Because Red Hat Enterprise Linux is a multiterminal operating system, it allows you to have more than one login session on the system console at a time using virtual consoles.
- ❑ By default, six virtual consoles are started when you boot Linux.
- ❑ You can switch between virtual consoles by pressing ALT-F1 to ALT-F6. By default, you start on the first virtual (ALT-F1) console screen.
- ❑ You can get to console mode from your X Window System session with CTRL-ALT-(F1 to F6). Return to the X Window System with ALT-F7.

Other Configuration Tools

❑ There are a number of non-network configuration files in the /etc/sysconfig directory.

❑ You can edit many of these files directly, or use GUI tools, which you can start with commands such as **redhat-config-date**, **redhat-config-keyboard**, **redhat-config-mouse**, and **redhat-config-services**.

SELF TEST

The following questions will help you measure your understanding of the material presented in this chapter. Read all the choices carefully, as there may be more than one correct answer. Choose all correct answers for each question. Don't focus exclusively on these questions. There are no longer any multiple choice questions on the Red Hat exams. These questions test your understanding of the chapter. Getting results, not memorizing trivia, is what counts on the Red Hat exams.

Adding, Deleting, and Modifying User Accounts

1. When deleting a user account using **userdel**, which command switch deletes that user's home directory?

   A. -d

   B. -r

   C. -h

   D. -a

The Basic User Environment

2. Where are individual users' configuration files for the KDE window manager stored?

   A. /usr/lib/X11/.kde

   B. ~/.kde

   C. /etc/X11/.kde

   D. /etc/skel/.kde

Red Hat Filesystem Basics

3. Which of the following is an advantage of a journaling filesystem such as ext3?

   A. It supports the use of VFAT for floppy disks.

   B. It collects filesystem information in /etc/filesystems.

   C. It allows you to read CDs.

   D. It minimizes the risk if power is lost.

Filesystem Management and the Automounter

4. To change the mount options for a local filesystem, which of the following files would you edit?

A. /etc/filesystems

B. /etc/fstab

C. /etc/group

D. /etc/mnttab

Using the Red Hat Package Manager Command and Utility

5. Which of the following commands correctly installs the package penguin-3.26.i386.rpm?

A. rpm -I penguin-3.26.i386.rpm

B. rpm -i penguin

C. rpm -i penguin-3.26.i386.rpm

D. rpm --install penguin.rpm

RPM Sources

6. Assume you have the rpm-build RPM installed. When you install a source RPMs, where will you find key files?

A. /usr/lib/rpm

B. /usr/src/rpm

C. /usr/src/redhat

D. /usr/src/redhat/rpm

Network Configuration

7. What information can you find in the /etc/sysconfig/network file?

A. Your computer's hostname

B. The devices used for your network connections

C. Chat scripts for PPP and SLIP connections

D. The status of the network

The Basic Boot Process

8. Upon boot, the kernel starts init. What does init start next?

    A. /etc/rc.d/init.d

    B. /etc/inittab

    C. /etc/rc.d/initdefault

    D. /etc/rc.d/rc.sysinit

Virtual Consoles

9. To switch to the fourth virtual console from another text console, which keys would you press?

    A. ALT-4

    B. ALT-F4

    C. CTRL-4

    D. CTRL-F4

Other Configuration Tools

10. What types of services can you configure with files in the /etc/sysconfig directory?

    A. All types of services. These files supplement, but do not replace any other configuration files.

    B. Only network services.

    C. Only critical services related to your hardware configuration.

    D. All runlevels.

LAB QUESTIONS

The Red Hat exams are unique based on their reliance on labs and hands-on demonstrations. With these questions, you're practicing the skills you need on both Red Hat exams.

Lab 1

In this exercise, you are going to experiment with two ways to manage services at different runlevels: the **chkconfig** command and the **redhat-config-services** utility, also known as the Service Configuration utility. The commands in this lab don't start or stop scripts immediately; just the next time you move your Linux system into runlevel 3.

1. Open the GUI. From a text command line interface, run the **redhat-config-services &** command. This allows you to use the same terminal window for other commands. Alternatively, click Main Menu | System Settings | Server Settings | Services.

2. The Service Configuration utility is a graphical tool for controlling the services that Linux starts and stops at each runlevel.

3. These next steps assume that the nfs service is already running and installed. If not, pick another service to add and remove (it does not matter which as long as you restore the original condition when you're done).

4. At the command line, run the **ls /etc/rc3.d/*nfs** command to find the priority number.

5. Remove the nfs service from runlevel 3 using the Service Configuration utility.

6. Switch back to the command line window and run the **chkconfig --list nfs** command to see if it has been deactivated in runlevel 3.

7. Restore the nfs start script with the following command:

   ```
   # chkconfig --level 3 nfs on
   ```

8. Switch back to the console window and run the **chkconfig --list nfs** command to verify that it is back.

9. Return to the Service Configuration utility, and click View | Refresh Service List to confirm that nfs is back on in runlevel 3.

10. Although the Red Hat Service Configuration utility provides a nice graphical interface, the **chkconfig** command is faster and more reliable, especially since X is not always available in an emergency or through remote login.

Lab 2

While the Red Hat User Manager provides a convenient interface to add new users, it's important for the exam to know the basic command line tools. Specifically, you can use the **useradd**, **usermod**, and **userdel** commands to add, modify, and delete user accounts.

1. Use the man pages for **useradd** (or just type **useradd** with no arguments for a simple help summary) to find the switches you need to add the following account with each of these attributes:

   ```
   login: brianr
   name: brian rite
   UID: 5010
   ```

```
GID: nobody
shell: /bin/bash
```

2. Change the passwd for brianr to RvRg49().

3. Open a different virtual terminal. Log in as brianr. What files are present in this new account? Exit from this login.

4. Remove the brianr account using the **userdel** command. Is the brianr home directory gone? What option would have done this for you?

Lab 3

In this lab, you'll configure the Automounter on your computer on an NFS connection. You'll need a second computer with Linux or Unix installed, and a shared NFS directory. You can use the shared NFS installation source created in Chapter 2 or any other shared NFS directory described in Chapter 9. A virtual machine such as a VMWare computer qualifies as a second computer.

1. Back up your current /etc/auto.master and /etc/auto.misc configuration files.

2. Open the /etc/auto.master configuration file in the text editor of your choice. Add or activate the command which applies the Automounter to the /misc directory.

3. Open the /etc/auto.misc configuration file. Use the example shown in this file to create an NFS entry, which points to the shared NFS directory on the second computer. For the purpose of this lab, set the name of the directory to test.

4. Restart the autofs server.

5. Try your connection. Run the following command:

```
# ls /misc/test
```

6. You should see the contents of the shared NFS directory. Run the following command. What do you see?

```
# ls /misc
```

7. Wait a while, at least the *timeout* specified in the /etc/auto.master configuration file.

8. Run the **ls /misc** command again. What happens?

9. Once you're satisfied with the result, restore the files you backed up in step 1.

Lab 4

In this lab, you'll observe what happens when you avoid mounting the /boot filesystem. This of course assumes that you have a computer configured with /boot mounted on a separate partition.

1. Back up your /etc/fstab configuration file to something you can easily remember, such as /etc/bak.fstab.

2. Run the **df** command and make a note of the mounted filesystems, especially the partition associated with /boot.

3. Open /etc/fstab in the text editor of your choice. You should have a line associated with the /boot directory. If you do not, *stop*, as you cannot continue with this lab. **Trying to continue with this lab under these circumstances will probably render your system unbootable.**

4. Comment out the line with the /boot directory. Add a # in front of that line. For example, your /etc/fstab /boot directory line might read something like:

```
# LABEL=/boot          /boot          ext3          defaults  1 2
```

5. Save /etc/fstab and reboot Linux.

6. Observe the results. Does Linux start normally?

7. Look at your boot directory. Are there any files missing? How did Linux boot without benefit of a vmlinuz kernel or a mkinird RAM disk file?

8. Run the **df** command and make a note of the mounted filesystems.

9. Open /etc/fstab again. Remove the comment field, the **#**, in front of the /boot directory line. Save /etc/fstab. This should restore your /etc/fstab to the original configuration.

10. Mount the /boot directory with the **mount /boot** command.

11. Open your GRUB configuration file, /boot/grub/grub.conf in your text editor.

12. Observe the line associated with the **root** variable. This should correspond to the default partition for the /boot directory. Note that GRUB does not require that a partition is mounted to access a file.

13. Reboot your system. Run the **df** command and compare the list of mounted filesystems to step 2. If they are the same, stop here. Otherwise, restore your /etc/fstab from the backup file, /etc/bak.fstab.

Lab 5

In this lab, you'll install a new package group with the **redhat-config-packages** command, also known as the Package Management utility. You'll need a remote network source with the Red Hat installation files. It can be the same network source that you used in Chapter 2 to install RHEL 3.

1. In the Red Hat GUI, open a command line interface.

2. Click Main Menu | System Settings | Add/Remove Applications to open the Package Management utility.

3. Try adding the software of your choice. When you're prompted for a CD, click Cancel and exit from the utility.

4. Mount the network installation source that you created in Chapter 2. For the purpose of this lab, create a /mnt/test directory, and then use that as the mount point.

5. Run the following command. If it doesn't start the Package Management utility, there may be a problem with the mount or the network source. See Chapter 2 for more information.

    ```
    # redhat-config-packages --tree=/mnt/test
    ```

6. Try adding the software of your choice. Now see if you're prompted for a CD.

SELF TEST ANSWERS

Adding, Deleting, and Modifying User Accounts

1. ☑ **B**. The **userdel -r** *username* command deletes the user as well as all of the files in the /home/*username* directory.

   ☒ **A**, **C**, and **D** are not real switches for the **userdel** command.

The Basic User Environment

2. ☑ **B**. The tilde (~) is the generic term for each user's home directory. When users are created, these files are transferred from /etc/skel to the right home directory.

   ☒ **A** and **C** are not valid locations for KDE configuration files. While the generic KDE configuration files are stored in /etc/skel, they do not belong to any particular user (**D**).

Red Hat Filesystem Basics

3. ☑ **D**. Journaling filesystems can speed recovery from a crash, which includes what can happen when power to your computer is lost.

   ☒ **A**, **B**, and **C** are incorrect. The ext3 filesystem is unrelated to VFAT (**A**). The /etc/filesystems file lists currently supported filesystem formats. While that includes ext3, filesystems are not collected by ext3 (**B**). CDs are formatted to the ISO9660 filesystem, not ext3 (**C**).

Filesystem Management and the Automounter

4. ☑ **B**. Information regarding filesystems, including mount options, is stored in /etc/fstab.

   ☒ **A**, **C**, and **D** are incorrect. The /etc/filesystems file lists currently supported filesystem formats (**A**). Group information and passwords are documented in /etc/group (**C**). /etc/mnttab (**D**) is an invalid filename.

Using the Red Hat Package Manager Command and Utility

5. ☑ **C, rpm -i penguin-3.26.i386.rpm**. When installing a package, the **-i** option is used, followed by the name of the RPM file.

   ☒ **D** is almost correct. It has an incomplete filename for the RPM, but it would otherwise work. **B** also does not use the full filename. An asterisk at the end would make it work (as in **penguin***), but this would install every package starting with the name penguin, so it may install more than you want. The **-I** option is invalid with rpm (**A**).

RPM Sources

6. ☑ C. When installing SRPMs, they are, by default, extracted into the /usr/src/redhat directory structure.
☒ A, B, and D are nonexistent files and directories.

Network Configuration

7. ☑ A. If networking is enabled, /etc/sysconfig/network activates networking, contains the hostname, and possibly NIS domain name information as well.
☒ This file does not identify the network device, nor will it contain status information or any chat scripts (**B**, **C**, and **D**).

The Basic Boot Process

8. ☑ D. init runs /etc/rc.d/rc.sysinit, which performs a number of tasks, including configuring the network and setting up keymapping, swapping, and the host name.
☒ A is a directory. **B**, /etc/inittab, is the init configuration file, which sets the runlevel at startup. However, /etc/inittab is not a script. While **C**, /etc/rc.d/initdefault is not a real filename, initdefault is a variable within /etc/inittab that determines the default runlevel of your system.

Virtual Consoles

9. ☑ B. Press ALT-F4. Each virtual console has an ALT-function key associated with it to move to that virtual console.
☒ A, C, and D normally do not do anything when you are at a regular virtual console.

Other Configuration Tools

10. ☑ A. You can configure Red Hat services of all types in the /etc/sysconfig directory.
☒ B, C, and D are all incorrect. Files in /etc/sysconfig are not limited to network services or hardware configuration. It has nothing to do with configuring runlevels.

LAB ANSWERS

Lab 1

1. To open a command line interface in the Red Hat GUI, right-click on the desktop. In the pop-up menu that appears, click New Terminal.

2. In the new terminal, open the Service Configuration utility. Run the applicable graphical tool in the background so you can still use this terminal window with the following command:

   ```
   # redhat-config-services &
   ```

3. Run the **ls /etc/rc3.d** command. Look for the nfs start script and record the current order number. If you see only a kill script for nfs, it is not active in runlevel 3. If you don't see it at all, you need to install the nfs-utils RPM.

4. Deactivate the nfs service from level 3. It's easy to do so in the Service Configuration utility. But you have to remember to save your changes with the File | Save Changes command.

5. Switch back to the console window and run **chkconfig** to see if it has been deactivated in runlevel 3. If it has, you should see the following result:

   ```
   # chkconfig --list nfs
   autofs    0:off   1:off   2:off   3:off   4:on   5:on   6:off
   ```

6. Now run the **chkconfig** command to reactivate the nfs service. Return to the Service Configuration utility. Add the nfs service back in with the following command:

   ```
   # chkconfig --level 3 nfs on
   ```

7. Now run the following **chkconfig** command to verify that nfs is active again in runlevel 3:

   ```
   # chkconfig --list nfs
   autofs    0:off   1:off   2:off   3:on   4:on   5:on   6:off
   ```

   This should show that the nfs is started in runlevel 3. You practice using the **chkconfig** command. One way is to redo this lab. Use the service of your choice. Make sure what you see in the GUI Service Configuration utility matches what you see. After each change with the **chkconfig** command, run the View | Refresh Service List command to make sure the GUI tool reflects your change.

Lab 2

1. To add the account, enter:

   ```
   # useradd brianr -u 5010 -g nobody -c 'brian rite' -s /bin/bash
   ```

2. Change the password:

   ```
   # passwd brianr
   ```

3. Open a new virtual console. For example, to open the second virtual console, press ALT-F1. If you're in the GUI, also press the CTRL key.

4. Log into the new account.

5. What files are there? Include all the hidden files to see the skeleton files copied over from the /etc/skel directory.

   ```
   $ ls -a
   ```

6. Remove the brianr account using the **userdel** command. Is the brianr home directory gone? What option would have done this for you?

   ```
   # userdel brianr      # leaves the home directory
   # userdel -r  brianr  # also removes home directory
   ```

7. Rerun these tasks in the Red Hat User Manager.

Lab 3

Configuring the Automounter on a shared NFS directory is easier than it looks. Before you begin, make sure that you can mount the shared NFS directory from the remote computer. If there's a problem, resolve those first before beginning this lab. Refer to Chapter 2 on creating an NFS Installation Server or Chapter 9 on NFS for more information. If there's no problem with a source on an NFS server with an IP address of 192.168.30.4, you should be able to mount it locally. For example, you can mount a shared remote NFS /mnt/inst directory on an existing empty local /mnt/test directory as follows:

```
# mount -t nfs 192.168.30.4:/mnt/inst /mnt/test
```

Configuring the Automounter is easier than it looks. But first, as with any of these experiments, it's important to back up any files that you're about to edit. In this case, those are the configuration files which govern the autofs daemon, /etc/auto.master and /etc/auto.misc.

One of the fortunate things about the RHEL 3 version of these files is that they contain tips and example commands that you can use and learn from as you work with the Automounter. Use them to your advantage. You can activate the standard commented command in the /etc/auto.master file to activate the Automounter on the /misc directory:

```
/misc    /etc/auto.misc    --timeout=60
```

This command sets a timeout of 60 seconds, depending on details specified in /etc/auto.misc. Activate this command (remove the #) and save your changes to /etc/auto.master.

Open /etc/auto.misc in your text editor. The example shown is easy to follow:

```
#linux    -ro,soft,intr    ftp.example.org:/pub/linux
```

Let's assume you're using your NFS installation server from Chapter 2, and that server is at IP address 192.168.30.4. In that case, you'd add the following command to this file:

```
test     -ro,soft,intr    192.168.30.4:/mnt/inst
```

Now you can restart the autofs server; the quickest way is with the following command:

```
# service autofs restart
```

Now when you test the result, you should be able to see the contents of your shared NFS directory.

```
# ls /misc/test
```

You can test the result in a different way. Before the timeout in /etc/auto.master expires, the following command should reveal the test subdirectory:

```
# ls /misc
test
```

After the timeout is complete, rerun the **ls /misc** command again. The test subdirectory should no longer be there, which tells you that the timeout specified in /etc/auto.master has expired. Please, retry this lab with other shared NFS directories. Remember to restore the original /etc/auto.master and /etc/auto.misc files when you're done.

Lab 4

Remember, you should not try this exercise if you don't have a separate line for the /boot filesystem in /etc/fstab. And this assumes that GRUB is your default bootloader.

This should be a self-explanatory exercise. Essentially, you're just making a minor modification to the /etc/fstab file. If you do it correctly, Linux should boot normally, even if it does not mount the /boot filesystem. The key is within the GRUB configuration file, as the **root** variable in /boot/grub/grub.conf doesn't require a mounted filesystem to read your vmlinuz kernel or your mkinird initial RAM disk files.

Lab 5

The point of this lab is to see how you can use the Package Management utility with a network installation source. You'll be able to install any additional package groups that you need. That can be much more efficient than using the **rpm** command to install the dozens of RPMs associated with some package groups.

The steps I've described work only if your connection to the NFS server works, as described in Chapter 2 as well as Lab 3.

5

Kernel, cron, and User Administration

I
n this chapter, you will learn how to set up the Linux startup shell configuration scripts so that users' sessions are configured according to your (and their) requirements. You will learn how to create and implement policies for managing disk usage—by user or by group.

Next, you will learn how to upgrade, configure, compile, and install your own custom kernels. You will learn about the advantages and disadvantages of monolithic and modular kernels. You have three different ways to customize and optimize your kernel configuration for size and functionality. You will also learn the recommended techniques for configuring and installing the kernel. Finally, you'll learn how to schedule the one-time and periodic execution of jobs.

For the Red Hat exams, the skills you learn in this chapter are important for the Installation and Configuration exam. As described in the Red Hat Exam Prep guide, you need to know how to manage accounts and set up the user environment.

INSIDE THE EXAM

Configuring Users

You need to know how to create and configure users on the Red Hat exams. This means that you need to know how to configure the environment associated with each user account—in configuration files and in user settings. You also need to know how to specify the configuration files associated with the default bash shell. Finally, you need to know how to limit the resources allocated to each user through quotas. These requirements are all explicitly cited in the Red Hat Exam Prep guide for both exams.

Managing Kernels

As a competent Linux administrator, you need to know how to install, patch, and recompile kernels. It's easy to install a new kernel from an RPM, which makes it a reasonable requirement on the RHCT and RHCE exams. However, the latest RHCE Exam Prep guide no longer explicitly requires that you need to know how to recompile the Linux kernel. Therefore, the long discussion on recompiling kernels is "only" important if you want the skills needed to become a Linux systems administrator.

CERTIFICATION OBJECTIVE 5.01

Shell Configuration Files

All system-wide shell configuration files are kept in the /etc directory. These files are bashrc, profile, and the scripts in the /etc/profile.d directory. These files and scripts are supplemented by hidden files in each user's home directory, as described in Chapter 4. Let's take a look at these files.

/etc/bashrc

The /etc/bashrc file is used for aliases and functions, on a system-wide basis. Open this file in the text editor of your choice. Read each line in this file. Even if you don't understand the programming commands, you can see that this file sets the following bash shell parameters for each user. For example:

- It assigns a value of umask, which creates the default permissions for newly created files. It supports one set of permissions for root and system users (with user IDs below 100), and another for regular users.

- It assigns a prompt, which is what you see just before the cursor at the command prompt.

The settings here are called by the .bashrc file in each user's home directory. The settings are supplemented by the .bash_history and .bash_logout files in each user's home directory.

/etc/profile

The /etc/profile file is used for system-wide environments and startup files. The following is the profile script from my copy of the RHEL 3 operating system. The first part of the file sets the PATH for searching for commands. Then it sets the PATH, USER, LOGNAME, MAIL, HOSTNAME, HISTSIZE, and INPUTRC variables, and finally it runs the scripts in the /etc/profile.d directory. You can check the current value of any of these variables with the **echo $*variable*** command.

```
# /etc/profile

# System wide environment and startup programs, for login setup
```

```
# Functions and aliases go in /etc/bashrc

pathmunge () {
  if ! echo $PATH | /bin/egrep -q "(^|:)$1($|:)" ; then
    if [ "$2" = "after" ] ; then
      PATH=$PATH:$1
    else
      PATH=$1:$PATH
    fi
  fi
}

# Path manipulation
if [ `id -u` = 0 ]; then
  pathmunge /sbin
  pathmunge /usr/sbin
  pathmunge /usr/local/sbin
fi

pathmunge /usr/X11R6/bin after

unset pathmunge

# No core files by default
ulimit -S -c 0 > /dev/null 2>&1

USER="`id -un`"
LOGNAME=$USER
MAIL="/var/spool/mail/$USER"

HOSTNAME=`/bin/hostname`
HISTSIZE=1000

if [ -z "$INPUTRC" -a ! -f "$HOME/.inputrc" ]; then
    INPUTRC=/etc/inputrc
fi

export PATH USER LOGNAME MAIL HOSTNAME HISTSIZE INPUTRC

for i in /etc/profile.d/*.sh ; do
    if [ -r "$i" ]; then
      . $i
    fi
done

unset i
```

/etc/profile.d/

Actually, /etc/profile.d is not a script, but a directory of scripts. As I just noted, /etc/ profile runs the scripts in this directory. Here is a partial listing of the files, which apply to the default bash shell:

```
-rwxr-xr-x   1 root     root        724 Aug 12 11:34 colorls.sh
-rwxr-xr-x   1 root     root        190 Sep  8 11:32 glib2.sh
-rwxr-xr-x   1 root     root         70 Sep 17 12:13 gnome-ssh-askpass.sh
-rwxr-xr-x   1 root     root        210 Sep 23 15:42 krb5.sh
-rwxr-xr-x   1 root     root         53 Mar 26  2003 lam.sh
-rwxr-xr-x   1 root     root       2595 Sep 26 00:39 lang.sh
-rwxr-xr-x   1 root     root        435 Sep  1 10:32 less.sh
-rwxr-xr-x   1 root     root         70 May  1  2003 pvm.sh
-rwxr-xr-x   1 root     root        181 Sep  1 11:01 vim.sh
-rwxr-xr-x   1 root     root        170 Jul 17 15:09 which-2.sh
```

By looking at the /etc/profile script, you can see that any script in this directory that ends with an "sh" and is set as an executable will be run when /etc/profile is executed.

EXERCISE 5-1

Securing Your System

We want to keep our system as secure as possible. One approach is to change the default permissions users have for new files and directories they make. We'll set all new files and directories to No Access to group or other members.

1. Back up your current /etc/bashrc file. If you want to cancel any changes that you make during this exercise, restore from the backup after the final step.

2. Edit the /etc/bashrc file. Two lines in the file set the umask. One of the two lines is selected depending on the if statement above them. See if you can determine which line gets executed for an average (non-root) user.

3. The **if** statement tests to see if the user ID (uid) and group ID (gid) are the same, and that the uid is greater than 99. If this is true, then the first umask is executed; otherwise, the second is executed. The second umask is for root and other key system accounts. The first is for users.

4. Change the first umask statement to exclude all permissions for groups and others. Use umask 077 to do the job.

5. Save and exit the file.

6. Log in as a nonprivileged user. Use the **touch** command to make a new empty file. Use **ls -l** to verify the permissions on that file.

7. Log in as root. Again, use the **touch** command to make a new empty file and use **ls -l** to verify the permissions on that new file.

You have just changed the default umask for all shell users. If you backed up your /etc/bashrc in step 1, you can now restore the original version of this file.

User Shell Configuration Files

As described in Chapter 4, each user gets a copy of the hidden files from the /etc/skel directory. As your users start working with their accounts, more configuration files are added to their home directories. Some are based on shells such as bash (.bash*); others draw their settings from the GUI desktops that you use, typically GNOME and KDE. I'll describe the GUIs in more detail in Chapter 6.

The default Linux shell is bash. However, if you or your users work with other shells, you'll find configuration files associated with those shells hidden in each user's home directory.

CERTIFICATION OBJECTIVE 5.02

Setting Up and Managing Disk Quotas

Quotas are used to limit a user's or a group of users' ability to consume disk space. This prevents a small group of users from monopolizing disk capacity and potentially interfering with other users or the entire system. Disk quotas are commonly used by ISPs, by Web hosting companies, on FTP sites, and on corporate file servers to ensure continued availability of their systems.

Without quotas, one or more users can upload files on an FTP server to the point of filling a filesystem. Once the affected partition is full, other users are effectively denied upload access to the disk. This is also a reason to mount different filesystem directories on different partitions. For example, if you only had partitions for your root (/) directory and swap space, someone uploading to your computer could fill up all of the space in your root directory (/). Without at least a little free space in the root directory (/), your system could become unstable or even crash.

You have two ways to set quotas for users. You can limit users by inodes or by kilobyte-sized disk blocks. Every Linux file requires an inode. Therefore, you can limit users by the number of files or by absolute space. You can set up different quotas for different filesystems. For example, you can set different quotas for users on the /home and /tmp directories if they are mounted on their own partitions.

Limits on disk blocks restrict the amount of disk space available to a user on your system. Older versions of Red Hat Linux included LinuxConf, which included a graphical tool to configure quotas. As of this writing, Red Hat no longer has a graphical quota configuration tool. Today, you can configure quotas on RHEL only through the command line interface.

on the **Job** *Learn to focus on command line tools. Red Hat used to make LinuxConf available as a graphical and console tool for a number of system administration functions, including quotas. While Red Hat may eventually create another GUI quota manager, don't count on it. And GUI tools have been known to crash. On the job, as well as on the exam, command line tools are the only sure way to address just about any Linux configuration issue. Besides, command line tools are faster, and time is often of the essence on the Red Hat exams.*

Quota Settings in the Kernel

By default, the Linux kernel as configured by Red Hat supports quotas. However, if you install and compile a new kernel from a remote source, you should make sure that this feature is active. The basic kernel configuration is stored in the /boot directory. For the default RHEL 3 system, you'll find the configuration in the config-2.4.21-4.EL file. If you've configured a custom kernel file, you'll find it listed under a different name.

To verify that quotas are enabled in the default RHEL 3 kernel, run the following command:

```
# grep CONFIG_QUOTA /boot/config-2.4.21-4.EL
```

There are three possible results. If you see the following, quota support is enabled:

```
CONFIG_QUOTA=y
```

Alternatively, if you see the following, quota support is not enabled:

```
CONFIG_QUOTA=n
```

If you don't see any output, then you haven't installed the kernel source files.

If you have a custom or upgraded kernel, use either the **make menuconfig** or **make xconfig** command to make sure support is enabled for quotas. The quota support option is located in the filesystem section. All you need to do is turn on quota support and then rebuild and install your new kernel. I'll describe this process in more detail later in this chapter.

The Quota Package

The quota RPM package is installed by default on RHEL 3, as well as Red Hat Linux 9. You can find out more about RPMs such as quota with the following command:

```
# rpm -qi quota
```

Assuming you haven't removed the quota RPM, you'll see the following description of the package which tells you that it includes a number of tools:

```
The quota package contains system administration tools for
monitoring and limiting user and or group disk usage per
filesystem.
```

You can find out more about these tools by reviewing a list of associated files. You can find a list of files installed through the quota RPM with the following command:

```
# rpm -ql quota
```

As you can see for yourself, the quota package includes the following commands:

- **/sbin/quotaon /fs**   Enables quotas for the /fs filesystem.
- **/sbin/quotaoff /fs**   Disables quota tracking.
- **/usr/sbin/edquota *name***   Edits the quota settings for user *name*. Can also be used to set defaults, or to copy quota settings from one user to another.
- **/usr/bin/quota**   Allows users to see their current resource consumption and limits.
- **/usr/sbin/repquota**   Generates a report of disk consumption by all users for a quota-enabled filesystem.

■ **/sbin/quotacheck**   Scans a filesystem for quota usage. Initializes the quota databases.

I've included the entire path to each command for your reference. But as discussed earlier in this book, I recommend that you normally work as the root user during the Red Hat exams. As the noted directories are all part of the root user's PATH, you don't need to specify the full path to each command. (You can verify the directories in your path with the **echo $PATH** command.)

The next step is to ensure that the quotas are active and checked when Linux boots on your system.

sysinit Quota Handling

The /etc/rc.sysinit script as described in Chapter 4 initializes Linux system services during the boot process. This script includes commands which start quota services. Specifically, this script runs both the **quotacheck** (to ensure that disk consumption usage records are accurate) and **quotaon** commands (to enable quotas on all filesystems indicated in /etc/fstab). You don't have to run these commands manually.

Quota Activation in /etc/fstab

As described in Chapter 4, the file /etc/fstab tells Linux which filesystems to mount during the boot process. The options column of this file configures how Linux mounts a directory. You can include quota settings in /etc/fstab for users and or groups.

on the **Job**   *Before you edit a key configuration file such as /etc/fstab, it's a good idea to back it up and save it to any boot or rescue disks that you may have. If your changes lead to a catastrophic failure, you can boot your system from a rescue disk and then restore the original configuration file.*

Here is a sample /etc/fstab before editing:

```
Device          Mount point     Filesys     Options                 dump Fsck
LABEL=/         /               ext3        defaults                  1    1
LABEL=/boot     /boot           ext3        defaults                  1    2
none            /dev/pts        devpts      gid=5,mode=620            0    0
none            /proc           proc        defaults                  0    0
none            /dev/shm        proc        tmpfs                     0    0
/dev/hda3       swap            swap        defaults                  0    0
/dev/hdd1       /home           ext3        defaults                  1    2
/dev/cdrom      /mnt/cdrom      udf,iso9660     noauto,owner,kudzu,ro 0    0
/dev/floppy     /mnt/floppy     auto        noauto,owner,kudzu        0    0
```

In this configuration, we may want to enable quotas on the root (/) and /home directory filesystems. You can tell Linux to start tracking user quotas by adding the keyword **usrquota** under the options column. Similarly, you can tell Linux to start tracking group quotas with the **grpquota** option. Use vi or your favorite text editor to update /etc/fstab.

In our example, we will add both user and group quotas to the /home directory filesystem:

```
Device              Mount point    Filesys    Options                            dump Fsck
LABEL=/             /              ext3       defaults                            1    1
LABEL=/boot         /boot          ext3       defaults                            1    2
none                /dev/pts       devpts     gid=5,mode=620                       0    0
none                /proc          proc       defaults                            0    0
none                /dev/shm       proc       tmpfs                               0    0
/dev/hda3           swap           swap       defaults                            0    0
/dev/hdd1    /home         ext3    exec,dev,suid,rw,usrquota,grpquota              1    2
/dev/cdrom          /mnt/cdrom     udf,iso9660      noauto,owner,kudzu,ro 0        0
/dev/floppy         /mnt/floppy    auto           noauto,owner,kudzu               0    0
```

If you edit the /etc/fstab file by hand, you'll need to ensure that the line you are editing does not wrap to the next line. If it does, the format for your /etc/fstab will be invalid and you may not be able to successfully boot Linux.

on the job   ***You can test changes to /etc/fstab by rebooting your computer or remounting a filesystem. For example, if you've just added usrquota and grpquota entries as shown to the /home directory filesystem, you can test it with the mount -o remount /home command.***

Quota Management Commands

The next step is to create quota files. For user and group quotas, you'll need the aquota.user and aquota.group files in the selected filesystem. You need these files before you can activate actual quotas. You no longer need to create those files; once you've remounted the desired directory, you can create them directly with the appropriate **quotacheck** command. For the /home directory described earlier, you'd use the following commands:

```
# mount -o remount /home
# quotacheck -avugm
```

The **quotacheck -avugm** command automatically scans /etc/mtab, which includes the mounted directories from /etc/fstab. The options for **quotacheck** are

- **-a**   Scans all filesystems with quotas enabled by checking /etc/mtab.
- **-v**   Performs a verbose scan.
- **-u**   Scans for user quotas.
- **-g**   Scans for group quotas.
- **-m**   Remounts the scanned filesystem.

This will check the current quota information for all users, groups, and partitions. It stores this information in the appropriate quota partitions. You should also find the aquota.user and aquota.group files in the configured directory. If you're configuring quotas on the /home directory, you can check that it worked with the following command:

```
# ls -l /home/aquota.*
```

Using edquota to Set Up Disk Quotas

To specify disk quotas, you need to run the **edquota** command. This edits the aquota.user or aquota.group file with the vi editor. In our example, we will pretend we have a user named nancy, and we want to restrict how much disk space she is allowed to use. We type the following command to edit their quota records:

```
# edquota -u nancy
```

This command launches the vi editor and opens the quota information for user nancy, as shown in Figure 5-1.

The quota information is formatted strangely. There are actually seven columns. The lines are wrapped. In this case, the filesystem with the quota is mounted on partition /dev/hdd1. There are soft and hard limits for both inodes and files. By default, soft and hard limits of 0 means that there are no limits for nancy.

FIGURE 5-1	Disk quotas for user nancy (uid 507):					
	Filesystem	blocks	soft	hard	inodes	soft
	hard					
Quota	/dev/hdd1	52	0	0	13	0
information	0					

We can see that nancy is currently using 52 blocks and has 13 files (inodes) on this partition. Each block takes up 1KB of space; thus, user nancy's files total 52KB. We want to set a limit so that nancy does not take more than 20MB of space with her files.

First, we need to elaborate on the meaning of soft and hard limits.

- **Soft limit**   This is the maximum amount of space a user can have on that partition. If you have set a grace period, then this will act as an alarm. The user will then be notified he is in quota violation. If you have set a grace period, you will also need to set a hard limit. A grace period is the number of days a user is allowed to be above the given quota. After the grace period is over, the user must get under the soft limit to continue.

- **Hard limit**   Hard limits are necessary only when you are using grace periods. If grace periods are enabled, this will be the absolute limit a person can use. Any attempt to consume resources beyond this limit will be denied. If you are not using grace periods, the soft limit is the maximum amount of available to each user.

In our example, we will set our user an 18MB soft limit and a 20MB hard limit. As shown in Figure 5-2, this is written as a number of 1KB blocks in the quota file.

Note that we have not limited user nancy's use of inodes. She is still able to use as many inodes (thus as many files) as she likes. To implement these quotas, we must save these settings. Assuming you're still using the default vi editor, the **:wq** command does this job nicely.

We will also give user nancy a seven-day grace period, if and when she exceeds the soft limit. She has that amount of time to get back under the soft limit. To set the grace period for all users, run the **edquota -t** command. The result should look similar to what you see in Figure 5-3.

Here, Linux has provided us with the default of seven days for both inodes and block usage. That is, a user may exceed his soft limit on either resource for up to seven days. After that, further requests by that user to use files will be denied. Our user

FIGURE 5-2	
Quotas with hard and soft limits	

```
Disk quotas for user nancy (uid 507):
  Filesystem                   blocks       soft       hard     inodes       soft
  hard
  /dev/hdd1                        52      18000      20000         13          0
  0
```

FIGURE 5-3

Quota grace
period

```
Grace period before enforcing soft limits for users:
Time units may be: days, hours, minutes, or seconds
 Filesystem                  Block grace period      Inode grace period
   /dev/hdd1                        7days                   7days
```

nancy would have to delete files to get her total disk block consumption under 18MB before she could create new files or grow existing files. You can edit the grace period directly, using vi commands. To activate the new grace period, just save the file.

There is a quirk to quota grace periods. When you use **edquota** and specify the grace period, you cannot have a space between the number and the unit (for example, **7days**, not 7 days). Fortunately, the quota system in RHEL 3 automatically fixes this problem.

on the
Job

In older versions of Red Hat Linux, a space between the number and the unit would lead to a quota error.

The **edquota** command allows you to use an already configured user's quota as a template for new users. To use this feature, you need to add the following switch and options, *-p configured_user* arguments:

```
# edquota -up nancy michael randy donna
```

This command will not provide any output, but it will take the quota configuration settings of user nancy and apply them to michael, randy, and donna. You can list as many users as you want to edit or apply templates to.

You can also set up quotas on a per-group basis. To do this, simply run **edquota** with the **-g *group_name*** argument. Here, *group_name* would need to be a valid group as specified in the /etc/group file.

```
# edquota -g nancy
```

This opens the block and inode quota for group nancy, as shown in Figure 5-4.

FIGURE 5-4

Group quota

```
Disk quotas for group nancy (gid 507):
 Filesystem              blocks      soft      hard     inodes      soft
   hard
   /dev/hdd1                52          0         0         13         0
     0
```

Automating Quota Settings

As an administrator, you'll want to maintain any quotas that you create. For that purpose, it's useful to run the aforementioned **quotacheck** command on a regular basis. As you'll see later in this chapter, that is easy to do through the cron system. A simple command in the right cron file automatically runs the **quotacheck** command on a regular basis. For example, the following command in the right cron file runs the **quotacheck** command at 4:00 A.M. every Saturday:

```
0 4 * * 6 /sbin/quotacheck -avug
```

You can also use the **edquota** command to apply quotas to all users on your system. For example, the following command applies the quotas that you've already set on user mj to all other real users on the system:

```
edquota -p mj `awk -F: '$3 > 499 {print $1}' /etc/passwd`
```

Note that this command lists the first column ($1) of /etc/passwd, which is the user name. And in keeping with the UIDs for regular Red Hat users (from the third column, $3, of /etc/passwd), this is limited to users with UIDs of 500 or higher. You can add this type of command to the appropriate cron file as well, which makes sure that the quotas are applied to all existing and new users.

Quota Reports

As an administrator, it can be useful to see reports on who is using the most disk space. You can generate reports on users, groups, or everybody on every partition. To view a report showing quota information for all, run the **repquota -a** command. You'll see a list of quotas for all users similar to what is shown in Figure 5-5.

If you have multiple filesystems with quotas, you can use the **repquota** command to isolate a specific filesystem. For example, if you wanted to view the quota report for the partition with the /home directory, you'd run the following command:

```
# repquota -u /home
```

Alternatively, if you wanted to view quota information on user nancy, run the following **quota** command:

```
# quota -uv  nancy
Disk quotas for user nancy(uid 507):
Filesystem  blocks  quota  limit   grace   files   quota   limit  grace
/dev/hdd1      52   18000  20000              13      0       0
```

An individual user can check his or her own usage with the **quota** command, but only the administrative root user can examine the quotas for other users.

Quotas on NFS Directories

The Network File System (NFS) allows users to share files and directories on a network with Linux and Unix computers. Users across the network mount a shared NFS directory from a specific computer. Users are normally in a single database in an NFS setup. Disk quotas can be applied to these users in virtually the same way as on a regular Linux computer. For example, if you create a local user called nfsuser, and you translate all remote requests to this user, then you need to set up quota restrictions for nfsuser on the mounted partition. This will limit the disk consumption of all incoming NFS users. See Chapter 9 for more about NFS.

FIGURE 5-5   A quota report

```
[root@Enterprise3 root]# repquota -a
*** Report for user quotas on device /dev/hdd1
Block grace time: 7days; Inode grace time: 7days
                      Block limits             File limits
User          used   soft    hard   grace   used  soft  hard  grace
-------------------------------------------------------------------
root      --    36      0      0              3     0     0
michael   --    52  18000  20000             13     0     0
donna     --    52      0      0             13     0     0
elizabeth --    52      0      0             13     0     0
nancy     --    52  18000  20000             13     0     0
randy     --    52  18000  20000             13     0     0


[root@Enterprise3 root]# []
```

EXERCISE 5-2

Configure Quotas

In this exercise, we will set up user quotas for one user on your system. These quotas will allow a soft limit of 80MB and a hard limit of 100MB for each user. No limits are to be placed on the number of inodes. Assume the /home directory is mounted on a separate partition. (If /home is not mounted separately, apply the commands to the top-level root directory /.) The first couple of steps should be formalities, as quotas should be active and installed by default. However, it's a good habit to check. To set up quotas in this exercise, use the following steps:

1. Check your kernel configuration for the CONFIG_QUOTA variable, using the /boot/config-2.4.21-4.EL file. It should be set to "Y." If not, proceed to the Lab Question at the end of this chapter for instructions on how to revise your kernel. If you're using a different version of Linux such as Red Hat Linux 9, substitute the /boot/config-* file associated with your kernel version.

2. Check to make sure that the quota package is installed. Install from the RHEL 3 installation source if required.

3. Add quotas to /etc/fstab. Add the usrquota variable to the Options column for the partition with the /home directory. Make sure the info stays on one line in /etc/fstab.

4. Activate the quotas. You can unmount and remount the /home directory, reboot Linux, or use the following command:

   ```
   # mount -o remount /home
   ```

5. Use the **quotacheck -avum** command to activate the quota files in the /home directory.

6. Make sure this command worked. Look for the aquota.user file in the /home directory.

7. Now you're ready to set up quotas for a specific user. If necessary, look up usernames in /etc/passwd. Use the **edquota -u *username*** command to edit the quotas for the user of your choice.

8. Under the soft and hard columns, change the 0 to 80000 and 100000, respectively. Remember, these files are set up for 1KB blocks. Save the file.

CERTIFICATION OBJECTIVE 5.03

The Basics of the Kernel

The kernel is the heart of the whole operating system. It manages communication with hardware, decides which processes to run, and provides each process with an isolated, virtual address space in which to run. The kernel is what your boot loader, GRUB or LILO, loads into memory. The kernel loads device driver modules. It also allocates hardware resources such as IRQ ports, I/O addresses, and DMA channels. When you recompile your kernel, you can

- Greatly improve the speed at which kernel services operate.
- Build in direct support for commonly used drivers.
- Configure the dynamic loading of appropriate drivers as modules.
- Lower the memory consumption of your kernel by removing unneeded components.
- Configure support for high-end hardware, such as memory above 4GB, hardware array controllers, symmetric multiprocessing (multiple CPU) support, and more.

In essence, you can customize the Linux kernel any way you want. The best way to do it is to make it fit every detail of your hardware. However, you may not need to be so picky. In many cases, where there's a small update to the kernel, all you need to do is install the updated kernel RPM.

Best Practices

You should compile your kernel with only the elements you need. The more you can leave out, the faster your whole system will run. For example, if you don't have a sound card, you can remove sound card support from your kernel. By removing unneeded devices, you will

- Decrease the size of the kernel.
- Provide a modest increase in speed for the devices that are present.

- Make more hardware resources (I/O addresses, IRQ ports, and so on) available for other hardware such as network cards, disk controllers, and more.

- Reduce the chance of hardware limits, such as those that may be based on the size of the compressed kernel.

Generally, it is a good idea to have device drivers compiled as modules for any equipment that you may add in the near future. For example, if you may use your Linux computer as a router, you'll need a second network card, and you can add support for that card to your kernel. For example, if you have a 3Com 3c595 network card installed but you also have some 3Com 3c905 cards in storage, then it may be a good idea to include the 3c905 module. That way, you will just have to swap in the new card and let the module load, causing minimum downtime.

Modules are kernel extensions. They are not compiled directly into the kernel but can be plugged in and removed as needed. When configured as a module, a hardware failure such as that of a network card will not cause the whole system to fail.

Kernel Concepts

You will need to understand some basic kernel concepts before you can compile your own kernel. Kernels can be organized as one big unit, or as a lot of interconnected pieces. Kernels are called up by boot loaders when you boot your computer.

Monolithic versus Modular

A *monolithic* kernel is a kernel where all the device modules are built directly into the kernel. *Modular* kernels have many of their devices built as separate loadable modules. Monolithic kernels can communicate with devices faster, since modular kernels can talk to the hardware only indirectly through a module table. Unfortunately, monolithic Linux kernels are huge. Bigger kernels reduce available RAM. In addition, some systems just can't boot a kernel that's too large.

There used to be advantages to a monolithic kernel. Linux once had problems loading modular kernels for some hardware. With a monolithic kernel, the drivers would already be there. But now modular kernels load new drivers a lot more reliably.

A modular kernel has greater flexibility. You can compile almost all your drivers as modules, and then each module can be inserted into the kernel whenever you need it. Modules keep the initial kernel size low, which decreases the boot time and improves overall performance. If Linux has trouble loading a kernel module, you can use the **modprobe** or **insmod** commands to load modules as needed.

Updating the Kernel

Updating the kernel is not as difficult as it looks. You should always keep a copy of your old kernel around in case you make a mistake. New kernels are handled by installing the newly built kernel in /boot and then adding another boot option to your boot loader configuration file (/etc/grub.conf or /etc/lilo.conf) for the new kernel. GRUB or LILO treats the new kernel as if it were an entirely new operating system.

If you install the new kernel directly from a Red Hat configured RPM, it updates your boot loader automatically.

If you do make a drastic mistake and the kernel doesn't boot, then you can simply reboot the server and select your old kernel at the GRUB or LILO prompt. You should also save your kernel configuration files so that you can easily copy to the newer kernels and use them as a guideline. This will be discussed in more detail later in this chapter.

Other RHEL 3 Kernels

There are a number of different kernels included with the RHEL 3 installation files. You can and should install the kernel best suited to your system. I briefly describe available RHEL 3 kernels in Table 5-1. The "EL" in each of these kernels refers to their customization for Red Hat Enterprise Linux. The version numbers shown is what was released with RHEL 3. If you've used the Red Hat update agent, your kernel version number may vary.

| TABLE 5-1 | Available Red Hat Enterprise Linux 3 Kernels (and Related Packages) |

Kernel RPM	Description
kernel-2.4.21-4.EL.athlon.rpm	Suitable for PCs with a single AMD Athlon CPU.
kernel-2.4.21-4.EL.i686.rpm	Designed for PCs with a single Intel CPU.
kernel-unsupported-2.4.21-4.EL.athlon.rpm	The Athlon kernel with additional unsupported modules.
kernel-unsupported-2.4.21-4.EL.i686.rpm	The Intel kernel with additional unsupported modules.
kernel-BOOT-2.4.21-4.EL.i386.rpm	Kernel used only during the RHEL 3 installation process.
kernel-hugemem-2.4.21-4.EL.i686.rpm	Supports multiple CPUs and systems with more than 4GB of RAM.

| TABLE 5-1 | Available Red Hat Enterprise Linux 3 Kernels (and Related Packages) *(continued)* |

Kernel RPM	Description
kernel-hugemem-unsupported-2.4.21-4.EL.i686.rpm	The *hugemem* kernel configured with additional untested kernel modules.
kernel-pcmcia-cs-3.1.31-13.i386.rpm	Adds PCMCIA (PC Card) modules to your current kernel.
kernel-smp-2.4.21-4.EL.athlon.rpm	The symmetric multiprocessing (SMP) kernel suitable for multi-CPU AMD Athlon systems. Also supports more than 4GB of RAM.
kernel-smp-2.4.21-4.EL.i386.rpm	The symmetric multiprocessing (SMP) kernel suitable for multi-CPU Intel systems. Also supports more than 4GB of RAM.
kernel-smp-unsupported-2.4.21-4.EL.athlon.rpm	The SMP kernel with additional untested kernel modules for Athlon CPUs.
kernel-smp-unsupported-2.4.21-4.EL.i386.rpm	The SMP kernel with additional untested kernel modules for Intel CPUs.
kernel-source-2.4.21-4.EL.i386.rpm	Includes the source code for the RHEL 3 kernel.

This is just a short list of kernels available for RHEL 3. As the Red Hat exams assume the use of standard PCs with a single CPU, I've limited the list in Table 5-1 to such kernels. For more information on RHEL 3 kernels available for multi-CPU or higher-end CPUs, refer to the RHEL 3 documentation available online from www.redhat.com/docs/manuals/enterprise/.

The /boot Partition

The Linux kernel is stored in the partition with the /boot directory. New kernels must also be transferred to this directory. By default, RHEL 3 configures a partition of about 100MB for this directory. This provides enough room for your current kernel plus several additional upgraded kernels.

The /proc Filesystem

The /proc directory is based on a virtual filesystem; in other words, it does not include any files that are stored on the hard drive. But it is a window into what the kernel sees of your computer. It's a good idea to study the files and directories in /proc, as it can help

A Red Hat Enterprise Linux 3 /proc directory

```
[root@Enterprise3 root]# \ls /proc/
1       1880  1950  2159  2245  2762  devices      ksyms     stat
1175    1903  1960  2170  2246  3     dma          loadavg   swaps
1182    1907  1969  2171  2254  4     driver       locks     sys
16      1908  1999  2174  2256  5     execdomains  mdstat    sysrq-trigger
1655    1909  2     2191  2261  6     fb           meminfo   sysvipc
1659    1910  2008  2216  2365  7     filesystems  misc      tty
1685    1911  2022  2218  2420  74    fs           modules   uptime
17      1912  2023  2223  2485  8     ide          mounts    version
1704    1913  2024  2230  2586  9     interrupts   mtrr
1772    1914  2025  2234  2655  apm   iomem        net
18      1915  2026  2236  2713  bus   ioports      partitions
1811    1916  2027  2238  2714  cmdline  irq       pci
1851    1922  2028  2241  2715  cpuinfo  kcore     self
1865    1941  2085  2243  2749  crypto   kmsg      slabinfo
[root@Enterprise3 root]# []
```

you diagnose a wide range of problems. Figure 5-6 shows the /proc from a typical RHEL 3 computer.

The numbered items are based on process IDs. For example, the process ID of init is 1. The files in this directory include the memory segments that make up the active process. The contents of each of these files include the active memory for that process.

The other items in the listing are files and directories that correspond to configuration information for components such as DMA channels or whole subsystems such as memory information.

Take a look at some of these files. For example, the /proc/meminfo file provides excellent information as to the state of memory on the local computer, as shown in Figure 5-7. It can help you determine if RHEL 3 is having trouble detecting all of the memory on your computer.

It can also help you measure the current memory state of your system. For example, if your system is overloaded, you'll probably find very little free swap space. The HugePage settings are associated with systems with over 4GB of RAM.

Now you can examine how Linux looks at your CPU in the /proc/cpuinfo file, as shown in Figure 5-8. In this particular case, the cpu family information is important; the number 6 in this figure corresponds to a 686 CPU. Some of this information is available through the **top** utility.

Many programs are available that simply look at the information stored in /proc and interpret it in a more readable format. The **top** utility is a perfect example. It reads the process table, queries RAM and swap usage and the level of CPU use, and presents it all on one screen.

FIGURE 5-7

Detected
memory
information

```
[root@Enterprise3 root]# cat /proc/meminfo
              total:    used:     free:  shared: buffers:  cached:
Mem:    128675840 126464000  2211840        0 14028800 63885312
Swap: 394805248 31461376 363343872
MemTotal:         125660 kB
MemFree:            2160 kB
MemShared:             0 kB
Buffers:           13700 kB
Cached:            51304 kB
SwapCached:        11084 kB
Active:            87704 kB
ActiveAnon:        49664 kB
ActiveCache:       38040 kB
Inact_dirty:           0 kB
Inact_laundry:     18908 kB
Inact_clean:        2208 kB
Inact_target:      21764 kB
HighTotal:             0 kB
HighFree:              0 kB
LowTotal:         125660 kB
LowFree:            2160 kB
SwapTotal:        385552 kB
SwapFree:         354828 kB
HugePages_Total:       0
HugePages_Free:        0
Hugepagesize:       4096 kB
[root@Enterprise3 root]# []
```

IP Forwarding

More importantly, there are kernel variables you can alter to change the way the kernel behaves while it's running. Sometimes it's appropriate to configure a Linux computer as a router between networks. By default, it does not forward TCP/IP information. You can confirm it with the following command:

```
# cat /proc/sys/net/ipv4/ip_forward
0
```

If your computer has two or more network cards, you may want to activate *IP forwarding* with the following command:

```
# echo 1 >> /proc/sys/net/ipv4/ip_forward
# cat /proc/sys/net/ipv4/ip_forward
1
```

FIGURE 5-8	Detected CPU information

```
processor       : 0
vendor_id       : GenuineIntel
cpu family      : 6
model           : 11
model name      : Intel(R) Pentium(R) III Mobile CPU        1200MHz
stepping        : 1
cpu MHz         : 1193.582
cache size      : 512 KB
fdiv_bug        : no
hlt_bug         : no
f00f_bug        : no
coma_bug        : no
fpu             : yes
fpu_exception   : yes
cpuid level     : 2
wp              : yes
flags           : fpu vme de pse tsc msr pae mce cx8 sep mtrr pge mca cmov pat pse
36 mmx fxsr sse
bogomips        : 2365.84

~
~
~
~
~
~
~
"/proc/cpuinfo" [readonly] 19L, 402C                      19,0-1        All
```

Preventing the Ping of Death

The following is another useful change to a proc kernel variable, which enables the use of TCP SYN packet cookies. These cookies prevent SYN flood attacks on your system, including the so-called "ping of death."

```
# echo 1 >> /proc/sys/net/ipv4/tcp_syncookies
```

Managing /proc Graphically

There is a Red Hat graphical tool that you can use to manage /proc directories. It's known as the Kernel Tuning tool, which you can start from a GUI command line with the **redhat-config-proc** command. For example, you can use it to set up IP Forwarding, as shown in Figure 5-9.

Tuning the kernel through /proc

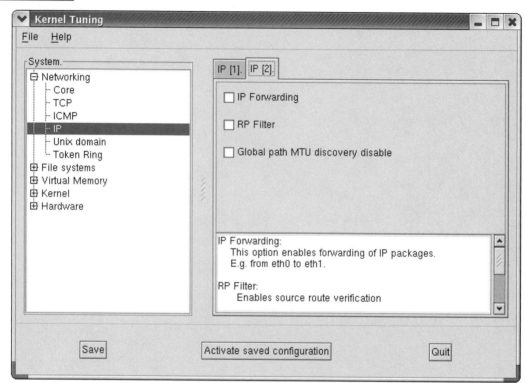

Understanding Kernel Modules

When you compile your kernel, you can set up a monolithic kernel with every driver that you might ever need. Unfortunately, such kernels are large, unwieldy, and take a lot of time to load. Generally, most Linux administrators use kernel modules. As described earlier, a *kernel module* is not compiled directly into the kernel but instead operates as a pluggable driver that can be loaded and unloaded into the kernel as needed.

e x a m
Ⓦatch   *If you're having problems*   *configuration utility. It is normally run*
with hardware related kernel modules,   *during the boot process, but you might*
one utility you can try is kudzu, the   *try running it again if you're having*
Red Hat hardware detection and   *a problem.*

To have the kernel dynamically load and unload kernel modules as needed, the kernel module loader, **kmod**, is used to control the loading and unloading of modules. For special parameters and options, edit the /etc/modules.conf file.

Most hardware modules are automatically detected. If you've just installed new undetected hardware, you could issue the following command:

```
# depmod -a
```

This will scan through your modules, find out what the different dependencies for all your modules are, and map them out to a file (modules.dep). This command also creates a number of other files in the /lib/modules/2.4.21-4.EL/ directory (if you've installed another kernel, the directory version changes accordingly).

RHEL 3 runs this command automatically through the /etc/rc.sysinit script. Once the **depmod** module scan is complete, you can load additional kernel modules. If that module has dependencies, then all the needed modules will automatically load first.

To load a module, you can use the **modprobe** command with the name of a specific driver:

```
# modprobe 3c503
```

In this example, the Ethernet module for a 3Com 503 network card requires the 8390 module to work properly. If **depmod** was run first, then 8390 would have loaded automatically before the 3c503 driver. If a dependency in the list fails during loading, then all modules will be automatically unloaded.

Alternatively, you can set up these modules in /etc/modules.conf. It should already be configured during the RHEL 3 installation process. Unfortunately, this work can be rather tedious. The following commands are accepted in this file:

- **alias**   Allows you to bind a name to a module.
- **options**   Allows you to specify options for a module.
- **install** *module command*   Use *command* instead of **insmod** on this module.
- **pre-install** *module command*   Run *command* before installing this module.
- **post-install** *module command*   Run *command* after installing this module.
- **remove** *module command*   Use *command* instead of **rmmod** on this module.
- **pre-remove** *module command*   Run *command* before loading this module.
- **post-remove** *module command*   Run *command* after loading this module.

Here is an example of what a common modules.conf file may look like:

```
alias eth0 pcnet32
alias usb-controller usb-uhci
options sb irq=5 io=0x220 dma=1
alias midi awe_wave
alias parport_lowlevel parport_pc
```

Here the eth0 device is bound to the pcnet32 module. To load the network card, you can then simply type **modprobe eth0** without knowing what card is in the computer. The next command sets the USB controller. The following two lines show the configuration of a soundblaster (sb) module. This information includes a specific IRQ port, I/O address, and DMA channel. The options line specifies these options and binds them to the sb alias. The sound card happens to be a Sound Blaster AWE 32 model card; therefore, the midi alias is bound to the awe_wave module. Finally, a parallel port module is bound to the parport_lowlevel alias.

The /etc/rc.sysinit script recognizes certain aliases and will load them if it finds them in this file. You need to specifically place the sound modules in modules.conf to have them automatically loaded. To have the sound modules automatically loaded during the Linux boot process without having to edit the /etc/rc.sysinit file, you can simply create an alias to sound and or midi in the modules.conf file.

To see what modules are loaded, you can type either

```
# cat /proc/modules
```

or

```
# lsmod
```

Both commands return output that looks something like the following:

```
Module              Size   Used by    Not tainted
nfs                92912   1   (autoclean)
ide-cd             35680   0   (autoclean)
cdrom              33696   0   (autoclean) [ide-cd]
smbfs              44528   1   (autoclean)
nfsd               85456   8   (autoclean)
lockd              59856   1   (autoclean) [nfs nfsd]
sunrpc             85692   1   (autoclean) [nfs nfsd lockd]
parport_pc         19076   1   (autoclean)
lp                  9028   0   (autoclean)
parport            37088   1   (autoclean) [parport_pc lp]
autofs             13364   0   (autoclean) (unused)
pcnet32            18080   1
```

```
mii                     3976   0   [pcnet32]
crc32                   3712   0   [pcnet32]
ipt_REJECT              4632   1   (autoclean)
ipt_state               1080   1   (autoclean)
ip_conntrack           27304   1   (autoclean) [ipt_state]
iptable_filter          2412   1   (autoclean)
ip_tables              15776   3   [ipt_REJECT ipt_state iptable_filter]
floppy                 58160   0   (autoclean)
microcode               4724   0   (autoclean)
keybdev                 2976   0   (unused)
mousedev                5524   1
hid                    22212   0   (unused)
input                   5888   0   [keybdev mousedev hid]
usb-uhci               26412   0   (unused)
usbcore                79392   1   [hid usb-uhci]
ext3                   91592   3
jbd                    52336   3   [ext3]
raid1                  14988   2
```

The module name is listed on the left, and its size is in the second column. The "Used by" column shows more detail on how the module is being handled. An autoclean message means that the kernel, using the kmod thread is taking care of the module and will handle removing it. If a module name, such as ext3, is listed in brackets, then the module depends on the module in brackets. In our example, jbd depends on the ext3 module.

The /lib/modules/kernel_version/ Directory Structure

All kernel modules are stored in the /lib/modules/*kernel_version*/ directory. When RHEL 3 is installed, *kernel_version*=2.4.21-4.EL. If you have recently compiled a new kernel and your modules are not loading properly, then you have probably forgotten to compile and install the modules. In the /usr/src/*kernel_version* source directory, run the following commands:

```
# make modules
# make modules_install
```

The first line compiles the modules, while the second places them under the proper directory tree. In this directory tree, different subdirectories represent different groupings. The following is a sample of a module directory:

```
# ls -l /lib/modules/2.4.21-4.EL/kernel/drivers
total 60
drwxr-xr-x     7 root      root          4096 Oct 23 15:22 addon
```

```
drwxr-xr-x    2 root     root         4096 Oct 23 15:22 block
drwxr-xr-x    2 root     root         4096 Oct 23 15:22 cdrom
drwxr-xr-x    8 root     root         4096 Oct 23 15:22 char
drwxr-xr-x    2 root     root         4096 Oct 23 15:22 ide
drwxr-xr-x    2 root     root         4096 Oct 23 15:22 input
drwxr-xr-x    2 root     root         4096 Oct 23 15:22 md
drwxr-xr-x    3 root     root         4096 Oct 23 15:22 message
drwxr-xr-x   10 root     root         4096 Oct 23 15:22 net
drwxr-xr-x    2 root     root         4096 Oct 23 15:22 parport
drwxr-xr-x    2 root     root         4096 Oct 23 15:22 pcmcia
drwxr-xr-x    5 root     root         4096 Oct 23 15:22 scsi
drwxr-xr-x    5 root     root         4096 Oct 23 15:22 sound
drwxr-xr-x    5 root     root         4096 Oct 23 15:22 usb
drwxr-xr-x    3 root     root         4096 Oct 23 15:22 video
```

Remember that each /lib/modules/*kernel_version* directory contains a modules.dep file that lists all the dependencies for all the modules within the directories. Each of these module directories includes a group of kernel modules for a common type of hardware. You might want to become familiar with where to find certain modules when needed. Here are some module types you can find under each directory:

- **addon**   High-end cards such as for server racks
- **block**   Block devices: parallel port ide drives, network block devices, XT disks, hardware raid devices
- **cdrom**   Non-ATAPI CD-ROM drivers: Mitsumi, Sony
- **char**   Miscellaneous input and serial devices
- **ide**   Hard disk drivers
- **input**   Input devices (keyboards, mice)
- **md**   raid devices
- **message**   Specialized I/O adapters
- **net**   Network modules: basic network cards, generic ppp, slip
- **parport**   Parallel port devices (not printers)
- **pcmcia**   Drivers used by the pcmcia cardmgr daemon (the actual cards use separate drivers)
- **scsi**   SCSI tape, RAID, and hard drive modules, video (special video modules for Linux)
- **sound**   Sound adapters

- **usb**   Universal Serial Bus hubs and devices
- **video**   Graphics adapters

All modules have .o for an extension (such as pcnet32.o). You do not need to specify the full name, just the first part of the module file (pcnet32). Once you know the directory structure, you can have the **modprobe** command load all modules for a certain category. For instance, if you are on a PC and you don't know the network card, you can simply type

```
modprobe -t net
```

This will attempt to load all modules in /lib/modules/*kernel_version*/net, stopping when a match is found. To remove a module such as pcnet32 and all its dependencies, you can type either

```
modprobe -r pcnet32
```

or

```
rmmod -r pcnet32
```

Either of these commands will remove the modules and all their dependencies, provided they are not in use by another module or not currently active. For example, if your network is active, you can't remove the network pcnet32 driver module. If you want to remove only the module and leave the other dependent drivers, run the **rmmod** command without the **-r** switch.

CERTIFICATION OBJECTIVE 5.04

New Kernels, the Easy Way

On the Red Hat exams, you may be expected to upgrade your kernel by installing the latest Red Hat kernel RPM. You may be able to patch an existing kernel. Whatever you do, you should make a boot disk associated with your new or upgraded kernel with the **mkbootdisk** command.

Before we begin, it's important to understand the way kernels are numbered.

Understanding Kernel Version Numbers

The version number associated with the RHEL 3 kernel may look a little confusing, but it tells you a lot about the history of the kernel. The standard RHEL 3 kernel is version 2.4.21-4.EL, formatted in a *majorversion.majorrevision.patch-build* format.

The first number (2) is the major version number. These are drastic changes to the kernel. Typically, older version software will *not* work in the newer version when this number changes. Kernel major version numbers are reserved for completely new kernel designs.

The second number (4) actually has two meanings. First, it indicates this is the fourth major revision of major version 2 of the kernel. Second, since it is an even number, it indicates that the kernel release is a stable release. If it were an odd number, it would be a developmental kernel, not suitable for production computers.

on the **Job**

While Linux kernel 2.6 has been officially released, Red Hat has already incorporated a number of associated features in the RHEL 3 kernel. To promote stability, Red Hat has no plans as of this writing to incorporate or offer a version of Linux kernel 2.6 for RHEL 3. This is consistent with the demands of the RHEL 3 customer base; most business customers want to stay away from the "bleeding edge."

The third number (21) is the patch version number for the kernel. These changes are typically small changes, bug fixes, security fixes, and enhancements. Generally, you can use the **zcat** command to increment one patch at a time. For example, if your current kernel is version 2.4.21, you can use the patch-2.4.22.gz file to upgrade your kernel to version 2.4.22.

The fourth number (-4.EL) is a number added by Red Hat. This is the fourth Red Hat build of Linux kernel 2.4.21, which incorporates features customized for Red Hat Enterprise Linux.

Some Linux software, such as firewalls, are associated with a specific Linux kernel. The requirements are associated only with the first two major numbers. For example, the older **ipchains** firewall command works only with version 2.2 and later kernels. In contrast, the **iptables** firewall commands require version 2.4 and later kernels.

Upgrading Kernels

During the lifetime of RHEL 3, you may find a security advisory which strongly suggests that you upgrade your Linux kernel. In this case, a Red Hat kernel RPM will be available through the Red Hat Network.

Watch *You won't have access to* *Red Hat Network for updates. However,* *the Internet during the Red Hat exams, and* *you may still be required to install an* *therefore, you may not be able to get to the* *upgraded kernel.*

Upgrading a kernel from a Red Hat RPM is fairly easy. Basically, all you need to do is install the new kernel with the appropriate **rpm** command. When properly configured, the RPM automatically upgrades your default boot loader as well. For example, say you've just downloaded the 2.4.21-4.1.EL kernel RPM from one of the FTP servers with Red Hat RPMs to the /tmp directory.

Watch *If you're told to upgrade* *newer kernels allows you to use the older* *a new kernel, you'll probably use the* *kernel, in case the new kernel does not* *rpm -i kernel.rpm command, and not rpm* *work for you.* *-U kernel.rpm. Installing (and not upgrading)*

Be careful. Install (**-i**), don't upgrade (**-U**) your new kernel. Otherwise, if you have a problem, you won't be able to go back to the old working kernel. Installing (**-i**) a new kernel with a command such as:

```
# rpm -i /tmp/kernel-2.4.21-4.1.EL.i386.rpm
```

installs the kernel, initial RAM disk, System.map, and config files automatically in the /boot directory. In addition, the RPM automatically adds a new stanza to your boot loader configuration file. For GRUB, the file is /etc/grub.conf.

Watch *The /etc/grub.conf* *configuration file is linked to the actual* *GRUB configuration file, /boot/grub* */grub.conf. You can open either filename* *in the text editor of your choice.*

Kernel Patches

Sometimes, all you need is a simple patch to a kernel. Patches usually work fairly well if you're upgrading from one patch version to the next higher version, such as from 2.4.21 to 2.4.22.

Kernel patches are easily available from Internet sites such as ftp.kernel.org. For example, if you want to upgrade from kernel version 2.4.21 to kernel version 2.4.22, download the patch-2.4.22.gz file from the Internet. Copy the patch to the /usr/src directory. Move to that directory, and run a command similar to the following to make the upgrade:

```
# zcat patch-2.4.22.gz | patch -p0
```

If it doesn't work, you'll see files with a .rej extension somewhere in your kernel source tree. Use a command such as **find** to check for such files. If you don't find any of these files, you can proceed with the **make clean**, **make menuconfig**, and **make dep** commands as described in the next section.

on the

job

Generally, it may not be advisable to patch a Red Hat built kernel on your Red Hat systems. Different build versions of Red Hat Enterprise Linux kernels often incorporate changes that are part of generic Linux kernel patches.

mkbootdisk

The **mkbootdisk** utility creates a boot disk customized for your configuration. This is basically a rescue disk. After creating this disk, you can use it to simply boot your system, or you can type **rescue** at the boot prompt. Whenever you upgrade or install a new kernel, you should upgrade your boot disk. It's a simple command; in most cases, all you need to do is specify the version number associated with the desired kernel as follows:

```
# mkbootdisk 2.4.21-4.1EL
```

This command automatically takes the kernel with the specified version number from the /boot directory and writes it with appropriate configuration information to the first floppy drive, /dev/fd0. Table 5-2 lists several other options that may come in handy when using **mkbootdisk**.

Here is another example of the **mkbootdisk** command:

```
# mkbootdisk --device /dev/fd1 --verbose --noprompt 2.4.21-4.1.EL
```

| TABLE 5-2 | mkbootdisk Command Switches |

Command	Description
--device *device file*	Specifies where to put the image.
--mkinitrdargs *args*	Passes arguments to **mkinitrd**.
--noprompt	Won't prompt to insert a disk.
--verbose	Normally, **mkbootdisk** has no output. This option turns the output on.

This command creates a boot disk on the *second* floppy drive. It does not suppress output, nor does it prompt for a disk to be inserted. It uses kernel version 2.4.21-4.1.EL. When you boot Linux with this disk, you can use it as a rescue disk. Just type **linux rescue** at the boot prompt.

on the job *By default, the first floppy drive on a PC is associated with /dev/fd0; the second floppy drive is associated with /dev/fd1.*

exam watch *A significant portion of the practical exam tests your ability to recover a system that has failed in some way. While I am prohibited by the Red Hat non-disclosure agreement from providing the exact nature of the problems, I can say that being able to use rescue disks is a very important Linux administration skill.*

Updating Your Boot Loader

If properly configured, the Red Hat kernel that you install should automatically update your boot loader. But as a RHCT or RHCE, you need to know how to check. If the code described in this chapter has not been added, you'll need to know how.

Whether you're using GRUB or LILO, it is advisable to keep your old kernel in case something goes wrong. So you'll be adding a stanza to either /etc/grub.conf or /etc/lilo.conf. In either case, the changes that you'll make will be as if you're setting up two different operating systems.

Updating GRUB

Look at your /etc/grub.conf file. If you have Linux on your system and use GRUB, you should already have a stanza that points to the appropriate locations for your original

Linux kernel and Initial RAM disk. For example, here is an excerpt from my RHEL 3 /etc/grub.conf file (which includes a dual-boot configuration with Microsoft Windows):

```
title Red Hat Enterprise Linux ES (2.4.21-4.EL)
    root (hd0,0)
    kernel /vmlinuz-2.4.21-4.EL ro root=LABEL=/
    initrd /initrd-2.4.21-4.EL.img
title DOS
    rootnoverify (hd0,1)
    chainloader +1
```

In Red Hat Enterprise Linux, the vmlinuz and initrd files are already in the /boot directory. Since you've copied the revised kernels to the same directory, all you need is a second stanza that points to your revised files. When I revised my kernel earlier in this chapter, my EXTRAVERSION variable in /usr/src/linux-2.4/Makefile was -4.ELcustom. The changes are in bold:

```
title Red Hat Enterprise Linux ES (2.4.21-4.EL)
    root (hd0,0)
    kernel /vmlinuz-2.4.21-4.EL ro root=LABEL=/
    initrd /initrd-2.4.21-4.EL.img
title Red Hat Enterprise Linux ES (2.4.21-4.ELcustom)
    root (hd0,0)
    kernel /vmlinuz-2.4.21-4.ELcustom ro root=LABEL=/
    initrd /initrd-2.4.21-4.ELcustom.img
title DOS
    rootnoverify (hd0,1)
    chainloader +1
```

Since you don't need to load /etc/grub.conf into the MBR, no further action is required. The resulting GRUB menu looks like Figure 5-10. Note how the original kernel is set as the default. If you've watched closely, you'll note that in /etc/grub.conf, the value of **default** was changed from 0 to 1. If you want to set the default to the new kernel, change the value of **default** back to 0.

Updating LILO

Alternatively, if you're using LILO as a boot loader, you'll need to revise /etc/lilo.conf. Add a stanza that points to the new kernel. Take a look at the following excerpt from /etc/lilo.conf:

```
image=/boot/vmlinuz-2.4.21-4.EL
    label=linux
    initrd=/boot/initrd-2.4.21-4.EL
```

```
read-only
append="root=LABEL=/"
```

From this information, you can see that the original kernel is called vmlinuz-2.4.21-4.EL. Assume LILO resides on the MBR and controls the boot process.

Now add another stanza for the new kernel.

```
image=/boot/vmlinuz-2.4.21-4.EL
        label=linux
        initrd=/boot/initrd-2.4.21-4.EL
        read-only
        append="root=LABEL=/"
image=/boot/vmlinuz-2.4.21-4.ELcustom
        label=linux
        initrd=/boot/initrd-2.4.21-4.ELcustom
        read-only
        append="root=LABEL=/"
```

FIGURE 5-10   GRUB menu with original and recompiled kernels

Save this file, then run the **lilo -v** command. The output should resemble the following:

```
LILO version 21.4-4, Copyright (C) 1992-1998 Werner Almesberger
'lba32' extensions Copyright (C) 1999,2000 John Coffman

Reading boot sector from /dev/hda
Merging with /boot/boot.b
Mapping message file /boot/message
Boot image: /boot/vmlinuz-2.4.21-4.EL
Mapping RAM disk /boot/initrd-2.4.21-4.EL
Added linux *
Boot image: /boot/vmlinuz-2.4.21-4.ELcustom
Added newLinux
Backup copy of boot sector in /boot/boot.0300
Writing boot sector.
```

When you reboot, LILO will wait for you to enter a label, in this case, either linux or newLinux.

e x a m

w a t c h   *Although there are references to both GRUB and LILO in the RHCT and RHCE exam curricula, Red Hat is focusing on GRUB and has "deprecated" LILO. Therefore, I believe you can expect to work with GRUB on the Red Hat exams.*

CERTIFICATION OBJECTIVE 5.05

Kernel Sources

One of the strengths of Linux is the ease with which you can customize your kernel to precisely meet your needs. But before you can start this process, you need the Linux kernel source code.

While references to recompiling the kernel have been removed from the Red Hat exam requirements, you may still need to find kernel modules and configuration files, which I cover in this section.

e x a m

w a t c h   *Fortunately, the Red Hat exams no longer specify requirements to recompile the Linux kernel. Nevertheless, it is a very important skill for any Linux administrator.*

The Kernel Source Tree and Documentation

Once installed, you can easily access the kernel source code through the /usr/src/linux-2.4 directory. Installation procedures are addressed in the following sections. Once the source code is installed, the /usr/src directory should look similar to the following:

```
# ls -l /usr/src/
total 12
drwxr-xr-x   2 root   root   4096 Jan 24  2003 debug
lrwxrwxrwx   1 root   root     17 Oct 23 16:12 linux-2.4 -> linux-2.4.21-4.EL
drwxr-xr-x  16 root   root   4096 Nov  7 15:56 linux-2.4.21-4.EL
drwxr-xr-x   8 root   root   4096 Nov  9 12:13 redhat
```

In this case, the physical directory is /usr/src/linux-2.4.21-4.EL, and there is a soft link called linux-2.4 that points to this directory.

Periodically, you may wish to upgrade your kernel. If you use Red Hat sources, the new RPM packages should automatically update the symbolic link from /usr/src /linux-2.4 to the real directory with the new kernel's source code (for example, sym-link it to linux-2.4.21-4.1.EL). If necessary, you could perform the same action with the following command:

```
# ln -s linux-2.4.21-4.1.EL linux-2.4
```

The /usr/src/linux-2.4 directory on my RHEL 3 computer includes the following files and directories:

```
arch              Documentation   kernel        README
configs           drivers         lib           REPORTING-BUGS
COPYING           fs              MAINTAINERS   Rules.make
COPYING.modules   include         MAKEFILE      scripts
CREDITS           init            mm            tmp_include_depends
crypto            ipc             net
```

Begin your study of the current kernel with the README file. While the instructions in this chapter work with the current configuration of RHEL 3 on my computer, details can change from kernel to kernel. Also, examine the Documentation directory. It contains everything you need, from information on setting up symmetrical multiprocessors to serial consoles.

The other directories mainly contain source code, and you probably won't need to spend time examining those files (unless you *really* want to see how TCP/IP works). There is also a hidden file, .config, that may be present in this directory. I'll describe this file in more detail later in this chapter.

The Kernel RPMs

If you don't see the directories mentioned in the preceding section, then you haven't installed your Linux kernel's source code. There are two ways to install the source code for your RHEL 3 system. You could access the Red Hat RPMs from CD or a network source and install the kernel RPM. Alternatively, you could install the packages through the **redhat-config-packages** utility. The following example is based on an installation from the appropriate Red Hat Installation CD:

```
# mount /mnt/cdrom
# rpm -Uvh /mnt/cdrom/RedHat/RPMS/kernel-source-*
```

Depending on the packages you've specified when you installed RHEL 3, this may be all you need. However, this command may bring up some error messages similar to the following:

```
error: Failed dependencies:
       gcc >= 2.96-98 is needed by kernel-source-2.4.21-4.EL
```

which suggests that you need to install some other RPM packages, as described in the next section.

Required RPMs

In order to build a kernel from the source code, you need to ensure you have all the RPMs necessary, not only for the kernel, but also for the tools needed to build the kernel. You can check your system to ensure you have the RPM packages described in Table 5-3. Many of these packages have a number of other dependencies.

If not, mount the appropriate Red Hat installation CDs or network installation source and install the needed packages with the **rpm -Uvh *packagename*** command. If the revision associated with your package and architecture are different, revise the package names accordingly.

The packages shown in Table 5-3 end with an * because version numbers do change frequently. In any case, the objective is to install these packages. For example, in order to install the tk package from a mounted CD, all you need is the **rpm -Uvh /mnt/cdrom/RedHat/RPMS/tk-*** command.

However, you'll also need to install any related dependent packages. For example, the kernel-source-* RPM requires the appropriate GNU C Compiler, which is the gcc-* RPM.

TABLE 5-3	Kernel Source RPMs

Package	Description
kernel-source-*	Kernel source files
glibc-kernheaders-*	Kernel header files
glibc-devel-*	Required for C libraries
cpp-*	C language preprocessor
ncurses-*	Required for menuconfig screen
ncurses-devel-*	Development libraries for ncurses
binutils-*	Required binary utilities
gcc-*	C language compiler
tcl-*	TCL scripting language—required for xconfig screen
tk-*	TK X Window widgets—required for xconfig screen

on the **Job**   *Wildcards such as an * are often also known as globbing.*

GUI Kernel Source Management

It can take time to load all of the RPMs required to compile and customize the Linux kernel. It can be difficult to remember to install every RPM. There is an alternative: the Red Hat Package Management utility. I'll show you how to use this tool to load the kernel source packages in Exercise 5-3.

EXERCISE 5-3

Loading the Kernel Source Graphically

In this exercise, we'll install the source code and associated files for the Linux kernel using the Red Hat Package Management utility. I'll assume that you're using the same network source that you created in Chapter 2. This exercise assumes that network source is on a remote computer with an IP address of 192.168.30.4. Substitute the IP address (or if you have a DNS server for your LAN, the hostname) for your network source computer. You'll need to start from the Linux GUI.

1. If you're not already in the Linux GUI, run the **startx** command.

2. Open a command line interface. Right-click on the desktop, and click New Terminal in the pop-up menu that appears.

3. At the command line interface, make a connection to the network source. I'm assuming that you have an active NFS connection, no firewall, and a local /mnt/inst directory. For the given source, run the following command (substitute your IP address or hostname, and preferred mount directory in this command):

   ```
   # mount -t nfs 192.168.30.4:/mnt/inst /mnt/inst
   ```

4. Start the Package Management utility. Point to the mounted network source (without the --tree option, the Package Management utility works from the installation CDs):

   ```
   # redhat-config-packages --tree=/mnt/inst
   ```

5. Select the Kernel Development package group for installation.

6. Click Update. The Package Management utility computes the dependencies, adding RPMs to the list of packages to be installed.

7. Once you see the Completed System Preparation window, click Continue.

8. The Package Management utility starts installing the packages you need to examine the source code and recompile the Linux kernel.

9. When installation is complete, click OK.

10. Click Quit to exit from the Package Management utility.

The Linux Kernel tar File

Alternatively, you can download the newest kernel from the Linux kernel home page at www.kernel.org. The version numbers are discussed in the next section. Once you have downloaded the kernel source, you will need to properly install it. For our example, we will assume you downloaded linux-2.4.22.tar.gz into the /usr/src/ directory.

```
# cd /usr/src
# mkdir linux-2.4.22
# rm linux-2.4
```

```
# tar xzvf linux-2.4.22.tar.gz
# ln -s linux-2.4.22 linux-2.4
```

Here we manually created a new directory for the kernel, removed the old link, and then uncompressed the tar.gz file. Then you can link linux-2.4 to the new directory created when you uncompress the tar.gz file.

on the job *Compressed tar files are shown in tar.gz format; they are also known as "tarballs."*

CERTIFICATION OBJECTIVE 5.06

Recompiling a Kernel

Fortunately, references to recompiling the Linux kernel have been removed from the Red Hat exam requirements. However, RHCEs in the real world are expected to know how to perform high-level tasks such as optimizing and recompiling the Linux kernel.

In this section, we'll start by looking at the kernel configuration file. Then we'll proceed with the different tools available to edit the kernel configuration. Finally, I'll show you the commands needed to compile your new configuration into the kernel, and show you the files this adds to the /boot directory and the settings it adds to the boot loader.

exam watch *References to recompiling the Linux kernel have been removed from the Red Hat Exam Prep guide and associated Red Hat prep courses. However, good Linux administrators know how to recompile the Linux kernel.*

The Kernel Configuration Scripts

After you've configured a kernel once, the configuration information is stored in a hidden file, /usr/src/linux-2.4/.config. It is structured as a listing of variables. Here are some entries from the .config file:

```
CONFIG_NETDEVICES=y
CONFIG_DUMMY=m
# CONFIG_SUNLANCE is not set
```

As you can see, there are three main types of variables in this file. The first command here compiles in direct support, the second entry compiles support as a module (the "m"), and the third is commented out, and is therefore not compiled into the kernel at all. You should never have to edit this file directly, as there are easier ways to configure your kernel.

Move to the directory with your kernel source files. If you've installed the RHEL 3 kernel-source RPM, you can use the /usr/src/linux-2.4 directory. If you've installed the latest kernel from www.kernel.org, it may be in the /usr/src/linux directory. Three tools can help you configure the kernel configuration file: **make config**, **make menuconfig**, and **make xconfig**.

Back Up Your Configuration

The default configuration for your current Linux kernel is stored in the /boot directory. For the default RHEL 3 system, it's stored in the config-2.4.21-4.EL file. Back up this file on another location such as a rescue floppy so that you can restore your current kernel configuration if all else fails.

You can use your current configuration as a baseline; the Linux kernel configuration tools will start with these settings. To do so with the current kernel, run the following command:

```
# cp   /boot/config-2.4.21-4.EL   /usr/src/linux-2.4/.config
```

Alternatively, there are a number of standard configuration files in the /usr/src/linux-2.4 /configs directory. If you want to start with one of these files, use the config file that corresponds most closely to your hardware. You can set that as the starting point for your configuration by copying it to the /usr/src/linux-2.4/.config file.

There is a default kernel configuration file in the /usr/src/linux-2.4/configs directory. It's associated with your CPU hardware; for example, if you have an Athlon CPU, you'll find it in a file named kernel-2.4.21-athlon.config. If your kernel version is different, the number changes accordingly.

make config

Once you're in the directory with the kernel source files (/usr/src/linux-2.4), you can call a simple script to configure a new kernel with the following command:

```
# make config
```

This script will prompt you through your different options. Figure 5-11 shows an excerpt from the output for this script.

FIGURE 5-11   Questions from the **make config utility**

```
( cd include ; ln -sf asm-i386 asm)
/bin/sh scripts/Configure arch/i386/config.in
#
# Using defaults found in .config
#
*
* Code maturity level options
*
Prompt for development and/or incomplete code/drivers (CONFIG_EXPERIMENTAL) [Y/n
/?]
*
* Loadable module support
*
Enable loadable module support (CONFIG_MODULES) [Y/n/?]
  Set version information on all module symbols (CONFIG_MODVERSIONS) [Y/n/?]
  Kernel module loader (CONFIG_KMOD) [Y/n/?]
*
* Processor type and features
*
Processor family (386, 486, 586/K5/5x86/6x86/6x86MX, Pentium-Classic, Pentium-MM
X, Pentium-Pro/Celeron/Pentium-II, Pentium-III/Celeron(Coppermine), Pentium-4, K
6/K6-II/K6-III, Athlon/Duron/K7, Opteron/Athlon64/Hammer/K8, Elan, Crusoe, Winch
ip-C6, Winchip-2, Winchip-2A/Winchip-3, CyrixIII/VIA-C3, VIA-C3-2) [Pentium-Pro/
Celeron/Pentium-II]
```

Here the kernel variables are listed in parentheses and the possible answers are in brackets. The default answer is in capital letters. If you type in a ?, you will see a help page explaining this option. Since several hundred questions are associated with this script, most administrators use one of the other two scripts to manage their Linux kernels.

make menuconfig

A nicer way to create the .config file is to use the **make menuconfig** command. This requires the ncurses RPM package. This opens a text-based, menu-driven system that classifies and organizes the changes that you can make to a kernel. Figure 5-12 illustrates the main menu associated with this command.

The nice thing about **menuconfig** is that it works very nicely over a remote text connection from other Linux computers (or perhaps that is dangerous!). Also, options appear at the bottom of the menu to load or save the configuration file from a different location.

FIGURE 5-12 The **make menuconfig** configuration menu

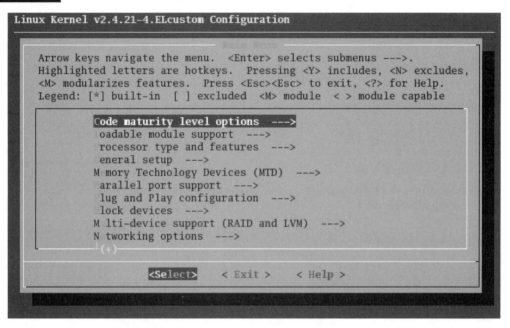

```
Linux Kernel v2.4.21-4.ELcustom Configuration

                              Main Menu
 Arrow keys navigate the menu.  <Enter> selects submenus --->.
 Highlighted letters are hotkeys.  Pressing <Y> includes, <N> excludes,
 <M> modularizes features.  Press <Esc><Esc> to exit, <?> for Help.
 Legend: [*] built-in  [ ] excluded  <M> module  < > module capable

              Code maturity level options  --->
              Loadable module support  --->
              Processor type and features  --->
              General setup  --->
            M mory Technology Devices (MTD)  --->
              Parallel port support  --->
              Plug and Play configuration  --->
              Block devices  --->
            M lti-device support (RAID and LVM)  --->
            N tworking options  --->
                  (+)

              <Select>     < Exit >     < Help >
```

make xconfig

The other way to make changes to the kernel is to use the X Window System. You can generate a graphical menu system to configure your kernel by running the **make xconfig** command. Figure 5-13 shows the **xconfig** main menu. You can also use **xconfig** to load or save the configuration from the file of your choice.

While this menu may look slightly different in different Linux distributions, the principles and basic options remain fairly constant. Each of the Kernel Configuration Options discussed on the following pages are presented for completeness. It is important for a Linux administrator to have a detailed understanding of the hows and whys about reconfiguring and recompiling the kernel.

FIGURE 5-13   The **make xconfig** configuration menu

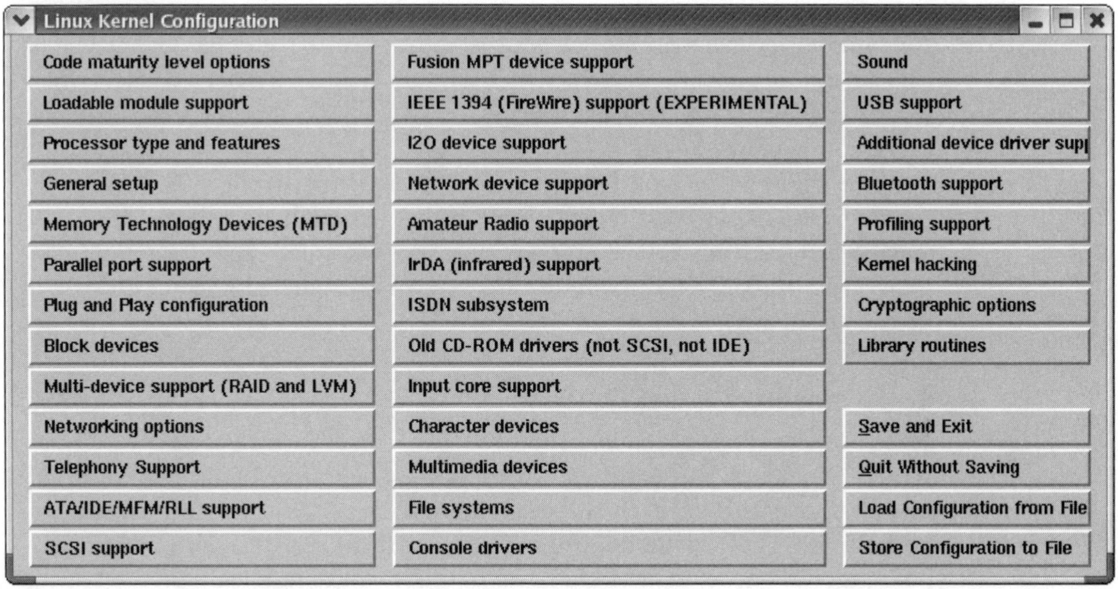

Code maturity level options	Fusion MPT device support	Sound
Loadable module support	IEEE 1394 (FireWire) support (EXPERIMENTAL)	USB support
Processor type and features	I2O device support	Additional device driver sup|
General setup	Network device support	Bluetooth support
Memory Technology Devices (MTD)	Amateur Radio support	Profiling support
Parallel port support	IrDA (infrared) support	Kernel hacking
Plug and Play configuration	ISDN subsystem	Cryptographic options
Block devices	Old CD-ROM drivers (not SCSI, not IDE)	Library routines
Multi-device support (RAID and LVM)	Input core support	
Networking options	Character devices	Save and Exit
Telephony Support	Multimedia devices	Quit Without Saving
ATA/IDE/MFM/RLL support	File systems	Load Configuration from File
SCSI support	Console drivers	Store Configuration to File

Understanding Kernel Configuration Options

To configure a kernel, you need to understand some of the main kernel configuration options. Each of the aforementioned kernel configuration tools includes help menus for just about every available option.

The Basic Kernel Configuration

If you're asked to change a setting such as CONFIG_EXPERIMENTAL, you don't have to search through different menus. You can find the governing menu using the information in the /boot/config-2.4.21-4.EL configuration file. As you can see in the file:

```
# Code maturity level options
#
CONFIG_EXPERIMENTAL=y
```

The CONFIG_EXPERIMENTAL variable can be found under the Code Maturity Level Options menu.

The Standard Red Hat Kernel Configuration

The standard RHEL 3 Linux kernel supports a wide variety of hardware and software. Almost every module that could be made is made. This is a big kernel, and numerous modules can be used for it with the standard installation. This is not a problem when you install RHEL 3, but it is highly recommended you streamline the standard kernel and remove unwanted modules.

In the following sections, I describe the different kernel configuration menus, section by section. However, since it appears that recompiling the kernel is no longer a requirement on the Red Hat exams, I do not provide any screenshots of additional menus. If you're interested in this level of detail, follow along on your Red Hat computer.

Code Maturity Level Options

The Code Maturity Level options allow you to incorporate experimental code in the kernel. Common examples include drivers for new hardware, esoteric filesystems, and network protocols. Experimental code is often also known as alpha level software. If you have obsolete code that you want to incorporate into your kernel, it also falls in this category, as newer kernels often omit support for older features.

The one option relates to the CONFIG_EXPERIMENTAL variable. It's enabled by default in RHEL 3.

Loadable Modules Support Options

The Loadable Module Support screen allows you to enable loadable modules. The kernel module loader will automatically load modules for most new hardware, when detected. As discussed earlier, loadable modules allow you to optimize the kernel. If you want to optimize the kernel, keep all of the options on this screen active.

Processor Type and Features

The Processor Type and Features menu in RHEL 3 supports a wide variety of CPUs.

General Setup Options

The General Setup Options menu includes some basic hardware and kernel configuration options. Many of these options are self-explanatory, and the defaults are generally acceptable. If you need more information, click the Help button associated with a specific kernel option.

On a network, you want networking support. Most computers have PCI cards, and the defaults give you full PCI support, using BIOS detection, documenting the detected cards in the /proc directory. Various types of hot-pluggable devices are now popular, including PCMCIA cards for laptops and PCI hotplug support for removable drives.

The System V IPC, BSD Process Accounting, and Sysctrl support parameters are all standard for current kernels. While Linux kernels are normally associated with ELF binaries, the other binaries may help with certain programs.

Memory Technology Devices

The options shown in the Memory Technology Devices menu allow you to set up Linux for basic "Flash" memory cards, including those that might be installed through a PCMCIA adapter. Unless you're planning to use some of these devices in the future, keep this option disabled.

Parallel Port Support

The options shown in the Parallel Port support menu are based on hardware that may be connected to your computer through a parallel port. This includes everything from printers through parallel port hard drives. Remember that it is normally best to avoid the Experimental options unless you are a developer working on supporting the associated drivers.

Plug and Play Configuration

The options shown under the Plug and Play Configuration menu activate basic plug and play support on your Linux computer. Generally, you should keep the defaults. While Linux plug and play does not handle all ISA and PCI devices, it does help you configure your computer for Linux.

Block Device Options

Under the Block Device Options menu, you can specify your floppy devices and nonstandard hard disks. You can specify support for parallel port ATAPI CD-ROMs, tape drives, and even ATAPI floppy drives. You can also enable loopback support and network block support (which lets you use a physical disk on the network as if it were a local disk). If you have any parallel port devices such as external CD-ROMs or hard drives, you could enable support for those here. You can also set up support for RAM disks under this menu.

Multidevice Support for RAID and LVM

If you're ever going to set up a RAID array of disks to help protect your data, you can enable that option in the Linux kernel under the Multidevice Support for RAID and LVM menu. If you ever want to put together a volume set, where a directory can span more than one partition on more than one physical hard disk, you can enable that option here as well.

While there is support for RAID-4 in the Linux kernel, it is not directly supported by RHEL 3 or currently available versions of Red Hat or Fedora Linux.

Networking Options

There are many options for networking in the Linux kernel. The Networking Options menu is extensive. It includes a substantial number of settings for different hardware devices, software settings, and more.

Telephony Support

Telephony support on a computer network uses special network cards to convert voice into the type of data that can be sent over a network. Linux offers some limited telephony support through the kernel as shown under the menu of the same name.

ATA/IDE/MFM/RLL Support

These acronyms all relate to various types of regular PC hard disk and CD drive interfaces. Normally, you shouldn't disable this kernel option unless all hard disk storage on your system is based on a SCSI interface. Even then, the flexibility of being able to install IDE devices is usually worth the extra code this adds to the kernel.

SCSI Support Options and Low-Level Drivers

You can enable SCSI hard disks, tape drivers, and CD-ROM support in this section. If you have a SCSI CD-ROM jukebox, or any other device that requires more than one SCSI Logical Unit Number (LUN), you may have to enable probing of all LUNs.

Near the bottom of the menu, you can configure verbose SCSI error reporting. You can also enable specific low-level SCSI support. Red Hat includes support for high-end hardware RAID-enabled SCSI host adapters, including 64-bit PCI adapters.

Fusion MPT Device Support

This menu supports modules associated with very high speed SCSI adapters, associated with hardware developed by LSI logic.

IEEE 1394 Support

The IEEE 1394 standard is more popularly known as FireWire or iLink. It's basically a very high speed hot plug and play hardware option, with data transfer speeds in the hundreds of Mbps. Linux support for IEEE 1394 standards is far from complete. Kernel support for any IEEE 1394 device is currently officially experimental. However, support for IEEE devices such as external hard drives are readily available, and configured as modules by default in RHEL 3.

I2O Device Support

The I2O specification, also known as Intelligent I/O, supports split drivers which can optimize communication performance between a device and the rest of your computer. Don't enable I2O haphazardly; it requires hardware that supports it.

Network Device Support

Linux supports a wide range of network cards. The Network Device Support menu allows you to enable support for the adapters you may need. Generally, you should enable support for only network devices that you're using now or may use in the future.

Amateur Radio Support

Linux supports connections to various amateur radios. Unless you plan to connect your computer to an amateur radio station in the future, there is no need to enable support for any of these devices.

IrDA Support

Linux supports Infrared connections, mostly for network support. The IrLAN protocol supports wireless access points. The IrNET protocol requires PPP. The IrCOMM protocol sets up port emulation, useful for setting up terminals and printers. For a list of supported infrared-port device drivers, click that button and activate the devices that you need.

ISDN Options

Integrated Services Digital Networks (ISDN) lines are a fairly popular high-speed digital option, especially outside of North America. Adding ISDN support allows you to use an ISDN card for inbound or outbound dialing connections. The ISDN device has a built-in AT-compatible modem emulator, autodial, channel-bundling, callback, and caller authentication without the need for an external daemon to be running. Under the ISDN Options menu, you can enable synchronous Point-to-Point Protocol (PPP) connections. The supporting isdn4k-utils RPM is installed by default on RHEL 3.

Older CD-ROM Support Options

If you have an older CD-ROM that is not an IDE or SCSI CD-ROM, then you need to enable special support for it in the Linux kernel, as shown when you click the "Old CD-ROM drivers (not SCSI, not IDE)" option. This section has many drivers for Mitsumi, Goldstar, Philips, Sony, Sound Blaster, and other old CD-ROM and disk types.

Input Core Support

The Input Core Support section configures support for various basic input devices: keyboards, mice, and joysticks. These devices are modular by default, which allows Linux to recognize these basic devices using plug and play detection.

Character Device Options

Character devices send their data in byte streams. Typical character devices range from serial ports to virtual consoles. The Character Devices submenu allows you to specify support for a wide variety of devices, including virtual terminals, serial ports, newer AGP video cards, mice, joysticks, non-SCSI tape drives, and more.

Multimedia Devices

The Multimedia Devices options support a wide range of video capture and AM/FM radio devices. Click each option (Video for Linux, Radio Adapters) for a list of drivers which you can enable. As always, it is best to keep what you enable to a minimum.

Filesystem Options

The File Systems subsection is a list of all the different types of filesystems Linux supports. Select the Quota option if you need to support quotas. You can also compile in the kernel Automounter to support remote filesystems.

Because Linux supports so many different hardware platforms, it includes support for a large number of filesystem types. However, because of the proprietary nature of some filesystems, the degree of support is variable. You'll note that support for a lot of filesystems in this menu is experimental; in fact, support for writing to NTFS filesystems may be dangerous!

Console Driver Options

Linux supports console drivers, which can set up text on most graphics systems, even when Linux doesn't detect the right cards or monitors. The Frame Buffer Support option supports video adapters that store images in frame buffers.

Sound System Support Options

A wide variety of sound cards are supported by RHEL 3, normally as modules. These cards range from the Ensoniq Audio PCI card to TV card mixers. You can also use these drivers for cards that emulate the appropriate hardware. Check the Sound submenu for the latest list of supported hardware for your kernel. If you have a card not named in the previous list, try to see if it emulates any card on the list. Many proprietary cards do emulate products from Sound Blaster or offer OPL/2 or OPL/3 compatibility.

USB Support

Linux supports a number of USB mass storage devices, input devices, printers, cameras and scanners, and even modems. Linux support for USB networking cards is still officially experimental. Linux support for USB is improving, although some USB drivers that you'll see in the USB support menu are still considered experimental as well. Unfortunately, this includes support for faster USB 2.0 standard drivers.

Additional Device Driver Support

As befits the name, the Additional Device Driver support menu allows you to configure the Linux kernel for a variety of hardware devices. These devices range from Gigabit Ethernet adapters to Storage Area Network devices.

Bluetooth Support

Bluetooth is a radio technology for short-range networks. You can configure a number of Bluetooth devices in the Linux kernel.

Profiling Support

Profiling support allows you to use the OProfile system to characterize the performance of your system. It is described in more detail at oprofile.sourceforge.net.

Kernel Hacking

Kernel hacking allows you to use the drivers you need to debug driver or related Linux kernel issues.

Cryptographic Options

The Cryptographic options support software associated with strong encryption in Linux. It's disabled by default in RHEL 3.

Library Routines

The Library Routines support compression in Linux. Unlike for Red Hat Linux 9, they are enabled by default for RHEL 3.

Compiling and Installing a Custom Kernel

After setting up all the options you want from one of the Kernel configuration programs, make sure to save your changes. The changes are saved in the appropriate .config file. Next, you can compile your kernel. Compiling a new kernel can be a long and tedious process. The following is a list of things you should do to successfully compile your kernel—*in order*:

1. If you haven't already done so, create a custom boot floppy disk with the following command. Test the floppy that's created.

   ```
   # mkbootdisk `uname -r`
   ```

2. Run the **cd /usr/src/linux-2.4** command to reach the proper directory. You'll need to run your commands to modify and compile the kernel in this directory. This assumes that you've installed the appropriate kernel-source RPM. In RHEL 3, this directory is linked to the directory with the source code, /usr/src/linux-2.4.21-4.EL.

3. Open /usr/src/linux-2.4/Makefile in a text editor. In RHEL 3, the EXTRAVERSION variable is already set to identify a custom kernel.

If necessary, change the value of this variable to uniquely identify your kernel. Record the value of this variable.

```
EXTRAVERSION= -4.ELcustom
```

4. Save your current kernel configuration file. It's stored in the /boot directory. For RHEL 3, it's the /boot/config-2.4.21-4.EL file. Have it ready with a rescue floppy in case disaster strikes. Copy it to the /usr/src/linux-2.4/.config file.

   a. Alternatively, you can start from a standard configuration file in the /usr /src/linux-2.4/configs/ directory. You can also run the **make oldconfig** command.

5. Run the **make mrproper** command to ensure your source files are in a consistent and clean state.

6. Now you can customize your kernel with one of the following three utilities: the **make config** command runs the text-based configuration script; the **make menuconfig** command runs a low-level graphical configuration script; and the **make xconfig** command starts the X Window System configuration tool.

7. Make any changes as required by your hardware and/or the RHCE exam. Before you exit from the kernel configuration utility, make sure to save your changes!

8. The **make dep** command will set up all your dependencies correctly. This takes the settings from /usr/src/linux-2.4/.config and pushes them down into the correct source code subdirectory. This will take some time, as there are nearly 1,500 possible kernel settings on a RHEL 3 system!

on the *job*

*The make dep **process took about 20 minutes on my computer with a 1.2GHz CPU.***

9. Run the **make clean** command to prepare the source code directories to build your new kernel.

10. The **make bzImage** command compiles the kernel and creates a gzip compressed kernel image file.

on the *job*

*The make bzImage **process took about 20 minutes on my computer with a 1.2GHz CPU.***

11. Now you need to build your modules (you did include kernel module support, didn't you?). Use **make modules** to build all your modules.

The make modules *process took about 50 minutes on my computer with a I.2GHz CPU.*

12. Now you need to install your newly made modules, which will install all your loadable modules into a new subdirectory of the /lib/modules/*kernelversion* directory. The *kernelversion* should correspond to the EXTRAVERSION variable in your Makefile. Use **make modules_install** to install your modules.

13. With our kernel now built, we need to move it to /boot before we can boot from it. Run the **make install** command to copy the new kernel and create a new Initial RAM Disk file (initrd) in the /boot directory. It also updates the default GRUB boot loader.

The make install **command copies your new kernel from the** *lusrlsrcllinux-2.4* *larchli386lboot* **to the** *lboot* **directory. It also uses the** *mkinitrd* **command to create a new Initial RAM disk in the** *lboot* **directory.**

14. Verify the changes to the /boot directory.

Building a kernel is an involved process, but it follows a standard pattern. It is very important that you become familiar with kernel construction procedures and troubleshooting. Refer to the following Scenario & Solution for some common problems encountered and their recommended solutions.

SCENARIO & SOLUTION

You looked under /usr/src/ but did not see the Linux kernel source code. What did you do wrong?	You did not install the kernel source code. Install the kernel-source and related RPMs or use the Red Hat Package Management utility to install the Kernel Development package group.
You configured the kernel as a monolithic kernel, but when you run **make bzImage**, it fails, saying the kernel is too big. What should you do?	You must reconfigure your kernel to use modules. There are limits on the size of a compressed kernel, so you should always build a modular kernel.
You can't find your new kernel.	Did you create an appropriate EXTRAVERSION variable in your Makefile? Did you use this variable throughout this process? If not, then you may not be able to correctly locate the kernel or its modules.

CERTIFICATION OBJECTIVE 5.07

The cron and at Systems

The cron system is essentially a smart alarm clock. When the alarm sounds, Linux runs the commands of your choice automatically. You can set the alarm clock to run at all sorts of regular time intervals. Alternatively, the at system allows you to run the command of your choice once, at a specified time in the future.

e x a m

ⓦ a t c h *Because cron always checks for changes, you do not have to restart cron every time you make a change.*

Red Hat configured the cron daemon, crond. By default, it checks a series of directories for jobs to run, every minute of every hour of every day. The crond checks the /var/spool/cron directory for jobs by user. It also checks for scheduled jobs for the computer under /etc/crontab and in the /etc/cron.d directory.

The behavior of the Linux cron is different from under Unix, where the cron daemon wakes up only when it needs to launch a program.

The System crontab and Components

The crontab file is set up in a specific format. Each line can be blank, a comment (which begins with #), a variable, or a command. Blank lines and comments are ignored.

When you run a regular command, the actions of the shell are based on environmental variables. To see your environmental variables, run the **env** command. Some of the standard variables in Red Hat Enterprise Linux include: HOME as your home directory, SHELL as the default shell, and LOGNAME as the username.

You can set different variables within the crontab file, or you can set environmental variables with the following syntax:

```
Variable=Value
```

Some variables are already set for you. For example, HOME is your home directory, SHELL is the user's default shell, and PATH is where the shell looks for commands. You can set these variables to different values in your crontab file. For example, the default /etc/crontab file includes the following variables:

```
SHELL=/bin/bash
PATH=/sbin:/bin:/usr/sbin:/usr/bin
MAILTO=root
HOME=/
```

Note that the values of PATH, MAILTO, and HOME are different from those for the standard environment variables.

on the job

The MAILTO variable can help you administer several Linux systems. The cron daemon sends output by e-mail. Just add a line like *MAILTO=me@somewhere.com* to route all cron messages associated with that file to that e-mail address.

e x a m

watch   *Note how the PATH variable in a crontab may be different from the PATH variable associated with your shell. In fact, the two variables are independent.*   *Therefore, you'll want to know the exact path of every command in your crontab. Specify the absolute path with the command if it isn't in the crontab PATH.*

Here is the format of a line in crontab. Each of these columns is explained in more detail in Table 5-4.

```
#minute, hour, day of month, month, day of week, command
*        *      *                month    *         command
```

If you see an asterisk in any column, cron runs that command for all possible values of that column. For example, an * in the minute field means that the command is run every minute during the specified hour(s). Take another example, as shown here:

```
1   5   3   4   *   ls
```

This line runs the **ls** command every April 3, at 5:01 A.M. The asterisk in the day of week column simply means that it does not matter what day of the week it is; crontab still runs the **ls** command at the specified time.

TABLE 5-4	Field	Value
Entries in a **crontab** Command Line	Minute	0-59
	Hour	Based on a 24-hour clock; for example, 23 = 11 P.M.
	Day of month	1-31
	Month	1-12, or jan, feb, mar, etc.
	Day of week	0-7; where 0 and 7 are both Sunday; or sun, mon, tue, etc.
	Command	The command you want to run

The crontab file is flexible. For example, a 7-10 entry in the hour field would run the specified command at 7:00 A.M., 8:00 A.M., 9:00 A.M., and 10:00 A.M. A list of entries in the minute field such as: 0,5,10,15,20,25,30,35,40,45,50,55 would run the specified command every five minutes. The cron daemon also recognizes abbreviations for months and the day of the week.

The actual command is the sixth field. You can set up new lines with a percent (%) symbol. This is useful for formatting standard input. The example that follows formats input for an e-mail message. Here is an example cron file:

```
# crontab -l
# Sample crontab file
#
# Force /bin/sh to be my shell for all of my scripts.
SHELL=/bin/sh
# Run 15 minutes past Midnight every Saturday
15 0 * * sat    $HOME/scripts/scary.script
# Do routine cleanup on the first of every Month at 4:30 AM
30 4 1 * *      /usr/scripts/removecores >> /tmp/core.tmp 2>>&1
# Mail a message at 10:45 AM every Friday
45 10 * * fri  mail -s "Project Update employees%Can I have a status
update on your project?%%Your Boss.%
# Every other hour check for alert messages
0 */2 * * * /usr/scripts/check.alerts
```

Setting Up cron for Users

Each user can use the **crontab** command to create and manage cron jobs for their own accounts. There are four switches associated with the **crontab** command:

- **-u** *user*   Allows the root user to edit the crontab of another specific user.
- **-l**   Lists the current entries in the crontab file.
- **-r**   Removes cron entries.
- **-e**   Edits an existing crontab entry. By default, crontab uses vi.

If you want to set up cron entries on your own account, start with the **crontab -e** command. It opens the vi editor, where you can add the variables and commands of your choice, similar to what you've seen in /etc/crontab.

EXERCISE 5-4

Create a cron Job

In this exercise, we will modify the basic Red Hat cron job settings to read a text file at 1:05 P.M. every Monday in the month of January. To do so, you'll need to create a directory for yearly cron jobs. To do this, use the following steps:

1. Log in as the root user.

2. Create a /etc/cron.yearly directory. Add a file called taxrem, which reads a text file from your home directory. A command such as the following in the taxrem file should suffice:

   ```
   cat ~/reminder
   ```

3. Make sure to add appropriate lines to the reminder file in your home directory.

4. Add an appropriate command to your /etc/crontab file. Based on the conditions described, it would read as follows:

   ```
   5 13 * 1 1 root run-parts /etc/cron.yearly
   ```

5. Save and exit.

Running a Job with the at System

Like cron, the at daemon supports job processing. However, you can set an at job to be run once. Jobs in the cron system must be set to run on a regular basis. The at daemon works in a way similar to the print process; jobs are spooled in the /var/spool/at directory and run at the specified time.

You can use the at daemon to run the command or script of your choice. For the purpose of this section, assume that user michael has created a script named 7e7 in his home directory to process some airplane sales database to another file in the same directory called sales.

From the command line, you can run the **at** *time* command to start a job to be run at a specified *time*. That *time* can be now, in a specified number of minutes, hours, or days, or at the time of your choice. I illustrate several examples in Table 5-5.

You can use one of the example commands shown in Table 5-5 to open an at job. It opens a different command line interface, where you can specify the command of your choice. Assume you're about to leave work, and want to start the job in an hour. From the conditions specified above, you'd run the following commands:

```
$ at now + 1 hour
at> /home/michael/7e7 > /home/michael/sales
at> Ctrl-D
```

The CTRL-D command exits the at command shell and returns to your original command line interface. To check the status of your jobs, so you can see if it will work, run the following job queue command:

```
$ atq
1         2004-4-12 17:18 a michael
```

If there's a problem with the job, you can remove it with the **atrm** command. For the output shown, you'd remove job number 1 with the following command:

```
$ atrm 1
```

TABLE 5-5　　Examples of the **at** Command

Time Period	Example	Description
Minute	at now + 10 minutes	Associated jobs will start in 10 minutes.
Hour	at now + 2 hours	Associated jobs will start in 2 hours.
Days	at now + 1 day	Associated jobs will start in 24 hours.
Weeks	at now + 1 week	Associated jobs will start in 7 days.
n/a	at teatime	Associated jobs will start at 4:00 P.M.
n/a	at 3:00 6/13/04	Associated jobs will start on June 13, 2004, at 3:00 A.M.

Securing cron and at

You may not want everyone to be able to run a job in the middle of the night. If there is a security flaw in your system, someone may download important data or worse, and it could be days before you discover the security breach.

As with network firewalls, you can allow or deny users the privilege of using cron. You can set up users in /etc/cron.allow and /etc/cron.deny files. If these files don't exist, cron usage is not restricted. If users are named in /etc/cron.allow file, all other users won't be able to use cron. If there is no /etc/cron.allow file, only users named in /etc/cron.deny can't use cron.

These files are formatted as one line per user; if you have the following entries in /etc/cron.deny and no /etc/cron.allow file, users elizabeth and nancy aren't allowed to set up their own cron commands:

```
elizabeth
nancy
```

You can secure access to the at system in the same way. The corresponding security configuration files are /etc/at.allow and /etc/at.deny.

CERTIFICATION SUMMARY

You can have great control over how your Linux installation is set up and configured. You can control almost all aspects of the user environment, as well as the details of your kernel. Any variables or system-wide functions you may need to run can be kept in the /etc/bashrc or /etc/profile script.

You can set up quotas to limit the user's disk usage. You can set up one quota per partition, and set soft and hard limits for users. With grace periods, you can set up a soft limit to give users an appropriate warning.

The easiest way to update a kernel is to install (and not upgrade it) from a Red Hat RPM. When you do, it automatically updates your boot loader files as needed.

Alternatively, the kernel can be optimized for your particular installation and hardware, and you have detailed control over its configuration. To make a modular kernel, you need to run six commands: **make mrproper, make config, make dep, make clean, make modules, make modules_install** and **make install**. If you are compiling a monolithic kernel, you will *not* need to run the last two module-related commands.

The cron and at daemons allow you to schedule jobs to run at any given time.

TWO-MINUTE DRILL

Here are some of the key points from the certification objectives in Chapter 5.

Shell Configuration Files

❏ All system-wide shell configuration files are kept in the /etc directory.

❏ /etc/profile is the system-wide startup shell script for bash users.

❏ All users have hidden shell configuration files in their home directories.

Setting Up and Managing Disk Quotas

❏ Quotas are used to limit a user's or a group of users' ability to consume disk space.

❏ Quotas are set on specific filesystems mounted to standard Linux formats.

❏ Quota support must be enabled in the kernel. By default, quotas are enabled in RHEL 3 kernels.

❏ Quotas have soft limits and hard limits. If both soft and hard limits are set, then a user can exceed his or her soft limit for a modest period of time.

❏ Users and groups may never exceed their hard limits.

The Basics of the Kernel

❏ The kernel lies at the heart of the operating system.

❏ You can recompile Linux kernels to minimize size and maximize efficiency.

❏ To optimize the Linux kernel, it is a best practice to compile kernels with only needed elements, and configure modules for most hardware.

❏ Modular kernels, with separate device modules, are more efficient than monolithic kernels, where device drivers are integrated into the kernel.

❏ If you're going to update your kernel, you should keep a copy of your current working kernel.

❏ There are a number of RHEL 3 kernels available for different types of CPU and levels of RAM.

❏ Linux kernels and related files are stored in the /boot directory.

❏ The /proc directory provides a window to what Linux sees in your computer.

❑ Changing the values of variables in the /proc directory can change the behavior of your running kernel. For example, setting **ip_forward = 1** enables routing.

❑ Kernel modules are managed by a special kernel thread, **kmod**. Additional settings can be configured through /etc/modules.conf.

❑ The **lsmod** command lists currently loaded modules; important related commands are **insmod**, **rmmod**, and **modprobe**.

❑ Basic RHEL 3 modules are stored in the /lib/modules/2.4.21-4.EL directory.

New Kernels, the Easy Way

❑ Kernel version numbers are organized in *major.minor.patch* format. Red Hat adds a build number to the Linux kernels that it builds from source code.

❑ It's fairly easy to install a Red Hat kernel from RPM, as long as you remember to install and not upgrade. This allows you to return to the current working kernel if you have a problem.

❑ Sometimes, what you need is a kernel patch, which supports upgrades of one patch version number. Unfortunately, patches are not always compatible with Red Hat built kernels.

❑ It's important to create a new boot floppy whenever you install a new kernel.

❑ When you install a Red Hat kernel from RPM, the process should automatically update your boot loader (GRUB or LILO).

Kernel Sources

❑ The kernel source tree is accessible through /usr/src/linux-2.4, which is normally linked to the actual directory with kernel source files.

❑ Kernel sources can be loaded from the kernel-source RPM or from a Linux kernel tarball downloaded from a site such as ftp.kernel.org.

Recompiling a Kernel

❑ Your current kernel configuration is stored in the config-*versionnumber* file in the /boot directory.

❑ You can modify kernel settings from the /usr/src/linux-2.4 directory with one of the following commands: **make config**, **make menuconfig**, or **make xconfig**. The last two lead to a long series of menus.

❑ Once you've made the proper backups and boot disks, set the EXTRAVERSION variable in your Makefile, run the **make mrproper** command, and placed current settings in /usr/src/linux-2.4/.config, you're ready to modify your kernel.

❑ Once you've settled on and saved your changes, run the **make dep**, **make clean**, **make bzImage**, **make modules**, **make modules_install**, and **make install** commands, you've compiled your new kernel, and it should be ready for use from the GRUB boot loader.

The cron and at Systems

❑ The cron system allows any user to schedule jobs so they run at given intervals.

❑ The at system allows users to configure jobs to run once at a scheduled time.

❑ The **crontab** command is used to work with cron files. Use **crontab -e** to edit, **crontab -l** to list, or **crontab -d** to delete cron files.

❑ The /etc/cron.allow and /etc/cron.deny files are used to control access to the cron job scheduler.

SELF TEST

The following questions will help you measure your understanding of the material presented in this chapter. Read all the choices carefully, as there may be more than one correct answer. Choose all correct answers for each question. This is just to test your understanding of the material; Red Hat no longer includes multiple choice questions on the RHCE or RHCT exams.

Shell Configuration Files

1. The system-wide file associated with the bash shell is:
   - A. /etc/shells.conf
   - B. /etc/startup.sh
   - C. /etc/profile
   - D. There is no system-wide shell startup file; all such files reside in individual user directories.

Setting Up and Managing Disk Quotas

2. You are running an ISP service and provide space for users' Web pages. You want them to use no more than 40MB of space, but you will allow up to 50MB until they can clean up their stuff. How could you use quotas to enforce this policy?
   - A. Enable grace periods; set the hard limit to 40MB and the soft limit to 50MB.
   - B. Enable grace periods; set the soft limit to 50MB and the hard limit to 40MB.
   - C. Enable grace periods; set the soft limit to 40MB, and the hard limit to 50MB.
   - D. None of the above.

3. If you wanted to configure quotas for everyone on the /home directory, what would you add to the options in /etc/fstab?
   - A. quota
   - B. usrquota
   - C. grpquota
   - D. userquota

The Basics of the Kernel

4. You are troubleshooting someone else's computer and are not sure what network card is inside it. You have checked the output from the **dmesg** command, but no network cards are listed,

and even though you have a bunch of compiled network modules, none are currently loaded. What could you do to load the unknown network device most quickly?

   A. Try loading each module manually.

   B. modprobe *

   C. Nothing. The kernel will load the module when you try to connect to the network.

   D. modprobe -t net

5. You can't find any modules in the /lib/modules/*kernel_version*/kernel/drivers (or similar) directories. Which of the following actions would set up these modules?

   A. Go into the /lib/modules/*kernel_version* directory and run the **make modules** command.

   B. Go into the /lib/modules/*kernel_version* directory and run the **make modules** and **make modules_install** commands.

   C. Go into the /usr/src/linux-2.4 directory and run the **make modules** command.

   D. Go into the /usr/src/linux-2.4 directory and run the **make modules** and **make modules_ install** commands.

New Kernels, the Easy Way

6. When you install an updated kernel from a Red Hat RPM, which of the following steps do you need to take?

   A. Add information on the new kernel in a GRUB stanza.

   B. Add a new Initial RAM disk to the /boot directory.

   C. Reconfigure the /usr/src/linux-2.4/.config file.

   D. None of the above.

Kernel Sources

7. You're not sure which kernel source tree is active for your Linux computer. Which of the following directories should be linked to that source tree?

   A. /usr/src/linux

   B. /usr/src/linux-2.4

   C. /usr/src/linux-2.4rh

   D. /usr/src

Recompiling a Kernel

8. When compiling a kernel, you've navigated to the /usr/src/linux-2.4 directory. Which of the following would not work with the **make** command to reconfigure your kernel?

   A. config

   B. menuconfig

   C. windowconfig

   D. xconfig

9. You have just compiled a new kernel with the **make bzImage** command. You need to copy the kernel and Initial RAM disk to the /boot directory. What is the most efficient way to make this happen?

   A. Copy the image from the /usr/src/linux/arch/i386/boot directory.

   B. Nothing. The **make bzImage** command automatically installs the kernel to the /boot directory.

   C. Install a revised Red Hat kernel RPM.

   D. After you've set up modules, run the **make install** command.

The cron and at Systems

10. You want to schedule a maintenance job to run from your home directory on the first of every month at 4:00 A.M. Which of the following cron entries runs the specified job at the specified time?

A.	0	4	1	*	*	~/maintenance.pl
B.	4	1	*	*	~/maintenance.pl
C.	0	4	31	*	*	~/maintenance.pl
D.	1	4	0	0	~/maintenance.pl

LAB QUESTIONS

If you're pressed for time with these labs, I suggest that you run Lab 3 first. As you've read in the chapter, recompiling the kernel takes a long time. If you have a slower computer, some of the commands required to recompile the kernel take a while to complete. You can use this time to log into a different terminal and run the other labs in this chapter.

Lab 1

In this first lab, we'll look at setting up automatic connections to a shared network directory. While this lab uses files described in Chapter 4, it is focused on shell configuration files. For the purpose of this lab, assume your username is vaclav and you're mounting a shared NFS /mnt/inst directory from a remote computer with an IP address of 192.168.30.4. You're going to mount it in vaclav's home directory, in a blank directory named inst.

1. Select the regular user of your choice. That user should have files such as .bashrc and .bash_logout.

2. Find a shared directory on a remote computer.

3. Set up a local directory for that user as a mount point.

4. Configure commands for that user to **mount** and **umount** that remote directory. Make sure those commands run only when that user logs into his or her account.

Lab 2

In this lab, we will test the quotas created in this chapter. You'll use the basic quota settings described in this chapter, and then copy files to fill up the home directory of a user who has a quota applied. The steps required for this lab are straightforward.

1. Set up quotas on the local computer. Use the criteria described earlier in this chapter. If you don't have a separate /home directory partition, you can set up quotas on the top-level root directory (/).

2. Once you've set quotas in your /etc/fstab configuration file, remember to remount the partition where you've created a quota. Alternatively, you could reboot Linux, but that would take time that you may not be able to spare during either of the Red Hat exams.

3. Set up a quota for the user of your choice. Remember, when you use the **edquota** command on a specific user, you can edit the quota file directly using vi editor commands. Configure a hard and a soft limit for that user.

4. Log in as the user with the quota. Copy some large files to the home directory of that user.

5. Continue the copying process until you see a warning message. When you do, run the **quota** command. What do you see? Is there anything in the output that gives you warning that you've exceeded the quota?

6. Copy some additional files until you see a "Disk quota exceeded" message. Run the **quota** command again. What do you see?

7. Delete some files from that user's home directory—at least enough to get the files under the quota limits.

Lab 3

This lab is more of a detailed kernel-building exercise than a typical lab in this book. The exercise will include concise steps on how to configure, install, and test a new kernel. While the Red Hat Exam Prep guide no longer specifies that you have to know how to recompile the kernel, it is something you will need to do at some point in time as a Linux system administrator. See the Lab Answer section at the end of this chapter for the exercise.

Lab 4

In this fourth lab, you'll be updating your kernel from another source. One proviso—this lab will work only if there is a Red Hat RPM kernel file that is a later version from what is already installed on your computer. If you're running RHEL 3, you can still download and use one of the Fedora development kernel RPMs for the purpose of this exercise. (While there are no guarantees, the Fedora development kernel available as of this writing works fine on my RHEL 3 computer. However, there have been reported issues with various video cards and printer configurations.)

1. Check download.fedora.redhat.com or one of the mirrors listed online at fedora.redhat.com /download/mirrors.html.

2. Download the new kernel to the /tmp directory.

3. Back up your current /etc/grub.conf configuration file, as well as the current files in your boot directory, in case something goes wrong.

4. Use the **rpm -ivh** *kernelfile* command to install the new kernel.

5. Observe the results. Check the files in /boot. Which files look like they're duplicated but with a different version number?

6. Check your boot loader file. Assuming it's GRUB, open the /etc/grub.conf file in a text editor. Change the *default* variable in this file to point to the new kernel. If it's LILO, remember to run **lilo** to record the change in the MBR.

7. Reboot your computer to test the new kernel.

SELF TEST ANSWERS

Shell Configuration Files

1. ☑ C. This is the system-wide shell script executed for all users.

   ☒ A and B are incorrect because there are no such files. While each user does get their own hidden configuration files in their home directories, they apply only to that user. D is incorrect because answer C is correct.

Setting Up and Managing Disk Quotas

2. ☑ C. Enable grace periods; set the soft limit to 40MB, and the hard limit to 50MB. This will warn users they are over their limit after the grace period, but will make sure they do not exceed the 50MB true maximum barrier.

   ☒ A is incorrect because the soft limit must be less than the hard limit. B is incorrect because it is actually the same as A. D is incorrect because C does the job.

3. ☑ B and C. The usrquota and grpquota options allow the configuration of quotas on the given filesystem on user and group bases.

   ☒ A and D are not valid options for /etc/fstab.

The Basics of the Kernel

4. ☑ D. The **modprobe -t net** command tries each module from the /lib/modules/*kernel_version* /kernel/drivers/net directory, until it reaches the end of the list or finds a module that works for a network interface.

   ☒ A, B, and C are incorrect. Linux needs to load the card module before you can connect to the network, so C is incorrect. You might try loading all modules manually, but that is not efficient, so A is incorrect. While the **modprobe *** would test all options, it is also not efficient, so B is also incorrect.

5. ☑ D. These commands together compile your modules and then place them in the appropriate directory trees. Because these are kernel-related commands, they have to be run from the /usr /src/linux-2.4 directory.

   ☒ A, B, and C are incorrect. The **make modules** command just compiles the modules, so A and C are not correct. The /lib/modules/*kernel_version* directory is the wrong place to apply these commands, so B is incorrect.

New Kernels, the Easy Way

6. ☑ **D,** None of the above. GRUB is automatically updated when you install a new Red Hat kernel from a Red Hat RPM; however, you may want to change the value of *default* in /etc/grub.conf. A new Initial RAM disk file, initrd-*versionnumber,* is also added to the /boot directory. You don't need to change /usr/src/linux-2.4/.config file unless you want to recompile this new kernel.

   ☒ **A, B,** and **C** are all not required and are therefore incorrect.

Kernel Sources

7. ☑ **B.** The /usr/src/linux-2.4 directory is normally soft-linked to the actual directory with the active kernel source files.

   ☒ **A, C,** and **D** all specify directories that aren't linked to the Linux kernel source tree. (However, the situation was different before Linux kernel version 2.4; answer A was correct for older Linux distributions, such as Red Hat Linux 7.0.)

Recompiling a Kernel

8. ☑ **C** is correct because there is no kernel configuration utility based on the **make windowconfig** command.

   ☒ **A, B,** and **D** are all incorrect. In the /usr/src/linux-2.4 directory, the **make config, make menuconfig,** and **make xconfig** commands all call kernel configuration utilities.

9. ☑ **D.** The **make install** command in RHEL 3 automatically loads the files and data related to your recompiled kernel in the /boot directory. It also installs a new Initial RAM disk and revises the GRUB boot loader.

   ☒ **A, B,** and **C** are all incorrect. While the recompiled kernel is stored in the directory noted in answer **A,** this action does not create an Initial RAM disk. **B** is incorrect as more action is required. **C** is incorrect as the revised Red Hat kernel RPM probably does not reflect your custom kernel configuration.

The cron and at Systems

10. ☑ **A.** The syntax for cron is minute, hour, day of month, month of year, weekday, and then the command. This answer corresponds to 4:00 A.M. on the first of every month.

    ☒ **B** executes at 4 minutes after 1 in the morning for every day. However, there are only four time fields, not five, so the entire line would be considered invalid. **C** is incorrect because it runs the job at 4:00 A.M. on the 31st of the month, and then only if the month has 31 days. **D** is incorrect because it executes the program at one minute after 4:00 A.M. And there are only four time values in this line, which makes it invalid.

LAB ANSWERS

Lab 1

This lab has two purposes: it is designed to help you understand mounted network directories and the login process. You can substitute the user, the shared network directory, and directories of your choice. But based on the premises in this lab, I would take the following steps:

1. Log in as user vaclav. Create the specified directory. For this lab, you would use the **mkdir /home/vaclav/inst** command.

2. Test the network connection. Mount the remote NFS directory on the directory that you just created. For this lab, use the following command:

    ```
    # mount -t nfs 192.168.30.4:/mnt/inst /home/vaclav/inst
    ```

3. Run the **mount** command by itself. If you've successfully mounted to the shared directory, you should see it at the end of the list of mounted directories.

4. Unmount the network connection. For this lab, you would use the following command:

    ```
    # umount /home/vaclav/inst
    ```

5. Add the commands specified from steps 2 and 4 to the local .bashrc and .bash_logout configuration files. Remember, since these files start with a dot, they are hidden.

6. Test the result. Log out and log back in. Check your mounted directories. If the command in .bash_logout does not work, you'll probably see the shared directory mounted multiple times.

Lab 2

The purpose of this lab is to get you some more practice with creating quotas for users. It's quite possible that you'll have to configure quotas on the Red Hat exams. While you may not have to test quotas in the way described in this lab, it will help you become familiar with the error messages that you'll see when you exceed a hard and then a soft quota limit.

Lab 3

Before we can build a new kernel, we have to ensure we have all the correct RPM packages. You could do so by checking a list of RPMs as described. Alternatively, you can start the Package Management utility with the **redhat-config-packages** command. From this GUI utility, make sure you have the Kernel Development package group installed. As with the rest of this chapter and the Red Hat exams, this assumes that you have a PC with a 32-bit Intel type CPU. The procedures for other CPUs vary and are not, as of this writing, covered on the Red Hat exams.

The following list of RPMs are associated with the source code:

```
kernel-source-*
glibc-kernelheaders-*
glibc-devel-*
cpp-*
ncurses-*
ncurses-devel-*
binutils-*
gcc-*
```

1. When you install RHEL 3, you've probably already installed most of these packages. Alternatively, it may be faster to install the Kernel Development package group using the Package Management utility. This utility automatically takes care of any dependencies.

2. Navigate to the /usr/src directory with the **cd /usr/src** command. Run the **ls -l** command. You should see a link between the linux-2.4 directory and the location of your source code files. In RHEL, that is by default the /usr/src/linux-2.4.21-4.EL directory.

3. Navigate to the /usr/src/linux-2.4 directory. You'll be running the remaining kernel configuration commands from this directory.

4. Set up a unique name for the kernel that you're about to modify. Open the Makefile file in a text editor. Look for the EXTRAVERSION variable. Red Hat adds this variable as a suffix to the recompiled kernel. Modify this variable as desired; save and exit from Makefile.

5. Jot down the value of the EXTRAVERSION variable here: _____

6. Determine the correct CPU on your hardware. Use the command

```
# cat /proc/cpuinfo
```

7. Jot down the CPU model name here: _____

8. Run the **ls /usr/src/linux-2.4/configs** command. You'll see a list of available default kernel configuration files. Find the file associated with your CPU. If your computer has more than one CPU, use the smp version of the kernel, if available. If your computer has more than 4 GB of RAM, use the hugemem version of the kernel, if available. Save it in the /usr/src/linux-2.4 /.config file.

9. Make sure you're in the /usr/src/linux-2.4 directory. Clean up any stray source code from previous kernel reconfigurations with the following command:

```
# make mrproper
```

10. Wait until the messages are complete. Problems are rare at this stage.

11. Next, it is time to configure your kernel, using one of the three major tools:

- **make config**   A line-by-line tool that gives you a choice with all kernel options
- **make menuconfig**   A text-based menu that allows you to select just the changes you want
- **make xconfig**   A GUI interface that works only in the X Window System

12. Set the processor type to match your hardware (for example, Pentium, Pentium II, Pentium III, Pentium IV).

13. Return to the kernel configuration tool of your choice. Turn off all unneeded devices. Some possible unneeded devices are in the following categories:

- ISDN Subsystem
- I2O
- Old CD-ROMs
- Amateur Radio
- Telephony Support
- Symmetric Multiprocessing Support
- MTR Memory Support

14. Be sure to turn on Kernel Loadable Modules support.

15. Save your changes and exit.

16. When you save the new configuration, the kernel configuration tool overwrites your /usr/src /linux-2.4/.config file.

17. Resolve all kernel dependencies (between sources) with the following command. This will produce a lot of output and may take several minutes.

```
# make dep
```

18. Prepare the source code directories to create the new kernel with the following command:

```
# make clean
```

19. Once your dependencies are resolved, it's time to build a new compressed kernel image, with the following command:

```
# make bzImage
```

20. This is the actual kernel build, which will take some time. You may take this opportunity to log into another terminal and run one of the other labs.

21. The easiest way to see if the kernel build worked is to run the following command immediately after the messages from **make bzImage** command stop:

```
# echo $?
0
```

22. If you got a 0, everything worked (success). Any other result indicates a failure during the kernel build process. In that case, go back and reconfigure your kernel to make a configuration that works.

23. Check for the existence of two new files. Run this command:

```
# ls -l System.map arch/i386/boot/bzImage
```

It should show you two files, a relatively small System.map and a much larger bzImage.

24. Make the loadable modules that will be used by this kernel:

```
# make modules
```

25. Install the new custom kernel files into their correct locations and update your boot loader so that it knows about your new kernel. The **make install** command should perform all of these tasks.

26. Check to see that the **make install** command worked. Based on the EXTRAVERSION variable that you set earlier, check your /boot directory. You should see at least a new initrd, System.map, and vmlinuz file in this directory, with this variable as a suffix. Otherwise, you'll need to copy these files yourself. Also, check your boot loader configuration file (/etc/grub.conf for the default GRUB boot loader).

27. If the **make install** command didn't put an initial RAM disk (initrd) into the /boot directory, you'll have to create one with the following command (if your version and EXTRAVERSION variables are different, revise this command accordingly):

```
# mkinitrd /boot/initrd-2.4.21-4.ELcustom1 2.4.21-4.ELcustom1
```

28. Congratulations, you have just installed a custom kernel on your new system. As long as you also have your original kernel in your boot loader menu, test it out!

29. Run the **reboot** command. You should see both kernels in the boot loader menu. Try your custom kernel!

Lab 4

Assuming everything works with the updated Red Hat RPM kernel package, you should not have to update anything, especially if your boot loader is GRUB. The steps described in the lab should help you confirm this through the appropriate configuration files on your RHEL 3 computer.

6

X Window System

One of the most important aspects of getting a Linux system up and running is configuring the user interface. As RHCEs and RHCTs are expected to configure computers for non-administrative users, the Red Hat exams test your ability to configure the X Window System. The *X Window System* is the foundation of the Linux graphical user interface (GUI). While the GUI plays an integral part of other operating systems such as Microsoft Windows, the X Window System on Linux is essentially just another application.

Many administrators don't even bother with the GUI; the command line interface is enough for most administrative purposes. However, regular users on a Linux workstation are more productive with the GUI and the multitude of X Window-based applications. If you are helping users migrate from Microsoft Windows to Linux, the X Window System allows you to provide a less intimidating environment.

Not all Linux computers require the X Window. For example, computers that are used as dedicated DHCP, DNS, or NFS servers generally don't serve as workstations for anyone and therefore don't need any sort of GUI. Many Linux gurus have a negative bias toward the GUI. While Red Hat and others have developed some helpful GUI tools, they are almost always "front ends," or programs that customize one or more commands at the command line interface.

But if you're administering a network of Linux computers for regular users, you'll need to know how to administer the X Window System, a skill that requires a basic understanding of the available desktops and graphical applications.

This chapter starts with the X Server, as configured on the local computer. It continues with X Clients, as generic applications that you can run from the local or a remote network computer. Once everything is configured, you're ready to take a step back to the start process for the X Window. It moves on to the two major Linux graphical desktops, and finally goes into an overview of a very few of the available graphical applications.

CERTIFICATION OBJECTIVE 6.01

X Server

The X Window System is designed as a flexible and powerful client/server-based system. In order to configure and troubleshoot the X Window interface, it is important you understand the client/server nature of the X Window System.

INSIDE THE EXAM

The Linux Graphical User Interface

The Red Hat exams test your ability to configure the X Window, presumably for non-administrative users. As stated in the Red Hat Exam Prep guide, RHCE candidates have to successfully complete *all* RHCT Troubleshooting and System Maintenance requirements, including configuring the X Window System and a desktop environment. Naturally, you need to know how to configure the X Window on a local computer. The X Window may fail if you have problems with the X Font Server.

This is a situation where it may be more efficient to use the Red Hat GUI X Window

Display Settings configuration tool, which you can start with the **redhat-config-xfree86** command. The language of the X Window configuration file is difficult to master. As time is of the essence on the Red Hat exams, you should use the method that does the job most quickly for you.

The X Window System can work over a network. Once properly configured, you can run GUI applications from a remote computer. To make this work, you need to understand modularity of the X Server and X Clients, as well as the way X Window security is managed on your network.

on the job

*I use the Display Settings tool and redhat-config-xfree86 **command** interchangeably; the command is the fastest way to start the tool.*

As you might have guessed from the terms *client* and *server*, the X Window System is designed to work in a networked environment. The client and server can both reside on your own computer or on separate computers on the network. In other words, not only can you run X applications on your system, you can run X applications on other computers on your network. The graphical displays from those remote applications are sent to your monitor.

In fact, X Window applications handle this task so well that, providing the network is fast enough, you really can't tell from a performance point of view which applications are running locally and which applications are running remotely.

When you configure the X Server, I'll show you the modularity of the system. In brief, components such as keyboards, mice, and monitors are configured separately and all become modular components of the X Server.

Different Meanings for Client and Server

Normally on a network, the local computer is the client, and the remote computer acts as the server. X Window Clients and Servers work on a different paradigm. The X Server controls the graphics on the local computer. The X Server draws images on your screen and takes input from your keyboard and mouse. In contrast, X Clients are local or remote applications such as **xclock** that you can run on the local X Server.

You can run an X Client locally or remotely. Local X Clients run on your workstation; remote X Clients run on the local X Server. When you run a remote X Window Client application, you start the program on a different computer and send its output to use the X Server on your local computer. Figure 6-1 illustrates a local X Server with one local and one remote X Client.

Before we can talk about running X Client applications, we need to look first at configuring an X Server on our system. While RHEL 3 normally configures most hardware configurations during the installation process, you need to know how to edit the X Window configuration file, directly in a text editor or with the Red Hat configuration tool (**redhat-config-xfree86**).

on the
job   *If you're in the GNOME or KDE desktops, you can also start the Red Hat Display Settings tool with the Main Menu | System Settings | Display command.*

Supported Hardware

If a Linux installation program does not successfully configure the X Window System, it can be difficult to configure the GUI on a Linux workstation. Fortunately, RHEL 3 comes with tools and drivers that make this job relatively painless and easy.

FIGURE 6-1

Running X
Window Clients
from remote or
local computers

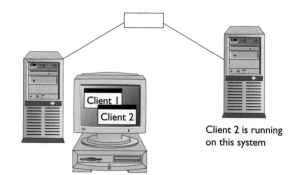

Client 1
Client 2

Client 2 is running
on this system

Your workstation running X-server
and one X-client (Client 1)

Both X-client applications get their imput
from the keyboard and mouse attached to
your workstation

But it all depends on the hardware. Linux may not always work with the latest and greatest video card or monitor. Many video cards and monitors include proprietary software; it may take some time before Linux developers are able to "reverse-engineer" these components. For the latest official information, check the Red Hat Hardware Compatibility List described in Chapter 1.

on the *Job* *Linux provides world-class support for graphics. The list of movie studios that use Linux to create feature films is impressive (Disney, DreamWorks, Industrial Light and Magic, Paramount, and so on). If you need motion-picture quality graphics support, you may want to consider some commercial alternatives to XFree86. Two are Metro-X from Metro Link (www.metrolink.com) and Accelerated-X from X-Inside (www.xinside.com).*

Hardware: X Server Selection

The X Window Server program shipped with RHEL 3 is an open-source X Server program called XFree86. The XFree86 Server supports hundreds of video cards and monitors. The best place to check to see whether your video card and monitor are supported is the Red Hat Hardware Compatibility List, currently available from hardware.redhat.com/hcl.

Alternatively, navigate to the XFree86 Web site at www.xfree86.org to find the latest support information. As installed, RHEL 3 uses the XFree86-4.3.0 package; you can find more about compatible hardware at www.xfree86.org/4.3.0/Status.html.

on the *Job* *As of this writing, RHEL 3 includes only the XFree86 (4.3.0) server. There may be a few video cards that require the older XFree86 server, version 3.3.x. Hopefully, these cases are now rare. If you find that you are unlucky in this way and cannot upgrade your video card, first try a standard VGA or VESA (also known as SVGA) configuration. As a last resort, download the older XFree86 Server from www.xfree86.org.*

Servers and XFree86

The latest version of XFree86 includes modules for different video servers. Unlike the XFree86 3.x series, this one doesn't require you to install different packages for each video server. Hardware support for most video servers is already there. If you learn of updates, changes are easy. Just add the module, and then point to it in the /etc/X11/ XF86Config configuration file.

If you are using an unsupported video card, support is also included for generic VGA devices. Most video cards and monitors will work with these X Servers.

Recent versions of Red Hat Linux included an /etc/X11/XF86Config-4 configuration file. When Red Hat removed support for XFree86 version 3.x servers, it changed the name of the default X Window configuration file to /etc/X11/XF86Config.

Tools for X Configuration

If you want to configure your X Window System, you have two options. You can edit the X Window configuration file directly, you can use the Red Hat Display Settings tool (**redhat-config-xfree86**), or you can install and configure the X Window during the installation process.

Older configuration tools, including xf86config, Xconfigurator, and XF86Setup, are not included with RHEL 3 (or Red Hat Linux 9).

Even if you didn't install any graphics software when you installed RHEL 3, you can still use the **redhat-config-xfree86** command. When you do, it starts its own default graphics mode if it detects a graphics driver.

Red Hat Display Settings Tool

The Red Hat Display Settings tool is a stand-alone program that you can run at any time from the command line. The basic routines which start with the **redhat-config-xfree86** command are also used by the Red Hat installation program if you choose to install and configure the X Window System at that time.

The **redhat-config-xfree86** program is a character-based, menu-driven interface that helps you to configure your video hardware. If you're starting from a text console, it automatically probes your video card and selects the appropriate X Server image. If **redhat-config-xfree86** cannot detect your graphics card, it allows you to select them from the list of supported video cards.

Running the Red Hat Display Settings Tool

It's easy to start the Red Hat Display Settings tool. Just type **redhat-config-xfree86** at a command line interface. It provides a simple GUI, even if you start it from a regular text console. When you start **redhat-config-xfree86**, you'll see the Display Settings window similar to that shown in Figure 6-2.

FIGURE 6-2

The Display
Settings tool,
started from
the text console

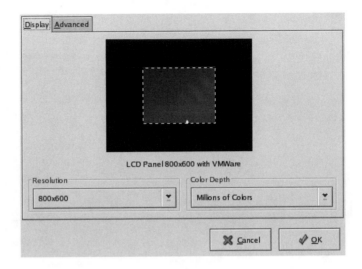

LCD Panel 800x600 with VMWare

Resolution

800x600

Color Depth

Millions of Colors

✗ Cancel   ✓ OK

on the

ʃob

While the look of the Display Settings tool is slightly different when started from the text console or the GUI, the functionality is identical.

If the Display Settings tool successfully identifies your hardware, you'll see it listed under the Display tab. In this case, it detected a VMWare graphics driver with a LCD monitor. You can now set the default resolution and color depth under the Display tab. You can change these settings by clicking on the associated drop-down text box. If your hardware supports it, you can configure:

- Monitor resolutions between 640×480 and 1920×1440.

- A color depth of 256, thousands, or millions of colors. Thousands corresponds to 16-bit color, and millions corresponds to 24- or 32-bit color, depending on the capability of your hardware.

But if you want to select a different hardware component, you can select it from a list. Click the Advanced tab, as shown in Figure 6-3.

You'll see options to configure your monitor and video card. Click the Configure button in the Video Card section. This should bring up the Video Card Settings dialog box shown in Figure 6-4. If the Probe Videocard option is active, the Display Settings tool may be able to configure your card for you. Otherwise, search through the list of video cards. If you do not see your graphics card here, it may not be supported. In this case, you have several options:

FIGURE 6-3

Display settings

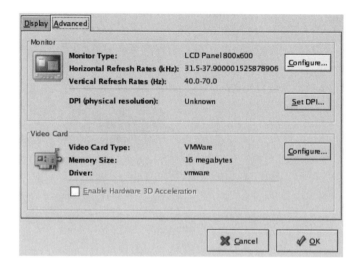

FIGURE 6-4

Selecting a
graphics card

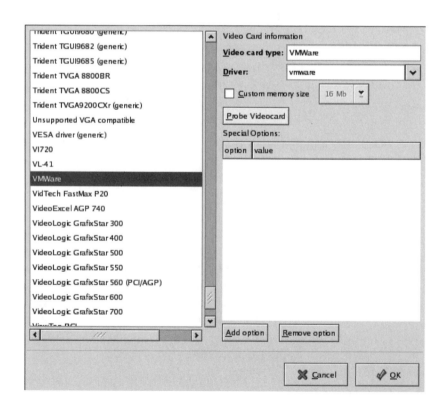

■ Select a video card similar to your model. Alternatively, you may find a generic server such as VESA driver (generic) that is compatible with your video card. Test and if necessary edit the /etc/X11/XF86Config file to complete your changes.

■ Check the Web for other Linux users who are running the X Window System with the same type of hardware. A useful database is available by searching through newsgroup messages at groups.google.com.

■ Use the Unsupported VGA compatible X Window Server.

■ Select one of the more generic cards. With the Custom Memory Size option, you can configure between 1MB and 128MB of video RAM. You can also add one of the many configuration options associated with the /etc/X11/XF86Config file.

■ Go to www.xfree86.org and download the latest drivers. You'll need to edit the /etc/X11/XF86Config file directly to point to this driver.

Once your selections are complete, click OK. This returns you to the Advanced tab. If your video card is so capable, you'll be able to activate the Enable Hardware 3D Acceleration option. Next, configure the Monitor. Click the Configure button in the Monitor section of the Advanced tab. This brings you to the dialog box shown in Figure 6-5.

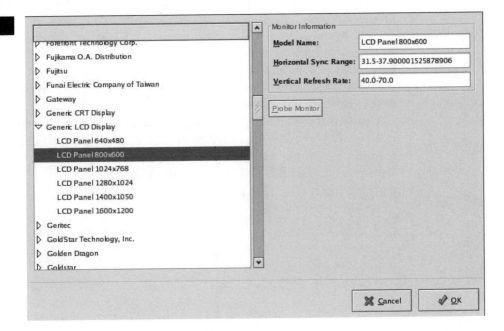

FIGURE 6-5

Selecting a monitor

If the Probe Monitor button is active, the Display Settings tool may be able to probe your hardware. Otherwise, select the option that most closely matches your monitor. If you don't see the make and model for your monitor, select one of the "generic" monitors. You can then customize the Horizontal and Vertical settings per your monitor's documentation.

Don't select Probe Monitor if you have an older monitor. And don't configure a horizontal sync or vertical refresh rate beyond the capability of your monitor. Otherwise, your video card may send signals that exceed the capability of your monitor. Especially on a laptop computer, the consequences can be rather costly.

Laptops

Configuring the X Window System to run on a laptop can be more challenging than configuring it to run on a desktop system. If you are planning to install Red Hat Enterprise Linux on a laptop, a good source for tips and additional information is the Linux on Laptops Web site at www.linux-laptop.net.

Configuring the X Window System

With some older or sensitive hardware, configuring the X Window System may be a risk. If the refresh rate that you set is too high, you could potentially damage your hardware. The refresh rate is the frequency at which your graphics card redraws images on your screen.

Refresh rates are expressed in terms of hertz (Hz). A refresh rate of 60 Hz means that an image is redrawn 60 times in one second. Computer monitors have both vertical and horizontal refresh rates. Modern monitors, known as multisync or multiscan monitors, automatically adjust to the vertical and horizontal refresh rates as driven by the graphics card. In either case, refresh rates vary from monitor to monitor.

Caution! If the monitor you configure does not match your actual hardware, it is possible for your video card to overtax your monitor, resulting in a blown monitor. This is a special concern with laptop computers. Laptop display screens are expensive; it is often more cost-effective to replace a laptop computer instead of replacing just the laptop display screen.

It's just as easy to overtax your monitor with any of the Microsoft Windows operating systems.

Using a Two-Button Mouse

The X Window System was designed to work with a three-button mouse. Many PCs come with only a two-button mouse. With the Mouse Configuration tool, you can configure your Linux to emulate the middle button in the GUI by pressing both buttons simultaneously.

Alternatively, if you have a mouse with a scrolling wheel, you may already have a middle mouse button. If you have a mouse of this type, try pressing the scroll wheel. If it clicks, RHEL 3 has probably already configured it as a middle mouse button.

In many cases, the Red Hat installation program automatically configures the scroll wheel. But if you have a problem, you may need to edit the /etc/X11/XF86Config file directly. The following is an excerpt from my version of this file. It describes the mouse settings, with the scroll wheel enabled.

```
Section "Input Device"
      Identifier "Mouse0"
      Driver     "mouse"
      Option     "Protocol" "IMPS/2"
      Option     "Device"   "/dev/psaux"
      Option     "ZAxisMapping" "4 5"
      Option     "Emulate3Buttons" "no"
EndSection
```

"Mouse0" helps identify the mouse in other parts of this configuration file. The driver is mouse; the device is /dev/psaux. The protocol, IMPS/2, is associated with a standard PS/2 mouse. And the ZAxisMapping variable translates motion from the wheel to standard software mouse buttons 4 and 5, which corresponds to up and down motion in the active window. Mouse buttons 4 and 5 exist in the software even if you have only two physical buttons on your mouse.

X Configuration Files

While there are a wide variety of X Window configuration files in the /etc/X11 directory, the primary X Window configuration file is XF86Config. It's instructive to read the associated man page carefully. It is well documented and includes a number of commented sample commands that can help you configure your system in a number of special ways. For example, it includes tips on how you can

- Configure different keyboards
- Set up multiple monitors, in what is known as a "multi-head" configuration

■ Disable switching from the GUI to other virtual terminals with the following command:

```
Option "DontVTSwitch" "on"
```

■ Disable the CTRL-ALT-BACKSPACE key sequence, which normally exits from the GUI, with the following command:

```
Option "DontZap" "on"
```

This is just a small sample of the things you can do with your X Window configuration. It's possible that you'll see a problem like this on the Troubleshooting and System Maintenance exam. You may also be asked to configure one of these options during the Installation and Configuration Exam.

Starting the X Window

The default server is linked to the **X** command. X is called up by the **startx** command. Both of these commands are located in the /usr/X11R6/bin directory. Examine the long listing for the **X** command. You'll see that it's linked to the version 4 all-in-one server package, XFree86:

```
# ls -l /usr/X11R6/bin/X
lrwxrwxrwx    1 root    root      7 Jul 30 07:33 /usr/X11R6/bin/X ->>
XFree86
```

The Display Settings tool normally writes its changes to /etc/X11/XF86Config. When the XFree86 X Server starts, it reads this file.

EXERCISE 6-1

X Server

In this exercise, you will start your X Server without a window manager. You'll then start an X Client application known as **xterm**. Some of the commands used in this exercise are covered later in the chapter. If the X Window System is not running, you can skip steps 1 and 3.

1. If the X Window System is running, change to a text console by pressing CTRL-ALT-F1.

2. If you see a login prompt, log in at the text console as root. Otherwise, press CTRL-C to stop the X Window.

3. If you logged in as root at the text console, stop the current X Window Server with the following command:

```
# init 3
```

4. Start the XFree86 X Server by typing the command:

```
# X &
```

Your X Server will start, but all you will see is a blank gray screen, with an "x" that represents your mouse cursor.

5. Switch back to your text console session by pressing CTRL-ALT-F1.

6. Type the following command:

```
# xterm -display localhost:0.0  &
```

(Note: **xterm** starts with a lowercase **x**, and there is only one hyphen before the display switch.)

7. Switch back to your X Window display by pressing ALT-F7.

You should now have an **xterm** terminal window. Select the window and enter commands at the **xterm** command line. Check out the contents of the /usr/X11R6/ bin directory. Try starting other X Client applications such as **xcalc** and **xclock** from the **xterm** command line. Reboot your system to return things to normal.

One last keystroke hint for X: pressing the CTRL-ALT-BACKSPACE keys sends a termination signal to the X Server. In some situations, the Linux GUI crashes and it's not possible to start a text console session by pressing CTRL-ALT-F1. In this case, the CTRL-ALT-BACKSPACE key combination can keep you from having to reboot your computer.

EXERCISE 6-2

Multiple X Servers

In this exercise, you will start two different X Servers. If the X Window System is not running, you can skip steps 1 and 3.

1. If the X Window System is running, change to a text console by pressing CTRL-ALT-F1.

2. If you see a login prompt, log in at the text console as root. Otherwise, press CTRL-C to stop X Window.

3. If you logged in at the text console, stop the current X Window Server by typing this:

```
init 3
```

4. Start the XFree86 X Server by typing the command:

```
# startx &
```

Your normal GUI will start.

5. Switch back to your text console session by pressing CTRL-ALT-F1. Return to your GUI by pressing ALT-F7. Switch back again to your text console session. (If these commands do not work, check for a DontVTSwitch option in your /etc/X11/XF86Config file.

6. Type the following command:

```
# startx -- :1 &
```

7. You should now have two different GUIs. Switch to the first GUI by pressing CTRL-ALT-F7. Return to the second GUI by pressing CTRL-ALT-F8.

8. Log out from both GUIs.

XF86Config in Detail

As you learn the intricacies of configuring the Linux X Window Server, it's worth some trouble to examine the /etc/X11/XF86Config file in detail. It's interesting to note that these files are almost identical with RHEL 3 on my VMWare computer and with Red Hat Linux 9 on my desktop computer. The only differences are associated with the different graphics hardware and monitor.

The first line is a comment that indicates whether your X Window system was last configured by the Red Hat installation program or the Display Settings tool. The two options are:

```
# XFree86 4 configuration created by pyxf86config
# XFree86 4 configuration created by redhat-config-xfree86
```

The first section binds the other sections together. In other words, you'll see sections later in this file, each associated with an Identifier variable: Screen0, Mouse0, Keyboard0, and DevInputMice.

```
Section "ServerLayout"
    Identifier      "Default Layout"
    Screen      0   "Screen0" 0 0
    InputDevice     "Mouse0" "CorePointer"
    InputDevice     "Keyboard0" "CoreKeyboard"
    InputDevice     "DevInputMice" "AlwaysCore"
EndSection
```

The next section identifies the location of RGB (red, green, blue) style colors for display in the X Window. It also identifies the standard TCP/IP port for the X Font Server. That provides a key clue: the X Font Server can communicate over a network. You may have problems if a firewall is blocking this port.

```
Section "Files"
    RgbPath     "/usr/X11R6/lib/X11/rgb"
    FontPath    "unix/:7100"
EndSection
```

The following section describes font and server extension modules. These are fairly standard; you can review a full list of possible modules in the /usr/X11R6/lib/ modules directory (or subdirectories).

```
Section "Module"
    Load    "dbe"
    Load    "extmod"
    Load    "fbdevhw"
    Load    "glx"
    Load    "record"
    Load    "freetype"
    Load    "type1"
    Load    "dri"
EndSection
```

Next, we'll look at a couple of different sections, both labeled InputDevice. The first configures your keyboard as a regular US keyboard with 105 keys. The second configures a PS/2 mouse, as described earlier. The Emulate3Buttons option, when active, configures the X Server to activate middle mouse button functionality when you click the left and right mouse buttons simultaneously.

```
Section "InputDevice"
    Identifier  "Keyboard0"
    Driver      "keyboard"
    Option      "XkbRules" "xfree86"
```

```
    Option      "XkbModel" "pc105"
    Option      "XkbLayout" "us"
EndSection

Section "InputDevice"
    Identifier  "Mouse0"
    Driver      "mouse"
    Option      "Protocol" "IMPS/2"
    Option      "Device" "/dev/psaux"
    Option      "ZAxisMapping" "4 5"
    Option      "Emulate3Buttons" "no"
EndSection
```

The following InputDevice is included by default, to support the simultaneous use of a USB mouse:

```
Section "InputDevice"
    Identifier  "DevInputMice"
    Driver      "mouse"
    Option      "Protocol" "IMPS/2"
    Option      "Device" "/dev/input/mice"
    Option      "ZAxisMapping" "4 5"
    Option      "Emulate3Buttons" "no"
EndSection
```

The following Monitor and Device sections are associated with the monitor that you configured during the installation process or with the **redhat-config-xfree86** command. Since no Monitor Vendor is specified, this is associated with some generic monitor.

```
Section "Monitor"
    Identifier  "Monitor0"
    VendorName  "Monitor Vendor"
    ModelName   "LCD Panel 800x600"
    HorizSync   31.5 - 37.9
    VertRefresh 40.0 - 70.0
    Option      "dpms"
EndSection

Section "Device"
    Identifier  "Videocard0"
    Driver      "vmware"
    VendorName  "Videocard vendor"
    BoardName   "VMWare"
```

```
        VideoRam        16384
    EndSection
```

As you can see, the Screen section associates the "Monitor" and "Device" as configured by Identifiers Videocard0 and Monitor0. If the Red Hat installation program or the Display Settings tool gives you the wrong DefaultDepth or inappropriate screen sizes (Modes), you can add them here.

```
Section "Screen"
    Identifier    "Screen0"
    Device        "Videocard0"
    Monitor       "Monitor0"
    DefaultDepth  24
    SubSection "Display"
            Depth    24
            Modes    "800x600" "640x480"
    EndSubSection
EndSection
```

Many graphics systems support the 3D direct rendering interface, as shown:

```
Section "DRI"
    Group    0
    Mode     0666
EndSection
```

CERTIFICATION OBJECTIVE 6.02

X Font Server

Assuming your X Server is properly configured, you should be able to start a GUI with the **startx** command. One of the things that could go wrong is with the X Font Server. The X Window System needs fonts. Linux manages fonts through the X Font Server. RHEL 3 manages the X Font Server with the **xfs** service script. Generally, you can't start the Linux GUI unless **xfs** is running. Many different fonts are normally available in the /usr/X1R6/lib/X11/fonts directory.

The X Font Server can be an Achilles' heel for X Window. A number of things can go wrong with **xfs**. If you can't start your X Window, check the status of your X Font Server with the following command:

```
# service xfs status
```

If the X Font Server is not running, you'll want to go through the following troubleshooting list:

- The **xfs** service could be stopped or dead. In this case, you may need to try restarting **xfs**.

- The **xfs** service might not be set to start in your current runlevel; you can inspect and change this with the appropriate **chkconfig** command.

- The filesystems with /tmp or /home could be full. The **xfs** service can't start if either of these filesystems is full. There may also be problems if /tmp is on a different physical hard disk from other X Window files.

on the
○ o b   *Do not confuse the X Font Server service script, xfs, with the filesystem with the same initials, which was developed for very large files by Silicon Graphics.*

- Fonts could be misconfigured in /etc/X11/XF86Config.

- Fonts could be missing from the default /usr/X1R6/lib/X11/fonts directory. For example, missing 100-dpi or 75-dpi fonts could cause applications in a Linux GUI to look strange.

Any of these problems could make it impossible for you to start a Linux X Window. In addition, if you've set up a default X Window login, these problems could keep you from getting to the graphical login manager.

EXERCISE 6-3

X Font Server

In this exercise, we'll look at the effect of a problem with the X Font Server on starting the GUI in Linux.

1. If you're in the GUI, exit from it. If you've configured RHEL 3 to start from the text login interface by default, that is easy. Just click Main Menu | Log Out, and click OK to confirm your logout from the GUI.

2. If you have configured RHEL 3 to start the GUI by default, you'll have to open up a command line interface. Right-click on the desktop. In the pop-up menu that appears, click New Terminal, and run the following command:

```
# init 3
```

3. Check on the status of your X Font Server. If your GUI works, it should be operational. Next, deactivate your X Font Server:

```
# service xfs status
xfs (pid 2560) is running . . .
# service xfs stop
Shutting down xfs:                       [OK]
#
```

4. Try starting the GUI again with the **startx** command. Watch what happens. Look for the "Fatal server" error message.

5. What other things could keep the X Font Server from starting on your computer? Think about elements such as the service configuration utility, or a full /tmp or /home filesystem. You may need to go through this process to diagnose problems during the Red Hat exams.

6. Restart the X Font Server.

CERTIFICATION OBJECTIVE 6.03

X Clients

Once you've configured a working X Server, you are (almost) ready to start connecting to various X Window Client applications. An X Window Client is an application program. This client uses your X Server's graphical services to display output. While one X Server process controls the display, you can run as many X Clients as your hardware resources, primarily RAM, will support. If your Linux system is part of a network, you may also start X Clients on other systems on the network and have those clients send their displays to your X Server.

X Clients exist for almost every basic application. There are X Clients for word processing, spreadsheets, games, and more. The Red Hat GUI configuration tools were developed as X Clients. There are even X Client versions of popular utilities such as the emacs editor.

Default X Clients

When you configure a workstation for most users, you'll be configuring their GUI. You may need to specify a default desktop such as GNOME or KDE. I'll describe these desktops later in this chapter. You may want to set up specific applications to start automatically on a   user's desktop. Settings for default X Clients are stored in each user's home directory, in various hidden directories. In RHEL 3, KDE configuration files are stored in each user's ~/.kde directory (where the tilde, ~, represents a Linux home directory). GNOME configuration files are stored in hidden directories such as ~/.gconf, ~/.gnome, and ~/.gnome2.

Towards the end of this chapter, I'll show you the GUI tools that you can use to help you configure a workstation quickly during the Red Hat exams.

X Clients and Command Line Options

Starting an X Client is very easy. When you start the X Window System for the first time on RHEL 3, it puts X Client icons on the desktop by default. You can start additional X Clients by selecting a program from a menu, or you can start an X Client from a command line terminal screen. Later, I'll show you how to set up default X Clients when you start the Linux GUI.

It's almost as easy to start running X Clients from remote servers. All you need to do is give permission. As discussed later in this chapter, the **xhost +*client*** command on your Linux computer allows a remote computer named *client* to run X Clients on your local X Server.

on the **job**

You may wish to reread and practice with the commands in this section after reading the next section on the Remote Display of X Applications.

X Clients are standard Linux applications, which you can start with commands such as **xclock, xeyes, xterm, xclipboard**, etc. If you choose to start an X Client from a command line, you can follow the command name with any number of options. Most X Clients understand a common set of options. These options are used to control such things as the size and location of the X Client's window, the font the application uses to display the text, and even the display on which the application should display its output. Table 6-1 lists some of the more useful options you can supply when you start an X Client from the command line.

The behavior of most of the command line options in Table 6-1 is self-descriptive, but we need to take a more detailed look at how some of the options work. We will examine the **-display** option in more detail when we look at running remote X Clients.

TABLE 6-1 Common X Client Command Line Options

Option	Example	Result
-display *server*:0.0	-display frodo:0.0	Send output to the X Server running on the computer named frodo.
-geometry *XSIZE×YSIZE+XOFF+YOFF*	-geometry 100×100+10+20	Specify the size and location of the window. In this case, we want a window 100×100 pixels in size, offset from the upper-left corner by 10 pixels horizontally and 20 pixels vertically.
-font *fontname*	-font lucidasans-14	Display text for this client using a specific font.
-background *color*	-background blue	Set the window background to blue.
-foreground *color*	-foreground white	Set the window foreground to white.
-title *string*	-title "My Window"	Place a title on the client window's title bar.
-bordercolor *color*	-bordercolor green	Make the window border green.
-borderwidth *pixels*	-borderwidth 5	Make the window border 5 pixels wide.

The **-geometry** option is used to specify both the size of the window that the X Client starts up in and the location of the window. Notice that the first two numbers, the *XSIZE* and the *YSIZE*, are separated by a lowercase "x." These two numbers specify the size of the client window in either pixels or characters, depending on the application. For example, if you are opening an **xterm** window, the size represents a terminal screen with *XSIZE* columns and *YSIZE* lines. If you are starting an **xclock**, the size represents a window *XSIZE×YSIZE* in pixels.

The next two numbers specify where you want the client window to appear on your display. The numbers are relative to the upper-left and lower-right corners of the desktop: +0+0 represents the upper-left corner, -0-0 represents the lower-right corner. These specs are shown in Table 6-2.

Therefore, for *XOFF+YOFF*, if you specify +10+10, the client is positioned 10 pixels from the left edge of the screen and 10 pixels from the top of the screen.

TABLE 6-2

X Client Geometrical Positioning

XSIZExYSIZE	Description
-0-0	Lower-right corner
-0+0	Upper-right corner
+0-0	Lower-left corner
+0+0	Upper-left corner

Alternatively, -10-10 positions the client 10 pixels from the right edge of the screen and 10 pixels up from the bottom of the screen.

The **-font** option specifies the font that the X Client should use to display text. The X Window System comes with a wide variety of both fixed and proportionally spaced fonts. The default list is located in the /usr/X11R6/lib/X11/fonts directory. This directory contains a number of subdirectories, each of which contains font files for the various types of fonts installed on your system.

Many of the X Client command line options enable you to specify colors for different parts of the client window. You can specify a simple color such as red, green, white, and black. Alternatively, you can specify a color by indicating the red, green, and blue components of the color:

```
# xclock -background RGB:FF/00/FF
```

xterm

One of the most useful X Clients is a program called **xterm**. As its name implies, **xterm** is an X Client application that creates a terminal window on your X display. So, after all the hard work you've gone through to get a nice windowing display, you're right back where you started, with a command line interface.

The difference is that now you can start up as many of these command line interfaces as you like, and you can switch between them with the click of a mouse. Since **xterm** is an X Client, you can even open terminal windows on other computers on your network and have them display to your desktop. You can start **xterm** either from a menu or from a command line prompt.

While the two major desktops include their own versions of **xterm**, Red Hat has configured gnome-terminal as the default command-line interface within the default GNOME desktop. It is what is started when you right-click on the desktop and select New Terminal from the pop-up menu.

on the
ʘ o b

In RHEL 3, the default GUI command line interface for the KDE desktop is konsole, which you can start when you right-click on the desktop and select Open Terminal from the pop-up menu. Functionally, you can run commands in konsole just as you can run commands within gnome-terminal.

CERTIFICATION OBJECTIVE 6.04

Remote Display of X Applications

One of the most powerful features of the X Window System is its networking support. The X Window System was designed to run in a networked environment. If you are a system administrator responsible for a number of RHEL 3 systems, you don't have to run to the server room every time you want to run a GUI administration tool. With the X Window System, you can connect to any number of systems and redirect the output from X Clients running on those systems back to the X Server running on your desktop.

Security

Before we configure clients and servers to transmit graphical applications, let's examine some of the basics of X Window security. When working with remote X applications, all other Linux security features are still in effect. You will still need a user account and password in order to connect to the remote system to start an X Client. You need to make sure that a firewall isn't blocking access.

Part of the job of the X Server running on your local computer is to listen for requests from X Clients that want to send their output to your display. Those requests can come from applications that are running on your local computer, or they can come from applications running on another computer on your network.

You need access control. Otherwise, anyone on your network can send the display from their X Clients to your computer. In a larger or a production network environment, you will want to limit access to your local X Server.

xhost Control

The Linux way to control access to your local X Server is with the **xhost** command. This command controls access by computer. In Table 6-3, I illustrate a number of examples of how you can use the **xhost** command to secure your X Server. You can substitute IP addresses for specific computer hostnames.

	Command	Description
TABLE 6-3		
	xhost	Show current security settings
Limiting Access to Your Local X Server	xhost +	Disable security; allow connections from any system
	xhost -	Enable security
	xhost +apps.xyz.com	Allow connection from apps.xyz.com
	xhost -apps.xyz.com	Disable connections from apps.xyz.com

e x a m

Ⓦatch *These xhost commands won't work unless you're running them from a command line terminal inside the Linux GUI. Otherwise, you'll get an error message like "unable to open display."*

The **xhost** command allows you to control X Server security on your computer. One more sophisticated alternative is the **xauth** command, which can use encryption to verify not just remote computers, but the permissions that you may grant to remote users. Access information for these other validation methods is stored in the hidden binary file ~/.Xauthority.

Before you can send X Clients from a remote computer, you need to set the **DISPLAY** variable. You can do so with a command such as **DISPLAY=localhost:0.0**. Then you can export that variable with the **export DISPLAY** command. Alternatively, you can combine the two commands with the following command:

```
# export DISPLAY=xserver:0
```

where *xserver* is the name of the remote computer where you want the X Client to be shown.

The second part of the **DISPLAY** line (0.0) requires further explanation. As described earlier, you can start multiple X Servers. When you are redirecting the output for an X Client, you must tell it not only which system to connect to but also which GUI display and which screen on that display to use. On most systems this will be servername, display 0, console 0 (written as *host*:0.0). The server portion of this entry can be a hostname, a fully qualified domain name, or an IP address. The following are all valid specifications for remote displays:

- desk:0.0
- desk.xyz.com:0.0
- 192.168.1.5:0

To summarize, there are three steps required before you can run X Clients from remote computers:

- Disable the firewall on the local computer, the X Server, with a command such as **service iptables stop**.
- Authorize connections from the remote computer. For example, for a remote computer named charlie, you'd run the **xhost +charlie** command.
- Log into the remote computer and export the **DISPLAY** variable.

xauth Control with ssh

But there's an easier way. Using the Secure Shell (**ssh**) described in Chapter 11, you can log into the remote client computer. You can then start X Clients such as **xterm** or even a Red Hat GUI tool such as the Security Level Configuration tool described in Chapter 10 with the **redhat-config-securitylevel** command. The GUI application opens automatically on the local computer.

You still need to authorize access from the local computer with an appropriate **xhost** command, as I've just described.

EXERCISE 6-4

Starting a Display from a Remote Client

In this exercise, we'll look at the steps required to run a display from a remote client. This assumes a basic knowledge of the Secure Shell, and its associated command, **ssh**. For more information on running the **ssh** command, see Chapter 11. You'll need two computers running Linux. While RHEL 3 is not required on both computers, you will need the Secure Shell installed on both. The Secure Shell service, **sshd**, should be running on the remote computer. You'll also need the root password for both computers. Assume the local computer is named Enterprise, and the remote computer is named cosmicc (which is short for Cosmic Charlie, my favorite Grateful Dead teddy bear).

1. On the Enterprise computer, start the X Window. If it isn't already open, use the **startx** command.

2. When the Linux GUI is open, right-click on the desktop. In the pop-up menu that appears, click New Terminal.

3. Log into the remote computer using the Secure Shell. To log in as root, use the following command. Enter the root password on the remote computer

when prompted. If you're asked if you want to set up a encryption key, type **yes**. This should log you into the remote computer.

```
# ssh root@cosmicc
root@cosmicc's password:
```

4. Now you can start the GUI applications of your choice. Start with some easy X Clients, such as **xterm**, **xclock**, and **xeyes**. Where do you see these clients displayed? If you have the GUI open on the remote computer, you can walk over there and check the other computer for yourself. Close whatever X Clients you open.

5. You should be able to run most of the Red Hat GUI utilities from the remote computer. Try some with commands such as **redhat-config-network**, **redhat-config-samba**, and **redhat-config-securitylevel**. You can now edit the configuration on the remote computer. Remember to close the GUI utilities that you open.

6. If you run any remote GUI configuration utilities, check the results in the appropriate configuration file.

Troubleshooting

The X Window System is very robust and stable, but occasionally problems can arise. You can try several things when you troubleshoot X Window problems:

■ Session managers create log files in your home directory such as ~/.xsession-errors. Check these log files as well as /var/log/messages and /var/log/XFree86.0.log for error messages from your X Server.

■ Check the **DISPLAY** environment variable to make sure it is set correctly. If you are running X Clients locally, they still use this variable. You can set it with this command:

```
export DISPLAY=localhost:0.0
```

or

```
export DISPLAY=:0.0
```

■ Make sure /usr/X11R6/bin is in your $PATH.

- Check for underlying system problems or network problems that could be causing problems with the X Window System.

- Check the X Font Server for problems described earlier in this chapter.

- Even if your X Server is not responding or you can't read the display, don't forget that you can switch to a text console to gain access to the system.

- If you are troubleshooting X Server problems on a remote system, try starting an X Client from your workstation using the remote X Server's display. Note that you will need appropriate X security access to run the following command:

```
# xclock -display remotesys:0.0
```

EXERCISE 6-5

Troubleshooting DISPLAY Problems

In this exercise, we will see what happens if you unset the **DISPLAY** variable.

1. Log into an X Window session. Run the **startx** command if required to do so.

2. Bring up a terminal window. Right-click on the desktop and click New Terminal from the menu that appears.

3. Start the **xclock** X Client using the following command:

```
# xclock  &
```

4. Unset your **DISPLAY** variable:

```
# unset DISPLAY
```

5. Start another **xclock**:

```
# xclock  &
```

6. You should get an error message saying that the X Client can't find your display. Reset the **DISPLAY** variable with the command:

```
# export DISPLAY=localhost:0.0
```

7. Try starting the **xclock** X Client again.

CERTIFICATION OBJECTIVE 6.05

Desktops and Window Managers

Part of the Linux GUI is a special type of X Client known as a *window manager*. Earlier in this chapter in Exercise 6-1, you started the XFree86 X Server with the **X** command. It turned your display into a blank electronic canvas. This is the default desktop display for XFree86, which is an uninteresting textured gray background. The default mouse pointer for the X Window display is a graphic representation of an "X."

Once XFree86 starts and you have this canvas on your screen, the X Server is ready to start serving X Clients. You will notice that the windows seem to be missing something. You could use the methods in the preceding section to set up various X Clients; for example, the **xclock -display localhost:0.0** command would lead to the screen shown in Figure 6-6.

Still, you don't have any of the useful features that you've come to expect in a GUI, such as borders, title bars, menu bars, and minimize/maximize buttons. For this purpose, you need a window manager. A window manager is a special type of X Client that can only run with an X Server. The window manager controls how other X Clients appear on your display. This includes everything from placing title bars and drawing borders around the window for each X Client application you start,

FIGURE 6-6

An X Client on a plain X Server

to determining the size of your desktop. In a nutshell, the window manager controls the look and feel of your GUI.

As is usually the case with all things Linux, you have multiple ways to accomplish the same task. RHEL 3 can be installed with several different window managers and desktops. The GNOME and KDE desktops include their own window managers. Your choice of window manager and desktop will drive the look, feel, and functionality of the Linux X Window System.

The GNOME and KDE Desktops

Two powerful virtual desktop environments that come with RHEL 3 are the GNOME (GNU Network Object Model Environment) desktop environment and KDE (the K Desktop Environment). The GNOME desktop, shown in Figure 6-7, is the default desktop for RHEL 3 and is the desktop you first see after installing the X Window System. The

FIGURE 6-7	The GNOME desktop

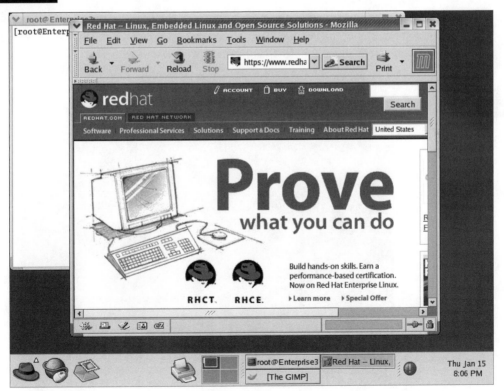

KDE desktop, shown in Figure 6-8, is the main alternate desktop system. KDE is the default for several other Linux distributions.

GNOME Features

The GNOME desktop includes support for the Common Object Request Broker Architecture (CORBA), which allows GNOME software components written in any language and running on different systems to work together. In addition, the GNOME developer community is also working on an architecture similar to Microsoft's Object Linking and Embedding (OLE) architecture that will allow one GNOME application to call and control another GNOME application.

One very nice feature of GNOME-compliant applications is that they are *session aware*; that is, when you quit an application, the application remembers the location in the document where you were last working and will reposition your cursor to that point when you restart the application.

Using GNOME

Many of the features of the GNOME interface will be familiar to you from other desktop environments. On the left side of the screen are icons representing files and applications that you can open by double-clicking them with the mouse. The GNOME desktop environment also provides you with several virtual desktops. Next to the application

FIGURE 6-8

The KDE desktop

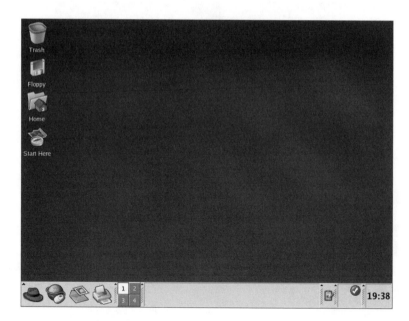

buttons on the right side of the panel is a pager you can use to move from one area of the desktop to another.

One of the key features of GNOME is the *panel*, which you can see at the bottom of the screen in Figure 6-7. The panel is the control center for most of your activities while you use GNOME. The button at the far left of the panel with the imprint of a red hat is the Main Menu button. Click this button, and you will see a list of menus and submenus which start applications. You can also launch configured applications from the panel by clicking the appropriate icon. The default buttons include Mozilla (the Web browser) and Evolution (the mail and schedule manager).

GNOME includes a number of applications, including graphics tools and an office suite, GNOME Office. As the default Red Hat desktop is GNOME, the remainder of this book will be based on this desktop environment. Nevertheless, the Red Hat exam requirements do not specify a preferred desktop; there should be no problems using KDE or the command line console to do everything that is required for the exam. You may be asked to configure either desktop on the Red Hat exams.

If you configure the default GNOME desktop for your users, you may want to configure GNOME in a special way. Normally, GNOME opens with a number of icons and possibly default applications such as nautilus. You can add more default applications such as a new terminal window or the **xcalc** calculator with the Sessions tool, which you can access via the Main Menu | Preferences | More Preferences | Sessions command.

KDE Features

The KDE desktop is built on the Qt C++ cross-platform GUI toolkit. This is another versatile way to create GUI applications for Linux.

Many of the features of KDE should also be familiar to you from other desktop environments. In fact, you can configure KDE to a look and feel that is quite similar to Windows 9*x*. As shown in Figure 6-8, it includes a Main Menu button, represented by the Red Hat in the lower-left corner of the desktop. Like GNOME, it includes pagers and buttons representing the open programs on the desktop.

Default Desktop

Once you've configured X Window, it's easy to start a Linux GUI. If it isn't already configured to start automatically, just run the **startx** command. This command, in the /usr/X11R6/bin directory, calls configuration files from your home directory. If these files don't exist, they are taken from the default directory for GUI configuration, /etc/X11.

To manage the default desktop, use the **switchdesk** command. For example, the following commands set the default desktop to KDE and GNOME, respectively:

```
# switchdesk KDE
# switchdesk GNOME
```

The **switchdesk** program creates two hidden files in your home directory, ~/.Xclients and ~/.Xclients-default, that are used to start your alternate desktop. You don't need to use **switchdesk**; once you have an ~/.Xclients-default file, you can edit it directly. It is a simple file; if your default desktop is KDE, this file has one line:

```
exec startkde
```

If your default desktop is GNOME, this file has a different line:

```
exec gnome-session
```

Alternatively, you can use **switchdesk** to set up twm, known as Tom's Window Manager. The version of twm in RHEL 3 includes just the same textured gray screen that you get with the **X** command. The ~/.Xclients-default file would include the following line:

```
exec /usr/X11R6/bin/twm
```

If you have other desktops or window managers installed, you can use those instead. When run at the command line, the **switchdesk** command can also let you set FVWM, Enlightenment, or WindowMaker as the default window manager. You'll see the new default the next time you run the **startx** command from a console command line interface.

EXERCISE 6-6

Desktops

Let's use the **switchdesk** command to explore the various desktops available in RHEL 3. It's also known as the Desktop Switching Tool.

1. The easiest way to make this work is if you've disabled any automatic login through the GUI. To do so, open a terminal window and run the **init 3** command.

2. Now enter the GUI with the **startx** command.

3. Open a terminal window in a GUI and run Main Menu | System Settings | More System Settings | Desktop Switching Tool. You can also open it from a GUI command line with the **switchdesk** command.

4. Your current desktop (probably GNOME) is selected. Try one of the other desktops (such as KDE, the other popular desktop for Linux).

5. Log out of your current session with the GNOME Main Menu | Log Out command.

6. Log back in again. This time you should see the KDE desktop.

7. Repeat step 3.

8. In the Desktop Switching Tool, try switching to twm.

9. Log out of KDE and run the **startx** command again. You should see that twm is a much more basic window manager. You'll need to log out again for your changes to take effect.

10. To exit from twm, left-click on the desktop. In the pop-up menu that appears, click Exit.

11. Run **switchdesk** from the command line. Select your favorite desktop. For example, if you want to make GNOME your default desktop again, run the **switchdesk gnome** command.

on the *Job*

Commercial Unix vendors like Sun Microsystems and Hewlett-Packard have officially endorsed GNOME and are working to make their proprietary versions of Unix (Solaris and HP-UX) fully GNOME-compliant. If you get comfortable with GNOME, you will find moving to Solaris or HP-UX much easier. Alternatively, several Linux distributions use KDE as their default desktop.

CERTIFICATION OBJECTIVE 6.06

The X Start Process

You can configure the X Window interface to start automatically when your system boots, or you can choose to start the X Window System manually. You can set up this option in the /etc/inittab configuration file. If you select a text login, you'll have to start the Linux GUI with the **startx** command. If you select a graphical login, you can also select the graphical login manager of your choice.

Text Login Mode

To access a Linux system, you need to log in. In other words, you identify yourself to the system with a username and a password. But this requires a login program. When you log into Linux at a regular command line interface, the **mingetty** command calls up a login program that prompts you for your username and password. Six **mingetty** terminals are configured through /etc/inittab.

There are six active runlevels in Linux. The two of concern here are runlevels 3 and 5. If you start Linux in runlevel 3, you get a text login. If you start Linux in runlevel 5, you get a graphical login screen.

It's easy to change the default boot mode from the command line to X Window. Just edit the /etc/inittab file. Go to the line with the initdefault variable. To make Linux start the X Window System automatically when Linux starts, use your favorite text editor and change the line in /etc/inittab that reads

```
id:3:initdefault:
```

to

```
id:5:initdefault:
```

Of course, you can reverse this process. This change does not take effect until you reboot. If you are running as the root user, you can also use the **init** command to switch between runlevel 5 and runlevel 3. Running this command:

```
# init 3
```

switches your display from X Window back to text terminal mode, whereas:

```
# init 5
```

switches you from text terminal mode to X Window. You can find more information on different runlevels and /etc/inittab in Chapter 4.

Display Managers: xdm, gdm, kdm

When you configure Linux to start from runlevel 5, you can log in through a special X Client, the *display manager*. The display manager is a fairly simple program; all it does is display a dialog box on the screen asking for your username and password. You can use any of three major display managers. The default display manager is the GNOME display manager, or gdm. To change your display manager, edit the **prefdm** shell script in the /etc/X11 directory, as shown in Figure 6-9.

Take the line that contains preferred= and add either kdm, gdm, or xdm for the KDE Display Manager, GNOME Display Manager, or X Display Manager, respectively. In the default RHEL 3 version of this file, it's on line 25.

How you start the X Window System affects its behavior. Assume you start X Window through one of the graphical display managers. When you exit an X Window session, you're returned to the same display manager. To continue, you would need to log in again.

The default behavior for the gdm window manager is to launch a GNOME session for you. The kdm window manager by default launches a KDE session. However, you can start GNOME or KDE from either login manager.

Both the GNOME and KDE environments use their own startup files. Through the use of option buttons, both the GNOME and KDE display managers allow you to choose the desktop environment you wish to start. From the GNOME display manager, click the Session menu. This starts a window where you can select from several desktop options, as shown in Figure 6-10.

FIGURE 6-9

Set your preferred display manager in /etc/X11/prefdm.

```
 5
 6 # shut down any graphical boot that might exist
 7 if [ -x /usr/bin/rhgb-client ]; then
 8     /usr/bin/rhgb-client -quit
 9 fi
10
11 # We need to source this so that the login screens get translated
12 [ -f /etc/profile.d/lang.sh ] && . /etc/profile.d/lang.sh
13
14 # Run preferred X display manager
15
16 # Try autologin first, if wanted...
17 if [ -f /etc/sysconfig/autologin -a -x /usr/sbin/autologin ]; then
18         if /usr/sbin/autologin; then
19                 exit 0
20         fi
21         # If autologin fails (bad permissions, etc.), we get here -
22         # time to start a real display manager.
23 fi
24
25 preferred=gdm
26 if [ -f /etc/sysconfig/desktop ]; then
27         . /etc/sysconfig/desktop
28         _if [ "$DISPLAYMANAGER" = GNOME ]; then
```

FIGURE 6-10

The GNOME
display manager,
gdm

From the KDE display manager, click the drop-down text box adjacent to Session Type, as shown in Figure 6-11. You can then select the desired desktop.

You can even set up the generic xdm window manager, which gives you the login screen shown in Figure 6-12.

FIGURE 6-11

The KDE display
manager, kdm

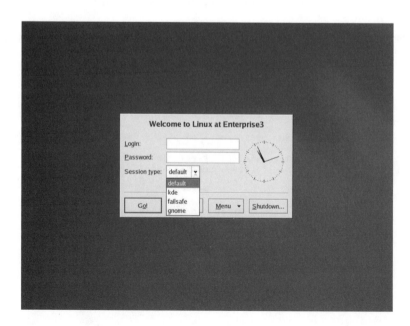

FIGURE 6-12

The xdm
login screen

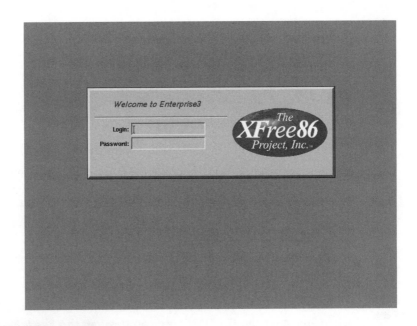

If the startx command doesn't successfully start the GUI from the command line in runlevel 3, check for a working xfs server in that runlevel. Unless you're already in runlevel 5, it doesn't matter if you've set xfs to start in runlevel 5.

If you log in using a display manager, X Window starts somewhat differently when compared to using **startx**. When you run **startx**, the X Window runs as a child process of your text-based login shell. Even though the X Window System is running, Linux is still at runlevel 3. After you exit the X Window System, you still have to log out of this shell to terminate your login session.

Analyzing startx

You've already seen that you can start the Linux GUI with the **startx** command. This starts the X Server and switches your display into graphics mode. It also runs through a series of configuration files which prompt Linux to start your selected desktop and other desired applications. In this section, we'll look at how **startx** actually works.

on the
ⓙob
The startx command is actually a shell script that serves as a front end to the xinit command. The default location for both the startx and xinit is the /usr/X11R6/bin directory.

There are a number of configuration files which can help you customize the behavior of your X Window session. These are hidden files that you can install into user's home directories. If **startx** doesn't find a particular configuration file in your home directory, it uses a default version of the same file. Let us start our analysis with two of the first lines in the **startx** script:

```
userclientrc=$HOME/.xinitrc
sysclientrc=/etc/X11/xinit/xinitrc
```

When you start the X Window System with the **startx** command, the **xinit** program looks for a file to run named .xinitrc in your home directory. If the **startx** command cannot find $HOME/.xinitrc, it will read the /etc/X11/xinit/xinitrc configuration script. This file, in turn, runs either the file $HOME /.Xclients or, if that file doesn't exist, /etc/X11/xinit/Xclients.

A typical ~/.xinitrc file includes commands that start various X Clients. (Remember, the tilde (~) represents the home directory.)

on the job

As described earlier in this chapter, you can also configure X Clients to start when you start the GNOME desktop through the Sessions utility. Settings are stored in each user's home directory, in the ~/.gnome2/session-manual file.

Let me illustrate a simple ~/.xinitrc file:

```
#!/bin/bash
xterm &
xclock -geometry 200x200-20+20 &
xcalc -geometry 300x300-20-20 &
exec twm
```

The first line sets bash as the shell for this script. The next line starts an **xterm** terminal client. The following line starts **xclock**, with a specific size and location. The line after that brings up an X Window calculator, also with a specific size and location. Notice that the first three command lines end with an ampersand (&). This is important; it tells the shell to run each command line and return control to the shell for this script. The final line uses the **exec** command to start the twm window manager. I illustrate the result in Figure 6-13; this supersedes any default desktop and X Clients which you may have otherwise configured.

FIGURE 6-13

A GUI as configured through ~/.xinitrc

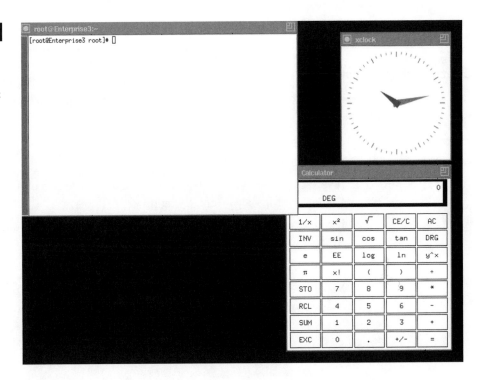

You can start other desktops through this file. You can substitute one of the following commands for **exec twm**:

```
exec gnome-session
exec startkde
```

You can create an ~/.xinitrc file with a text editor of your choice. Once you've saved the file, **startx** executes the commands in this file, with the results shown in Figure 6-13.

EXERCISE 6-7

Customizing the startx Process

In this exercise, we will configure the X Window System to use a customized .xinitrc file.

1. If the X Window System is running, change to a text console by pressing CTRL-ALT-F1.

2. If you see a login prompt, log in at the text console as root. Otherwise, press CTRL-C to stop the current X Window.

3. If you logged in at the text console, stop the current X Window Server with the following command:

   ```
   # init 3
   ```

4. Make sure you're in your home directory. Use your favorite text editor to create a .xinitrc file. If you're not sure what to do, use the sample file shown in the previous section.

5. Start the X Window System with the following command:

   ```
   startx
   ```

   Your X Window session should automatically start the applications in your .xinitrc file.

6. Exit from the twm desktop. Left-click on the desktop to bring up the twm main menu and click Exit.

7. If you want to restore your original desktop settings, to allow you to start GNOME or KDE with the **startx** command, remove the .xinitrc file from your home directory.

Now that you have seen how X Window Clients and the X Window Server work together, refer to the following Scenario & Solution for some common situations you may encounter, along with their solutions.

SCENARIO & SOLUTION

I'm having problems getting XFree86 to run on my hardware.	Check the Red Hat hardware support site. Run **redhat-config-xfree86**.
I want to use a different desktop environment.	Use the **switchdesk** command to change your desktop environment.
I want to stop the X Window System without rebooting Linux. When I try logging out, all I see is a graphical login manager.	Use the **init 3** command to change the system runlevel to runlevel 3.
I'm having problems starting an X Client.	Check that the **DISPLAY** variable is properly set with the following command: # **export DISPLAY=localhost:0.0** Check for underlying network problems. Check X security problems.
My X Window display is acting strangely and I can't log in.	Switch to a virtual console and log in. Check the error logs. See if your X Font Server (**xfs**) is running. If it isn't, check for errors in ~/.xsession-errors and /var/log/messages. Make sure your /tmp and /home directory partitions are not full. As a last resort, rerun **redhat-config-xfree86**.

CERTIFICATION OBJECTIVE 6.07

Basic Graphical Applications

At the last revision to the Red Hat Exam Prep guide, Red Hat added a couple of prerequisite skills: configuring e-mail clients and working with Web browsers. Therefore, it is reasonable to expect to have to install browsers, configure e-mail clients, and similar applications on a desktop computer during the Red Hat exams.

Overview

There is a wide variety of graphical applications available for RHEL 3. Most are accessible through the Red Hat Main Menu button in the lower-left corner of the GNOME and KDE desktop environments.

Red Hat has modified its version of the GNOME and KDE desktops with the "Bluecurve" theme. It has partially standardized the look and feel of both desktops. The Main Menu button in the lower-left corner of these desktops has a different look in other Linux distributions. In GNOME, the Main Menu button is a foot; in KDE, it's a big "K."

Red Hat has modified the Main Menu options that you see in both desktops. The results are similar, though not identical. Many of the menu options are the same in the Red Hat version of the GNOME and KDE desktops.

Browsers

The default Web browser in the RHEL 3 GNOME and KDE desktops is Mozilla. You can start it in either desktop environment by clicking on the icon with the mouse and globe adjacent to the Main Menu button.

One of the prerequisites in the Red Hat Exam Prep guide is that you need to know how to use the Mozilla Web browser to access regular and secure sites on the Internet. While this is an elementary skill, you don't have to know how to use a Web browser to administer a Linux operating system.

There are a number of other Web browsers available in RHEL 3, including KDE's Konqueror. If you don't know how to use a Web browser in Linux, I suggest that you refer to a basic guide to Linux, such *Red Hat Linux Administration: A Beginner's Guide* by Michael Turner and Steve Shah (McGraw-Hill/Osborne, 2003).

Configuring E-mail Clients

There are graphical and text e-mail clients available on RHEL 3. The default graphical e-mail client in RHEL 3 is Evolution, which is functionally similar to Microsoft's Outlook. You can start this program by clicking on the icon with an envelope and stamp. By default, it's next to the Mozilla icon in the taskbar.

When you first start Evolution, it prompts you for your e-mail information, including your name, e-mail address, and mail server type. If you're configuring a POP (Post Office Protocol) or IMAP (Internet Message Access Protocol), you're also prompted for incoming and outgoing mail server addresses, as well as login information as required for each server. Finally, you're asked to set your time zone.

Configuring Default Clients

It's easy to add default clients for a user. If you're configuring a GNOME system, you can do so with the Session utility. As described earlier, you can open it by clicking

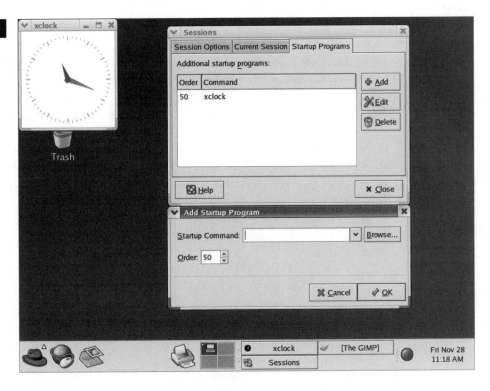

FIGURE 6-14

Configuring
default GNOME
clients

Main Menu | Preferences | More Preferences | Sessions. In the Sessions window,
click the Startup Programs tab. As shown in Figure 6-14, the **xclock** program is already
in the list. If you click Add, that starts the Add Startup Program window, where you
can add the additional startup programs of your choice.

Alternatively, you can use the .xinitrc file described earlier. As the Sessions utility
does not work on KDE, that is the only option if you're configuring X Clients to
start when you run the KDE desktop.

CERTIFICATION SUMMARY

The X Window System provides a state-of-the-art graphical user interface and offers
features not found in other GUI environments. Although the X Window System can
be complicated, you should be able to configure it during the RHEL 3 installation
process. Alternatively, the Red Hat Display Settings tool simplifies the setup or
reconfiguration process.

One of the key parts of the X Window system is the X Font Server. If it isn't running,
or the /tmp or /home directory partitions are full, you can't run the Linux GUI.

The X Window system works as client and server. X Clients and X Servers can be located on different computers on a network. You can set it up with appropriate **xhost**, **DISPLAY**, and firewall commands. If you prefer, you don't have to worry about your firewall, as you can bypass it through the Secure Shell.

The look and feel of the X Window interface is determined by your choice of desktop. RHEL 3 comes with several desktop environments, including GNOME, KDE, and twm. The GNOME desktop interface is the default for RHEL 3.

You can customize the GUI start process in a number of ways. You can configure a default login manager. With an appropriate .xinitrc file, you can set up X Clients to start when you run the **startx** command. Plus, if you create an .xinitrc file and then run the **switchdesk** command, Linux modifies the .xinitrc file. Alternatively, you can run the Sessions utility to configure X Clients in the GNOME desktop.

TWO-MINUTE DRILL

Here are some of the key points from the certification objectives in Chapter 6.

X Server

❏ The X Server is the software that manages the graphics display on the local computer, which includes your monitor/graphics adapter, keyboard, and mouse.

❏ X Servers work with local and remote X Clients to keep your display up to date. X Servers send inputs from the keyboard and mouse to X Clients. Then X Clients send instructions to the X Server to update the graphics on the monitor.

❏ You can configure the X Server during the RHEL 3 installation process. You can also configure or modify the configuration using the Red Hat Display Settings tool.

❏ The X Server configuration is stored in the /etc/X11/XF86Config file.

X Font Server

❏ If your X Font Server is not running, you won't be able to start the Linux GUI. Make sure it's set to run in your current run level, and that the /tmp and /home directory partitions are not full.

X Clients

❏ RHEL 3 supports a great number of X Client programs. These include terminal emulators, desktop accessories (such as the File Manager), and more.

❏ You can send the display of an X Client program to a remote system by using the **-display** option.

Remote Display of X Applications

❏ By default, X Clients sends display output to the local computer.

❏ You can send display output to other computers with the **-display** command line option.

❑ The local system must be willing to accept your remote X Client. You can run the **xhosts +remotepc** command to accept remote X Clients from the computer named remotepc.

❑ You can log into the remote client using the Secure Shell.

❑ You can set the **DISPLAY** environment variable on the X Client computer to direct all display output to a remote X Server.

Desktops and Window Managers

❑ The X Window System just gives you a blank electronic canvas. The look and feel of a GUI is provided by the window manager and desktop.

❑ The two main desktop environments are GNOME and KDE.

❑ You can use **switchdesk** from a terminal window or the command line interface console to select your default desktop.

The X Start Process

❑ You can configure the X Window interface to start automatically, or you can start it manually from the command line console with the **startx** command.

❑ You can customize the **startx** process by configuring X Clients in the ~/.xinitrc or the Sessions manager.

❑ You can set up graphical logins with the X display manager, the KDE display manager, or the GNOME display manager.

Basic Graphical Applications

❑ The default RHEL 3 Web browser is Mozilla. The default graphical e-mail client is Evolution.

SELF TEST

The following questions will help you measure your understanding of the material presented in this chapter. Read all the choices carefully, as there may be more than one correct answer. Don't focus exclusively on these questions. There are no longer any multiple choice questions on the Red Hat exams. These questions exclusively test your understanding of the chapter. While the topics in this chapter are "prerequisites," it is okay if you have another way of performing a task. Getting results, not memorizing trivia, is what counts on the Red Hat exams.

X Server

1. Which of the following is true about the X Window System?

   A. The X Server runs on your workstation; X Clients run on your workstation or on other computers on the network.

   B. If an X Server is running on your workstation, then X Client applications running on your computer cannot send their output to an X Server running on another system on the network.

   C. An X Client application gets its input from the keyboard and mouse attached to the same X Server where the client is sending its output.

   D. Aside from the steps necessary to start the remote application, there is no difference between running an X Client locally and running one remotely.

2. You performed a new install of RHEL 3 and chose not to configure the X Window System. Your system is now active, and you can log into a command prompt. How do you go about configuring the X Window System?

   A. Use the vi editor and modify the /etc/X11/XF86Config file.

   B. Run the **redhat-config-xfree86** command.

   C. Run the **xf86config** command.

   D. Reinstall RHEL 3.

X Font Server

3. You're having trouble starting the GNOME desktop environment, and you suspect the problem is with the X Font Server. Which of the following commands will tell you if it's running properly?

   A. service xfont status

   B. service xfs status

   C. service xfonts status

   D. service gnome status

X Clients

4. You want to start an **xterm** X Client that is 80 columns wide by 30 lines high from the command line and position it in the upper-right corner of your display when it starts. What command would you use?

  A. xterm -geometry +0-0 -font 80×30

  B. xterm -geometry 80×30-0+0

  C. xterm -geometry 80+30+0+0

  D. xterm -display 80×30-0+0

Remote Display of X Applications

5. You log into a remote system with the Secure Shell with the intention of starting several remote X Clients to send their output to your local display (admin1.xyz.com). What can you do to make this easier?

  A. Use the **-display admin1.xyz.com** option.

  B. Create a **DISPLAY** variable with this command:

      `DISPLAY=admin1.xyz.com:0.0`

  C. Create a **DISPLAY** variable with this command:

      `export DISPLAY=admin1.xyz.com`

  D. Create a **DISPLAY** variable with this command:

      `export DISPLAY=admin1.xyz.com:0.0`

6. You're trying to gain Secure Shell access to another computer on your LAN so you can run X Clients from the remote system. That computer is refusing access. Neither computer has a firewall. What can you do on that remote computer so it will accept your **ssh** command inputs?

  A. Restart the Secure Shell with the **/etc/rc.d/init.d/sshd restart** command.

  B. Enable the Secure Shell in the /etc/ssh.conf configuration file.

  C. Disable firewalls on the network.

  D. Restart xinetd with the **/etc/rc.d/inet.d/xinetd restart** command.

Desktops and Window Managers

7. When you installed RHEL 3, you configured the X Window System but chose to log on in text mode. You have been starting the X Window System with the **startx** command and everything is working fine. In the future, you want to boot Linux directly into the GUI. How would you make this happen?

    A. Edit /etc/inittab and replace the **id:3:initdefault** command with **id:5:initdefault**.

    B. Run **redhat-config-xfree86**.

    C. Change the /etc/X11/prefdm link.

    D. Execute the **runlevel 5** command.

8. Your system is using the xdm display manager. You want to use the GNOME display manager (gdm). How can you do this?

    A. Change the /etc/X11/prefdm shell script and define a value for the variable named **preferred**.

    B. Run **redhat-config-xfree86**.

    C. Edit /etc/X11/XF86Config.

    D. Use the GNOME Control Panel to change the display manager.

The X Start Process

9. You would like to automatically start up the **xclock** application whenever you start the GNOME desktop with the **startx** command. Which of the following methods can you use?

    A. Create or edit the file ~/.Xdefault and add this command:

```
xclock &
```

    B. Use the Sessions utility and add the **xclock** command to the Startup tab.

    C. Edit /etc/X11/XF86Config and add this command:

```
xclock -geometry 200x200-0+0 &
```

    D. Create or edit the file .xinitrc in your home directory and add the following command. Make sure the last command in this file is **exec twm**.

```
xclock &
```

Basic Graphical Applications

10. Which of the following is true about the default GNOME and KDE desktop environments in RHEL 3?

    A. The basic Red Hat utilities can only be found through the GNOME desktop.

    B. The basic Red Hat utilities can only be found through the KDE desktop.

    C. You can configure GNOME and KDE with the Red Hat Display Settings tool.

    D. You can use the same menus in GNOME and KDE to start many Red Hat configuration utilities.

LAB QUESTIONS

Lab 1

You want to upgrade the video card in your Linux system. Your old video card is slow and doesn't have enough display memory to provide you with the resolution and color depth you require. You have obtained a new ATI 32MB Radeon card (I'm using this product for example purposes only). What steps might you follow to replace your old card with your new card?

Lab 2

You want to see what happens when there are problems starting the Linux GUI. With RHEL 3, the XFree86 Version 4.x server is configured by default. The configuration of the X Server is stored in the /etc/X11/XF86Config configuration file. Before Linux starts the X Server, it reads this file. To do so, you'll want to back up your current /etc/X11/XF86Config file, delete it, and then reboot your computer into runlevel 5. You can restore it after the lab is complete.

Lab 3

For this lab, you'll need two Linux computers connected over a network. You'll need a shared NFS directory from the local computer. You can use the same directory that you may have used in Chapter 2 to share the RHEL 3 installation files. Start a Secure Shell connection between the two computers. Start the GUI on the local computer, and use the Secure Shell to log in remotely to the other computer. Finally, set and export an appropriate **DISPLAY** variable. You can then see what happens when you start X Clients from the remote computer.

Once you do, run the Red Hat root password program from the remote computer. Make changes to the password. When you log out and try to log back into the remote computer, you should be able to confirm that the root password on the remote computer has changed.

Lab 4

In this lab, you'll set up a GUI workstation. It'll start with the xdm login manager, and automatically start GNOME, open the Mozilla Web browser, and start a gnome-terminal session when you boot this Linux computer.

SELF TEST ANSWERS

X Server

1. ☑ **A, C,** and **D. A** is correct because the X Server runs on the local computer with the graphics hardware, while X Clients may run locally or remotely. **C** is correct because the X Server sends keyboard and mouse inputs to local or remote X Clients. **D** is also correct because remote X Clients interact with the X Server in the same way as a local X Client.

    ☒ **B** is incorrect because there simply is no such restriction.

2. ☑ **B.** You should use the Display Dettings tool any time you need to make changes to your X Window configuration.

    ☒ **A** is possibly correct assuming you understand enough about the XF86Config file to make the necessary changes. From experience, I would suggest you only edit this file if you have an (almost) working configuration you only wish to fine-tune. **C** refers to an X configuration tool that is not available in RHEL 3. **D** is extreme. The only justification for this might be if you performed a custom install and perhaps neglected to include all the components of the X Window System. Even if this is the case, you can still install the needed RPMs from the command line.

X Font Server

3. ☑ **B.** The X Font Server service is **xfs**. You can check the status of this service with the **service xfs status** command.

    ☒ **A, C,** and **D** are incorrect because these are not valid services for RHEL 3.

X Clients

4. ☑ **B.** The correct option is **-geometry 80×30-0+0**. Since you are creating a terminal window, the size specification 80×30 refers to the number of columns and lines. The offset specification -0+0 specifies that the right border of the **xterm** window should be offset 0 pixels from the right edge of the display and that the top border of the **xterm** window should be offset 0 pixels from the top of the display.

    ☒ **A** is incorrect because the **-font** option is used to specify the default font for the window, not the window location. **C** is incorrect because the window size is specified by the 80×30 format. **D** is incorrect because **-display** is the wrong switch for sizing and positioning the **xterm** window.

Remote Display of X Applications

5. ☑ **D.** X Client applications use the **DISPLAY** environment variable to determine where to send their output. It must be an environment variable, so you must use the **export** command to create it.

   ☒ **A** suggests using the **-display** option to every remote X Client you wish to start. While this is not the easiest way to do it, it could work. To make the option effective, though, you would have to write it as **-display admin1.xyz.com:0.0**. **B** is incorrect because it makes a variable called **DISPLAY** with the correct value, but it neglects to export the variable. **C** is not quite correct. While you do export **DISPLAY**, this answer does not identify the X graphics display and the screen (0.0).

6. ☑ **A.** The Secure Shell is normally enabled by default in RHEL 3. However, there are a number of reasons why it may not be on; this command restarts it.

   ☒ **B** is incorrect because there is no /etc/ssh.conf configuration file. **C** is incorrect because standard firewalls should not block the Secure Shell. **D** is incorrect because the Secure Shell in RHEL 3 is not a xinetd "Super Server" process. For more information on the Secure Shell, see Chapter 11.

Desktops and Window Managers

7. ☑ **A.** The easiest way to change the default runlevel for your Linux system is to change the initdefault setting in /etc/inittab to runlevel 5. You could then enter the **init 5** command to change to runlevel 5 immediately.

   ☒ **B** is incorrect because the Red Hat Display Settings tool cannot change /etc/inittab. **C** is incorrect because this just configures the preferred display manager. **D** is incorrect because the **runlevel** command is used to report on the previous and current runlevels, not to set the new default runlevel.

8. ☑ **A.** The file /etc/X11/prefdm is a script that starts your preferred display manager. By default, the variable named **preferred** is not set, so if your default runlevel is 5, Red Hat launches gdm (the GNOME display manager). To force a different display manager, set the **preferred** variable to either kdm (for the KDE display manager) or xdm (for the X display manager).

   ☒ **B** is incorrect because the Red Hat Display Settings tool does not set the preferred display manager. **C** is incorrect because the preferred display manager is not set in XF86Config. **D** is incorrect because there is no such option in the GNOME Control Panel.

The X Start Process

9. ☑ **B.** You can configure X Clients to start automatically in GNOME with the Sessions utility.

☒ **A** is incorrect because .Xdefault is not used to start X Clients when you start the GUI. **C** is incorrect because the XF86Config file is used to configure the X Server to the correct hardware settings, not launch a user's favorite applications. **D** is incorrect because the **exec twm** command starts Tom's Window Manager, not the GNOME desktop.

Basic Graphical Applications

10. ☑ **D.** Red Hat has configured both GNOME and KDE so you can find many Red Hat configuration utilities through the same GUI menus.

☒ **A** and **B** are incorrect as you can find basic Red Hat configuration utilities, using the Main Menu button, in both the GNOME and KDE desktops. **C** is not correct as you can only configure the X Server with the Red Hat Display Settings tool.

LAB ANSWERS

Lab I

1. Before you stop Linux on your computer, you should configure it so it no longer attempts to start the X Server when Linux boots. This is controlled by the initdefault line in the /etc/inittab file. Edit this file and change the second field from 5 (Multi-User With X Support) to 3 (Multi-User With No X Support). You could use vi, pico, or any other suitable text editor to do this job.

2. Perform an orderly shutdown on your system at a safe time. Use the **shutdown -h now** command.

3. Now that the system is off, replace your video card.

4. Start your computer and boot into RHEL 3. During the boot process, the Red Hat **kudzu** command automatically probes for new hardware. If this probe finds your new video card, you can configure it when prompted.

5. If **kudzu** fails to find your new hardware, you should log in as root and run the Red Hat Display Settings tool.

6. The Red Hat Display Settings tool should correctly identify your new hardware. You should select the correct amount of display memory (32MB) and the graphics resolutions and color depths you desire. If it does not, you can configure it manually using the available settings.

7. Test the result. Run the **startx** or **init 5** command to start the Linux GUI.

Lab 2

1. Back up /etc/X11/XF86Config to a safe location such as your home directory.

2. As the root user, delete or rename the /etc/X11/XF86Config file.

3. Open /etc/inittab in your favorite text editor. Look at the line with initdefault. Change the number right before this variable from a 3 to a 5 if required.

4. When you reboot your computer, observe what happens when Linux tries to find the default login display manager.

5. Restore your original settings.

If you are interested in more experiments, try deactivating the X Font Server. Run the **chkconfig xfs off** command. Change your initdefault in /etc/inittab from 3 to 5 again. Restart your computer and observe what happens.

Lab 3

For this lab, you'll need two Linux computers connected over a network. You'll need a shared NFS directory from the local computer. You can use the same directory that you may have used in Chapter 2 to share the RHEL 3 installation files. You'll start a Secure Shell connection between the two computers. You'll start the GUI on the local computer, and use the Secure Shell to log in remotely to the other computer. Finally, you'll set and export an appropriate **DISPLAY** variable. You can then see what happens when you start X Clients from the remote computer.

Once you do, run the Red Hat GUI firewall program from the remote computer. Make changes to the firewall, and see what happens. Finally,

1. On the local computer, start the GUI. If you're currently at the text interface, you can do so with the **startx** command.

2. Open a command line interface. Assuming you're using the default GNOME desktop, right-click on the desktop and click New Terminal in the pop-up menu that appears.

3. In the new terminal, confirm any currently exported directories with the **showmount -e** command. Based on /etc/exports, select a directory that is set as writable. Use the techniques described in Chapter 9 if required to make it so. You'll be connecting back to one of these directories from your remote computer.

4. Authorize access from the remote computer. For example, if you're connecting to a computer named desktop2, run the following command (you can substitute the IP address):

   ```
   # xhost +desktop2
   ```

5. Connect to the remote computer using the Secure Shell. Assuming the remote computer is named desktop2, run the following command:

   ```
   # ssh root@desktop2
   ```

   (If you have a problem making the connection, you may need to go to the remote computer and activate the Secure Shell service with the **service sshd start** command. You can also substitute the IP address for the computer name.)

6. Enter the root password on the remote computer when prompted.

7. Set and export the **DISPLAY** variable on the remote computer. Make sure it points to the local computer. If the local computer is named desktop1, you would use the following command:

   ```
   # export DISPLAY=desktop1:0.0
   ```

8. Now try running the **redhat-config-rootpassword** command. If successful, you'll be changing the root password on the remote computer.

9. Log out of the remote computer. Log back in using the **ssh** command from step 5. Did the root password change?

10. Restore the original root password on the remote computer. Reset the display variable on the remote computer with the following command:

    ```
    # export DISPLAY=localhost:0.0
    ```

Lab 4

1. Since you're setting up this workstation for a user, you'll want it to start automatically in the GUI. To do so, open the /etc/inittab file in a text editor, and make sure the initdefault variable is set to runlevel 5 as follows:

   ```
   id:5:initdefault
   ```

2. Make sure you don't have other settings defined in the local home directory, in the ~/.xinitrc file.

3. As you want to start with the xdm login manager, you'll want to set it as the preferred login manager in the /etc/X11/prefdm file. You can do it by setting the **preferred** variable as shown:

   ```
   preferred=xdm
   ```

4. Make sure that GNOME is the default desktop. If you see an .Xclients-default file, it should contain the following line:

   ```
   exec gnome-session
   ```

5. If you don't see this line, or the file does not exist, you can set it up and make GNOME the default desktop with the following command:

   ```
   # switchdesk gnome
   ```

6. Now reboot your computer. From the command line, you can just run the **reboot** command. Alternatively, if you're already in GNOME, click Main Menu | Log Out and select the Reboot option.

7. If you've taken the steps described, you should now see the xdm login manager. Log in through that interface.

8. Now in GNOME, click Main Menu | Preferences | More Preferences | Sessions. This opens the Sessions utility.

9. Click the Startup Programs tab. Click Add. This opens the Add A New Session window.

10. Enter the **gnome-terminal** command and click OK.

11. Repeat step 9.

12. Enter the **mozilla** command in Add A New Session window and click OK.

13. Click Close in the Session window.

14. Log out of GNOME, and log back in.

15. You should now see the GNOME desktop with the **gnome-terminal** command line interface and Mozilla Web browser.

7

Linux Sharing
Services

U nix was developed by AT&T in the late 1960s and early 1970s, and was freely distributed among a number of major universities during those years. When AT&T started charging for Unix, a number of developers tried to create clones of this operating system. In one of these efforts, Linux was developed in the early 1990s.

Many of these same universities were also developing the network that evolved into the Internet. With current refinements, this makes Linux perhaps the most Internet-friendly network operating system available. The extensive network services available with Linux are not only the tops in their field, they create one of the most powerful and useful Internet-ready platforms available today at any price.

Currently, Apache is the most popular Web server on the Internet. According to the Netcraft (www.netcraft.com) survey, which tracks the Web server associated with virtually every site on the Internet, Apache is currently used by more Internet Web sites than all the other Web servers combined. Naturally, Apache is included with RHEL 3.

RHEL 3 also includes a number of other services which I discuss in this chapter. These services include the Squid Proxy Server, which caches frequently used pages

INSIDE THE EXAM

Clients and Servers

On both exams, you'll need to configure a workstation on a network; this includes connecting to all types of network services. On the RHCE exam, you'll configure the corresponding network servers. In this chapter, you'll configure Web (HTTP/ HTTPS), Web proxy, FTP, and various mail services. You need to know how to do the following five things with each of these services:

1. Install the RPM packages or package groups required by the service.

2. Configure the service to start automatically when you reboot Linux.

3. Set up the service for basic operation on your network.

4. Configure security by hosts and users for the service.

5. Use log files, service specific tools, and more to troubleshoot service problems.

If you're studying for the RHCT exam, read though this chapter. Part of the chapter addresses the network clients such as **lftp**, Web server, and e-mail that you may configure during your exam.

on a dedicated server. There is the Very Secure FTP (vsFTP) daemon, which provides both basic and secure FTP server services. With vsFTP, you can secure users, directories, subdirectories, and files with various levels of access control.

Other standard services in the Linux/Unix world are e-mail services using the sendmail SMTP server and the POP and IMAP e-mail client services. These are the de facto standards for e-mail on the Internet.

This chapter deals with the basic concepts surrounding the use of these services, and a basic level of configuration. In all cases, the assumption is that your network settings are correct and functioning properly. If you're having problems with your network configuration, read Chapter 3.

As for the RHCE exam, you may have to configure or troubleshoot any of the services discussed in this chapter. So as you read this chapter and look through the configuration files and exercises, be willing to experiment. And practice, practice, practice what you learn.

CERTIFICATION OBJECTIVE 7.01

Apache

Apache is by far the most popular Web server today. Based on the HTTP daemon (**httpd**), it provides simple and secure access to all types of content, based on the regular HTTP protocol, as well as its secure cousin, HTTPS.

Apache is based on the server code developed by the National Center for Supercomputing Applications (NCSA). It included so many "patches" it became known as "a patchy" server. The Apache Web server continues to advance the art of the Web and provides one of the most stable, secure, robust, and reliable Web servers available. This server is under constant development by the Apache Software Foundation (www.apache.org).

While there are numerous other Web servers available, Apache is the only one described in the current curricula for RH133 and RH300. One alternative Web server is Tux, which you can configure separately. You can also configure it to work with Apache to optimize service for certain types of Web sites.

Apache is a service; basic Apache clients are Web browsers. Therefore, only those concerned with the RHCE should read this section. This provides the briefest of overviews on Apache. For more information, read the documentation online at httpd .apache.org/docs-2.0/, or *Apache Server 2.0: The Complete Reference* by Ryan Bloom (McgrawHill/Osborne, 2002).

e x a m

w a t c h

If you're studying for the exam using Red Hat Linux 9, the version numbers of Apache RPM packages are slightly different. However, if you're careful, the results should be the same (as per the Red Hat Exam Prep guide, we're configuring the service for basic operation). There are defaults in some of the Red Hat Linux 9 versions of the Apache configuration files that you'll have to change or comment out in order to follow the discussion in this section.

Apache 2.0

Red Hat Enterprise Linux includes the latest major release of Apache. The version included with RHEL 3 is httpd-2.0.46-25.ent. While there are major differences with Apache version 1.3.x if you're a Web administrator or developer, the differences with respect to the RHCE exam are fairly straightforward. It supports the configuration for regular (HTTP) and secure (HTTPS) web services. Both are specified as requirements in the Red Hat Exam Prep guide.

- **New packages** If you're installing Apache from the Red Hat Installation RPMs, all the package names have changed. As you'll see in the following section, most start with httpd. Strangely enough, the username associated with Apache services is now apache.

- **Modular directive files** Basic directives, such as those based on Perl, PHP, or the Secure Socket Layer, are now configured separately in the /etc/httpd /conf.d directory.

- **Revised variables** Some variables have changed in the httpd.conf configuration file. For example, Apache listens for computers that are looking for Web pages on port 80. You can now change that port with the **Listen** variable.

- **Virtual hosts** Apache configuration is now normally based on virtual hosts, which allows you to host multiple Web sites on the same Apache server, using a single IP address.

You may see some of these characteristics if you use Apache 1.3.x; some of these features have been "backported" from Apache version 2.0.x.

Installation

The RPM packages required by Apache are included in the Web Server package group. As you'd have to install a total of 33 RPM packages, it's probably more efficient to install these packages using the Red Hat Package Management utility. If you selected the Web Server package group with its defaults when you installed RHEL 3, you can continue to the next section.

e x a m

ⓦ**a t c h**

If you know which of the 33 RPM packages you want to install, it may be slightly faster to install the Apache packages *with the* rpm *command. However, if you use the Package Management utility, you can do other things while Apache is being installed.*

Unless you have the Installation CDs available, you should start the Package Management utility, pointing to the networked source for the RHEL 3 installation files. If it's mounted on the /mnt/inst directory, you'd use the following command from a Linux GUI command line interface:

```
# redhat-config-packages --tree=/mnt/inst
```

For more information on this command, see Chapter 4.

Once the Package Management utility is open, select the Web Server package group. It's easiest to accept the defaults. As shown in Figure 7-1, when you select this package group, you'll be installing 27 RPM packages. In Red Hat Linux 9, there are fewer RPMs in the Web Server package group; the defaults still suffice.

Starting on Reboot

Once Apache is installed, you'll want to make sure it starts the next time you boot Linux. If it doesn't start when the person who grades your Red Hat exam reboots your computer, you may not get credit for your work on the Apache service.

The most straightforward way to make sure Apache starts the next time you boot Linux is with the **chkconfig** command. You'll need to set it to start in at least runlevels 3 and 5, with a command such as:

```
# chkconfig --level 35 httpd on
```

FIGURE 7-1

Installing from
the Package
Management
utility

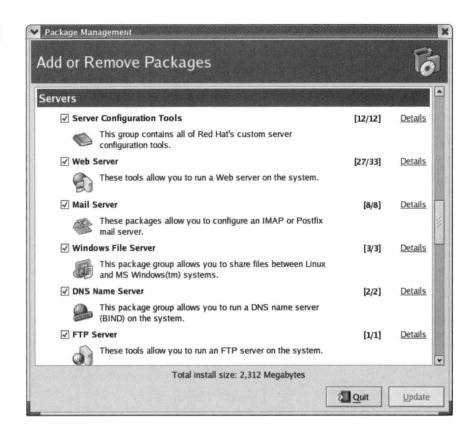

To see if the **chkconfig** command worked, use the **--list** switch:

```
# chkconfig --list httpd
```

Normally to start services, it's best to use the associated script in the /etc/rc.d/init.d directory. There is an **httpd** script in that directory. However, Apache often starts and stops more gracefully with the following commands:

```
# apachectl stop
# apachectl start
```

Once you've got Apache running, start a Web browser and enter a URL of http://localhost. If Apache installation is successful, you should see the screen in Figure 7-2.

When you read the screen, you will see that RHEL 3 looks for Web page files in the /var/www/html directory. You can verify this with the DocumentRoot variable

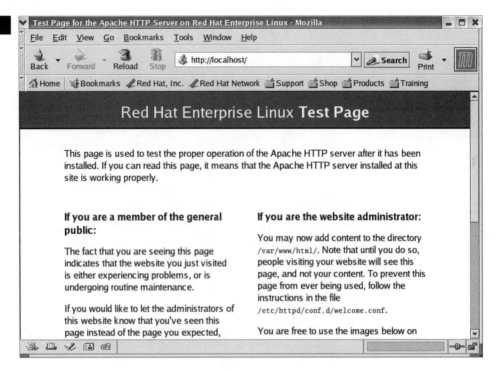

FIGURE 7-2

The default
Apache Web
page

in the main Apache configuration file. If you want to create a custom error page, you
can set it in the /etc/httpd/conf.d/welcome.conf file.

EXERCISE 7-1

Installing the Apache Server

In this exercise, you'll be installing all of the packages generally associated with the
Apache server. Then you'll test and activate the result so that the Apache daemon,
httpd, is active the next time you reboot Linux.

1. Open the GUI in your computer. If you aren't already in a graphical login
   manager, you can do so with the **startx** command.

2. Open a command line interface in the GUI. In the default GNOME desktop,
   right-click on the desktop and click New Terminal in the pop-up menu that
   appears. (In KDE, the Open Terminal command works as well.)

3. Mount to the source of RHEL 3 installation files. Refer to Chapter 2 for more information. For the purpose of this exercise, we'll assume that you're mounting on the local /mnt/entr directory.

4. Start the Red Hat Package Management utility. Make sure it reads from the RHEL 3 installation files with the following command:

```
# redhat-config-packages --tree=/mnt/entr
```

5. Locate the Web Server package group. Select it if required.

6. Click Update. When you see the Completed System Preparation window, you may notice that there are more packages on the list than you selected in the Web server package group. Click Continue.

7. When you see the Update Complete window, click OK. Click Quit to exit the Package Management utility.

8. Back in the command line window, run the following command to see if Apache is already configured to start in any runlevels:

```
# chkconfig --list httpd
```

9. Now, use the following command to make sure Apache starts in runlevels 3 and 5 the next time you boot Linux:

```
# chkconfig --level 35 httpd on
```

10. Start the Apache service with the following command:

```
# /etc/rc.d/init.d/httpd start
```

11. Start a Web browser such as Mozilla or Konqueror. Navigate to http://localhost. You should see the default Apache Web page for Red Hat Enterprise Linux.

12. Close your Web browser.

The Apache Configuration Files

There are two key configuration files for the Apache Web server: httpd.conf in the /etc /httpd/conf directory and ssl.conf in the /etc/httpd/conf.d directory. The default version of these files create a generic Web server service you can further customize and optimize, as desired. There are other configuration files, as shown in Figure 7-3, in two directories: /etc/httpd/conf and /etc/httpd/conf.d.

FIGURE 7-3

FIGURE 7-3

Apache
configuration files

```
[root@Enterprise3 root]# \ls -l /etc/httpd/conf
total 72
-rw-r--r--    1 root     root     35168 Sep 25 09:31 httpd.conf
-rw-r--r--    1 root     root     12959 Sep 25 09:31 magic
lrwxr-xr-x    1 root     root        37 Oct 23 16:12 Makefile -> ../../../usr
/share/ssl/certs/Makefile
drwx------    2 root     root      4096 Oct 23 16:12 ssl.crl
drwx------    2 root     root      4096 Oct 23 16:12 ssl.crt
drwx------    2 root     root      4096 Sep 25 09:31 ssl.csr
drwx------    2 root     root      4096 Oct 23 16:12 ssl.key
drwx------    2 root     root      4096 Sep 25 09:31 ssl.prm
[root@Enterprise3 root]# \ls -l /etc/httpd/conf.d
total 44
-rw-r--r--    1 root     root       517 Sep  8 09:17 authz_ldap.conf
-rw-r--r--    1 root     root      1800 Sep  8 10:07 perl.conf
-rw-r--r--    1 root     root       459 Sep  5 13:04 php.conf
-rw-r--r--    1 root     root      1276 Jul  3 06:14 python.conf
-rw-r--r--    1 root     root       180 Sep 25 09:31 README
-rw-r--r--    1 root     root        96 Mar 24  2003 squirrelmail.conf
-rw-r--r--    1 root     root     11316 Sep 25 09:31 ssl.conf
-rw-r--r--    1 root     root       333 Aug  2 06:17 webalizer.conf
-rw-r--r--    1 root     root       299 Sep 25 09:31 welcome.conf
[root@Enterprise3 root]#
```

on the *Job*

Previous versions of Apache, 1.3.x and below, required two other Apache configuration files in the same directory, access.conf and srm.conf. Even though these files were essentially blank in later versions of Apache 1.3.x, they were still required. These files are no longer required in any way in Apache 2.x.

The generic configuration file is httpd.conf. If you're required to configure a Secure Web server on the RHCE exam, you'll also need to configure the ssl.conf configuration file.

Basic Apache Configuration for a Simple Web Server

As described earlier, Apache looks for Web pages in the directory specified by the DocumentRoot variable. In the default httpd.conf file, this variable points to the /var /www/html directory.

In other words, all you need to get your Web server up and running is to transfer Web pages to the /var/www/html directory. The default DirectoryIndex variable looks for an index.html Web page file in this directory. You can test this for yourself by copying the default Mozilla home page file, index.html, from the /usr/share/doc/HTML directory.

If you have an **iptables** firewall on your computer, you'll need to disable it at least for TCP/IP port 80. Chapter 10 describes this process in detail.

The base location of configuration and log files are determined by the ServerRoot variable. The default value from httpd.conf is:

```
ServerRoot "/etc/httpd"
```

You'll note that the main configuration files are stored in the conf and conf.d subdirectories of the ServerRoot. If you run the **ls -l /etc/httpd** command, you'll find that Red Hat links /etc/httpd/logs to the directory with the actual log files, /var/log/httpd.

Analyzing the Default Apache Configuration

Apache comes with a well-commented set of default configuration files. In this section, we'll look at the key commands in the httpd.conf configuration file, in the /etc/httpd /conf directory. Browse through this file in your favorite text editor or with a command such as **less**. Before we begin our analysis, keep two things in mind:

- If you configure Apache with the Red Hat HTTP tool (**redhat-config-httpd**), it overwrites any changes that you may have made with a text editor.
- The main Apache configuration file incorporates the files in the /etc/httpd /conf.d directory with the following directive:

```
Include conf.d/*.conf
```

There are a couple of basic constructs in httpd.conf. First, directories, files, and modules are configured in containers. The beginning of the container starts with the name of the directory, file, or module to be configured, contained in directional brackets (< >). Examples of this include:

```
<Directory "/var/www/icons">
<Files ~ "^\.ht">
<IfModule mod_mime_magic.c>
```

The end of the container starts with a forward slash. For the above examples, the end of the container would be:

```
</Directory>
</Files>
</IfModule>
```

Next, Apache includes a substantial number of directives, which are commands that Apache can understand that have some resemblance to English. For example, the ExecCGI directive allows executable CGI scripts.

Apache Security

You can modify the httpd.conf configuration file to secure the entire server or manage security on a directory-by-directory basis. Directory controls secure access by the server, as well as users who connect to the Web sites on the server. To explore the basics of Apache security, start with the first default active line in httpd.conf:

```
ServerTokens OS
```

This line looks deceptively simple; it limits what readers see about your Web server when you browse to a nonexistent page. If you don't use this command, outsiders can see if you've loaded modules such as Perl, Python, and PHP. Sharing this knowledge can make your system more vulnerable. You can restrict access to the root directory on your Web server, as shown below:

```
<Directory />
    Options FollowSymLinks
    AllowOverride None
</Directory>
```

This configures a very restrictive set of permissions. The **Options FollowSymLinks** line supports the use of symbolic links for Web pages. The **AllowOverride None** line disables any .htaccess files. Otherwise, .htaccess can allow others to administer your server, starting from your computer's root directory.

You can improve this further by limiting access to all but desired users, such as those within your company, by adding the following commands to the <Directory /> container:

```
        Order deny,allow
        Deny from all
```

The next excerpt limits access to /var/www/html, which corresponds to the default DocumentRoot variable:

```
<Directory /var/www/html>
    Options Indexes FollowSymLinks
    AllowOverride None
    Order allow,deny
    Allow from all
</Directory>
```

You'll note that the **Options** directive has changed; the **Indexes** setting allows readers to see a list of files on your Web server if there is no index.html file in the DocumentRoot directory. The **Order** and **Allow** lines shown here allow all users to access the Web pages on this server.

Finally, the **Listen** directive defines the IP address and TCP/IP port for this server. For example, the default shown here means that this server will work with every computer that requests a Web page from any of the IP addresses for your computer on the standard TCP/IP port, 80.

```
Listen 0.0.0.0:80
```

If you have more than one IP address on your computer, you can use this directive to limit this Web server to one specific IP address. For example, if you've set up an intranet on this Web server, you could use the IP address that connects to your private network here.

If you're also setting up secure Web services, there's a second **Listen** directive in the ssl.conf file in the /etc/httpd/conf.d directory. The data from this file is automatically incorporated into your Apache configuration. It includes the following directive, which points to the default secure HTTP (HTTPS) port for TCP/IP, 443:

The Red Hat Exam Prep guide suggests that you need to be ready to configure a regular HTTP and a secure HTTPS Web server.

```
Listen 0.0.0.0:443
```

Virtual Hosts

Another useful feature of Apache 2.0 is its ability to manage Web sites using a single IP address. You can do so by creating multiple virtual hosts on the same Web server. You can configure virtual hosts for regular Web sites in the main Apache configuration file /etc/httpd/conf/httpd.conf. In that way, you can link multiple domain names such as www.example.com and www.mommabears.com to the same IP address on the same Apache server.

on the job *The www.example.com domain name cannot be registered and is officially reserved by the Internet society for documentation.*

If you're required to create a virtual host for a secure Web site, you'll need a second NameVirtualHost directive *for the HTTPS port, 443. These settings are already available in /etc/httpd/conf.d /ssl.conf.*

You can also create multiple secure Web sites which conform to the HTTPS protocol, by configuring virtual hosts in the /etc/httpd/conf.d/ssl.conf configuration file. While the details vary, the basic directives that you'd use in this file are the same.

Section 3 of the default httpd.conf includes sample commands which you might use to create one or more virtual hosts. To activate the Virtual Host feature, you'll want to activate this line. If you're using a name-based host, leave the asterisk after this directive. Otherwise, set the IP address for your interface.

```
#NameVirtualHost *:80
```

It's often more reliable to substitute the IP address, as it avoids the delays sometimes associated with name resolution through a DNS server.

You should already know that TCP/IP port 80 is the default for serving Web pages. If you want to direct all requests to IP address 192.168.30.2 on port 80, you can substitute <VirtualHost 192.168.30.2:80> for the first line shown below:

```
#<VirtualHost *>
#      ServerAdmin webmaster@dummy-host.example.com
#      DocumentRoot /www/docs/dummy-host.example.com
#      ServerName dummy-host.example.com
#      ErrorLog logs/dummy-host.example.com-error_log
#      CustomLog logs/dummy-host.example.com-access_log common
#</VirtualHost>
```

Don't forget to uncomment the commands shown by removing the # in front of each line. As you can see, it includes a number of directives from the main part of the configuration file. Here are the highlights of this container:

- You'll want to substitute the Web server IP address and TCP/IP port for the asterisk (*) in the <Virtual Host *> command. The standard HTTP port is 80; the standard HTTPS port is 443.

- Error messages are sent to the e-mail address defined by ServerAdmin.

- The Web pages can be stored in the DocumentRoot directory.

- Clients can call this Web site through the ServerName.

- The ErrorLog and CustomLog files use the *relative* log directory—relative to the ServerRoot. In other words, you can find these files in the /etc/httpd/logs directory. As noted earlier, this directory is linked to /var/logs/httpd.

Substitute the IP addresses, domain names, directories, and e-mail addresses of your choice. Create the DocumentRoot directory if required. You can test the syntax of what you've done with the following command:

```
# httpd -t
```

and Apache will verify your configuration or identify specific problems. When you run this command on the default configuration, you'll get the following message:

```
httpd: Could not determine the server's fully
qualified domain name, using 127.0.0.1 for ServerName
Syntax OK
```

This message is nothing to worry about during initial testing; it just notes that you haven't set a fully qualified domain name for the overall Web server through the **ServerName** directive.

Secure Virtual Hosts

If you're configuring a secure Web server, which conforms to the HTTPS protocol, Red Hat provides a different configuration file for this purpose: ssl.conf in the /etc/httpd /conf.d directory. If you don't see this file, you need to install the mod_ssl RPM. Before you begin editing this file, make sure the following **Listen** directive is active:

```
Listen 0.0.0.0:443
```

Later in this file, pay attention to the <VirtualHost _default_:443> container. You'll need to make sure that all of the directives between this line and the </VirtualHost> line at the end of the file are included in some way. If you accidentally leave out some of these commands, you'll end up with a nonworking Web server. You can replace _ **default_** in the VirtualHost container with the IP address of your local secure server.

Follow the same guidelines as described for the regular virtual host. Ideally, you should configure a DocumentRoot in a different directory. You'll also need to add an index.html file to this directory. One possible DocumentRoot directive is:

```
DocumentRoot /www/secure/dummy-host.example.com
```

You'll also need to add a ServerName directive, pointing to the secure HTTP port, 443. For the previously noted Virtual Host domain, that would lead to the following directive:

```
ServerName dummy-host.example.com:443
```

A Basic Web Page

You may need to create some index.html files. You could use Apache's default Web page. You can change this or any other Web page with a text- or HTML-specific editor. If you need to create a simple Web page during the exam, you don't have to use HTML tags. The Red Hat exams aren't intended to test your knowledge of HTML code.

Alternatively, you may be able to create a basic index.html page on the RHCE exam, as a simple text file. For example, you might save the following line in the text editor of your choice as index.html. You could then copy it to the appropriate DocumentRoot directory.

```
This is a simple Web page
```

Checking Syntax

You can also check the work that you've done to create virtual hosts with the following command:

```
# httpd -S
```

Assuming there were no problems, you should be able to start your Web server and connect to your local service with a browser request. (This command does not work in Red Hat Linux 9.)

Be prepared to create multiple Web sites on an Apache Web server using virtual hosts. If you're required to do so on your exam, create a separate VirtualHost container for this purpose.

The beauty of VirtualHost containers is that you can repeat the process. With name-based virtual hosting, you can set up as many Web sites on your Apache server as your computer can handle. All you require is one IP address. When you set up your new VirtualHost container, make sure to revise at least the ServerName, the locations of the log files, and the DocumentRoot.

Host-Based Security

You can add the **Order, allow,** and **deny** directives to regulate access based on hostnames or IP addresses. This basic command reads the **deny** directive first:

```
Order deny,allow
```

You can **deny** or **allow** from various forms of hostnames or IP addresses. For example, the following directive denies access from all computers in the osborne.com domain:

```
Deny from osborne.com
```

It's preferable to use IP addresses, so communication with a DNS server does not slow down your Web server. The following example directives use a single IP address;

alternatively, you can set up the 192.168.30.0 subnet in partial, netmask, and CIDR (Classless InterDomain Routing) notation:

```
Deny from 192.168.30.66
Allow from 192.168.30
Deny from 192.168.30.0/255.255.255.0
Allow from 192.168.30.0/24
```

User-Based Security

You can limit access to your Web sites to authorized users with passwords. As I'll describe shortly, these passwords can be different from the regular password database on your Linux computer.

If you want to configure User-based security for the virtual Web site described earlier, you'll need to set up a <Directory> container for the directory specified by the DocumentRoot. In this case, it's /www/docs/dummy-host.example.com. You'll want several commands in the <Directory> container:

- To set up basic authentication, you'll need an **AuthType Basic** command.
- To describe the site to requesting users, you can include an **AuthName** *"some comment"* command.
- To refer to a Web server password database named /etc/httpd/webpass, you'll need a **AuthUserFile /etc/httpd/webpass** command.
- To limit the site to a single user named engineer1, you could add a **Require user engineer1** command.
- Alternatively, to limit the site to a group as defined in /etc/httpd/webgroup, you'd add the **AuthGroupFile /etc/httpd/webgroups** command. You'll also need a **Require group Design** command, where Design is the name of the group specified in webgroups.

Here's an example of code that I've added after the <Virtual Host> container:

```
<Directory "/www/docs/dummy-host.example.com">
    AuthType Basic
    AuthName "Internal Use Only"
    AuthUserFile /etc/httpd/webpass
    Require user michael
</Directory>
```

When properly configured, the next time you try accessing the dummy-host .example.com Web site in the Mozilla browser, you're prompted for a username and password, as shown in Figure 7-4.

FIGURE 7-4

A secured
Web site

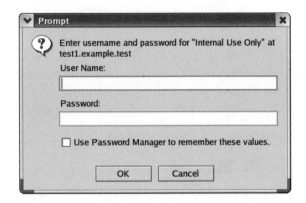

Configuring Web Passwords

To configure passwords for a Web site on your server, you need to create a separate
database of usernames and passwords. As the **useradd** and **passwd** command is used
for regular users, the **htpasswd** command is used to set up usernames and passwords for
your Web server.

For example, if you want to create a database file named webpass in the /etc/httpd
directory, you'd start with the following command:

```
# htpasswd -c /etc/httpd/webpass engineer1
```

The **-c** switch creates the specified file, and the first user is engineer1. You're prompted
to enter a password for engineer1. Users in the webpass database do not have to have a
regular account on your Linux computer.

Once you've created the database file, you can add to it without the **-c** switch; for
example, the following command prompts you for a password for drafter1 before adding
it to your webpass database:

```
# htpasswd /etc/httpd/webpass drafter1
```

To set up access for more than one user, you'll also need a group file. For the example
described in the previous section, you can set up a webgroup file in the same directory
with the following line of users:

```
Design: engineer1 drafter1 lead1
```

Web Access to Home Directories

One useful option through Apache is access to users' home directories. If you change
the following directive from **UserDir disable** to:

```
UserDir public_html
```

anyone will have access to Web pages that a user puts in his or her ~/public_html directory. For example, if you have a user named michael, he can create a /home/michael /public_html directory, and add the Web pages of his choice.

However, this requires a bit of a security compromise; you need to make michael's home directory executable for all users. This is also known as 701 permissions, which you can configure with the following command:

```
# chmod 701 /home/michael
```

Control Through .htaccess

There is a way to override inherited permissions in any subdirectory. If you're willing to set the following command in the <Directory> containers of your choice:

```
AllowOverride Options
```

you can configure .htaccess files to override previously set permissions. In this way, you can customize permissions on different virtual hosts. For example, you can configure an intranet site limited to your employees and an Internet site for general access on the same Apache server.

You can store an .htaccess file in every Web directory. While you can configure all types of Apache directives in this file, the Red Hat Exam Prep guide suggests that all you need to do is configure host-based and user-based security for the service.

Options and .htaccess

There are many ways to activate the **Options** directive. The simplest two are **Options None** and **Options All**. They would do the following:

None	For no custom options in force
All	Allows all options except **MultiViews**

You can also set finer options with keywords. Some examples include:

ExecCGI	Permits Web pages to run CGI scripts
FollowSymLinks	Permits symbolic links to directories outside of DocumentRoot
Includes	Allows server-side includes
Indexes	Permits FTP-style directory indexing

The **Indexes** directive controls directory indexing, which is the name for file lists that are generated automatically by Apache.

Executable Files in Apache

You have many different ways to set up Apache resources. Some might be available in different languages, different media types, or more. When you set up multiple resources, Apache can choose depending on the browser-supplied preferences for media type, languages, character set, and encoding.

You can use the **ScriptAlias** variable for directories with executable CGI files. An **Alias** variable essentially links one file or directory to another. The **ScriptAlias** variable links the default cgi-bin directory to /var/www/cgi-bin. You can set up CGI scripts in a different directory and change the reference accordingly.

```
ScriptAlias /cgi-bin/ "/var/www/cgi-bin"

<Directory /var/www/cgi-bin>
    AllowOverride None
    Options None
    Order allow,deny
    Allow from all
</Directory>
```

This excerpt from the default /etc/httpd/conf/httpd.conf file first identifies the directory with server scripts. The user apache is allowed to run these scripts. Permissions for others are adjusted through the <Directory /var/www/cgi-bin> container. The **AllowOverride None** command prevents regular users from changing permissions/settings in that directory. Otherwise, smarter users could read the CGI files in your directory, potentially compromising the security of your Web server. The **Options None** line prevents other users from running CGI scripts in the given directory. The **Order allow,deny** command sets up authorization checks; **Allow from all** lets all users run scripts in this directory.

The **Alias /manual "/var/www/manual"** command allows clients to read documentation stored in the /var/www/manual directory. If the name of your Web site is www.example.com, the alias allows clients to read the documentation by navigating to www.example.com/manual.

The **Alias /icons/ "/var/www/icons"** command identifies a directory for icons on your Web site. If the name of your Web site is www.example.com, you can set up the icons in HTML code on your page in the www.example.com/icons directory. You can then store the icons on your computer in the /var/www/icons directory.

Finally, you can add access control for any other directories available via your Web interface. Just wrap the directory you wish to control in a <Directory /*path/to/dir*>. . . </Directory> container and set the access restrictions you need. The command shown below applies the **Deny** directive first:

```
<Directory /path/to/your/directory/goes/here/>
    Options Indexes FollowSymLinks
    Order deny,allow
    Deny from .evil.crackers.net
    Allow from .yourdomain.net
</Directory>
```

Apache Log Files

As described earlier, the log files in httpd.conf are configured in the /etc/httpd/logs directory. It's linked to /var/logs/httpd. Access to your Web server is logged in the access_log file; errors are recorded in the error_log file. If you want more detail about your Web site for tuning or statistical reasons, you can have the Web server generate more information, generate separate log files for each virtual Web site, and create new log files at different frequencies (such as daily, weekly, or monthly).

There are standard log file formats. For more information, take a look at the **LogFormat** directive as shown in Figure 7-5. Four different formats are shown: combined, common, the referrer (the Web page with the link used to get to your site), and the agent (the user's Web browser). The first two **LogFormat** lines include a number of percent signs followed by lowercase letters. These variables determine what goes into the log.

You then use the CustomLog directive to select a location for the log file (for example, logs/access_log) and which log file format you wish to use (for example, common). For more information on log files and formats, refer to httpd.apache.org /docs-2.0/logs.html.

on the
job

Some Web hit log analyzers have specific requirements for log file formats. For example, the popular Open Source tool awstats (advanced Web Stats) requires the combined log format. It will fail to run if you leave the default common format. Awstats is a great tool for graphically displaying site activity. You can download it from a site such as www.sourceforge.net.

FIGURE 7-5

Customized
Apache logs

```
LogLevel warn

#
# The following directives define some format nicknames for use with
# a CustomLog directive (see below).
#
LogFormat "%h %l %u %t \"%r\" %>s %b \"%{Referer}i\" \"%{User-Agent}i\"" combine
d
LogFormat "%h %l %u %t \"%r\" %>s %b" common
LogFormat "%{Referer}i -> %U" referer
LogFormat "%{User-agent}i" agent

#
# The location and format of the access logfile (Common Logfile Format).
# If you do not define any access logfiles within a <VirtualHost>
# container, they will be logged here.  Contrariwise, if you *do*
# define per-<VirtualHost> access logfiles, transactions will be
# logged therein and *not* in this file.
#
# CustomLog logs/access_log common
CustomLog logs/access_log combined
```

Apache Troubleshooting

When you install the right Apache packages, the default configuration normally creates a running system. But if you're setting up a real Web site, you probably want more than just the test page. Before you start changing the configuration, back up the httpd.conf Apache configuration file. If something goes wrong, you can then always start over. Some Apache errors fall into the following categories:

- **Error message about an inability to bind to an address**   Another network process may already be using the default http port (80). Alternatively, your computer is running httpd as a normal user (not the user apache) with a port below 1024.

- **Network addressing or routing errors**   Double-check your network settings. For information on configuring your computer for networking, see Chapter 4.

- **Apache isn't running**   Check the error message when you use the **apachectl** command to start or restart the Apache server. Check the error_log in the /var /log/httpd directory.

■ **Apache isn't running after a reboot**   Run **chkconfig --list httpd**. Make sure Apache (httpd) is set to start at runlevels 3 and 5 during the boot process with the following command:

```
# chkconfig --level 35 httpd on
```

■ **You need to stop Apache**   Send the parent process a **TERM** signal, based on its PID. By default, this is located in /var/run/httpd.pid. You kill Apache with a command such as:

```
#kill -TERM `cat /var/run/httpd.pid`
```

Alternatively, you can use the **apachectl stop** command.

EXERCISE 7-2

Updating a Home Page

In this exercise, you'll update the home page associated with your Web site on the Apache server. You can use these techniques to copy the actual HTML formatted pages that you'll need for your Web site.

1. Start the Apache Web server with the default configuration.

2. Copy an HTML file such as /var/www/error/noindex.html to /var/www/html /index.html.

3. Edit the file /var/www/html/index.html.

4. Change the title of the page to reflect your personal or corporate name.

5. Use a Web browser such as Mozilla to connect to localhost (or 127.0.0.1).

on the
❶ o b   *Apache administration is a necessary skill for any Linux system administrator. You should develop the ability to install, configure, and troubleshoot Apache quickly. You should also be able to set up and customize virtual Web sites, which will make you a more effective Webmaster. You can test your skills using the exercise that follows.*

EXERCISE 7-3

Set Up a Virtual Web Server

In this exercise, you'll set up a Web server, with a virtual Web site. You can use this technique with different directories to set up additional Web sites on the same Apache server.

1. Back up your httpd.conf file.

2. Add a virtual Web site for the fictional company SnoBard, called www .snobard.net.

3. Create a DocumentRoot directory called /snobard. (Don't forget to create this directory on your system as well.)

4. Open the /snobard/index.html file in your text editor. Add a simple line in text format such as:

   ```
   This is the placeholder for the SnoBard Web site.
   ```

5. Save this file.

6. Open the browser of your choice. Test access the configured Web site (www.snobard.com) and the Web site on the localhost computer.

The Red Hat httpd Configuration Tool

Red Hat has recently introduced its own graphical configuration tool for Apache, **redhat-config-httpd**, which you can install from the RPM of the same name. Before using this tool, back up your current /etc/httpd/conf/httpd.conf configuration file. Any changes that you make with this tool overwrite this file.

You will find that **redhat-config-httpd** is a straightforward tool, with four different tabs that can help you configure the httpd.conf configuration file. You can also open this tool in the GUI with the Main Menu | System Settings | Server Settings | HTTP command. However, you cannot use it to edit the ssl.conf configuration file, and therefore should not use it to create a secure (HTTPS) Web server.

However, it may be useful to practice creating virtual hosts with this utility, so I've described the tabs shown in Figure 7-6 here:

- **Main** The Main tab allows you to set basic parameters for your Apache server, including the ServerName, the Webmaster e-mail address, and the **Listen** variable.

- **Virtual Hosts** The Virtual Hosts tab permits you to set the properties for different Web sites that you host on your Apache server. This includes the DocumentRoot, basic HTML filenames and locations, SSL support, basic log file configuration, CGI script variables, and default directories.

- **Server** The Server tab enables you to set the basic lock and PID files, as well as the user and group associated with the httpd service. In most cases, you should not have to change these settings.

- **Performance Tuning** The Performance Tuning tab allows you to set basic connection parameters.

Even if you do master this tool for configuring a regular Web server, you'll still need to manually edit the ssl.conf file to create a secure Web server. And I believe that it's easier to learn and faster to edit the Apache configuration file, /etc/httpd/conf/httpd .conf, directly in a text editor. Remember, time may be of the essence when you take the RHCE exam.

FIGURE 7-6

The Apache configuration tool, Main tab

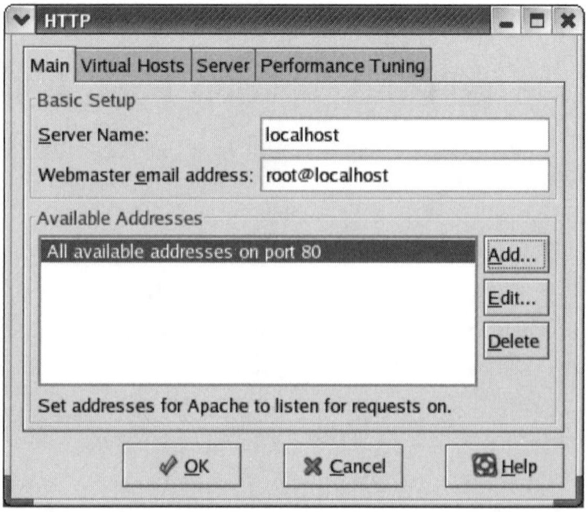

CERTIFICATION OBJECTIVE 7.02

Easy Squid Configuration

Squid is a high-performance HTTP and FTP caching proxy server. It is also known as a Web proxy cache. It can make your network connections more efficient. As it stores data from frequently used Web pages and files, it can often give your users the data they need without having to look to the Internet.

Studies on very busy networks suggest that a Squid server can reduce the size, or bandwidth, of your Internet connection by 10–20 percent. That can lead to considerable savings for larger offices.

Squid conforms to the original Harvest Cache architecture and uses the Inter-Cache Protocol (ICP) for transfers between participating peer and parent/child cache servers. It can be used either as a traditional caching proxy or as a front-end accelerator for a traditional Web server. Squid accepts only HTTP requests, but speaks FTP on the server side when FTP objects are requested. You can join the worldwide hierarchy of Harvest Cache sites; see www.ircache.net for more information.

Required Packages for Squid

There is one Squid RPM package, squid-2.5.STABLE3-3.3E. It is installed by default when you install the Web Server package group. So if you've installed Apache and have not tinkered with the defaults, the Squid RPM should also be installed on your computer. This RPM package installs a substantial number of files and scripts; some of the key files include the following:

- **/etc/rc.d/init.d/squid**   Start/stop script
- **/etc/squid/**   Configuration directory
- **/usr/share/doc/squid-2.5.STABLE3**   Documentation, mostly in HTML format
- **/usr/lib/squid/**   Support files and internationalized error messages
- **/usr/sbin/squid**   Main Squid daemon
- **/var/log/squid/**   Log directory
- **/var/spool/squid/**   Cache directory (Hundreds of MB and maybe more in many hashed directories)

There are minor differences between the versions of Squid on RHEL 3 and Red Hat Linux 9. The changes that you'll make are identical; however, the locations of each command that you'll change or add vary slightly.

Starting Squid on Reboot

The Squid Web Proxy is not started by default on RHEL 3. To do so, you'll want to activate it using a command such as **chkconfig** or the Service Configuration utility described in Chapter 4. The easiest way to set Squid to start the next time you boot Linux is with the following command:

```
# chkconfig --level 35 squid on
```

When the Squid Proxy Server starts for the first time, the **/etc/rc.d/init.d/squid start** script starts the Squid daemon. Squid runs as a caching proxy server on port 3128. You can then set up Web browsers on your LAN to point your computer to Squid on port 3128 instead of an external network such as the Internet. In that way, Squid would get the first chance at serving the needs of users on your network.

Configuration Options

You can configure and customize the way Squid operates through its configuration file, /etc/squid/squid.conf. The default version of this file includes a large number of comments that can help you tune and secure Squid. Since it has more than 3,000 lines, this isn't the easiest file to review. However, you only need to add three lines to this file before you activate Squid. For example, if the name of the local computer is Enterprise, you'd add the following line:

```
visible_hostname Enterprise
```

Next, to support regular Web (HTTP) access, you'll need to set the http_access variable to allow some arbitrary name:

```
http_access allow local_net
```

Next, you'll need to add your local network to the Squid Access Control List. This particular command line uses the local_net setting that you just created, and adds the IP addresses of a private network that I've used:

```
acl local_net src 192.168.30.0/255.255.255.0
```

Now you can save your changes and exit from the squid.conf configuration file. You can then create the basic cache directories in /var/spool/squid with the following command:

```
# squid -z
```

Finally, start the Squid service for the first time with the appropriate **service** command:

```
# service squid start
```

While you're unlikely to have a chance to configure more than one computer with Squid during the RHCE exam, its power is in connecting the cache from multiple servers. You can configure this with the *cache_peer* lines, which specify parent and sibling Squid cache servers. If your Linux computer is part of a group of Squid servers in a Harvest Cache, these lines allow your Squid servers to check these other Squid servers before going to the Internet.

Squid first checks its own cache and then queries its siblings and parents for the desired object such as a Web page. If neither the cache host nor its siblings have the object, it asks one of its parents to fetch it from the source. If no parent servers are available, it fetches the object itself.

on the
🄾o b

Squid can greatly improve the performance of a corporate intranet. If your company has many employees who surf the Net, a Squid server can reduce your network connection costs by decreasing the bandwidth you need for your Internet connection.

EXERCISE 7-4

Configuring Squid to Act as a Proxy Server

This exercise assumes you have a LAN. One of the computers on the LAN is also a server that is connected to the Internet. It also assumes that you've already installed the Squid RPM. Then you can configure Squid to act as a proxy for Web and FTP service for your LAN.

1. Open the Squid configuration file, /etc/squid/squid.conf, in a text editor.

2. Add the name of your computer to this file. Add the following command near the comments associated with **visible_hostname**:

```
visible_hostname computername
```

3. Add an **http_access** command to allow access from your local network. You can set an arbitrary name of your choice for the network, but you'll need to

use it in the command afterwards. Locate the command near the other **http_access** commands in this file.

```
http_access allow lan_net
```

4. Configure access from your LAN to Squid with an appropriate **acl** command. The following command allows access from your **lan_net** with an IP network address of 172.168.30.0:

```
acl local_net src 172.168.30.0/255.255.255.0
```

5. Save your changes and exit.

6. Stop the Squid service if it isn't already running with the **service squid stop** command.

7. Create Squid swap directories with the **squid -z** command.

8. Start the Squid service with the **service squid start** command.

9. Configure a test client such as a Web browser to use your Squid service.

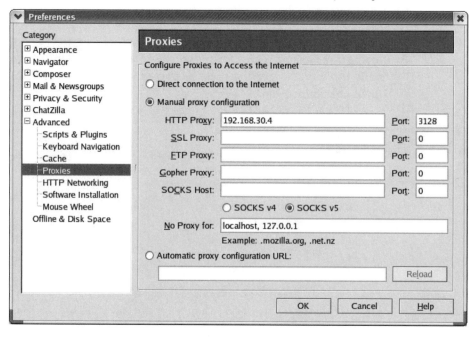

10. Test your client by using both HTTP and FTP addresses in the browser address. Use it to retrieve files from various sites on the Internet, such as www.redhat.com and ftp.kernel.org.

CERTIFICATION OBJECTIVE 7.03

The Very Secure FTP Service

FTP, the File Transfer Protocol, is one of the original network applications developed with the TCP/IP protocol suite. It follows the standard model for network services, as FTP requires a client and a server. The FTP client is installed by default on most operating systems, including Red Hat Enterprise Linux. If you've installed the FTP Server package group, you've installed the default Red Hat FTP Server, the very secure FTP (vsFTP) daemon. But before we begin, let's look at FTP clients.

on the *Job*   *Red Hat no longer includes alternate FTP servers such as WU-FTP. When you install vsFTP on your computer, you're installing the same FTP server used on ftp.redhat.com.*

FTP Client (lftp)

The original FTP client software was a basic command line, text-oriented client application that offered a simple but efficient interface. Most Web browsers offer a graphical interface and can also be used as an FTP client.

Any FTP client allows you to view the directory tree and files. Using **ftp** as a client is easy. You could use the **ftp** command to connect to a server such as ftp.redhat.com with the following command:

```
# ftp ftp.redhat.com
```

The FTP client listed in the Red Hat Exam Prep guide is **lftp**. You can use it to connect to the FTP server of your choice. It automatically attempts an anonymous login. It also supports command completion, which can especially help you access files and directories with longer names.

Figure 7-7 illustrates a typical **lftp** session to ftp.redhat.com. As you can see, **lftp** uses a number of typical bash commands. The command completion feature lists available subdirectories. I've navigated to the directory with RHEL 3 Source RPMs.

Another advantage of **lftp** is that it can handle all of the basic upload and download commands of a regular FTP client. Some of these commands are described in Table 7-1.

```
[root@Enterprise3 root]# lftp ftp.redhat.com
lftp ftp.redhat.com:~> ls
drwxr-xr-x    6 ftp        ftp          4096 Nov 11 16:18 pub
lftp ftp.redhat.com:/> cd pub/
contrib/  redhat/  up2date/
lftp ftp.redhat.com:/> cd pub/redhat/
ccm/    edk/      interchange/  mirror-tools/  support/
ccvs/   gnupro/   linux/        rhdb/          tux/
lftp ftp.redhat.com:/> cd pub/redhat/linux/
1.0/  2.1/    4.1/  5.1/  6.1/  7.1/  8.0/    code/       preview/
1.1/  3.0.3/  4.2/  5.2/  6.2/  7.2/  9/      current@    rawhide/
2.0/  4.0/    5.0/  6.0/  7.0/  7.3/  beta/   enterprise/ updates/
lftp ftp.redhat.com:/> cd pub/redhat/linux/enterprise/3/en/os/i386/SRPMS/
cd ok, cwd=/pub/redhat/linux/enterprise/3/en/os/i386/SRPMS
lftp ftp.redhat.com:/pub/redhat/linux/enterprise/3/en/os/i386/SRPMS>
```

Almost all commands in FTP mode are run at the remote host, similar to a Telnet session. You can also run commands locally from the FTP prompt. When you start the command with an exclamation point (!), you can run regular shell commands.

This is only a subset of the commands available through **lftp**. Typing the **help** command will give you a full list of the available commands. The command **help** *cmd* yields a brief description of the command itself.

Command	Description
cd	Changes the current working directory at the remote host
ls	Lists files at the remote host
get	Retrieves one file from the remote host
mget	Retrieves many files from the remote host with wildcards or full filenames
put	Uploads one file from your computer to the remote host
mput	Uploads a group of files to the remote host
pwd	Lists the current working directory on the remote host
quit	Ends the FTP session
!ls	Lists files on your host computer in the current directory
lcd	Changes the local host directory for upload/download
!pwd	Lists the current working directory on local host computer

One graphical FTP client for Linux is GNOME FTP (GFTP). GNOME FTP provides an easy-to-use GUI interface to FTP. It also offers these features:

■ Restartable transfers

■ Multiple independent transfers

■ Download file queuing

■ Transferring whole directory trees (recursive transfers)

■ Drag-and-drop transfer activation

■ Session names and settings

And with GFTP you don't even need to know a single FTP command. If you have installed the gftp RPM, you can start the GFTP client from a GUI command line with the **gftp** command. Alternatively, you can start it from the Red Hat GNOME or KDE desktop with the Main Menu | Internet | More Internet Applications | gFTP command.

Installing the Very Secure FTP Server

The only FTP server included with RHEL 3 is vsFTP. In fact, it's the only RPM that's part of the FTP Server package group. If it isn't already installed, you probably won't have to bother with the GUI package management utility. This package has few dependencies, and should be installed automatically when you install RHEL 3. Assuming you've connected to the NFS installation share described in Chapter 2, you'd run the following command:

```
# rpm -Uvh /mnt/inst/RedHat/RPMS/vsftpd-1.2.0-4.i386.rpm
```

In the following sections, I'll show you how to start the vsFTP service the next time you reboot your computer, how it's already configured by default, and how to secure it by user. If you want to limit access to vsFTP by computer or network, you'll have to use the tcp_wrappers system, with its hosts.allow and hosts.deny files in the /etc directory, as described in Chapter 10.

Starting on Reboot

Once vsFTP is installed, you'll want to make sure it starts the next time you boot Linux. If it doesn't start when the person who grades your Red Hat exam reboots your computer, you may not get credit for your work configuring an FTP server.

The most straightforward way to make sure the FTP server starts the next time you boot Linux is with the **chkconfig** command. You'll need to set it to start in at least runlevels 3 and 5, with a command such as:

```
# chkconfig --level 35 vsftpd on
```

To see if the **chkconfig** command worked, use the **--list** switch:

```
# chkconfig --list vsftpd
```

If you want to start the vsFTP server, just start the service script with the following command:

```
# service vsftpd start
```

Basic FTP Server Configuration

As you've seen in Chapter 2, the vsFTP server is very easy to configure. Once you've started the daemon and modified any current firewalls, it's ready for use. By default, remote users can log in anonymously or with a username on the local computer. The sequence is straightforward. Assume you have a vsFTP server on a computer named Enterprise3. To connect anonymously using the **lftp** client, you'd run the following command:

```
# lftp Enterprise3
```

This opens a connection in the /var/ftp directory. It looks like a top-level root directory to the **lftp** client. Alternatively, if you wanted to connect to the account of user michael, you'd add just a little more:

```
# lftp -u michael Enterprise3
```

This opens a connection to the /home/michael directory. Unfortunately, the default is dangerous, as users who log in with a real username can navigate to the top-level root directory.

vsFTP Server Security

So now you know that vsFTP can be dangerous. But you can help secure your system by configuring vsFTP to disable logins from regular users. Naturally, you can configure vsFTP through the vsftpd.conf configuration file, in the /etc/vsftpd directory.

The commands in this file are straightforward. I urge you to read the file for yourself; the comments make many of the commands self-explanatory. Let's examine just a few of these commands in Table 7-2. I've focused on those commands that you might change to enhance the security of your system. The commands in the default vsftpd.conf file are just a small fraction of the commands that you can use. You can review the RHEL 3 Reference Guide available online at www.redhat.com/docs/manuals/enterprise for detailed information.

By default, vsFTP is configured to disable logins from sensitive users such as root, bin, and mail. The **userlist_enable=YES** command points to a list of disabled users in /etc/vsftpd.user_list. As vsFTP also uses Pluggable Authentication Modules (PAM) for security, it also disables the users in /etc/vsftpd.ftpusers. The list of users in the default versions of this file are identical.

If you want regular users to log into your FTP server, you should add the **chroot_local_user=YES** command. This helps secure your system by keeping regular users from navigating to your top-level root directory (/).

A couple of useful features for users help welcome them to your server. The following command provides a message for users who are logging into your system:

```
ftpd_banner=Welcome to blah FTP service
```

TABLE 7-2   Some vsFTP Server Configuration Commands

Command	Description
anonymous_enable=YES	If you don't want anonymous access, you'll have to set this to NO.
local_enable=YES	If you don't want regular users to log in, comment this out by adding a pound (#) character.
write_enable=YES	If you don't want remote users writing to your directories, comment out this command.
#chroot_list_enable=YES	If you set **chroot_local_user=YES** (see discussion that follows), you can configure users who are allowed to roam through your directories by activating this command.
pam_service_name=vsftpd	Configures Pluggable Authentication Module (PAM) security. For more information, see Chapter 10.
userlist_enable=YES	Don't change this! This keeps users such as root from logging into your system.
tcp_wrappers=yes	Supports the use of security commands in /etc/hosts.allow and /etc/hosts.deny. See Chapter 10.

This next message looks for a .message file in each directory and sends it to the client:

```
dirmessage_enable=YES
```

Unfortunately, these messages don't work for users who log into your system using a client such as **lftp**.

Access by root and many service users are disabled by default. If you try to log in as root using **lftp**, it will look like you're connected. But when you try to do something as root, you'll see messages delaying your commands "before reconnect."

EXERCISE 7-5

Configuring a Basic FTP Server

In this exercise, you'll install and activate a basic vsFTP server on your RHEL 3 computer. While you should ideally also have a second computer, it isn't absolutely necessary here.

1. Check your system to see if the vsFTP server is installed. The easiest way is with the following command:

   ```
   # rpm -q vsftpd
   ```

2. If it isn't already installed, use the techniques discussed in earlier chapters to install the vsFTP RPM package on your computer.

3. Activate the vsFTP server with the **service vsftpd start** command.

4. Make sure this server is automatically activated the next time you boot Linux with the following command:

   ```
   # chkconfig --level 35 vsftpd on
   ```

5. Log into the vsFTP server as a regular user. You should preferably log in from a remote computer.

6. Once you're logged in, run the **cd ..** command twice (remember the space between the command and the two dots). Explore the local directory. You should see a danger here, as this is the root directory for the FTP server computer.

7. Close the FTP client session.

8. If you're concerned about the security issues, deactivate the vsFTP server. The best way to secure FTP is to uninstall the vsFTP server. However, if you need a vsFTP server, work with the lab at the end of the chapter.

Mail Services

If you have Linux installed on your computer, you can set up a powerful mail server. Perhaps the most common mail server on the Internet is sendmail, which may already be installed on your RHEL 3 computer. Once it is installed and configured, you can set up sendmail as your own personal mail server (subject to the limitations of your ISP). One alternative to sendmail that is installed on RHEL 3 is known as postfix.

on the Job

A number of alternatives to sendmail are not covered in this book; they include procmail, mail.local, exim, and uucp.

When you install sendmail and/or postfix, you also get huge and difficult-to-read configuration files. Do not be intimidated. There are only a few entries you are ever likely to have to change. A mail server has three major components, as described in Table 7-3. You need all three of these components to have a fully functional mail system.

On your Linux computer, you can configure your mail transfer agent (sendmail or postfix) for various outbound services, such as forwarding, relaying, method of transport (such as TCP or UDP), lists of computers with other MTAs, optional aliases, and spooling directories.

TABLE 7-3	Abbreviation	Meaning	Examples
Mail Server Components	MTA	Mail transfer agent	sendmail, postfix, qmail
	MUA	Mail user agent	mail, Mozilla, elm
	MDA	Mail delivery agent	procmail, maildrop

E-mail systems are heavily dependent on name resolution. While you could handle name resolution through /etc/hosts on a small network, any mail system that requires Internet access needs access to a fully functional DNS server.

The sendmail and postfix systems use SMTP to send e-mail. But that is only one end of the mail system. You also need to configure POP and or IMAP to receive e-mail.

SMTP

SMTP, the Simple Mail Transfer Protocol, has become one of the most important service protocols of the modern era. Much of the Internet-connected world lives and dies by e-mail and relies on SMTP to deliver it. SMTP is a *protocol*, a set of rules for transferring data used by various Mail Transfer Agents. The default SMTP program for RHEL 3 is sendmail; the alternate is postfix.

Installing Mail Server Packages

The RPM packages associated with sendmail and postfix are both part of the Mail Server package group. It includes only eight RPM packages, as described in Table 7-4. You can install them with the **rpm** command or the Red Hat Package Management utility. You may not need to install all of these packages on your exam; read your requirements carefully!

Time is of the essence on the Red Hat exams. Since you may not need all of these packages, it may be faster to install these with the **rpm** command, especially if you're

TABLE 7-4	Mail Server Package Group RPMs

RPM Package	Description
sendmail	Installs the most popular mail server of the same name
imap	Supports both the IMAP and the POP incoming e-mail protocols
sendmail-cf	Adds a number of templates that you can use to generate your sendmail configuration file
spamassassin	Installs a program which you can start from sendmail or postfix to minimize spam
squirrelmail	Installs a Web-based e-mail server
postfix	Includes an alternative to sendmail
redhat-switch-mail redhat-switch-mail-gnome	Adds a GUI method for switching between sendmail and postfix

configuring your Linux computer from the text console. It takes time to start the GUI. On the other hand, once you've started the installation process, you can work on other exam requirements while the Package Management utility is installing your Mail Server packages. For more information on the Package Management utility, see Chapter 4.

If all that you're asked to configure from Table 7-4 during your Red Hat exam is sendmail, all that you would need to install is the sendmail and sendmail-cf RPM packages. And sendmail should already be installed by default, since it is part of the Base package group.

on the job *You can find a list of RPMs associated with each package group for an Intel 32-bit CPU installation in the /usr/share/comps/i386/comps.xml file.*

sendmail

The sendmail daemon is configured from a directory of files in /etc/mail and a directory of configuration files in /usr/share/sendmail-cf. There are two basic configuration files: sendmail.cf for incoming mail and submit.cf for outgoing mail. I describe the key configuration files in /etc/mail in a bit of detail here.

- **sendmail.cf**   The main sendmail configuration file.
- **sendmail.mc**   A macro which you can edit and then generate a new sendmail.cf file.
- **access**   Supports outgoing access control to your sendmail server. The default version of this file supports access from the local computer. You can add hostnames or networks to this list, with a message to REJECT with an error message, DISCARD without an error message, or RELAY to accept and send the e-mail.
- **domaintable**   Allows you to map different domains. For example, if you've changed your domain name from Compaq.com to HP.com, people might still send e-mails to addresses such as michael@Compaq.com. The following line would forward that e-mail to michael@HP.com.

    ```
    Compaq.com    HP.com
    ```

- **helpfile**   Supports help commands when you manage your mail server from the sendmail prompt, which you can access with the **telnet localhost 25** command.
- **local-host-names**   Allows you to add hostnames or aliases for your computer as a sendmail server. Enter one alias per line in this file.

- **mailertable**   Rarely used.
- **Makefile**   Supports compiling the sendmail.mc file.
- **spamassassin**   A directory which includes configuration files that can help you minimize spam. If you want to configure it on locally received e-mail, add the following line to /etc/procmailrc:

```
INCLUDERC=/etc/mail/spamassassin/spamassassin-default.rc
```

- **statistic**   Collects statistics on sendmail usage in binary format. You can read it with the **mailstats** command.
- **submit.cf**   The main outgoing sendmail configuration file.
- **submit.mc**   A macro which you can edit and then generate a new submit.cf file.
- **trusted-users**   Lists special users which can send e-mail without warnings. For example, you saw e-mail addresses in the Apache configuration file; if you include the apache user in this list, it can send messages to your Web server administrators without generating sendmail warning messages.
- **virtusertable**   Supports e-mail forwarding; if you have users outside your network who use your sendmail server, you can enter individual e-mail addresses or domains for allowed users.

If you don't see some of these files or directories, you may not have both sendmail RPM packages installed: sendmail and sendmail-cf. Use the **rpm -q** *packagename* command to check if you have these packages installed, and install them as required.

Configuring sendmail for Basic Operation

When sendmail starts, it reads the /etc/sendmail.cf and /etc/submit.cf files. The sendmail.cf file is a long (around 1,800 lines) file that may seem difficult to decipher but includes a wealth of helpful comments. The submit.cf file is nearly as long. This file provides detailed rules (organized into rulesets) on how sendmail should process e-mail addresses, filter spam, talk to other mail servers, and more.

This file is extremely complex and uses cryptic syntax. Fortunately, most of the directives included in this file are standards that you don't need to change. Many are required by various Internet agreements relating to e-mail address, mail transfer agents, and more.

Red Hat tries to simplify this process with a smaller file, /etc/mail/sendmail.mc, which contains only the most relevant configuration directives. It is composed entirely of macros that define key sendmail.cf settings. Once you've configured this file, you can use the **make** command to compile a new, custom sendmail.cf file. However, the default RHEL 3 version of this file is still over 140 lines long. Remember, the Red Hat Exam Prep guide only requires that you configure the service for basic operation. Therefore, I'll highlight those commands that you may want to change or modify for that purpose.

While older versions of the submit.mc file required work, the default versions included with RHEL 3 (or Red Hat Linux 9) should work on the local computer without changes. Unless you're on an IPv6 network, you can focus entirely on the sendmail.mc file. If you are on an IPv6 network, you'll need to change the loopback address in the last line as described in a comment in the file.

The sendmail.mc file is made up of directives (macros) used to create content for sendmail.cf. (Other related .mc files follow the same criteria and use many of the same commands). These macros do the following:

- Add comments to aid in comprehension
- Define key variables and values
- Enable or disable features
- Create variables with specific settings

The most basic macro is **dnl**, which tells **m4** to delete from this point through to the end of the line. It is used to comment out descriptive text or disable a feature that would otherwise be included.

The **include** directive instructs the **make** command to read the contents of the named file and insert it at the current location in the output. This is how additional configuration information (needed by sendmail but not relevant to mail configuration) is kept separately from settings you may wish to change.

The **define** directive sets files or enables features that you wish to use. In the preceding example, you set the path to your e-mail name user ALIAS_FILE as (/etc /aliases), identify where procmail lives (PROCMAIL_MAILER_PATH), and provide the path for the official database of e-mail users—in this case, in virtualusertable.db.

The **FEATURE** directive enables specific features. For example, you use **FEATURE** to set accept_unresolvable_domains. This allows you to accept mail where you can't figure out the domain of the user who sent the e-mail. Specifically, an unresolvable domain refers to a case where it isn't possible to find a domain name through a reverse

IP address lookup. If you don't have reliable DNS access, you may need this feature, or else your sendmail configuration may refuse a lot of valid e-mail.

DAEMON_OPTIONS directly controls the SMTP daemon. In the default case, you do not accept any mail from outside your own system (note the loopback address on this line).

You'll notice unusual quote characters in most of these lines. The command inside parentheses starts with a back quote (`` ` ``) and ends with a single quote (`'`).

Configuring and Securing sendmail

In this section, you'll modify the sendmail.mc configuration file. Back it up first! You only need to make a couple of adjustments to get your system ready for use on the Internet. By default, the following line limits sendmail use to the local computer:

```
DAEMON_OPTIONS(`Port=smtp,Addr=127.0.0.1, Name=MTA')dnl
```

You can allow other computers to use your sendmail server by commenting out this line. As described earlier, this requires a **dnl** command. The result would be:

```
dnl DAEMON_OPTIONS(`Port=smtp,Addr=127.0.0.1, Name=MTA')dnl
```

Next, if you have reliable DNS access, comment out the **FEATURE** directive that allows you to **accept_unresolvable_domains**. This blocks spammers who use just an IP address or spammers who fake their domain name to hide themselves.

```
FEATURE(`accept_unresolvable_domains')dnl
```

But that's not enough. If you want to allow remote computers or networks access to your sendmail server, you'll need to add their names or addresses to the /etc/mail/access file. For example, if you wanted to allow access to the 192.168.30.0 domain, you'd add the following line to that file:

```
192.168.30          RELAY
```

It's also important to add names associated with your network's e-mail addresses, such as mail.example.com and www.example.com. Watch the notation; unlike other services, there is no dot (.) at the end of the address. It covers all computers on the 192.168.30.0 network. Alternatively, you could designate the example.com domain, or a specific computer name or IP address.

Back up the current sendmail.cf file. Then you can generate a new sendmail.cf file with the following command:

```
# cp /etc/mail/sendmail.cf /root
# make -C /etc/mail/
```

Now you can reconfigure your e-mail clients such as Mozilla or even Microsoft Outlook Express to send outgoing e-mail through your sendmail server. You'll need to set your sendmail computer domain name or IP address as the SMTP outgoing mail server.

on the
job

In previous versions of sendmail, all you needed to do was process sendmail.mc; it was therefore sufficient to use the m4 macro command. But you may be processing more files. The make -C /etc/mail command shown processes all files in the /etc/mail directory.

Configuring sendmail to Start at Reboot

Now start or restart sendmail to make sure it reads your new sendmail.cf configuration file:

```
# chkconfig sendmail --level 35 on
# service sendmail restart
```

Your sendmail (SMTP) service should now be up and running and ready to accept mail from any (valid) source.

Troubleshooting sendmail

When name resolution is not working on your network, sendmail doesn't know where to send your outbound e-mail. These messages are placed in a queue that tries to resend your e-mail at regular intervals. Other mail forwarders and relay hosts on the Internet provide the same functionality if a network segment is not working. As an administrator, you need to monitor this queue. If it gets overloaded, you may wish to reconfigure messages for that network to be sent at more irregular times. See the following code for an example of a problem message:

```
# mail
Mail version 8.1 6/6/93.  Type ? for help.
"/var/spool/mail/root" 1 messages 1 new
>N  1 MAILER-DAEMON@localh  Wed Dec 3 08:55  60/1914   "Returned mail: see tr"
&      # simply press <ENTER> key to see each message
Message 1:
From MAILER-DAEMON@localhost.localdomain  Wed Dec  3 08:55:39 2002
Date: Wed, 3 Dec 2003 08:55:39 -0500
From: Mail Delivery Subsystem <MAILER-DAEMON@localhost.localdomain>
To: root@localhost.localdomain
MIME-Version: 1.0
Content-Type: multipart/report; report-type=delivery-status;
        boundary="DAA03153.938948139/localhost.localdomain"
```

```
Subject: Returned mail: see transcript for details
Auto-Submitted: auto-generated (failure)
This is a MIME-encapsulated message
--DAA03153.938948139/localhost.localdomain
The original message was received at Wed, 3 Dec 2003 08:55:39 -0500
from Enterprise3
—-- The following addresses had transient non-fatal errors —--
<michael@mommabears.cob>
      (reason: 550 Host unknown)
  —-- Transcript of session follows —--
550 5.1.2 <michael@mommabears.cob>... Host unknown
(Name server: mommabears.cob: host not found)
..
(additional details deleted)
..

& d       # delete current read buffer
& q       # quit mail
#
```

In the previous example, the destination name server (mommabears.cob) could not be resolved (it is mommabears.com). Consequently, sendmail notifies the sender (root@localhost.localdomain) that the mail could not be delivered.

In this case, the problem is straightforward: you've specified a nonstandard domain. However, you may get a similar error for one of the following reasons:

- No DNS server available, if so required in sendmail.mc.

- Access from a computer not listed or specifically denied in the /etc/mail/access configuration file.

- Some firewall blocking access. You can configure a firewall to allow incoming e-mail through TCP/IP port 25. You can find more information about this in Chapter 10.

Configuring and Activating postfix

You can configure the postfix mail server as a substitute for sendmail. The configuration files are stored in the /etc/postfix directory. The main configuration file, main.cf, is somewhat simpler than sendmail.cf, as it includes around 600 lines. Back up this file and open it in a text editor. There are several things that you need to configure in this file to get it working:

- Activate and modify the following **myhostname** command to point to the name of your computer:

```
#myhostname = host.domain.tld
```

- Activate and modify the following **mydomain** command to reflect the domain name or IP network of your system (if you substitute your IP network, use the same format as illustrated for the sendmail.mc file):

```
#mydomain = domain.tld
```

- The following two commands set postfix to listen to only the local computer. Activate and deactivate the following commands to remove that limitation:

```
#inet_interfaces = all
inet_interfaces = localhost
```

- Activate and modify the following **mynetworks** command to point to the IP network address that you want to serve:

```
#mynetworks = 168.100.189.0/28, 127.0.0.0/8
```

Configuring postfix to Start at Reboot

Now start or restart postfix to make sure it reads your new /etc/postfix/main.cf configuration file:

```
# chkconfig postfix --level 35 on
# service postfix restart
```

Your postfix service should now be up and running and ready to accept mail from any (valid) source.

Mail Clients

One of the prerequisite skills for the Red Hat exams is to configure an e-mail client. This should be easy for anyone who has used Linux for any length of time. In fact, the process for graphical Linux clients such as Evolution or Mozilla is quite similar to the process for various Microsoft e-mail clients. But as you've seen earlier in this section, there are text-based mail clients as well.

Command Line Mail

To test your mail system, you can use the built-in command line **mail** utility, a simple text-based interface. The system keeps each user's mail in a system directory. Once users read a message, they can reply, forward, or delete it. If they do not delete the message before quitting the **mail** utility, the system stores the message in the /var/mail directory, in a file named after the applicable username.

You can certainly use any of the other mail readers, such as mutt, or the e-mail managers associated with different GUI Web browsers to test your system. Other mail readers store messages in different directories. For example, pine would create and store messages for user mj in the /home/mj/mail directory.

To send mail to another user, you can use the **mail** command line utility. There are two basic methods for using **mail**. First, you can enter the subject and then the text of your message. When you're done, press CTRL-D and then enter another addressee in the Cc: line, if desired. When you press ENTER, the message is sent and the **mail** utility stops and sends you back to the command line.

```
$ mail Michael
Subject: Test Message
Sent and received
Cc: mjang@example.com
$
```

Alternatively, you can redirect a file as the text of an e-mail to another user. For example, the following command sends a copy of /etc/hosts to the root user, with the Subject name of "hosts file":

```
$ mail root@localhost -s 'hosts file' < /etc/hosts
```

Reading Mail Messages

By default, the mail system doesn't open unless you actually have e-mail in your in box. Once it is open, you'll see a list of new and already read messages. To read a specific message, enter the number of the message and press ENTER. If you press ENTER with no argument, the mail utility assumes you want to read the next unread message. To delete a mail message, use the **d** command after reading the message, or use **d#** to delete the message numbered #.

Mail Group "Alias" Lists

If you have a distribution list of people for the same e-mail, you can set it up in the /etc /aliases file. By default, it's set up to forward e-mail from pseudo-accounts such as system and apache to root. You can change it by adding a group list similar to the following:

```
groupname:  user01, user02, othergroupname
```

You can then run the **newaliases** command to compile this database. Then all you need to do is name the group of users as addressees for your e-mail.

POP

The sendmail and postfix services provide their own incoming e-mail support. If you've started them on your server, you won't need to activate the ipop3d service. You can enable the ipop3d service by editing the /etc/xinetd.d/ipop3 configuration file.

The Post Office Protocol (POP) is one of the two major mail delivery protocols. It includes some basic commands that allow you or an e-mail client to send and retrieve messages. A mail service can be configured to be a central depository for incoming mail messages from any other MTA service. Client applications then download the mail messages off the POP server for processing at the local host. The ipop3d service handles all requests.

on the **Job**

You can configure user accounts that are only designed to service POP user accounts, where users log in and receive mail only, and no interactive service is provided. Just set up the appropriate mail client in the login configuration sequence for a given user.

IMAP

The IMAP service is the other major mail delivery protocol. While POP downloads all e-mail to the client, an IMAP server maintains all mail messages on the server, as a database. IMAP is commonly used by businesses that service users who log in from different locations. It's also the most common mail delivery protocol for Web-based mail services.

Installing, Configuring, and Securing POP and IMAP

Both POP3 and IMAP4 servers are part of one Red Hat RPM package: imap-2002d-2 .i386.rpm. Install it as required. No special configuration is needed. It includes SSL support; it's also one of the xinetd "super servers." These packages are configured in the /etc /xinetd.d directory. POP3 service is configured through the ipop3 file; IMAP4 service is configured through the imap and imaps files. All of these are disabled by default with the following line:

```
disable = yes
```

You can enable it in one of two ways: edit the file directly to change this line to **disable = no**. Alternatively, the following command activates the POP3 service:

```
# chkconfig ipop3 on
```

CERTIFICATION SUMMARY

You can configure a number of network sharing services on your RHEL 3 computer. Apache is the most important Web server on the Internet. Squid allows you to save bandwidth. The very secure FTP daemon allows you to let users transfer files to and from your server efficiently and securely. Mail services enable you to set up e-mail send and receive functions on your network.

Apache was developed from the NCSA Web server. Once the appropriate packages are installed, you have a structure and sample Web pages in the /var/www/html directory, based on the /etc/httpd/conf/httpd.conf configuration file. The httpd.conf file is organized in containers. You can create virtual hosts for multiple Web sites on your computer, even if you have only one IP address.

Squid is a proxy server that allows a network to filter its HTTP and FTP traffic through a cache. Requests are taken from the cache when possible. This reduces the load between the LAN and the Internet, reducing your network costs. When users access cached files, they get better performance from the external network.

FTP has two parts: the client and the server. FTP clients such as **ftp** and **lftp** are available from the command line. Red Hat includes one FTP server, the very secure FTP service. You can configure it in detail through the /etc/vsftpd/vsftpd.conf configuration file.

Red Hat includes two mail servers with RHEL 3: sendmail and postfix. Both rely on SMTP to send e-mail over the Internet. The sendmail service includes difficult-to-read configuration files: sendmail.cf and submit.cf, both in the /etc/mail directory. Fortunately, you can configure these files through easier-to-read macro files, sendmail.mc and submit.mc. postfix is somewhat easier to configure directly through its own configuration file, /etc/postfix/main.cf. Red Hat also provides a variety of e-mail clients, including **mail**, mutt, and the mail clients that come with the various Web browsers that are also available for Linux. These clients either use POP or IMAP protocols to receive e-mail.

Because RHCE is a performance-based exam, it is important to practice all the skills discussed in this chapter. You may need to use these skills on the exam!

TWO-MINUTE DRILL

Here are some of the key points from the certification objectives in Chapter 7.

Apache

❑ Red Hat Enterprise Linux 3 includes the Apache Web server, which is currently used by over twice as many Internet Web sites as all other Web servers combined.

❑ Web services are an easy way to provide simple, secure access to many types of documents. The Apache Web server provides both normal and secure Web services using the HTTP and HTTPS protocols.

❑ With Apache 2.0, you can configure multiple Web sites on your server, even if you have only one IP address. This is possible through the use of virtual hosts.

Easy Squid Configuration

❑ Squid is a high-performance HTTP and FTP caching proxy server.

❑ The main Squid configuration file is long, but all you need to do in /etc/squid /squid.conf is configure the following parameters: **visible_hostname**, **http_access**, and **acl**.

❑ Squid can refer requests to sibling and parent proxy servers. If the request still isn't available, a parent proxy server refers the request to the Internet.

❑ Once Squid is configured, you can set each computer on the LAN to browse Web pages to the proxy server on port 3128.

The Very Secure FTP Service

❑ The FTP, or File Transfer Protocol, service includes a client and a server. RHEL 3 includes the command line **ftp** and **lftp** clients.

❑ RHEL 3 includes the vsFTP server. The default configuration allows anonymous and real user access.

❑ You can customize vsFTP through the /etc/vsftpd/vsftpd.conf configuration file. It also uses authentication files in the /etc directory: vsftpd.ftpusers, vsftpd.user_ list, and vsftpd.chroot_list.

Mail Services

❑ RHEL 3 includes sendmail and postfix, two mail servers that you can use to support sending and receiving e-mail.

❑ The main sendmail configuration file is /etc/mail/sendmail.cf. It's easier to configure sendmail through its macro file, /etc/mail/sendmail.mc.

❑ You can customize the computers allowed to access your sendmail server through the access and virtusertable files in the /etc/mail directory.

❑ The postfix server is easier to configure through configuration files in the /etc/postfix directory. In fact, you can configure the main.cf file directly.

❑ Different mail clients can receive e-mail using the POP or IMAP protocols. Mail clients such as **mail** and mutt are available at the command line. GUI mail clients are also available, usually as part of a Web browser package.

SELF TEST

The following questions will help you measure your understanding of the material presented in this chapter. Read all the choices carefully, as there may be more than one correct answer. Don't focus exclusively on these questions. There are no longer any multiple choice questions on the Red Hat exams. These questions exclusively test your understanding of the chapter. While the topics in this chapter are "prerequisites," it is okay if you have another way of performing a task. Getting results, not memorizing trivia, is what counts on the Red Hat exams.

Apache

1. Which of the following Apache directives give you the base directory for configuration and log files?

   A. ServerRoot

   B. DocumentRoot

   C. Options

   D. UserDir

2. How would you configure a virtual host as a secure server?

   A. Set up password protection on the DocumentRoot.

   B. Configure security in /etc/httpd/conf/httpd.conf.

   C. Create a Virtual Host container in /etc/httpd/conf.d/ssl.conf.

   D. Add the contents of the ssl.conf file to the httpd.conf configuration file.

3. Once you've modified httpd.conf, which of the following commands should you use to reread this file?

   A. service httpd restart

   B. service apache reload

   C. apachectl reload

   D. apachectl restart

4. Which of the following commands creates a password file and configures a password for user elizabeth?

   A. .htpasswd elizabeth

   B. htpasswd -c /etc/httpd/passwords elizabeth

   C. passwd elizabeth

   D. service htpasswd elizabeth /etc/httpd/passwords

Easy Squid Configuration

5. Which of the following commands in the squid.conf file is used to point to the network IP address served by Squid?

   A. visible_hostname

   B. http_access allow

   C. acl

   D. squid -z

6. Which of the following commands should you use before starting Squid for the first time? This command configures the Squid cache directories.

   A. visible_hostname

   B. http_access allow

   C. acl

   D. squid -z

The Very Secure FTP Service

7. Which of the following commands should you disable if you don't want users logging into their accounts through the vsFTP server?

   A. local_enable = yes

   B. anonymous_enable = yes

   C. nopriv_user = ftpsecure

   D. chroot_local_user = yes

8. Which of the following commands should you enable if you want to keep regular users from getting to the top-level root directory (/) on your computer?

   A. local_enable = yes

   B. anonymous_enable = yes

   C. nopriv_user = ftpsecure

   D. chroot_local_user = yes

Mail Services

9. Which of the following directives would you disable in /etc/mail/sendmail.mc to allow your sendmail server to serve more than just the local computer?

   A. FEATURE(`mailertable',`hash -o /etc/mail/mailertable.db')dnl

   B. FEATURE(`virtusertable',`hash -o /etc/mail/virtusertable.db')dnl

    C. LOCAL_DOMAIN(`localhost.localdomain')dnl

    D. DAEMON_OPTIONS(`port=smtp,Addr=127.0.0.1, Name=MTA')dnl

10. Which of the following commands should you add to /etc/mail/access if you want to set up service to the 10.11.12.0 network?

    A. 10.11.12.0/24   RELAY

    B. 10.11.12   RELAY

    C. 10.11.12.   RELAY

    D. 10.11.12.0/255.255.255.0 RELAY

LAB QUESTIONS

Lab 1

In this first lab, you'll install and configure Apache to start and run automatically the next time you boot your computer. You'll also configure the default Mozilla Web browser home page as the default home page for the local computer.

Lab 2

In this second lab, you'll configure two Web sites on the local Apache server. Call them big.example.big and small.example.small. Don't forget to create the directories that you need, as well as set up these Web sites on your DNS server or /etc/hosts file. Make sure your Web sites are accessible to users from remote computers on your network. Add an appropriate index.html file to the DocumentRoot for each Web site. Simple Web pages, such as a single line of text, are acceptable.

Lab 3

Continuing on with Apache, now configure secure versions for each of your two Web sites. Make sure that there are appropriate directories available for each secure Web site.

Lab 4

Set up a Squid proxy server on your computer. Set up access to your LAN on the 10.11.12.0 /255.255.255.0 network. Assign appropriate values to **acl, http_access,** and **visible_hostname**. Set up the cache directories for Squid. Make sure it starts now and automatically the next time you reboot your computer.

Lab 5

Configure an FTP server for your computer. Make sure to allow only anonymous access. Don't allow anonymous users to upload to your server. Enable messages when users access your /var/ftp and /var/ftp/pub directories. Add an appropriate one-line message to each directory. Test the result, preferably from a remote computer. Make sure to start the vsFTP server now, and see that it starts automatically the next time you reboot your computer.

Lab 6

Set up a sendmail mail server for your network. First, make sure to disable local-only access in the /etc/mail/sendmail.mc file. Add your network to the /etc/mail/access file. Test the result, preferably from a remote computer on your network. Configure Mozilla to read your e-mail. You can set it up to read e-mail without downloading it from the server (even if it's a POP3 server). Make sure to start the sendmail server now, and see that it starts automatically the next time you reboot your computer.

SELF TEST ANSWERS

Apache

1. ☑ **A** is correct. The **ServerRoot** directive sets the default directory for the Apache server. Any files and directories not otherwise configured—or configured as a relative directory—are set relative to ServerRoot.

☒ **B, C,** and **D** are incorrect. The DocumentRoot is the root directory for each Web site. The **Options** directive is used to set exceptions to document permissions. The **UserDir** directive supports access to Web sites from users' home directories.

2. ☑ **C** is correct. The Red Hat Apache configuration supports the creation of secure servers in /etc/httpd/conf.d/ssl.conf. You can configure virtual hosts for your secure Web site in the same way as you can in /etc/httpd/conf/httpd.conf.

☒ **A, B,** and **D** are incorrect. Password protection on a Web site is unrelated to a secure Web site using the HTTPS protocol. While you can configure a secure Web site in httpd.conf, the configuration file designed for this purpose is ssl.conf. For the same reason, you should not add the contents of ssl.conf to httpd.conf.

3. ☑ **D** is correct. The **apachectl** command is the preferred method to control the Apache service.

☒ **A, B,** and **C** are incorrect. While the **service** command is generally used to control Linux services, it does not control Apache gracefully. The name of the Apache service is httpd. And there is no **apachectl reload** command.

4. ☑ **B** is correct. The **htpasswd** command sets up passwords. The **-c** switch is required to create a new file to store passwords.

☒ **A, C,** and **D** are incorrect. The .htpasswd file is not a command. The **passwd** command isn't used for Web server usernames or passwords. The **service** command has nothing to do with passwords.

Easy Squid Configuration

5. ☑ **C** is correct. The **acl** command in squid.conf can be used to specify the network to be served by Squid.

☒ **A, B,** and **D** are incorrect. The **visible_hostname** command is used to identify the local computer. The **http_access** command can be used to actually configure Squid for the network of your choice. The **squid -z** command sets up the directories for the Squid cache.

6. ☑ **D**. See answer 5 for the reasons.

☒ **A, B,** and **C** are incorrect. See answer 5 for the explanation.

The Very Secure FTP Service

7. ☑ **A** is correct. The **local_enable** command allows local users to log in remotely to their home directories. Disabling this command disables this functionality.

   ☒ **B, C,** and **D** are incorrect. The **anonymous_enable = yes** command supports access by the anonymous user. The **nopriv_user = ftpsecure** command is already disabled in the default version of vsftpd.conf; it defines an unprivileged user. The **chroot_local_user = yes** command does not keep users with local accounts from logging in, it just keeps them from accessing the root directory of your computer.

8. ☑ **D** is correct. See answer 7 for the reasons.

   ☒ **A, B,** and **C** are incorrect. See answer 7 for the explanation.

Mail Services

9. ☑ **D** is correct. The **DAEMON_OPTIONS** directive in the default sendmail.mc file prevents access to anything but the local computer.

   ☒ **A, B,** and **C** are incorrect. Answers **A** and **B** refer to database files which allow you to configure access to other computers, therefore you should not disable these commands. Answer **C** just identifies the domain name of the local computer.

10. ☑ **B** is correct. This is the required format in the /etc/mail/access configuration file.

   ☒ **A, C,** and **D** are incorrect. These options do not conform to the required format in /etc/mail /access.

LAB ANSWERS

Lab 1

First, make sure the Apache Web server is installed. If an **rpm -q httpd** command tells you that it is missing, you haven't installed the Web Server package group. The most efficient way to do so is with the Red Hat Package Management utility, only accessible through the Linux GUI.

To configure Apache to start, you'll want to run the **apachectl start** command. To make sure it starts the next time you boot your computer, you'll want to run the **chkconfig --level 35 httpd on** command.

Once Apache is installed, you should be able to access it by opening a browser and navigating to http://localhost. You can see in the default Apache configuration file that the DocumentRoot is located in /var/www/html. The default Mozilla home page is located at /usr/share/doc/HTML/index.html. You can copy that index.html file to the /var/www/html directory, and test the result by navigating once again to http://localhost. If you did not copy the other files associated with the default Mozilla home page, you'll be missing some icons.

Lab 2

This lab requires that you create two virtual hosts in the main Apache configuration file, /etc/httpd /conf/httpd.conf. To do so, you should do the following:

1. Set the **NameVirtualHost** directive to the IP address and port (80) serving your intended network audience.

2. Add a VirtualHost container with the same IP address.

3. Assign the ServerAdmin to the e-mail address of this Web site's administrator.

4. Configure a unique DocumentRoot directory.

5. Set the first ServerName to big.example.big.

6. Add **ErrorLog** and **CustomLog** directives, and set them to unique filenames in the /etc/httpd /logs directory. With the default ServerRoot, you can use a relative logs directory, such as:

   ```
   ErrorLog logs/big.example.big-error_log
   ```

7. Make sure to close the VirtualHost container.

8. Repeat the process for the second Web site, making sure to set the second ServerName to small.example.small.

9. Close and save the httpd.conf file with your changes.

10. Create any new directories that you configured with the **DocumentRoot** directives.

11. Create index.html text files in each directory defined by your new **DocumentRoot** directives. Don't worry about HTML code; a text file is fine for the purpose of this lab.

12. Make sure these domain names are configured in your DNS server or in /etc/hosts. For example, you could add the following lines to /etc/hosts:

    ```
    192.168.30.2 big.example.big
    192.168.30.2 small.example.small
    ```

13. Disable any firewall on your computer. Alternatively, you can use the Security Level Configuration tool (**redhat-config-securitylevel**) utility to allow HTTP data through your firewall; see Chapter 10 for more information on this process.

14. Finally, make sure to run the **apachectl restart** command to reread the httpd.conf configuration file, so Apache reads your changes.

15. Now you can test the result in the browser of your choice. If it works, the big.example.big and small.example.small domain names should direct you to the index.html files that you created for each Web site.

Lab 3

The basics of this lab are straightforward. You'll need to repeat the same basic steps as you performed in Part 2; you're just editing the /etc/httpd/conf.d/ssl.conf configuration file. However, there are a few things to be concerned about:

- Make sure that the top **VirtualHost** directive points to the IP address that you're using for your Web server.
- Set up the DocumentRoot in a directory different from a regular Web server.
- Configure the ErrorLog and CustomLog separately; it can help to associate it with the name of the secure Web site.

Continuing on with Apache, now configure secure versions for each of your two Web sites. Make sure that there are appropriate directories available for each secure Web site.

Lab 4

First, Squid is automatically installed when you install the Web server package group. To configure a Squid proxy server for your network, you'll need to configure /etc/squid/squid.conf. Assume the name of your computer is myproxy, and you're arbitrarily assigning mylan as the name for your LAN. If your network IP address is not 10.11.12.0, substitute accordingly. In this file, you'll need to add the following lines:

```
visible_hostname=myproxy
acl mylan src 10.11.12.0/255.255.255.0
http_access allow mylan
```

Next, you'll need to set up the Squid directories with the following command:

```
# squid -z
```

Finally, to configure Squid to start, you'll want to run the **service squid start** command. To make sure it starts the next time you boot your computer, you'll want to run the **chkconfig --level 35 squid on** command.

But you'll also need to activate proxy server access in client applications such as Web browsers. Remember that you can do so by pointing your browsers to port 3128.

Lab 5

The vsFTP server is part of a one-RPM package group. So if you have not installed this server during the installation process, the quickest thing to do is to connect to your installation source (CD or network), and install it from that location. For example, if the source is mounted on /mnt/source, you'd install it with the following command:

```
# rpm --Uvh /mnt/source/RedHat/RPMS/vsftpd-1.2.0-4.i386.rpm
```

This also installs configuration files in the /etc and /etc/vsftpd directories. The main configuration file is /etc/vsftpd/vsftpd.conf. Based on the RHEL 3 default version of this file, you can make the following changes. To allow only anonymous access, comment out the following line:

```
local_enable=yes
```

Anonymous users are already prevented from uploading files to your server. You could enable it by activating the **anon_upload_enable=yes** command. By default, messages are already enabled for directory access on an FTP server, courtesy of the following command:

```
dirmessage_enable=yes
```

Actually configuring a message is a matter of creating a text file, and saving it as .message in the desired directories, /var/ftp, and /var/ftp/pub. You could add a simple line such as "root directory for the FTP server" or "main download directory."

Finally, to configure the Red Hat FTP server to start, you'll want to run the **service vsftpd start** command. To make sure it starts the next time you boot your computer, you'll want to run the **chkconfig --level 35 vsftpd on** command.

Lab 6

The sendmail mail server is part of the Mail Server package group. It is automatically installed when you install RHEL 3. You could install related packages using the Package Management utility, or you could install the sendmail-cf RPM package.

To disable local-only access in the /etc/mail/sendmail.mc file, comment out the following line. Unlike most Linux configuration files, you'll want to add a **dnl** at the start of this line:

```
DAEMON_OPTIONS(`Port=smtp,Addr=127.0.0.1, Name=MTA')dnl
```

The **dnl** at the end of the line does not affect the command to its left. Next, you'll want to enable support through /etc/mail/access. If you want to support your LAN with this server, and its network address is 10.11.12.0, you'd add the following command line to /etc/mail/access:

```
10.11.12                RELAY
```

You can test the result from the e-mail client of your choice. It's easiest to use a client such as Mozilla. Netscape users should find this browser to be familiar; it uses the Netscape code, which has been released under an open source–style license. If you're not familiar with Mozilla, you can open it by clicking on the globe icon adjacent to the Main Menu icon in the lower-left corner of the desktop. Once Mozilla is open, click Window | Mail & Newsgroups to open the Mozilla mail management utility. If this is the first time you've opened the Mozilla mail management utility, the Account Wizard prompts you to add the information associated with your e-mail account. Otherwise, click the Add Account button.

You'll need to know the name of your incoming mail server, whether it conforms to the POP3 or IMAP4 protocols, and the name (and password) of your account. You presumably already know the name of the outgoing mail server, the name of the computer with the sendmail server that you just configured.

8

Linux Network Services

R ed Hat Enterprise Linux 3 supports direct communication with the various Microsoft Windows operating systems. Microsoft networking is based on the Common Internet File System (CIFS), which was developed from the Server Message Block (SMB) protocol. Samba was developed as a freely available SMB server for all Unix-related operating systems, including Linux, and has been upgraded to support CIFS.

Samba interacts with CIFS so transparently that Microsoft clients cannot tell your Linux server from a genuine Windows NT/2000/XP/2003 server, and with Samba there are no server, client, or client access licenses to purchase. If you can learn to edit the main Samba configuration file from the command line interface, you can configure Samba quickly. RHEL 3 includes a GUI alternative, the Samba Server Configuration utility.

INSIDE THE EXAM

Samba

If you're taking the RHCE exam, you definitely have to know how to configure Samba as a server and as a client. While there is no direct reference to Samba in the RHCT requirements, the spirit of the exam suggests that you need to know how to set up a Linux computer as a client on a network. While Samba clients are relatively easy to use, there is no reference to Samba client software in the Red Hat curricula related to the RHCT exam.

Once you configure a Samba server, you can use Samba clients on Linux just as easily as you can use Microsoft's Network Neighborhood or My Network Places. While I can't tell you what I saw on the RHCE exam, you don't need a Microsoft Windows computer to confirm that you've configured Samba properly.

CUPS

CUPS is something that you may expect to configure on the RHCT and RHCE exams. You'll need to know how to configure a CUPS printer locally and to be shared on a network. You need to know how to connect to a remote printer through CUPS. And finally, you'll want to learn how to manage CUPS print queues.

Printing is a fundamental service for all operating systems. The default for RHEL 3 is CUPS, which has replaced the Line Print Daemon. CUPS supports autoconfiguration of shared network printers and includes a Web interface configuration tool. Red Hat has also customized its own graphical configuration tool. It also provides connectivity to several other network print services via their native protocols.

As for the RHCE exam, you may have to configure or troubleshoot any of the services discussed in this chapter. So as you read this chapter and look through the configuration files and exercises, be willing to experiment. And practice, practice, practice what you learn.

CERTIFICATION OBJECTIVE 8.01

Samba Networking

Microsoft's CIFS was built on the Server Message Block (SMB) protocol. SMB was developed in the 1980s by IBM, Microsoft, and Intel as a way to share files and printers over a network.

As Microsoft has developed SMB into CIFS, the Samba developers have upgraded Samba accordingly. Samba services provide a stable, reliable, fast, and highly compatible file and print sharing service that allows your computer to act as a client, a member server, or even a Primary Domain Controller (PDC) on Microsoft-based networks. While Samba does not include every feature built into the latest Microsoft networks, I have confidence that it will in the near future.

SMB network communication over a Microsoft-based network is also known as NetBIOS over TCP/IP. Through the collective works of Andrew Tridgell and the Samba team, Linux systems provide transparent and reliable SMB support over TCP/IP via a package known as Samba. You can do four basic things with Samba:

- Share a Linux directory tree with Windows and Linux/Unix computers
- Share a Windows directory with Linux/Unix computers
- Share a Linux printer with Windows and Linux/Unix computers
- Share a Windows printer with Linux/Unix computers

Samba emulates many of the advanced network features and functions associated with the Win9x/ME and NT/2000/XP operating systems through the SMB protocol. Complete information can be found at the official Samba Web site at www.samba.org. It is easy to configure Samba to do a number of things on a Microsoft-based network, for example:

- Participate in a Microsoft Windows 9x–style Workgroup or an NT/2000/XP Domain as a client, member server, or even a Primary Domain Controller
- Share user home directories
- Act as a WINS (Windows Internet Name Service) client or server
- Link to or manage a workgroup browse service
- Act as a Master Browser
- Provide user/password and share security databases locally, from another Samba server, or from a Microsoft NT 4 Primary Domain Controller
- Configure local directories as shared SMB filesystems
- Synchronize passwords between Windows and Linux systems
- Support Microsoft Access Control Lists

While Samba can do more, you get the idea. Samba features are configured through one very big file, smb.conf, in the /etc/samba directory. As this file may intimidate some users, Red Hat's Samba Server Configuration tool (**redhat-config-samba**) provides an easier interface. RHEL 3 does not include the Samba Web Administration Tool, so don't expect it to be available on the Red Hat exams.

RHEL 3 includes the newly released Samba version 3.0. This includes a number of features over and above the version of Samba included with Red Hat Linux 9 (2.2.7). Despite this change, you can use the same basic steps (for the most part) to configure a Samba client and/or a Samba server on your computer.

Installing Samba Services

If you selected the Windows File Server package when you installed RHEL 3, then the Samba RPM packages should already be installed. These are the four Samba RPM packages that you need:

- The samba RPM package includes the basic SMB server software for sharing files and printers.

- The samba-client RPM package provides the utilities needed to connect to shares from Microsoft computers.

- The redhat-config-samba package installs the Red Hat Samba Server Configuration utility.

- The samba-common RPM package contains common Samba configuration files. While it isn't a part of the Windows File Server package group, it is installed as a dependency if you install that package group.

It's easy to start the Samba Server Configuration tool. You can do so from a command line interface in the GUI with the **redhat-config-samba** command. Alternatively, you could click Main Menu | System Settings | Server Settings | Samba. Either command opens the utility, as shown in Figure 8-1.

Configuring Samba to Start

Configuring Samba to start when Linux boots is a straightforward process. You'll want to configure Samba to start in runlevels 3 and 5, and then start the Samba server. You can do so with the following two commands:

```
# chkconfig --level 35 smb on
# service smb start
```

e x a m

Watch   *If you're using Red Hat Linux 9 to study for the exam, you'll want to use an upgraded version of Samba. You can set it up on Red Hat Linux 9 using the RHEL 3 source RPMs available online*   *from ftp.redhat.com (or mirrors). Use the commands described in Chapter 4 to compile binary RPMs from source. You can then install the RHEL 3 version of Samba on your Red Hat Linux 9 computer.*

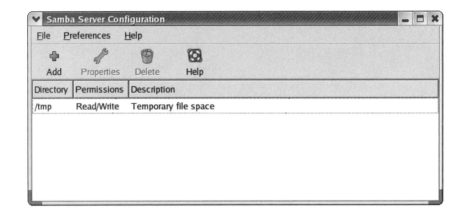

Some Samba Background

Samba services provide interoperability between the Microsoft Windows and Linux /Unix computers. Before you begin configuring Samba, you need a basic understanding of how Microsoft Windows networking works with TCP/IP.

The original Microsoft Windows networks were configured with computer hostnames, known as NetBIOS names, limited to 15 characters. These unique hostnames provided a simple, flat hostname system for the computers on a LAN. All computer identification requests were made through broadcasts. This overall network transport system is known as NetBEUI, which is not "routable." In other words, it does not allow communication between two different LANs. As a result, the original Microsoft-based PC networks were limited in size to 255 nodes.

While Microsoft networks could use the Novell IPX/SPX protocol stack to route messages between networks, that was not enough. As the Internet grew, so did the dominance of TCP/IP. Microsoft adapted its NetBIOS system to TCP/IP with SMB. Since Microsoft published SMB as an industry-wide standard, anyone could set up their own service to work with SMB.

One of the nice features of Windows networks is the browser service. All computers register their NetBIOS names with one "elected" master browser, the keeper of the database of network-wide services. In fact, a browse database is maintained by some "elected" host for every protocol running on the network. For instance, if the NetBEUI, IPX/SPX, and TCP/IP protocols were installed on a host, then three duplicate browse databases were required—one per protocol, as the services available may differ between protocols.

Name Resolution: WINS

WINS was designed as a dynamic, centralized, and robust service. It was supposed to become a viable alternative to DNS. Each WINS server maintained a central database with multiple records for all machines. On a large network, this was a big data file.

WINS needs about three to ten data records for each computer. Naturally, this is cumbersome for larger networks. This is another reason why Microsoft is phasing out WINS.

What About Samba?

This is where Samba fits in. Samba on Linux provides all the Windows networking services available on any Windows TCP/IP client or server. To configure Samba, you simply need to know the name of your NT/2000/XP/2003 Domain or Windows 9x/ME–style Workgroup, and configure the parameters accordingly for your Linux workstation or server to match the settings on the local Microsoft network.

Fortunately, Samba comes with extensive online documentation (with examples) available in the smb.conf configuration file. The following lists some of the key Samba commands and files:

```
/usr/sbin/smbd        - main SMB service daemon
/usr/sbin/nmbd        - NetBIOS name service daemon
/etc/samba/smb.conf   - SAMBA's primary configuration file
/usr/bin/smbclient    - connects to SMB shares, ftp-like syntax
/usr/bin/smbmnt       - mounts SMB shares on a designated directory
/usr/bin/smbumount    - unmounts a SMB shared directory
/usr/bin/testparm     - tests validity of /etc/samba/smb.conf file
/etc/rc.d/init.d/smb  - daemon start and stop control script
smbfs                 - file system extension to mount SMB shares on
                        directories; use with the mount -t command.
/usr/bin/smbprint     - a script to print to a printer on an SMB host
/usr/bin/smbstatus    - lists current SMB connections for the local host
```

Samba Has Two Daemons

You need two daemons to run Samba: smbd and nmbd, both located in /usr/sbin. Both are configured through the /etc/samba/smb.conf configuration file. It's easy to check the syntax of this large configuration file with the **testparm** command. If problems arise, this program produces error messages to help you correct them.

Configuring Samba as a Client

There are two types of clients that you can configure through Samba. One connects to directories shared from Microsoft Windows servers or Samba servers on Linux/Unix. The second connects to shared printers from one of the same two types of servers.

When you have installed the samba-common RPM package, you've installed the Samba client commands that you need to find browse lists and mount shared directories locally.

Checking Samba File and Print Services

If you want to browse shared directories from a Linux computer, you'll want to know how to use **smbclient**. This can help you test connectivity to any SMB host on a Windows- or Samba-based Linux/Unix computer. You can use **smbclient** to check the directories and printers that are shared from remote computers on your network. For example, the **smbclient** command shown in Figure 8-2 checks shared directories and printers from a remote Linux-based Samba PDC.

As you can see, I've specified two arguments with the **smbclient** command: **-L** allows you to specify the name of the Samba server, and **-U** allows you to specify a username

FIGURE 8-2	

List of shared directories and printers from a remote PDC

```
[root@Enterprise3 root]# smbclient -L //cosmicc -U donna
Password:

        Sharename       Type        Comment
        ---------       ----        -------
        netlogon        Disk        Network Logon Service
        tmp             Disk        Temporary file space
        registry        Disk        Disabing Encryption
        inst            Disk        Red Hat Linux 9 CD files
        inst-1          Disk        Enterprise Inst Directory
        IPC$            IPC         IPC Service (PDC - from a Samba Server)
        ADMIN$          Disk        IPC Service (PDC - from a Samba Server)
        WinPrint1       Printer
        LinuxHP         Printer
        WinClass1       Printer
        WinPrint2       Printer
        donna           Disk        Home Directories

        Server                  Comment
        ---------               -------
        ALLACCESS               Windows XP Pro Workstation
        COSMICC                 PDC - from a Samba Server

        Workgroup               Master
        ---------               -------
        GRATEFUL                COSMICC
[root@Enterprise3 root]#
```

on the remote computer (or the PDC for the domain). If the command reaches the Samba server, you're then prompted for the appropriate password.

Alternatively, you can browse shared Samba directories using the graphical Nautilus client. In the Linux desktop, click Main Menu | Home Folder. This opens the Nautilus file manager with a list of files in your home directory. In the Location text box, enter

```
smb:///
```

If you're connected to a network with Windows and or Samba-enabled Linux computers, you'll see an icon associated with connected workgroups and or domains. Click on the workgroup or domain of your choice. You should see a list of Windows and Samba-enabled Linux computers on that workgroup or domain.

Select the computer of your choice. You'll be prompted for a username and password on the remote computer. Once entered, you'll get a list of shared directories, as shown in Figure 8-3.

FIGURE 8-3

Browsing remote shared directories

Mounting Shared Samba Directories During Login

You can also configure automated mounting during the login process. In the first lab of Chapter 5, you saw how to configure connections to shared NFS directories. You can use the same process with shared Samba directories.

Specifically, you can configure commands to mount a shared directory for an individual user in the .bashrc file, and set up a command to unmount that directory in the .bash_logout file. Both files are stored in each user's home directory.

There's one drawback: unless you're willing to add the shared directory to your /etc/fstab file, or you're limiting yourself to the root user, you can't use the **mount** command. There is an option: the **smbmnt** and **smbumount** commands. Once you've set them up to be executable for all with the following commands, you can add them to individual users' .bashrc and .bash_logout files:

```
# chmod u+s /usr/bin/smbmnt
# chmod u+s /usr/bin/smbumount
```

These commands set the SUID bit, which I described briefly in Chapter 1 and use in Chapter 11. Once the SUID bit is set, you can mount shared Samba directories as a regular user. Now when you log in as a regular (not root) user, you can mount and unmount a Samba share named inst from a computer named cosmic on the /home /michael/shared directory with the following commands:

```
$ smbmnt //cosmicc/inst /home/michael/shared -o username=michael
$ smbumount /home/michael/shared
```

With the first command, you're prompted for a password for user michael on the cosmicc computer. In other words, user michael gets to enter two passwords: first to log into his local account, second to authorize a connection to the shared directory. Alternatively, if user michael's password is a2b3c4d5, you could use the following command:

```
$ smbmnt //cosmicc/inst /home/michael/shared -o username=michael%a2b3c4d5
```

Once you've verified that they work, you can add these commands to user's .bashrc and .bash_logout files. If you're configuring this for the root user, you'll need to use the corresponding **mount** commands:

```
# mount -o username=michael //cosmicc/inst /root/shared
# umount /root/shared
```

You can add user michael's password in the same way as shown for the **smbmnt** command. Once you're satisfied with the result, you can add these commands to the root user's .bashrc and .bash_logout files.

Alternatively, if your users log in through GNOME, you can set up the same **mount** command through the Sessions utility. As discussed in Chapter 6, you can start this utility by clicking Main Menu | Preferences | More Preferences | Sessions. Figure 8-4 illustrates the previous command, with a password, added to the graphical startup programs list for the root user.

Client Configuration for Print Services

There is a simple option line in the /etc/samba/smb.conf file that shares all local printer systems as if this were another Windows host.

In /etc/samba/smb.conf, printer configurations start with the section heading named [printers]. Using the same share options used for directories, Samba can create a shared print service for each installed print queue. These print shares are available to Microsoft clients when users install network printers. For more information on the [printers] share, please read the next section.

Once shared, you can use a service such as CUPS to connect to these shared printers. In fact, I'll show you how this is done with the Red Hat Printer Configuration utility later in this chapter.

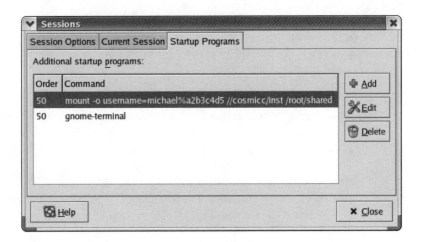

FIGURE 8-4

Using Startup Programs to connect to a shared Samba directory

Configuring a Samba Server

If you want to configure a Samba server, you'll need to edit the main Samba configuration file, /etc/samba/smb.conf. This file is long and includes a number of commands that require a good understanding of Microsoft Windows networking. Fortunately, the default version of this file also includes helpful documentation with suggestions and example configurations that you can use.

You can edit this file directly, or you can create directory shares using Red Hat's Samba Server Configuration utility. It's useful to study the original /etc/samba/smb.conf file. Once you see how the file is structured, back it up. Try editing the file directly. Try changing the file with the Samba Server Configuration utility (which I describe in the next section). Test the result by restarting the Samba server with the following command:

```
# service smb restart
```

To help you with this process, I've copied the RHEL 3 version of this file. The following code is essentially a complete view of this file. I've replaced the comments in the file with my own explanations. You might want to browse your own /etc/samba/smb.conf file as well.

e x a m

⍵atch
    As stated in the Red Hat exam guide, RHCEs must be able to configure various services, including *Samba, for basic operation. I go into detail on the smb.conf file that, in my opinion, goes beyond basic operation.*

The smb.conf file includes two types of comment lines. The hash symbol (#) is used for a general text comment. This is typically verbiage that describes a feature. The second comment symbol is the semicolon (;), used to comment out Samba directives (which you may later wish to uncomment in order to enable the disabled feature).

on the
ⓙob   *Because of the dimensions of the book, the length of code lines is limited. In a few cases, I've modified the code lines slightly to meet this limit, without changing the intent of any command in this configuration file.*

```
# This is the main Samba configuration file. You should read the
# smb.conf(5) manual page in order to understand the options listed
# here. Samba has a huge number of configurable options (perhaps
```

```
# too many!) most of which are not shown in this example
#
# comments deleted
# NOTE: Whenever you modify this file you should run the command
# "testparm" to check that you have not made any basic syntactic
# errors.
```

Global Settings

Remember, time is of the essence on the RHCE exam. While you should be aware of what you can do with all of the different global settings, change as little as possible. The less you change, the less that can go wrong. Perfect configuration files are not required. Configuration files that meet the specific requirements of your exam are.

In smb.conf, the global settings, which define the overall attributes of your server, follow the first set of comments. This section starts with the following two lines:

```
#======================= Global Settings ============================
[global]
```

Now we'll examine the critical global settings. First, with respect to the **workgroup** variable, this Samba server will become a member of that Microsoft Workgroup or Domain. The default Samba workgroup is Workgroup. If you know Microsoft Windows, you'll recognize it as the name of the default peer-to-peer workgroup. The same variable is used if you're joining this computer to a Microsoft-style Domain.

```
# workgroup = NT-Domain-Name or Workgroup-Name
    workgroup = MYGROUP
```

Next, it's a good idea to add a NetBIOS name for your computer to this file. This becomes what other clients see in network browse lists such as those shown from Network Neighborhood/My Network Places and the **smbclient** command. The command that follows becomes the comment shown with the browse list:

```
# local computer NetBIOS name
    netbios name = cosmicc
# server string is the equivalent of the NT Description field
    server string = Samba Server
```

If you activate the **hosts allow** command, you can limit access to the specified network. The following default would limit access to the networks with the 192.168.1.0 and 192.168.2.0 network IP addresses, as well as the local computer (127.):

```
;    hosts allow = 192.168.1. 192.168.2. 127.
```

These default printer settings are required to share printers from this Samba server. You'll want to change the printing command as shown to enable cooperation with CUPS, as shown. (CUPS is an allowed value despite the comments in the default RHEL 3 version of this file.)

```
printcap name = /etc/printcap
load printers = yes
;   printing = bsd
printing = cups
```

If you want to configure a special guest account, you can activate this command, as long as you add a pcguest user with the **useradd** command described in Chapter 4.

```
;   guest account = pcguest
```

This command sets up log files for every computer that connects to this Samba server. For example, if a computer named allaccess connects to this Samba server, you can find a log of its access problems in /var/log/samba/allaccess.log. The log file is limited to 50Kb.

```
log file = /var/log/samba/%m.log
max log size = 50
```

The **security** command may be a bit confusing. This command means that connections check the local password database. It is appropriate if you're configuring this computer as a PDC.

```
security = user
```

If you want to configure this computer as a member server on a Domain, you'll want to use a password database from a PDC. Strangely enough, in that case, you would substitute the following command:

```
security = domain
```

on the
Job

If you just want to set up this computer as a workstation that happens to share directories on a Microsoft Domain, you'll need to set up the computer as a member server on that Domain.

Alternatively, if you just want to use a database from another computer that is not a PDC, you'd substitute the following command:

```
security = server
```

Finally, if you're configuring this computer on a peer-to-peer workgroup, you want to substitute the following command:

```
security = share
```

There are four basic authentication options: **share**, **user**, **server**, and **domain**. The default is **user**; in this case, you'll want to make sure the Samba usernames and passwords that you create match those on individual Windows NT/2000/XP systems on your network.

If you use the **server** authentication option, you can name another Samba server to carry the database of usernames and passwords.

If you use the **domain** authentication option, you can name an NT/2000/XP domain controller. You can set up a Samba server as a domain controller as well, emulating the functionality of a Windows domain controller.

on the Job

With Samba version 3.0, you can now configure a Samba-enabled Linux computer as a member server on an Active Directory network. If that's what you want, set up security = *ads.*

If you've set up **security = domain** or **share**, you'll want to activate this command with the name of the password server:

```
;    password server = <NT-Server-Name>
```

Linux is case sensitive. If you want to disable the case sensitivity for usernames and passwords of up to eight characters, activate these commands:

```
;    password level = 8
;    username level = 8
```

Encryption is enabled by default for Microsoft Windows computers, unless you have a network with operating systems older than Windows 95 (pre-OSR2) or Windows NT 4 (before Service Pack 3). Therefore, you'll want to activate these commands. I'll describe how you can set up the Samba password file later in this chapter.

```
;    encrypt passwords = yes
;    smb passwd file = /etc/samba/smbpasswd
```

If you've configured the same usernames for your Microsoft and Linux computers, activate the following commands. They help synchronize the passwords on the different accounts.

```
;    unix password sync = Yes
;    passwd program = /usr/bin/passwd %u
```

```
;   passwd chat = *New*UNIX*password* %n\n \
;  *ReType*new*UNIX*password* %n\n \
    *passwd:*all*authentication*tokens*updated*successfully*
```

If the usernames on your Linux computers aren't identical to your Windows usernames, you'll need to activate a database of matching usernames in the following database:

```
;   username map = /etc/samba/smbusers
```

You can customize the local Samba configuration by the computer (machine) client that connects by activating the following command. Configuring these computer-specific command files is complex, and I suspect is beyond configuring "the service for basic operation."

```
;   include = /etc/samba/smb.conf.%m
```

Configuring socket options also takes trial and error and requires more than the "basic operation" configuration skills specified in the Red Hat Exam Prep guide.

```
    socket options = TCP_NODELAY SO_RCVBUF=8192 SO_SNDBUF=8192
```

If your computer is connected to more than one network, you can specify the networks served by your Samba server here:

```
;   interfaces = 192.168.12.2/24 192.168.13.2/24
```

If you want to keep your browse list synchronized with other LANs, you can specify those computers or networks here:

```
;   remote browse sync = 192.168.3.25 192.168.5.255
```

If other computers are having trouble finding the browse list, you can tell Samba to share the list with specific computers or subnets:

```
;   remote announce = 192.168.1.255 192.168.2.44
```

Unless you specifically designate this computer to be a local master, Samba participates in browser elections like any other Microsoft Windows computer, using the **os level** that you designate. Alternatively, if you don't already have a Domain Controller acting as a browse master, you can give the responsibility to the Samba server. Or if you just want to make it easier for the local computer to win the browser election, activate the **preferred master** command.

```
;    local master = no
;    os level = 33
;    domain master = yes
;    preferred master = yes
```

If you have Windows 95 computers on your network, you'll want to activate this command. Remember, many Windows 95 computers can't handle encryption.

```
;    domain logons = yes
```

The following commands set up Microsoft command line batch files by computer and user. The command afterwards stores Microsoft user profiles on the local Samba server. That means these commands can't be tested on the Red Hat exams unless you have access to a Microsoft Windows computer. Since I can't tell you what's on the Red Hat exams, it is up to you to determine whether it's practical to have separate Microsoft Windows computers available during those exams.

```
;    logon script = %m.bat
;    logon script = %U.bat
;    logon path = \\%L\Profiles\%U
```

If you have multiple browse methods, you can set the order used by your Samba server to search for other computers. This particular command looks to the WINS (Windows Internet Name Service) server first, followed by any available lmhosts file; if both options fail, a broadcast request for names is sent to the network.

```
; name resolve order = wins lmhosts bcast
```

If you activate the following command, Samba activates a WINS server on the local computer:

```
;    wins support = yes
```

Alternatively, you can point the local computer to a remote WINS server on the network; of course, you'd have to substitute the IP address for w.x.y.z.

```
;    wins server = w.x.y.z
```

If there are non-WINS capable computers on the network, such as Linux computers without the Samba server software, you can activate this command:

```
;    wins proxy = yes
```

on the job

Adding Linux to a Microsoft Windows NT/2000/XP network can be made easier by configuring the Samba service to look like another Windows host on the network. You can configure the Samba server to act as a WINS client of the WINS server, share files and printers just like all the other Windows hosts, and participate in the browser service.

If you change this setting to **yes**, name searches can go through available DNS databases.

```
dns proxy = no
```

The remaining commands are fairly self-explanatory; however, I've never changed these settings, as changes to these variables can cause trouble with file transfers.

```
# Case Preservation can be handy - system default is _no_
# NOTE: These can be set on a per share basis
;  preserve case = no
;  short preserve case = no
# Default case is normally upper case for all DOS files
;  default case = lower
# Be very careful with case sensitivity - it can break things!
;  case sensitive = no
```

on the job

If you want to set up a Samba server to use a Microsoft Windows database of usernames and passwords, you'll need to activate the winbindd *daemon. With the right commands in smb.conf, you can also set up Microsoft users and groups with the UIDs and GIDs of your choice on your Linux system.*

Share Settings

Share settings are organized into *stanzas*, which are groups of commands associated with a share name. (With respect to stanzas, some believe that well-constructed configuration code is like good poetry.) The first four lines in this section define the [homes] share, which automatically shares the home directory of the logged in user. Remember, RHEL 3 includes Samba version 3.0. Every user gets access to their own home directory; the **browsable = no** command keeps users away from each other's home directory.

There is no default /homes directory. It's just a label. You don't need to supply a home directory, because Samba will read the user's account record in /etc/passwd and /etc/shadow to determine the directory to be shared.

By default, this does not allow access to unknown users (**guest ok = no**). If you prefer, you can limit the systems that can use this share (**hosts allow** = ?, and **hosts deny** = ?).

```
#============================== Share Definitions =============
[homes]
    comment = Home Directories
    browseable = no
    writable = yes
```

e x a m

ⓦ **a t c h**   *If you forget the meaning of a specific Samba variable, you can find more information with the* man smb.conf *command.*

Those of you who are familiar with Red Hat Linux 9 may note that it supports Samba version 2.2.7. The basic [homes] directory share is the same; however, you may notice that the Samba version 2.2.7 version of this file in Red Hat Linux 9 includes three more variables:

- **valid users = %S**   By default, all users with a local account can access their home directory using this share; this command adds the name of the service.

- **create mode = 664**   Sets permissions when you create or copy files to your home directory through this share. The default, and thus what happens in the default RHEL 3 smb.conf file, corresponds to a create mode of 744. This gives the file owner rwx permissions, and other users on that computer read-only permissions. I explain the concept of Linux file permissions briefly in Chapter 1.

- **directory mode = 775**   Similar to create mode; sets permissions when you create directories through this share. The default for RHEL 3 if you don't specify a **directory mode** is 755.

If you activate the commands in the following stanza, you can set up a netlogon share for Microsoft Windows workstations. As there are no netlogon shares even for Samba-enabled Linux workstations, this section requires a Microsoft Windows computer to verify functionality. If you believe that you'll have access to a Microsoft Windows computer during the Red Hat exams, you'll want to study this section carefully.

```
# Un-comment the following and create the netlogon directory for
# Domain Logons
; [netlogon]
;    comment = Network Logon Service
;    path = /home/netlogon
;    guest ok = yes
;    writable = no
;    share modes = no
```

This next stanza configures profiles for Microsoft Windows workstations. As these profiles become a part of a Microsoft Windows registry when you log on to one of those workstations, you're unlikely to configure this section in a network of Linux-only computers. Make your own judgment on whether you might have to configure this section during the RHCE exam.

```
# Un-comment the following to provide a specific roving profile
# share; the default is to use the user's home directory
;[Profiles]
;    path = /home/profiles
;    browseable = no
;    guest ok = yes
```

The [printers] stanza normally works as is, to allow access by all users with accounts on your computer or domain. If you want to limit access to specific users, see the [fredsprn] stanza later in this default file. While the spool directory (/var/spool/samba) is not browsable, the associated printers are browsable by their NetBIOS names. When you configure a printer later in this chapter, the name you designate automatically becomes the NetBIOS name.

```
# NOTE: If you have a BSD-style print system there is no need to
# specifically define each individual printer
[printers]
   comment = All Printers
   path = /var/spool/samba
   browseable = no
# Set public = yes to allow user 'guest account' to print
   guest ok = no
   writable = no
   printable = yes
```

If you activate the [tmp] share, it's a standard location for people to download and share files; all users get write access to this share.

```
# This one is useful for people to share files
;[tmp]
;    comment = Temporary file space
;    path = /tmp
;    read only = no
;    public = yes
```

The following stanza, as suggested by the comment, configures the /home/samba directory to be shared by the group named staff. You can configure this group in /etc

/group or through the Network Information System (Chapter 10). And you need to configure special ownership and permissions for /home/samba, as described in the User Private Group scheme in Chapter 11.

```
# A publicly accessible directory, but read only, except for people
# in the "staff" group
;[public]
;    comment = Public Stuff
;    path = /home/samba
;    public = yes
;    read only = yes
;    write list = @staff
```

If you activate the following stanza, it would configure a printer exclusively for one user. The default RHEL 3 smb.conf file has an error in this file; it lists the path to Fred's home directory as /homes/fred.

```
# A private printer, usable only by fred. Spool data will be
# placed in fred's home directory. Note that fred must have
# write access to the spool directory,
# wherever it is.
;[fredsprn]
;    comment = Fred's Printer
;    valid users = fred
;    path = /home/fred
;    printer = freds_printer
;    public = no
;    writable = no
;    printable = yes
```

This stanza configures a directory for Fred's exclusive use. I'm not sure why it's included in the Samba configuration file, as the user fred would already have a home directory on this computer. A better location for the **path**, which you need to create, is within the /home directory.

```
# A private directory, usable only by fred. Note that fred
# requires write access to the directory.
;[fredsdir]
;    comment = Fred's Service
;    path = /usr/somewhere/private
;    valid users = fred
;    public = no
;    writable = yes
;    printable = no
```

You can also set up directories by workstation; the **%m** variable is replaced by the name of the computer (machine) that connects to the Samba server. A better location for the path is the /home/pc/%m directory.

```
# The %m gets replaced with the machine name that is connecting.
; [pchome]
;   comment = PC Directories
;   path = /usr/pc/%m
;   public = no
;   writable = yes
```

The following stanza is slightly different from the [tmp] share. Once connected, the only user that connects is a guest. Unless you've configured a guest user, this defaults to the user nobody.

```
# A publicly accessible directory, read/write to all users. Note
# that all files created in the directory by users will be owned
# by the default user, so any user with access can delete any
# other user's files. Obviously this directory must be writable
# by the default user. Another user could of course be specified,
# in which case all files would be owned by that user instead.
; [public]
;   path = /usr/somewhere/else/public
;   public = yes
;   only guest = yes
;   writable = yes
;   printable = no
```

Finally, this is another variation on the User Private Group scheme, which creates a group directory. Unlike the [public] stanza, this share is private.

```
# The following two entries demonstrate how to share a directory so
# that two users can place files there that will be owned by the
# specific users. In this setup, the directory should be writable
# by both users and should have the sticky bit set on it to prevent
# abuse. Obviously this could be extended to as many users as required.
; [myshare]
;   comment = Mary's and Fred's stuff
;   path = /usr/somewhere/shared
;   valid users = mary fred
;   public = no
;   writable = yes
;   printable = no
;   create mask = 0765
```

To summarize, the settings for each shared directory start with a section name, such as [tmp]. This section name contains the name that will be seen by Microsoft clients only if the service is set to be browseable (**browseable = yes**).

There are a number of variables in smb.conf that are not spelled correctly, such as browseable. In some cases, the correct spelling (browsable) also works. They are still accepted Samba variables, and generally should be spelled per the Samba defaults, not standard written English.

Joining a Domain

If you've configured a Samba server, and it's not the PDC for your network, you'll need to set it to join the domain. Essentially, you're configuring an account on the Domain Controller for the network. As long as there's one domain on this network, it's easy to do with the following command:

```
# net rpc join -U root
```

This assumes that root is the administrative user on the PDC; if you're joining a domain governed by a Microsoft Windows computer, the administrative user is *administrator*. If successful, you're prompted for the root password on the remote PDC. An account for the local computer is added to the PDC's user database in /etc/password.

If you're using Red Hat Linux 9 with Samba 2.2.7, the net rpc command is not available. You'll either have to upgrade or use the smbpasswd -j domainname -r domaincomputer -U root command.

Configuring Samba Users

You could set up identical usernames and passwords for your Microsoft Windows and Samba-enabled Linux computers. However, this is not always possible. For example, Microsoft usernames often start with a capital letter, which is not allowed for a Linux username. In that case, you'll want to set up a database of Samba users and passwords which correspond to current Microsoft usernames and passwords on your network.

If you're comfortable with the command line interface, the quickest way to set up Samba users is with the **smbadduser** and **smbpasswd** commands. Remember, you can create a new Samba user only from valid accounts on your Linux computer.

Managing Samba Users

You can set up Samba users on a list independent from your Linux users who have accounts on your Linux system. The Samba development team chose to do this because

- There is no reason to grant Samba access to all Linux users.

■ You may wish to manage user access via Windows NT/2000/XP, so Linux wouldn't necessarily even know about your Samba users.

■ Samba user authentication may involve clear text passwords (for compatibility with Windows 95 and Windows 3.1). This could potentially compromise your Linux system.

To support these features, you can set up separate user accounts in the /etc/samba directory, in the smbusers and smbpasswd files. Two steps are required to make and enable a new Samba user:

1. Create a Samba user entry by name and add a password for the user. Samba users can be created only from the current users on your Linux system.

2. Enable Samba access for the new user.

If the username that you want does not yet exist, create it with the **useradd** **username** command. Then you can set that user up as a Samba user with the **smbpasswd** command. Use the following command; you're prompted to enter a password. That password can be different from the password used to log in directly to that Linux computer.

```
# smbpasswd -a newUser
New SMB password:
Retype SMB password:
#
```

Next, to enable Samba access for this user, run the following command:

```
# smbpasswd -e newUser
Enabled user newUser
#
```

Changes made by **smbpasswd** are passed to the Samba server to be copied to the system with the username and password database for your network.

on the
job

The smbadduser command is no longer available in Samba 3.0, which is included with RHEL 3.

If you've configured Samba as a PDC for your network, the /etc/passwd file should govern the basic usernames and passwords for your system. You can use the **mksmbpasswd.sh** script to add all passwords to the /etc/samba/smbpasswd configuration file.

The **smbpasswd** command is powerful in RHEL 3; it includes a number of switches that you should learn, as described in Table 8-1.

	smbpasswd Switch	Description
TABLE 8-1	-a *username*	Adds the specified username to /etc/samba/smbpasswd.
Various smbpasswd Commands	-d *username*	Disables the specified username; thus disables that password from Microsoft networking.
	-e *username*	Enables the specified username; opposite of **-d**.
	-r *computername*	Allows you to change your Windows or Samba password on a remote computer. Normally goes with **-U**.
	-U *username*	Normally changes the username on a remote computer, if specified with the **-r** switch.
	-x *username*	Deletes the specified username to /etc/samba/smbpasswd.

If you need to configure different usernames and passwords for your Linux and Microsoft computers, you'll need to edit them directly into the /etc/samba/smbusers file—or you can use the Samba Server Configuration utility which I describe shortly.

EXERCISE 8-1

Using Home Directories

In this exercise, you'll learn about the basic home directory share. You'll need at least two computers, one of which should be a Samba server. The other can be a Linux or Microsoft Windows workstation. You'll connect to the Samba server from the workstation, and access the files in your home directory on the Samba server.

1. Install and configure Samba to start using the methods described earlier in this chapter.

2. Open the /etc/samba/smb.conf configuration file. Look for the current value of **workgroup**.

3. Make sure that the computers on your network have the same value of **workgroup**. If your computer is on a domain, set **workgroup** to the name of the domain. If you don't already have a WINS server on this network, you'll also want to activate the **wins support = yes** command.

4. Test the syntax of your Samba configuration file with the **testparm** command (I'll describe how this works shortly).

5. Read and address any problems that you might see in the output from the **testparm** command. Fix any syntax problems with your smb.conf configuration file.

6. Set up the root user on the server in the Samba database with the following commands (enter an appropriate password when prompted):

```
# smbpasswd -a root
# smbpasswd -e root
```

7. Make Samba reread the smb.conf file with the following command:

```
# service smb reload
```

8. Now go to a remote Linux or Microsoft Windows workstation on the same Domain or Workgroup.

9. If you can browse the list of computers from the Samba server with the following command, browsing and probably WINS is working properly. (Alternatively, from a Microsoft Windows computer, you should see a list of computers in the Network Neighborhood or My Network Places window.)

```
# smbclient -L sambaserver -U root
```

10. Enter the root username on the remote Samba server.

11. If you're on a Linux computer, use the **smbmnt** or **mount** command (depending on whether you're regular or a root user) to configure the remote [homes] directory share on an empty local directory. For example, as the root user, you could mount on the local /mnt/share directory with the following command:

```
# mount -o username=root "//sambaserver/homes" /mnt/share
```

12. Test the result. Can you browse your home directory on the remote computer?

The Red Hat Samba Server Configuration Utility

RHEL 3 includes Red Hat's graphical configuration tool for Samba, **redhat-config-samba**, which you can install from the RPM of the same name. Before you use this tool to modify your configuration, back up the files in your /etc/samba directory.

Also known as the Samba Server Configuration utility, you can use this tool to set basic global parameters and configure shared directories. You can start it from a GUI

command line with the **redhat-config-samba** command, or you can click Main Menu |
System Settings | Server Settings | Samba. You've seen the basic tool back in Figure 8-1.

You will find that this tool is straightforward to use. You can configure general Samba
settings such as security level and workgroup through the Preferences | Server Settings
command. The Add button enables you to set up a new share. The Preferences | Samba
Users command allows you to modify the smbusers and smbpasswd files in the /etc
/samba directory.

You can also use this tool to configure Samba usernames and passwords. In other
words, you can use this tool to configure your smb.conf file as well as Samba usernames
and passwords through the smbusers and smbpasswd files. Naturally, these files are
stored in the /etc/samba directory.

There are drawbacks to the Samba Server Configuration utility. For example, you
can't use it to edit all global parameters or share printers. You can't use it to set a Samba
member server to join a domain.

Note that the Samba Server *special printer shares, to join a domain, to*
Configuration utility may not do everything *control samba services, your fastest option*
you need. To configure most global settings, *is to work from the command line interface.*

Global Settings

To see what the Samba Server Configuration utility can do to the global settings in the
smb.conf configuration file, click Preferences | Server Settings. As you can probably
guess from Figure 8-5, the basic settings set the **workgroup** and **server string** variables.
The workgroup variable can represent the name of a Workgroup or Domain; in this
case, Grateful is the name of my network domain.

FIGURE 8-5

Samba Server
basic settings

Server Settings
Basic Security
Workgroup: grateful
Description: samba server
Cancel OK

When you use this utility and assign default variables, it erases the variable from your smb.conf file. For example, if you set the **workgroup** name to Workgroup, this utility erases the **workgroup** command line from smb.conf. Therefore, it's an excellent idea to back up smb.conf before using the Samba Server Configuration utility.

In contrast, the Security tab supports a few more settings, as you can see in Figure 8-6. The entries are fairly straightforward. If you want more information on these variables, refer to the discussion on smb.conf earlier in this chapter:

- Authentication Mode sets the **security** value in /etc/samba/smb.conf. The default is **user**.

- Authentication Server sets up the location of the **password server**. There is no default.

- Encrypt Passwords is associated with the variable of the same name. The default is **yes**.

- Guest Account is associated with the variable of the same name. The default in RHEL 3 is **nobody**.

on the **job**

If you've selected a default, you may still see the variable in the smb.conf file in comments. Alternatively, you may see the variable in an unexpected location relative to the default comments.

Share Settings

Click the Add button. This opens the Create Samba Share window shown in Figure 8-7. The Basic tab helps you define the basic parameters associated with the share:

- Directory defines the directory that you want to share, using the **path** variable. The share name is taken from the last part of the directory name. For example, if you're sharing the /usr/share/to/path1, Samba designates [path1] as the share name.

- Description allows you to define the comment that users can see in the browse list.

- Basic permissions lets you set **writable** as yes or no; read only (**writable=no**) is the default. (This is another case where two spellings for the same variable are acceptable; writeable is also an acceptable spelling in smb.conf.)

The Access tab is simpler; it allows you to limit access to specific users from the smbpasswd configuration file. In other words, you can only limit access to users from

FIGURE 8-6

Samba Server
security settings

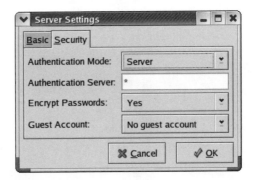

the Samba password database. Once you've clicked OK, the Samba Server Configuration
tool automatically updates the smb.conf configuration file.

Samba Users

The Samba Server Configuration tool also allows you to configure Samba users, based
on the users already present in your /etc/passwd configuration file. Unfortunately, it
can only use local password databases as of this writing. However, that's good enough to
configure Microsoft usernames on this computer. To add Samba users from the Samba
Server Configuration tool, click Preferences | Samba Users. This opens the Samba Users
window shown in Figure 8-8.

As you can see, this window includes a list of currently configured Samba users.
Click Add User. This opens the Create New Samba User window shown in Figure 8-9,
where you can:

- Select an existing username from /etc/passwd.
- Enter the corresponding Microsoft Windows username.
- Set up a password for that Samba user. It can be different from that user's
  Linux password.

FIGURE 8-7

Basic components
of Create Samba
Share

FIGURE 8-8

Current
Samba users

Click OK when you're done. Naturally, you can also change the Windows username and password for each Samba user, or even delete Samba users with the Edit User and Delete User buttons. Click OK to exit from the Samba Users window.

Creating a Public Share

Now let's create a public access share for use with the entire network. First, create the /home/PublicShare directory for this purpose. Click Add to open the Create Samba Share window. Enter the directory that you want to share, /home/PublicShare, in the directory text box. Enter an appropriate description and select Read/Write access. In the Access tab, select the Allow Access To Everyone option. Click OK and exit from the Samba Server Configuration tool with the File | Quit command.

FIGURE 8-9

Adding another
Samba user

Now, you'll have to finish the task directly from the text editor. The instructions so far add the following commands in the /etc/samba/smb.conf configuration file:

```
[PublicShare]
     comment= Shared Public Directory
     path = /home/PublicShare
     writeable = yes
     guest ok = yes
```

Now you want to modify these commands. The [PublicShare] should be accessible to all users with a Linux account on your computer. It should also deny access to guest users and others. You want to provide access to anyone in your domain (.myCompany.com), and you want to deny access to everyone in the suspect domain (which we'll call evil.crackers .com). Finally, your shares should be browseable to valid users.

You'll want to change the last command in this stanza. As **guest ok = no** is the default, you can just erase the command, or replace it as shown:

```
guest ok = no
```

To provide access to all users in the given domain, I'd add the following command:

```
hosts allow = .myCompany.com
```

If you wanted to deny access to one specific computer on that network, you could add **EXCEPT guest.myCompany.com** to the end of this command. Alternatively, if this domain is on the 192.168.99.0 network, you could use one of the following commands:

```
hosts allow = 192.168.99.
hosts allow = 192.168.99.0/255.255.255.0
```

---

e x a m

w a t c h   *The digit '1' in front of the 777 directory permission string in the* chmod *command is known as the "sticky bit." By enabling the sticky bit, you are saying that anyone can do anything in the directory (because of the 777 permission value) but only to files they make! Otherwise, any user could delete or rename any file in your PublicShare, regardless of the file's owner.*

You could specifically deny access to computers with a command such as the following:

```
hosts deny = evil.crackers.com
```

Or you could substitute IP addresses in the same format as with the **hosts allow** command. You've defined the share attributes in the Samba smb.conf configuration file. But you need to modify the directory associated with the share with the following command, which includes the "sticky bit":

```
# chmod 1777 /home/PublicShare
```

Testing Changes to /etc/samba/smb.conf

After making any changes to /etc/samba/smb.conf, it is always a good idea to test your system before putting it into production. You can do a simple syntax check on the Samba configuration file with the **testparm** test utility, as shown in Figure 8-10. This does not actually check to see if the service is running or functioning correctly, it checks only basic text syntax and command stanzas.

FIGURE 8-10

Testing smb.conf syntax

```
[root@Enterprise3 root]# testparm | more
Processing section "[homes]"
Processing section "[printers]"
Processing section "[tmp]"
Processing section "[samba]"
Processing section "[PublicShare]"
Load smb config files from /etc/samba/smb.conf
Loaded services file OK.
Server role: ROLE_DOMAIN_MEMBER
Press enter to see a dump of your service definitions
# Global parameters
[global]
        workgroup = GRATEFUL
        server string = samba server
        security = DOMAIN
        password server = 192.168.30.4
        log file = /var/log/samba/%m.log
        max log size = 50
        socket options = TCP_NODELAY SO_RCVBUF=8192 SO_SNDBUF=8192
        dns proxy = No
        printing = cups

[homes]
--More--
```

EXERCISE 8-2

Configuring Samba with Shares

In this exercise, you'll be configuring Samba to do something useful, sharing a directory and any configured printers. For this purpose, you can't do anything with the Samba Server Configuration tool; therefore, you'll need to edit the /etc/samba/smb.conf file directly in a text editor.

1. Install the Samba RPMs or Windows File Server Package Group as described earlier in this chapter.

2. Create a /home/ftp/public directory. Change ownership to the ftp user and group, with full permissions (770).

3. Open the /etc/samba/smb.conf file in a text editor.

4. Configure Samba to share all installed print queues to all users. Normally, the default [printers] stanza in smb.conf should suffice. However, as you're about to create a guest account, you'll want to add the last command shown here:

```
[printers]
      comment = All printers
      path = /var/spool/samba
      browseable = no
      printable = yes
guest ok = yes
```

5. Configure Samba to share as public, in read-only mode, the /home/ftp/pub directory tree. In the Share Definitions section, you could add the following commands:

```
[pub]
      comment = shared FTP directory
      path = /home/ftp/pub
```

6. Allow guest access to all public shares. In smb.conf, this means adding the following line to the [pub] stanza:

```
      guest ok = yes
```

7. Since you're about to create a guest account, you'll need to activate the following command in smb.conf:

```
; guest account = pcguest
```

8. Create a guest account for pcguest, associate it with an unused UID and GID 600. Set the password to be "anonymous." While you can do this with the Red Hat User Manager discussed in Chapter 4, the quickest way to do this is with the following commands:

```
# useradd pcguest -u 600
# passwd pcguest
```

9. Create separate log files for each computer host that connects. This is already active by default with the following command:

```
log file = /var/log/samba/%m.log
```

10. If you have a WINS server configured, authorize Samba to participate as a WINS client. Use the IP of that WINS server. While you don't want to enable the **wins support** command, you do want to point the **wins server** command to the IP address of your WINS server (I've added a random IP address):

```
wins server = 10.11.12.13
```

11. Write and save your changes to the smb.conf file.

12. You can see if Samba is already running with the **service smb status** command. If it's stopped, you can start it with the **service smb start** command. If it's running, you can make Samba reread your configuration file with the following command:

```
# service smb reload
```

This final option allows you to change your Samba configuration without disconnecting users from your Samba server.

CERTIFICATION OBJECTIVE 8.02

Print Services

RHEL 3 comes with one print service, the Common Unix Printing System (CUPS). It's the successor to the Line Print Daemon (LPD), which is no longer offered with

RHEL 3 or Fedora Linux. However, Red Hat includes software that allows you to use a number of LPD commands to monitor and maintain printers.

You can configure printers directly through the CUPS configuration files in the /etc/cups directory. Alternatively, RHEL 3 includes two quality GUI tools that you can use to configure local and remote printers on your network. One is a Web-based interface, and Red Hat is focusing its efforts on its own Printer Configuration utility.

CUPS is the Linux/Unix implementation of the Internet Print Protocol (IPP). I expect IPP to become a fairly universal standard for printer configuration sometime in the future, even for Microsoft and Apple computers.

Installing and Starting CUPS

CUPS and a number of print databases are installed with the Printing Support package group. It includes ten RPM packages which appear unrelated. If you haven't already installed this package group during the RHEL 3 installation process, it's likely most efficient to install it using the Red Hat Package Management utility described in Chapter 4. If you want to learn to install the packages on your own, review the packages in the Package Management utility or the /usr/share/comps/i386/comps.xml file.

It's easy to start and configure CUPS to start when Linux boots on your computer. The **cups** service script works like most of the other services on RHEL 3. In other words, you can start it with the following command:

```
# service cups start
```

Naturally, by substituting **restart**, **stop**, or **reload** for **start**, you can restart or stop the CUPS service, or reload the CUPS configuration files.

CUPS Configuration Files

There are a number of printer configuration files in the /etc/cups directory. Each of these files include a substantial number of commands and comments. I'm going to summarize some key commands in these files, which are listed in Table 8-2.

While I still believe that it's best in general to edit configuration files directly, the commands associated with CUPS can be difficult to learn. Several of the files in /etc /cups don't include the same quality of comments as other services. And the Red Hat configuration tool provides the functionality that you need—it's considerably better than the functionality of the Samba Server Configuration tool, for example.

TABLE 8-2	CUPS Configuration Files

CUPS Configuration File	Description
/etc/cups/classes.conf	Specifies different classes of printers. A print *class* can include several printers; when you print to a print class, CUPS sends your print job to the first available printer in that class, as specified here.
/etc/cups/client.conf	Sets the default CUPS server for this computer; it can be local or another remote print server.
/etc/cups/cupsd.conf	The main CUPS configuration file.
/etc/cups/mime.convs	Includes file format filters, such as images and documents.
/etc/cups/mime.types	Sets file types that can be processed through CUPS printers.
/etc/cups/printers.conf	Documents printers configured by the CUPS Web-based tool.
/etc/cups/pstoraster.convs	Includes a conversion filter which supports PostScript printers.
/etc/printcap	Adds a list of printers for sharing; used by Samba.

The Red Hat Printer Configuration Tool

The main Red Hat Printer Configuration tool works well. You can start it with the **redhat-config-printer** command, or you can click Main Menu | System Settings | Printing. Either option opens the utility shown in Figure 8-11. It is a "front end" that can help you configure the files in the /etc/cups directory.

You can use this tool to manage printers. It can configure print queues to local ports or through remote systems:

- Local CUPS ports
- Remote Unix/Linux LPD print services
- Shared Windows printers
- Novell NCP print queues
- HP JetDirect print servers

on the **Job**

Red Hat has developed a text-mode version of the Printer Configuration tool. You can start it from the text console with the redhat-config-printer-tui *command.*

Previous versions of Red Hat used the **printtool** GUI printer manager and the **printconf-gui** utility. These commands now are "front-ends" which have been

FIGURE 8-11

Red Hat's Printer
Configuration
utility

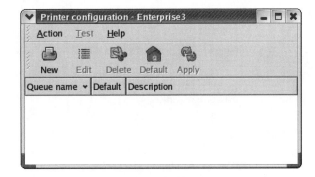

reconfigured to start the Printer Configuration tool. You should be able to use this tool to connect to just about any type of printer available on your network.

Now let's try defining a local printer. Click Add. This should automatically start the Add a New Print Queue wizard, as shown in Figure 8-12.

Click Forward. In the Queue name screen shown in Figure 8-13, designate a name and comment for the printer. When you share printers over a network, the name and comment can help you identify the printer. The printer name must be one word. Click Next to continue.

If you selected a local printer, the next step is to select a printer port. The normal default is the first printer port, /dev/lp0. This corresponds to LPT1: in the Microsoft world. You might see /dev/usb/lp0 for a printer on a USB port. This is the default option shown in Figure 8-14.

FIGURE 8-12

Starting
the printer
configuration
process

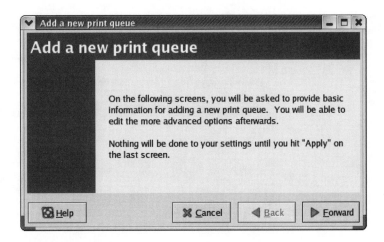

FIGURE 8-13

Naming the
printer

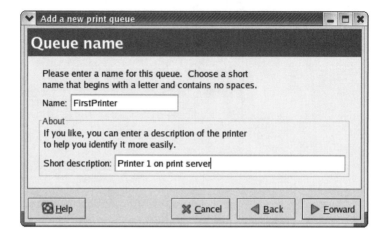

Alternatively, if you're configuring a printer over a network, click the Select A Queue Type drop-down text box. You'll get to choose between printers shared on several different types of networks, as described at the start of this section. If you select a network option, the window changes to allow you to enter network information. For example, if you select a Networked CUPS (IPP) printer, the window changes to Figure 8-15.

In this setup, you'll need the hostname or IP address of the print server, the name of the printer, and any required usernames and passwords to authorize access to that network printer. Once you've identified the printer location, click Forward. There

FIGURE 8-14

Selecting
the printer
connection

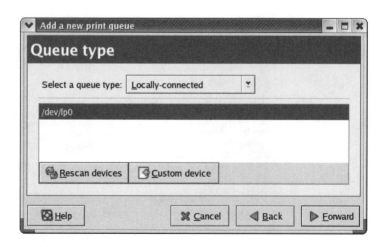

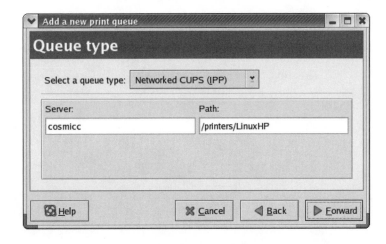

FIGURE 8-15

Configuring a
CUPS network
printer

may be a slight delay as the tool looks through the network. Now you can select
a printer manufacturer and driver, as shown in Figure 8-16.

There are two steps here. First, click the drop-down text box where you see Generic
(Click To Select Manufacturer). You'll be able to choose between several dozen
manufacturers. Once you select a manufacturer, the screen changes to a database of
printer models associated with that manufacturer. Select a driver and then click Forward.

Before the Printer Configuration tool creates a print queue, it documents what it's
about to do. If you're satisfied with the configuration, click Apply. This returns you to
the main Printer Configuration menu shown previously in Figure 8-11, and an offer
to print a test page. You have to select Yes to apply changes.

FIGURE 8-16

Selecting a driver

> **Add a new print queue**   _ □ ✗
>
> ## Printer model
>
> Select the printer manufacturer and model.   Notes...
>
> | Generic (click to select manufacturer)   ▾ |
>
> 48 pin
> 9-pin 136 Col
> 9-pin 80 Col
> PostScript Printer
>
> 🅗 Help   ✗ Cancel   ◀ Back   ▶ Forward

FIGURE 8-17

Sharing a
CUPS printer

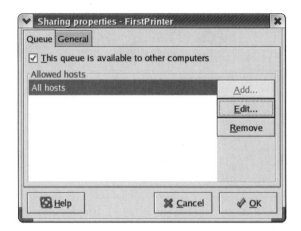

FIGURE 8-17

Sharing a
CUPS printer

The main Printer Configuration menu should now include the name of your printer.
To write these changes to the configuration files in the /etc/cups directory, as well as
/etc/printcap, click the Apply button.

If you have trouble here, you may not have shared the CUPS printer at the server.
To do so at the server, highlight the name of the printer that you want to share. Right-
click on it and select Sharing in the pop-up menu that appears. This opens the Sharing
Properties window named for the printer on the server. Under the Queue tab shown
in Figure 8-17, activate the "This queue is available to other computers" option. This
works with the Printer Configuration tool included with RHEL 3 and Red Hat Linux 9.

The Line Print Daemon Commands

Even though RHEL 3 uses CUPS, you can still control your print system with LPD
commands. Three major commands are associated with the **lpd** service: **lpr**, **lpq**, and
lprm. They are used to add print requests, list queued print requests, and remove print
requests, respectively. One more command can help you administer one or more print
queues: **lpc**.

lpc: Line Print Control

To view all known queues, run the **lpc status** command; it implements the result shown
in Figure 8-18. As you can see, the output helps you easily scan all configured print
devices and queues.

on the
job

*The lpc command that comes with CUPS does not support starting or stopping
of print queues.*

FIGURE 8-18	```[root@CosmicC root]# lpc status```

Status of
configured
printers

```
[root@CosmicC root]# lpc status
LinuxHP:
        printer is on device 'parallel' speed -1
        queuing is enabled
        printing is enabled
        1 entries
        daemon present
WinPrint1:
        printer is on device 'parallel' speed -1
        queuing is enabled
        printing is enabled
        4 entries
        daemon present
WinPrint2:
        printer is on device 'parallel' speed -1
        queuing is enabled
        printing is enabled
        no entries
        daemon present
[root@CosmicC root]#
```

lpr: Line Print Request

Any user can use **lpr** to send print requests to any local print queue. You can **lpr** any files to a queue, or you can redirect any output via **lpr**. If you wanted to print to the queue named color, you'd use a command such as **lpr -Pcolor** *filename*. Note there is no space between the **-P** switch and the name of the queue.

lpq: Line Print Query

Note that your printer is no longer printing requests. Now let's queue up a new job. Issue these commands:

```
# lpq
WinPrint1 is ready and printing
Rank    Owner   Job  Files                   Total Size
active  root    373  smbprn.000486.6JkBaq    10240 bytes
1st     root    374  smbprn.000487.6JkBaq    10240 bytes
2nd     root    376  smbprn.000488.6JkBaq    10240 bytes
```

FIGURE 8-19

GNOME Print
Manager

Now you can delete the jobs of your choice by using the **lprm** command and job number:

```
# lprm 376
```

GUI Front-Ends

RHEL 3 includes two GUI front-ends on the GNOME desktop. They run one of the commands noted in this section and format it into a graphical interface. To view the printers that you've configured on the GUI, click Main Menu | System Tools | Print Manager. One example is shown in Figure 8-19.

Each of these printers may have a print queue. For example, Figure 8-20 illustrates

FIGURE 8-20

Typical print
spool

Document	Owner	Job Number	Size	Time Submitted
smbprn.000354.6JkBaq	root	282	10240 bytes	Sun 07 Dec 2003 09:55:00 PM EST
smbprn.000355.Mt5ZV7	root	283	10240 bytes	Sun 07 Dec 2003 09:55:14 PM EST
smbprn.000356.UoEuHe	root	284	10240 bytes	Sun 07 Dec 2003 09:55:21 PM EST
passwd	remroot	285	92160 bytes	Sun 07 Dec 2003 09:56:14 PM EST
passwd	root	287	3072 bytes	Sun 07 Dec 2003 10:17:35 PM EST
passwd	remroot	288	92160 bytes	Sun 07 Dec 2003 10:27:14 PM EST

6 jobs in queue "LinuxHP"

the result after double-clicking on the LinuxHP print icon. You can review the print jobs waiting in the spool to print on the LinuxHP printer.

The CUPS Web-Based Interface

Another way to configure CUPS is through the Web-based interface. Open up the browser of your choice on the local Linux computer. Direct it to the http://localhost:631 address to get to the main CUPS configuration menu. There are seven options atop the Administration menu:

- **ESP**   Brings you to the Easy Software Products home page at www.easysw.com. CUPS is officially one of their products, licensed under the Linux GPL.

- **Administration**   A basic interface that allows you to set up classes of printers, manage print jobs, and add or manage printers. You can also administer these features through the Classes, Jobs, or Printers options.

- **Classes**   Enables you to set up groups of printers together.

- **Help**   Provides extensive documentation.

- **Jobs**   Enables you to view and manage active print jobs.

- **Printers**   Enables you to manage existing printers and set up new printers.

- **Software**   Enables you to review the current version and upgrade if appropriate.

You can manage Classes, Jobs, and Printers from the Administrative menu. You can read the Help section on your own, and software upgrades to CUPS are not covered in this book. The heart of CUPS is in the Administrative menu. If you click on it, you're prompted to enter your administrative root username and password.

One drawback to CUPS is that RHEL 3 does not support the same extensive database of printers as you see in the Red Hat Printer Configuration tool. On the other hand, the Red Hat tool does not support the creation of printer classes.

on the
Ĵob

Other Linux distributions don't include Red Hat's Printer Configuration tool. Many do include extensive printer databases in the CUPS Web-based tool.

CUPS Administration

Once you've entered your administrative credentials, you'll see the Admin setup page shown in Figure 8-21. There are three sections here. Classes enable you to configure a group of printers together. When you use a specific class, CUPS directs your print job to the first available printer in this class. Jobs help you manage the print jobs currently in the print queue. Printers allow you to add new printers and manage existing printers.

As the Red Hat Printer Configuration tool is superior (in my opinion, on a Red Hat computer), I won't explain the Add Printer menu in this book. However, if you want to create a printer class, the CUPS Web-based tool is the easiest way to go. As described earlier, a CUPS printer class allows you to print to a group of printers. CUPS then selects the first available printer in that class.

FIGURE 8-21   CUPS Admin menu

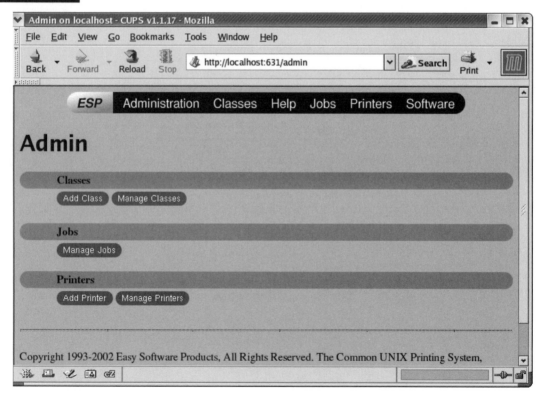

To proceed, click Add Class. You're taken to a menu where you need to fill in three text boxes, as shown in Figure 8-22:

- **Name**   The name of the printer class. If you want to print to this printer group, you'll call or connect to this printer class name.
- **Location**   Must be set to the name or IP address of the local print server.
- **Description**   Allows you to add the comment of your choice to help identify the printer class.

After you click Continue, you'll get to include one or more configured printers in your printer class. Do so, and click Continue. The CUPS Web-based tool now creates a print class, as shown in Figure 8-23.

FIGURE 8-22   Configuring a printer class

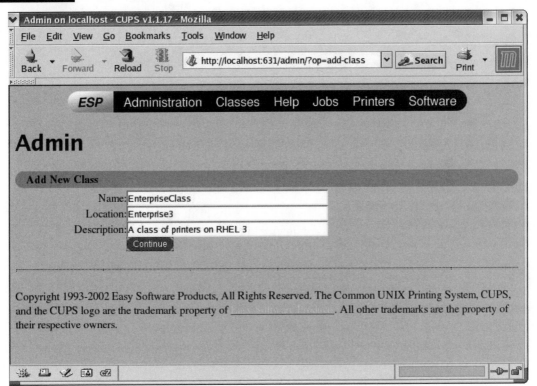

FIGURE 8-23 Your new printer class

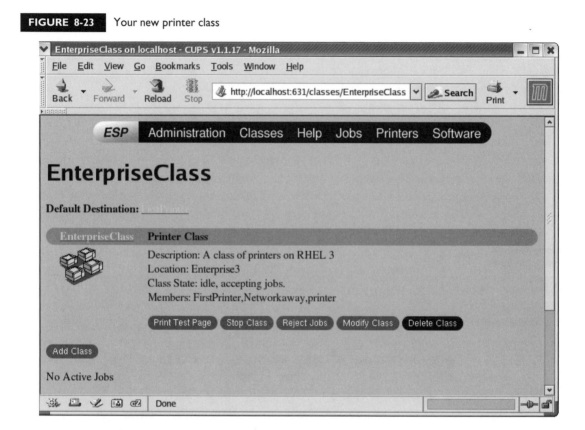

Verifying CUPS Sharing

Once you've configured security for a CUPS printer, you can verify it in /etc/cups /cupsd.conf. The security commands in this file are fairly straightforward. By default, access to a CUPS printer is limited to the local computer with a stanza such as:

```
<Location /printers/printer>
    Order Deny,Allow
    Deny From All
    Allow From 127.0.0.1
    AuthType None
</Location>
```

If you configure a CUPS printer to be shared with the world, you'll see one more command in the stanza. For example, printer2 is shared with the world because of the command in bold:

```
<Location /printers/printer>
     Order Deny,Allow
     Deny From All
     Allow From 127.0.0.1
     AuthType None
Allow From All
</Location>
```

Naturally, you can limit access to specific IP address networks. For example, to limit access to the 192.168.30.0 LAN, you'd substitute the following command for **Allow From All**:

```
Allow From 192.168.30.0/255.255.255.0
```

You can also substitute computer or domain names. For example, the following command allows access from the example.com domain:

```
Allow From *.example.com
```

You can't configure these limits using the Red Hat Printer Configuration utility (**redhat-config-printer**). If you want to set up host-based security in this way, you'll have to edit the cupsd.conf configuration file directly.

CERTIFICATION SUMMARY

A number of important network client services are associated with Red Hat Enterprise Linux 3. Two of them are Samba and CUPS. Samba sets up interoperability between Microsoft Windows and Linux/Unix computers. CUPS allows printers to be set up locally or over the network.

Samba allows a Linux computer to appear like any other Microsoft computer on a Microsoft Windows–based network. Samba is based on the Server Message Block protocol, which allows Microsoft computers to communicate on a TCP/IP network. It has evolved as Microsoft has adapted SMB to the Common Internet File System.

The main Samba configuration file, /etc/samba/smb.conf, includes separate sections for global settings and share definitions. The Red Hat Samba Server Configuration tool is a GUI tool that makes it easier to configure smb.conf. Changes to smb.conf can be easily tested with the **testparm** utility.

Linux includes the Common Unix Printing System (CUPS). With CUPS, the configuration files are stored primarily in the /etc/cups directory. However, it also includes a list of printers in /etc/printcap to accommodate sharing through Samba. You can edit the CUPS configuration files directly, with Red Hat's Printer Configuration tool or the CUPS Web-based interface.

Because RHCE is a performance-based exam, it is important to practice all the skills discussed in this chapter. You may need to use these skills on the exam!

TWO-MINUTE DRILL

Here are some of the key points from the certification objectives in Chapter 8.

Samba Networking

❑ Samba allows Microsoft Windows computers to share files and printers across networks, using the Server Message Block (SMB) protocol on the TCP/IP protocol stack.

❑ Samba includes a client and a server. Variations on the **mount -t, smbfs,** or **smbmnt** command allow you to connect to a Microsoft Windows shared directory.

❑ The main Samba configuration file is /etc/samba/smb.conf. You can configure it in a text editor or a GUI tool such as the Samba Server Configuration tool.

❑ Samba allows you to configure your Linux computer as a member of a Microsoft Windows 9x–style Workgroup or Domain.

❑ Samba allows you to configure your Linux computer as a Microsoft Windows server. It can also provide Microsoft browsing, WINS, and Domain Controller services, even on an Active Directory network.

Print Services

❑ The Printer Configuration tool, which you can start with the command **redhat-config-printer,** can be used to configure most popular printers in /etc/printcap.

❑ CUPS provides a Web-based interface similar to Samba's SWAT. Once enabled, you can get to this interface in your browser by navigating to http://localhost:631.

SELF TEST

The following questions will help you measure your understanding of the material presented in this chapter. Read all the choices carefully, as there may be more than one correct answer. Choose all correct answers for each question. Don't focus exclusively on these questions. There are no longer any multiple choice questions on the Red Hat exams. These questions test your understanding of the chapter. Getting results, not memorizing trivia, is what counts on the Red Hat exams.

Samba Networking

1. A group that prefers Microsoft servers has set up a Windows 2000 server to handle their file and print sharing services. This server correctly refers to a WINS server on 192.168.55.3 for name resolution and configures all user logins through the PDC on 192.168.55.8. If you're configuring the PDC, what options do you have to configure in the local Samba configuration file?

    A. domain master = yes

    B. wins support = yes

    C. password server = 192.168.55.3

    D. security = user

2. Which of the following files or commands is not a component of the Samba file-sharing service?

    A. /usr/bin/smbd

    B. /usr/bin/nmbd

    C. /usr/bin/smbclient

    D. /etc/samba/smb.conf

3. You made a couple of quick changes to your Samba configuration file and you need to test it quickly for syntax errors. Which command should you run?

    A. smbmount

    B. smbclient

    C. smbfs

    D. testparm

4. You are asked to share the HR downloadable documents to Microsoft Windows users who are not that familiar with FTP and want a shared drive connection. Which of the following commands forces the Samba service to reread the configuration file—without having to disconnect your Microsoft users or restarting the service?

    A. testparm

    B. /etc/smb.conf

C. /etc/rc.d/init.d/smb reload

D. service smb restart

5. Microsoft Windows users are complaining that they cannot see the shared Human Resources directory of documents, [hrdocs], in their Network Neighborhood diagram. Which of the following options should you delete from the [hrdocs] stanza in smb.conf?

A. read only = yes

B. browseable = yes

C. guest ok = yes

D. printable = yes

6. Which of the following files can you configure with **mount** or **smbmnt** style commands on a user-by-user basis?

A. /home/.bashrc

B. ~/.bash_logout

C. /etc/fstab

D. /boot/.bashrc

7. Based on the following code, which of the following things do you need to do to limit access to the following [tmp] share in /etc/samba/smb.conf to the local network, with a network IP address of 192.168.99.0?

```
# This one is useful for people to share files
[tmp]
    comment = Temporary file space
    path = /tmp
    read only = no
    public = yes
```

A. A firewall on any connections to outside networks which blocks at least Samba ports.

B. Add the following command to the stanza:

```
local only = yes
```

C. Add the following command to the stanza:

```
hosts allow = 192.168.99.
```

D. Make sure the **password server** command points to the PDC on your network.

Print Services

8. You want to look at your current printer configuration in a GUI desktop interface. What command might you use to start a GUI printer configuration tool?

A. redhat-printer-config

B. redhat-config-printer

C. printconf-gui

D. lprsetup

9. You have a group of printers that you want to configure as a printer class. Which of the following tools can you use?

A. Direct editing of /etc/cups/classes.conf

B. Red Hat's Printer Configuration tool

C. The CUPS Web-based tool

D. Direct editing of /etc/printcap

10. Which of the following commands can you use to remove a print job with a known job number from the print queue?

A. lpr

B. lpc

C. lpq

D. lprm

LAB QUESTIONS

Lab 1: Configuring Samba

Part 1: Installing and Starting Samba

1. Ensure that all four components of the Samba service are correctly installed. What RPMs did you install and how did you install them?

2. Use one of the service management tools available to you to ensure that the Samba services are configured to start correctly when you boot Linux. What tool did you use?

3. Start Samba services now. You can use either the service management script located directly in /etc/rc.d/init.d, or you can use the "service" startup tool. How did you start your Samba service?

4. Verify that Samba services are now running. How did you do this?

Part 2: Configuring Samba's Global Settings

1. You'll use Red Hat's Samba Server Configuration tool to configure your Samba service. Start this tool. If you didn't log in as the root user, did something happen before the tool started?

2. Configure the Samba global settings. You will provide Workgroup services to your users. Set the Workgroup name to something appropriate for your company.

3. Can you limit access to your company's domain name (such as example.com) through this tool? If you have to edit the Samba configuration file directly, what do you have to do?

4. Can you prevent access to evil.cracker.com through this tool? If you have to edit the Samba configuration file directly, what do you have to do?

5. Commit your changes. What do you need to do to make Samba reread the configuration file?

Part 3: Configuring File Shares

1. Open the main Samba configuration file.

2. Navigate to the predefined [homes] share.

3. Ensure that the [homes] share is available only to hosts on your example.com network.

4. Ensure that the share is writable to authenticated users but not available to guest users.

5. Commit your changes.

6. Create a new share called [public].

7. Change the path to the public share to /home/public.

8. Configure the public share so anyone in your domain can access the share.

9. Create the /home/public directory as required. Change the permissions to this directory to 1777.

10. Why do you set permissions to 1777?

11. Commit your changes.

Part 4: Setting Up Printer Shares

1. Your Linux server has many printers defined. You want to offer access to them to your desktop client users. Enable access to the generic printers share now.

2. Again, restrict access to your print shares to members of your example.com domain.

3. Commit your changes.

Part 5: Verifying the smb.conf File

1. You want to verify your changes. Start a terminal window. Run the syntax tester tool on your Samba configuration tool. What program did you use?

2. Review the /etc/samba/smb.conf file. Look over each section including the [globals] section. Ensure that all updates are correct and reflect the requirements previously stated. Go back and make changes, if necessary. Commit all changes.

3. Again, go back and make revisions if the test program indicates problems with the smb.conf file.

Part 6: Starting the Samba Servers

1. Navigate to a command line interface.

2. Start the Samba server. Which daemons does it start?

3. If possible, go to a Microsoft Windows computer on your network. Use a Microsoft browsing tool such as Network Neighborhood or My Network Places in Windows Explorer. See if you can connect to the Samba public share. Alternatively, you can go to another Linux computer and browse Nautilus by navigating to smb:///.

4. Congratulations! You have just configured your Samba server to share files with your local workgroup.

Part 7: Persistency Check

It is important for your server (and critical to pass the RHCE exam) that any changes you make to your server should be persistent. This means that changes should be active when you reboot Linux. Perform an orderly reboot of your server now and verify that Samba starts when you boot Linux.

1. How did you make your changes persistent?

2. What command did you use to perform an orderly shutdown?

Lab 2: Creating a Printer

In this lab, you'll want to use the Red Hat Printer Configuration utility to connect a printer to your Linux system. The printer can be local or remotely connected through your LAN. As you'll want to create a printer class, you'll need more than one printer.

If you have only one physical printer, you can set up multiple print queues with different printer names. CUPS sees each print queue as if it were a separate printer.

Once you've created multiple printers, open a GUI Web browser. Navigate to http://localhost:631. Click the Class link and then click Add Class. Follow the prompts to create a printer class with the printers that you've configured.

Once you've created a new printer class, inspect the result in the /etc/cups/classes.conf configuration file. Check the contents of your /etc/printcap file. What are the names of the printers that you see? Are there any surprises in the list?

If you have a Microsoft Windows computer on your network, activate the Samba service if required. Check the printer names as shown in the browse list. Are there any surprises on this list?

SELF TEST ANSWERS

Samba Networking

1. ☑ **D.** If you're configuring a PDC, you'll want the **security = user** command in the local /etc/samba/smb.conf file.

   ☒ **A** is incorrect because being a Browse Master is not a requirement for a PDC. **B** is incorrect because the WINS server is on a different computer. **C** is incorrect because the local computer is the PDC, which keeps the password database.

2. ☑ **C.** This is a tricky question. **smbclient** is a client command; it is not part of the service that provides Samba file shares.

   ☒ **A, B,** and **D** are all components that are either daemons (**smbd** and **nmbd**) that manage the service or are the server's configuration file (smb.conf).

3. ☑ **D. testparm** is the smb.conf configuration file syntax and semantics checker.

   ☒ **A** is wrong because **mount -t smbfs** is used by the root user to make remote SMB shares available to Linux. It wouldn't test your local configuration. **B** is wrong because **smbclient** is the Linux SMB client program for accessing Samba services on the network. **C** is incorrect because smbfs is the filesystem type used when a Samba share is mounted through the **mount** command or via /etc/fstab.

4. ☑ **C.** This is one way to tell Samba to reload the configuration file without restarting. This is a little tricky, as I've been using the **service** command instead of the /etc/rc.d/init.d directory path.

   ☒ **A** is incorrect because **testparm** is just a syntax checker for smb.conf. **B** is incorrect because smb.conf is just the Samba configuration file (albeit in the wrong location; for RHEL 3, it should be /etc/samba/smb.conf). Finally, **D** is incorrect because it disconnects users and restarts the service.

5. ☑ **B.** A share must be marked as browseable before it will show up in a Microsoft tool such as Network Neighborhood or My Network Places.

   ☒ **A, C,** and **D** are all incorrect. While you probably should make a share that contains Human Resource documents read-only, it's not required to make the share browseable. Making a share accessible to authorized users is not related to whether guests are allowed to read the share. Making the share printable does not affect whether the share is browseable.

6. ☑ **B.** The .bash_logout file in users' home directories (~) is a good place to include **umount** and **smbumount** commands.

   ☒ **A, C,** and **D** are all incorrect. There is no .bashrc file in the /home directory, at least not for individual users. The /etc/fstab file is a good place to configure mounted directories for all users simultaneously. The default /boot directory does not include a .bashrc file and is an inappropriate location for such.

7. ☑ **A and C.** A firewall can effectively block communication to a Samba server from an outside network. And the given **hosts allow** command limits access to the given network; no additional **hosts deny** command is required.

☒ **B and D** are both incorrect. There is no **local only** command in smb.conf. And the location of the PDC does not affect the security of your Samba server.

Print Services

8. ☑ **B and C.** The **redhat-config-printer** and **printconf-gui** commands, when run in the GUI desktop, start the Red Hat Printer Configuration tool.

☒ **A** is wrong because there is no such command as **redhat-printer-config**. **D** is wrong because there is no such file as lprsetup.

9. ☑ **A and D; or C.** If you know the language associated with CUPS configuration files, you can set up a printer class by directly editing the /etc/cups/classes.conf file. You'll need to add the name of the printer class to the /etc/printcap list. Alternatively, you can configure a printer class through the CUPS Web-based tool.

☒ **B** is incorrect because, as of this writing, Red Hat's Printer Configuration Tool does not support the creation of a print class.

10. ☑ **D.** The **lprm** command can be used to remove a print job with a known job number from the print queue.

☒ **A, B,** and **C** are all incorrect. The **lpr** command prints a job. The **lpc** command checks the status of your printers. The **lpq** command checks the status of the default printer.

LAB ANSWERS

Lab I

The first chapter lab on Samba is designed to be easy to follow. However, you'll need explicit Linux knowledge to complete some specific steps. Answers to these steps can be found in the following:

Part I

Step 1: You've installed the Windows File Manager package group, which includes the samba-client, samba, and redhat-config-samba RPMs. These RPMs depend on the samba-common RPM, which you'll also need to install.

Step 2: You can use the **chkconfig --level 35 smb on** command or the Service Configuration utility described in Chapter 4 to make sure Samba starts the next time you boot Linux.

Step 3: Use the **service smb start** command to begin the Samba service.

Step 4: One way to verify Samba is to look for the existence of the **smbd** and **nmbd** processes in the process table. Use **ps aux | grep mbd** to see if these processes are present. Another way is with a service command such as **service smb status**.

Part 2

Step 1: To use the Samba Server Configuration tool, you'll need the root password.

Step 2: Many administrators stick with the default Microsoft Windows workgroup name of WORKGROUP. You can find it in the output from the **smbclient -L //**_clientname_ command.

Step 3: If you want to limit access to your Samba server, you can't do it through the Samba Server Configuration tool. You'll want to set up the **hosts allow** command in /etc/samba/smb.conf.

Step 4: If you want to restrict access from a specific computer to your Samba server, you can't do it through the Samba Server Configuration tool. You'll want to set up the **hosts deny = evil crackers.com** command in /etc/samba/smb.conf.

Step 5: When you exit the Samba Server Configurator, or save the smb.conf file, you can make Samba read the changes with the **service smb reload** command. But before committing the changes, you should test them with the **testparm** command.

Part 3

Step 1: Open the main Samba configuration file, /etc/samba/smb.conf, in a text editor.

Step 2: Navigate to the [homes] share in the last half of this file.

Step 3: Unless there is a limitation in the Globals part of this file, you can limit the [homes] share with the **hosts allow = example.com**. Commit your changes. Restart or reload smb under the Status menu or with the appropriate **service** command.

Step 4: Add a **guest ok = no** to the [homes] stanza.

Step 5: Save the changes you've made so far.

Step 6: At the end of the file, start a [public] stanza. Add an appropriate comment for the stanza.

Step 7: Set **path = /home/public**. Save your changes to the smb.conf file.

Step 8: Make sure to set **hosts allow = example.com**.

Step 9: Set permissions for the public share, with the following commands:

```
# mkdir /home/public
# chmod 1777 /home/public
```

Create a new directory, /home/public; configure that share in SWAT and call it public. Set the hosts allow setting in SWAT under the Shares menu, and list the domain associated with your network. Deny to all others.

Step 10: The 777 aspect of permissions grants read, write, and execute/search permissions to all users (root, root's group, and everyone else). The 1 at the beginning of the permission value sets the sticky bit. This bit, when set on directories, restricts users from deleting or renaming files they don't own.

Step 11: Commit your changes with the **service smb reload** command.

Part 4

Step 1: Open your /etc/samba/smb.conf configuration file. Navigate to the [printers] stanza. The default version of this stanza should already enable access to all users who connect.

Step 2: In this stanza, use the **hosts allow** command as before.

Step 3: Commit your changes by closing and saving the smb.conf file, and then running the **service smb reload** command.

Part 5

Step 1: You can use the Samba syntax checker, **testparm**, to make sure there are no glaring problems to your Samba configuration file.

Step 2: This is more of an exercise; if you don't have any problems, you might want to deliberately add some to your smb.conf file and rerun **testparm** again. It's helpful to be familiar with different kinds of Samba syntax issues. Don't forget to restore a working version of the smb.conf file!

Part 6

Step 1: Again, this is more of an exercise than a lab. The steps are generally self-explanatory. If your Samba configuration is successful, you should be able to review browseable shares from a Microsoft Windows computer on the same LAN.

Part 7

Step 1: To complete many Linux configuration changes, you need to make sure that the service will start automatically when you reboot your computer. In general, the key command is **chkconfig**. In this case, the **chkconfig --level 35 smb on** command sets up the **smbd** daemon to become active when you boot Linux into either runlevel 3 or runlevel 5.

Step 2: The command you should always use to perform an orderly shutdown is **shutdown -r now**.

Lab 2

Starting the Printer Configuration utility is easy. One way in the GUI is to click Main Menu | System Settings | Printing. Then you can click the Add button to start what is known in the Microsoft world as a configuration wizard. If you like, you can create two different print queues with the same printer. Just repeat the same process, using a different printer name.

Open the Web browser of your choice. The default is Mozilla, which you can start in the GNOME desktop by clicking the globe icon adjacent to the Main Menu icon. You can then navigate to http:// localhost:631.

Once the CUPS Web-based tool opens, you can click the Classes or the Manage Printer Classes link. Click Add Class in the Class Web page. Enter the root username and password when prompted.

Enter the single-word name of your choice for the printer class name. Add the name or IP address of the computer in the Location text box. Enter the comment of your choice in the Description text box. Click Continue; select more than one computer as members of the printer class. Click Continue; once your new printer class is confirmed, you can close the browser.

You should now see the printer class and member printers in the /etc/cups/classes.conf file. You'll find a list of printers in /etc/printcap; you'll find the names of any configured printers *and* printer classes in this file. You should also see the list of printers in /etc/printcap in any Microsoft Windows Network Neighborhoods or My Network Places that is connected to the same network. This assumes that you've activated a Samba server on the local print server computer, of course.

9

Network Management

More complex networking services in Red Hat Enterprise Linux require more advanced administration methods. While graphical tools such as the Network Configuration tool are available to assist in configuring all aspects of Linux networking, the best way to configure networking is by practicing with the key command line utilities and associated configuration files.

This chapter starts with a discussion of the Domain Name System (DNS). DNS is a service that translates human-readable domain names such as www.mommabears.com to IP addresses such as 209.197.248.180, and vice versa. Next, this chapter continues to a description of the Network File System (NFS), which is a powerful and versatile way of sharing filesystems between servers and workstations. DHCP allows a Linux computer to serve dynamic IP addresses. Finally, the section on keeping servers in sync demonstrates how you can set up a RHEL 3 computer to synchronize with a central time server.

INSIDE THE EXAM

More Network Services

Both Red Hat exams require that you configure a Linux workstation as a client on a network. On a network with Linux computers, that naturally includes using DNS servers, connecting to shared NFS directories, and taking IP address information from DHCP servers.

The RHCE exam requires that you configure Linux servers on a network. The Red Hat Exam Prep guide suggests that you can expect to configure DNS and NFS servers during the exam. While DHCP servers aren't explicitly listed in the Red Hat Exam Prep guide, they are listed in the Red

Hat curriculum for the RHCE exam (in the RH300 course outline).

In this chapter, the NFS and NTP services should be installed automatically with RHEL 3. I proceed to tell you about the packages required for the DNS and DHCP services. For each service, you'll need to remember to use a command such as **chkconfig** to make sure it starts the next time you boot Linux. It also will help you get full credit for the work you do on the Red Hat exams. I show you how to configure each service for basic operation. However, for a detailed discussion on how to secure these services, you'll need to read Chapter 10.

As you learn about these network services, you're learning about the services that you might configure and/or troubleshoot on the Red Hat exams. Take the time you need to understand the configuration files associated with each of these services, and practice making them work on your Linux computer. In some cases, two computers running Linux will be useful to practice what you learn in this chapter.

CERTIFICATION OBJECTIVE 9.01

DNS/BIND

DNS is the Domain Name System, which maintains a database that can help your computer translate domain names such as www.redhat.com to IP addresses such as 216.148.218.197. As no individual DNS server is large enough to keep a database for the entire Internet, they can refer requests to other DNS servers.

DNS is based on the **named** daemon, which is built on the BIND (Berkeley Internet Name Domain) package developed through the Internet Software Consortium. More information is available from the BIND home page at www.isc.org/products/BIND. Red Hat Enterprise Linux 3 (and Red Hat Linux 9) includes BIND version 9.2. While this version of BIND supports the use of the /usr/sbin/rndc configuration interface, RHEL 3 still includes sample files based on the older /etc/named.conf configuration file. However, you can use the **rndc** command to manage DNS operation, in the same way that you used **apachectl** to manage the Apache server.

You can configure a DNS server by directly editing the DNS configuration files. Alternatively, you can configure a DNS server using the Red Hat Domain Name Service configuration tool. Careful use of both tools can help you learn more about DNS.

exam

ⓦatch *I've found the Red Hat Domain Name Service tool to be less than reliable. It sometimes aborted unpredictably on my installations of* *RHEL 3. In other words, the only reliable way to configure DNS on your RHEL 3 computer is by direct editing of configuration files.*

You can set up four different types of DNS servers:

- A master DNS server for your domain(s), which stores authoritative records for your domain.
- A slave DNS server, which relies on a master DNS server for data.
- A caching-only DNS server, which stores recent requests like a Proxy server. It otherwise refers to other DNS servers.
- A forwarding-only DNS server, which refers all requests to other DNS servers.

*redhat-config-bind **is the successor to** bindconf. **Red Hat Enterprise Linux 3 includes a link from** bindconf **to** redhat-config-bind.*

DNS Packages

If you're just configuring your Linux computer as a DNS client, you can skip this section. The basic DNS client configuration files are automatically installed with even a minimal installation of RHEL 3.

On the other hand, if you're configuring your Linux computer as a DNS server, you'll need to install the packages associated with the DNS Name Server package group. You can do so with the Red Hat Package Management utility described in Chapter 4. However, there are only four RPM packages associated with DNS:

- **bind**   Includes the basic name server software, including /usr/sbin/named.
- **bind-utils**   Contains tools such as **dig** and **host** that allow you to ask a DNS server for more information about a specific Internet host. It should already be installed in any minimum installation of RHEL 3.
- **caching-nameserver**   Allows you to set up a local cache of a remote DNS server to speed access from the computers on your network to a remote network such as the Internet.
- **redhat-config-bind**   A GUI configuration tool useful for adding host and reverse address lookup data. It's not officially a part of the DNS Name Server package group.

Naturally, these tools are easy to install from any Red Hat network installation source that you may have created in Chapter 2. Different options and commands for installing RPMs from a remote installation source are described in Chapter 4.

The DNS Configuration Files

There are DNS configuration files required to configure your Linux computer as a client and as a server. There are two DNS client configuration files: /etc/hosts and /etc /resolv.conf. They are fairly straightforward, as described in the next section.

There are a number of additional configuration files that support the use of DNS as a server, as described in Table 9-1. You may have to create some of these files as you configure DNS.

In the following sections, I'll show you how to configure the files that you need for a working DNS server. But first, you should know how to configure your computer as a DNS client. One thing to remember is that all of the files in /var/named include

TABLE 9-1   DNS Server Configuration Files

DNS Configuration File	Description
/etc/sysconfig/named	You can set up different configuration and data file directories through this file.
/etc/named.conf	The main DNS configuration file. Incorporates /etc/named.custom, and calls data files in the /var/named directory.
/etc/named.custom	If you use the Red Hat DNS configuration tool, you can include additional settings in this file.
/etc/rndc.key	The authentication key required to support requests to the DNS server.
/var/named/0.0.127.in-addr.arpa.zone	The reverse zone file for the localhost computer.
/var/named/*netaddr*.in-addr.arpa.zone	The reverse zone file for the LAN; on an IPv4 network, it's the first three octets, written backwards. For example, for a network address of 192.168.30.0, the reverse zone file is 30.168.192.in-addr .arpa.zone.
/var/named/*domain*.zone	A database for a *domain* such as example.com.
/var/named/localhost.zone	The zone file for the localhost computer.
/var/named/named.ca	A list of root DNS servers on the Internet.
/var/named/named.local	A reverse zone record for the localhost.
/var/named/named.stats	Statistics from your DNS server.

a dot at the end of each domain name. For example, /var/named/localhost.zone lists the local computer as:

```
localhost.
```

In contrast, the domain names in /etc/named.conf and /etc/named.custom do not have dots at the end of their domain names.

A DNS Client

When your computer looks for another computer on a TCP/IP network such as the Internet, it typically looks in two places: /etc/hosts and any DNS servers that you've set up for your network. The order is determined by a single line in /etc/host.conf. The default is:

```
order hosts,bind
```

When your computer searches for another, this line tells your computer to search first through your /etc/hosts database. The following line in my /etc/hosts is what drives a Web browser address to my local IP address:

```
127.0.0.1    Enterprise3    localhost.localdomain    localhost
```

While you could theoretically also configure every computer on the Internet in your /etc/hosts configuration file, it's not realistic. However, if your LAN is small, you could add the IP address and hostname of each computer on your network in the /etc/hosts file. You could then duplicate this file on each computer on your LAN. Then you could use an external DNS server, provided by your ISP, for Internet access.

It's easy to configure a Linux computer as a DNS client. You may have already done so during the RHEL 3 installation process. If you have a working DHCP server, it probably provided you with the settings you need as a DNS client. Alternatively, you can configure your computer as a DNS client with the Red Hat Network Configuration utility described in Chapter 4. You can even configure your computer directly through your /etc/resolv.conf file. It's easy to do; the following version of this file lists two DNS servers on the Internet:

```
nameserver 207.217.120.83
nameserver 207.217.126.81
```

If you want to add or change the DNS servers for your computer, you can open this file directly in the text editor of your choice.

In the following section, you'll get a chance to learn about DNS nameserver configuration files from the ground up. Many of the lessons associated with a caching-only name server apply to slave and master DNS servers.

on the **Job**   *As with a number of Samba variables, "name server" and "nameserver" are both in common use with respect to servers that conform to Domain Name Service (DNS), and I use both variations throughout the book.*

A Forwarding-Only Name Server

This first type of DNS server is simple. It requires a single command in the /etc/named.conf configuration file. As you can see, it's straightforward; I've set it to refer to the DNS servers that I had configured as a client:

```
options {
     directory "/var/named";
     forward only;
     forwarders {
          207.217.120.83;
          207.217.126.81;
     };
};
```

You can activate this configuration once you've activated this DNS server. With this configuration, any computer that looks to the local DNS server is forwarded to the IP addresses shown.

If the data can't be found in those DNS servers, it's up to those servers to ask others for the information. The alternative is to use the /var/named/named.ca file described later in this chapter.

A Caching-Only Name Server

When you request a Web page such as www.osborne.com, your network asks the configured DNS server for the associated IP address. This is usually known as a name query. If the DNS server is outside your network, this request can take time. If you have a caching-only name server, these queries are stored locally, which can save significant time while you or others on your network are browsing the same sites on the Internet.

When configuring a caching-only name server, the first step is to look at the /etc /named.conf configuration file. An abbreviated version of this file, configured for a caching name server, is shown in Figure 9-1.

The **directory** command tells your DNS server where to look for data files. All other files specified in named.conf are located in the /var/named directory. The /etc /named.conf file continues with the **controls** command, which allows you to use the **rdnc** command to control DNS. The next three **zone** commands support access to various domains:

- The first zone "dot" refers regular requests to /var/named/named.ca, the list of root servers for the Internet.
- The second zone, for localhost, sets the forward zone for the local computer.
- The third zone is a reverse zone for the local computer.

FIGURE 9-1

/etc/named.conf, configured for a caching nameserver

```
// generated by named-bootconf.pl

options {
        directory "/var/named";
        // query-source address * port 53;
};

//
// a caching only nameserver config
//
controls {
        inet 127.0.0.1 allow { localhost; } keys { rndckey; };
};
zone "." IN {
        type hint;
        file "named.ca";
};

zone "localhost" IN {
        type master;
        file "localhost.zone";
        allow-update { none; };
};

zone "0.0.127.in-addr.arpa" IN {
        type master;
        file "named.local";
        allow-update { none; };
};

include "/etc/rndc.key";
```

on the **Job**

If you have an older hardware firewall, it might expect DNS communication on TCP/IP port 53. If it does, you'll want to activate the query-source address * port 53 command.

named.ca

If your DNS servers don't have the IP address for a domain name in its database, it can refer to other databases. By default, it refers to the /var/named/named.ca file, which is a list of the root DNS servers for the Internet. An excerpt is shown in Figure 9-2. This list changes from time to time and must be maintained. I include a shell script that you can use to maintain this file later in this section.

FIGURE 9-2

The root DNS servers are stored in named.ca

```
;          This file holds the information on root name servers neede
d to
;          initialize cache of Internet domain name servers
;          (e.g. reference this file in the "cache  .  <file>"
;          configuration file of BIND domain name servers).
;
;          This file is made available by InterNIC
;          under anonymous FTP as
;               file                    /domain/named.cache
;               on server               FTP.INTERNIC.NET
;
;          last update:     Nov 5, 2002
;          related version of root zone:    2002110501
;
;
; formerly NS.INTERNIC.NET
;
.                            3600000   IN  NS   A.ROOT-SERVERS.NET.
A.ROOT-SERVERS.NET.          3600000       A    198.41.0.4
;
; formerly NS1.ISI.EDU
;
.                            3600000       NS   B.ROOT-SERVERS.NET.
B.ROOT-SERVERS.NET.          3600000       A    128.9.0.107
;
; formerly C.PSI.NET
;
.                            3600000       NS   C.ROOT-SERVERS.NET.
C.ROOT-SERVERS.NET.          3600000       A    192.33.4.12
;
; formerly TERP.UMD.EDU
;
.                            3600000       NS   D.ROOT-SERVERS.NET.
D.ROOT-SERVERS.NET.          3600000       A    128.8.10.90
"/var/named/named.ca" 79L, 2499C
```

FIGURE 9-3

The localhost
.zone DNS
data file

```
$TTL    86400
$ORIGIN localhost.
@                       1D IN SOA       @ root (
                                        42              ; serial (d. adams)
                                        3H              ; refresh
                                        15M             ; retry
                                        1W              ; expiry
                                        1D )            ; minimum

                        1D IN NS        @
                        1D IN A         127.0.0.1
```

localhost.zone

The default /var/named/localhost.zone file is shown in Figure 9-3. It incorporates a basic DNS entry for the local computer, which you can use as a template for other computers on your network.

Reverse Lookups with named.local

The /var/named/named.local file provides a reverse-lookup record for your computer, as localhost. As shown in Figure 9-4, the PTR record (on the last line in the file) is 1, which associates the loopback address, 127.0.0.1, with your computer.

Configuring a Simple Domain

Return to the /etc/named.conf configuration file. With what we know about DNS configuration files, we can create a Master DNS server. Assume that you've defined a simple domain for the computers on your network; call it example.com.

FIGURE 9-4

The named.local
reverse DNS file

```
$TTL    86400
@       IN      SOA     localhost. root.localhost.  (
                                        1997022700 ; Serial
                                        28800       ; Refresh
                                        14400       ; Retry
                                        3600000     ; Expire
                                        86400 )     ; Minimum
                IN      NS      localhost.

1       IN      PTR     localhost.
```

The example.com domain is a generic domain that can't be assigned on the Internet. You can therefore use this domain name on your private network (assuming that you don't have a domain of your own).

Look at the zone "0.0.127.in-addr.arpa" IN line near the bottom of the sample file. This says that the zone 0.0.127.in-addr.arpa will be defined, that the localhost is the master server (**type master**) for that zone, associated data is stored in a **file** called named.local, and no other DNS server is allowed to "update" or change the IP address associated with the localhost (**allow-update { none; }**).

Not all characters are allowed in hostnames. DNS can read only regular letters, numbers, and the hyphen (-) character. Unlike Linux, DNS does not distinguish between upper- and lowercase characters; for example, Mail.Example.Com is equivalent to mail.example.com.

Now you can add your network to your DNS server. Start by inserting a new zone section in the /etc/named.conf file, before the **include "/etc/rndc.key";** command. (If you're also going to use Red Hat's GUI Domain Name Service tool, you should *instead* add this information to /etc/named.custom.)

```
zone "example.com" IN {
    type master;
    file "example.com.zone";
};
```

Note again that we do not use a period at the end of any address in /etc/named.conf. If you want to create a slave server, the information that you'd enter is similar:

```
zone "example.com" IN {
    type slave;
    file "slave.example.com.zone";
    masters {
            192.168.30.5
              };
};
```

The task for a slave server is easier; it periodically checks with the master DNS server, in this case the computer with an IP address of 192.168.30.5. When it does, it automatically reads the master DNS server data and creates the slave.example.com.zone file in the /var/named directory.

Creating a Zone File

If you're creating a master DNS server, you'll need to create a zone file. Based on the configuration so far, this will be an example.com.zone file in the /var/named directory. I've created one for my own network, as shown in Figure 9-5.

Now let's decipher some of the language in this file:

$TTL 3D means that the default Time To Live (TTL) for data on this DNS server is three days. It's also common to have a TTL of 86400, which corresponds to the number of seconds in a day. You can specify individual TTLs for each entry in this file.

The SOA (Start Of Authority) record is the preamble to all zone files. It describes the zone where it comes from (a computer called enterprise3.example.com), the administrator e-mail for this DNS server (hostmaster@example.com). The SOA record command line also specifies a number of other parameters:

- Serial number is based on the date and version number. Based on the one shown in Figure 9-5, this database file is the first one created for this server on February 12, 2004.

- The refresh frequency determines how long the local DNS *slave* server waits before checking for updates from any master DNS servers.

- The retry frequency specifies how often the local DNS slave server retries contacting the master server.

- If there is no response from a DNS master server before the end of the expiration period, the local server stops accepting requests for the given domain.

- The Time To Live is the minimum amount of time other DNS servers should keep the local zone information in their remote cache.

The NS is the Name Server resource record, which refers to the name of the DNS server computer, which in this case is enterprise3.example.com.

The MX is the Mail Exchange record, which directs e-mail information to a particular computer, in this case, mail.example.com. Some number such as what's shown is required with any MX record.

In my example.com.zone file shown in Figure 9-5, I also have entries for three computers in this DNS zone. Each is associated with an A (address) record, its IP

FIGURE 9-5	

An example
.com.zone file

```
;
;  Zone file for Mike's example.com domain
;
;  This is the full database file for this particular zone
;      (which is typically a LAN or a network domain)
;
$TTL 3D
@      IN      SOA     enterprise3.example.com. hostmaster.example.com. (
                      200402121      ; serial number = today's date + rev number
                      8H             ; refresh frequency (8 hours)
                      2H             ; retry frequency (2 hours)
                      4W             ; expiration period for data (4 weeks)
                      3D )           ; Time to live of at least three days

       IN      NS      enterprise3.example.com.    ; Specifying the nameserver

       IN      MX      10  mail.example.com.       ; See below for actual server

allaccess   IN      A       192.168.30.1
enterprise3 IN      A       192.168.30.2
entwks3     IN      A       192.168.30.5

mail        IN      CNAME   enterprise3
ftp         IN      CNAME   enterprise3
www         IN      CNAME   enterprise3
```

address. The final three entries specify canonical names (CNAME) for specific computers. For this zone file, www.example.com is also known as enterprise3.example.com.

CNAME allows you to assign several names to each computer. In this case, mail, ftp, and www are all aliases for the enterprise3 computer. A CNAME is not a legal hostname for an e-mail address. For example, admin@ftp.example.com won't work based on the example.com.zone file shown. However, it is something you can use on your network as an outgoing mail server.

If you have more than one mail server, you can add a number before the name of each MX computer. For example, based on the following commands:

```
        IN      MX      10      mail.example.com.
        IN      MX      20      mail2.example.com.
```

any e-mail directed to this domain is first sent to mail.example.com.

Save this file and restart named with the **service named restart** command. Examine the results with the **host -l example.com** command. I've shown the result from my zone file in Figure 9-6.

FIGURE 9-6

Listing a working
DNS zone

```
[root@Enterprise3 root]# host -l example.com
example.com SOA enterprise3.example.com. hostmaster.example.com. 200402121 28800
 7200 2419200 259200
example.com name server enterprise3.example.com.
example.com mail is handled by 10 mail.example.com.
allaccess.example.com has address 192.168.30.1
enterprise3.example.com has address 192.168.30.2
entwks3.example.com has address 192.168.30.5
ftp.example.com is an alias for enterprise3.example.com.
mail.example.com is an alias for enterprise3.example.com.
www.example.com is an alias for enterprise3.example.com.
example.com SOA enterprise3.example.com. hostmaster.example.com. 200402121 28800
 7200 2419200 259200
[root@Enterprise3 root]#
```

The Reverse Zone

Now programs can convert the names in your-domain.com to real IP addresses. You're ready for the next step: a *reverse zone* file, which allows a DNS server to convert backwards, from an IP address to a hostname. Reverse zone lookups are used by many servers of different kinds (FTP, IRC, WWW, and others) to decide if they even want to talk to a computer asking for information. It's a common way for a mail server to check if an e-mail has come from a valid domain. Therefore, for full access to all Internet services, you need a reverse zone. Start by adding another zone to the /etc/named.conf configuration file:

```
zone "30.168.192.in-addr.arpa" IN {
        type master;
        file "example.com.rr.zone";
        allow-update { none; };
};
```

This is similar to the 0.0.127.in-addr.arpa zone as described in /etc/named.conf. I've created an example.com.rr.zone file in the /var/named directory for the computers on my network, as shown in Figure 9-7.

Once again, restart **named** and examine the output of **host -l your-domain.com**. If the results do not look similar to the actual zone file, look for error messages in /var/log/messages.

on the
job

Reverse zones can be used by several different services, such as sendmail and Apache. The reverse zone DNS database allows a server to verify if the name of a requesting computer matches its IP address, which can keep crackers from trying to "spoof" your system.

FIGURE 9-7				
	$TTL	3D		
	@	IN	SOA	enterprise3.example.com. hostmaster.example.com. (
A reverse DNS				200402121 ; serial number
zone file				28800 ; refresh frequency
				14400 ; retry frequency
				3600000 ; expriation period
				3D ; minimum TTL
		IN	NS	enterprise3.example.com
	1	IN	PTR	allaccess.example.com
	2	IN	PTR	enterprise3.example.com
	5	IN	PTR	entwks3.example.com
	~			
	"example.com.rr.zone" 12L, 587C			

Starting named

Make sure your computer is connected to a network. Now you can start your DNS server through the **named** daemon with the **service named start** command. View the syslog message file (usually called /var/log/messages) with the **tail -f /var/log/messages** command. If there are problems, you'll see error messages here.

If there are any error messages, the **named** daemon will display the file with the error. Stop the service with the **service named stop** command and check the applicable configuration files.

Now test the setup. Use the **dig** command to examine your work. For example, if you use **dig** to look up the address of www.redhat.com, you'll see something like the output shown in Figure 9-8.

The **dig** command asks your DNS server to look for the www.redhat.com server. It then contacts one of the name server computers listed in /etc/resolv.conf. If that doesn't work, it goes to one of the name servers listed in the named.ca file and makes its requests from there. The request may be passed on to other DNS servers. Therefore, it can take some time before you see an answer.

Once you're satisfied with your configuration, you'll want to make sure that DNS starts the next time you reboot Linux. Naturally, that may be the only way that you would get full credit for your work on the RHCE exam. The following command makes sure that the **named** daemon starts the next time you boot Linux in the standard login runlevels:

```
# chkconfig --level 35 named on
```

FIGURE 9-8

DNS query
using dig

```
[root@Enterprise3 root]# dig www.redhat.com

; <<>> DiG 9.2.2 <<>> www.redhat.com
;; global options:  printcmd
;; Got answer:
;; ->>HEADER<<- opcode: QUERY, status: NOERROR, id: 31616
;; flags: qr aa rd ra; QUERY: 1, ANSWER: 2, AUTHORITY: 3, ADDITIONAL: 3

;; QUESTION SECTION:
;www.redhat.com.                        IN      A

;; ANSWER SECTION:
www.redhat.com.         600     IN      A       216.148.218.197
www.redhat.com.         600     IN      A       216.148.218.195

;; AUTHORITY SECTION:
redhat.com.             600     IN      NS      ns1.redhat.com.
redhat.com.             600     IN      NS      ns2.redhat.com.
redhat.com.             600     IN      NS      ns3.redhat.com.

;; ADDITIONAL SECTION:
ns1.redhat.com.         300     IN      A       66.187.233.210
ns2.redhat.com.         600     IN      A       66.77.185.41
ns3.redhat.com.         600     IN      A       63.240.14.66

;; Query time: 214 msec
;; SERVER: 207.217.126.81#53(207.217.126.81)
;; WHEN: Wed Jan 21 10:39:01 2004
;; MSG SIZE  rcvd: 166

[root@Enterprise3 root]# []
```

Common DNS Pitfalls

DNS is an Internet-wide database of domain names and IP addresses. If you want your DNS server to participate, make sure the information that goes into the database is up to date and properly formatted. Many network outages can be traced to poorly administered DNS servers. A few examples of common DNS errors are described in the following sections.

Timing

Sometimes, all you need to do is wait a while. Whenever a change is made in a DNS database, it takes some time before the change is noted (a.k.a. propagated) to other DNS servers on the Internet. Therefore, whenever you change something such as the IP address associated with a Web server, it's advisable to keep the old IP address available for that Web server until the new IP address has time to propagate.

The Serial Number Wasn't Incremented

The single most common DNS error occurs when an administrator makes updates to a zone file, restarts DNS, and notices that no one else on the Internet knows about the updates. If another DNS server doesn't detect a new serial number on a zone file, it assumes the file is the same, and sticks with its cache. No data is taken from the update, and other DNS servers don't get the revised information.

When you update a zone file, update the serial number. It's best done with the current date in the format shown in the examples (four-digit year, two-digit month, and two-digit date, followed by a one-digit increment number). If you've updated the DNS more than once today, increment the last number as well.

The Reverse Zone Isn't Delegated

Not all network administrators have control over their DNS servers. Some administrators contract with an ISP for this service.

Now assume you're that ISP administrator. You'll need to assign this customer a range of IP addresses for their domain name. Then you'll need to assign the domain name and IP addresses to a specific DNS "zone of authority."

Next, you'll also need to set up the reverse zone. For example, if you assign the 192.168.1. network (192.168.1. is short for the IPv4 network address of 192.168.1.0), you'll need to add NS records in the forward zone, and PTR records in the reverse zone.

on the **job** *From an end-user perspective, DNS might be considered the glue that holds the Internet together. Pay special attention to the nuances of the configuration files, so that network-wide problems are avoided.*

The Red Hat DNS Configuration Tool

Red Hat has created a number of excellent GUI configuration tools. They are "front-ends" which can help many administrators create the configuration files that they need. Unfortunately, I do not believe that the Red Hat Domain Name Service tool should be included in this category. As of this writing, Red Hat has incorporated changes into a different RPM package optimized for Fedora Linux; this updated RPM package, system-config-bind, is not supported by Red Hat through an enterprise subscription.

In any case, it is best if you learn how to configure Linux services, including DNS, directly from the configuration files. As a Linux systems administrator, you may not always have access to the GUI. You may need to administer servers remotely, which makes GUI configuration difficult at best.

If you want to try the Red Hat Domain Name Service configuration tool shown in Figure 9-9, back up your DNS configuration files first: /etc/named.conf, /etc/named .custom, and the files in the /var/named directory. In RHEL 3, this is based on the redhat-config-bind RPM.

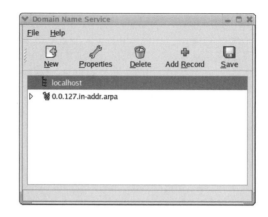

The Red Hat
Domain Name
Service
configuration tool

Keep It Working

Assuming you're running your own DNS, you also need to keep the /var/named/named.ca file up to date. The easiest way to do this is by using **dig**, which is also known as the DNS Information Groper. If your DNS is working properly and is connected to the Internet, you can run commands such as **dig www.osborne.com**.

Let us analyze the **dig** command further. First, run **dig** with no arguments. You will get information from the local named.ca file. Then use this command to query one of the listed root servers with a command such as **dig a.ROOT-SERVERS.NET**. The output should resemble a named.ca file. Save it to a file with a command such as **dig @a.root-servers.net.ns > named.ca.new** and replace the old named.ca file. Remember to reload the **named** daemon after replacing the named.ca file.

Alternatively, the following script can be run automatically to update named.ca. The text of the base script is also available in the DNS-HOWTO available from the Linux Documentation Project at www.tldp.org. At the time of this writing, the base script in the HOWTO is still written for BIND 8. If you're using this file, change all of the "root.hints" filenames to "named.ca", and then replace the mail-alias "hostmaster" with a working e-mail address.

Once you're satisfied with the configuration, you can set up a crontab entry to run this script on a monthly basis in the /etc/cron.montly directory.

```
#!/bin/sh
 #
 # Update the nameserver cache information file once per month.
 # This is run automatically by a cron entry.
 #
 # Original by Al Longyear
```

```
# Updated for bind 8 by Nicolai Langfeldt
# Miscellaneous error-conditions reported by David A. Ranch
# Ping test suggested by Martin Foster
#
(
echo "To: hostmaster <hostmaster>"
echo "From: system <root>"
echo "Subject: Automatic update of the named.ca file"
echo

PATH=/sbin:/usr/sbin:/bin:/usr/bin:
export PATH
cd /var/named

# Are we online?  Ping a server on the Internet
case 'ping -qnc 1 www.redhat.com' in
  *'100% packet loss'*)
        echo "The network is DOWN. named.ca NOT updated"
        echo
        exit 0
        ;;
esac

dig @A.ROOT-SERVERS.NET . ns > named.ca.new 2>>&1

case 'cat named.ca.new' in
  *Got answer*)
        # It worked
        :;;
  *)
        echo "The named.ca file update has FAILED."
        echo "This is the dig output reported:"
        echo

        cat named.ca.new
        exit 0
        ;;
esac

echo "The named.ca file has been updated to contain the following
    information:"
echo
cat named.ca.new

chown root.root named.ca.new
```

```
      chmod 444 named.ca.new
      rm -f named.ca.old
      mv named.ca named.ca.old
      mv named.ca.new named.ca.hints
      /etc/rc.d/init.d/named restart
      echo
echo "The nameserver has been restarted to ensure that the update
   is complete."
   echo "The previous named.ca file is now called
   /var/named/named.ca.old."
   ) 2>>&1 | /usr/lib/sendmail -t
   exit 0
```

EXERCISE 9-1

Set Up Your Own DNS Server

Following the example files shown previously, set up your own DNS server. Set it up to serve the domain called rhce.test. As long as your domain is private, it doesn't matter that rhce.test does not match the standard domain name types such as .com or .net.

1. Edit the /etc/named.conf file to reflect the configuration files that you plan to use. Name the zone file rhce.test.zone and set it to be a master domain.

2. Edit the file /var/named/rhce.test.zone and place the proper zone information in it. Start by adding in the header with the serial number and expiration information.

3. Add the SOA resource record (RR) with a proper administrative e-mail address contact.

4. Add NS and MX RRs for the domain. Use the 192.168.*.* address range. If you're configuring an actual TCP/IP network with static IP addresses, feel free to use the assigned IP addresses on your network.

5. Add several hosts to the zone file. Use WWW, FTP, and mail for a few.

6. Save the zone file and then restart named with the **service named restart** command.

7. Use the **dig** command to check the rhce.test domain. If it works, you have a working DNS server.

CERTIFICATION OBJECTIVE 9.02

Network File System (NFS)

The Network File System (NFS) is the standard for sharing files and printers on a directory with Linux and Unix computers. It was originally developed by Sun Microsystems in the mid-1980s. Linux has supported NFS (both as a client and a server) for years, and NFS continues to be popular in organizations with Unix- or Linux-based networks.

You can create shared NFS directories directly by editing the /etc/exports configuration file, or you can create them with Red Hat's NFS Configuration tool. As you need an NFS server before you can configure an NFS client, I describe how to create NFS servers first.

NFS Server Configuration and Operation

NFS servers are relatively easy to configure. All that is required is to export a filesystem, either generally or to a specific host, and then mount that filesystem from a remote client. I've shown you how to configure an NFS server to install RHEL 3 over a network. In this chapter, you'll learn the basics of NFS server configuration and operation.

Required Packages

Two RPM packages are closely associated with NFS: portmap and nfs-utils. They should be installed by default in RHEL 3. Just in case, you can use the **rpm -q** *packagename* command to make sure these packages are installed. The **rpm -ql** *packagename* command provides a list of files installed from that package. The nfs-utils package includes a number of key files. The following is not a complete list:

- /etc/rc.d/init.d/nfs (control script for NFS)
- /etc/rc.d/init.d/nfslock (control script for lockd and statd)
- /usr/share/doc/nfs-utils-1.0.5 (documentation, mostly in HTML format)
- Server daemons in /usr/sbin: rpc.mountd, rpc.nfsd
- Server daemons in /sbin: rpc.lockd, rpc.statd
- Control programs in /usr/sbin: exportfs, nfsstat, nhfsgraph, nhfsnums, nhfsrun, nhfsstone, showmount
- Status files in /var/lib/nfs: etab, rmtab, statd, state, xtab

The portmap RPM package includes the following key files (also not a complete list):

- /etc/rc.d/init.d/portmap (control script)
- /usr/share/doc/portmap-4.0 (documentation)
- Server daemon in /sbin: portmap
- Control programs in /usr/sbin: pmap_dump, pmap_set

Configuring NFS to Start

Once configured, you can set up NFS to start during the Linux boot process, or you can start it yourself with the **service nfs start** command. NFS also depends on the portmap package, which helps secure NFS directories that are shared through /etc/exports. Because of this dependency, make sure to start the portmap daemon before starting NFS, and don't stop it until after stopping NFS.

on the **Job** *Remember that both the portmap and nfs daemons must be running before NFS can work.*

The nfs service script starts the following processes:

- **rpc.mountd**   Handles mount requests
- **nfsd**   Starts an nfsd kernel process for each shared directory
- **rpc.rquotad**   Reports disk quota statistics to clients

If any of these processes are not running, NFS won't work. Fortunately, it's easy to check for these processes. Just run the **rpcinfo -p** command. As with other service scripts, if you want it to start when RHEL 3 boots, you'll need to run a command such as:

```
# chkconfig --level 35 nfs on
```

Alternatively, you can use the Red Hat Service Management utility described in Chapter 4 to make sure NFS starts the next time you boot RHEL 3.

Configuring NFS for Basic Operation

NFS is fairly simple. The only major NFS configuration file is /etc/exports. Once configured, you can export these directories with the **exportfs -a** command. Each line in this file lists the directory to be exported, the hosts it will be exported to, and the options that apply to this export. You can export a given directory only once. Take the following examples from an /etc/exports file:

```
/pub                    (ro,sync) someone.mylocaldomain.com(rw,sync)
/home                   *.mylocaldomain.com(rw,sync)
/opt/diskless-root      diskless.mylocaldomain.com(rw,no_root_squash,sync)
```

In the preceding example, the /pub directory is exported to all users as read-only. It is also exported to one specific computer with read/write privileges. The /home directory is exported, with read/write privileges, to any computer on the .mylocaldomain.com network. Finally, the /opt/diskless-root directory is exported with full read/write privileges (even for root users) on the diskless.mylocaldomain.com computer.

All of these options include the sync flag. This requires all changes to be written to disk before a command such as a file copy is complete. This is a fairly new change, which Red Hat first implemented on Red Hat Linux 8.0.

Be very careful with /etc/exports; one common cause of problems is an extra space between expressions. For example, if you type in a space after the comma in **(ro,sync)**, your directory won't get exported, and you'll get an error message.

Wildcards and Globbing

In Linux network configuration files, you can specify a group of computers with the right wildcard. This process in Linux is also known as *globbing*. What you do for a wildcard depends on the configuration file. The NFS /etc/exports file uses "conventional" wildcards;

for example, *.mydomain.com specifies all computers within the mydomain.com domain. In contrast, /etc/hosts.deny is less conventional; .mydomain.com, with the leading dot, specifies all computers in that same domain.

For IPv4 networks, wildcards often require some form of the subnet mask. For example, 192.168.0.0/255.255.255.0 specifies the 192.168.0.0 network of computers with IP addresses that range from 192.168.0.1 to 192.168.0.254. Some services support the use of CIDR (Classless Inter-Domain Routing) notation. In CIDR, since 255.255.255.0 masks 24 bits, CIDR represents this with the number 24. If you're configuring a network in CIDR notation, you can represent this network as 192.168.0.0/24. For details, see the discussion for each applicable service in Chapters 7 through 11.

Activating the List of Exports

Once you've modified /etc/exports, you need to do more. First, this file is simply the default set of exported directories. You need to activate them with the **exportfs -a** command. The next time you boot RHEL 3, if you've activated **nfs** at the appropriate runlevels, the nfs start script automatically runs the **exportfs -r** command, which synchronizes exported directories. You can see this for yourself in the /etc/rc.d/init.d /nfs script.

When you add a share to /etc/exports, the **exportfs -r** command adds the new directories. However, if you're modifying, moving, or deleting a share, it is safest to first temporarily unexport all filesystems with the **exportfs -ua** command before reexporting the shares with the **exportfs -a** command.

Once exports are active, they're easy to check. Just run the **showmount -e** command on the server. If you're looking for the export list for a remote NFS server, just add the name of the NFS server. For example, the **showmount -e enterprise3** command looks for the list of exported NFS directories from the enterprise3 computer. If this command doesn't work, you may have blocked NFS messages with a firewall.

NFS Server Configuration Tool

Naturally, as it is easy to configure /etc/exports, the Red Hat NFS Server Configuration tool is easy to use and is reliable. To start this tool, type the **redhat-config-nfs** command in a GUI terminal, or click Main Menu | System Settings | Server Settings | NFS. This opens the NFS Server Configuration window shown in Figure 9-10. After you go through these steps, you'll see how much simpler it is to add a line to /etc/exports.

FIGURE 9-10

NFS Server
Configuration

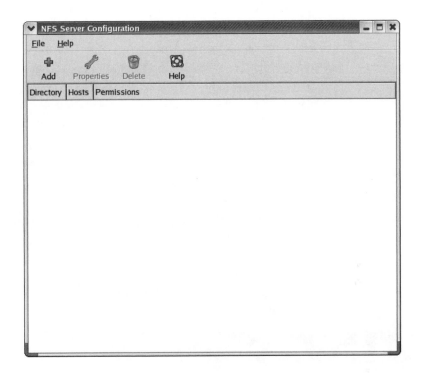

To add a shared NFS directory, take the following steps:

1. Click Add or File | Add NFS Share. This opens the Add NFS Share window
   shown in Figure 9-11.

2. Under the Basic tab, add the directory that you want to share. If you want to
   limit access to a specific host or domain, add the appropriate names to the

FIGURE 9-11

The Add NFS
Share window

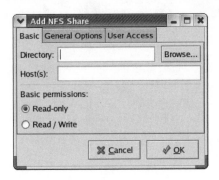

Host(s) text box. If you want to allow access to all users, enter an asterisk (*). Set read-only or read/write permissions as desired. Click the General Options tab.

3. Under the General Options tab, you can set several parameters for this share, as described in Table 9-2. Note that **sync** is the only option that's active by default. The default is sufficient unless you receive specific instructions for an NFS share on your exam. Click the User Access tab.

4. Under the User Access tab, you can set different parameters for remote users, as defined in Table 9-3.

5. Once you've finished configuring your shared NFS directory, click OK. The directory is automatically exported with the **exportfs -r** command and, as long as you aren't blocking access with firewalls, should now be ready for use.

6. If you have problems, check for firewalls. Check for limitations in /etc/hosts.allow and /etc/hosts.deny. For more information on firewall management, read Chapter 10. If necessary, use the **service nfs stop** and **service nfs start** commands to restart the NFS service. If there are still problems, you may find more information in your /var/log/messages file.

e x a m
ⓦatch

If you use Red Hat's NFS Server Configuration tool, don't forget to activate NFS at the appropriate runlevels (3 and 5) so your shared directories are available when your exam proctor reboots your computer to see what you've done.

TABLE 9-2   NFS Tool General Options

Parameter	Corresponding /etc/exports Command and Explanation
Allow connections from ports 1024 or higher	**insecure** As this sends NFS requests above ports 1024, it is not blocked by most firewalls.
Allow insecure file locking	**insecure_locks** If you have an older NFS client, this does not check user permissions to a file.
Disable subtree checking	**no_subtree_check** If you export a subdirectory such as /mnt/inst, this does not check higher level directories such as /mnt for permissions.
Sync write operations on request	**sync** Data is written upon request. Active by default.
Force sync of write operations immediately	**no_wdelay** Data is written to the share immediately.

TABLE 9-3   NFS Tool User Access Options

Parameter	Corresponding /etc/exports Command and Explanation
Treat remote root user as local root	**no_root_squash** Remote root users get root privileges on the shared directory.
Treat all client users as anonymous users	**all_squash** All remote users are mapped as an anonymous user. In RHEL 3, that user is nfsnobody, which you can see in /etc/passwd.
Specify local user ID for anonymous users	**anonuid=***userid* Allows you to map remote users to a specific user ID such as pcguest.
Specify local group ID for anonymous users	**anongid=***groupid* Allows you to map remote groups to a specific group ID such as pcguest.

Unfortunately, the NFS Server Configuration tool does not activate NFS at the appropriate runlevels for the next time you boot Linux.

NFS Client Configuration and Operation

Now you can mount a shared NFS directory from a client computer. The commands and configuration files are similar to those used for any local filesystem.

Mounting an NFS Directory from the Command Line

Before doing anything elaborate, you should test the shared NFS directory from a Linux or Unix client computer. But first, you should check for the list of shared NFS directories. If you're on an NFS server computer named enterprise3, the command is easy:

```
# showmount -e
```

This command assumes that the NFS server is local. If you don't see a list of shared directories, review the steps described earlier in this chapter. Make sure you've configured your /etc/exports file properly. Remember to export the shared directories. And your NFS server can't work if you haven't started the NFS daemon on your computer.

If you're on a remote NFS client computer and want to see the list of shared directories from the enterprise3 computer, run the following command:

```
# showmount -e enterprise3
```

If it doesn't work, there are a couple of more things that you'll need to check: firewalls and your /etc/hosts or DNS server. If you have a problem with your /etc/hosts or DNS server, you can substitute the IP address of the NFS server. You'll see output similar to the following:

```
Export list for enterprise3
/mnt/inst *
```

Now if you want to mount this directory locally, you'll need an empty local directory. Create a directory such as /mnt/remote if required. You can then mount the shared directory from the enterprise3 computer with the following command:

```
# mount -t nfs enterprise3:/mnt/inst /mnt/remote
```

This command mounts the /mnt/inst directory from the computer named enterprise3. This command specifies the use of the NFS protocol (**-t nfs**), and mounts the share on the local /mnt/remote directory. Depending on traffic on your network, this command may take a few seconds. Be patient! When it works, you'll be able to access files on /mnt /inst as if it were a local directory.

NFS and /etc/fstab

You can also configure an NFS client to mount a remote NFS directory during the boot process, as defined in /etc/fstab. For example, the following entry in a client /etc/fstab mounts the /homenfs share from the computer named nfsserv, on the local /nfs/home directory:

```
## Server: Directory  Mount Point  Type  Mount Options    Dump Fsckorder
nfsserv:/homenfs       /nfs/home    nfs   soft,timeout=100 0    0
```

Alternatively, an automounter, such as autofs or amd, can be used to dynamically mount NFS filesystems as required by the client computer. The automounter can also unmount these remote filesystems after a period of inactivity. For more information, see Chapter 4.

Client-Side Helper Processes

When you start NFS as a client, it adds a few new system processes, including:

- **rpc.statd** Tracks the status of servers, for use by rpc.lockd in recovering locks after a server crash
- **rpc.lockd** Manages the client side of file locking

Diskless Clients

NFS supports diskless clients, which are computers without a hard drive. A diskless client may use a boot floppy or a boot PROM to get started. Then, embedded commands can mount the appropriate root (/) directory, swap space, the /usr directory as read-only, and other shared directories such as /home in read/write mode. If your computer uses a boot PROM, you'll also need access to DHCP and TFTP servers for network and kernel information.

Red Hat Enterprise Linux 3 includes features that support diskless clients. While not listed as part of the current Red Hat exam requirements or related course outlines, I would not be surprised to see such requirements in the future. You can find out more about how this works with the Network Installation and Diskless Environment tool, which you can start with the Main Menu | System Settings | Server Settings | Network Booting Service command.

Quirks and Limitations of NFS

NFS does have its problems. An administrator who controls shared NFS directories would be wise to take note of these limitations.

Statelessness

NFS is a "stateless" protocol. In other words, you don't need to log in separately to access a shared NFS directory. Instead, the NFS client normally contacts rpc.mountd on the server. The rpc.mounted daemon handles mount requests. It checks the request against currently exported filesystems. If the request is valid, rpc.mounted provides an *NFS file handle* (a "magic cookie"), which is then used for further client/server communication for this share.

The stateless protocol allows the NFS client to wait if the NFS server ever has to be rebooted. The software waits, and waits, and waits. This can cause the NFS client to hang as discussed later.

This can also lead to problems with insecure single-user clients. When a file is opened through a share, it may be "locked out" from other users. When an NFS server is rebooted, handling the locked file can be difficult. The security problems can be so severe that NFS communication is blocked even by the default Red Hat Enterprise Linux firewall.

In theory, the recent change to NFS, setting up sync as the default for file transfers, should help address this problem. In theory, locked-out users should not lose any data that they've written with the appropriate commands.

Absolute and Relative Symbolic Links

If you have any symbolic links on an exported directory, be careful. The client interprets a symbolically linked file with respect to its own local filesystem. Unless the mount point and filesystem structures are identical, the linked file can point to an unexpected location, which may lead to unpredictable consequences.

You have a couple of ways to address this issue. You can take care to limit the use of symbolic links within an exported directory. Alternatively, NFS offers a server-side export option (**link_relative**) that converts absolute links to relative links; however, this can have counter-intuitive results if the client mounts a subdirectory of the exported directory.

Root Squash

By default, NFS is set up to **root_squash**, which prevents root users on an NFS client from gaining root access to a share on an NFS server. Specifically, the root user on a client (with a user ID of 0) is mapped to the nfsnobody unprivileged account.

This behavior can be disabled via the **no_root_squash** server export option in /etc/exports. In that case, root users who connect from a client gain root privileges on the shared NFS directory.

NFS Hangs

Because NFS is stateless, NFS clients may wait up to several minutes for a server. In some cases, an NFS client may wait indefinitely if a server goes down. During the wait, any process that looks for a file on the mounted NFS share will hang. Once this happens, it is generally difficult or impossible to unmount the offending filesystems. You can do several things to reduce the impact of this problem:

- Take great care to ensure the reliability of NFS servers and the network.

- Avoid mounting many different NFS servers at once. If several computers mount each other's NFS directories, this could cause problems throughout the network.

- Mount infrequently used NFS exports only when needed. NFS clients should unmount these clients after use.

- Set up NFS shares with the **sync** option, which should at least reduce the incidence of lost files.

- Don't configure a mission-critical computer as an NFS client, if at all possible.

- Keep NFS mounted directories out of the search path for users, especially that of root.

- Keep NFS mounted directories out of the root (/) directory; instead, segregate them to a less frequently used filesystem such as /nfs/home or /nfs/share.

Soft Mounting

Consider using the **soft** option when mounting NFS filesystems. When an NFS server fails, a soft-mounted NFS filesystem will fail rather than hang. However, this risks the failure of long-running processes due to temporary network outages.

In addition, you can use the **timeo** option to set a timeout interval, in tenths of a second. For example, the following command would mount /nfs/home with a timeout of 30 seconds:

```
# mount -o soft,timeo=300 myserver:/home /nfs/home
```

Inverse DNS Pointers

An NFS server daemon checks mount requests. First, it looks at the current list of exports, based on /etc/exports. Then, it looks up the client's IP address to find its hostname. This requires a reverse DNS lookup.

This hostname is then finally checked against the list of exports. If NFS can't find a hostname, rpc.mountd will deny access to that client. For security reasons, it also adds a "request from unknown host" entry in /var/log/messages.

File Locking

Multiple NFS clients can be set up to mount the same exported directory from the same server. It's quite possible that people on different computers end up trying to use the same shared file. This is addressed by the file locking daemon service.

NFS has historically had serious problems making file locking work. If you have an application that depends on file locking over NFS, test it thoroughly before putting it into production.

Filesystem Nesting

It is impossible to export two directories in the same filesystem if one is inside the other. For example, /usr and /usr/local cannot both be exported unless /usr/local is mounted on a separate partition from /usr.

Performance Tips

You can do several things to keep NFS running in a stable and reliable manner. As you gain experience with NFS, you might monitor or even experiment with the following:

- Eight kernel NFS daemons, which is the default, is generally sufficient for good performance, even under fairly heavy loads. If your NFS server is busy, you may want to add additional NFS daemons through the /etc/rc.d/init.d/nfs script. Just keep in mind that the extra kernel processes consume valuable kernel resources.

- NFS write performance can be extremely slow, particularly with NFS v2 clients, as the client waits for each block of data to be written to disk.

- You may try specialized hardware with nonvolatile RAM. Data that is stored on such RAM isn't lost if you have trouble with network connectivity or a power failure.

- In applications where data loss is not a big concern, you may try the **async** option. This makes NFS faster because **async** NFS mounts do not write files to disk until other operations are complete. However, a loss of power or network connectivity can result in a loss of data.

- Hostname lookups are performed frequently by the NFS server; you can start the Name Switch Cache Daemon (nscd) to speed lookup performance.

on the
ꝏob   *NFS is a powerful file-sharing system. But there are risks associated with NFS. If an NFS server is down, it could affect your entire network. It's also not sufficiently secure to use on the Internet. NFS is primarily used on secure LAN/WAN networks.*

NFS Security

NFS includes a number of serious security problems and should never be used in hostile environments (such as on a server directly exposed to the Internet), at least not without strong precautions.

Shortcomings and Risks

NFS is an easy-to-use yet powerful file-sharing system. However, it is not without its problems. The following are a few security issues to keep in mind:

- **Authentication**   NFS relies on the host to report user and group IDs. However, this can expose your files if root users on other computers access your NFS shares. In other words, data that is accessible via NFS to *any user* can potentially be accessed by *any other* user.

■ **Privacy**   Not even Secure NFS encrypts its network traffic.

■ **portmap infrastructure**   Both the NFS client and server depend on the RPC portmap daemon. The portmap daemon has historically had a number of serious security holes. For this reason, portmap is not recommended for use on computers that are directly connected to the Internet or other potentially hostile networks.

Security Tips

If NFS *must* be used in or near a hostile environment, you can do some things to reduce the security risks:

■ Educate yourself in detail about NFS security. If you do not clearly understand the risks, you should restrict your NFS use to friendly, internal networks behind a good firewall.

■ Export as little data as possible, and export filesystems as read-only if possible.

■ Use root squash to prevent clients from having root access to exported filesystems.

■ If an NFS client has a direct connection to the Internet, use separate network adapters for the Internet connection and the LAN. Use the right firewall commands (**iptables** or **ipchains**) to block the routing on the TCP and UDP ports associated with portmapper, mountd, and nfsd.

■ Use a firewall system such as **iptables** or **ipchains** to deny access to the portmapper, mountd, and nfsd ports, except from explicitly trusted hosts or networks. The ports are

```
111    TCP/UDP    portmapper    (server and client)
745    UDP        mountd        (server)
747    TCP        mountd        (server)
2049   TCP/UDP    nfsd          (server)
```

Use a port scanner to verify that these ports are blocked for untrusted network(s).

EXERCISE 9-2

NFS

This exercise requires two computers, one set up as an NFS server, the other as an NFS client. On the NFS server:

1. Set up a group named IT for the Information Technology group in /etc/group.

2. Create the /MIS directory. Assign ownership to the MIS group with the **chgrp** command.

3. Set the SGID bit on this directory to enforce group ownership.

4. Update /etc/exports file to allow read and write for your local network. Run the following command to set it up under NFS.

   ```
   # exportfs -a
   ```

5. Restart the NFS service.

On an NFS client, take the following steps:

6. Create a directory for the server share called /mnt/MIS.

7. Mount the shared NFS directory on /mnt/MIS.

8. List all exported shares from the server and save this output as /mnt/MIS /thishost.shares.list.

9. Make this service a permanent connection in the /etc/fstab file. Assume that the connection might be troublesome and add the appropriate options, such as soft mounting.

10. Reboot the client computer. Check to see if the share is properly remounted.

11. Test the NFS connection. Stop the service on the server, and then try copying a file to the /mnt/MIS directory. While the attempt to copy will fail, it should not hang the client.

12. Restart the NFS server.

13. Edit /etc/fstab again. This time assume that NFS is reliable, and remove the special options that you added in step 4.

14. Reboot the client computer. Test the service with the new settings.

Now test what happens when you shut down the server. The mounted NFS directory on the client should hang when you try to access the service. Restart the server service and see if your client service resumes.

Using the NFS Server Configuration tool

In this exercise, you'll use the options associated with the NFS Server Configuration tool to experiment with creating a shared directory in /etc/exports. While it's best and usually fastest to edit a Linux configuration file directly, Red Hat GUI configuration tools such as the NFS Server Configuration tool can help you learn about different options for Linux services.

1. Open a GUI on a RHEL 3 computer. If not already open, you can do so with the **startx** command.

2. Start the NFS Server Configuration tool. You can run **redhat-config-nfs** from a command line interface, or click Main Menu | System Settings | Server Settings | NFS.

3. In the NFS Server Configuration tool, click Add. This opens the Add NFS Share window with the Basic tab. Set up a share for your home directory. Share it with one specific host on your LAN, with read-only permissions.

4. Click the General Options tab. Select the options of your choice. It does not matter what you select; the purpose of this lab is to demonstrate the effect of the NFS Server Configuration tool on the /etc/exports file.

5. Click the User Access tab. Select the options of your choice.

6. Click OK. The settings you choose are saved in /etc/exports.

7. Open a command line window. Right-click on the desktop and select New Terminal from the pop-up menu that appears.

8. Open the /etc/exports file in the text editor of your choice. What is the relationship between the options you selected in the NFS Server Configuration tool and the command options associated with your home directory in /etc /exports? Close the /etc/exports file.

9. Back in the NFS Server Configuration tool, highlight the line associated with your home directory, and then click Properties. This opens the Edit NFS Share window with the settings that you just created.

10. Make additional changes under the three tabs in this window. After you click OK, check the results in /etc/exports. What happened?

11. If you don't want to actually export your home directory, highlight the appropriate line in the NFS Server Configuration tool and click Delete. What happens to /etc/exports?

12. Exit from the NFS Server Configuration tool.

CERTIFICATION OBJECTIVE 9.03

DHCP

There are two protocols that allow a client computer to get network configuration information from a server: DHCP (Dynamic Host Configuration Protocol) and bootp. DHCP works if you have a DHCP server on the local network. The bootp protocol is required if you're getting information from a DHCP server on another network.

DHCP servers can simplify and centralize network administration if you're administering more than a few computers on a network. They are especially convenient for networks with a significant number of mobile users. The bootp protocol is essentially just a way to access a DHCP server on a remote network.

As of this writing, Red Hat does not include any GUI tool to configure a DHCP server. You'll have to do your work in this section from the command line interface.

exam
watch

While DHCP knowledge is not explicitly listed in the current Red Hat Exam Prep guide, it is a part of the associated curriculum. Based on their outlines, the RHCT course, RH133, teaches you how to configure a DHCP client. The RHCE course, RH300, teaches you how to configure a DHCP server. It is important for any network administrator to know DHCP. You'll have to make your own decision regarding whether you'll need to study how to create a DHCP server for your exam.

Installing DHCP Packages

As with most network services, DHCP has a client and a server. These are based on the dhcp-3.0pl2-6.14 and dhclient-3.0pl2-6.14 RPM packages. The dhclient RPM package should be installed by default. The dhcp RPM package is installed by default with the Network Server package group. Install them if required.

on the
Job
Red Hat seems to change the commands and packages related to the DHCP client frequently. Recent versions of Red Hat have used dhcpcd *and* pump *as DHCP client commands. If you are using a different version of Red Hat Linux, make sure you've installed the right packages and are using the right commands.*

DHCP Server Configuration

A DHCP server sends messages to multiple computers on a LAN. This is also known as a multicast. It should be enabled by default in RHEL 3. You can confirm this with the **ifconfig** command. The output should resemble Figure 9-12, which includes a MULTICAST setting for the active network card.

If you don't see MULTICAST associated with your network card, someone has compiled this feature out of your kernel. For more information on the kernel management process, see Chapter 5.

Now configure the DHCP server daemon, **dhcpd**, by creating or editing the /etc /dhcpd.conf configuration file. Normally, this file allows the DHCP server to randomly assign IP addresses from a specific range. If you don't already have an /etc/dhcpd.conf file, you can start with the dhcpd.conf.sample file in the /usr/share/doc/dhcp-3.0-pl2

FIGURE 9-12	
Active network interfaces MULTICAST	

```
[root@Enterprise3 root]# ifconfig
eth0      Link encap:Ethernet  HWaddr 00:0C:29:1C:1E:9E
          inet addr:192.168.30.2  Bcast:192.168.30.255  Mask:255.255.255.0
          UP BROADCAST RUNNING MULTICAST  MTU:1500  Metric:1
          RX packets:1961 errors:0 dropped:0 overruns:0 frame:0
          TX packets:415 errors:0 dropped:0 overruns:0 carrier:0
          collisions:0 txqueuelen:1000
          RX bytes:762485 (744.6 Kb)  TX bytes:40639 (39.6 Kb)
          Interrupt:11 Base address:0x10c0

lo        Link encap:Local Loopback
          inet addr:127.0.0.1  Mask:255.0.0.0
          UP LOOPBACK RUNNING  MTU:16436  Metric:1
          RX packets:412 errors:0 dropped:0 overruns:0 frame:0
          TX packets:412 errors:0 dropped:0 overruns:0 carrier:0
          collisions:0 txqueuelen:0
          RX bytes:29010 (28.3 Kb)  TX bytes:29010 (28.3 Kb)

[root@Enterprise3 root]#
```

directory. The lines that start with a hash mark (#) are comments in the file. Let's analyze this sample file in detail:

- **ddns-update-style interim** With this command, the RHEL 3 DHCP server conforms as closely as possible to the new Dynamic DNS standard, where the DNS database is updated when the DNS server renews its DHCP lease. It is "interim" because the standards for DDNS are not complete as of this writing.

- **ignore client-updates** A good setting if you don't want to allow users on client computers to change their hostnames.

- **subnet 192.168.0.0 netmask 255.255.255.0** Describes a network with an address of 192.168.0.0 and a subnet mask of 255.255.255.0. This allows you to assign addresses in the range 192.168.0.1–192.168.0.254 to different computers on this network. Naturally, if you've configured a different network IP address, you'll want to change these settings accordingly.

- **option routers** Lists the default router. You can add additional **option routers** commands if you have more than one connection to an outside network. This information is passed to DHCP clients as the default gateway, which supports access to outside networks such as the Internet. Naturally, you'll want this command to reflect the IP address for the gateway for your network.

- **option subnet-mask** Specifies the subnet mask for the local network.

- **option nis-domain** Notes the server that provides the NIS shared authorization database. If you've configured NIS on your network, you'll want to substitute the name of your domain for domain.org. Otherwise, you should comment out this command.

- **option domain-name** Adds the domain name for your network. If your domain name is different, you'll want to change this command accordingly.

- **option domain-name-servers** Notes the IP address for the DNS server for your network. You can add more commands of this type to specify additional DNS servers.

- **option time-offset** Lists the difference from Greenwich Mean Time, also known as UTC (a French acronym), in seconds.

- **option ntp-servers** Notes any Network Time Protocol (NTP) servers for keeping the time on the local computer in sync with UTC. I describe NTP in more detail later in this chapter.

- **option netbios-name-servers** Adds the location of any Windows Internet Naming Service (WINS) servers for your network. As this is a Microsoft service, I only refer to it briefly in my description of Samba in Chapter 8.

- **option netbios-node-type 2** Peer-to-peer node searches, associated with WINS.

- **range dynamic-bootp 192.168.0.128 192.168.0.254** Notes the assignable IP addresses to remote networks, using the bootp protocol. (Drop the dynamic-bootp for a local network.) Remember the space between the IP addresses! (Don't use the 192.168.0.255 address in the sample dhcpd.conf file.)

- **default-lease-time** Specifies the lease time for IP address information, in seconds.

- **max-lease-time** Specifies the maximum lease time for IP address information, in seconds.

- **next-server** Notes the boot server for network computers. If you don't have any network computers, you can comment out this entire stanza.

You can also assign a specific IP address to a computer based on a client's Ethernet address. Just add an entry similar to the following to /etc/dhcpd.conf:

```
host dragonfire {
    hardware ethernet 08:00:12:23:4d:3f;
    fixed-address 192.168.0.201;
}
```

This assigns the IP address 192.168.1.201 to a client named dragonfire with the Ethernet hardware address 08:00:12:23:4d:3f.

Naturally, you'll want to modify this file accordingly for your particular network. For example, if you've configured computers on the example.com network described earlier in this chapter, you'll want to substitute example.com and the associated IP addresses in your /etc/dhcpd.conf file. I've done this for my network in Figure 9-13.

 on the job

To assign an IP address to a specific network card on a specific computer, you need the hardware address, which can be found via the ifconfig command.

DHCP can be customized for individual computers. You can set up static IP addresses for servers. Once you're ready, start the dhcpd service with the following command:

```
# service dhcpd start
```

FIGURE 9-13

Sample DHCP
configuration file

```
ddns-update-style interim;
ignore client-updates;

subnet 192.168.30.0 netmask 255.255.255.0 {

# --- default gateway
        option routers                  192.168.30.113;
        option subnet-mask              255.255.255.0;

        option nis-domain               "example.com";
        option domain-name              "example.com";
        option domain-name-servers      192.168.30.2;

        option time-offset              -18000; # Eastern Standard Time
#       option ntp-servers              192.168.1.1;
#       option netbios-name-servers     192.168.1.1;
# --- Selects point-to-point node (default is hybrid). Don't change this unless
# -- you understand Netbios very well
#       option netbios-node-type 2;

        range dynamic-bootp 192.168.30.128 192.168.30.254;
        default-lease-time 21600;
        max-lease-time 43200;

        # we want the nameserver to appear at a fixed address
        host ns {
                next-server enterprise3.example.com;
                hardware ethernet 00:0C:29:1C:1E:9E;
                fixed-address 192.168.30.2;
        }
}
"/etc/dhcpd.conf" 31L, 865C                                    29,1-8         All
```

By default, this starts a DHCP server, which listens for requests on the eth0 network
card. Alternatively, to have a DHCP server listen on the eth1 network interface, run
the following command:

```
# service dhcpd start eth1
```

If these commands don't get a response, you probably haven't created a /etc/dhcpd.conf
configuration file.

You can watch the DHCP server in action. Stop the DHCP server with the **service
dhcpd stop** command. You can then restart it in the foreground with the following
command:

```
# /usr/sbin/dhcpd -d -f
```

Start another Linux/Unix client. Make it look for another DHCP lease with the **dhclient -r** and **dhclient** commands, then watch the console of the server. You'll see a number of DHCP communication messages on the server that illustrates the process of leasing an IP address to a client.

on the job

Another easy way to get the MAC address for a given client is to watch the DHCP server messages.

Once you've configured your DHCP server to your satisfaction, remember to activate it at the appropriate runlevels. For example, the following command activates the DHCP daemon when you boot Linux into runlevels 3 and 5:

```
# chkconfig --level 35 dhcpd on
```

DHCP and Microsoft Windows

In order for the DHCP server to work correctly with picky DHCP clients such as Microsoft Windows 9*x*, the server needs to send data to the broadcast address: 255.255.255.255. Unfortunately, Linux insists on changing 255.255.255.255 into the local subnet broadcast address. The mixed message results in a DHCP protocol violation, and while Linux DHCP clients don't notice the problem, Microsoft DHCP clients do. Normally, such clients can't see DHCPOFFER messages and therefore don't know when to take an IP address offered from the DHCP server. If you're configuring a DHCP server for a network with Microsoft Windows computers, run the following command:

```
# route add --host 255.255.255.255 dev eth0
```

where eth0 is the name of the NIC that connects the server to the network.

Client Configuration

You can set up DHCP as a client using the **dhclient** command, or you can use the Red Hat Network Configuration tool (which you can also start with the Main Menu | System Settings | Network command). Alternatively, configuring a DHCP client at the command line is not difficult (and I believe is faster on the Red Hat exams). Make sure that the /etc/sysconfig/network configuration file includes the following line:

```
NETWORKING=yes
```

Next, make sure that the /etc/sysconfig/network-scripts/ifcfg-eth0 script contains the following lines (if you're using a different network device, modify the appropriate file in /etc/sysconfig/network-scripts directory):

```
BOOTPROTO='dhcp'
ONBOOT='yes'
```

The next time you reboot, your network configuration should look for DHCP address information automatically from the DHCP server for your network.

on the **J o b** *There is a subtle difference in the Linux names for the DHCP client and server. The DHCP server daemon is dhcpd; the DHCP client daemon is dhclient. If you're experienced with older versions of Red Hat Linux, this can get even more confusing, as obsolete DHCP client daemons were named dhcpcd and pump.*

Alternatively, you can use the Network Configuration tool from a GUI to configure DHCP. You can also start it from a GUI terminal console with the **redhat-config-network** command. When the tool opens, select your network card and click Edit. You should see a window similar to what is shown in Figure 9-14.

If you want to use DHCP on this computer, select the "Automatically obtain IP address settings with" option. You'll then get to choose between getting IP address information from a DHCP server on your local network, using bootp to get IP address information from a remote network, or going through a dialup connection, such as to an ISP. Once you've activated the changes, restart the network daemon with the **service network restart** command. Your network card will then look for IP address information from a DHCP server.

DHCP Client Troubleshooting

If the DHCP client configuration instructions in this chapter are not working, there may be a problem with the way the network is set up on your Linux computer. For example:

- The NIC is not configured properly. See Chapter 4 for information on reconfiguring your network card.
- If the computer is still having problems finding a DHCP server, check your firewall. If port 67 or 68 is blocked, your computer won't be able to get a message to the server.

on the **J o b** *The gateway daemon, starting with Red Hat 8.0, is zebra, which is now part of the quagga RPM. The gated and zebra RPM packages are now obsolete.*

FIGURE 9-14

Configuring your
network card

DHCP

To run this exercise, you'll need two different computers: a DHCP server and a DHCP client on the same LAN.

1. Open /etc/dhcpd.conf. Configure the server with an IP address range of 192.168.11.11–192.168.11.15 and with a network mask of 255.255.255.0. (If you want to use a different private IPv4 address subnet, substitute accordingly.)

2. Configure the client computer to use DHCP. Restart the network service on the client and record the IP address that it gets.

3. Add gateway and DNS server options with IP addresses of 192.168.11.254 and 12.34.45.56, respectively. If you already have a gateway and a DNS server, substitute the appropriate IP addresses. Restart the DHCP service. Restart networking on the client to make it renew the lease on the IP address.

CERTIFICATION OBJECTIVE 9.04

Keeping Servers in Sync

A number of companies keep servers in different time zones around the world. This allows users to select the server closest to them, maximizing network performance. As a Linux administrator, it may be your responsibility to make sure that all of these servers are on the same time. You can set up time synchronization on a centralized server through the Network Time Protocol (NTP).

The Network Time Protocol

NTP works by synchronizing a computer to UTC, through a connection to a time server. The current time is distributed through a hierarchy of NTP servers, through TCP/IP port 123. One point worth noting is that NTP will never run a system clock backward. If the clock on your computer is fast, NTP slows down the clock until it is in sync with UTC.

NTP Configuration

The configuration file for NTP is /etc/ntp.conf. In RHEL 3, it is already preconfigured to use your computer as a time server. But synchronizing your computer with your computer's hardware clock may not be enough.

To see how the default works, open the /etc/ntp.conf file in a text editor. You'll find a server that is listed with the **fudge** command. The default server is listed at IP address 127.127.1.0. While this isn't the normal "loopback" IP address, it is still within the "loopback" subnet; therefore, this address points right back at your computer. Alternatively, you can set it to one of the standard time servers described at www.eecis .udel.edu/~mills/ntp/servers.html.

Another way to synchronize your computer is to use the Red Hat Date/Time Properties tool to set NTP. You can start it in two ways. You can enter the **redhat-config-date** command in a GUI console, or click Main Menu | System Settings | Date & Time. This opens the Date/Time Properties dialog box shown in Figure 9-15.

When you select the Enable Network Time Protocol option and set a time server, ntpd is started and the name of the server is added to /etc/ntp.conf. If you want to set NTP to work after a reboot, you still need to make sure it starts the next time you reboot your computer with the appropriate **chkconfig** command.

FIGURE 9-15

Date/Time
Properties

CERTIFICATION SUMMARY

Networking services are an integral part of Red Hat Enterprise Linux. DNS, NFS, DHCP, and NTP are a few of the services that you can configure for this operating system.

DNS provides a database of domain names and IP addresses that help Web browsers and more find sites on the Internet. It's a distributed database, where each administrator is responsible for his or her own zone of authority. The diagnostic tool for DNS is now **dig**. You can also use the more traditional **nslookup** command, but it has been deprecated.

NFS allows you to share filesystems between Linux and Unix computers. This is a powerful method of controlling data and distributing I/O load, but there are many security concerns involved with its use. Be careful when setting up an NFS share on an unprotected network.

DHCP allows a network administrator to manage IP address assignments of the computers on a LAN from a centralized server. DHCP requires some specialized setup on both the client and the server; however, it is easy to maintain once it is configured.

NTP allows you to set up any computer to be synchronized to a central time standard, based on UTC.

✓ TWO-MINUTE DRILL

Here are some of the key points from the certification objectives in Chapter 9.

DNS/BIND

❑ DNS, the Domain Name System, includes a database of computer names and IP addresses.

❑ DNS is based on the Berkeley Internet Name Domain (BIND), using the named daemon.

❑ Critical DNS configuration files include /etc/named.conf and the files in the /var/named directory.

❑ Caching-only DNS servers store requests and their associated IP addresses on a computer.

❑ Every time you change DNS, remember to update the serial number in your zone file. Otherwise, other DNS servers don't realize that you've changed anything.

Network File System (NFS)

❑ NFS is the standard for sharing files and printers between Linux and Unix computers.

❑ Key NFS processes are rpc.mountd for mount requests, rpc.rquotad for quota requests and nfsd for each network share.

❑ NFS shares are configured in /etc/exports and activated with the **exportfs -a** command.

❑ Clients can make permanent connections for NFS shares through /etc/fstab.

❑ If an NFS server fails, it can "hang" an NFS client. When possible, avoid using NFS on mission-critical computers.

❑ NFS and portmap have security problems. Limit their use when possible to secure internal networks protected by an appropriate firewall.

DHCP

❑ DHCP (Dynamic Host Configuration Protocol) allows a client computer to obtain network information (such as an IP number) from a server.

❏ The bootp protocol allows a client computer to access a DHCP server on a remote network.

❏ DHCP servers are configured through /etc/dhcpd.conf.

❏ Remember that the DHCP server daemon is dhcpd; the DHCP client daemon is dhclient.

Keeping Servers in Sync

❏ You can keep the time on a server in sync with UTC using the Network Time Protocol (NTP).

❏ The configuration file for NTP is /etc/ntp.conf.

❏ The Red Hat Date/Time Configuration tool is a GUI utility that can help you configure /etc/ntp.conf.

SELF TEST

The following questions will help you measure your understanding of the material presented in this chapter. Read all the choices carefully, as there may be more than one correct answer. Choose all correct answers for each question. Don't focus exclusively on these questions. There are no longer any multiple choice questions on the Red Hat exams. These questions test your understanding of the chapter. Getting results, not memorizing trivia, is what counts on the Red Hat exams.

DNS/BIND

1. Which of the following commands check the setup of the database on your DNS server?

   A. dnscheck

   B. BIND

   C. dig

   D. resolve

2. You have added the addresses for several new servers into your primary DNS server. The zone files are formatted properly, and you've restarted the daemon called *named*. You advertise the new servers, and your help desk immediately starts getting calls that no one outside your domain can see the new servers. What is the most likely cause?

   A. Your servers are not connected to the network.

   B. The serial number was not incremented in the zone file.

   C. Someone has changed the zone files without your knowledge.

   D. The users at the other end are having ISP problems.

3. Which is an example of a properly formatted MX record?

   A. MX 10.mail.domain.com.

   B. MX mail.domain.com.

   C. MX 10 mail.domain.com

   D. MX 10 mail.domain.com.

4. Where will you find the database files associated with your DNS server?

   A. /etc/named

   B. /var/named

   C. /etc

   D. /var/bind

Network File System (NFS)

5. In the /etc/exports file, if we want to export the /data directory as read-only to all hosts and grant read and write permission to the host superv in domain.com, what is the proper entry?

   A. /data (rw,sync) superv.domain.com(ro,sync)

   B. /data (ro,sync) superv.domain.com(rw,sync)

   C. /data (ro,async) *.domain.com(rw,async)

   D. /data superv.domain.com(rw,async)

6. When Linux boots, what configuration file does Linux use to see what NFS shares to mount?

   A. /etc/exports

   B. /etc/nfs.conf

   C. /etc/fstab

   D. /nfs/conf

7. Your company has just suffered an external security breach. As a result, the security group in your department has tightened the screws on all the servers, routers, and firewalls. Up until this point, all user data had been mounted over NFS, but now, nothing works. What happened?

   A. The crackers erased the data from your NFS shared directories, and they erased the backups as well.

   B. The NFS ports are no longer allowed through the necessary firewalls.

   C. The two problems are unrelated. Make sure you have the disk space you need on your servers.

   D. The filesystem is no longer shared from the server.

8. You're experiencing problems with NFS clients for various reasons, including frequent downtime on the NFS server and network outages between NFS clients and servers. Which of the following steps can help address this problem?

   A. Remove all firewalls on individual computers inside your network.

   B. Avoid setting up mission-critical computers as NFS clients.

   C. Always make sure the portmap daemon is active before starting NFS.

   D. Configure NFS with "soft" mounts.

DHCP

9. You add a new workstation to your dhcpd.conf file. You're in a hurry to finish, so you save and go to lunch. When you return, your phone mail is full of user complaints that they can't access

the Internet, but the local network is fine. You surmise that you accidentally changed something in the dhcpd.conf file. What is the most likely cause?

A. A missing **routers** command.

B. The subnet mask was changed.

C. The IP range was thrown off.

D. The broadcast address was changed.

Keeping Servers in Sync

10. Which are proper keywords that can be used in an ntp.conf file?

A. server

B. client

C. sibling

D. child

LAB QUESTIONS

Lab 1

Your internal network is growing, and you're having trouble keeping up with the different workstations that are being added to your network on a regular basis. You use the good.example.com subdomain for your internal network, and you've named your computers for your departments, such as engr1 through engr10.good.example.com.

Your mail server is named postal, your Web server is named www, your FTP server is named ftp. You want to configure a DNS server on the computer named names. What do you need to do?

While you may not have enough information in this lab to create a complete and working file, you should be able to figure the outline of what you need to do, with the possible exception of specific IP addresses.

Lab 2

You'll need two Linux computers for this lab: one as an NFS server, a second as an NFS client. Let's call these computers nfssvr.example.com and nfsclient.example.com. On the server, you'll want to share the /home directories, and provide write permissions to the client computer. On the client, you'll want to set up the /home directory from the NFS server to be mounted the next time you boot that client computer.

Lab 3

You'll also need two Linux computers for this lab: one as a DHCP server, a second as a DHCP client. Using the DHCP server created earlier in this chapter, set up a static IP address for the computer of your choice. You'll want to assign a specific name for that server, precious.example.com, and a special IP address on the 10.11.12.0 network, 10.11.12.13. Assume that you've already set up the example.com network as well as an appropriately configured DNS server.

Lab 4

Your network has more than 500 hosts with users in three major groups wanting to share their files within their groups. There are also 30 Windows XP clients in the publishing department that cannot use the Linux OS for their proprietary software needs. Everything is time-critical, as the outputs are related to stock quotes and therefore need to be synchronized to the same clock. What should you do?

SELF TEST ANSWERS

DNS/BIND

1. ☑ **C.** **dig** checks the configuration of the DNS server against the resolv.conf file.

   ☒ **A, B,** and **D** are incorrect. Neither **dsncheck** nor **resolve** are valid commands. BIND refers to the Berkeley Internet Name Domain, the basis for the DNS software.

2. ☑ **B.** Make absolutely sure that the serial number at the top of the zone file is changed each time you revise a zone file. Otherwise, other DNS servers won't know that anything has changed in your domain, and won't update their databases.

   ☒ **A** might be correct if something strange happened to your server, but the original server name still works internally, so your service is still connected to the network. **C** and **D** are also not likely scenarios, as root access is needed locally to edit the DNS configuration files and your ISP may or may not know the addresses of your server clients.

3. ☑ **D.** Make sure the preference is defined, and the trailing "." is included at the end of the record.

   ☒ **A, B,** and **C** are incorrectly formatted.

4. ☑ **B.** By default, the database files associated with a DNS server are stored in the /var/named directory.

   ☒ **A, C,** and **D** are incorrect. There are no default /etc/named or /var/bind directories, and only the standard DNS configuration files, named.conf and named.custom, are stored in the /etc/directory. While you could reconfigure /etc/named.conf to point to different directories for DNS database files, the default is /var/named.

Network File System (NFS)

5. ☑ **B.** This answer exports the filesystem as read-only to all users; it then specifies the computer that gets read/write permission.

   ☒ **A** provides read/write to all general hosts and gives the superv.domain.com computer read-only access. **C** provides read-only to all but allows all computers on the domain.com subnet to have read/write access. **D** gives read/write access only to the superv.domain.com computer. The **sync** and **async** options can both be appropriate under different circumstances.

6. ☑ **C.** /etc/fstab can be configured with all the necessary information for a computer to mount a shared NFS directory.

   ☒ **A** refers to /etc/exports, which lists the exported NFS directories. However, it does not itself mount an NFS directory. **B** and **D** are nonexistent files.

7. ☒ **B.** Ports 111, 745, 747, and 2049 must be open through firewalls to allow NFS to function. Since the security problems associated with NFS may have been to blame for the break-in, it is a good idea to restrict its use to isolated or protected subnets.

☒ While **A**, **C**, and **D** are all possibilities you should check for, the most likely culprit is **B**.

8. ☑ **A**, **B**, **C**, and **D** are all to some extent correct. Ideally, you should be able to set NFS on computers inside a "trusted" network, which means that you can remove firewalls on computers inside that network. If you avoid setting up mission-critical computers on NFS, you'll have fewer problems with NFS. The portmap daemon has to be running before NFS can work. To some extent, **D** is the best answer, because it can help an NFS client cope with downtime on an NFS server.

☒ None of the answers are incorrect.

DHCP

9. ☑ **A.** The lack of a router declaration in /etc/dhcpd.conf would keep your hosts from getting the gateway address, which is required to access the Internet from an internal network.

☒ **B**, **C**, and **D** would probably cause a general network outage.

Keeping Servers in Sync

10. ☑ **A** is correct. In /etc/ntp.conf, a server is an alternate time server.

☒ **B**, **C**, and **D** are incorrect. The **client**, **sibling**, and **child** commands are not relevant in the ntp.conf file.

LAB ANSWERS

Lab 1

While you could subcontract out the task to an ISP, it's easy to create a DNS server for your internal network. The basic files are already available on RHEL 3. All you need to do is modify these files and add appropriate zone files to your /var/named directory. As there are problems with the Red Hat DNS Server Configuration tool, I'll describe the basics on how you can set up a DNS server by directly editing the appropriate configuration files. Assume that you're using the 10.11.12.0/255.255.255.0 network addresses for your LAN.

First, you'll need to modify the default /etc/named.conf configuration file. It's best to start by backing up this file. You'll need to add stanzas that refer to a zone and a reverse zone file. The stanzas are straightforward:

```
zone "good.example.com" IN {
    type master;
    file "good.example.com.zone";
};

zone "12.11.10.in-addr.apra" IN {
    type master;
    file "good.example.com.rr.zone";
    allow-update { none; }
};
```

Next, you can create the good.example.com.zone and good.example.com.rr.zone files in the /var/named directory. These files will contain a database of local and reverse local computer names and IP addresses for your LAN.

In the good.example.com.zone file, you'll want to create the forward database for your DNS server. It'll contain the records for your domain as well as the administrator e-mail address. There's not enough information in the problem to set up a full file, but the following principles apply.

You need to start the zone file with a general Time To Live (TTL) variable; for example, the following command sets a standard TTL (4 days) for data on this DNS server:

```
$TTL 4D
```

You'll need a Start Of Authority (SOA) record with the name of the DNS server and your administrative e-mail address. The format of the e-mail address is a little strange; the following line sets an e-mail address of admin@good.example.com. It also sets a serial number based on the date, a refresh (16 hours) and a retry frequency (4 hours), an expatriation period (2 weeks), as well as a TTL (4 days). Do note the dot at the end of each name:

```
@   IN   SOA    names.good.example.com. admin.good.example.com. (
                200402121
                16H
                4H
                2W
                4D
```

Now you can specify the computers associated with the DNS and mail servers:

```
IN   NS    names.good.example.com.
IN   MX    10 postal.good.example.com.
```

Finally, you can specify the different computers on your network. While no specific IP addresses are given, you know that you have computers with the following names that you'll have in the good.example .com.zone file. I've added arbitrary IP addresses on the given IPv4 network. You'll have to find the proper IP addresses for yourself with **ifconfig** commands on each computer:

```
engr1    IN    A    10.11.12.1
engr2    IN    A    10.11.12.2
engr3    IN    A    10.11.12.3
engr4    IN    A    10.11.12.4
engr5    IN    A    10.11.12.5
engr6    IN    A    10.11.12.6
engr7    IN    A    10.11.12.7
engr8    IN    A    10.11.12.8
engr9    IN    A    10.11.12.9
engr10   IN    A    10.11.12.10
ftp      IN    A    10.11.12.11
www      IN    A    10.11.12.12
postal   IN    A    10.11.12.13
```

Finally, to make sure that the DNS server works the next time you boot this Linux computer, you'll want to set it to run at the appropriate runlevels with a command such as the following:

```
# chkconfig --level 35 named on
```

Lab 2

This lab is the first step towards creating a single /home directory for your network. Once you get it working on a single client/server combination, you can set it up on all clients and servers. You can then use the NIS server described in Chapter 10 for a single Linux/Unix database of usernames and passwords for your network. On the NFS server, you'll want to take the following steps:

1. Set up some users and special files that you'll remember in some of the user's home directories on the server. The details are not important—just make a note of what you've done.

2. Share the /home directory in /etc/exports. You'll want to share it with the nfsclient.example .com client. You can do this in this file with the following command:

   ```
   /home nfsclient(rw,sync)
   ```

3. Export this directory with the following command:

   ```
   # exportfs -a
   ```

4. Restart the NFS service:

```
# service NFS stop
# service NFS start
```

5. Make sure that the exported /home directory shows in the export list. On the local server, you can do this with the following command:

```
# showmount -e
```

6. If you have problems with any step in this process, make sure you don't have extra spaces in /etc/exports and that the NFS service is actually running with the **service nfs status** command. You may also want to check your firewall and make sure the appropriate services described in this chapter are running with the **rpcinfo -p** command.

7. Remember to make sure that the NFS server starts automatically the next time you boot that computer. One way to do so is with the following command:

```
# chkconfig --level 35 nfs on
```

Now on the NFS client, you'll want to take the following steps to connect to the shared /home directory:

8. First, you'll want to make sure that you can see the shared /home directory. If your DNS server is not working in any of these commands, you can substitute the IP address of the appropriate computer:

```
# showmount -e nfssvr.example.com
```

9. Now you'll want to mount the share that is offered on the local /home directory:

```
# mount -t nfs nfssvr.example.com:/home /home
```

10. Check to see that the mounting has worked. If it did, you'll see the NFS mount in the output to the **mount** command.

11. Now look through the mounted /home directory for the special files that you created in step 1. If you find them from the NFS client, you've succeeded in creating and connecting to the /home directory share.

12. To make the mount permanent, you'll want to add it to your /etc/fstab file. Once you've added a command such as the following to that file, the Linux client automatically mounts the shared /home directory from the NFS server.

```
nfssvr.example.com:/home    /home    nfs    soft,timeout=100  0  0
```

Lab 3

Assuming you've read the chapter, you've seen the template in the dhcpd.conf.sample configuration file for a static IP address:

```
host ns {
     next-server marvin.redhat.com
     hardware ethernet 12:34:56:78:AB:CD;
     fixed-address 207.175.42.254;
   }
```

As described in the chapter, the **next-server** command is associated with the boot server for this computer; since there is no boot server mentioned, you won't need this command. To set up the DHCP server, take the following steps:

1. On the DHCP server computer, open the /etc/dhcpd.conf file. If this file doesn't exist, you haven't yet created a DHCP server on this computer.

2. Set up a new host in the DHCP configuration file:

   ```
   host precious {
   ```

3. On the DHCP client, run the **ifconfig** command to find the hardware address associated with that computer's Ethernet network card. For the purpose of this exercise, assume it's AB:CD:EF:12:34:56; the host command line continues as follows:

   ```
   hardware ethernet AB:CD:EF:12:34:56
   ```

4. Finally, you can complete this line by setting up the static IP address that you want to assign to the DHCP client computer:

   ```
   fixed-address 10.11.12.13
   }
   ```

5. Save your changes to the /etc/dhcpd.conf configuration file. Restart the DHCP server daemon with the following command:

   ```
   # service dhcpd restart
   ```

6. Now proceed to the DHCP client, the precious.example.com computer. You can release any current DHCP client with the following command:

   ```
   # dhclient -r
   ```

7. Finally, you can see if the DHCP client actually takes the static IP address from the DHCP server with the following commands:

   ```
   # dhclient
   # ipconfig
   ```

Lab 4

You need to configure a few services on your central host. NIS can be used to manage all the users so that all hosts use the same user IDs. Then configure a central server with Samba and NFS and sufficient disk space for the four groups, restricting each service to members of each group only. Use NTP to synchronize the NFS server to an Internet time server, if available, and then have all the other hosts synchronize their time to the NFS server host on an hourly basis. As NIS is covered in the next chapter, I don't go into additional detail here.

10

Systems Administration and Security

As a Red Hat Enterprise Linux systems manager, you probably wear several hats, one of which is security manager. This is especially true if you work for a small company. Even if you work for a large organization that has a dedicated network or systems security staff, most of the administrators are probably responsible for other operating systems. You're probably responsible for security policies on your Linux systems.

You may spend very little time thinking about Linux security, or it may turn out to be a full-time job. The level of security you choose to configure depends on many factors, including the purpose of the system and the overall security policies of your company or organization, as well as the size and number of computers in the company.

For example, a Red Hat Enterprise Linux workstation at home does not require as much security as a secure Red Hat Enterprise Linux server that is being used to process credit card orders for a Web site.

Red Hat Enterprise Linux comes with a large and varied assortment of tools for handling security. This includes tools for managing the security on individual Linux computers and tools for managing security for an entire network of systems, both Linux and otherwise. In this chapter, we look at some of the tools provided by RHEL 3 for managing security. We start out by looking at tools for controlling access to individual Linux host systems, then we look at tools for securing networks.

on the
ⓙob

You'll need to know how to protect your computer and network. Sometimes this means you'll turn off, deactivate, or even uninstall a service. Other times, you'll set specific levels of security for different users. You can even regulate the type of traffic coming in, going out, and being transferred through your computer.

You have different ways to secure your system and network. The Network Information System (NIS) and the Lightweight Directory Access Protocol (LDAP) can provide a common database of authentication and configuration files for your network. The PAM (Pluggable Authentication Module) system lets you configure how users are allowed to log in or access different services. System logging often provides the clues that you need to solve a lot of problems. The Extended Internet Services Daemon (xinetd) governs a lot of services that do not have their own individual daemons. IP aliases allow you to set up more than one IP address on a specific network card. With **iptables**, you can set up firewalls to accept or block many different kinds of network traffic. Network Address Translation allows you to protect computers inside your network by hiding their address information.

INSIDE THE EXAM

Systems Administration and Security

RHCT candidates need to know how to configure a client to directory services such as NIS and LDAP. They will also want to read the System Logging section to learn how to troubleshoot a number of basic problems. However, most of this chapter is focused on RHCE requirements. While not part of the Red Hat Exam Prep guide, NIS servers are included in the RHCE prep course outline, RH300.

With respect to the RHCE exam, focus on security. Remember to remove unneeded services to minimize the ways crackers can break into your system. Learn the PAM system, and how it allows you to customize security for different services and utilities—even by user. Understand how to implement tcp_wrappers to secure xinetd services. Learn the **iptables** command in detail. Practice with this command. Experiment with the results from remote clients.

CERTIFICATION OBJECTIVE 10.01

Configuring Directory Clients and NIS Servers

By default, access to a Linux computer requires a valid username and password. One problem with a large network of Linux systems is that "normally" each user requires an account on every Linux computer.

There are two services which allow you to set up one centrally managed database of usernames and passwords for Linux and Unix computers. These services are NIS and LDAP. With each of these services, you can maintain one password database on an NIS or LDAP server and configure the other systems on the network as clients. When a user logs into an NIS or LDAP client, that system first checks its local password file, usually /etc/passwd. If it can't find your username, it looks up the corresponding file on the server.

I'll start by showing you how to configure NIS and LDAP clients. First, I'll show you how you can configure these clients using the command line interface and then use the Red Hat Authentication Configuration tool.

NIS Client Configuration

It's fairly simple to configure an NIS client on a network. Assuming you have an NIS server, you need to do three things. First, specify the server and domain name in /etc/yp.conf. Next, make sure the **ypbind** client service starts the next time you boot Linux. Finally, make sure the /etc/nsswitch.conf file looks to the NIS service for at least the username and password database.

The change to the /etc/yp.conf configuration file is simple. All you need is a command such as the following, which specifies the name of the NIS domain as nisdomain, and the name of the NIS server as enterprise3:

```
domain nisdomain server enterprise3
```

Making sure that the **ypbind** client service starts the next time you boot Linux is a simple matter. Just as with other Linux services, you can make sure it starts at the appropriate runlevels with a command such as the following:

```
# chkconfig --level 35 ypbind on
```

Finally, making sure your computer looks for the NIS server for key files means modifying the /etc/nsswitch.conf configuration file. For example, to make sure your computer looks to the NIS server for the username and password database, you'll want to configure the following commands in that file (you can add other services such as **ldap** to the list):

```
passwd:    files nis
shadow:    files nis
group:     files nis
```

This assumes that you're using the standard version of NIS that's included with RHEL 3, NIS version 2.

One command you need to know about when running an NIS client is **yppasswd**. All users can manage their NIS password with this command.

LDAP Client Configuration

If you want to configure your RHCE 3 computer as an LDAP client, you'll need the openldap-clients, openldap, and nss_ldap RPM packages. The openldap-clients RPM is a default part of the System Tools package group. The other two packages should be installed by default on your RHEL 3 computer.

To configure an LDAP client, you'll need to configure two different ldap.conf configuration files: in the /etc and the /etc/openldap directories. While both files can get quite complex, for the purposes of the exam, I'll keep the definitions simple.

/etc/ldap.conf

The default version of the /etc/ldap.conf file includes a number of different commands and comments. To set up your RHEL 3 computer as an LDAP client, you'll need to be concerned with four commands in this file, as described in Table 10-1.

/etc/openldap/ldap.conf

You'll need to specify the HOST and BASE variables in this file, just as you did in the /etc/ldap.conf configuration file. Based on the parameters in the previous section, this leads to the following two commands:

```
HOST 127.0.0.1
BASE dc=example,dc=com
```

If your LDAP server is not on the local computer, and your domain is not example.com, you'll need to substitute accordingly.

TABLE 10-1   Some /etc/ldap.conf Parameters

Command	Description
host 127.0.0.1	Specifies the IP address for the LDAP server. This particular command assumes the LDAP server is on the local computer.
base dc=example,dc=com	Sets the default **base** distinguished name, in this case, example.com.
ssl start_tls	Required if you want Transport Layer Security (TLS) support to encrypt passwords that are sent to the LDAP server.
pam_password md5	Supports the MD5 encryption scheme for passwords.

The Name Service Switch File

The Name Service Switch file, /etc/nsswitch.conf, governs how your computer searches for key files such as password databases. You can configure it to look through NIS and LDAP server databases. For example, when an NIS client looks for a computer hostname, it might start with the following entry from /etc/nsswitch.conf:

```
hosts: files nisplus nis dns
```

This line tells your computer to search through name databases in the following order:

1. Start with the database of hostnames and IP addresses in /etc/hosts.
2. Next, search for the hostname in a map file based on NIS+ (NIS Version 3).
3. Next, search for the hostname in a map file based on NIS (Version 2).
4. If none of these databases includes the desired hostname, refer to the DNS server.

You can configure the /etc/nsswitch.conf configuration file to look at an LDAP server for the desired databases. For example, if you want to set up a centralized username and password database for your network, you'll need to configure at least the following commands in /etc/nsswitch.conf:

```
passwd:   files ldap
shadow:   files ldap
group:    files ldap
```

You can configure a number of additional files in an LDAP or NIS centralized database; however, the details are beyond the scope of this book.

Configuring Clients with the Red Hat Authentication Tool

If you're not familiar with NIS or LDAP, it may be simpler to configure your computer as a client using the Red Hat Authentication Configuration tool. In the RHEL 3 GUI, you can start it with the **redhat-config-authentication** command or click Main Menu | System Settings | Authentication. This opens the Authentication Configuration tool shown in Figure 10-1.

If you've gone through the First Boot process described in Chapter 2, you may have already configured your computer using this tool. You can set your computer to check an NIS and an LDAP server for usernames and passwords.

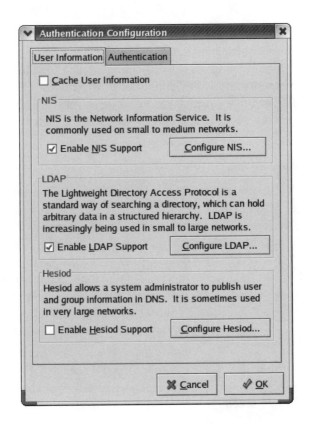

FIGURE 10-1

Authentic
Configuration

If you select Enable NIS Support, click the Configure NIS button. You'll need to enter the name of the NIS domain, as well as the name or IP address of the computer with the NIS server. Make any desired changes and click OK.

If you select Enable LDAP Support, click the Configure LDAP button. Make any desired changes and click OK. You'll need to enter the following information:

- If you want to use Transport Layer Security to encrypt the passwords sent to the LDAP server, activate the Use TLS To Encrypt Connections option.

- Enter the domain name for your server in LDAP format in the LDAP Search Base DN text box. For example, if your domain is my-domain.com, enter the following:

```
dc=my-domain.dc=com
```

- Specify the location of the LDAP server. If it's the local computer, you can use the 127.0.0.1 IP address.

Under the Authentication tab, you can also specify the use of LDAP support for PAM-aware applications.

Once you've made your changes, click OK; it may take a few seconds for the Authentication Configuration tool to write the changes to the noted configuration files before it closes. If you've set up an NIS client, it automatically sets the **ypbind** service to start at appropriate runlevels the next time you boot Linux.

NIS Services

If you want to set up an NIS server on your computer, you'll need to install the ypserv RPM. It's a part of the Network Servers package group. You'll also need the yp-tools RPM, which should already be installed by default on a RHEL 3 computer. You can verify and install these RPM packages using the techniques described throughout the book.

NIS clients and NIS servers are organized in NIS domains. In contrast, LDAP clients rely on the LDAP server database. You can have multiple NIS domains on a single network, but clients and servers can belong to only one domain. If you are using NIS, you can find out the name of your NIS domain by using this command:

```
# domainname
```

If this returns a blank or (none), you'll need to define the NIS domain name for your system. It's easy to do; for example, the following command assigns the name nisdomain to your system:

```
# domainname nisdomain
```

NIS domains are different from BIND domains. In fact, for security reasons, your NIS domain name should be different from your BIND domain name. If you are coming from the world of Microsoft Windows servers, NIS domains are analogous to LAN Manager domains.

NIS provides you with more than a shared authorization database. With NIS, you can provide shared access to any kind of information. By default, NIS under RHEL 3 shares the following files:

- /etc/passwd
- /etc/group
- /etc/hosts

- /etc/rpc
- /etc/services
- /etc/protocols

You can configure NIS to share other files as well. This is easy to configure in the NIS configuration file, /var/yp/Makefile.

NIS services require at least one *NIS master server*. This is where the centralized NIS database files, known as *maps*, are stored. NIS changes require an update to the map on the master server. You can have only one NIS master server per NIS domain.

For larger networks, you may also want an *NIS slave server*. NIS slaves take copies of the NIS maps from the master server. NIS clients can then get their configuration files from either the master server or a slave server. You can have multiple NIS slave servers on a network.

NIS clients are systems that use information from an NIS server. NIS clients don't store any information that is contained in the NIS databases; whenever that information is needed, it is retrieved from a server.

on the **Job** *You may notice that most NIS commands start with yp. This is a holdover from the previous name of NIS when it was known as the Yellow Pages service.*

Starting the NIS Service

Once you have edited the configuration files for your computer and network, you can start the NIS service. You can do so with the **ypinit** command in the /usr/lib/yp directory. This command has two key switches: **-m** is used to create a master NIS server; **-s** is used to create a slave NIS server. The process is straightforward. When you run the command to set up a master NIS server, you're prompted to enter the different hosts on the NIS domain. Here's what happened when I ran the command on my Enterprise3.example.com computer:

```
# /usr/lib/yp/ypinit -m

At this point, we have to construct a list of the hosts
which will run NIS servers. Enterprise3.example.com is
in the list of NIS server hosts. Please continue to add
the names for the other hosts, one per line. When you are
done with the list, type a <control D>.
        next host to add:  Enterprise3.example.com
        next host to add:
```

As you can see, the process is straightforward. Once I complete the list with a CTRL-D, I'm asked to verify the list. Once I confirm, the NIS server takes a few minutes to build a database based on the files specified in /var/yp/Makefile. Once complete, you'll see a message to the effect:

```
Enterprise3.example.com has been set up as an NIS master server.
```

If you see errors, make sure that the NIS server daemon, ypserv, is running properly with the **service ypserv status** command.

You can now join this NIS domain from the NIS clients of your choice.

NIS Components on Red Hat Enterprise Linux

Once you've started the NIS Service, the /usr/lib/yp directory includes the utilities you need to configure and manage NIS services. The **ypinit** program can configure an NIS server. Table 10-2 lists the files that you can use to configure an NIS server.

Although NIS was designed to enable you to manage security by controlling who has access to the systems on your network, NIS is not a very secure product. Anyone who knows your NIS domain name and can connect to your network can read all the information stored in your NIS databases, such as /etc/passwd.

TABLE 10-2   Key NIS Configuration Files and Commands

File	Description
/usr/lib/yp/ypinit	A shell script to build initial database maps in /var/yp; **ypinit -m** builds the databases for a master server.
/var/yp/Makefile	The main NIS configuration file. Edit this file to control which maps are shared via NIS. You should edit this file and run the **make** command in the /var/yp directory.
/usr/lib/yp/makedbm	Converts text database files to NIS maps. Called by /var/yp/Makefile.
/usr/sbin/ypserv	NIS server daemon. You should use a command such as **chkconfig** to make sure this starts the next time Linux boots on your computer.
/usr/sbin/yppasswdd	NIS password change daemon. You need to activate this service before users can change their NIS passwords with the **yppass** command. Use a command such as **chkconfig** to make sure this starts the next time Linux boots on your computer.
/etc/ypserv.conf	Another NIS server configuration file.
/var/yp/securenets	Controls which systems can access NIS databases.

NIS Access Control

You can do a couple of things to help protect your NIS database. The /var/yp/securenets file can control who can connect to your NIS server. While it isn't installed by default, this file is easy to create and configure. Only two lines are required for a LAN. You may notice that the lines appear backwards, as they specify IP network masks followed by network addresses:

```
255.0.0.0       127.0.0.1
255.255.255.0   192.168.0.0
```

The first line allows access from the local computer. The second line allows access from all of the computers with IP addresses on the 192.168.0.0 network. In RHEL 3, there's a template for this file, with comments, available in the /usr/share/doc/ypserv-2.8 directory.

on the
job
One security risk to keep in mind if you use NIS is that anyone with access to the root account on any system that uses NIS can use the su - username command (note the space on both sides of the hyphen) to work with any account in your NIS database.

CERTIFICATION OBJECTIVE 10.02

Basic Host Security

A network is only as secure as the most open system in that network. Although no system can be 100 percent secure, you can follow certain basic host measures to enhance the security on any given system and, consequently, your network. When devising security measures, you have to plan for two types of security violations: user accidents and break-ins.

Accidents happen because users lack adequate training or are unwilling to follow procedures. If security is too burdensome, productivity may suffer, and your users will try to get around your rules. Password security falls into this category.

When a cracker breaks into your system, some crackers may be looking for secrets such as credit card information. Others may just want to bring down your system. You can do several things to keep your network secure. Monitor Red Hat errata for the latest issues. With the **up2date** tool, you can keep your Red Hat system updated with the latest packages.

As you'll see later in this chapter, you can manage your computer's response to certain requests through the /etc/hosts.allow and /etc/hosts.deny files. You can set up protection within the kernel through firewalls based on **iptables** or **ipchains**. One simple way to promote security is to uninstall as many network access programs as possible.

e x a m

ⓦatch

While this section does not directly relate to Red Hat exam requirements, it is fundamental to the way you secure your system and network. I believe that anyone who wants to be an RHCE should be already following the principles described in this section.

Password Security

Good password security is important. Good passwords include a combination of letters, numbers, and even punctuation that isn't easily guessed. Good password security requires users to change their password on a regular basis.

e x a m

ⓦatch

On the Red Hat exams, follow the instructions carefully for any users and passwords. You do want to make sure that the person grading your exam can get into your accounts!

Password security also means disabling or deleting unused accounts. These accounts are a common way for a cracker to try to break into your system.

You can also check system log files for suspicious activity. Login records are kept in a database in /var/log/wtmp. While you can't read this file directly, you can use the utmpdump command to make this file readable. For example, the **utmpdump /var/log/wtmp** command lists recent login activity. Take a look at Figure 10-2. Note the login from IP address 172.132.4.8. If you don't have any users from a computer with that IP address, you have a reason for concern.

Security Updates

Another step you can take to keep your RHEL 3 system secure is to install the latest errata releases from Red Hat. These contain patches or fixes for problems in applications or the operating system that could result in security violations. A list of the latest errata is available as of this writing at www.redhat.com/apps/support/errata.

FIGURE 10-2

Suspicious
login activity

```
[5] [01997] [4   ] [           ] [              ] [2.4.21-4.EL      ] [0.0.0.0
    ] [Tue Dec 30 13:10:04 2003 EST]
[5] [01998] [5   ] [           ] [              ] [2.4.21-4.EL      ] [0.0.0.0
    ] [Tue Dec 30 13:10:04 2003 EST]
[6] [01996] [3   ] [LOGIN     ] [tty3          ] [                 ] [0.0.0.0
    ] [Tue Dec 30 13:10:04 2003 EST]
[6] [01999] [6   ] [LOGIN     ] [tty6          ] [                 ] [0.0.0.0
    ] [Tue Dec 30 13:10:04 2003 EST]
[5] [01999] [6   ] [           ] [              ] [2.4.21-4.EL      ] [0.0.0.0
    ] [Tue Dec 30 13:10:04 2003 EST]
[6] [01997] [4   ] [LOGIN     ] [tty4          ] [                 ] [0.0.0.0
    ] [Tue Dec 30 13:10:04 2003 EST]
[6] [01998] [5   ] [LOGIN     ] [tty5          ] [                 ] [0.0.0.0
    ] [Tue Dec 30 13:10:04 2003 EST]
[6] [01994] [1   ] [LOGIN     ] [tty1          ] [                 ] [0.0.0.0
    ] [Tue Dec 30 13:10:04 2003 EST]
[6] [01995] [2   ] [LOGIN     ] [tty2          ] [                 ] [0.0.0.0
    ] [Tue Dec 30 13:10:04 2003 EST]
[7] [01994] [1   ] [root      ] [tty1          ] [                 ] [0.0.0.0
    ] [Tue Dec 30 13:26:58 2003 EST]
[7] [02147] [/0  ] [root      ] [pts/0         ] [:0.0             ] [172.32.4.8
    ] [Tue Dec 30 13:30:35 2003 EST]
[7] [02147] [/1  ] [root      ] [pts/1         ] [:0.0             ] [0.0.0.0
:
```

Red Hat provides a built-in service to check for updates called **up2date** that you can configure if your computer is directly connected to the Internet. Just run **up2date** from a command line in the X Window of your choice. If you haven't already done so, you'll need to register the settings on your computer. Then follow the prompts; **up2date** connects to rhn.redhat.com for updates. With Red Hat Enterprise Linux 3, this assumes you've already configured your system for updates through rhn.redhat.com.

Delete Extra Services

One simple way to promote security on your system is to delete the packages associated with network services that you aren't going to use. For example, a cracker can't use Samba to break into your system if the Windows File Server package group is not installed. Any firewall or other configuration that you may add to the service still means that you are theoretically vulnerable to an attack through that service. If you're not going to use a network service, you may want to remove the associated RPM packages.

To review currently installed network services, check the /etc/xinetd.d and /etc /rc.d/init.d directories.

CERTIFICATION OBJECTIVE 10.03

The Pluggable Authentication Module (PAM) System

RHEL 3 uses the Pluggable Authentication Modules (PAM) system to check for authorized users. PAM includes a group of dynamically loadable library modules that govern how individual applications verify their users. You can modify PAM configuration files to suit your needs.

PAM modules are documented in the /usr/share/doc /pam-0.75/txts directory. For example,	*the functionality of the pam_securetty.so module is described in the README.pam_ securetty file.*

PAM was developed to standardize the user authentication process. For example, the **login** program uses PAM to require usernames and passwords at login. Open the /etc/pam.d/login file. Take a look at the first line:

```
auth   required   pam_securetty.so
```

This line means that root users can log in only from secure terminals as defined in the /etc/securetty file.

on the job *In older versions of Red Hat Linux, the full path to the PAM module was required. It is now understood that these modules are stored in the /lib /security directory.*

The configuration files shown in the /etc/pam.d directory are named after applications. These applications are "PAM aware." In other words, you can change the way users are verified for applications such as the console login program. Just modify the appropriate configuration file in the /etc/pam.d directory.

Pluggable Authentication Modules (PAM) and Associated Files

The PAM system divides the process of verifying users into four separate tasks. These are the four different types of PAM modules:

- **Authentication management (auth)** Establishes the identity of a user. For example, a PAM **auth** command decides whether to prompt for a username and or a password.

- **Account management (account)** Allows or denies access according to the account policies. For example, a PAM **account** command may deny access according to time, password expiration, or a specific list of restricted users.

- **Password management (password)** Manages other password policies. For example, a PAM **password** command may limit the number of times a user can try to log in before a console is reset.

- **Session management (session)** Applies settings for an application. For example, the PAM **session** command may set default settings for a login console.

The code shown in Figure 10-3 is an example PAM configuration file, /etc/pam.d /login. Every line in all PAM configuration files is written in the following format:

```
module_type  control_flag  module_path  [arguments]
```

The **module_type**, as described previously, can be **auth**, **account**, **password**, or **session**. The **control_flag** determines what PAM does if the module succeeds or fails. The **module_path** specifies the location of the actual PAM module file. Finally, as with regular shell commands, you can specify arguments for each module.

The **control_flag** field requires additional explanation. It determines how the configuration file reacts when a module flags success or failure. There are four different control flags, as described in Table 10-3.

To demonstrate how control flags work, take a look at the commands from the /etc/pam.d/reboot configuration file:

```
auth    sufficient    pam_rootok.so
```

The first **auth** command checks the pam_rootok.so module. If the root user runs the reboot command, the **control_flag** is **sufficient**, the other **auth** commands in this file are ignored. Linux runs the reboot command. This is explained in the README.pam_ rootok file in the /usr/share/doc/pam-0.75/txts directory.

```
auth    required    pam_console.so
```

FIGURE 10-3

The PAM /etc
/pam.d/login
module

```
#%PAM-1.0
auth       required      pam_securetty.so
auth       required      pam_stack.so service=system-auth
auth       required      pam_nologin.so
account    required      pam_stack.so service=system-auth
password   required      pam_stack.so service=system-auth
session    required      pam_stack.so service=system-auth
session    optional      pam_console.so
~
~
~
~
~
~
~
~
~
~
~
~
~
~
"/etc/pam.d/login" 8L, 329C
```

The second **auth** command is run only for nonroot users; it just governs the console parameters at the command line interface. As described in the README.pam_ console file, you can find more information about this module with the **man pam_console** command.

```
#auth    required    pam_stack.so service=system-auth
```

TABLE 10-3   PAM Control Flags

control_flag	Description
required	If the module works, the command proceeds. If it fails, go to the next command in the configuration file—but the command will still fail.
requisite	Stop the process if the module fails.
sufficient	If the module works, the login or other authentication proceeds. No other commands need be processed.
optional	PAM ignores module success or failure.

The third line is commented out by default. If you make this line active, it refers to the system-auth configuration file, which requires root user privileges. Remote users who know your root password are still allowed to reboot your computer.

```
account    required    pam_permit.so
```

The module associated with the **account** command (pam_permit.so) accepts all users, even those who've logged in remotely. In other words, this configuration file would allow any root user, local or remote, to reboot your Linux computer.

Alternatively, you might add the pam_securetty.so module, which would keep remote users from rebooting your system. This module is described in more detail earlier in this chapter.

on the
job

While it's not normal to allow just any user to shut down a corporate server, you may want to do so on a Linux workstation. In this way, users can shut down their own laptop or desktop without having to know the root account.

PAM Configuration Example: /etc/pam.d/login

This section refers back to the /etc/pam.d/login configuration file shown in Figure 10-3. When a user opens a text console and logs in, Linux goes through this configuration file line by line. As previously noted, the first line in /etc/pam.d/login:

```
auth    required    pam_securetty.so
```

limits root user access to secure terminals as defined in the /etc/securetty file. The next line brings the login program through the following service, system-auth, which also happens to be a PAM configuration file.

```
auth    required    pam_stack.so service=system-auth
```

Essentially, this calls the **auth** commands in the /etc/pam.d/system-auth configuration file shown in Figure 10-4. This sets up environment variables and allows different users to log in.

```
auth    required    pam_nologin.so
```

The last **auth** line from /etc/pam.d/login checks the /etc/nologin file.

```
account    required    pam_stack.so service=system-auth
password   required    pam_stack.so service=system-auth
```

FIGURE 10-4

The /etc/pam.d/system-auth configuration file

```
#%PAM-1.0
# This file is auto-generated.
# User changes will be destroyed the next time authconfig is run.
auth        required      /lib/security/$ISA/pam_env.so
auth        sufficient    /lib/security/$ISA/pam_unix.so likeauth nullok
auth        required      /lib/security/$ISA/pam_deny.so

account     required      /lib/security/$ISA/pam_unix.so

password    required      /lib/security/$ISA/pam_cracklib.so retry=3 type=
password    sufficient    /lib/security/$ISA/pam_unix.so nullok use_authtok md5
shadow
password    required      /lib/security/$ISA/pam_deny.so

session     required      /lib/security/$ISA/pam_limits.so
session     required      /lib/security/$ISA/pam_unix.so
~
~
~
~
~
~
~
"/etc/pam.d/system-auth" 15L, 688C
```

The **account** and **password** commands in /etc/pam.d/login also refer to the /etc/pam.d/system-auth configuration file. For more information, refer to the **account** command in /etc/pam.d/system-auth:

```
account   required    /lib/security/$ISA/pam_unix.so
```

exam watch

If the /etc/nologin file exists, regular users are not allowed to log into your console. Any regular user that tries to log in gets to read the contents of /etc/nologin as a message.

This refers to the pam_unix.so module in the /lib/security directory. The value of $ISA is normally null (empty), so you can ignore this variable. The pam_unix.so module sets up the normal username and password prompts.

For more information on the /etc/pam.d/login password command, you'll need to refer to the three **password** commands in /etc/pam.d/system-auth:

```
password required   /lib/security/$ISA/pam_cracklib.so retry=3 type=
password sufficient /lib/security/$ISA/pam_unix.so nullok use_authok md5
```

```
shadow nis
password required   /lib/security/$ISA/pam_unix.so
```

The first command from this list sets a maximum of three retries. The next command allows the use of null (zero-length) passwords, prompts the user for a password (**use_ authok**), encrypts passwords using the MD5 algorithm, supports the *shadow* password suite described in Chapter 1, and allows the use of NIS passwords.

Finally, there are two **session** commands in the /etc/pam.d/login file:

```
session    required    pam_stack.so service=system-auth
session    optional    pam_console.so
```

The first command refers to the /etc/pam.d/system-auth configuration file, which can allow you to set limits on individual users through /etc/security/limits.conf. The second command manages file permissions while users are logged onto your Linux computer.

EXERCISE 10-1

Configuring PAM

In this exercise, you can experiment with some of the PAM security features of Red Hat Enterprise Linux 3.

1. Make a backup copy of /etc/securetty with the following command:

   ```
   # cp /etc/securetty /etc/securetty.sav
   ```

2. Edit /etc/securetty and remove the lines for tty3 through tty11. Save the changes and exit.

3. Use ALT-F3 (CTRL-ALT-F3 if you're running X Window) to switch to virtual console number 3. Try to log in as root. What happens?

4. Repeat step 3 as a regular user. What happens? Do you know why?

5. Use ALT-F2 to switch to virtual console number 2 and try to log in as root.

6. Restore your original /etc/securetty file with the following command:

   ```
   # mv /etc/securetty.sav /etc/securetty
   ```

One thing to remember is that the /etc/securetty file governs the consoles from where you can log into Linux as the root user. Therefore, the changes that were made do not affect regular (non-root) users.

Securing PAM by User

In this section, you'll learn how to configure PAM to limit access to specific users. The key to this security feature is the pam_listfile.so module in the /lib/security directory. As described earlier, there are four settings in each PAM configuration command. To make sure that command respects what you do with this module, the first parts of the command should be:

```
auth required pam_listfile.so
```

The way PAM limits user access is in the last part of the command—in the details. For example, if you added the following line to a PAM configuration file, access to the associated tool would be limited to any users listed in /etc/special:

```
auth required pam_listfile.so onerr=succeed item=user \
sense=allow file=/etc/special
```

A backslash in a command line "escapes" the meaning of the next character; in the previous command, file=/etc/special is appended to the end of the command line. Due to limits in the format of this series, I've had to change the spacing of some lines and add backslashes to others.

To understand how this works, it's time to break this command into its component parts. You already know the first three parts of the command from the previous section. The switches that are shown are associated with the pam_listfile.so module, as described in Table 10-4. Based on the topic matter for the exam, this table is limited; for full details, see README.pam_listfile in the /usr/share/doc/pam-0.75/txts directory.

TABLE 10-4   Switches for the pam_listfile.so Module

pam_listfile Switch	Description
onerr	If there is a problem, tell the module what to do. The options are **onerr=succeed** or **onerr=fail**.
item	You can use this switch to limit access to a terminal (**tty**), users in a specific file (**user**), groups (**group**), or more.
sense	If the item is found in the specified **file**, take the noted action. For example, if the user is in /etc/special, and **sense=allow**, then this command allows use of the specified tool.
file	Configures a file with a list, such as **file = /etc/special**.

Thus, for the specified command, (**onerr=succeed**) an error returns success, (**item=user**) based on a specific list of users. If the user is in the specified list (**file=/etc/special**), allow that user (**sense=allow**) to access the specified tool. To see how this works, run through the steps in the following exercise.

e x a m
ⓦ a t c h
Make sure you understand how Red Hat Enterprise Linux handles user authorization through the /etc/pam.d configuration files. When you test these files, make sure you create a backup of *everything in PAM before making any changes, because any errors that you make to a PAM configuration file can disable your system completely (it is that secure).*

EXERCISE 10-2

Using PAM to Limit Access

You can also use the Pluggable Authentication Module system to limit access to regular users. In this exercise, you'll limit access by adding one or more users to the /etc/nologin file. It should work hand-in-hand with the default /etc/pam.d/login security configuration file, specifically the following line:

```
auth   required  pam_nologin.so
```

1. Look for an /etc/nologin file. If it doesn't already exist, create one with a message such as:

   ```
   I'm sorry, access is limited to the root user
   ```

2. Access another terminal with a command such as CTRL-ALT-F2. Try logging in as a regular user. What do you see?

CERTIFICATION OBJECTIVE 10.04

System Logging Configuration

An important part of maintaining a secure system is keeping track of the activities that take place on the system. If you know what usually happens, such as understanding when users log into your system, you can use log files to spot unusual activity. Red Hat Enterprise Linux 3 comes with several utilities you can use to monitor activity on a system. These utilities can help you identify the culprit if there is a problem.

RHEL 3 comes with two logging daemons. The kernel log daemon service, klogd, logs kernel messages and events. The syslog daemon, syslogd, logs all other process activity. You can use the log files that syslogd generates to track activities on your system. If you are managing multiple Red Hat Enterprise Linux systems, you can configure the syslogd daemon on each system to log messages to a central host system.

Both daemons are typically active by default, and they both can be activated by the /etc/rc.d/init.d/syslog script. Once these daemons start, the syslog daemon examines /etc/syslog.conf to find the logging options that you may have configured.

System Log Configuration File

You can configure what syslogd records through the /etc/syslog.conf configuration file. As shown in Figure 10-5, it includes a set of rules for different facilities: auth, auth-priv, cron, daemon, kern, lpr, mail, mark, news, security, syslog, user, and uucp.

Each facility is associated with several different levels of logging, known as the priority. In ascending order, log priorities are: debug, info, notice, warn, err, crit, alert, emerg. There's also a generic "none" priority which logs all messages at all levels.

For each facility and priority, log information is sent to a specific log file. For example, take the following line from /etc/syslog.conf:

```
*.info;mail.none;news.none;authpriv.none;cron.none   /var/log/messages
```

This line sends log information from all of the given facilities to the /var/log/messages file. This includes:

- All facility messages of info level and higher
- All log messages related to mail, news, authpriv (authentication), and cron

FIGURE 10-5

The syslog.conf log
configuration file

```
# Log all kernel messages to the console.
# Logging much else clutters up the screen.
#kern.*                                                 /dev/console

# Log anything (except mail) of level info or higher.
# Don't log private authentication messages!
*.info;mail.none;news.none;authpriv.none;cron.none          /var/log/message
s

# The authpriv file has restricted access.
authpriv.*                                              /var/log/secure

# Log all the mail messages in one place.
mail.*                                                  /var/log/maillog


# Log cron stuff
cron.*                                                  /var/log/cron

# Everybody gets emergency messages
*.emerg                                                        *

# Save news errors of level crit and higher in a special file.
uucp,news.crit                                          /var/log/spooler

# Save boot messages also to boot.log
local7.*                                                /var/log/boot.log


#
# INN
#
news.=crit                                       /var/log/news/news.crit
news.=err                                        /var/log/news/news.err
news.notice                                      /var/log/news/news.notice
"/etc/syslog.conf" 33L, 937C
```

You can use the asterisk as a wildcard in /etc/syslog.conf. For example, a line that starts with *.* tells the syslog daemon to log everything. A line that starts with auth.* means you want to log all messages from the auth facility.

By default, syslogd logs all messages of a given priority or higher. In other words, a cron.err line will include all log messages from the cron daemon at the err, crit, alert, and emerg levels.

Most messages from the syslog daemon are written to files in the /var/log directory. You should scan these logs on a regular basis and look for patterns that could indicate a security breach.

Managing Logs

Logs can easily become very large and difficult to read. By default, the logrotate utility creates a new log file on a weekly basis. You can also configure /etc/logrotate.conf to compress, mail, and remove desired log files. By default, the cron daemon runs logrotate on a regular basis, using the configuration files located in the /etc/logrotate.d directory. As you can see in Figure 10-6, this process works fairly well; five or more weeks of logs are kept for a number of log facilities.

The Red Hat Log Viewer

There is a new Red Hat GUI tool that can help you scan though applicable logs. It can be helpful if you don't remember the locations of the key log files and don't remember to look through /etc/syslog.conf for those locations. In the GNOME Desktop, you can start this tool from the console with the **redhat-logviewer** command or click Main Menu | System Tools | System Logs. Either option opens the tool shown in Figure 10-7.

However, this package took several minutes to load on my computer, time that you might not have during the Red Hat exams. As the Red Hat Log Viewer simply provides a front end, it's best if you know the files you need in the /var/log directory.

For example, you can review the information shown in Figure 10-7 simply by looking through the latest mail log files in the /var/log directory. And as of this writing, the regular text log files provide more complete information. On the other hand, the Red Hat Log Viewer does include warning and trouble icons that can help you identify

FIGURE 10-6
A typical set of log files in /var/log

```
[root@Enterprise3 root]# \ls /var/log/
boot.log      ksyms.3       redhat-config-network.1   squid
boot.log.1    ksyms.4       rpmpkgs                   up2date
boot.log.2    ksyms.5       rpmpkgs.1                 up2date.1
boot.log.3    ksyms.6       rpmpkgs.2                 up2date.2
cron          lastlog       rpmpkgs.3                 up2date.3
cron.1        maillog       sa                        vbox
cron.2        maillog.1     samba                     wtmp
cron.3        maillog.2     scrollkeeper.log          wtmp.1
cups          maillog.3     secure                    xdm-errors
dmesg         messages      secure.1                  xferlog
gdm           messages.1    secure.2                  XFree86.0.log
httpd         messages.2    secure.3                  XFree86.0.log.old
kdm.log       messages.3    spooler                   XFree86.1.log
ksyms.0       news          spooler.1                 XFree86.setup.log
ksyms.1       quagga        spooler.2
ksyms.2       redhat-config-network   spooler.3
[root@Enterprise3 root]#
```

FIGURE 10-7

Red Hat System
Log Viewer

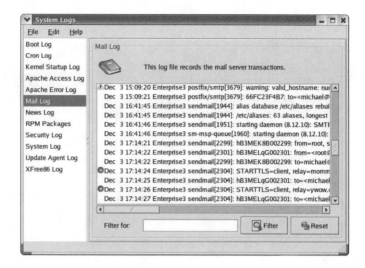

problems with specific services. Different log files and their functionality are shown in Table 10-5. This is based on the previously described configuration of the /etc/syslog.conf file. All files shown are in the /var/log directory. As you can see, the System Log tool does not cover all log files.

TABLE 10-5   Standard Red Hat Log Files

Log Files	Label in the System Log Tool	Description
boot.log	Boot Log	Associated with services that start and shut down process
cron	Cron Log	Based on scripts run by the cron daemon
cups/	Not included	Directory of printer access, page, and error logs
dmesg	Kernel Startup Log	Basic boot messages
gdm/	Not included	Directory of messages associated with starting via the GNOME Display Manager; includes login failures
httpd/	Apache Access Log Apache Error Log	Directory of log files associated with the Apache Web server
ksyms	Not included	Messages binding kernel modules (kallsyms for Linux Kernel 2.6)
maillog	Mail Log	Log messages related to the sendmail and postfix mail servers
messages	Not included	Messages from other services as defined in /etc/syslog.conf

TABLE 10-5	Standard Red Hat Log Files *(continued)*

Log Files	Label in the System Log Tool	Description
news/	News Log	Directory of log messages related to the Internet Network News (INN) service
quagga/	*Not included*	Directory of routing messages
redhat-config-network	*Not included*	Actions taken through the Red Hat Network Configuration tool
rpmpkgs	RPM Packages	Current list of installed RPM packages
sa/	*Not included*	List of memory usage information
samba/	*Not included*	Directory of access and service logs for the Samba server
scrollkeeper.log	*Not included*	Log related to GNOME documentation
secure	Security Log	Lists login and access messages
spooler	*Not included*	Print spool log
squid/	*Not included*	Directory of files related to Squid Proxy Server access, cache, and storage
up2date	Update Agent Log	Lists actions taken when you've updated your server using the Red Hat Update Agent (up2date)
wtmp	*Not included*	List of logins, in binary format; can be read with the **utmpdump** command
xdm-errors	*Not included*	Messages associated with the X Display Manager
xferlog	*Not included*	Log of files transferred from other computers, such as via FTP
XFree86	XFree86 Log	Messages during Linux GUI start process
XFree86.setup.log	*Not included*	Setup messages for the X Window System; may include configuration problems

EXERCISE 10-3

Checking Logs

In this exercise, you'll inspect the log files on your computer to try to identify different problems. You'll use the Red Hat System Log viewer, and inspect log files directly.

1. Restart your Linux computer. Log in as the root user. Use the wrong password once. Log in properly as the root user.

2. Open a GUI desktop interface.

3. Open the Red Hat System Log Viewer. Click Main Menu | System Tools | System Logs. Depending on the speed of your computer and the size of your logs, this may take a few minutes.

4. In the System Logs window, navigate to the Security Log area in the left pane. Scroll to the bottom of the screen. You should see a red "X" with a "FAILED LOGON" message.

5. In a console, navigate to the /var/log directory and open the file named secure. Navigate to the same "FAILED LOGON" message.

6. Look through the other logs in the System Logs window and close this tool. Close the secure file.

CERTIFICATION OBJECTIVE 10.05

The Extended Internet Services Daemon (xinetd)

Linux typically supports network communication between clients and servers. For example, you can use Telnet to connect to a remote system. The Telnet client on your computer makes a connection with a Telnet server daemon on the remote system. This section assumes that you have the default RHEL 3 krb5-workstation RPM package, which includes a more secure version of Telnet.

on the **Job**

If you're working with Red Hat Linux 9, you can also work with the telnet-server RPM. Some of the commands with this older Telnet server are different from what you see here.

To establish the connection on a TCP/IP network, a client application needs the IP address of the server, and the *port number* associated with the server daemon. All common TCP/IP applications have a standard port number; some examples are shown in Table 10-6.

Port Number	Service
21	FTP
23	Telnet
25	SMTP (outgoing mail)
80	HTTP
443	HTTPS (secure HTTP)
631	Internet Printing Protocol (CUPS configuration)

TABLE 10-6

Typical TCP/IP
Port Numbers

If you don't specify the port number, TCP/IP assumes that you're using the default port for the specified service. Clients can't connect unless the corresponding server is running on the remote system. If you are managing a server, you may have a number of server daemons to start when Linux is booted.

The xinetd (which stands for Extended Internet Services Daemon) program can start a number of these server daemons simultaneously. The xinetd program listens for connection requests for all of the *active* servers with scripts in the /etc/xinetd.d directory. There's a generic configuration file for xinetd services, /etc/xinetd.conf. The scripts in the /etc/xinetd.d directory also function as service specific configuration files.

Generic xinetd Configuration

The generic configuration for xinetd services is stored in the /etc/xinetd.conf file. It's short and fairly straightforward, so we can analyze it line by line. First, there are a number of default settings that are started with the following command:

```
defaults
```

This allows services such as POP3 to retain their default TCP/IP ports (110). This is followed by:

```
instances = 60
```

which limits the number of active services for a particular service; in this case, no more than 60 users can be logged into your Kerberos Telnet server simultaneously. The following line means that log messages are sent as specified in /etc/syslog.conf.

```
log_type = SYSLOG authpriv
```

The following line means that for each successful logon to a xinetd service, the name (or IP address) of the remote computer and the process ID (PID) are sent to the appropriate log file.

```
log_on_success = HOST PID
```

The next line means that whenever there is a failed attempt to log on to an xinetd service, the name (or IP address) of the remote computer and reason is sent to the appropriate log file.

```
log_on_failure = HOST
```

The **cps** command prevents attempts to "flood" any xinetd service; this line limits connections to 25 per second. If this limit is exceeded, xinetd waits 30 seconds before allowing a remote user to try again.

```
cps = 25 30
```

Finally, the last line supports the use of the other configuration files specified in the /etc/xinetd.d directory.

```
includedir /etc/xinetd.d
```

Sample xinetd Configuration

Each file in the /etc/xinetd.d directory specifies a particular service you want to allow xinetd to manage. By default, scripts in this directory are disabled. The following code shows a sample of the /etc/xinetd.d/krb5-telnet configuration file, with this service disabled:

```
# default: on
# description: The telnet server serves telnet sessions; it uses \
#       unencrypted username/password pairs for authentication.
service telnet
{
    flags           = REUSE
    socket_type     = stream
    wait            = no
    user            = root
    server          = /usr/Kerberos/sbin/telnetd
    log_on_failure  += USERID
    disable         = yes
}
```

TABLE 10-7	Standard Parameters for xinetd Configuration Files

Field	Description of Field Entry
flags	Supports different parameters for the service; REUSE is a default which supports continuous use of the service. Options include IPv6 to set this as a service for those types of networks.
socket_type	Specifies the communication stream.
wait	Set to yes for single-threaded applications, or no for multithreaded applications.
user	Account under which the server should run.
group	Group under which the server should run.
server	The server program.
only_from	Hostname or IP address allowed to use the server. CIDR notation (such as 192.168.0.0/24) is okay.
no_access	Hostname or IP address not allowed to use the server. CIDR notation is okay.
log_on_failure	If there's a failed login attempt, this specifies the information sent to a log file.
disable	Yes by default, which disables the service.

This is a typical /etc/xinetd.d configuration file. The variables (and a few additional variables that you can use) are described in Table 10-7. This is a versatile configuration file; other fields are described in the man pages for xinetd.conf. Read this man page; the only_from and no_access fields may be of particular interest.

You have two ways to activate a service. You can edit the configuration file directly by changing the disable field from no to yes. Then make the xinetd daemon reread the configuration files with the **service xinetd reload** command.

Alternatively, you can use the **chkconfig** *servicename* **on** command, which automatically makes this change and makes xinetd reread the configuration file.

e x a m

w a t c h
CIDR notation is based upon Classless Inter-Domain Routing. Under CIDR, you do not need to specify the full IPv4 subnet address; 192.168.0.0
/255.255.255.0 is the same as 192.168.0.0 /24. As of this writing, the Red Hat exams do not require any detailed understanding of IPv6 addresses.

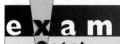

e x a m

watch   *Always remember to make sure that a service will be active after a reboot. The chkconfig servicename on command is one way to do this for xinetd services.*

Otherwise, anything you configure may not work after your computer is rebooted—and you may not get credit for how you configured that service on your exam.

EXERCISE 10-4

Configuring xinetd

In this exercise, you will enable the Telnet service using xinetd. Attempt to establish a Telnet session using the command **telnet localhost**. If you're successful, Telnet is already enabled; disable it first with the **chkconfig krb5-telnet off** command.

1. Edit /etc/xinetd.d/telnet and change the value of disable from yes to no.

2. Tell xinetd to reread its configuration file using the command:

   ```
   # service xinetd reload
   ```

3. Try the **telnet localhost** command again. It should work.

4. Use the **chkconfig** command to disable Telnet. Try connecting to the Telnet server again. Do you have to restart or reload xinetd?

5. What happens when you use **chkconfig** to enable Telnet? Does it change the /etc/xinted.d/telnet configuration file?

Security by User or Host

The best way to prevent a cracker from using a service is to remove it completely from your Linux system. However, you may want to keep a service loaded because you're planning to use it in the near future.

You can achieve some measure of security by disabling or removing unused services in the /etc/xinetd.d directory. But you need to take other measures to protect yourself against attacks through enabled services. With xinetd, you have two approaches. You can set up fields in individual /etc/xinetd.d configuration files to block computers by hostname or IP address. Alternatively, you can block access to specific users, computers, or even networks through the hosts.allow or hosts.deny files in the /etc directory. This system is known as tcp_wrappers, which is enabled by default.

When xinetd receives a network request for a service, it passes the request on to tcp_wrappers. This system logs the request and then checks its access rules. If there are no limits on the particular host or IP address, tcp_wrappers passes control back to xinetd to start the needed service.

The key files are hosts.allow and hosts.deny. The philosophy is fairly straightforward; clients listed in hosts.allow are allowed access; clients listed in hosts.deny are denied access. When xinetd receives a request, the tcp_wrappers system takes the following steps:

1. It searches /etc/hosts.allow. If tcp_wrappers finds a match, it grants access.

2. It searches /etc/hosts.deny. If tcp_wrappers finds a match, it denies access.

3. If the host isn't found in either file, access is automatically granted to the client.

You use the same access control language in both /etc/hosts.allow and /etc/hosts.deny to tell tcp_wrappers which clients to allow or deny. The basic format for commands in each file is as follows:

```
daemon_list : client_list
```

The simplest version of this format is:

```
ALL : ALL
```

This specifies all services managed by xinetd and makes the rule applicable to all hosts on all IP addresses. If you set this line in /etc/hosts.deny, all access is prohibited to all services. However, you can create finer filters. For example, the following line:

```
telnetd : 192.168.1.5
```

in /etc/hosts.allow allows the client with an IP address of 192.168.1.5 to connect to your system through Telnet. The same line in /etc/hosts.deny would prevent the computer with that IP address from using Telnet to connect to your system. You can specify clients a number of different ways, as shown in Table 10-8.

As you can see in Table 10-8, there are two different types of wildcards. ALL can be used to represent any client or service. The dot (.) specifies all hosts with the specified domain name or IP network address.

TABLE 10-8	Sample Commands in /etc/hosts.allow and /etc/hosts.deny

Client	Description
.example.com	Domain name. Since this domain name begins with a dot, it specifies all clients on the example.com domain.
172.16.	IP address. Since this address ends with a dot, it specifies all clients with an IP address of 172.16.x.y.
172.16.72.0/255.255.254.0	IP network address with subnet mask. CIDR notation not recognized.
ALL	Any client, any daemon.
user@linux1.example.com	Applies to the specific user on the given computer.

You can set up multiple services and addresses with commas. Exceptions are easy to make with the EXCEPT operator. See the following excerpt from a /etc/hosts.allow file for an example:

```
#hosts.allow
ALL :.example.com
telnetd : 192.168.25.0/255.255.255.0 EXCEPT 192.168.25.73
in.pop3d, in.tftpd : 192.168.1.10
```

The first line in this file is simply a comment. The next line opens ALL xinetd services to all computers in the example.com domain. The following line opens the Telnet service to any computer on the 192.168.25.0 network, except the one with an IP address of 192.168.25.73. Then, the POP3 and TFTP services are opened to the computer with an IP address of 192.168.1.10.

The code that follows contains a hosts.deny file to see how lists can be built to control access.

```
#hosts.deny
ALL EXCEPT in.tftpd : .xyz.com
telnetd : ALL EXCEPT 192.168.1.10
ALL:ALL
```

The first line in the hosts.deny file is a comment. The second line denies all services except TFTP to computers in the .xyz.com domain. The third line states that the only computer that is allowed to access our Telnet server has an IP address of 192.168.1.10. Finally, the last line is a blanket denial; all other computers are denied access to all services controlled by tcp_wrappers.

TABLE 10-9	Field	Description	Field	Description
tcp_wrappers Operators	%a	Client address	%h	Client hostname
	%A	Host address	%H	Server hostname
	%c	Client information	%p	Process ID
	%d	Process name	%s	Server information

You can also use the **twist** or **spawn** command in /etc/hosts.allow or /etc/hosts.deny to access shell commands; primarily they're intended to send messages, track access, and log problems. For example, take the following line in a /etc/hosts.deny file:

```
telnetd : .crack.org : twist /bin/echo Sorry %c, access denied
```

This sends a customized error message for Telnet users on the crack.org domain. Different operators such as **%c** are described in Table 10-9. Some of these operators may be able to help you track the intruder.

EXERCISE 10-5

Configuring tcp_wrappers

In this exercise, you will use tcp_wrappers to control access to network resources. Since tcp_wrappers is enabled by default, you shouldn't have to make any modifications to /etc/xinetd.conf.

1. Verify that you can telnet to the system using the address localhost.
2. Edit /etc/hosts.deny and add the following line (don't forget to write the file):
   ```
   ALL : ALL
   ```
3. What happens when you try to telnet to the address localhost?
4. Edit /etc/hosts.allow and add the following line:
   ```
   telnetd : 127.0.0.1
   ```
5. Now what happens when you try to telnet to the address localhost?
6. If you have other systems available to you, try restricting access to the Telnet service using some of the other tcp_wrappers rules.
7. Undo your changes when finished.

CERTIFICATION OBJECTIVE 10.06

Firewall Policies

A firewall sits between your company's internal LAN and an outside network. A firewall can be configured to examine every network packet that passes into or out of your LAN. When configured with appropriate rules, it can filter out those packets that may pose a security risk to your system. To understand how *packet filtering* works, you have to understand a little bit about how information is sent across networks.

Before you send a message over a network, the message is broken down into smaller units called *packets*. Administrative information, including the type of data, the source address, and destination address, is added to each packet. The packets are reassembled when they reach the destination computer. A firewall examines these administrative fields in each packet to determine whether to allow the packet to pass.

Red Hat Enterprise Linux 3 comes with everything you need to configure a system to be a firewall. Three basic Linux firewall commands are available: **ipfwadm**, **ipchains**, and **iptables**. The first command, **ipfwadm**, was associated with Linux kernel 2.0.x and is now generally obsolete. The **ipchains** command was developed for Linux kernel 2.2.x and is still in active use, even on Linux distributions based on Linux kernel 2.4.x. But the default is **iptables**, which is available by default for RHEL 3.

e x a m

ⓦatch   *The Linux 2.4.x kernel firewalling subsystem is also known as the netfilter/iptables project. The current RH300 course refers to netfilter. The Red Hat firewall tools create iptables (IP version 4) commands. Therefore, I've focused this section on iptables.*

on the ⓙob   *RHEL 3 also includes a firewall command for IPv6 networks, ip6tables.*

Configuring iptables

The philosophy behind **iptables** is based on "chains." These are sets of rules applied to each network packet. Each rule does two things: it specifies the conditions a packet must meet to match the rule, and it specifies the action if the packet matches.

Before you can set up **iptables** commands, you need to make sure that the appropriate modules are part of your Linux kernel. Check your current rules. Run the **iptables -L** command to list the current chains. If you see error messages similar to the following:

```
iptables: Incompatible with this kernel
```

you'll need to upgrade your modules. Use the **rmmod *modulename*** command to delete any **ipchains**-related modules. Then use the **insmod ip_tables** command to add the **iptables** kernel module. Now you're ready to start configuring **iptables** rules.

The **iptables** command uses the following basic format:

```
iptables -t tabletype <action/direction> <packet pattern> -j <what to do>
```

Now let us analyze this command, step by step. First there is the **-t *tabletype*** switch. There are two basic *tabletype* options for **iptables**:

- **filter**   This sets a rule for filtering packets.
- **nat**   This configures Network Address Translation, which is discussed in the last section of this chapter.

The default is **filter**; if you don't specify a **-t *tabletype***, the **iptables** command assumes that you're trying to affect a filtering rule. Next is the **<*action/direction*>**. There are four basic actions associated with **iptables** rules:

- **-A (--append)**   Appends a rule to the end of a chain.
- **-D (--delete)**   Deletes a rule from a chain. Specify the rule by the number or the packet pattern.
- **-L (--list)**   Lists the currently configured rules in the chain.
- **-F (--flush)**   Flushes all of the rules in the current **iptables** chain.

If you're appending to (**-A**) or deleting from (**-D**) a chain, you'll want to apply it to network data traveling in one of three directions:

- **INPUT**   All incoming packets are checked against the rules in this chain.

- **OUTPUT**   All outgoing packets are checked against the rules in this chain.
- **FORWARD**   All packets being sent to another computer are checked against the rules in this chain.

Next, you need to configure a *<packet pattern>*. Your firewall checks every packet against this pattern. The simplest pattern is by IP address:

- **-s** *ip_address*   All packets are checked for a specific source IP address.
- **-d** *ip_address*   All packets are checked for a specific destination IP address.

Packet patterns can be more complex. In TCP/IP, packets are transported using the TCP, UDP, or ICMP protocol. You can specify the protocol with the **-p** switch, followed by the destination port (**--dport**). For example, the **-p tcp --dport 80** extension prevent users outside your network from looking for an HTTP connection.

Once the **iptables** command finds a packet pattern match, it needs to know what to do with that packet, which leads to the last part of the command, **-j** *<what to do>*. There are three basic options:

- **DROP**   The packet is dropped. No message is sent to the requesting computer.
- **REJECT**   The packet is dropped. An error message is sent to the requesting computer.
- **ACCEPT**   The packet is allowed to proceed as specified with the **-A** action: **INPUT**, **OUTPUT**, or **FORWARD**.

We will look at some examples of how you can use **iptables** commands to configure a firewall. The first step is always to see what is currently configured, with the following command:

```
# iptables -L
```

If **iptables** is properly configured, it should return chain rules in three different categories: **INPUT**, **FORWARD**, and **OUTPUT**.

Let's look at some examples. The following command defines a rule that rejects all traffic from the 192.168.75.0 subnet, and it sends a "destination unreachable" error message back to any client that tried to connect:

```
# iptables -A INPUT -s 192.168.75.0/24 -j REJECT
```

This rule stops users from the computer with an IP address of 192.168.25.200 from "pinging" your system (remember that the **ping** command uses the ICMP protocol):

```
# iptables -A INPUT -s 192.168.25.200 -p icmp -j DROP
```

The following command guards against TCP SYN attacks from outside our network. Assume that your network IP address is 192.168.1.0. The exclamation point (!) inverts the meaning; in this case, the command applies to all IP addresses except those with a 192.168.1.0 network address (and a 255.255.255.0 subnet mask).

```
# iptables -A INPUT -s !192.168.1.0/24 -p tcp -j DROP
```

Then, if you wanted to delete the rule related to the **ping** command in this list, use the following command:

```
# iptables -D INPUT -s 192.168.25.200 -p icmp -j DROP
```

The default rule for **INPUT, OUTPUT,** and **FORWARD** is to **ACCEPT** all packets. One way to stop packet forwarding is to add the following rule:

```
# iptables -A FORWARD -j DROP
```

Maintaining Netfilter Rules

Once you've added the **iptables** commands of your choice, the following command saves your new firewall configuration to a file:

```
# service iptables save
```

This saves your chains in the /etc/sysconfig/iptables configuration file. The **iptables** service script then reads this file, if it is active for the appropriate runlevel when you start Linux. You can configure **iptables** so that it is active for all network runlevels (2, 3, 4, and 5) with the **chkconfig** command, as follows:

```
# chkconfig --level 2345 iptables on
# chkconfig --list iptables
iptables        0:off   1:off   2:on    3:on    4:on    5:on    6:off
```

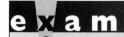

<table>
<tr><td>Knowing how to secure a Red Hat Enterprise Linux system against unauthorized access is critical.</td><td>Be sure you understand the concepts and commands discussed in this chapter.</td></tr>
</table>

The Red Hat Firewall Configurator

You can automate the process of configuring a firewall. RHEL 3 includes the Security Level Configuration tool. You can start it with the **redhat-config-securitylevel** command, or by clicking Main Menu | System Settings | Security Level. This is a straightforward tool, as shown in Figure 10-8.

If you've installed RHEL 3 before, this menu should look familiar; the choices are identical to those shown during the standard RHEL 3 installation process. There is a similar text-based version of this tool, which you can start with the **redhat-config-securitylevel-tui** or **lokkit** commands.

Red Hat has changed this tool for RHEL 3; there are no longer three security levels available. You can enable or disable a firewall for your computer. The default firewall loosely corresponds to the "High Security" firewall that you could have configured for Red Hat Linux 9.

- The default RHEL firewall blocks all inbound request traffic unless requested from within the network. For example, DNS replies are allowed.

- No security disables any rules that you've previously created using the Red Hat Firewall Configurator. It does not delete any rules that you've created directly with the **iptables** command.

FIGURE 10-8

The Security Level Configuration tool

You can create exceptions to each rule. First, firewalls are not applied to "Trusted Devices." Therefore, if you have multiple network card on your computer, you can apply firewall rules only to one network card—say, on the card that is directly exposed to the Internet.

As shown in Figure 10-8, you can allow incoming traffic to a number of services. For example, if you select WWW (HTTP), others can connect to a Web server on your computer. With the available settings, you can also allow incoming connections to

- A Web server, by activating the WWW (HTTP) option.
- An FTP server such as the vsFTP service, by activating the FTP option.
- A Secure Shell (SSH) service, by activating the SSH option. This is a common method for administering remote Linux computers; you'll read more about SSH in Chapter 11.
- Telnet, by activating the Telnet option. This also works with the Kerberos-based Telnet service described earlier in this chapter.
- Mail services through the sendmail or Postfix services described in Chapter 7, by activating the Mail (SMTP) option.

The settings that you create are documented in /etc/sysconfig/iptables. But there may be more firewall rules. You may have added some firewall chains with an **iptables** command.

In this case, the text-based version of this tool is more customizable. As you can see in Figure 10-9, you can use the "Other Ports" text box to allow data to come through using other incoming TCP/IP ports.

For example, if you wanted to allow secure Web communication through your firewall, you could enter the following line in the Other Ports text box:

```
443:udp,443:tcp
```

This opens communication through the TCP/IP ports associated with Secure Web services, and is equivalent to the following **iptables** commands:

```
# iptables -A INPUT -p udp --dport 443 -j ACCEPT
# iptables -A INPUT -p tcp --dport 443 -j ACCEPT
```

FIGURE 10-9

Customizing the use of the Red Hat Security Level tool in text mode

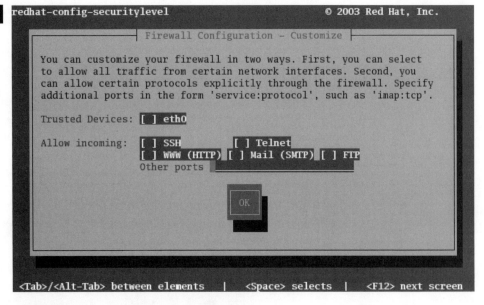

CERTIFICATION OBJECTIVE 10.07

Network Address Translation

Network Address Translation (NAT) lets you hide the IP address of the computers on your network that make a connection to the Internet. NAT replaces the source address with the IP address of the firewall computer, which also serves as a gateway between your network and the Internet. The source address is cached on the gateway, so it knows which computer made the request.

When the firewall receives data such as a Web page, the process is reversed. As the packets pass through the firewall, the originating computer is identified in the cache. The header of each packet is modified accordingly before the packets are sent on their way.

This approach is useful for several reasons. Disguising your internal IP addresses makes it harder for someone to break into your network. NAT allows you to connect computers to the Internet without having to have an official IP address for each computer. This allows you to use the private IP addresses discussed in Chapter 1 on your internal LAN. In the Linux world, this process is known as IP masquerading.

IP Masquerading

Red Hat Enterprise Linux supports a variation of NAT called *IP masquerading*. IP masquerading allows you to provide Internet access to multiple computers with a single officially assigned IP address. IP masquerading lets you map multiple internal IP addresses to a single valid external IP address.

Connecting multiple systems to the Internet using IP masquerading is a fairly straightforward process. Your firewall computer will need one network card to connect to your LAN, and a second network card for the Internet. This second network card can be a telephone modem, or it can be connected to a cable "modem" or DSL adapter. This configuration requires that you do the following:

- Assign your official IP address to the network card that is directly connected to the Internet.
- Assign computers on your LAN one of the private IP addresses described in Chapter 1.
- Reserve one private IP address for the network card on your firewall that is connected to the LAN.
- Use **iptables** to set up IP masquerading.
- Enable IP forwarding on the firewall computer.
- Configure the computers on your LAN with the IP address of your firewall computer as their Internet gateway.

Let us take a careful look at when a message comes from a computer on a LAN, through a firewall, to the Internet. When a computer on your LAN wants a Web page on the Internet, it sends packets to the firewall. The firewall replaces the source IP address on each packet with the firewall's official IP address. It then assigns a new port number to the packet. The firewall caches the original source IP address and port number.

When a packet comes in from the Internet to the firewall, it should include a port number. If your firewall can match it with the port number assigned to a specific outgoing packet, the process is reversed. The firewall replaces the destination IP address and port number with the internal computer's private IP address and then forwards the packet back to original client on the LAN.

The next step in the process is to use **iptables** to enable masquerading. The following command assumes that eth1 represents the network card that is directly connected to the Internet, and that your LAN has a network address of 192.168.0.0/24:

```
# iptables -t nat -A POSTROUTING -s 192.168.0.0/24 -o eth1 -j MASQUERADE
```

The following command enables FTP access through your firewall:

```
# modprobe -a ip_conntrack_ftp ip_nat_ftp
```

Similar modules are available in your kernel directory, in the following subdirectory:

```
/usr/src/linux-2-4/net/ipv4/netfilter
```

But there is one more thing. IP masquerading does not work unless you've enabled IP forwarding, as described in the next section.

IP Forwarding

IP forwarding is more commonly referred to as *routing*. Routing is critical to the operation of the Internet or any IP network. Routers connect and facilitate communication between multiple networks. When you set up a computer to find a site on an outside network, you need a gateway address. This corresponds to the IP address of your router on your LAN.

A router looks at the destination IP address of each packet. If the IP address is on one of its LANs, it routes the packet directly to the proper computer. Otherwise, it sends the packet to another gateway closer to its final destination. To be able to use a Red Hat Enterprise Linux system as a router, you must enable IP forwarding in the /etc/sysctl.conf configuration file by changing:

```
net.ipv4.ip_forward = 0
```

to

```
net.ipv4.ip_forward = 1
```

These settings take effect the next time you reboot your system. Until you reboot, you can enable forwarding directly in your kernel with the following command:

```
echo 1 > /proc/sys/net/ipv4/ip_forward
```

Now that you have seen some of the security capabilities of Red Hat Enterprise Linux, refer to the following Scenario & Solution for some possible scenario questions and their answers.

SCENARIO & SOLUTION	
You have installed an e-mail server on your corporate network, and you want to restrict access to certain departments. Each department has its own subnet.	Use the /etc/hosts.deny file in the tcp_wrappers package to block e-mail access (**ipop3d**) to the unwanted subnets.
You have only one official IP address, but you need to provide Internet access to all of the systems on your LAN. Each computer on the LAN has its own private IP address.	Use **iptables** to implement IP masquerading. Make sure IP forwarding is active.
You have a LAN of Linux and Unix computers, and want to implement a single authentication database of usernames and passwords for the network.	Implement NFS file sharing on the network. Set up an NIS server. Set up the other computers on your LAN as NIS clients.
You want to modify the commands associated with halting and rebooting your computer so they're accessible only to the root user.	Set up the appropriate Pluggable Authentication Module configuration files in /etc/pam.d to use the system-auth module.

CERTIFICATION SUMMARY

One of the basic functions of a Red Hat Enterprise Linux system administrator is to protect a Linux computer and a network from inside and outside attacks. RHEL 3 includes a variety of tools that can help you establish a secure computing environment.

RHEL 3 includes powerful tools for securing networks from outside attack. You can use centralized account management with an NIS service. Log files can be configured to collect data from any number of services. Pluggable Authentication Modules can help you configure how individual services verify usernames and passwords. The Extended Internet Services daemon, xinetd, governs the services configured through the /etc/xinetd.d directory.

With tcp_wrappers and **iptables** at your disposal, you can create a firewall which can protect your RHEL 3 system as well as the computers on your LAN. Firewalls require a computer with at least two network cards. Routing must be enabled on that computer. The firewall can include IP masquerading to hide the IP addresses of the computers inside your LAN.

✓ TWO-MINUTE DRILL

The following are some of the key points from the certification objectives in Chapter 10.

Configuring NIS Clients and Servers

❏ NIS allows you to configure one centrally managed username and password database with other Linux and Unix systems on your LAN.

❏ With NIS, you maintain one password database on an NIS server and configure the other systems on the network to be NIS clients.

❏ You can configure NIS to share other configuration files, including many of those in the /etc directory.

❏ The NIS server stores the centralized NIS database files, which are also known as maps.

❏ You can have only one NIS master server per NIS domain.

Basic Host Security

❏ Password security requires good passwords from your users.

❏ You can check for suspicious login activity with the **utmpdump /var/log/wtmp** command.

❏ Many security updates are available through Red Hat errata releases.

❏ The best way to promote security is to delete the packages associated with services that you do not need.

The Pluggable Authentication Module (PAM) System

❏ Red Hat Enterprise Linux uses the Pluggable Authentication Modules (PAM) system to check for authorized users.

❏ PAM modules are called by configuration files in the /etc/pam.d directory. These configuration files are usually named after the service or command that they control.

❏ There are four types of PAM modules: authentication, account, password, and session management.

❏ PAM configuration files include lines that list the module_type, the control_ flag, the path to the actual module, followed by arguments such as system-auth.

❏ PAM modules are well documented in the /usr/share/doc/pam-0.75/txts directory.

System Logging Configuration

❑ Red Hat Enterprise Linux includes two logging daemons: **klogd** for kernel messages and **syslogd** for all other process activity. Both are activated by the syslog service script.

❑ You can use log files generated by the syslogd daemon to track activities on your system.

❑ Most log files are stored in /var/log.

❑ You can configure what is logged through the syslog configuration file, /etc/syslog.conf.

The Extended Internet Services Daemon (xinetd)

❑ xinetd is the Extended Internet Services Daemon, which acts as a "super-server" for a number of other network services, such as IMAP, POP, and Telnet.

❑ Individual services have their own management scripts in the /etc/xinetd.d directory.

❑ Most xinetd services are disabled by default.

❑ You can activate an xinetd service with the appropriate **chkconfig** command, or by directly editing its xinetd script.

❑ xinetd listens for connection requests from client applications.

❑ When xinetd receives a connection request, it starts the server associated with the TCP/IP port, then waits for other connection requests.

❑ Red Hat Enterprise Linux comes with a package known as libwrap or tcp_wrappers. This package, which is enabled by default, allows you to limit access to various xinetd services.

❑ You configure the access rules for tcp_wrappers through the /etc/hosts.allow and /etc/hosts.deny configuration files.

❑ Clients listed in /etc/hosts.allow are allowed access; clients listed in /etc/hosts.deny are denied access.

❑ Services can also be configured in /etc/hosts.allow and /etc/hosts.deny. Remember to use the actual name of the daemon, such as telnetd.

Firewall Policies

❑ Firewalls can secure an internal network as a packet filter that controls the information that comes in, goes out, and is forwarded through the internal network.

❑ The current firewall configuration utility is **iptables**, which has replaced **ipchains**.

❑ The **iptables** utility retains a number of elements of **ipchains**. **iptables** directives are sets of rules, chained together, which are compared and then applied to each network packet.

❑ Each rule sets conditions required to match the rule, and then specifies the action taken if the packet matches the rule.

❑ Use the **service iptables save** command to save any chains that you configure in the /etc/sysconfig/iptables configuration file.

Network Address Translation

❑ NAT modifies the header in packets coming from a LAN. It replaces the source address with the public address of the firewall computer, with a random port number.

❑ Linux supports a variation of NAT called IP masquerading.

❑ IP masquerading allows you to provide Internet access to multiple computers with a single officially assigned IP address.

❑ With IP masquerading, messages for the network are sorted by the random port number. The original source address is taken from the cache and added to the packet, so the message gets to the right computer.

❑ A firewall computer needs at least two network cards: one on the LAN, and the other on an external network such as the Internet.

❑ IP forwarding is more commonly known as routing.

❑ Routing is critical to the operation of the Internet or any IP network.

❑ To enable IP forwarding, edit /etc/sysctl.conf and change the line net.ipv4.ip_forward = 1.

❑ To enable IP forwarding immediately, type the **echo 1 > /proc/sys/net/ipv4/ip_forward** command.

SELF TEST

The following questions will help you measure your understanding of the material presented in this chapter. Read all the choices carefully, as there may be more than one correct answer. Choose all correct answers for each question. Don't focus exclusively on these questions. There are no longer any multiple choice questions on the Red Hat exams. These questions test your understanding of the chapter. Getting results, not memorizing trivia, is what counts on the Red Hat exams.

Configuring NIS Clients

1. You have a network with 50 Linux workstations and five Linux servers. Most of the workstations are in public areas, and your users need to be able to log in from any workstation on the network. What is the most efficient way to satisfy this requirement?

    A. Keep a master copy of /etc/passwd on one of the servers, and do a backup and restore of that copy to all the workstations every evening.

    B. Set one of the servers up to be an NIS server. Arrange another server to be an NIS slave server. Make the workstations NIS clients.

    C. Set the workstations up to be NIS clients.

    D. Create a common account on every workstation and give each person the password to this account.

2. How would you set up the workstations to be NIS clients?

    A. Edit /etc/passwd and add the **USE_NIS** command at the end of the file.

    B. Start the ypbind daemon, and configure it to start the next time you boot Linux.

    C. Add a command to /etc/xinetd.conf to start the ypbind daemon.

    D. Run the Red Hat Authentication Configuration Utility and enable NIS.

Basic Host Security

3. Which of the following measures is the most effective way to prevent attacks through various network services?

    A. Disable a service in the appropriate /etc/xinetd.d configuration file.

    B. Block service requests with the appropriate commands in /etc/hosts.deny.

    C. Use a firewall to drop all requests to unneeded services.

    D. Uninstall unneeded network services.

The Pluggable Authentication Module (PAM) System

4. What are the four areas associated with Pluggable Authentication Modules?

 A. Authentication management, account management, session management, and password management

 B. Authentication management, account management, network management, and password management

 C. Authentication management, account logging, session management, and password management

 D. Authentication management, account management, session management, and firewall management

5. You are editing the PAM configuration file by adding a module. How would you indicate the authentication process should immediately terminate and succeed if the module succeeds?

 A. Make sure the module is either an auth module or a password module, since these must always succeed.

 B. Use the required control flag.

 C. Use the sufficient control flag.

 D. It doesn't matter; the authentication process always stops as soon as a module fails.

System Logging Configuration

6. Assume you normally work from a user account called sysadm. How might you configure your Red Hat Enterprise Linux 3 System to notify you whenever there is a serious problem with the kernel?

 A. Edit /etc/syslog.conf and add an entry such as this:

```
kern.err          root,sysadm
```

 B. Recompile the kernel to include error notification and specify sysadm as the user to be notified.

 C. Write a C program to monitor the /proc/err directory and send any messages that appear there to sysadm.

 D. Edit /etc/syslog.conf and add an entry such as this:

```
*.*               root,sysadm
```

The Extended Internet Services Daemon (xinetd)

7. You are using the xinetd program to start services. How could you limit access to Telnet access to clients on the 192.168.170.0 network?

    A. Edit /etc/xinetd.d/telnet and add this line

```
DENY EXCEPT 192.168.170.0.
```

    B. Edit /etc/hosts.allow and add this line:

```
telnetd : 192.168.170.0/255.255.255.0
```

    C. Edit /etc/hosts.deny and add this line:

```
telnetd : 192.168.170.0/255.255.255.0
```

    D. Edit /etc/hosts.deny and add this line:

```
telnetd : ALL EXCEPT 192.168.170.0/255.255.255.0
```

Firewall Policies

8. You have just recently connected your organization's network to the Internet, and you are a little worried because there is nothing other than your router standing between your network and the Internet. You have a spare 400 MHz PC with 256MB of RAM that just happens to have two Ethernet cards. You also have a mixture of systems on your network that includes Macintosh, Windows 98, and Linux. What might you do to alleviate your concerns?

    A. Nothing, you're not advertising the systems on your LAN via DNS, so no one will ever find them.

    B. Install RHEL 3 on the spare PC and use **iptables** to set it up as a firewall.

    C. Install RHEL 3 on the spare PC and use tcp_wrappers to set it up as a firewall.

    D. Install Linux on all systems on your network.

9. Consider the following command:

```
# iptables -A INPUT -s 192.168.77.77 -j REJECT
```

What effect will this have when the client with an IP of 192.168.77.77 tries to connect to your system?

    A. No effect at all.

    B. Access will be denied, and the client computer won't get any message on what happened.

    C. Access will be denied, and the client application will get a message that the target destination is unreachable.

    D. You will receive a notification message on the system console.

Network Address Translation

10. You are setting up a small office and would like to provide Internet access to a small number of users, but you don't want to pay for a dedicated IP address for each system on the network. How could Linux help with the problem?

    A. Assign the official IP address to a Linux system and create accounts on that system for all of the office personnel.

    B. Install Linux and configure it for IP forwarding.

    C. Install a Linux router.

    D. Use the Linux system to connect to the Internet; then use **iptables** to set up IP masquerading.

LAB QUESTIONS

Lab 1

You have a growing network of Linux computers, and have to maintain users and passwords on each of these computers on a daily basis. You're having to update administrative files such as /etc/passwd on a number of computers. What can you do to simplify your task?

Lab 2

You want to set up a RHEL 3 computer as a secure Web server. To keep that system secure, you'll want to configure an appropriate firewall, and disable any services that you don't need. What should you do?

Lab 3

You want to make sure even the root user has to enter the root password when opening Red Hat administrative tools. You can do this by modifying the appropriate file in the /etc/pam.d directory. Try this out with the Red Hat Security Configuration tool.

Lab 4

In this lab, you'll see how you can limit access to specific users through the PAM listfile module. In this lab, you'll limit access to the Secure Shell that's covered in Chapter 11. Assume that you have four users on your system: michael, donna, randy, and nancy, and want to limit access to randy and nancy. What do you need to do to make this happen?

Lab 5

You want to set up Telnet service on your internal LAN, accessible only to one specific IP address. You want to block access from outside the LAN. Assume that your LAN's network address is 192.168.1.0, and the IP address of the computer that should get access is 192.168.1.33. For the purpose of this lab, feel free to substitute the IP address of a second Linux computer on your network. What do you do?

Lab 6

You want to set up a secure Web server on your corporate LAN that supports inbound requests from your LAN and the Internet, but you do not want any of these requests from the Internet to get into your intranet. What can you do?

SELF TEST ANSWERS

Configuring NIS Clients

1. ☑ **B.** This is an ideal situation for NIS, where you can set up a single database of usernames and passwords.

   ☒ **A** is incorrect because it is labor intensive and would lead to many password and database inconsistencies. **C** is incorrect because you need at least one NIS server. **D** is incorrect because this is obviously an insecure way to run a network.

2. ☑ **D.** Although you can configure NIS clients manually, the easier way is to use the Red Hat Authentication Configuration utility.

   ☒ **A** is incorrect because this is invalid syntax. **B** is incorrect because you need to do more than start ypbind; you also need to configure the NIS domain. **C** is incorrect because ypbind is an independent service that you need to start from the /etc/rc.d/init.d directory.

Basic Host Security

3. ☑ **D.** The most effective way to prevent an attack through a network service is to make sure that it is not installed.

   ☒ **A**, **B**, and **C** are all incorrect. Since the service is still installed on the system, it is still at least theoretically possible to attack through that service.

The Pluggable Authentication Module (PAM) System

4. ☑ **A.** PAM breaks the authentication process into these four areas.

   ☒ **B**, **C**, and **D** are not the four areas associated with PAM.

5. ☑ **C.** The sufficient flag is used to indicate the authentication process should end immediately if the module succeeds.

   ☒ **A** is incorrect because any PAM module can fail and the authorization process can continue. **B** is incorrect because failure would be delayed until any other modules of the same type have been checked. **D** is incorrect because the control flag determines when the authorization process terminates.

System Logging Configuration

6. ☑ **A.** Although **D** might seem like a good choice, this would also show you all messages from every facility. It would be very difficult to pick out just the kernel messages from everything else that would be coming to your screen.

☒ **B** and **C** are obviously incorrect because there is too much effort involved. **D** is also incorrect, as explained earlier.

The Extended Internet Services Daemon (xinetd)

7. ☑ **D.** Although **B** would allow the requested access, since no other configuration has been done for tcp_wrappers, /etc/hosts.deny will be empty, so other clients will be allowed access by default. The best choice is to restrict all access to the telnet daemon and then make an exception for clients in the requested subnet.

☒ **A** is incorrect because the syntax is wrong. **C** is incorrect because it would result in Telnet access being denied to the 192.168.170.0 network.

Firewall Policies

8. ☑ **B.** Your best choice would be to take the unused PC and turn it into a firewall using Linux and **iptables**. If you use a router to connect to the Internet, then your firewall system sits between your LAN and the router. This results in a two-node network consisting of the router and one of the network interfaces in your firewall that serves as a DMZ between the Internet and your LAN. You assume that any traffic on this side of the firewall is potentially unsafe.

☒ **A** is incorrect because this is a poor way to secure a network. **C** is incorrect because although you might also want to use tcp_wrappers as part of your security strategy, it is designed to secure individual computers, not an entire network. Although **D** is a good option in principle, it won't necessarily make your network more secure.

9. ☑ **C.** Because the target is set to **REJECT**, the client will receive an error message. If the target was set to **DENY**, the client would not get any error message.

☒ **A, B,** and **D** do not describe what happens with this firewall when the client with an IP address of 192.168.77.77 tries to connect to your system.

Network Address Translation

10. ☑ **D.** If you need to connect several systems to the Internet but have only one official IP address to use, IP masquerading is the perfect solution.

☒ **A** is incorrect unless your users want to telnet to a single system and use a command line interface. **B** and **C** are essentially the same answer and are both incorrect because a router will not help in this situation.

LAB ANSWERS

Lab 1

You can set up an NIS server to maintain a common database of usernames and passwords. This should include at least the basic password database files, such as /etc/passwd, /etc/group, /etc/shadow, and /etc/gshadow, as defined in the /var/yp/Makefile configuration file.

Before you can set up an NIS server, you need to make sure you have the packages that you need, specifically the ypserv and yp-tools RPM packages. You can check and install these packages using the **rpm** command, as described throughout the book. Once installed, you'll want to start the **ypserv** service in the /etc/rc.d/init.d directory. You'll also want to use the **chkconfig** command to make sure this service starts the next time you boot this computer.

You'll need to set up an NIS domain name with the **domainname** command. You can then configure the NIS master server with the following command:

```
# /var/lib/yp/ypinit -m
```

This command assumes the local computer should also be configured as an NIS client on the given network. You're then prompted to enter the hostnames of other computers that you want to add to the NIS domain.

On a larger network, it can be helpful to have a backup for the NIS master server. If the NIS master server hostname is NISmaster, you can set this up with the following command:

```
# /var/lib/yp/ypinit -s NISmaster
```

You can then set up clients by configuring the ypbind service on each computer on the NIS domain. Make sure that the ypbind service starts the next time each computer restarts with a command such as:

```
# chkconfig --level 35 ypbind on
```

Lab 2

If you want to set up a RHEL 3 computer as a secure Web server, it's a straightforward process. You'll want to set up a firewall to block all but the most essential ports. This should include TCP/IP ports 80 and 443, which allow outside computers to access your regular and secure Web services.

The easiest way to set this up is with the text-mode Red Hat Security Level configuration tool, which you can start with the **lokkit no change to this in RHEL?**or **redhat-config-securitylevel-tui** commands (**lokkit** is now a "front-end" to **redhat-config-securitylevel-tui**). Once you're in the Red Hat tool, take the following steps:

1. Enable the firewall. This configures a basic set of firewall rules that prohibits access except for requests that come from inside the firewall.

2. Click Customize. This opens the Firewall Configuration – Customize window. In the Allow Incoming section, activate the WWW (HTTP) option. This allows outside access to your regular Web site.

3. In the Other Ports text box, type the following, which opens the ports associated with a standard secure Web service:

   ```
   443:tcp,443,udp
   ```

4. Click OK. Click OK again to exit from the Firewall Configuration tool.

5. Enter the following command to check your resulting firewall.

   ```
   # iptables -L
   ```

6. Once you've configured a Web service as described in Chapter 7, you'll be able to access both the regular and secure Web servers from remote computers.

Lab 3

To make lab work, you'll need to modify the Security Level Configuration tool using the redhat-config-securitylevel file in the /etc/pam.d directory. Open this file in the text editor of your choice. The first two commands allow users to start this tool automatically:

```
auth    sufficient    pam_rootok.so
auth    sufficient    pam_timestamp.so
```

The first command checks if you're the root user. The second command checks to see if you've opened the given tool recently, based on the conditions of the pam_timestamp module. If you deleted (or commented out) these commands, all users, including the root user, will have to enter the root password when opening this tool. To do so, take the following steps:

1. Open the Red Hat Security Level Configuration tool in a command line in your GUI. Make sure it opens normally. When it does, close it without making any changes to your current firewall.

2. Back up the current PAM module for the Security Level Configuration tool to your home directory:

   ```
   # cp /etc/pam.d/redhat-config-securitylevel ~
   ```

3. Open the file in /etc/pam.d in the text editor of your choice. Comment out the first two commands in this file.

4. Save the file. If you're not already logged into the GUI as the root user, log out of the GUI. Log back into the GUI as root.

5. Try opening the Red Hat Security Level Configuration tool. Click Main Menu | System Settings | Security Level. What happens?

Lab 4

To limit access to a PAM configured tool to specific users, you need a bit of help from the PAM listfile.so module, /etc/security/pam_listfile.so. With the following steps, I'm assuming that you need to configure the four specified users; you can configure existing users of your choice.

1. Create the users michael, donna, randy, and nancy. Set up passwords for these users. There are a number of ways to do so; I believe the simplest is with the following commands. Naturally, you'll need to enter an appropriate password for each user when prompted.

   ```
   # useradd michael; passwd michael
   # useradd donna; passwd donna
   # useradd nancy; passwd nancy
   # useradd randy; passwd randy
   ```

2. Navigate to the /etc/pam.d directory. Look to see if the sshd file exists; if not, you'll have to install it from the openssh-server RPM. While the technique is described in Chapter 11, it is no different from the technique used to install other services throughout this book. It should already be installed by default on a RHEL 3 server computer.

3. Open the /etc/pam.d/sshd file in the text editor of your choice. By default, the first two commands should look like:

   ```
   auth required    pam_stack.so service=system-auth
   auth required    pam_nologin.so
   ```

4. After the final **auth** command, enter the **auth** command that you need to point to a file with allowed users. (You could certainly use the **sense=deny** switch and configure a file with disallowed users.)

   ```
   auth required pam_listfile.so onerr=succeed item=user \
   sense=allow file=/etc/special
   ```

5. Since you want users nancy and randy to have access to the Secure Shell service, you'll want to add their usernames to the /etc/special configuration file, one username per line.

6. Try logging into the Secure Shell service with a prohibited username such as michael:

   ```
   # ssh michael@localhost
   ```

7. If you haven't logged into the Secure Shell service before from this computer, you'll be prompted to verify the authenticity of the unknown computer. Since it's the local computer, you can assume it's reasonably safe; type **yes** and press ENTER.

8. Enter user michael's password. What happens? Can you get access?

9. Press CTRL-C to exit from the Secure Shell login process. Try again with donna's username and password. What happens? Is this what you expected?

10. Try again with the allowed users.

11. What happens if you return to the /etc/pam.d/sshd file and change **sense=allow** to **sense=deny**?

Lab 5

When you set up any xinetd service such as Telnet, there are several steps in the process. You'll need to modify the xinetd Telnet configuration file, and set up filtering in one of three ways: in the /etc/xinetd.d/telnet configuration file, through tcp_wrappers, or the appropriate firewall commands:

1. First, you want to enable Telnet. Make sure that the krb5-telnet RPM is installed.

2. Activate Telnet. Use the **chkconfig telnet on** command to revise the /etc/xinetd.d/telnet configuration script.

3. Edit the /etc/xinetd.d/telnet configuration file. Add the **only_from = 192.168.1.33** line. (If you have another computer on your network with a private IP address, substitute accordingly in all steps in this lab.)

4. Save the configuration file and reload the xinetd service script with the **service xinetd reload** command. Try accessing Telnet from the local computer. What happens?

5. Try accessing Telnet from the computer with the IP address of 192.168.1.33. What happens? Try again from a different computer on your LAN.

6. Restore the previous /etc/xinetd.d/telnet configuration file. Don't forget to reload the xinetd service script with the **service xinetd reload** command.

7. Edit /etc/hosts.deny. Add the **telnetd : ALL EXCEPT 192.168.1.33** line.

8. Try accessing Telnet from the computer with the IP address of 192.168.1.33. What happens? Try again from a different computer on your LAN.

9. Restore the previous /etc/hosts.deny file.

10. Save any existing **iptables** chains. Back up /etc/sysconfig/iptables, if that file currently exists to ~/bak.iptables.

11. Flush current firewall rules with the **iptables -F** command.

12. Block the Telnet port, 23, for all IP addresses except 192.168.1.33 with the **iptables -A INPUT -s ! 192.168.1.33 -p tcp --dport 23 -j DROP** command.

13. Try accessing the Telnet server from the computer with the IP address of 192.168.1.33. What happens? Try again from a different computer on your LAN.

14. Flush current firewall rules with the **iptables -F** command.

15. Restore any previous firewall rules with the **iptables-restore < ~/bak.iptables** command.

16. Bonus Lab: Repeat these commands for other services and networks.

Lab 6

Scenario 1: Cost is not an object. This means you can build a DMZ using two firewalls and a separate Web server, all running Linux. You should have the Web server dedicated only to the Web. You configure two more Linux hosts, each with two network cards, and essentially isolate the intranet behind one firewall. You then put the Web server in the middle, placing the second firewall between the Web server and the Internet. You configure the firewall on the intranet with IP masquerading to ensure anonymity for all your intranet hosts.

Scenario 2: You have one old computer available, and the Web server is a separate computer. Use your one computer as the firewall between you and the Internet and only forward HTTP packets to the Web server IP address directly; use NAT for all intranet requests going out to the Internet for HTTP and FTP. Disallow all other services.

11

Operational Administration Recovery and Security

The themes of this chapter are *security* and *recovery*. These are two critical concepts for the Red Hat exams. This continues the discussion of system security started in the last chapter, with a look at secure ways to run certain network services and a Red Hat Enterprise Linux–specific way of configuring file security.

This chapter includes a description of setting up security with groups. You can set up special groups on an RHEL 3 computer. You can set up a common directory for the users in these groups.

INSIDE THE EXAM

Installation and Configuration

Part of this chapter can help you with the skills you need on the Red Hat Installation and Configuration exams. One of the basic foundations of Linux is that most services have their own special accounts. While the User Private Group scheme isn't explicitly mentioned in the Red Hat Exam Prep guide, it is part of the prep courses (RH133, RH300) for both RHCT and RHCE exams. The RHCT prep course does also cover **anacron** and **tmpwatch**, so it's possible that you'll see those services on both exams.

Troubleshooting and System Maintenance

When you read this chapter, focus on the requirements associated with the Red Hat Troubleshooting and System Maintenance exams. Perhaps the most important Linux administrative skill is knowing how to rescue a damaged system. RHCTs need to know how to boot from the GRUB menu into different runlevels. RHCEs also need to know how to rescue a system using the first RHEL 3 installation CD. If you're planning to take the Red Hat exams, learn how to diagnose boot problems. Create a few more of your own, and learn the symptoms. It may help you avoid frustration and solve problems quickly during the RHCE Troubleshooting and System Maintenance exam. Finally, as Logical Volume Management is becoming more important on Red Hat systems, you need to know how to add, remove, and resize logical volumes on the RHCE exam.

Next, you'll learn about two different administrative processes. The **anacron** service can help you make sure that cron jobs that are missed when your RHEL 3 computer is powered down are run. The **tmpwatch** script is a standard cron job that can help you maintain your temporary directories.

You'll also examine one of the most fundamental fears of any systems administrator: what to do when a system will not boot. When the inevitable happens, knowing the right things to look for and having some tricks up your sleeve may possibly help you avoid a potential nightmare and a major loss of service for your users. Understanding these tools is fundamental to getting through troubleshooting scenarios on the Red Hat exams.

Finally, you'll look at how to manage and extend the Logical Volumes that you created in Chapters 2 and 3. With this skill in hand, you can expand full volumes such as the /home directory, as needed.

CERTIFICATION OBJECTIVE 11.01

Services and Special Users

Programs that run on Linux are all processes. When Red Hat Enterprise Linux starts on your computer, it first starts a special process known as init. The init process then starts other basic processes required for a working Linux system, including the shell, the basic user consoles, startup daemons, and more. Because it needs the authority, init runs as root; in other words, it runs with the privileges of the root user.

Interestingly enough, most other services, especially network daemons, do not run under the root user ID. This is one important way Linux protects your network security.

Suppose you have configured a system to start several network services running under the root user ID. Even if you loaded the latest security patches, the risk is still high. If a cracker stumbles upon your system and is able to break in, he or she can quickly get root access through the service daemon.

To circumvent problems like this, RHEL 3 normally configures services to run under their own user accounts. If a cracker does succeed in breaking into one daemon, the damage is limited because the service is running as a normal, unprivileged user. Alternatively, some services can be run through the nobody account. Figure 11-1 shows a typical /etc/passwd file. Notice that most common network services have their own user accounts.

```
root:x:0:0:root:/root:/bin/bash
bin:x:1:1:bin:/bin:/sbin/nologin
daemon:x:2:2:daemon:/sbin:/sbin/nologin
adm:x:3:4:adm:/var/adm:/sbin/nologin
lp:x:4:7:lp:/var/spool/lpd:/sbin/nologin
sync:x:5:0:sync:/sbin:/bin/sync
shutdown:x:6:0:shutdown:/sbin:/sbin/shutdown
halt:x:7:0:halt:/sbin:/sbin/halt
mail:x:8:12:mail:/var/spool/mail:/sbin/nologin
news:x:9:13:news:/etc/news:
uucp:x:10:14:uucp:/var/spool/uucp:/sbin/nologin
operator:x:11:0:operator:/root:/sbin/nologin
games:x:12:100:games:/usr/games:/sbin/nologin
gopher:x:13:30:gopher:/var/gopher:/sbin/nologin
ftp:x:14:50:FTP User:/var/ftp:/sbin/nologin
nobody:x:99:99:Nobody:/:/sbin/nologin
rpm:x:37:37::/var/lib/rpm:/sbin/nologin
vcsa:x:69:69:virtual console memory owner:/dev:/sbin/nologin
nscd:x:28:28:NSCD Daemon:/:/sbin/nologin
sshd:x:74:74:Privilege-separated SSH:/var/empty/sshd:/sbin/nologin
rpc:x:32:32:Portmapper RPC user:/:/sbin/nologin
rpcuser:x:29:29:RPC Service User:/var/lib/nfs:/sbin/nologin
nfsnobody:x:65534:65534:Anonymous NFS User:/var/lib/nfs:/sbin/nologin
"/etc/passwd" 37L, 1680C
```

EXERCISE 11-1

Verifying that Services Have Their Own Accounts

In this exercise, you will verify that certain system and network services run with their own accounts. You should try this exercise on a system that is configured to offer various network services. At a shell prompt, issue the following command:

```
# ps aux --headers | less
```

What account is the Web server service (httpd) running under? What account is the xfs service running under?

CERTIFICATION OBJECTIVE 11.02

Red Hat User Private Group Scheme

One major difference between Red Hat Enterprise Linux 3 and non–Red Hat Linux or Unix distributions is how new users are assigned to groups. A Linux group allows its members to share files. Unfortunately, that also means everyone in the same primary group has access to the home directories of all other group members. Users may not always want to share the files in their home directories with others. For example, if you're setting up an ISP, your users pay for their privacy.

On the other hand, Red Hat Enterprise Linux normally gives each user a unique user ID and group ID in /etc/passwd. This is known as the *user private group* scheme. As users get exclusive access to their own groups, they don't have to worry about other users reading the files in their home directories.

Standard and Red Hat Groups

Traditionally, users are assigned to one or more groups such as users in /etc/group. For example, you might configure accgrp for the accounting department and infosys for the information systems department in your company.

If you have access to one of these other versions of Unix or Linux, check the third and fourth fields in /etc/passwd. Many users will have the same fourth field, which represents their *primary* group. Then, when you create a new user, each account receives a unique user ID but shares the same group ID with other users in the acct group. Users can still belong to other groups as well.

In RHEL 3, each user gets their own special private group by default. As you probably noticed in Chapter 4, user IDs and group IDs by default start at 500, match, and proceed in ascending order.

By default in RHEL 3, all regular users have a **umask** of 0002. If you are coming from a traditional Unix environment, you may be concerned. With the traditional user/group scheme, any member of that user's primary group will automatically have write access to any file that the user creates in his home directory.

This is the advantage behind the user private group scheme. Since every user account is the only member in its own private group, having the **umask** set to 002 does not affect file security. This provides advantages for systems such as Internet Service Providers, where you don't want users to have access to each other's files.

Shared Directories

Most people work in groups. They may share files. You can give a group of users access to a specific user's home directory or you can set up a shared directory for a group.

When you configure a shared directory, you can set up a group owner, and then add the users you need to that group, through the /etc/group configuration file. When you set the group ID bit (SGID) on this directory, any file created in this directory inherits the group ID. Assuming you have set appropriate permissions, all members of this group can then access files in that the directory.

There are several basic steps required to create a useful shared directory. For example, assume you want to set up a shared directory, /home/accshared, for the accountants in your organization. To set this up, you'll want to take the following steps:

1. Create the shared directory:

   ```
   # mkdir /home/accshared
   ```

2. Create a group with the users in your accounting department. Give it a group ID that doesn't interfere with existing group or user IDs. One way to do this is to add a line such as the following to your /etc/group file. You could also create this kind of group using the Red Hat User Manager described in Chapter 4. Note that the name of this new group is accgrp.

   ```
   accgrp:x:5000:stewardh,jamiec,davidw,debl,callend,vanessar
   ```

3. Set up appropriate ownership for the new shared directory. The following command prevents any specific user from taking control of the directory, and assigns group ownership to accgrp.

   ```
   # chmod 2770 /home/accshared
   ```

Any user who is a member of the accgrp group can now create files in the /home /accshared directory. Any files generated will then be associated with the accgrp group ID, and all users listed as members of accgrp in the /etc/group file will have read, write, and execute access to the /home/accshared directory.

What makes this possible are the permissions that you've assigned to the /home /accshared directory: 2770. Let's break this down into its component parts.

The first digit (2) is the *set group ID bit*, also known as the *SGID bit*. When you set the SGID bit for a directory, any files created in that directory automatically have their group ownership set to be that of the group owner of the directory. There are two ways to set the SGID bit for the /home/accshared directory:

```
chmod g+s /home/accshared
```

or alternatively:

```
chmod 2770 /home/accshared
```

Setting the SGID bit solves the problem of making sure all files created in a shared directory belong to the correct group—as long as the **umask** is set properly.

The remaining digits are basic knowledge for any experienced Linux or Unix user. The 770 sets read, write, and execute permissions for the user and group that owns the directory. But since the user owner is nobody, the group owner is what counts. In other words, members of the accgrp group gain read, write, and execute permissions to files created in this directory.

Otherwise, users who are members of accgrp and belong to another primary group would have to remember to use the **chgrp** command on every file they put in /home/accshared. While clumsy, that command allows other users in that group to access the file.

EXERCISE 11-2

Controlling Group Ownership with the SGID Bit

In this exercise, you will create new files in a directory where the SGID bit is set.

1. Add users called test1, test2, and test3. Check the /etc/passwd and /etc/group files to verify that each user's private group was created:

```
# useradd test1; passwd test1
# useradd test2; passwd test2
# useradd test3; passwd test3
```

2. Edit the /etc/group file and add a group called tg1. Make the test1 and test2 accounts a member of this group. You could add the following line to /etc/group directly or use the Red Hat User Manager:

```
tg1::9999:test1,test2
```

Before you proceed, make sure the group ID you assign to group tg1 (in this case, 9999) is not already in use.

3. Create a shared director for the tg1 group:

```
# mkdir   /home/testshared
```

4. Change the user and group ownership of the shared directory:

```
# chown   nobody.tg1   /home/testshared
```

5. Log in as test1 and test2 separately. Change the directory to the testshared directory and try to create a file. Two ways to do so are with the following commands. What happens?

```
$ date >> test.txt
$ touch abcd
```

6. Now as the root user, set group write permissions on the testshared directory.

```
# chmod 770 /home/testshared
```

7. Log in again as user test1, and then try to create a file in the new directory. So far, so good.

```
$ cd /home/testshared
$ date >> test.txt
$ ls -l test.txt
```

8. Now check the ownership on the new file. Do you think other users in the tg1 group can access this file?

```
$ ls -l
```

9. From the root account, set the SGID bit on the directory:

```
# chmod g+s  /home/testshared
```

10. Switch back to the test1 account and create another file. Check the ownership on this file. Do you think that user test2 can now access this file?

```
$ date >> testb.txt
$ ls  -l
```

11. Now log in as the test2 account. Go into the /home/testshared directory, create a different file, and use **ls -l** to check permissions and ownership again.

12. Switch to the test3 account and check whether you can or cannot create files in this directory, and whether you can or cannot view the files in this directory.

CERTIFICATION OBJECTIVE 11.03

anacron and tmpwatch

There are two cron jobs which are critical for basic system administration. The anacron RPM package makes sure that cron jobs are run on computers that may be powered down during the night. The tmpwatch RPM configures cron jobs which removes files from various /tmp directories that have not been accessed in a specified number of hours.

exam
Watch

As of this writing, anacron is listed as part of the RHCT prep course (RH133). It is therefore an implicit part of the requirements for both Red Hat exams. However, the anacron RPM package is not included as part of RHEL 3. There's an open request to add it to RHEL 3; see bug 103691 at bugzilla.redhat.com for more information. You'll have to make your own judgment on whether to study anacron for your exam. Watch for changes in the Red Hat Exam Prep guide and RH133 syllabus. In my opinion, anacron is still an excellent tool for Linux administrators.

anacron

Some of the cron jobs described in Chapter 5 are essential to the smooth operation of a RHEL 3 computer. And if you add backup jobs to the cron directories, you want to make sure the backups are always executed. For example, if there is a power failure when you schedule a backup job, you may never know that the backup wasn't created—at least until you need the backup that you don't have.

Since the anacron RPM is not included with RHEL 3, you'll need to get the RPM from a different source, such as the Red Hat Linux 9 or Fedora Linux installation files. If it is included on your Red Hat exam, you should be able to install it from some readily available source, as you won't have access to the Internet during your exam. Therefore, all I'll say for the purposes of this book is that you can download the anacron RPM from a source such as ftp.redhat.com or a mirror site such as those specified at www.redhat.com/download/mirror.html.

Once installed, the **anacron** command checks the jobs of your choice, based on the settings in the /etc/anacrontab configuration file. The default version of this file is straightforward. The first two lines set the SHELL and PATH for commands in the remainder of the file:

```
SHELL=/bin/sh
PATH=/usr/local/sbin:/usr/local/bin:/sbin:/bin:/usr/sbin:/usr/bin
```

The following three commands run the cron scripts in the noted directories:

```
1    65    cron.daily    run-parts /etc/cron.daily
7    70    cron.weekly   run-parts /etc/cron.weekly
30   75    cron.monthly  run-parts /etc/cron.monthly
```

These commands are in the following format:

```
period delay job-identifier command
```

In this format, **anacron** checks the jobs in the *job-identifier* directory every *period* (in days). If one or more jobs in this directory have not been run, the *command* is executed after the given *delay* (in minutes).

In other words, if you've installed the anacron RPM, RHEL 3 runs the **anacron** service every time Linux boots on your computer. Take the last command in this list. The **anacron** service checks the commands in the /etc/cron.monthly directory. If they have not been run for 30 days, **anacron** waits 75 minutes, and then executes the **run-parts /etc/cron.monthly** command, which executes the scripts in the /etc /cron.monthly directory.

tmpwatch

As its name implies, the **tmpwatch** script is normally run on directories such as /tmp and /var/tmp. The **tmpwatch** script works recursively, so if you specify the top-level directory in a tree, **tmpwatch** will search through the entire directory tree looking for files to remove.

The following **tmpwatch** command deletes all files in the /tmp directory that haven't been accessed in the past week (168 hours = 7 days × 24 hours/day):

```
# tmpwatch 168 /tmp
```

While you can run the **tmpwatch** command from the command line, it is often more practical to set it up to be run by the cron daemon on a regular basis. It's run as a script on a daily basis, in the /etc/cron.daily directory. By default, RHEL 3 configures the first two commands in **tmpwatch** to delete files in /tmp and /var/tmp every 10 and 30 days, respectively:

```
/usr/sbin/tmpwatch 240 /tmp
/usr/sbin/tmpwatch 720 /var/tmp
```

The final command deletes formatted manuals, which are cached and stored in various /var/cache directories, every 30 days.

```
for d in /var/{cache/man,catman}/{cat?,X11R6/cat?,local/cat?}; do
    if [ -d "$d" ]; then
        /usr/sbin/tmpwatch -f 720 $d
    fi
done
```

EXERCISE 11-3

Clearing an Imaginary /db Directory

In a bizarre twist of fate, a runaway process has just created 200 temporary files in /db that it did not remove. You could remove them manually, or you can let **tmpwatch** delete all the files that are more than one hour old. Note that this removes all files over an hour old, not just these imaginary files, so this should *not* be done on a production server directory. If you already have a directory named /db, do *not* use it. If necessary, create a separate directory just for the purpose of this exercise.

```
# cp /etc/* /db    # copying a large number of files to /db
# ls /db | wc -w   # how may files need to be removed
```

Wait at least an hour.

```
# tmpwatch 1 /db
# ls /db           # files should be gone
```

Alternatively, you can copy or extract files from an older backup or tar archive to the /db directory, and have **tmpwatch** delete them. If they are all more than seven days old, then use 168 as the waiting period. You could even try various times to see which files are deleted.

CERTIFICATION OBJECTIVE 11.04

The linux rescue Environment

At some point in your career as a Red Hat Enterprise Linux administrator, maybe even on the Red Hat exams, you're going to be faced with a system that will not boot. It will be up to you to determine the cause of the problem and implement a fix. Sometimes, the problem may be due to hardware failure: the system in question has a bad power supply or has experienced a hard disk crash.

Quite often, however, the failure of a system to boot can be traced back to the actions of a user: you, the system administrator! When you are editing certain system configuration files, typographical errors can render your system unbootable.

Any time you plan to make any substantial modifications to your system or change key configuration files, back them up first. Then, after making changes, you should actually reboot your system rather than assume that it will boot up the next time you need a reboot. It's much better to encounter problems while you can still remember exactly which changes you made. It is even better if you can go back to a working configuration file.

w a t c h

Know every detail that you can about the linux rescue *environment for the RHCE exam.*

To prepare for boot failures, you should make sure you have a valid boot floppy for your system. But boot floppies can be lost. So it's also important to know how to use the Red Hat installation boot disk or CD to get to the Linux Rescue environment, first discussed in Chapter 2. Refer to that chapter for more information on creating a installation boot disk.

While most of this section applies to the RHCE exam, the RHCT part of the Exam Prep guide suggests that you need to know how to boot Linux into different runlevels, which you can learn about near the end of this part of this chapter.

A mkbootdisk Boot Floppy

When you installed RHEL 3, the last screen may have asked whether you wanted a boot disk. If you answered No to this prompt, you can still create a valid boot floppy for your computer using the **mkbootdisk** command. This command reads the selected kernel images in /boot and the default boot loader, GRUB or LILO, to create a LILO-style boot image on a floppy disk. For example, if the current version of the RHEL 3 kernel is 2.4.21-4.EL, use this command:

```
#  mkbootdisk  2.4.21-4.EL
```

You may be able to fix a few problems with this boot disk, such as an accidentally deleted master boot record, by booting from your boot disk.

The **mkbootdisk** command in Red Hat Enterprise Linux 3 may not work as described. In a desktop environment, it worked perfectly. On my notebook computer, however, it created a syslinux.cfg file on the floppy, with the following two lines at the end of the file:

```
      append initrd=initrd.img ro
   ro root=/dev/hda2
```

This actually causes a kernel panic. You can find out more in the Red Hat bug database at bugzilla.redhat.com. In this database, bug number 109834 suggests that this is also a problem on Red Hat Linux 9. But as shown in this bug and in bug 116446, the syslinux.cfg file is easily fixed. In this case, I'd combine these two lines into the following:

```
append initrd=initrd.img ro root=/dev/hda2
```

With this fix, the associated boot disk will now work.

If the kernel can't locate the root filesystem, or if the root filesystem is damaged, the Linux kernel will issue a kernel panic with messages similar to the following:

```
Creating root device
Mounting root filesystem
kjournald starting. Commit interval 5 seconds
EXT3-fs: mounted filesystems with ordered data mode.
pivotroot: pivot_root (/sysroot,/sysroot/initrd) failed: 2)
Freeing unused kernel memory: 272k freed
Kernel panic: No init found. Try passing init= option to kernel
```

Although this may look very bad the first time you encounter it, often the problem can easily be fixed from the **linux rescue** environment with a little bit of work. Other problems may also require the use of the **linux rescue** environment, as described in the following section.

Installation Disk Rescue Mode

As discussed in Chapter 3, you can start Linux in rescue mode from the Red Hat Enterprise Linux installation CD or boot disk. When you type **linux rescue** at the installation boot prompt and go through the steps, the installation disks install a compact version of a root filesystem. As this information has to fit on two 1.44MB floppy disks, it includes a minimal set of utilities that will allow you to mount a disk and either repair the problem with the disk or edit the broken files on the disk.

w a t c h   *The RHCE portion of the Red Hat Exam Prep guide explicitly states that you need to know how to boot into* linux rescue *mode from the first RHEL 3 installation CD.*

To boot into rescue mode, first boot your system either using your boot floppy or directly with the first installation CD in a bootable CD-ROM drive, as shown in Figure 11-2.

If you've booted from the first RHEL 3 installation CD, you have two options at the boot prompt: you can type **linux rescue** or **linux rescue askmethod** and press ENTER. If you may not need access to the installation RPMs, or have booted from the RHEL 3 boot floppy, linux rescue is sufficient. If you may need the installation RPMs, linux rescue **askmethod** allows you to connect to the network

FIGURE 11-2

Booting into
linux rescue
mode

FIGURE 11-2

Booting into
linux rescue
mode

installation server that you used in Chapter 2—and that may be available to you
during the Red Hat exams.

When booting from the RHEL 3 1.44 MB boot floppy, the linux rescue *command is*
functionally equivalent to the linux rescue askmethod *command when booting*
from the first RHEL 3 installation CD.

When you run the **linux rescue askmethod** command, it's as if rescue mode isn't
working; you're taken through the first steps of RHEL 3 installation process in text

mode. You'll need to enter a language, a keyboard type, and the location of the RHEL 3 installation files, as shown in Figure 11-3.

Next, you're asked to configure an IP address, network mask, gateway, and primary (DNS) nameserver for on the local computer. Follow any relevant instructions on your exam carefully. Then, as described in Chapter 2, you're asked to point to the network installation server name or IP address, as well as the directory which contains the Red Hat installation files. Once the files associated with the **linux rescue** environment are loaded, you'll see the screen shown in Figure 11-4.

As you can see, you now have three options. I address each option in detail in the following sections:

- **Continue** will search through and mount the available filesystems.

- **Read-Only** performs the same tasks as Continue, except all filesystems that are found are mounted read-only.

- **Skip** does not try to look through the available filesystems. Instead, it proceeds directly to a root shell prompt.

FIGURE 11-3

Connecting to a network source

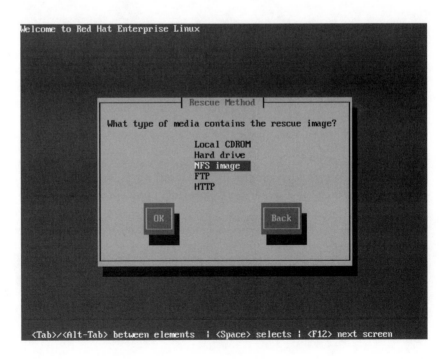

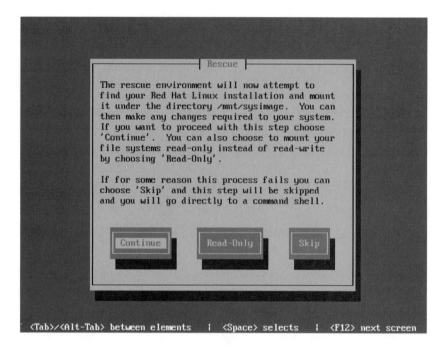

FIGURE 11-4

Three choices in
the **linux rescue**
environment

Standard linux rescue Environment

When you select Continue from the screen shown in Figure 11-4, you're taken through
the standard **linux rescue** environment. The rescue files search for your root directory
(/) filesystem. If found, your standard root directory (/) is mounted on /mnt/sysimage.
All of your other regular filesystems are subdirectories of root; for example, your /etc
directory will be found on /mnt/sysimage/etc.

Not all of your filesystems may mount properly. You may see error messages such as:

```
Error mounting filesystem on sdb1: Invalid argument
```

This suggests that at least the filesystem that you would normally mount on /dev/sdb1
isn't working for some reason. If the **linux rescue** environment can mount your root
directory (/), you'll see a message noting that your system has been mounted, as shown
in Figure 11-5.

Click OK. You should see the following prompt messages:

```
Your system is mounted under the /mnt/sysimage directory.

When finished please exit from the shell and your system will reboot.

sh-2.05b#
```

The linux rescue Environment

FIGURE 11-5

The **linux rescue** environment has found your root directory (/)

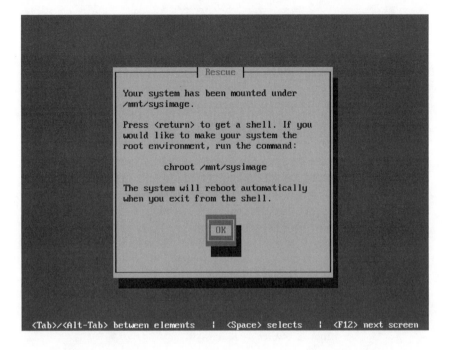

You'll use the **chroot /mnt/sysimage** command shortly. Now you can work on repairing any files or filesystems that might be damaged. First, check for unmounted filesystems. Run a **df** command. The output should look similar to Figure 11-6.

Compare the result to the /mnt/sysimage/etc/fstab configuration file. If some filesystem is not mounted, it may be configured incorrectly in the fstab file. Alternatively, the label associated with a partition may not match the filesystem shown in your fstab file. For example, to find the label associated with /dev/sda1, run the following command:

```
# e2label /dev/sda1
```

FIGURE 11-6

Labels, filesystems, and partitions

```
sh-2.05b# df
Filesystem           1K-blocks     Used Available Use% Mounted on
rootfs                    6120     2468      3302  43% /
/dev/root.old             6120     2468      3302  43% /
192.168.30.4:/mnt/inst
                       6756712  4228736   2184752  66% /mnt/source
/dev/hda2              3644800  2921256    538396  85% /mnt/sysimage
/dev/hda1              101089      15036     80834  16% /mnt/sysimage/boot
/dev/hdd1             1031800      34328    945060   4% /mnt/sysimage/home
sh-2.05b#
```

which should return the name of a filesystem to be mounted on that partition such as /boot.

Sometimes an unmounted filesystem just needs a little cleaning; remember, a command such as the following cleans the /dev/sdb1 partition.

```
# fsck /dev/sdb1
```

The **fsck** command works only on an unmounted filesystem. For example, if you get a message such as:

```
WARNING!!! Running e2fsck on a mounted filesystem may cause
SEVERE filesystem damage.
```

unmount the subject filesystem such with a command such as **umount /dev/sdb1**. If that doesn't work, restart the rescue process. When you get to the screen shown in Figure 11-4, select Skip and read the "No Mount **linux rescue** Environment" section later in this chapter.

Remember the message in Figure 11-5? It includes an important clue. All you need to do to restore the original filesystem structure is to run the following command:

```
# chroot /mnt/sysimage
```

When you use the rescue disk, your standard root directory (/) is actually mounted on the /mnt/sysimage directory. This command resets your standard root directory (/), so you don't have to go to the /mnt/sysimage subdirectory.

When you've made your changes, run the **sync** command, twice, to make sure any changes you've made are written to disk. Type the **exit** command, twice. Linux *should* automatically run the **sync** command again when you exit, making sure any changes are written to disk. Then it stops, allowing you to reboot or restart your computer.

on the
j o b

*Normally, it should not be necessary to run the sync **command. However,** running it several times does make sure that any pending data is actually written to your floppy and hard disks.*

Read-Only linux rescue Environment

When you select the Read-Only option shown in Figure 11-4, you'll get the same basic prompt. There is little difference between regular and read-only rescue mode. The rescue system attempts to do everything that it would under regular mode, except all partitions are mounted read-only.

This is appropriate if you have a large number of mounted filesystems; it can help you cull through what is and isn't working with less risk of overwriting key configuration files.

No Mount linux rescue Environment

When you select the Skip option shown in Figure 11-4, the installation files loads a minimal root image from into a RAM disk created by the kernel, and takes you to a root shell prompt (#) as shown:

```
When finished, please exit from the shell and your system will reboot.
-/bin/sh-2.05b#
```

At this point, you have access to a basic set of commands. You can mount filesystems, create directories, move files, and edit files using vi. You can apply the **fdisk** and **fsck** commands to various hard disks and partitions. A few other basic commands are also available.

The greatest difficulty in operating from the rescue environment is that you are working with a minimal version of the Linux operating system. Many of the commands you are used to having at your disposal are not available at this level. If your root partition has not been completely destroyed, you may be able to mount this partition to your temporary root directory in memory and access commands from there.

But you may need a little help identifying the partitions on your system. As I'll show you shortly, the **fdisk -l /dev/hda** command lists the configured partitions on the first IDE hard drive. You can create a new directory such as /mnt/sysimage, mount a partition such as /dev/hda2 on that directory, and check the result with the following commands:

```
# mkdir /mnt/sysimage
# mount /dev/hda2 /mnt/sysimage
# ls /mnt/sysimage
```

If you can verify that you've mounted the standard root directory (/) filesystem on the /mnt/sysimage directory, you can run the **chroot /mnt/sysimage** command. You can then have full access to the commands and configuration files available under that mounted partition.

on the
job

If you mount partitions from your hard drive in rescue mode and then make changes to files on those partitions, remember to use the sync *command. This writes your files to disk so the information isn't lost if you hit the power button on your computer. Alternatively, a* umount *command applied to any partition also writes data to disk.*

Booting into a Different Runlevel

At the boot loader prompt, you can start Linux at a different runlevel. This may be useful for two purposes. If your default runlevel in /etc/inittab is 5, your system normally boots into the GUI. If you're having problems booting into the GUI, you can start RHEL into the standard text mode, runlevel 3.

One other option to help rescue a damaged Linux system is *single-user mode*. This is appropriate if your system can find at least the root filesystem (/). Your system may not have problems finding its root partition and starting the boot process, but it may encounter problems

ⓦ a t c h   *In the current Red Hat Exam Prep guide, it states that RHCTs (and therefore also RHCEs) should be able to boot systems into different runlevels. The method is described in this section.*

such as damaged configuration files or an inability to boot into one of the higher runlevels. When you boot into single-user mode, your options are similar to the standard **linux rescue** environment where the system has already been mounted and the **chroot /mnt/sysimage** command has been applied.

To boot into a different runlevel, first let us assume that you're using the default RHEL 3 boot loader, GRUB. In that case, press P (lower case) to enter the GRUB password if required. Press A (lower case) to modify the kernel arguments. When you see a line similar to

```
grub append> ro root=LABEL=/
```

add one of the following commands (shown in bold) to the end of that line:

```
grub append> ro root=LABEL=/ single
grub append> ro root=LABEL=/ 1
grub append> ro root=LABEL=/ init=/bin/sh
```

Alternatively, if you're using LILO, the **linux single** command will do nicely. Any of these commands will boot Linux into a minimal runtime environment, and you will receive a bash shell prompt (bash#).

Naturally, you can use the same technique to boot into another runlevel; for example, to boot from the GRUB boot loader into runlevel 3, navigate to where you can modify the kernel arguments, and add the following command to the end of the following line:

```
grub append> ro root=LABEL=/ 3
```

on the **job** *The terms boot loader and bootloader are used interchangeably. For the purpose of this book, I've used the term "boot loader," as that seems to be the direction of the Red Hat documentation. However, the term "bootloader" is still common even in Red Hat documentation.*

When you boot into single-user mode, no password is required to access the system. Running your system in single-user mode is somewhat similar to running a system booted into rescue mode. Many of the commands and utilities you normally use are unavailable. You may have to mount additional drives or partitions and specify the full pathname when running some commands.

When you have corrected the problem, you can reboot the system. Alternatively, you can type the **exit** command to boot into the default runlevel as defined in /etc/inittab, probably runlevels 3 or 5.

on the **job** *In single-user mode, any user can change the root password. You do not want people rebooting your computer to go into single-user mode to change your root password. Therefore, it's important to keep your server in a secure location. Alternatively, you can password-protect GRUB to keep anyone with physical access to your computer from booting it in single-user mode.*

Troubleshooting the Boot Process

Although there are potentially many things that will cause a system not to boot, they can roughly be categorized as either hardware problems or software and configuration problems. The most common hardware-related problem you will probably encounter is a bad hard disk drive; like all mechanical devices with moving parts, these have a finite lifetime and will eventually fail. Fortunately, the Red Hat exams do not require you to address hardware failures.

Software and configuration problems, however, can be a little more difficult. At first glance, they can look just like regular hardware problems.

In addition to knowing how to mount disk partitions, edit files, and manipulate files, you will need to know how to use several other commands in order to be able to fix problems from rescue mode or single-user mode. The most useful of these are the **df**, **fdisk**, and the **fsck** commands. To diagnose a problem, you need to know how these commands work at least at a rudimentary level.

df

The Linux **df** command was covered briefly in Chapter 3. When you use **df**, you can find mounted directories, the capacity of each partition, and the percentage of each partition that's filled with files. The result shown back in Figure 11-6 illustrates the result in kilobytes. There are a couple of simple variations; the following commands give the result in megabytes and inodes:

```
# df -m
# df -i
```

fdisk

The Linux **fdisk** command was covered briefly in Chapter 3. When you use **fdisk**, you can find the partitions you have available for mounting. For example, the **fdisk -l /dev /hda** command lists available partitions on the first IDE hard disk:

```
# fdisk -l /dev/hda

Disk /dev/hda: 15.0GB, 15020457984 bytes
240 heads, 63 sectors/track, 1940 cylinders
Units = cylinders of 15120 * 512 = 7741440 bytes
    Device   Boot    Start     End      Blocks   Id   System
/dev/hda1      *        1       949     7174408+   b   Win95 FAT32
/dev/hda2             950       963      105840    83   Linux
/dev/hda3             964      1871     6864480    83   Linux
/dev/hda4            1872      1940      521640     f   Win95 Ext'd (LBA)
/dev/hda5            1872      1940      521608+   82   Linux swap
```

Looking at the output from **fdisk**, it's easy to identify the partitions configured with a Linux format, /dev/hda2, /dev/hda3, and /dev/hda5. Given the size of each partition, it is reasonable to conclude that /dev/hda2 is associated with /boot, and /dev/hda3 is associated with root (/).

For simple partitioning schemes, this is easy. It gets far more complicated when you have lots of partitions, as in this next example. You should always have some documentation available that clearly identifies your partition layout within your filesystem:

```
# fdisk -l /dev/hda
Disk /dev/hda: 26.8 GB, 26843545600
255 heads, 63 sectors/track, 3263 cylinders
Units = cylinders of 16065 * 512 = 8225280 bytes

    Device   Boot    Start     End      Blocks   Id   System
/dev/hda1      *        1        13     104391    83   Linux
/dev/hda2              14       268    2048287+    b   Win95 FAT32
```

```
/dev/hda3      269     396  1028160    83  Linux
/dev/hda4      397    3263  23029177+   f  Win95 Ext'd (LBA)
/dev/hda5      397    1097  5630751    83  Linux
/dev/hda6     1098    1734  5116671    83  Linux
/dev/hda7     1735    1989  2048256    83  Linux
/dev/hda8     1990    2244  2048256    83  Linux
/dev/hda9     2245    2372  1028218+   83  Linux
/dev/hda10    2373    2499  1020096    82  Linux swap
/dev/hda11    2500    2626  1020096    83  Linux
/dev/hda12    2627    2753  1020096    83  Linux
/dev/hda13    2754    2880  1020096    83  Linux
/dev/hda14    2881    3007  1020096    83  Linux
/dev/hda15    3008    3134  1020096    83  Linux
/dev/hda16    3135    3236  1020096    83  Linux
```

In this example, it's easy to identify the Linux swap partition. Since /boot partitions are small and normally configured toward the front of a drive, it's reasonable to associate it with /dev/hda1.

However, that is just a guess; some trial and error may be required. For example, after mounting /dev/hda2 on an empty directory, you would want to check the contents of that directory for the typical contents of /boot.

e2label

Based on the previous example, you probably could use a little help to identify the filesystems associated with the other partitions. That's where the **e2label** command can help. When you set up a new filesystem, the associated partition is normally marked with a label. For example, the following command tells you that the /usr filesystem is normally mounted on /dev/hda5.

```
# e2label
Usage: e2label device [newlabel]
# e2label /dev/hda5
/usr
```

dumpe2fs

You can get a lot more information on each partition with the **dumpe2fs** command, as shown in Figure 11-7.

The **dumpe2fs** command not only does the job of **e2label** but also tells you about the format, whether it has a journal, and the block size. Proceed further down this list, and you'll find the locations for backup superblocks, which can help you use the **fsck** or **e2fsck** commands to check select the appropriate superblock for your Linux partition.

| **FIGURE 11-7**<br><br>The **dumpe2fs** command gives a lot of information. | ```
dumpe2fs 1.32 (09-Nov-2002)
Filesystem volume name:   /boot
Last mounted on:          <not available>
Filesystem UUID:          ae6d740d-25fb-40d2-b2e7-a5585f8345af
Filesystem magic number:  0xEF53
Filesystem revision #:    1 (dynamic)
Filesystem features:      has_journal filetype needs_recovery sparse_super
Default mount options:    (none)
Filesystem state:         clean
Errors behavior:          Continue
Filesystem OS type:       Linux
Inode count:              26104
Block count:              104391
Reserved block count:     5219
Free blocks:              86052
Free inodes:              26057
First block:              1
Block size:               1024
Fragment size:            1024
Blocks per group:         8192
Fragments per group:      8192
Inodes per group:         2008
Inode blocks per group:   251
--More--
``` |

on the **job**   *fsck is a "front end" for* e2fsck, *which is used to check partitions formatted to the ext2 and ext3 filesystems.*

Filesystem Check—fsck

You should also know how to use the **fsck** command. This command is a front end for most of the filesystem formats available in Linux, such as ext2, ext3, reiserfs, vfat, and more. This command is used to check the filesystem on a partition for consistency. In order to effectively use the **fsck** command, you need to understand something about how filesystems are laid out on disk partitions.

When you format a disk partition under Linux using the **mkfs** command, it sets aside a certain portion of the disk to use for storing *inodes*, which are data structures that contain the actual disk block addresses that point to file data on a disk. The **mkfs** command also stores information about the size of the filesystem, the filesystem label, and the number of inodes in a special location at the start of the partition called the *superblock*. If the superblock is corrupted or destroyed, the remaining information on the disk is unreadable. Because the superblock is so vital to the integrity of the data on a partition, the **mkfs** command makes duplicate copies of the superblock at fixed intervals on the partition, which you can find with the **dumpe2fs** command described earlier.
```

The **fsck** command checks for, and corrects problems with, filesystem consistency by looking for things such as disk blocks that are marked as free but are actually in use (and vice versa), inodes that don't have a corresponding directory entry, inodes with incorrect link counts, and a number of other problems. The **fsck** command will also fix a corrupted superblock. If **fsck** fails due to a corrupt superblock, you can use the **fsck** command with the **-b** option to specify an alternative superblock. For example, the command:

```
#  fsck -b 8193 /dev/hda5
```

tells **fsck** to perform a consistency check on the filesystem on disk partition /dev/hda5, using the superblock located at disk block 8193.

---

e x a m

w a t c h

Get to know the key commands and the associated options for checking disks and partitions: fdisk, e2label, dumpe2fs, and fsck.

Practice using these commands to check your partitions—on a test computer! (Some of these commands can destroy data.)

Boot Loaders

There are two boot loaders, GRUB and LILO. While you may be more familiar with LILO, Red Hat Enterprise Linux has adapted GRUB as the default boot loader. One of the benefits is that any changes that you make to the GRUB configuration file, /boot /grub/grub.conf, need not be written to your hard disk's Master Boot Record (MBR). However, if your MBR has been overwritten by an MS-DOS or Windows NT/2000/2003 boot loader, you can tell your BIOS to look for GRUB with the **grub-install** command. For example, if the /boot directory is on the first SCSI hard drive, you would run the following command:

```
# grub-install /dev/sda
```

Alternatively, if you are using LILO, you need to run the **lilo** command whenever you rebuild your Linux kernel or change the disk partition associated with the /boot directory. Otherwise, LILO may not be able to find your boot files. In this case, you will have to use the **linux rescue** environment to fix the problem.

In either case, errors to the boot loader configuration file are a common problem that can keep Linux from booting properly.

Missing Files

You may find corruption in some key files or commands such as **mount** or **init**. If you do, one option is to reload the files from the original RPMs. For example, if the **mount** command were to be corrupted or erased, you can reload it from the mount RPM.

When you boot your system into the **linux rescue** environment, using a network source, you have access to those network source files in the /mnt/source directory. After your computer boots into the **linux rescue** environment, you'll want to take the following steps:

1. Run the **df** command. You should see how the **linux rescue** environment mounted your partitions. You should also see your network source on the /mnt/source directory.

2. Copy the mount RPM from the /mnt/source directory. This allows you to reinstall the mount RPM later with files in the correct locations. Use the following command:

   ```
   # cp /mnt/source/RedHat/RPMS/mount-*.rpm /mnt/sysimage/root/
   ```

3. Run the following **chroot** command to move into the standard directory tree:

   ```
   # chroot /mnt/sysimage
   ```

4. Install the mount RPM, forcing installation over current files.

   ```
   # rpm -Uvh --force /root/mount-*.rpm
   ```

5. Check the status of the **mount** command.

   ```
   # rpm -Vf /bin/mount
   ```

If you see no output, you'll know that there is no longer a problem with the **mount** command. (You can also use this command at the start of the process to see if there is a problem.) You should now be able to run the **exit** command twice to reboot your computer—and at least this problem should be solved.

Places to Look First

Two places where you are likely to make errors that result in an unbootable system are in the boot loader and filesystem configuration files, /boot/grub/grub.conf and /etc/fstab. In each case, identifying the wrong partition as the root partition (/) can lead to a kernel panic. Other configuration errors in /boot/grub/grub.conf can also cause a kernel panic when you boot Linux. Whenever you make changes to these files, the only way to test them out is to reboot Linux.

The following scenarios and solutions list some possible problems and solutions that you can have during the boot process, and possible associated solutions. It is far from comprehensive. The solutions that I've listed work on my computer, as I've configured it. There may be (and often is) more than one possible cause. **These solutions may not work for you on your computer or on the Red Hat exams. To know what else to try, you need more experience.**

To get the equivalent of more experience, try additional scenarios as proposed in the following Scenario & Solution. Once you're familiar with the **linux rescue** environment, test these scenarios. For the first scenario shown, change the name of the grub.conf file so it can't be loaded. See what it does on your system. Use the **linux rescue** environment to boot into RHEL 3 and use the noted solution to fix your system. Two of the possible error messages are shown in Figure 11-8 and Figure 11-9.

| **FIGURE II-8**<br><br>One possible<br>error message | ```
Configuring kernel parameters:                        [  OK  ]
Setting clock  (localtime): Thu Jan  8 13:17:09 EST 2004   [  OK  ]
Loading default keymap (us):                          [  OK  ]
Setting hostname Enterprise3.example.com:             [  OK  ]
Initializing USB controller (usb-uhci):               [  OK  ]
Mounting USB filesystem:                              [  OK  ]
Initializing USB HID interface:                        [  OK  ]
Initializing USB keyboard:                            [  OK  ]
Initializing USB mouse:                               [  OK  ]
Checking root filesystem
fsck.ext2: /:
The superblock could not be read or does not describe a correct ext2
filesystem.  If the device is valid and it really contains an ext2
filesystem (and not swap or ufs or something else), then the superblock
is corrupt, and you might try running e2fsck with an alternate superblock:
    e2fsck -b 8193 <device>

Is a directory while trying to open /
                                                    [FAILED]

*** An error occurred during the file system check.
*** Dropping you to a shell; the system will reboot
*** when you leave the shell.
Give root password for maintenance
(or type Control-D to continue): _
``` |
```

FIGURE 11-9

A second possible
error message

```
 Booting 'Red Hat Enterprise Linux ES (2.4.21-4.EL)'

root (hd0,1)
 Filesystem type is ext2fs, partition type 0x83
kernel /vmlinuz-2.4.21-4.EL ro root=LABEL=/

Error 15: File not found

Press any key to continue..._
```

FIGURE 11-9

A second possible
error message

Summary of the linux rescue Environment

If you have a problem during the boot process, get as much information as you can. Use the experience that you have to recognize or diagnose the problem. Then boot into your system using a different method, confirm and then fix the problem (naturally, that's the hard part).

The easiest way to boot into an unbootable system is with a customized boot disk. Alternatively, you may be able to boot into your system at a different runlevel such as 1 or 3. If that is not available or appropriate to your problem, you'll also need to know how to use the **linux rescue** environment to rescue a system, using the following basic steps:

e x a m

⚆atch   *Whenever you're working in rescue mode or single-user mode, always remember to run the sync command to save changes to your drives before halting or rebooting your system.*

1. Boot using a Red Hat Enterprise Linux installation floppy or the first installation CD.

2. Know the location of your installation files, such as from a CD or over a network. You are taken to single-user mode.

3. At the rescue shell prompt, use **fdisk -l** *diskdevice* to identify your partitions.

4. If filesystem problems are suspected or indicated, run **fsck** on the afflicted partitions.

5. If the problem is with a configuration file:

    a. Create (a) temporary mount point(s), if necessary.

    b. Mount the appropriate partition(s), if necessary.

    c. Use the vi editor to fix the problem in the broken file(s).

6. Sync your changes to the drive.

7. Type the **exit** command as needed to restart the system.

SCENARIO & SOLUTION

When you boot RHEL 3, you see a grub> prompt in place of the standard GRUB boot menu.	You may have a problem that prevents the boot loader from reading the GRUB configuration file, grub.conf. The file may be missing or corrupt.
When you boot your computer, you see the following message: "Missing operating system"	Your Master Boot Record (MBR) has been erased, and you'll need to go into the Linux rescue environment and run **grub-install /dev/hda** (or /dev/sda) to reload GRUB on the MBR.
During the boot process, you see the following message: "Cannot open file '/proc/mounts' for reading (no such file or directory)"	You may have a problem with a corrupt **mount** command. You'll need to reload it from the mount RPM.
You see the following prompt: init-2.05b#	Check the current directory tree. If you see the standard directories, your **init** command may be corrupt. Try reloading it from the SysVinit RPM.
You see the following message: "INIT: No inittab file found"	This is straightforward—there is something wrong with your /etc/inittab file; it may be erased. You'll want to go into the **linux rescue** environment and restore it from backup or the initscripts RPM.
You see a message such as what's shown in Figure 11-8.	You may have a problem with the integrity of the /etc /fstab file. Start the **linux rescue** environment, check the integrity of /etc/fstab. If there is still a problem, run the steps described earlier to check the superblock and more. (For more experience, try including additional errors in /etc/fstab.)
You see a message similar to what's shown in Figure 11-9. Take careful note of the last file cited in the message.	RHEL 3 has encountered some problem when reading the grub.conf configuration file. Start the Linux rescue environment and check this file. Alternatively, check the files noted in grub.conf referenced in the /boot directory. For example, you can create a new initrd file with the **mkinitrd** command. (For more experience, try introducing other errors in the /boot directory.)
When you boot RHEL 3 into runlevel 5, you don't see a graphical login screen; a text login screen flashes periodically.	You may have some problem with the X Font Server. Boot into a different runlevel that does not require the X server, such as 1, 2, or 3. Check the **xfs** service script to see that it's set to run in runlevel 5. If yes, check for related error messages.
You see a Welcome to Kudzu screen during the boot process; afterwards, it stops after detecting a network card.	This is symptomatic of a problem with one of the boot scripts, such as /etc/inittab or /etc/rc.d/rc.sysinit. Boot into the **linux rescue** environment and check the files associated with the boot process.

EXERCISE 11-4

Performing an Emergency Boot Procedure

To do this exercise, you should have a test system at your disposal. Any data on the computer where you do this procedure is at risk. In this exercise, you will "break" your system by purposely misconfiguring a file and then reboot into the **linux rescue** environment to fix the problem. You'll be configuring a boot option in your GRUB menu which makes Linux look for boot files in the wrong partition.

1. Install the mkbootdisk RPM from a network source if required:

   ```
   # rpm -q mkbootdisk
   # rpm -Uvh /mnt/inst/RedHat/RPMS/mkbootdisk*
   ```

2. Even if you already have a boot disk, make one. Insert a floppy into the disk drive and type the following (the `uname -r` command switch includes the version number of the current kernel):

   ```
   # mkbootdisk `uname -r`
   ```

3. Edit the file /boot/grub/etc/grub.conf and make a copy of your boot stanza. Title this stanza badboot. Change the location of the root device to point to an invalid partition. For example, if your original grub.conf looks like this:

   ```
   default=0
   timeout=10
   splashimage=(hd0,0)/grub/splash.xpm.gz
   title Red Hat Enterprise Linux ES (2.4.21-4.EL)
           root=(hd0,0)
           kernel /vmlinuz-2.4.21-4.EL ro root=LABEL=/
           initrd /initrd-2.4.21-4.EL.img
   ```

   your new version should look like this:

   ```
   default=0
   timeout=10
   splashimage=(hd0,0)/grub/splash.xpm.gz
   title Red Hat Enterprise Linux ES (2.4.21-4.EL)
           root=(hd0,0)
           kernel /vmlinuz-2.4.21-4.EL ro root=LABEL=/
           initrd /initrd-2.4.21-4.EL.img

   title badboot
           root=(hd0,1)
           kernel /vmlinuz-2.4.21-4.EL ro root=LABEL=/
           initrd /initrd-2.4.21-4.EL.img
   ```

4. Reboot your system. In the GRUB menu, select badboot. GRUB will return a "File not found" message.

5. Since you left a valid boot stanza, your system isn't really broken. To fix the problem, however, you're going to boot into rescue mode. Insert your first RHEL 3 installation CD, and reboot the system. At the prompt, type **linux rescue askmethod**.

6. Proceed through the first steps of the Red Hat Enterprise Linux installation process.

7. When you see the Rescue menu, select Skip. None of your partitions will be mounted.

8. Although you know the source of the problem, once you boot into rescue mode, you should familiarize yourself with some of the repair utilities:

```
-/bin/sh-2.05b# fdisk  -l
   Device  Boot    Start       End    Blocks   Id  System
/dev/hda1    *         1        13    104391   83  Linux
/dev/hda2             14       474  3702982+   83  Linux
/dev/hda3            475       522   385560    82  Linux swap
```

The output of the following command will vary.

```
-/bin/sh-2.05b# fsck  -y  /dev/hda1
fsck 1.32 (09-Nov-2002)
WARNING: couldn't open /etc/fstab: No such file or directory
e2fsck 1.32 (09-Nov-2002)
/boot: clean, 47/26104 files, 18339/104391 blocks
```

9. Create (a) temporary mount point(s) for your /boot and root directory (/) partitions, and mount those partitions (if they are not already mounted). If the output from **fdisk -l** is different for you, revise the mounted devices accordingly.

```
-/bin/sh-2.05b# mkdir /tmpmnt
-/bin/sh-2.05b# mkdir /tmpmnt/boot
-/bin/sh-2.05b# mount /dev/hda1 /tmpmnt/boot
```

10. Edit the bad stanza in grub.conf and fix the problems:

```
-/bin/sh-2.05b# vi /tmpmnt/boot/grub/grub.conf
```

11. Your new version should look like this:

```
title badboot
        root=(hd0,0)
        kernel /vmlinuz-2.4.21-4.EL ro root=LABEL=/
        initrd /initrd-2.4.21-4.EL.img
```

12. Save your changes to the grub.conf file.

13. Unmount any mounted partitions and **sync** your changes:

    ```
    # umount /dev/hda1
    # sync
    ```

14. Remove any boot media from your disk drives. Type **exit** to unmount all drives and restart the system. You should now be able to boot from the badboot stanza.

CERTIFICATION OBJECTIVE 11.05

The Secure Shell Package

Red Hat Enterprise Linux 3 installs the Secure Shell (SSH) packages by default, using the openssh-server, openssh-clients, and openssh RPMs. The Secure Shell and Secure Copy programs, **ssh** and **scp**, are replacements for the **rsh**, **telnet**, and **rcp** programs. They encrypt communication between different computers. The secure daemon, sshd, listens for all inbound traffic on port 22. The SSH configuration files are located in the /etc/ssh directory.

The Secure Shell daemon works because it encrypts messages. RHEL 3 incorporates SSH version 2, which includes an enhanced key exchange algorithm.

Basic Encrypted Communication

Basic encryption in computer networking normally requires a private key and a public key. You keep the private key and send the public key to others. When they want to send data to you through SSH, their messages are encrypted with the public key. Your computer can descramble the message with the private key.

Encryption keys are based on random numbers. The numbers are so large (typically 512 bits or more), the chance that someone will break into your system, at least with a PC, is quite small in the foreseeable future. Private and public encryption keys are based on a matched set of these random numbers.

Private Keys

Your private key (essentially a file with your special number) must be secure. When you enable an application, it can attach the key to your messages. Anything you send—say, from your e-mail account—can then be digitally signed and encrypted. The public key is added to the end as part of your signature. Only the recipient will be able to decrypt the message.

Public Keys

Your public key value is just that, publicly available. A central authority such as Verisign, Globalsign, or Thawte provides public access to public keys they have created. If they generate a private key for you, they'll keep a secure copy on their system. You can just attach your public key to the e-mail, or the end users can publicly retrieve it from the Web site associated with the central authority.

The example shown in Figure 11-10 lists the directories and files associated with SSH usage as well as a public key that has been added to your "keyring."

This key is like a password used to encrypt your data. Imagine trying to remember the 1024-bit number expressed in hexadecimal value as shown below. That is why the applications save this value for you, on a "public keyring." You can add as many public keys from other users, sites, and services as you wish.

```
3081 8902 8181 00D4 596E 01DE A012 3CAD 51B7
7835 05A4 DEFC C70B 4382 A733 5D62 A51B B9D6
29EA 860B EC2B 7AB8 2E96 3A4C 71A2 D087 11D0
E149 4DD5 1E20 8382 FA58 C7DA D9B0 3865 FF6E
88C7 B672 51F5 5094 3B35 D8AA BC68 BBEB BFE3
9063 AE75 8B57 09F9 DCF8 FFA4 E32C A17F 82E9
7A4C 0E10 E62D 8A97 0845 007B 169A 0676 E7CF
5713 1423 96E0 8E6C 9502 0301 0001
```

Your private key is similar, *but you must keep it private*, or this whole system fails. Keeping it private means no one should have access to your PC. If your PC is public, secure your system with a passphrase (password), as shown in Figure 11-11, in order to use this key.

FIGURE 11-10

A public key

```
[root@Enterprise3 root]# ls .ssh/
id_dsa  id_dsa.pub  identity  identity.pub  known_hosts
[root@Enterprise3 root]# cat .ssh/id_dsa.pub
ssh-dss AAAAB3NzaC1kc3MAAACBAOC9nj2/VnRoQ1MoYzE1ULkaX3cH2YB1QB/H4TYsgXjxKyisv6eZ
/lujSoA3vUfQixeJ8Vf67+sswRoOzDIP1qV61D2tgueyN8s4YTOXx68qoOJfppabVuHl/Jw+O21d+YDH
oXNJAL4xWqCTe8mc2Fee1NVa3tasqQJ4+CA5WJkPAAAAFQCcSbdGnxO6EkoYqkLiXzCgNWqjbQAAAIBL
xSPrCX9yr6g6hUDiBf5iSGuXvjVCen47IRgukebFCnoWrDaD+5BfSz9ep7ompgZZGiZqsiEZTHJKRzu+
pZOzJGbLWKvnrzQz6OZCkk4L8cQbfAs8xgVcpLGM5wjVX2dtwcFIAPIfsdq/mXTOdHfehvO+EMxvL3GS
04cifu6gqAAAAIEAhbgY2XZ1cdg1utzz6GB5OIeChErEYsH2frd1TOGiXg5fm2W3XBTKQPuNBHsmIXD4
pnnO612qQoj8KMxojMQwd+9w2dMO/cNV+OZPtO/iwMK/qOBBiPksZUrz4Ij/hlL4HuaQxmgNKCTD2KT9
qYrg2MfjhjcqGIjoR1z1uL/xrfs= root@Enterprise3.example.com
[root@Enterprise3 root]#
```

FIGURE 11-11

Generating
encryption keys

```
[root@Enterprise3 root]# ssh-keygen -t dsa
Generating public/private dsa key pair.
Enter file in which to save the key (/root/.ssh/id_dsa):
Enter passphrase (empty for no passphrase):
Enter same passphrase again:
Your identification has been saved in /root/.ssh/id_dsa.
Your public key has been saved in /root/.ssh/id_dsa.pub.
The key fingerprint is:
ec:0d:48:0c:5b:38:6d:a0:31:c1:f2:c7:fb:b5:d3:e5 root@Enterprise3.example.com
[root@Enterprise3 root]# ssh-keygen -t rsa1
Generating public/private rsa1 key pair.
Enter file in which to save the key (/root/.ssh/identity):
Enter passphrase (empty for no passphrase):
Enter same passphrase again:
Your identification has been saved in /root/.ssh/identity.
Your public key has been saved in /root/.ssh/identity.pub.
The key fingerprint is:
94:f7:2d:10:48:6b:c3:07:b2:1c:42:e7:11:30:81:c3 root@Enterprise3.example.com
[root@Enterprise3 root]#
```

How to Generate Your Keys

There are a few SSH-oriented utilities you need to know about:

- **sshd** The daemon service; this must be running for inbound Secure Shell client requests.

- **ssh-agent** A program to hold private keys used for RSA authentication. The idea is that the **ssh-agent** command is started in the beginning of an X session or a login session, and all other windows or programs are started as clients to the ssh-agent program.

- **ssh-add** Adds RSA identities to the authentication agent, ssh-agent.

- **ssh** The Secure Shell command, **ssh**, is a secure way to log in to a remote machine, similar to Telnet or rlogin. To make this work, you need a private key on the server and a public key on the client. Take the public key file, identity.pub or id_dsa.pub, created later in this section. Copy it to the client. Place it in the home directory of an authorized user, in the ~/.ssh/authorized_keys or ~/.ssh/authorized_keys2 file.

- **ssh-keygen** A utility that will create your keys for you. The **ssh-keygen** **-t** *keytype* command will create the keys you desire. The *keytype* can be dsa (Digital Secure Algorithm) or rsa1 (RSA Security). The commands work as shown in Figure 11-11.

All you need to do is transfer the public key, with the .pub extension, to an authorized user. It's important to add a passphrase to protect that digital signature. In the worst case, a cracker could use this file to effectively steal your identity.

Why Use SSH?

The Internet is a public network. If you're connected to the Internet, anyone in the world could conceivably access your computer through this public network. All that is needed is Internet access from an anonymous location. In other words, a skilled cracker may be able to capture your passwords from a computer in a public library.

In contrast, private networks are used for security applications. Merchants who dial into a central server to check authorized credit card numbers are connecting to a private network. Access to such private networks can be expensive.

Unix and the network that became the Internet started in an educational setting, where there is a premium on the free exchange of information. While the resulting openness of the Internet is good, it can present security challenges. The original Unix tools developed for networks were not designed with security in mind.

These tools include **telnet**, **ftp**, and the "r" (remote) commands (**rlogin**, **rcp**, **rsh**). These utilities pass all information, including login names and passwords, across the network in clear text format. Anyone with a simple protocol analyzer such as Ethereal can find your password in this way. The Ethereal output shown in Figure 11-12 highlights one of the letters in a Telnet password on my private LAN (it's an "e"). The other Telnet packets contain the other letters and/or numbers of the password.

This is the Kerberos version of the Telnet server discussed in Chapter 7. While it's more secure than the older Telnet server, you can still find the clear text password using a tool such as Ethereal.

on the **!** Job *We do not in any way endorse the cracking of passwords. However, as a system administrator, you do need to know your vulnerabilities. If you can trace clear text passwords on your own network, you are at risk.*

The Secure Shell utilities were an answer to this problem, using high encryption standards. The Secure Shell tools replaced their insecure brethren and provided full encryption of all data between the hosts that is very hard to break, even by the "brute force" method.

FIGURE 11-12

It's easy to decipher a clear text password.

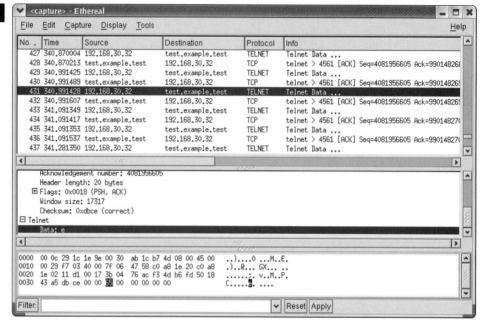

Brute Force Decryption

All computer data, including passwords, can be broken down into bits and bytes—in other words, 1s and 0s. If you can see the pattern of bits and bytes, you can decipher the password.

By convention, every character is associated with 7 of the 8 bits in a byte. Now assume you have 8 characters in a password. This makes for a 56-bit password. All you need to do to find the password is to compare it with every possible combination of bits and bytes. In other words, one of the bit-based values between 0 and 2^{56} (72,057,594,037,927,936) represents your password.

While this may seem like a large number, it is in fact trivial for a higher-end PC, which could decipher such a password in a matter of hours. This suggests that the older standard for secure HTTP Web pages, 40-bit encryption, is not very secure. On the other hand, the higher-level 128-bit-encrypted browsers are a lot more secure. It would take more than a few years for the latest PCs to break through such encryption.

By default, the **ssh-keygen** command creates encryption keys with 1024 bits. Breaking into such systems is beyond the capabilities of the latest PCs using brute force methods.

Lost Passphrase on Private Keys

Unfortunately, if you lose the passphrase on your private encryption key, there is no way to recover. You would need to start over, which means you would need to create a new set of keys and send your new public key to all concerned for them to replace your old public key.

PGP (Pretty Good Privacy)

E-mail has become a standard fixture in everyday business; e-mail security is a significant issue. One of the current standards for managing e-mail security is known as PGP (Pretty Good Privacy), developed by Phil Zimmerman. Like SSH, PGP provides a private- and public-key system for e-mail clients. The public key is usually attached to the end of the data, as shown in the next example.

The Linux implementation of PGP is known as GPG, the Gnu Privacy Guard. GPG is an implementation of the OpenPGP standard. Both standards are now common ways people and companies protect their correspondence.

```
******************************************************************
To:   Dreg (SD444466)
From: The SANS NewsBites service
*************************
---BEGIN PGP SIGNED MESSAGE---
Hash: SHA1
... (text removed)

Please feel free to share this with interested parties via e-mail (not
on bulletin boards).  For a free subscription, (and for free posters)
e-mail sans@sans.org with the subject: Subscribe NewsBites
...
-----BEGIN PGP SIGNATURE-----
Version: GnuPG v1.0.4 (BSD/OS)
Comment: For info see http://www.gnupg.org

iD8DBQE63beV+LUG5KFpTkYRAu/WAJ0fUwoQFUOETTd+wAbe1L784S3PDwCfULr0
DXDk20qZotKDLMfjLz1Gty4=
=K1Av
-----END PGP SIGNATURE-----
```

Notice in the previous listing that the BSD/OS (Berkeley Software Distribution/Operating System) is also using GPG, which is also known as GnuPG.

Validating RPMs with GPG

If you download an RPM from the Internet and would like to verify that it is an official unadulterated Red Hat RPM, GPG can help. All you need is the Red Hat Enterprise Linux public key. It's available from at least three different locations:

- Each Red Hat Enterprise Linux installation CD, in the main directory, in the RPM-GPG-KEY file

- On a standard Red Hat Enterprise Linux 3 installation, in /usr/share/rhn /RPM-GPG-KEY

- Online from www.redhat.com

First, you need to import the key. For example, if you want to import the key from the Red Hat installation CD, mounted on /mnt/cdrom, run the following command:

```
# rpm --import /mnt/cdrom/RPM-GPG-KEY
```

Now you should find the RPM-enabled key in the /var/lib/rpm/Pubkeys file. Next, you can verify the package's PGP-encrypted checksum using the **rpm -vK packagename** command. For example, if you wanted to verify the openoffice RPMs on a downloaded installation CD, run the following command:

```
# rpm -vK /mnt/cdrom/RedHat/RPMS/setup-*
```

on the **Ĵob**

Older versions of Red Hat Linux (and RHEL 2.1) used the gpg –import *keyfile command to download the Red Hat public GPG key. This is no longer possible with the advent of RPM version 4.1.*

CERTIFICATION OBJECTIVE 11.06

Managing Logical Volumes

Red Hat often waits a while before including software in its Linux distributions. I believe this practice promotes the interests of stability. This practice extends to Logical Volume Management (LVM). As a RHCE, you need to know how to add, remove, and resize Logical Volumes (LV).

You learned to create logical volumes during the installation process in Chapter 2, and after RHEL 3 is installed in Chapter 3. If you've created and mounted any Logical Volumes on your RHEL 3 computer, they should be readily available in the /etc/fstab configuration file. For example, I have a fairly generic LV for the /home directory on a different RHEL 3 computer, and it shows as the following command line in /etc/fstab:

```
/dev/Volume00/LogVol00   /home   ext3   defaults   1 2
```

Alternatively, you should be able to find the same basic information with the **vgscan** command. You can verify configured volume groups (VG) with the **vgdisplay** command. For example, Figure 11-13 illustrates the configuration of logical volume Volume00.

Before Logical Volumes are useful, you need to know how to add another LV. For example, if you've added more users, and they need more room than you have on the /home directory, you may need to add more LV for other filesystems, or resize the current /home directory Logical Volume.

Linux can't read /boot files if they're installed on a Logical Volume.

If you haven't added an LV before, you'll need to set up the basic files and the kernel LVM module, lvm-mod. To do so, run the **vgscan** command. This creates the /etc/lvmtab configuration file and adds the lvm-mod module. The next time you boot Linux, the /etc/rc.d/rc.sysinit file finds your /etc/lvmtab file and automatically loads the lvm-mod module.

FIGURE 11-13

Configuration of a Logical Volume (LV)

```
[root@Enterprise3a root]# vgdisplay Volume00
--- Volume group ---
VG Name               Volume00
VG Access             read/write
VG Status             available/resizable
VG #                  0
MAX LV                256
Cur LV                1
Open LV               1
MAX LV Size           255.99 GB
Max PV                256
Cur PV                2
Act PV                2
VG Size               1.71 GB
PE Size               4 MB
Total PE              438
Alloc PE / Size       275 / 1.07 GB
Free  PE / Size       163 / 652 MB
VG UUID               nSvJ9E-76ZC-hAOC-wFgj-j31I-ZUCh-zCO6pc


[root@Enterprise3a root]#
```

Adding Another Logical Volume

Adding another LV is a straightforward process. I've described it in some detail in Chapter 3, so I only summarize the steps here. For example, if you've just added a fourth SCSI hard drive, it's known as device /dev/sdd. If you need more Logical Vvolumes for the /tmp directory, you'd follow these basic steps:

1. Add the new hard drive.

2. Configure the new hard drive with partitions using a command tool such as **fdisk**. Make sure the hex code for the LVM partition(s) corresponds to the Linux LVM format. It's code 8e within **fdisk**. Alternatively, you can dedicate all space on the new hard drive as a Physical Volume (PV) with the **pvcreate /dev/sdd** command.

3. If you've created separate partitions, you can dedicate the space of a specific partition to a PV. If you don't already have an empty logical volume, you'll need to create more than one. For example, for the first partition /dev/sdd1, you can do this with the following command:

   ```
   # pvcreate /dev/sdd1
   ```

4. Next, you'll want to create a Volume Group (VG) from two or more empty, properly configured partitions (or drives). One way to do this, assuming you have an empty /dev/sdc3 partition, is with the following command:

   ```
   # vgcreate Volume01 /dev/sdc3 /dev/sdd1
   ```

5. Before proceeding, you should inspect the VG with the **vgdisplay** command. I've illustrated an example back in Figure 11-13.

6. You should now be able to add another LV with the **lvcreate** command. For example, the following command takes 20 Physical Extents (PE) for the new LV, LogVol01:

   ```
   # lvcreate -l 20 Volume01 -n LogVol01
   ```

7. You've added a new logical volume. Naturally, you'll need to format and mount a directory on this LV before you can use it. For the example shown, you would use the following commands:

   ```
   # mkfs -j /dev/Volume01/LogVol01
   # mount -t ext3 /dev/Volume01/LogVol01 /tmp
   ```

Removing Logical Volumes

Removing an existing LV requires a straightforward command. The basic command is **lvremove**. If you've created an LV in the previous section and want to remove it, the basic steps are simple:

1. Save any data in directories that are mounted on the LV.

2. Unmount any directories associated with the LV. Based on the example in the previous section, you would use the following command:

   ```
   # umount /dev/Volume01/LogVol01
   ```

3. Apply the **lvremove** command to the LV with a command such as:

   ```
   # lvremove /dev/Volume01/LogVol01
   ```

4. You should now have the PEs from this LV free for use in other LVs.

Resizing Logical Volumes

If you have an existing LV, you can add a newly created PV to extend the space available on your system. All it takes is appropriate use of the **vgextend** and **lvextend** commands. For example, if you want to add PEs to the VG associated with the aforementioned /home directory, you could take the following basic steps:

1. Back up any data existing on the /home directory.

2. Unmount the /home directory from the current logical volume.

3. Extend the VG to include the new hard drive or partitions that you've created. For example, if you wanted to add /dev/sdd1 to the /home VG, you would run the following command:

   ```
   # vgextend Volume00 /dev/sdd1
   ```

4. Make sure the new partitions are included in the VG with the following **vgdisplay** command:

   ```
   # vgdisplay Volume00
   ```

5. Extend the current LV to include the space you need. For example, if you wanted to extend the LV to 2000MB, you'd run the following command:

   ```
   # lvextend -L2000M /dev/Volume00/LogVol00
   ```

   The **lvextend** command can help you configure LVs in KB, MB, GB, or even TB. For example, you could get the same result with the following command:

   ```
   # lvextend -L2G /dev/Volume00/LogVol00
   ```

6. Reformat and remount the LV, using commands described earlier:

```
# mkfs -j /dev/Volume00/LogVol00
# mount -t ext3 /dev/Volume00/LogVol00 /home
```

CERTIFICATION SUMMARY

As you've seen in the past two chapters, there are many facets to system security. Making sure that network services run under nonprivileged accounts helps minimize the risks associated with outside attack.

By default, Red Hat Enterprise Linux assigns unique user and group ID numbers to each new user. This is known as the User Private Group scheme. This scheme allows you to configure special groups for a specific set of users. The users in the group can be configured with read and write privileges in a dedicated directory, courtesy of the SGID bit.

Two key cron jobs are anacron and tmpwatch. The anacron system, once installed from an outside source, automatically runs jobs that did not run while a RHEL 3 computer was turned off. The tmpwatch system is used to clear files from specified directories on a regular basis.

One of the most valuable skills you can have as a RHEL 3 systems administrator is knowing how to rescue a system. Some configuration problems can prevent a system from booting. Others can keep you from logging in. Key tools to manage configuration problems include: a boot disk from the **mkbootdisk** command, the **linux rescue** environment from a Red Hat installation floppy or CD, and single-user mode at the GRUB or LILO prompt. The **linux rescue** environment loads basic utilities and attempts to remount your directories on /mnt/sysimage. Key tools for managing problems include **fdisk**, **fsck**, **e2label**, and **dumpe2fs**.

Any network that is connected to an insecure network such as the Internet is vulnerable. The OpenSSH server can help you set up encrypted communication between computers. Encryption uses private and public keys. Whether you're using SSH or GPG, the default 1024-bit encryption scheme provides a "reasonable" level of security.

Finally, you need to know how to add, remove, and resize Logical Volumes (LV). Once you've configured partitions properly, you can add an LV with appropriate use of the **pvcreate**, **vgcreate**, and **lvcreate** commands. You can remove an LV with the **lvremove** command. You can resize an LV with the help of the **vgextend** and **lvextend** commands.

✓ TWO-MINUTE DRILL

Here are some of the key points from the certification objectives in Chapter 11.

Services and Special Users

❑ When Red Hat Enterprise Linux starts on your computer, it triggers a special process known as init, which then opens the other basic processes required for a working Linux system.

❑ Many services have their own user ID, as shown in /etc/passwd; alternatively, some services can run under the nobody account.

❑ Service user IDs are not for real users.

Red Hat User Private Group Scheme

❑ Red Hat's user private group scheme configures users with their own unique user and group ID numbers.

❑ With appropriate SGID permissions, you can configure a shared directory for a specific group of users.

❑ Setting the SGID bit ensures that all files created in a shared directory belong to the correct group.

❑ Setting the SGID bit is easy; use **chown** to set nobody as the user owner, and the name of the group as the group owner. Then run the **chmod 2770** command on the shared directory.

anacron and tmpwatch

❑ The **anacron** service includes a special cron job which runs jobs that were supposed to be run while a computer is powered down.

❑ The **tmpwatch** command (/usr/sbin/tmpwatch) is used to remove files that have not been accessed in a specified number of hours.

The linux rescue Environment

❑ Rescue disks aren't always available. Be prepared to use the **linux rescue** environment from a Red Hat installation CD.

❑ One good boot disk customized for your system can be created with the **mkbootdisk** command.

❑ When you start the **linux rescue** environment, be able to access the Red Hat installation files.

❑ The **linux rescue** environment may be able to mount your filesystems on /mnt /sysimage. It will provide a minimum set of commands such as **fdisk** and **fsck**, and utilities such as vi.

❑ If your filesystems are properly mounted, you can access documents such as man pages normally after a **chroot /mnt/sysimage** command.

❑ Linux may not be able to mount all of your filesystems.

❑ Some mount points fail because of bad labels. Check the label on a specific partition with the **e2label** command.

❑ The **fsck** command is used to check the filesystem on a partition for consistency.

❑ The **dumpe2fs** command can provide a lot of information about each partition, including the label, the journal, and the block size.

❑ One alternative to the **linux rescue** environment is single-user mode. You can even boot from GRUB into other runlevels such as 3 and 5.

❑ Common problem files that can prevent Linux from booting include /boot /grub/grub.conf and /etc/fstab.

The Secure Shell Package

❑ The OpenSSH command utilities—sshd, ssh, ssh-keygen, ssh-add, and ssh-agent—provide secure remote services over any network connections.

❑ Encryption is based on private and public keys.

❑ You can keep your private key secure with a passphrase.

❑ Public keys are shared with others so that they can communicate with you through SSH.

❑ As it is easy to decipher traffic, even passwords, from **telnet**, **ftp**, and the "r" commands, it is best to use SSH on any publicly accessible network.

❑ PGP, Pretty Good Privacy, is the way much e-mail is encrypted today.

❑ The Linux implementation of PGP is GPG.

❑ You can validate the signature of any RPM using the **rpm -vK** *packagename* command.

Managing Logical Volumes

❑ To add an LV, you need to know how to use the **pvcreate**, **vgcreate**, and **lvcreate** commands.

❑ To remove an LV, you need to know how to use the **lvremove** command.

❑ To resize an LV, you need to know how to use the **vgextend** and **lvextend** commands.

SELF TEST

The following questions will help you measure your understanding of the material presented in this chapter. Read all the choices carefully, as there may be more than one correct answer. Choose all correct answers for each question. Don't focus exclusively on these questions. There are no longer any multiple choice questions on the Red Hat exams. These questions test your understanding of the chapter. Getting results, not memorizing trivia, is what counts on the Red Hat exams.

Services and Special Users

1. You are setting up a Red Hat Enterprise Linux system and are adding several new services. What can you do to make sure your system is more secure from outside attack?

   A. Create individual accounts for each service.

   B. Pick a really secure password for the root account.

   C. Run services under their own accounts, or alternatively, the nobody account.

   D. Make sure the system is stored in a secure room.

Red Hat User Private Group Scheme

2. You've just issued the following command: **chown nobody.developgrp /home/developer**. How would you set the SGID bit on this directory?

   A. chmod 2775 /home/developer

   B. chgrp 2775 /home/developer

   C. chmod 775 /home/developer

   D. chmod g+s /home/developer

anacron and tmpwatch

3. What are the normal uses of the **tmpwatch** command script?

   A. To monitor the system for break-in attempts

   B. To clean up unused user account directories

   C. To scan system-wide temporary directories and clean up old temporary files

   D. To monitor the /tmp directory for the appearance of certain files

The linux rescue Environment

4. The junior system administrator at your site has just come to you to report a suspected bad hard drive on the system he was working on. Whenever he tries to boot the system, he gets a kernel panic with a message saying the root partition cannot be found. What is the most likely cause?

    A. The hard drive has crashed.

    B. The I/O bus is going bad.

    C. Intermittent RAM problems are masquerading as disk problems.

    D. The junior system administrator was modifying a system configuration file and has managed to configure the system so that it will not boot.

5. How can you boot a damaged Linux system in order to perform repairs?

    A. Boot from your system's custom boot floppy.

    B. Boot into the **linux rescue** environment.

    C. Boot into single-user mode. To do so, add the word **single** to the end of the kernel command line in GRUB.

    D. Boot into runlevel 4.

6. You are a consultant and are helping a client who has managed to render his system unbootable. You have booted into rescue mode, but the client doesn't have any documentation on the partition layout on his disk drive. What can you do?

    A. Use the **fdisk -l** command to display the partition table for installed drives.

    B. Reinstall Linux.

    C. Use the **fsck** command and look for the superblock.

    D. Use the **fdisk** command in interactive mode.

7. You are trying to boot a system and keep receiving a message about a corrupted partition. You manage to boot into rescue mode. From this point, what might you do to fix the problem?

    A. Use **fdisk** and delete the partition, then add it back.

    B. Use the **fdisk -l** command.

    C. Run **grub-install** to rebuild the boot block on the BIOS.

    D. Run the command **fsck -b 8193**.

8. Where are some likely places for configuration errors that can prevent your system from booting? (Choose all that apply.)

    A. /boot/grub/grub.conf

    B. /etc/fstab

    C. /etc/passwd

    D. /boot

The Secure Shell Package

9. When you set up a set of secure RSA keys for Secure Shell access, what should you do?

   A. Run **ssh-keygen -t dsa1**, and then enter a passphrase for your public key.

   B. Run **ssh-keygen -t rsa**, and then enter a passphrase for your private key.

   C. Run **ssh-keygen -t dsa1**, and then enter a passphrase for your private key.

   D. Run **ssh-keygen -t rsa1**, and then enter a passphrase for your private key.

Managing Logical Volumes

10. If you already have added PEs to your VG and want to add room to your LV with your /var directory, what command would you use to increase the size of that LV? Assume that you've backed up any essential data from /var, and the volume names stated in the answers are correct.

   A. vgextend Volume00 /dev/hdd1

   B. lvcreate -L2000M /dev/Volume00/LogVol00

   C. lvextend -L2000M /dev/Volume00/LogVol00

   D. vgcreate Volume00 /dev/hdc1 /dev/hdd1

LAB QUESTIONS

Lab 1

In this lab, you'll create a private directory for a group of engineers designing some galleys. You'll want to create a group named galley for the engineers named mike, rick, terri, and maryam. They'll want to share files in the /home/galley directory. What do you need to do?

Lab 2

In this lab, you'll configure the tmpwatch script in /etc/cron.daily to delete files from the /var/log /httpd directory on a periodic basis. You're doing this because the data that comes through your Web server is overwhelming your system. Unless you delete older files from this directory on a periodic basis, the data will crowd out the space needed by your users. Presumably, you're doing this until your new hard disk array is ready in a few weeks.

Lab 3

For this exercise, use a test computer. Do not use a production computer. Do not use a computer where any data might be important to you. If something goes wrong, and you are unable to restore from a backup, you may need to reinstall Linux. This exercise assumes that you're using the default Red Hat Enterprise Linux boot loader, GRUB.

Navigate to the /boot directory. Change the name of the initrd-*versionnumber*.img file. Make sure it's something easy to remember such as initrd-*versionnumber*.bak. Reboot Linux. As GRUB goes through the boot sequence, it will probably stop when it can't find your Initial RAM Disk (initrd) file, similar to what is shown in Figure 11-14.

Now that your boot loader isn't working, what do you do? Can you try to start Linux in single-user mode?

Lab 4

Your company bought another competitor on the opposite coast recently, just as the new corporate application was being deployed everywhere, so you sent the app to them, too. They use a Unix host for this application on their network. You need to be able to connect to this host for maintenance purposes on the new system-wide application you deployed. Both networks have Internet access.

Lab 5

In this lab, you'll create new PEs, and use them to increase the size of a configured LV. You're doing this for the LV used by the /var directory. Because of the increasing demands of your Web site, you need more room for the /var directory for your Web site data. Assume your /etc/fstab configuration file includes the following line:

```
/dev/Volume00/LogVol00   /var   ext3   defaults   1 2
```

You've created PEs from the /dev/sde and /dev/sdf hard drives, and have just added another SCSI hard drive, /dev/sdg. Assume you've backed up the data that you need from the /var directory.

FIGURE 11-14	
A boot failure	

```
    Booting 'Red Hat Enterprise Linux ES (2.4.21-4.EL)'

root (hd0,0)
 Filesystem type is ext2fs, partition type 0x83
kernel /vmlinuz-2.4.21-4.EL ro root=LABEL=/
    [Linux-bzImage, setup=0x1400, size=0x12c9d1]
initrd /initrd-2.4.21-4.EL.img

Error 15: File not found

Press any key to continue..._
```

SELF TEST ANSWERS

Services and Special Users

1. ☑ **A** and **C**. You should run network services under their own accounts or the nobody account. If a cracker does find a security hole, the damage will be limited to that service.

   ☒ **B** and **D** are incorrect. **B** is a good idea, but most outside crackers get root account privileges through security holes they find in programs or services. **D** is always a good idea but does nothing to protect your system from attacks from the outside, such as from the Internet.

Red Hat User Private Group Scheme

2. ☑ **A** and **D**. Both commands will set the SGID bit. Answer **D** is sometimes more appropriate, as it does not affect the permissions for the owner or others.

   ☒ **B** is incorrect, as **chgrp** does not modify SGID bits, and **C** is incorrect because it does not include the proper value for the SGID bit (2*xyz*).

anacron and tmpwatch

3. ☑ **C**. The **tmpwatch** command is usually run periodically by the cron daemon. It recursively searches through temporary directories and removes files that have not been accessed for a fixed amount of time.

   ☒ **A**, **B**, and **D** are incorrect. While **tmpwatch** does not monitor break-in attempts, you may be able to do this by creating /var/log/tmp using the system logging service (**A**). While it is a good idea to clean up unused account directories (**B**), you may not want to delete directories of people who are just on vacation. The **tmpwatch** command utility (**D**) does not monitor any directory for the appearance of specific files.

The linux rescue Environment

4. ☑ **D**. In a situation like this, the cause is most likely human error.

   ☒ **A**, **B**, and **C** are incorrect. If you have a kernel panic, then you know that your PC has checked its hardware and run through its initial BIOS checks. Therefore, you know that the hard disk is not bad (**A**), the I/O bus still works (**B**), and RAM was detected (**C**).

5. ☑ **A**, **B**, and **C** are correct procedures to boot a damaged Linux system in order to perform repairs.

   ☒ **D** is incorrect. By default, Red Hat Enterprise Linux does not use runlevel 4.

6. ☑ **A** is a good starting point, which will allow you to determine what partitions are available. Alternatively, **D** will give you some clues as to partition sizes. In addition, you could then try the **e2label** command; if you're fortunate, you'll see the labels associated with actual mounted partitions such as /boot or /home. One other approach is to just mount each partition, look at the file contents, and deduce what filesystem it represents.

   ☒ **B** and **C** are incorrect. Reinstallation is a last resort (**B**), would take too much time, and isn't allowed on either Red Hat troubleshooting exams. The **fsck** command might tell you the name of the partition (**C**), but you may end up waiting a long time.

7. ☑ **D**. Try running the **fsck** command with an alternative superblock, such as 8193, 16385, and so on. You can use the **dumpe2fs** command to help determine the appropriate superblock size.

   ☒ **A** might fix the problem but would have the unfortunate side effect of deleting all the data on the partition. **B** would just list the configured partitions, and **C** does not do anything to fix your existing partitions.

8. ☑ **A**, **B**, and **D**. Any typo in the /boot/grub/grub.conf or /etc/fstab files can make a good system unbootable. Any time you make changes that affect the files in /boot, you should make sure grub.conf reflects these changes.

   ☒ **C** is incorrect. The /etc/passwd file contains user authentication information and does not affect how Linux boots on your computer.

The Secure Shell Package

9. ☑ **D**. RSA keys are configured by the **ssh-keygen -t rsa1** command. A passphrase can be used to protect your private key.

   ☒ **A**, **B**, and **D** are incorrect. As of this writing, there are no dsa1 key options for the **ssh-keygen** command; even if there are, it would work with Digital Signature Algorithm keys (**A**, **C**). The **rsa** option is currently obsolete (**D**).

Managing Logical Volumes

10. ☑ **C**. The **lvextend** command extends the scope of the LV to the size specified with the -L switch, in this case, 2000MB.

   ☒ **A**, **B**, and **D** are incorrect. The **vgextend** command adds more PEs from a newly configured partition to a current VG. It may be required before you increase the size of the LV, but does not address the question. The **lvcreate** command creates a new LV. It does not increase the size of an LV, as stated in the question. The **vgcreate** command creates a new VG, which is not directly related to the question.

LAB ANSWERS

Lab 1

This is a straightforward process, using the following basic steps:

1. Create accounts for mike, rick, terri, and maryam if required. You can use the **useradd** command, edit the /etc/passwd file directly, or work through the Red Hat User Manager.

2. Set up a group for these users. Configure a group ID outside the range of your regular users with a line such as:

    ```
    galley::10000:mike,rick,terri,maryam
    ```

3. Create the /home/galley directory. Give it proper ownership and permissions with the following commands:

    ```
    # mkdir /home/galley
    # chown nobody.galley /home/galley
    # chmod 2770 /home/galley
    ```

Lab 2

In this lab, you'll want to set up a command in the tmpwatch script in the /etc/cron.daily directory, which deletes files that haven't been accessed for a certain number of hours. The commands in the default version of this script can help guide you in this process. For example, if you wanted to delete files that haven't been accessed in more than 30 calendar days, you just need to translate this into the equivalent number of hours. Thus, all you need to do is add the following command to the noted script:

    ```
    /usr/sbin/tmpwatch 720 /var/log/httpd
    ```

Lab 3

As you practice learning about Linux for the RHCE exam, it's important to know how GRUB works. By default, it requires an initial RAM disk file, initrd-*versionnumber*.img. If GRUB can't find this file, it'll give you the error shown in Figure 11-14. Since your computer does not boot, you'll need to boot with a rescue disk before you can fix the initrd file. Remember to make sure that the filename matches the name shown in /boot/grub/grub.conf *exactly*.

You can repeat this process with the vmlinuz file or the root directive in grub.conf. Make sure to have backups of key files so you can restore your original configuration. When you repeat this process, what happens after you select a kernel from the GRUB menu? Do you see a different error? Is it associated with a different file?

Understanding these answers can help you learn to use GRUB messages to better diagnose specific problems with Linux.

Lab 4

If you need access now, and both systems are connected to the Internet, you can set up SSH for secure communications. If the other network does not already have it installed, have them download it from the Internet, install it, and then create an account for you.

The basic steps which are outlined here may vary with the version of Unix used on the other network.

Get the OpenSSH utility source from the Net and put it into a specific directory. Since RPMs are not yet made for Unix, you'll need to unpack a "tarball." You can then unpackage the files in the tarball and use the files in the resulting directory to compile and configure a Secure Shell server. Once it is configured, set up private and public keys.

If you don't need immediate access, you could, alternatively, configure a computer with Linux and a Secure Shell server. Send the computer to the administrator of the remote Unix network. Have them add it to their network, and you can check the problem from your site securely. The application is running on the Linux computer that you sent. (Alternatively, you can even set up OpenSSH on Microsoft Windows, as described earlier in this chapter.)

Lab 5

If you've just added the new hard drive, you'll need to set up partitions or use the entire hard drive for PEs. Based on the premises of the lab, you have the entire SCSC /dev/sdg hard drive available, so you can just allocate this entire hard drive as PEs with the following command:

```
# pvcreate /dev/sdg
```

The next step is to extend the VG, Volume00, to include the newly configured PEs. You can do so with the following command:

```
# vgextend Volume00 /dev/sdg
```

With the additional PEs at your disposal, you can increase the size of the LV allocated to the /var directory. For example, if you wanted to increase the size to 2GB, you could run the following command:

```
# lvextend -L2G /dev/Volume00/LogVol00
```

A

About the CD

T he CD-ROM included with this book comes with two complete pencil-and-paper RHCE practice exams that are accessible in Linux with the Web browser of your choice. The CD also contains the electronic version of the book. You may browse the electronic book or pencil-and-paper exams directly from the CD from a Linux or a Microsoft Windows computer.

There are no longer any multiple choice questions on the Red Hat exams. You can read the sample exams in a Web browser on a Linux computer. Whatever format you select, we suggest that you print out the exam questions before trying the sample exams.

Using the CD in Linux

The exams and e-book are accessible in Linux. The exams are available on the CD in the mnt/cdrom/RHCE/exams directory. The e-book is accessible through the Linux PDF reader, **xpdf**. You can start it from the Linux GUI with the **xpdf** command, or you can click Main Menu | Graphics | PDF Viewer. When **xpdf** opens, click **o**, the PDF Viewer open command, and navigate to the /mnt/cdrom/Programs/eBook directory to open the e-book chapter of your choice. Please note that these directories assume that you've mounted your CD on the /mnt/cdrom directory.

System Requirements

If you have Red Hat Enterprise Linux 3 installed, you'll need the xpdf-* RPM package. It is normally installed by default. The xpdf-* RPM is also available on Red Hat Linux 9 and Fedora Core. The standard graphical hardware requirements for RHEL 3 are sufficient to open and read the files on the CD.

Running the CD in Microsoft Windows

We understand that as an Red Hat exam candidate, you may be using Linux as your only operating system. If you have Microsoft Windows installed, and if your computer CD-ROM drive is configured to autorun, the CD-ROM will automatically start up upon inserting the disk. From the opening screen, you may browse the electronic book or view the RHCE practice exams using the Windows interface. There is no additional benefit if you're reading the CD from Microsoft Windows.

System Requirements

If you have Microsoft Windows installed, the software requires Windows 98 or higher and Internet Explorer 5.0 or above. The electronic book requires Adobe Acrobat Reader.

Electronic Book

The entire contents of the Study Guide are provided in PDF, which you can read in Linux or Microsoft Windows. We've previously described how you can read PDF files using the Linux **xpdf** reader. For Microsoft Windows users, Adobe's Acrobat Reader has been included on the CD.

Help

A help file is provided through the help button on the main page in the lower-left corner.

Removing Installation(s)

This section applies only to Microsoft Windows computers. If Real Player has been installed on your system and you want to remove Real Player, use the Add/Remove Programs icon from your Control Panel. If you have purchased any LearnKey training for Microsoft Windows, you may also remove the LearnKey training program from this location.

Technical Support

For questions regarding the technical content of the electronic book, please visit www.osborne.com or e-mail customer.service@mcgraw-hill.com. For customers outside the 50 United States, e-mail international_cs@mcgraw-hill.com.

LearnKey Technical Support

For technical problems with the software (operation), and for questions regarding LearnKey Online Training, please visit www.learnkey.com or e-mail techsupport@ learnkey.com.

Glossary

~ The tilde (~) represents the home directory of the current user.

Address Resolution Protocol (ARP)   A protocol that maps an IP address to the hardware address on a network card.

anacron   The **anacron** service, while not included with RHEL 3, is part of the RHCT prep course as of this writing (and is therefore required knowledge for RHCEs). It runs **cron** jobs that could not run while a server was powered down.

Apache Web server   The Apache Web server provides both normal and secure Web services. Apache is controlled by the **httpd** daemon.

apachectl   The **apachectl** command is the preferred method to start and stop an Apache server.

arp (Address Resolution Protocol) command   The **arp** command is used to view or modify the kernel's ARP table. Using **arp**, you can detect problems such as duplicate addresses on the network. Alternatively, you can use **arp** to add the required entries from your LAN.

at   The **at** command is similar to **cron**, but it allows you to run a job on a one-time basis.

authentication   The way Linux checks the login rights of a user. Linux and Unix users are normally authenticated through use of a username and password, checked against /etc/passwd and related files.

Automounter   The Automounter can be configured to mount local and network directories on an as-needed basis. It's configured in /etc/auto.master and /etc/auto.misc.

BIND (Berkeley Internet Name Domain)   BIND is the Unix/Linux software that is used to set up a Domain Name System (DNS) service. The associated daemon is **named**.

/boot   The directory with the main files required to boot Linux, including the Linux kernel and initial RAM disk. By default, /boot is mounted on a separate partition.

BOOTP   A TCP/IP protocol that sends IP address information from a remote DHCP server.

caching-only name server   A caching-only name server performs many of the functions of a DNS server. It stores the IP address associated with recent name searches, for use by other computers on your LAN.

chage   The **chage** command manages the expiration date of a password.

chains   Chains are **iptables** (or **ipchains**) commands that are linked together. These are linked rules that are applied to each network packet that passes through a Linux firewall computer. **iptables** is the standard for RHEL 3.

chgrp   The **chgrp** command changes the group that owns a file.

chkconfig   The **chkconfig** command manages runlevel service information. It can activate or deactivate services. It can also customize services at specific runlevels.

chmod   The **chmod** command changes the permissions on a file.

chown   The **chown** command changes ownership on a file.

CIFS (Common Internet File System)   CIFS is the Microsoft name for advances in its networking software. It's also covered by the latest version of Samba, 3.0, which is included with RHEL 3.

client   A client is a computer that accesses information or resources from a server.

CNAME (canonical name)   The CNAME is a way to assign several different names to a computer in a DNS database. For example, you can set up www as an alias for the computer with your Web server. CNAME records cannot be assigned to a mail server (MX) or a Start of Authority (SOA) record.

cron   A service which runs jobs on a periodic basis. It's configured in /etc/crontab; by default, it executes jobs in the /etc/cron.hourly, /etc/cron.daily, /etc/cron.weekly, and /etc/cron.monthly directories.

crontab   Individual users can run the **crontab** command to configure jobs that are run periodically.

CUPS (Common Unix Printing System)   CUPS is the default print service for RHEL 3.

daemon   A process such as the Web service (**httpd**) or X font server (**xfs**) that runs in the background and executes as required.

/dev   The directory with device files, used to represent hardware and software components.

DHCP (Dynamic Host Configuration Protocol)   DHCP clients lease IP addresses for a fixed period of time from a DHCP server on a local network. The BOOTP protocol allows DHCP clients to get IP address information from a remote DHCP server. The DHCP server daemon is **dhcpd**; the DHCP client daemon is **dhclient**.

Disk Druid   Anaconda's hard disk management program. While the functionality is similar to **fdisk**, it is easier to use. However, Disk Druid is available only during the Linux installation process.

display manager   A Linux display manager includes a dialog box for your username and password. Three major display managers are used in RHEL 3: **gdm** (GNOME), **kdm** (KDE), and **xdm**.

dmesg   The **dmesg** command lists the kernel ring buffer, the initial boot messages.

DNS (Domain Name System)   This service maintains a database of domain names such as www.redhat.com and IP addresses such as 206.132.41.202. If the domain name is not in the local database, DNS is normally configured to look to other, more authoritative DNS servers. The associated daemon is **named**.

dumpe2fs   The **dumpe2fs** command provides a lot of information about the format of a partition.

e2label   The e2label command associates a device with a filesystem directory.

edquota   The **edquota** command edits the quota for a user or a group.

emacs   The emacs editor is a popular text editor, which can be run from a text console.

environment   Each user's environment specifies default settings such as login prompts, terminals, the PATH, mail directories, and more.

/etc/fstab   The /etc/fstab configuration file defines default mounted directories.

/etc/inittab   The /etc/inittab configuration file sets the default runlevel and starts key processes such as terminal gettys.

/etc/X11/prefdm   The /etc/X11/prefdm configuration file specifies the preferred GUI display manager.

exportfs   The **exportfs** command allows shared NFS directories to be shared with a network.

fdisk   A standard disk partition command utility, which allows you to modify the physical and logical disk partition layout.

Fedora Linux   The successor to the freely available version of Red Hat Linux; more information on this Linux distribution is available online at fedora.redhat.com.

filesystem   Filesystem has multiple meanings in Linux. It refers to mounted directories; the root directory (/) filesystem is formatted on its own partition. It also refers to file formats; Linux partitions are typically formatted to the ext3 filesystem.

Filesystem Hierarchy Standard   The official way to organize files in Unix and Linux directories. The top level directory is known as the root directory (/); users' home directories are configured in /home.

find   The **find** command searches for a desired file through a given directory and its subdirectories.

fips   The First Interactive Partition Splitter, **fips**, allows you to split existing VFAT partitions.

firewall   A hardware or software system that prevents unauthorized access over a network. Normally used to protect a private LAN from attacks through the Internet.

firstboot   The process that starts when you've configured RHEL 3 during installation to boot into the GUI (runlevel 5).

fsck   The **fsck** command checks the filesystem on a Linux partition for consistency.

FTP (File Transfer Protocol)   A TCP/IP protocol designed to optimize file transfer between computers.

gateway   A route from a computer to another network. A default gateway address is the IP address of a computer or router that connects a LAN with another network such as the Internet.

getty   A getty is a terminal program, which includes prompts for a login and a password. Virtual console gettys are configured through the **mingetty** program via /etc/inittab.

GNOME (GNU Network Object Model Environment)   GNOME is the default GUI desktop for Red Hat Enterprise Linux.

GPG (GNU Privacy Guard)   GPG is an implementation of the OpenPGP standard included with Red Hat Linux.

group ID   Every Linux group has a group ID, as defined in /etc/group.

GRUB (Grand Unified Bootloader)   The default boot loader for RHEL 3.

grub-install   The **grub-install** command makes your BIOS look for your GRUB boot loader.

home directory   The home directory is the login directory for Linux users. Normally, this is /home/*user*, where *user* is the user's login name. It's also represented by the tilde (~) in any Linux command.

ICMP (Internet Control Message Protocol)   A protocol for sending error /control messages. Associated with the **ping** command.

ifconfig   The **ifconfig** command is used to configure and display network devices.

init   The **init** process is the first Linux process called by the kernel. This process starts other processes that compose a working Linux system, including the shell.

Internet Print Protocol (IPP)   The Internet Print Protocol (IPP) is the evolving standard for printers shared over networks. It's being adapted by all major operating systems; the Linux implementation is CUPS.

IP forwarding   IP forwarding is where data is forwarded between computers or networks through your computer.

iptables   The **iptables** command is the basic command for firewalls and masquerading.

KDE   A GUI for Linux and Unix computers. Also known as the K Desktop Environment.

kernel   The kernel is the heart of any operating system. It loads device drivers. You can recompile a Linux kernel for additional drivers, for faster loading, and to minimize the required memory.

kernel module   Kernel modules are pluggable drivers that can be loaded and unloaded into the kernel as needed. Some loaded kernel modules are shown with the **lsmod** command.

Kickstart   Kickstart is the Red Hat automated installation system, which allows you to supply the answers required during the installation process. When properly configured, a kickstart floppy can allow you to start your computer and install RHEL 3 automatically from a network source.

LDP (Linux Documentation Project)   The LDP is a global effort to produce reliable documentation for all aspects of the Linux operating system. Its work is available online at www.tldp.org.

lftp   The **lftp** command starts a slightly more flexible FTP command line client.

Lightweight Directory Access Protocol (LDAP)   The Lightweight Directory Access Protocol allows you to keep authentication information on a central server on your network.

locate   The **locate** command searches through a default database of files and directories.

logrotate   The **logrotate** command utility allows you maintain log files. By default, RHEL 3 uses the **cron** daemon to rotate, compress, and remove various log files.

lpq   You can use the **lpq** command to view print jobs still in progress.

lpr   You can use the **lpr** command to send print requests.

lprm   You can use the **lprm** command to remove print jobs from the queue.

logical extent (LE)   A logical extent (LE) is a chunk of disk space that corresponds to a physical extent (PE).

logical volume (LV)   A logical volume (LV) is composed of a group of LEs.

Logical Volume Management (LVM)   Logical Volume Management (LVM) allows you to set up a filesystem on multiple partitions.

lvcreate   The **lvcreate** command creates a logical volume (LV) from a specified number of available PEs.

lvremove   The **lvremove** command is functionally opposite to the **lvcreate** command.

masquerading   Masquerading enables you to provide Internet access to all of the computers on a LAN with a single public IP address.

MBR (Master Boot Record)   The first sector of a bootable disk. Once the BIOS cycle is complete, it looks for a program on the MBR, which then looks at a boot loader configuration file such as grub.conf to see how to start an operating system.

mkbootdisk   The **mkbootdisk** command can create a boot disk, customized for your system.

mkfs   The **mkfs** command can help you format a newly configured partition.

mount   The **mount** command can specify mounted partitions, or attach local or network partitions to specified directories.

NAT (Network Address Translation)   NAT is a feature associated with firewall commands such as **iptables,** which connects computers inside your LAN to the Internet while disguising their true IP addresses. NAT modifies IP packet headers. The process is reversed for return messages. Closely related to masquerading.

netstat   The **netstat** command can display connectivity information for your network cards. For example, the **netstat -r** command is used to display the routing tables as stored in your kernel.

Network Time Protocol (NTP)   The Network Time Protocol allows you to synchronize your computer with a central timeserver. You can do this on RHEL 3 with the Date/Time Configuration tool.

NFS (Network File System)   NFS is a file-sharing protocol originally developed by Sun Microsystems; it is the networked filesystem most commonly used for networks of Linux and Unix computers.

NIC (Network Interface Card)   A NIC connects your computer to a network. A NIC can be anything from a Gigabit Ethernet adapter to a telephone modem.

NIS (Network Information System)   NIS allows you to share one centrally managed authorization database for the Linux and Unix systems on your network.

PAM (Pluggable Authentication Module)   PAM separates the authentication process from individual applications. PAM consists of a set of dynamically loadable library modules that configures how an application verifies its users before allowing access.

PATH   A shell variable that specifies the directories (and in what order) the shell automatically searches for input commands and files.

PGP (Pretty Good Privacy)   A technique for encrypting messages, often used for e-mail. It includes a secure private- and public-key system similar to RSA. The Linux version of PGP is known as GPG.

physical extent (PE)   A chunk of disk space created from a PV for LVM.

physical volume (PV)   An area of space for an LVM, which usually corresponds to a partition or a hard drive.

Primary Domain Controller (PDC)   A PDC is the governing server on a Microsoft Windows NT 4 network. You can configure RHEL 3 with Samba to function as a PDC.

/proc   /proc is the Linux *virtual* filesystem. *Virtual* means that it doesn't occupy real disk space. /proc files are used to provide information on kernel configuration and device status.

public/private key   Encryption standards such as PGP, GPG, or RSA are based on public/private key pairs. The private key is kept on the local computer; others can decrypt it with the public key.

pvcreate   The **pvcreate** command allows you to configure PEs from a properly configured partition.

quota   In Linux, a quota can limit users and or groups by number of inodes or disk space. Quotas can include hard and soft limits.

RAID (Redundant Array of Independent Disks)   RHEL 3 supports software RAID. You can use Anaconda to set up software RAID 0, 1, and 5 arrays. You can also set up RAID arrays using the **fdisk** and **mkraid** commands, as well as by configuring /etc/raidtab. Also known as Redundant Array of Inexpensive Disks.

RAID 0   A RAID 0 array requires two or more partitions or hard drives. Reads and writes are done in parallel, increasing performance, filling up all partitions or hard drives equally. RAID 0 includes no redundancy; if any partition or hard drive in the array fails, all data in the array is lost.

RAID 1   A RAID 1 array requires two or more partitions or hard drives. RAID 1 is also known as mirroring, because the same information is written to both partitions. If one disk is damaged, all data will still be intact and accessible from the other disk.

RAID 5   A RAID 5 array requires three or more partitions. Parity information is striped across all partitions. If one disk fails, the data can be rebuilt. It can be automatically written to a spare disk.

Red Hat Certified Engineer (RHCE)   Perhaps the most elite certification available for Linux systems administrators. Designed to qualify Linux administrators with significant experience in configuring Linux LANs with Red Hat Enterprise Linux 3.

Red Hat Certified Technician (RHCT)   Another elite certification for newer Linux administrators. Designed to qualify Linux administrators with significant experience in configuring Linux workstations with RHEL 3. RHCEs must also meet all RHCT requirements.

Red Hat Hardware Compatibility List   The Red Hat Hardware Compatibility List (HCL) specifies all hardware that has been tested on systems running the various Red Hat operating systems. Red Hat provides installation support for any hardware that is listed as "support " on their HCL.

Red Hat Package Manager (RPM)   The Red Hat Package Manager system sets up software in discrete packages. The associated **rpm** command allows you to add, remove, and upgrade packages.

redhat-config-*   Red Hat has created a series of GUI configuration tools to help configure a number of different systems and services. You can start them with a number of different commands that start with **redhat-config-***. While it's usually faster to directly configure a configuration file, not every experienced administrator knows every detail of every major configuration file. I've summarized the tools described in this book in Table G-1.

| TABLE G-1 | Red Hat Configuration Tools |

Command	Description
redhat-config-authentication	Supports client computers on NIS, LDAP, and Samba password databases. Also known as the Authentication Configuration tool.
redhat-config-bind	Configures a DNS server. Also known as the Domain Name Service configuration tool.
redhat-config-date	Sets the clock, and supports synchronization with a remote time server. Can also be started with **redhat-config-time**. Also known as the Date/Time Properties configuration tool.
redhat-config-httpd	Allows you to configure an Apache Web server. Also known as the HTTP configuration tool.
redhat-config-kickstart	Configures a file to automatically install RHEL 3. Also known as the Kickstart Configurator.
redhat-config-mouse	Lets you select a mouse or pointing device.
redhat-config-network	Starts the Network Configuration tool, which can help you configure the network interfaces on your system.
redhat-config-nfs	Allows you to configure exported NFS directories with a wide variety of permissions. Also known as the NFS Server Configuration tool.
redhat-config-packages	Opens the Red Hat Package Management tool, which allows you to manage the software on your system by RPM package or package group.
redhat-config-printer	Starts the Red Hat Printer Configuration tool, which can configure local printers as a server, or connections to remote printers.
redhat-config-proc	Allows you to configure kernel parameters in the /proc directory.
redhat-config-rootpassword	Lets the root user change his or her password.
redhat-config-samba	Starts the Samba Server Configuration tool, which allows you to share directories over a Microsoft Windows–based network.
redhat-config-securitylevel	Opens the Security Level Configuration tool, which allows you to set up a firewall.
redhat-config-services	Starts the Service Configuration tool, which is effectively a front-end for the **chkconfig** command.
redhat-config-users	Allows you to configure users and groups with the Red Hat User Manager.
redhat-config-xfree86	Opens the Display settings tool, which allows you to configure the graphics card and display.

refresh rate   This is the rate at which the image you see on your screen is redrawn, in hertz (Hz).

reverse (inverse) zone   A DNS reverse (inverse) zone can be required by some servers, such as Apache and sendmail, to make sure an IP address points to a real computer. If the reverse zone hostname does not match the IP address, the server might not respond.

rndc   The **rndc** command is used to manage the operation of a DNS server; it's preferred to commands such as **service named start**.

root   This word has multiple meanings in Linux. The root user is the default administrative user. The root directory (/) is the top-level directory in Linux. The root user's home directory, /root, is a subdirectory of the root directory (/).

router   A computer that transfers messages between LANs. Computers that are connected to multiple networks often serve as routers.

runlevel   RHEL 3 includes six available runlevels, as defined in /etc/inittab. Key runlevels include 1, single-user mode; 3, text login; and 5, GUI login.

Samba   The Linux and Unix implementation of the Server Message Block protocol and the Common Internet File System. Allows computers that run Linux and Unix to communicate with computers that are running Microsoft Windows operating systems.

secure Virtual Hosts   You can configure multiple secure Virtual Hosts on a single Apache server using the secure configuration file, /etc/httpd/conf.d/ssl.conf.

sendmail   A standard e-mail server application. Most Internet e-mail uses sendmail.

server   A computer that controls centralized resources such as files and printers. Servers can share these resources with client computers on a network.

SGID   The SGID bit sets common group ID permissions on a file or directory.

Shadow Password Suite   The Shadow Password Suite creates an additional layer of protection for Linux users and groups in the /etc/shadow and /etc/gshadow files.

showmount   The **showmount** command lists the shared directories from an NFS server.

single-user mode   When you start RHEL 3 in single-user mode, you're automatically logged in as the root user, without networking or most services. If your Linux system has boot problems, single-user mode may allow enough access to fix the problem.

smbmount and smbumount   The **smbmount** and **smbumount** commands, when properly configured, allow regular users to mount directories shared over a Microsoft Windows network through Samba.

SMTP (Simple Mail Transfer Protocol)   A TCP/IP protocol for sending mail. sendmail uses SMTP.

SOA (Start of Authority)   In a DNS database, the SOA record is the preamble to all zone files. It describes the zone, the DNS server computer (such as ns.*your-domain*.com), the responsible administrator (such as hostmaster@your-domain.com), the serial number associated with this file, and other information related to caching and secondary DNS servers.

soft limit   Associated with user quotas. Specifies the maximum amount of space a user can have on a partition. Soft limits can be configured with grace periods.

spec file   Spec files are associated with SRPMs. You can modify an SRPM spec file to change the way an RPM package is built.

Squid   Squid is a high-performance HTTP and FTP caching proxy server.

SRPM (source RPM)   SRPMs include the source code required to build a binary RPM package. SRPMs are installed with the **rpm -i** command, which installs SRPM files within the /usr/src/redhat directory. You can then use the **rpmbuild** command to create a binary RPM.

SUID   The SUID bit sets common user ID permissions on a file or directory.

superuser   The superuser represents a regular user who has taken root user privileges. Closely associated with the **su** and **sudo** commands.

swap space   Linux uses swap space for less frequently used data that would otherwise be stored in RAM. It is normally configured in Linux in a swap partition.

TCP/IP (Transmission Control Protocol/Internet Protocol)   TCP/IP is a suite of communications protocols for internetwork communication. It is primarily used as the communication system for the Internet.

Telnet   A terminal emulation program that allows you to connect to remote computers. RHEL 3 includes the Kerberos version of the Telnet server, as configured through the /etc/xinetd.d/krb5-telnet configuration file.

tmpwatch   The **tmpwatch** command removes files that have not been accessed in a specified number of hours. The default daily **tmpwatch** script checks files in the /tmp and /var/tmp directories.

Very Secure FTP (vsFTP)   The Very Secure FTP service is the default FTP server for RHEL 3.

umask   The **umask** command defines default permissions for newly created files.

user ID (UID)   Every Linux user has a user ID, as defined in /etc/passwd.

usermod   The **usermod** command modifies different settings in /etc/passwd, such as expiration date and additional groups.

vgcreate   Creates a volume group (VG) from two or more physical volumes (PV) for LVM.

vi   The vi editor is a basic Linux text editor. While other editors are more popular, vi may be the only editor you have available in the **linux rescue** environment.

Virtual Hosts   You can configure multiple Web sites on a single Apache server, by configuring a number of Virtual Hosts in your /etc/httpd/conf/httpd.conf configuration file.

volume group (VG)   A collection of physical volumes (PV) in LVM.

window manager   The window manager is a special type of X client, which controls how other X clients appear on your display.

WINS (Windows Internet Name Service)   WINS provides name resolution on Microsoft networks; it can be activated on Samba.

X client   An X client is an application that uses the X server services to display output.

X Display   The X Display is a console and a virtual window. By default, there are six virtual consoles configured with Linux; the X Display is associated with virtual console number seven.

X Font Server   The X Font Server, **xfs**, has to run before you can start the Linux GUI.

X server   The X server is the part of the X Window System that runs on your desktop. The X server draws images on your screen, takes input from your keyboard and mouse, and controls access to your display.

X Window System   The GUI for Linux is also known as X Window. Unlike other applications, the X Window System is a layered application.

XFree86   The XFree86 server is the default X server for RHEL 3.

xhost   The **xhost** command can be used to allow other hosts to access your X server. In other words, you can configure remote X clients to send their display to the local X server.

xinetd daemon   The **xinetd** "super-server" daemon controls connections to servers in the /etc/xinetd.d directory such as the Kerberos Telnet server and POP3 e-mail.

ypbind   The NIS client service is **ypbind**.

ypserv   The NIS server service is **ypserv**.

zebra   The RHEL 3 gateway daemon is **zebra**, which you need to activate before your computer can be configured as a router.

INDEX

Symbols

! (exclamation point), running shell commands, 454
* (asterisk) wildcard, 22, 623
/ (backslash), 620
? (question mark) wildcard, 22
[ ] (brackets) wildcard, 22
~ (tilde), representing home directory with, 16

A

A (address), DNS resource records, 554–555
absolute paths, 17
access control
    allow directive and, 436, 439–440
    controlling access to executable files, 443–444
    deny directive and, 439–440
    NIS and, 611
    order directive and, 436, 439
    PAM and, 620–621
    xhost and, 391–393
access.conf, 433
account (account management) command, PAM, 615, 617–618
accounts, user. See user accounts
acl command, 452
ACPI (Advanced Configuration and Power Interface), 53
Additional Device Driver support menu, kernel options, 345
address (A), DNS resource records, 554–555
Address Resolution Protocol (ARP), 268
Administration Tools, package groups, 106–107
administrative (root) account. See root user (/)
administrative commands, 21–22

Advanced Configuration and Power Interface (ACPI), 53
alias command, 221
Alias variable, Apache Web server, 443
aliases
    /etc/bashrc and, 297
    mail groups and, 468–469
allow directive, access control, 436, 439–440, 443
Amateur Radio Support menu, kernel options, 343
amd command, 570
Anaconda installation program, 94
anaconda-ks.cfg file, 189, 191–195, 197
anacron
    executing backups with, 669–670
    overview, 663
    self test, answers, 710
    self test, questions, 706
    two-minute drill, 703
Apache configuration tool.
    See redhat-config-httpd
Apache Web server, 427–448
    basic configuration, 433–434
    configuration files, 432–433
    controlling access to executable files, 443–444
    host-based security, 439–440
    httpd configuration tool, 447–448
    installing, 431–432
    log files, 444–445
    as network installation server, 90–91
    overview, 427
    permissions inheritance and, 442–443
    RPM packages for, 429
    security configuration, 435–436
    self test, answers, 477
    self test, questions, 473
    starts on boot up, 429–430
    troubleshooting, 445–446

    two-minute drill, 471
    updating home page, 446
    user-based security, 440–442
    versions, 428
    virtual hosts, 436–439
    as virtual server, 447
applications, Linux. See X Clients
ARP (Address Resolution Protocol), 268
arp utility, 268–269
asterisk (*) wildcard, 22, 623
asyn option, NFS, 574
at system
    running cron job and, 352–353
    security and, 354
    self test, answers, 364
    self test, questions, 360
    two-minute drill, 357
ATA/IDE/MFM/RLL Support menu, kernel options, 342
auth (authentication management) command, PAM, 615–617
authconfig command, 194
authentication
    NFS, 574–575
    PAM and, 614
    Samba server options, 497
Authentication section, Kickstart Configurator, 202–203
AuthName command, 440
Authoring and Publishing, package groups, 102
AuthType Basic command, 440
autofs daemon, 241, 244–245, 570
automated installation. See Kickstart
Automatically Resolve Dependencies option, Kickstart, 203
Automounter, 241–245
    activating, 243–244
    configuring, 244–245
    /etc/auto.master file and, 242
    /etc/auto.misc file and, 242–243
    NFS filesystems, 570
    overview, 241

HTTPS (Secure HTTP)
    Apache based on, 427
    ssl.conf and, 448
    virtual hosts and, 436
Hz (hertz), refresh rates, 378

I

I/O (input/output) addresses, 47, 52
I2O Device Support menu, kernel
    options, 343
ICMP, 638
ICP (Inter-Cache Protocol), 449
IDE (Integrated Drive Electronics)
    ATA/IDE/MFM/RLL Support
        menu, 342
    /boot directory and, 162
    hard drive options, 48
    partitions, 74, 76
IEEE 1394 (FireWire or iLink), 48, 55
IEEE 1394 Support menu, kernel
    options, 343
ifconfig command
    assigning IP addresses to network
        cards, 581
    configuring network devices, 266
    multicast and, 579
    network adapters and, 39
    switches, 267
ifdown command, 265
ifup command, 265
iLink, 48, 55, 343
IMAP (Internet Mail Access Protocol)
    configuring, 469–470
    e-mail client configuration, 410
    overview, 42
include directive, 463
incremental backups, 34
Indexes directive, 443
inherited environments, shells, 26
init command, 689
init process, 663, 686
init x command, 161
INN (Internet Network News), 104
Input Core Support menus, kernel
    options, 344
input devices, 344
input/output (I/O) addresses, 47, 52
insert mode, vi, 7
insmode command, 312

install mode, 249–250
installation. *See also* partitions
    automating. *See* Kickstart
    basic partitioning, 121–122
    boot disks, 112, 131–132, 136
    boot loader configuration, 128–129
    boot options during, 113–114
    bootable CD-ROMs, 113
    custom. *See* custom installation
    date/time configuration, 134
    disk space requirements, 108
    diskette images, 112–113
    filesystems, 109–110
    firewall configuration, 129–130
    first boot configuration, 133–134
    FTP Server configuration, 117, 119
    graphics system configuration,
        132–133
    HTTP Server configuration,
        117–118
    IP address configuration, 116
    keyboard selection, 116
    languages, 116, 130
    license agreement, 134
    LVM partitioning, 125–128
    methods, 111
    network computers,
        configuring, 129
    network-based.
        See network installation
    NFS Server configuration, 116–118
    overview, 73–75
    package group installation, 130–131
    partitioning servers, 139–142
    partitioning with Disk Druid,
        119–122
    preparation for, 56–58
    RAID partitioning, 123–125
    registration process, 135
    self test, answers, 152–153
    self test, questions, 147–149
    sound cards configuration, 135
    time zone selection, 130
    two-minute drill, 144–146
    types of, 114, 116
    user account configuration, 135
    validating, 160–161, 206, 208, 213
    video card and monitor
        configuration, 132
    workstation configuration, 138–139

installation CD-ROMs
    download process, 85–87
    Fedora Linux, 84
    overview, 82
    Red Hat Linux 9, 84
    RHEL 3, 83
    self test, answers, 152
    self test, questions, 146
    source RPMs, 83
    third-party Red Hat Linux
        distributions, 83–84
    two-minute drill, 144
Installation Method options, Kickstart
    Configurator, 201
installation scripts, Kickstart, 204
installation troubleshooting, 157–160
    bash shell for, 158–159
    consoles available during
        installation, 158
    hardware, 159–160
    log files, 157
    partitions, 160
    self test, answers, 213
    self test, questions, 208
    software, 160
    two-minute drill, 206
Installation Troubleshooting
    consoles, 156
instant messaging, gaim, 101
Integrated Drive Electronics.
    See IDE (Integrated Drive Electronics)
Intel communications channels, 46–47
Intelligent I/O, 343
Inter-Cache Protocol (ICP), 449
Internet Mail Access Protocol. *See* IMAP
    (Internet Mail Access Protocol)
Internet Network News (INN), 104
Internet Printing Protocol (IPP), 22,
    107, 517
IP addresses
    assigning to network cards, 581
    blocking computers by, 631–634
    configuring during installation, 116
    defining networks, 38
    network installation and, 92–94
    numbers and classes and, 37
    translating domain names to, 544
    virtual hosts and, 437
IP forwarding, 316, 643
IP masquerading, 642–643

INTERNATIONAL CONTACT INFORMATION

AUSTRALIA
McGraw-Hill Book Company
Australia Pty. Ltd.
TEL +61-2-9900-1800
FAX +61-2-9878-8881
http://www.mcgraw-hill.com.au
books-it_sydney@mcgraw-hill.com

CANADA
McGraw-Hill Ryerson Ltd.
TEL +905-430-5000
FAX +905-430-5020
http://www.mcgraw-hill.ca

GREECE, MIDDLE EAST, & AFRICA
(Excluding South Africa)
McGraw-Hill Hellas
TEL +30-210-6560-990
TEL +30-210-6560-993
TEL +30-210-6560-994
FAX +30-210-6545-525

MEXICO (Also serving Latin America)
McGraw-Hill Interamericana Editores
S.A. de C.V.
TEL +525-1500-5108
FAX +525-117-1589
http://www.mcgraw-hill.com.mx
carlos_ruiz@mcgraw-hill.com

SINGAPORE (Serving Asia)
McGraw-Hill Book Company
TEL +65-6863-1580
FAX +65-6862-3354
http://www.mcgraw-hill.com.sg
mghasia@mcgraw-hill.com

SOUTH AFRICA
McGraw-Hill South Africa
TEL +27-11-622-7512
FAX +27-11-622-9045
robyn_swanepoel@mcgraw-hill.com

SPAIN
McGraw-Hill/
Interamericana de España, S.A.U.
TEL +34-91-180-3000
FAX +34-91-372-8513
http://www.mcgraw-hill.es
professional@mcgraw-hill.es

UNITED KINGDOM, NORTHERN,
EASTERN, & CENTRAL EUROPE
McGraw-Hill Education Europe
TEL +44-1-628-502500
FAX +44-1-628-770224
http://www.mcgraw-hill.co.uk
emea_queries@mcgraw-hill.com

ALL OTHER INQUIRIES Contact:
McGraw-Hill/Osborne
TEL +1-510-420-7700
FAX +1-510-420-7703
http://www.osborne.com
omg_international@mcgraw-hill.com

Sound Off!

Visit us at **www.osborne.com/bookregistration** and let us know what you thought of this book. While you're online you'll have the opportunity to register for newsletters and special offers from McGraw-Hill/Osborne.

We want to hear from you!

Sneak Peek

Visit us today at **www.betabooks.com** and see what's coming from McGraw-Hill/Osborne tomorrow!

Based on the successful software paradigm, Bet@Books™ allows computing professionals to view partial and sometimes complete text versions of selected titles online. Bet@Books™ viewing is free, invites comments and feedback, and allows you to "test drive" books in progress on the subjects that interest you the most.

Prepare

Get the books that show you not only what—but *how*—to stud

MCSE/MCSA Implementing a Windows Server 2003 Infrastructure Study Guide
(Exam 70-291)
MCCAW & LIND
0-07-222566-1
$49.99
Available: October 2003

MCSE Windows Server 2003 Active Directory Infrastructure Study Guide (Exam 70-294)
SUHANOVS
0-07-222319-7
$49.99
Available: October 2003

MCSE Planning a Windows Server 2003 Network Infrastructure Study Guide *(Exam 70-293)*
BARTLEY
0-07-222325-1
$49.99
Available: November 2003

MCSE Designing Security for a Windows Server 2003 Network Study Guide *(Exam 70-298)*
GOODWIN
0-07-222747-8
$49.99
Available: December 2003

- **100% complete coverage** of all official objectives for each exam
- **Exam Readiness checklist** at the front of each book
- **Step-by-step exercises** are linked to MasterSims and CertCams on the CD-ROM—so you can watch, listen, and try the exercises live
- **Inside the Exam** sections in every chapter highlight key exam topics covered
- **Simulated exam questions** match the format, tone, topics, and difficulty of the real exam

On the CD-ROMs
- MasterExam Practice Tests
- MasterSim Labs
- CertCam Videos
- Complete Electronic Book
- LearnKey Video Training
- Flash card study program for your PC or Pocket PC